THE FUTURE OF TRADITION

THE FUTURE OF TRADITION

Customary Law, Common Law and Legal Pluralism

LEON SHELEFF

Tel Aviv University

FRANK CASS

LONDON • PORTLAND, OR

First published in 2000 in Great Britain by
FRANK CASS PUBLISHERS
Newbury House, 900 Eastern Avenue
London IG2 7HH

and in the United States by
FRANK CASS PUBLISHERS
c/o ISBS, 5804 N.E. Hassalo Street
Portland, Oregon, 97213-3644

Website: www.frankcass.com

British Library Cataloguing in Publication Data

Sheleff, Leon
The future of tradition: customary law, common law and legal pluralism
1. Multiculturalism 2. Pluralism (Social sciences)
3. Indigenous peoples – Legal status, laws, etc.
4. Indigenous peoples – Politics and government
I. Title
323.1'1

ISBN 0-7146-4953-8 (cloth)

Library of Congress Cataloging-in-Publication Data

Sheleff, Leon.
The future of tradition: customary law, common law, and legal pluralism / Leon Sheleff.
p. cm.
Includes bibliographical references and index.
ISBN 0–7146–4953–8 (cloth). – ISBN 0–7146–8012–5 (pbk.)
1. Customary law. 2. Indigenous peoples – Legal status, laws, etc. 3. Indigenous peoples – Social life and customs. 4. Legal polycentricity. I. Title.
K282.S53 1999
340.5–dc21 99–20646
CIP

Printed in Great Britain by
The Book Company, Ipswich, Suffolk

Contents

Part V: Conclusions

Preface

The writing of this book has been an odyssey in more ways than one – it has been a learning experience in the sense of trying to understand the culture of indigenous or tribal people in different parts of the world, and the political and social history of the countries in which they struggle to maintain their identity and dignity; it has entailed utilizing sabbatical leave to travel to different parts of the globe in an encounter with both new climes and old nostalgic memories; it has involved an intellectual challenge of collecting information and ideas, pondering over their meaning and significance, and formulating interpretations and appraisals; it has entailed exposure to fascinating written material and has facilitated stimulating contacts, some ongoing, some fleeting, with a wide range of people in diverse circumstances.

While true to the standards of academic research, it contains an underlying personal element – of birth and initial education in a land then wracked by the tragedy of racism and apartheid, and now, as an outsider, of paying respect, indirectly through this work, to the people of this special, almost unique, 'rainbow' nation, as they build their destiny anew, for it was long ago in South Africa that I first became aware of many of the issues that I have probed in this work. This book is also the fruition of earlier, more theoretical, endeavours involved in expressing different aspects of human rights and searching for a sociological perception of the role of law in society, in which customary law seems to provide a potential synthesis between what I have termed 'social cohesion and legal coercion' – of obligatory rules emanating upwards from the people and not imposed by external dictate.

During this journey over the past decade, I have benefited from fruitful discussions with many people, including students, to whom the facts and thesis have been presented in formal lectures and seminars. Amongst colleagues and friends who have listened and responded or helped and encouraged in various ways, I would like to mention in particular Tom Bennett, the late Gerald Gordon, Nancy Gordon, Sally Frankental, and the late Jack Simons (all of Cape Town), Louis Waller and Arie Frieberg (of Melbourne), Ian McDuff (of Wellington), Malcolm Feeley (of Berkeley), Riaz Hassan (of Adelaide), Gidon Kessel (of Beer-Sheva), and Natan

Lerner, Chava Shachor-Landau and Moshe Shokeid (of Tel-Aviv). At the institutional level, my thanks go to the Law Faculty of Monash University, the Center for the Study of Law and Society at the University of California at Berkeley, the Department of Criminology at Melbourne University, and the Kaplan Centre for Jewish Studies at the University of Cape Town, all of which provided me with space and facilities, as well as a pleasant environment conducive to work.

Others who have been helpful, include Aviam Soifer, Allie Dubb, Peter Skalnik, the late Roberta Kevelson, Pamela Dutton, Robert Leslie, Paul Nkwi, and Justice Durie. I am also grateful for the opportunity that was provided me to present and test my ideas in seminar presentations and informal discussions at the Sociology Department at Flinders University, the Law Faculty at Waitaki University, the Sociology Department at the University of Papua New Guinea, and the Department of Anthropology at the University of Cape Town, as well as at the Institute of Oriental and Orissan Studies in Cuttack, India, where I made my initial foray into this area at a conference on 'Tribal Society in a Changing World', held in 1988. My thanks to members of these academic units for their helpful comments, as also to my research assistants, Tamar Goldschmidt-Arad and Merav Afek, for their diligence, to typists, Sylvia Weinberg, Roslyn Langbart and Beryl Baleson, for their efficient and pleasant assistance, and to sundry colleagues, librarians and administrative staff at Tel Aviv University for their continuous support and interest. *The Israel Yearbook on Human Rights,* edited by Yoram Dinstein, also published early articles on the topic, based on work presented at a symposium held at the Law Faculty.

I end with the hope that beyond its academic value, this book may also contribute to the welfare of those living in tribal communities, who are involved in a constant striving to retain and express the culture and customs that were carved out by earlier generations and bequeathed to them as living links in an endless chain – and may help others to be more tolerant of their strivings, more understanding of the motivations spurring them on, and more respectful of the manifestations that emerge.

Finally, I dedicate this book to the members of my own extended family, spread out in four different continents, for their hospitality and encouragement during the years of research and writing.

PART I: BACKGROUND

-1-

Custom-Made Law

Social life is dependent on the capacity of people to create rules to guide them in their everyday activities. The rules themselves, in normal situations, will represent a common denominator of shared values and practices which may be enumerated in different ways – within a comprehensive prior framework in the form of legislation, by retroactive announcement while dealing with a particular issue that requires solution in the form of adjudication, or by the general acknowledgment and acceptance of agreed and known norms of behavior.

The usual manner in which concrete expression is given to most rules is through a state with its legislative and judicial organs, and generally accepted means of according recognition to prevalent customary practices. However, there are also situations, in which rules of an obligatory or strongly persuasive nature are created without the formal procedures of parliament, courts, and other constituted bodies that characterize a state. In some countries, a certain degree of formality may attach to them, in others they may be mainly amorphous.

Thus, although one of the main characteristics of a state is its power to make laws, yet, however extensive its power, however entrenched its sovereignty, however exclusive its claims, there will always be patterns of behavior that will follow the contours of norms that are extra-legal, there will always be subjects who will respond to obligatory demands that stem from non-governmental sources, there will always be interactions that will be determined and disputes that will be resolved by standards and procedures that emanate directly from the life of the people and the reality of their society.

Governmental authorities may choose to ignore such manifestations or they may decide to accommodate themselves to them by recognition in one form or another. But any comprehensive understanding of the legal system of a society must take due account of those normative structures which exist at its margins and possess, for some at least of the citizens, obligatory force.

There is increasing jurisprudential awareness of this situation, and various writers have attempted to incorporate a description of these processes into their theoretical framework. These jurists have attempted to provide a countervailing influence to the more positivistic theories of law that have for so long dominated in the philosophy of law, and that have focused concern so insistently on the formality and the certainty of law, and the sovereignty and the unity of its sources.

In contrast, schools of thought such as living law, legal realism or historical jurisprudence have collated examples of people carving out their rules, that are deeply embedded in the very fiber of their community life, attuned to its possibilities, and responsive to their needs. In the course of time, these rules take on a form and vitality of their own, and coalesce into a coherent, yet flexible, code of conduct.

The history of law is replete with such examples of 'people law-making', of *vox populi* making itself heard above the din of formal proclamations. But such processes are not just relics of the past; they are an ongoing fact of social life, often providing practical guidance for daily interactions and effective solutions for problematic situations in a more satisfying manner than that provided by the formal legal system. Indeed, the law itself, in its full and august splendor, often develops out of such customary practices. This was certainly the basis of Karl von Savigny's contention that law was, or rather should be, no more than the summation of prior binding rules, an expression of the *volksgeist*, of the spirit of the people.

Customs, then, have always played a significant role in the formation of law. This is widely acknowledged in the case of the legal system of the common law, where the judicial imprimatur of customary practices constituted the bulk of the law in the early stages of its growth, the term itself, 'common', indicating those customs that, over the years, had broken out of a local mould and become widely accepted throughout the realm. In France, too, there are distinctions from its earlier legal history between the *lex coutoume* (customary law) and the *lex ecrit* (the written law). In the German areas, there are descriptions of how ritual processes emerged by which the people would, in a question-and-answer catechism, make known to the rulers what the customs were in a particular field, before the latter would then incorporate them into their own official legal system.

There were also certain areas that were deliberately left outside of the legal system so as to allow for a maximum degree of responsiveness to changing situations in a specialized area – the most notable being the law that grew up around the law merchant, and still finds some continuation in private international law in the modern world. Public international law is another field where customary practices were gradually accorded growing support from individual states, until they came to have a binding status, some of them even receiving an additional affirmation as being of an immutable nature (the *ius cogens*).

But, of course, the most striking example of the role of custom in rule-making is in the pre-state period, where societies, despite lacking formalized institutions for enacting and enforcing the law, nevertheless created means of conveying to their members the parameters of desired behavior, and the scope of the obligations that devolved upon them and the rights that accrued to them. The term, tribe, is widely used to define such pre-state societies, for instance, the Teutonic tribes from northern Europe that engaged in military struggle and cultural rivalry against the empire that had developed out of the city-state that was Rome.

While the results of the military struggle were inconclusive, there were more definitive consequences to the cultural rivalry – the tribes were absorbed into the larger Roman empire, accompanied by their religious conversion to Christianity, their assimilation into the pattern of centralized state institutions, and their acceptance, especially from the eleventh century onwards, of the Roman law as a founding framework for a comprehensive legal system.

Thus, the convulsions of the Middle Ages seemed to have led either to the demise of tribes in western civilization, or consigned them to the peripheries of its empire. As tribe became state, so custom became law; yet, in the interstices of the society, customary practises continued to hold their appeal – and, apart from being received, as noted, into the corpus of the law through judicial recognition, persisted also without any such official incorporation, as variously described by different non-positivistic theories of law.

A leading American jurist, Justice Oliver Wendell Holmes, pithily distilled the essence of the law when he said, in a much-quoted phrase, 'The life of the law has not been logic, it has been experience': it may equally be said that the logic of life is not law but custom, an appreciation of the manner in which people will strive for the ultimate realization of their democratic right to express themselves as autonomous beings – by moving beyond the formal reaches of the law to lay down the rules that will govern their lives, beyond that which is contained in enacted codes, judicial pronouncements and learned treatises. Tribes may no longer exist in Europe, but they bequeathed to its people the compelling and persuasive power of custom as a source of authoritative rules.

These historical processes of Europe have been repeated throughout the world – firstly, where states or empires have emerged through the amalgamation of several peoples, or tribes, or the absorption of one by the other; second, where the colonial expansion led to European states imposing their rule and much of their law on people, many of whom were as yet stateless, and were then termed tribes. As colonialism came to an end, these conquered territories became states in their own right, searching in many respects for their own historical antecedents (for instance, taking on names that linked up with flourishing periods of the past), but moulded largely – in their institutions, ceremonials and, of special import, their legal systems – on the model of their former colonial rulers.

The inevitable question arose as to how to relate to infra-state groupings within these new states; in some cases, the problem was of a settler majority and a minority of indigenous people, in other cases, the problem was of nation-building by placing the demands and needs of the state above those of local population groups. But these local infra-state affiliations, with their bonds of allegiance and belonging, with their localized rules and rituals, continue to survive.

Two issues emerge – firstly, to what extent the all-encompassing state is able to concede the validity of the varied local customs and to share its rule-making and rule-enforcing power with local communities; second, to what extent the history of Europe is designed to serve as the role-model for other parts of the world in the present day? That is, whether the loose associations of people, such as the tribe, are doomed to surrender their own unique qualities and to be absorbed within larger state frameworks, or whether they may retain their inner vitality and corporate existence, and as such, to continue to shape some of the rules by which their members will conduct their lives; whether their customs that will doubtless subsist in one way or another, as part of some living law, will be sustained also by some conscious recognition as being of a defined and differentiated group, or whether they will be shorn of such support.

In a word, the question is whether or not the tribes of today, however defined and however named, may perhaps escape the fate of European tribes, and so continue to be the font out of which customary law may continue to grow and to change? In probing this, it is necessary to examine the manner in which the modern state is able to divest itself of some of the exclusive sovereignty that has so characterized it in the past; on the one hand to forgo claims not to be subject to any rules extraneous to the body politic, and on the other hand to forgo claims to have sole control over the legal parameters of social behavior.

Recent years have seen a move toward legal pluralism as an inevitable concomitant of social and cultural pluralism. In the final analysis such legal pluralism will most likely entail a certain degree of shared sovereignty; but any such suggestion clearly opens up possibilities of conflict between the different sources of legal authority. While pluralism offers prospects of a mosaic of different cultures in coexistence, with parallel legal frameworks, it also presents the danger of a clash of conflicting norms (between state law and customary practices). A true pluralistic society must learn to cope with such conflicts – searching for a *modus vivendi* that will allow the state to preserve social order (one of its prime tasks), while yet assuring its citizens of their legal rights to believe in and practice their own different ways of life.

In a sense this latter factor is really a pristine form of democracy, with norms being determined at the grass-roots level, by the people, sensitive to every nuance of their everyday needs, and respectful of the accumulated traditions of the past and their meaning for the present. But while many of these norms may be easily recognized and integrated, there are always likely to be some norms that are in violation of state law and general societal norms. The challenge is to seek reconciliation of the conflict; it is a challenge also to the nature of state sovereignty, and to the possibility of creating a meaningful pluralistic society.

Pluralism in the Modern World

Standardized concepts of a world neatly divided into independent states, each clearly differentiated by precisely drawn lines on a map, each presumed to possess absolute power within the designated area, presents a shallow, and ultimately false, picture of modern social and political reality. An earlier idea of sovereignty, which sanctioned total authority for the governing bodies to rule over the inhabitants of the territory under their control, has only limited value in a world of both increasing concern for the universal nature of human rights sparked by international and regional bodies and non-governmental organizations (NGOs), and of increasing activity and intervention in the economic area, spearheaded and symbolized by the proliferation of multinational companies.

The very term 'nation-state' has become – perhaps always was – a misnomer, as there are only a limited number of states in which there is any synchronism between the political fact of a state and the social fact of a nation. Most states are multinational (or multiethnic or multitribal), either by design (the result of immigration policies for sparsely populated areas) or by history (the consequences of past conquests or more subtle intermingling). Perhaps the most brash example of the artificial nature of many states is the outcome of the 'scramble for Africa', in which European colonial powers, towards the end of the nineteenth century, laid down artificial boundaries, based on military power, missionary presence and trading parameters, which have become, with only minor and insignificant alterations, the sacrosanct boundaries of independent countries, rendered ever more inflexible by the pronouncements of Africa's political leaders and the policies adopted by its continental organizations, such as the OAU.[1]

Yet, whatever the present-day fallacies and the flaws of yesteryear, the state is still the dominant factor in the modern world as we know it, and will probably remain so into the foreseeable future. But this very fact makes ever more urgent the need to understand its changing nature and its ongoing limitations. Indeed, the very colonial powers that once laid down the borders in the continent of Africa, have recently embarked on a pioneering effort to co-operate in a new-style community of nations, based on a willingness to restrict the totality of their sovereignty and to make both their legislative and judicial organs subject to a certain amount of regional surveillance in certain defined matters. The ultimate outcome of the present endeavors is unknown, but whatever emerges will have repercussions in other regions, and most certainly on the meaning of standard concepts in political and social science. One certain consequence is that geopolitical frameworks are no longer to be considered monolithic. The emerging pattern is one of pluralism – social, political and legal.[2]

It is in this context that I wish to examine the nature of customary law in the modern state: specifically the manner in which the traditional beliefs and practice of tribal groupings may be recognized by state authorities.

I have used the term 'tribe,' even though it has become a problematical one – and do so for a number of reasons, not least of which is the want of a better nomenclature. Like the word 'state' the word 'tribe' is undergoing reassessment, and there seems to be a growing number of persons, in political and academic life, who are eschewing its use, arguing that its limitations outweigh its clarificatory capacity, and that it is an imposed categorization enunciated by outsiders and attuned to their own convenience and not to objective reality. Even if there is some truth to these assertions, they often ignore the problematics that attach to all of the proposed alternative terms, problematics that are, it should be stressed, no different from those of much social science terminology – ranging from those of the aforementioned 'sovereign state' to the issue of what is a religion or a language or a race.

For instance, there is, we have been told, no such thing as tribe, partly because there is no clear-cut distinction allowing for meaningful categorization, as though there were no problems relating to, for example, religion: when is a religion only a cult, or should Catholicism be differentiated from Protestantism;[3] or language: when is a language only a dialect or how to categorize Pidgin or Creole.[4] These are issues that shall be dealt with in a subsequent chapter – but, at this stage, it is necessary only to emphasize the reluctance to use the term 'tribe.' For instance, the most touted alternative, indigenous people, is based directly on past imperialism – far more so than tribe, for it is applicable only in those states in which there is a dominant settler population. Thus, for example, in India, which does officially recognize the existence of tribes, partly for the purpose of what is known elsewhere as affirmative action programs on their behalf, all of its people are indigenous;[5] in this context those known as tribes are given certain privileges to offset some of the handicaps from which they suffer in the modern world.

In fact, the very use of the term 'indigenous' allows some countries that have 'tribal people' to deny, because of the semantics, their very existence, maybe thereby undermining the possibility of having their rights recognized as a minority group with legitimate claims on the majority population.

Perhaps there is a need for the use of a new word – but that seems a task of Sisyphean proportions, given the very looseness of the kind of population that is associated with the term 'tribal groupings' or 'indigenous people' – or any of the alternative suggestions, for example, fourth world, first nation, aboriginal, clan or descent group. Worse still are the attempts to ignore the uniqueness of tribal people, in terms of the very possibility of assuring them of their most basic rights – of land, religion, social ritual, by subsuming them under other categories, such as language, nation or ethnic group. In fact, the prevalent suggestion of ethnicity instead of tribalism, is perhaps the most problematical of all – both vague in its conceptualization and often specifically related either to the European continent, with its variegated population, or to the consequences of European, imperialistic, experience – as where Italian, Irish or Greek ethnicity is applied to immigrant groups only in the 'new world', and not to the home base.[6]

The solution may well be in trying to move beyond the old anthropological and political categories, and to see 'tribe' in sociological terms, as the embodiment of a *gemeinschaft*, as representing those qualities, which Tönnies[7] tried to describe as the alternative to a *gesellschaft* society, with the latter both most noted in the western world, and about which he also expressed reservations.

In any event, these are matters that will occupy us later on; for the moment it is necessary to clarify what it is that the book attempts to do. I wish to adopt an overall sociological perspective to examine the utilization of modern law to determine the nature of the rights of 'tribal' people to follow their way of life according to those beliefs and practices that form the essence of their culture as an entity, and thereby forge the character of their members. But the work will focus not so much on the nature of the tribe *per se* as on the manner in which modern states respond to the challenge posed inevitably by the existence of such groups within the purview of their governmental authority.

For indeed, tribal culture, while struggling for its own very viability in the modern world, poses also deep existential challenges for the modern state – from the degree of toleration the state is prepared to display towards deviant behavior (not in the sense of being negative, but of being a minority or marginal phenomenon[8]), through the extent of the pluralism they wish to encourage, to the vexed question of the rights of minorities in an all-powerful state, as recognized by its laws, its constitutional guarantees, earlier treaty provisions or more recent international conventions; since the latter rarely refer to tribe as such, the question becomes whether tribes are entitled to the same rights (at the least) that have been vouchsafed to other minority groups, based on language, religion or ethnicity.[9] Beyond that, the question arises whether the specific problems of tribes can always be resolved by relating to them as though they were no more than minorities of the type mentioned. Calling a tribe an ethnic group does not guarantee it all the rights it seeks, which often are different from, and go beyond, those that are claimed for ethnic groups – or religious or language groups.

There are also deep ideological issues at stake in terms of the rights of minorities, often part of a communitarian vision of the nature of the state and its law, now being increasingly urged as no less valid or vital than the traditional liberal accent on the individual.[10] It is, in fact, not just the state and the individual which may be in conflict with each other, (therefore necessitating the guarantee of rights to the individual), but the group (whether tribe, language, religion, ethnicity) and the individual, or group and state, or most pertinently, even a tripartite combination of state, group and individual.

Thus, to use the European model of the Council of Europe, an individual may sue the state, of which he is a citizen or inhabitant, in the European Commission of Human Rights,[11] for refusing to allow a practice (for example, polygamy), which is considered legitimate by the group of which he is a member. Or in another context, a divorcee may lodge a petition at the United Nations that her rights as a woman are being violated since she, or her progeny, is being denied membership of her tribe because it was lost automatically on the occasion of her marriage to a non-member of the tribe. Inevitably, questions arise – is this unfair (unconstitutional even) discrimination against women, if a man marrying outside the tribe does not suffer similar consequences? What happens to the woman if she gets divorced – is she entitled to regain her lost membership?[12]

It must be stressed that issues of this nature do not normally arise in connection with ethnicity, because it is a looser concept, but may, and do, arise in connection with religion, or even language. While the specific issue was the right to reside within tribal lands, the bigger theoretical issue is of how groups determine membership, a problem that is a constant source of tension for nations, religious groups and other social categories, especially where certain legal consequences flow from such membership.

This issue of group membership certainly caused a great deal of agitation for the state of Kenya in 1985, as for several months, the meaning and implications of tribal membership were extensively and minutely examined in the courts of law as the nation anxiously awaited the outcome of the litigation, in which the widow and children of a deceased man fought a legal battle against his brothers as to where he would be buried – in an urban cemetery, close to the home of his widow and children, or in the ancestral tribal burial-site.[13] The issue was not just one of geographical placement, but had to do with how an urbanized Kenyan, married to a member of another tribe, both basically cut off from their tribal past, educating their children to a 'detribalized' way of life, might effectively and legitimately terminate tribal membership, and how he and his wife and children could ensure that the ultimate act of burial would be in accordance with their wishes – both as to rites performed at the funeral and as to the placement of the grave. In this case, as in so many others, the final dispensation was made by a state court; the decision itself, as will be discussed in detail in a later chapter, being in favor of the tribe.

The case became a *cause célèbre* in Kenya, described daily in extensive media coverage, and carefully analyzed in subsequent academic discussion. The issue here was clearly a clash of tribal rites and personal rights – the differentiation was certainly not based merely on the language spoken, or the loose amalgam of an ethnic group, but as tribe *per se.*

Thus, whatever theoretical arguments may be advanced for the denial of tribe as a social category, they may well founder on the reality of concrete and real personal problems that have to be resolved pragmatically; and often in a court of law.

One cannot ignore the existence of a problem whose solution is bound up with legal interpretations as to the nature of tribal membership. In any event the issue itself is not unique to tribalism. In other contexts, similar issues of affiliation arise as to burial (the wishes of parents as against the wishes of a young widow or widower, let us say, with no children and likely to marry again) or the question of citizenship (with far-reaching implications where fidelity to one state might constitute treason to another, as in a war situation)[14] or religion (known, for instance, in Israel as the 'who is a Jew?' question,[15] on the basis of which, preferential treatment in the secular matter of conferring citizenship on an immigrant, is given to Jews – immediate, if so wanted, as against a waiting period of several years for non-Jews; the question once arose as to whether this would include a person born a Jew, but who had been converted to Christianity, and had indeed become a Catholic monk, but who continued to see himself as a member of the Jewish 'people' into which he had been born).[16]

At issue then is a whole host of problems connected with tribes over facts that are, at one and the same time, in some respects unique to a tribal situation, and in others, paralleled with similar problematics in relation to other categories used in the social sciences and in everyday life – of membership, rituals, right to live, place of burial, care of children, protective status, punitive practices for deviant acts, rites of passage, and so on.

Furthermore, the very term 'customary law' raises serious issues; on the one hand, those related to the well-worn question of whether custom constitutes law, or is some lesser breed of obligatory behavior; on the other hand, the fact that even in the most sophisticated system of law, custom is generally regarded as one of the recognized sources of law, most particularly in the common law, which basically grew out of customary practices (incorporated into the law by judicial decree). There are many differences between the customs of the tribe and the customs of the common law, but the similarities are far more pertinent for an understanding of the role of customary law in a modern state.

In fact, it is perhaps not custom, that is the most problematic concept, but the nature of law itself, and the different interpretations that have been applied to it. Indeed the negation of custom was made initially at a time when, at least in England, the dominant jurisprudential approach was that of positivism, as expounded particularly by John Austin, who defined law in strict terms as the command of the sovereign, and linked it to a formal written law.[17]

Austin's ideas no longer have the same dominance over jurisprudential thinking, nor does positivism have the same theoretical rigidity. Thus a leading thinker such as H. Hart adopts a far more open and flexible approach. In differentiating between primary and secondary rules, Hart facilitates the incorporation of tribal custom within the framework of law, even though there is some ambiguity in his position as he writes also on occasion of pre-law.[18] He also sees customary law as being uncertain, static and inefficient, qualities, which (as will be shown) do not really reflect the nature of customary law, and perpetuate some of the myths surrounding it.

However, more important are the non-positivistic theories, ranging from the older historical jurisprudence (which has direct and positive pertinence for customary law, especially as presented by Savigny)[19] to the various twentieth-century theories that are linked, in one way or another, to sociological jurisprudence,[20] though generally moving beyond in their innovative perspectives – for instance, the approach of those such as Eugen Ehrlich who speaks of the 'living law' to describe the manner in which, for the most part and for the bulk of the population, rights and obligations are determined by the norms of consensus behavior, and not necessarily by legal fiat.[21] There is surely no better example of 'living law' than the customary law of tribal communities; and when tribal custom is given some formal degree of recognition, as occurred in many cases in Africa and America, then its development, while formalized to an extent, remains very much within the descriptive framework of legal realism,[22] particularly of the American variety, where it is the ongoing 'loose' practices of lower courts (in many respects akin to the chief's or tribal courts) where the law finds its most frequent and relevant expression.

In other words, far from the customary law of tribal groupings being some sort of unique manifestation, it becomes an example of tendencies that exist in all forms of law, tendencies which form an integral aspect of the very essence of law, at least as described by those theorists who are more attuned to social factors in the formation of legal systems. These tendencies are actually most marked in the common law countries with its accent on the role of custom, even if rather strictly defined, and of judge-made law.

In this respect, tribal or customary law is no less precisely represented nor less formally recognized, than the use of law in magistrates courts, and similar judicial frameworks (for example, arbitration tribunals), which are integral parts of all modern legal systems.[23]

Thus, we see state courts often forced to examine and to try to understand customary law in order to make a determinative judicial decision, a process which becomes even more marked where customary courts are actually set up by law, thereby giving certain validity to the customary system, but also sometimes giving power beyond what customary practices traditionally allowed; or even appointing people (bureaucrats) to adjudicate, when they are not sufficiently familiar with the customary rules, or necessarily attuned to the underlying sentiments of the people.[24]

This is where the issue of chief becomes so critical,[25] since some degree of the general criticism applied to the tribe stems from the dominant role accorded some chiefs during colonial times, as an essential part of the policy of indirect rule,[26] whereby the most efficacious and least burdensome means of controlling the population was seen to be through manipulative utilization of local leaders, often artificially appointed, or else given added power.

In fact, of course, custom should ideally emerge from the people, with the task of judge or chief or headman being to sense the feelings and wishes of the community, the verdict being then an emanation of a consensus that continually determines norms, applying them to future similar situations in the same way as judges apply precedent, or, occasionally laying down new norms, in the same way that judges indulge in 'judicial law-making'.[27] And it is the common law, among modern sophisticated legal systems, that most notably uses such procedures.

Yet only a few writers have drawn attention to this overlap in approach of the common law and the structure of much tribal customary law. Of those who have, James Zion has stressed the importance of this perspective in examining North American Indian law.[28] He writes:

> This discussion is concerned with the Indians of North America ... and the common law systems of the United States and Canada. Since these two nations largely follow the common law tradition, it makes sense to speak to Indian law in terms of that method. This method of analysis is also useful in the international law context because many of its principles are based upon an international common law. This is not a matter of yet another imposition of alien forms of analysis on Indian cultures because the analysis is aimed at the non-Indian who needs to be convinced that Indians indeed have their own law. The comparison between Anglo-European common law and Indian common law demonstrates that Indian law has foundations which are understandable to the non-Indian.

> For the purpose of a rational discussion of Indian customary law, it is best to use the term 'Indian Common Law'. Indian government, law and daily life are founded upon long-standing and strong customs, and since the stated rationale for the English Common Law is that it is a product of custom, that approach may be used for Indian law as well.
>
> Indians have every right to assert that their law stands on the same footing as the laws of the United States and Canada. It is unfortunate that the term 'custom' implies something that is somehow less or of lower degree than 'law'. There are connotations that a 'custom' is somehow outside the 'law' of government, which is powerful and binding. This is an ethnocentric view.[29]

In another geographic area, southern Africa, dealing with a different legal situation and with 'tribes' that are different in many respects from the Indians of North America, Tom Bennett has also written persuasively of the commonalities of custom and law, this time, however, with a stress on the interconnection between the laws and the customs as merely an example of the conflict of laws,[30] involving almost identical issues to those that arise whenever legal systems come into contact with another, whether across political borders (the usual case, hence the term also private international law) or within those borders where parallel systems of law are, for one reason or another, in simultaneous operation.

For Bennett, given the equal status of both systems, the problem of how to accord recognition to customary law becomes largely a technical problem, (albeit a complex and sophisticated one at that) of the conflict of laws, one of the most difficult branches of the law. Bennett writes that

> Implicit in the conflict of laws is recognition of cultural (or socio-economic) differences, whether via the medium of the territorial state (as in private international law) or via membership of a group of people. Many African people have abandoned or are abandoning their traditional way of life in favour of what can be broadly conceived as a Western lifestyle. The conflict of laws takes cognizance of this and purports to define the circumstances in which it would be proper to apply the appropriate legal system for the solution of a dispute. It does not purport to apply legal systems on a general basis, but instead, operates on a case-by-case basis in terms of particular sets of facts ... The conflict of law pays due respect to all legal systems and thus, indirectly, pays regard to the personal inclinations of the people whose legal systems are involved.[31]

Like Zion, Bennett notes the constricted manner in which much discussion of conflict of laws takes place. Generally conflict of law is considered in terms of private international law, as referring to a clash based on geographical differentiation, where the legal systems of two or more states are possibly operative, and it is the task of the jurist to determine which law will be made applicable.

For this reason Bennett prefers the term 'conflict of personal laws'. In a footnote he refers to the use of a Dutch scholar, Kollewijn, of the term 'intergentiel' when discussing 'The effect of the Western influence on native civilization in the Malay archipelago'.[32] This Dutch term, notes Bennett, 'can be translated into English as "interracial" or "intertribal".' However, Bennett sees this term as being 'too limited for it excludes systems of law derived from religions, such as Islam and Judaism'.[33]

In a sense this seems closer to Antony Allott's use of the term, noted by Bennett of 'internal conflict of laws',[34] that is, internal to one geographical unit, generally the state. However, as Bennett also notes, internal conflicts of law often occur within a state because of regional differences based on federal constitutional arrangements, which are clearly vastly different from the personal basis of religion, community, or tribe.[35]

Bennett goes on to describe the historical background to the use of personal law, from the time of the Roman Empire up until modern times, when the rise of the idea of nationalism and formation of the state led to allegiance and status being determined primarily by geographical circumstances, and not cultural ones.

In fact, one of the key issues posed for the modern state by customary law is the extent to which account can be taken of systems of law, which are not always directly linked to a demarcated territory, or where the boundaries of the territory are rather amorphous and ambiguous.

As a solution to this problem, a suggestion has been made for a bicultural jurisprudence, one which will bypass standard judicial thought and allow for two legal systems to coexist. Ian Macduff describes an emerging model, based on New Zealand's desire to reconcile the differences between Maori law and the law of the state.[36] In some of the claims for rights being made by the Maori community there is, he notes, a challenge to the 'assumptions of universality and singularity of a legal system'. In these circumstances, 'Biculturalism is not merely a moral aspiration; it becomes a principle for the recognition of rights.'[37]

This approach emerges from much debate that has taken place in recent years, as to the rights of the Maori people as a minority group in New Zealand. It represents an attempt to give meaningful content to the Treaty of Waitangi of 1840, by which the Maoris are purported to have ceded the land to the British, but it is specifically the meaning of that treaty and the intent of the parties, and their understanding of each other, that is now being reassessed.[38]

However, while the concept of a bicultural jurisprudence is an interesting one, its terminology is too narrowly focused on the New

Zealand situation – of Maoris as a group *vis-à-vis* the white settlers, known as Pakeha. It perhaps even ignores possible future demands to be made by increasing numbers of migrants from neighboring Pacific island states. Elsewhere, the legal issue goes under the rubric of multiculturalism; of parallel systems of law in coexistence within one geographical framework and has been more broadly expressed as legal pluralism – which allows for a situation of several systems operating in unison with accepted rules as to how to settle the inevitable conflicts that arise.[39] However, what seems to be possibly unique about the New Zealand situation is its hint of parity between the two systems of law, instead of the older approach which involved formal recognition by the dominant political group as part of a concession, based not so much on respect for cultural traditions, but on the presumed convenience of indirect rule. The general commitment to parity between the two groups, Maori and Pakeha, finds a certain symbolic expression in the 1987 legislation,[40] recognizing the Maori language as an official national language, together with English.

In many instances in the past, even when some recognition of customary law was granted, it was almost always hedged around with reservations, and certainly always placed in a subordinate position to the dominant state law.[41] Inevitable 'repugnancy' clauses made acceptance of specific customs contingent on their compatibility with western norms, that they should not be 'repugnant' to western perceptions. Of course, it could be claimed that the dominance of state law is inherent in the nature of things – that other legal systems exist only on sufferance and with the acquiescence of the dominant legal systems, that of the state. However, if a true pluralism is to emerge, it will have to recognize a broader perspective, one that will see customary law (or other non-state systems of rules) as an integral and important part of the total legal framework of the state – just as, for instance, the state legal systems in the countries of the European Economic Community, are presumed to be in harmony with the law of the community: neither is really in a dominant position, for while the Community has precedence over state law in some areas, the bulk of law is still that of the state, given the many areas still in its exclusive jurisdiction.[42] It is this kind of partnership which is envisaged as desirable for a pluralistic system of law, one with room for both state and customary law.

Instead of the paternalism that tolerated a marginal alternative, there is the prospect of a pluralism that will actively seek out a viable partnership. The common law itself is the end product of a long historical process, which saw parallel systems of law developing, often initially in conflict and rivalry, while carving out their sphere of influence. For centuries the law of England developed through active judicial law-making in both the common law courts and in the courts of equity. While the latter were presumed to provide solutions that were beyond the scope of the ordinary courts of law, the truth is that there were also ulterior motives in the creation of the courts of equity – not just the search for justice and equitable solutions, but also a counterpart to the growing independence and power of the ordinary courts. It was only in 1873 that the two parallel systems of law were formally united by the Act of Judicature.[43]

However, even before this, other countries under the dominance of the English political power and the influence of its legal system, had incorporated standards of equity directly into the common law – as, for instance, in the United States, where it was formally announced that principles of equity would be used in the courts of law, even in the absence of special courts of equity.[44]

The use of equity in the common law opens up a host of possibilities for creative law-making – and indeed, as Ralph Newman[45] shows in his wide-ranging overview of the concept – equity is almost always an aspect of a vital legal system. Equity allows for larger considerations of justice, fairness and decency; similarly, the Romans recognized a *ius honorarium* – of individualistic decisions adapted to the solution of specific law-problems – side by side with the broader *ius civile*.[46] A legal system, then, under normal circumstances, takes account both of custom (norms that are widely accepted) and of equity (specific decisions aimed at just decisions). Consideration of the customs of tribes is certainly consonant with such an approach.

In this work we shall seek to examine how much the rights of tribal people have been respected, how closely the law has allowed their customs to be recognized, and how often principles of equity have been used in pursuance of these aims.

Part of the problem lies in the fact that some customs are *prima facie* incompatible with some of the basic rights enshrined in constitutions or elaborated in theorizing about the rule of law and human rights in general – thus the clash between some tribal practices pertaining to the role and status of women, and feminist principles of equal rights for women, or the ongoing issue as to polygamous marriages in cultural frameworks that raise the concept of monogamy almost to a sacrosanct principle, or serious differences as to common beliefs relating *inter alia*, to child care, where an accepted tribal custom of circumcision or scarification comes to be seen as child abuse, particularly in a climate of heightened sensitivity to the rights and needs of the young.[47]

But issues of this nature cannot be handled mechanistically within a legal context of constitutional rights or legal provisions. Interpretation of constitutional and legal rules is often dependent on the overall social context in which decisions are made, or the specific ideological propensities of the decision maker. These are never more pronounced than when differing value systems are in contact and in conflict.

Tribal customs often touch on the most sensitive sentiments of those – legislators, policy-makers, judges, academicians, field-workers, administrators – who have to determine whether or not to allow legitimacy to customs that might run counter to the overall norms of the society. One response is to attempt to eradicate them, for example, legislation banning polygamous marriages or forbidding the payment of what is called (perhaps incorrectly) bride-price, or the imposition of an expansive blanket ban on the use of drugs, including peyote, even if used as an important sacrament in religious ritual.

Alternatively, the custom may be ignored, but not without certain consequences flowing – for instance, where no action is actually taken against a polygamous marriage (or where it is even given indirect and partial recognition), but with all sorts of implications and complications for the rights of the wife and the children in various legal situations, such as intestate succession, or where there is a refusal to grant tax exempt status to religions that use peyote as part of their sacramental ceremonies.

But since the law, in all its majesty, cannot always succeed in its aims of attaining a minimum degree of conformity, nor is it always able to totally ignore deviant practices, sooner or later, confrontation of one sort or another becomes likely. It is then that the true values of a society will often be tested; on the one hand, as to how strong or meaningful or rational are its overall norms, on the other hand as to how sincere is its commitment to a pluralistic value-system, if such indeed be its underlying value-premises. Whereas in the past, it was the former issue that was of major concern, today, the latter consideration is becoming of major importance. This is because of a bench-mark change in societal perceptions – where most countries are moving from earlier conceptions of a unified value-system, based on ideas of assimilation or of the melting-pot,[48] to an approach that allows for diversity and speaks in terms of varying degrees of pluralism, an approach that encourages toleration for differing customs, including possibly ones perceived by the dominant culture to be deviant.

This is perhaps easier for older and more mature states, than it is for the newer states, still in the first decades of independence and still actively involved in the process of nation-building, often intent on breaking down old barriers of differentiation, continually aware of particularistic allegiances that might well undermine the struggle to forge a national unity and a national identity.

So, for instance, tribal identity is minimized, so that national allegiance may be enhanced. The very term tribe is superseded by alternatives such as language group, or ethnic group or community, as though the older countries of Europe have not known language strife or ethnic community strife, recently indeed rampant throughout Eastern Europe and noted also elsewhere, for example, in Northern Ireland, or the Basque country in northern Spain, or the French island of Corsica.

The truth of the matter is that some, at least, of the socio-legal issues that confront newer states cannot, in my opinion, be satisfactorily resolved, except by an acknowledgment of the fact that the issue is tribal – and not simply one of language, ethnicity, or religion.

Since it cannot be denied that certain dangerous and divisive manifestations have emerged from tribalism it might be well to recall the distinction made by a leading African politician, Tom Mboya of Kenya, between what he termed 'positive' and 'negative' tribalism, the former to be retained and fostered, the latter to be thwarted and removed.[49] Mboya himself did not deal in detail with the issue of custom *per se,* but stressed rather the various manifestations of tribal identity in a political context – negative tribalism, for instance, was not specific tribal customs, but the role of nepotism and corrupt practices linked to familial contacts, generally (and perhaps paradoxically), in the urban areas outside of tribal territory.

Writing at an early stage of independence for African countries, he concedes that

> to anyone concerned with African unity, tribalism presents one of the major problems. We discussed at length this problem at the All-African People's Conference in 1958, the question of traditional rulers, the problems of language and customs. We concluded that, if governments tried to destroy tribal culture and customs, language and ethnical groupings, they would create such a vacuum that the African might find he had nothing to stand upon and become a most bewildered person in the modern world. We thought it essential to isolate what you might call 'negative tribalism' from tribalism in the form of customs and culture.
>
> Let me state the positive contribution of tribalism first. At this stage of economic emancipation, with many more Africans moving into the money economy, they have to decide whether to allow themselves to be completely uprooted from all their past beliefs. I believe it unwise to destroy this African structure of interdependence within the community where each man knows he has certain responsibilities and duties and where there are certain sanctions against those who do not fulfill expectations: there is, for instance, inherent generosity within a tribe or clan.

After describing various aspects of tribal life, he continues,

> People have done their worst in outlawing tribalism, and never differentiating what was positive and worth preserving. Missionaries taught Africans to despise their tribal culture, telling them it was in conflict with the modern world. No effort was made to trace what was good, or to point out to the potential leaders of a community how some customs could be modified to suit the changes in the world.

> People were simply taught European social behaviour without any reference to African custom...The question is whether we can develop within Africa a system which reflects the African personality, but is at the same time a growing system in which a man does not have to cling to tribal customs in the raw and primitive sense.[50]

It is this approach that lay at the base of philosophical ideas seeking a specific African approach to social life, such as Negritude[51] or African Socialism, as espoused by Leopold Senghor.[52] With the years these lodestar ideas have lost their luster, perhaps a dull reflection of the malaise – political, economic, social – that has gripped so much of Africa as the original excitement of throwing off the shackles of colonialism has subsided, and the daily struggle for survival becomes an all-encompassing reality. One doubts that this malaise stems from tribal life. If anything, in other parts of the world a revival has taken place in recent years – as will be discussed later – in Australia among the Aborigines, in New Zealand among the Maoris, in the United States among the Amerindians, in Canada among the latter and the Inuit.[53] Will these groupings be encouraged to seek a revival of their damaged culture, after they have been made into marginal minorities in their own land, while those, in Africa, who have been accorded full independence as nations will, by virtue of the inexorable onward path of progress, lose their traditional culture? This would be an incomprehensible paradox.

Even so, social reality may impose its demands on political developments; firstly, that so many people still live in their tribal areas, still influenced by tribal life, still conversant with tribal customs, and secondly that tribal identity continues to maintain some hold over many who have physically departed their ancestral heartland.

Indeed, as many researchers have pointed out, tribal identity often becomes of greater importance in the urban areas, as migrants seek help;[54] sometimes this was legitimate and positive, when given within the framework of social welfare considerations, but often was negative, when exploited for the purpose of gaining favored treatment or as a ploy for political power. But here again this negative aspect is not one unique to or inherent in the nature of tribalism, but a common pattern noted in many places where ethnic links intrude on politics and become a basis for power (as in Tammany Hall-style politics in the United States),[55] or where there is glib talk of a Catholic vote, a Jewish vote or a Black vote.[56]

The issue of positive or negative tribalism is, in many respects, what underlies much of the involvement of states with the varied customs with which they deal. A key issue to be explained is the attitudes displayed by the various state authorities towards those customs which differ from the overall norms of the society.

During the period of colonial dominance, the British authorities worked out a formula which was to be a guide in making such determination – a recognition of tribal customs subject to the power to withhold such recognition, where the custom was considered to be 'repugnant' to natural justice, public polity, equity, conscience, or similar factors. It was within such a framework that colonial administrators and adjudicators were allowed to probe the possibility of allowing or disallowing various tribal customs.[57]

In Africa, there are still independent countries that use a similar formula to limit the extent of tribal practices considered to be unacceptable to the interests of a modern state. In a sense, what is at stake are questions of equity – is it equitable, is it fair, humane, decent, to allow a particular practice? How much latitude can a dominant culture allow to its minority groups, whatever the basis of that minority status – religious, ethnic, linguistic, tribal?

For the first three examples there are at least guidelines, laid down in international documents, and in many cases, also constitutional provisions.[58] But tribal groupings are generally omitted, it being the assumption that either they are irrelevant, or they are subsumed within one of the other categories.[59] Yet while the nature of the problems bear much similarity, there are unique aspects of tribal groupings that require special consideration. This may be seen in some of the initiatives being displayed by organizations of tribal or indigenous people or working mainly on their behalf – where suggestions for preservation of rights often encompass factors ignored when dealing with other groups, such as language, religion or ethnicity.[60]

Indeed, one of the major tribal issues is uniquely specific to the tribe as such, and often goes to the heart of the rights of the tribal group – the right to the land, and all that such a right means to them in terms of the capacity to preserve their culture. In some countries, particularly where there is a large settler population, this is a key factor in the present concerns and struggles. There are countries where dispensation as to land was determined by treaty: others where areas of land were set aside for tribespeople; or instances where the entire land was claimed in terms of total denial of prior control by the original inhabitants.

Indeed, it is specifically with regard to this problem that the concepts of the aboriginal communities and the settlers from overseas are so drastically at odds, the former with a loose concept of territory, sovereignty and ownership, revering the natural ecology, stressing communal values, including the possession of land; the latter, focusing on political sovereignty (in its old conceptualization), deeds registration of land and individual ownership.[61]

An alternative solution was delineation of reserved areas for exclusive tribal use; in the United States, for instance, treaties were often signed between the federal government and the various tribes, an act, which in purely legal terms raises clearly the possibility of self-determination for the tribes, since treaties are signed between independent entities. Furthermore the Indians in their tribal lands were initially not considered as citizens of the United States.[62]

The special status of the Cherokee tribe, for instance, was formally recognized by the Supreme Court when the tribe sought the Court's protection against the legislative plans of the state of Georgia to deny the tribe its rights and powers, as granted by the Federal Government.[63] In the years since other tribes have, with limited degrees of success, sought redress in the judicial system.

It is as tribes primarily, and not other social categories, that their rights are determined. In many instances, the underlying rationale of the tribal framework was to forestall any attempt at the local level, by the various states, to violate the rights of the tribes.

In fact, sovereignty is perhaps the key factor at issue between some of the tribal communities of the world and the states in which they live. Recent years have seen an increasing awareness of past injustices, and present needs and demands, with every prospect of pluralistic societies of one kind or another arising, and with creative attempts to redefine the meaning of sovereign power.[64] There are also states where it is the very existence of tribal groups that is at issue. In countries still striving to build up a national identity, tribal affiliation is often seen as being a divisive factor leading to possible fragmentation.

But, however much the political leaders of the new modern states may wish to minimize the tribal past, its traditions live on. They impinge on national life not just in tribal strife, but in the family tragedy of a legal battle as to how and where a deceased man can be buried; they affect the individual not just as he seeks nepotistic favors from a fellow tribesperson, but as he goes about his daily life, entering into binding agreements with others; they have repercussions not just when tribal affiliation may tend to undermine national cohesion, but when performance of a tribal custom might be inconsistent with the state laws.

Further, there are, in any case, some independent countries which have made specific provision for specialized courts, some of which carry the name tribal courts and are a continuation of pre-independence frameworks; others go under a variety of names – community courts, village courts and so on – and are entrusted with resolving disputes according to local customs.[65]

Yet, in a provocative book, one of Africa's leading social scientists, Ali Mazrui, presently with academic tenure in the United States, argues for, and basically predicts, the coming demise of the tribal system.[66] The tribal system is indexed in his book *The African Condition*, but for the exact pagination, the reader is referred to two other references, one being 'Africa', the other being 'humiliation'. The former is no more than an *en passant* statement about tribe, in fact one of several others scattered throughout the book (though not indexed): the latter is a 3-page treatment, at the end of a chapter entitled 'The Cross of Humiliation', which is aimed at explaining the 'nature of humiliation' suffered by Black people.[67]

Mazrui uses tribalism as a counterpoint to racism, contending that just as tribalism was eradicated in Europe, so will racism be eliminated there. He then shows the connection between the two terms, and then goes on to distinguish between 'two forms of human solidarity', one based on 'biological relationship' among the members of a group, the second based on 'an economic relationship ... real or assumed', of which, he claims, the clearest example is 'class consciousness', whether of workers or of employers.[68] Arising out of this contrast he claims that:

> the history of the world so far seems to indicate a decline in the power of biological solidarity, and a rise in the influence of economic forms of unity.
>
> Tribalism, in the sense of a larger group that sees itself as having been descended from a particular tribal ancestor, has almost disappeared in the western world as a whole.
>
> The question arises whether the fate of these other forms of biological solidarity – the extended family, the clan and the tribe – will also befall racism and race consciousness as the last political bulwarks of the mythology of kith and kin.
>
> In Europe, tribalism was almost the first to go among these forms of biological alignments; racism may well be the last to go. In Africa, on the other hand, racism is likely to end first, following the liberation of southern Africa. But tribalism may last much longer, though ultimately also doomed to extinction in the generations that will follow.[69]

Mazrui believes that the preferable advanced human relations of the future will emerge when tribalism, as one of the examples of biological connection, will disappear; relationships based on economics will replace them, even though here the future is of constant class struggle. And so, for Mazrui, going beyond Marxist thought, 'The ultimate destination for humankind is not a classless society, but a detribalized society, at least in the sense of the final elimination of all forms of political and economic allegiances based on the solidarity of kith and kin.'[70]

What Mazrui ignores is the fact that tribe is far more than a biological connection leading to economic interaction. It has other aspects that are far more important; as a framework for cultural expression, for sociological identity, for religious beliefs, for ties linked to geographical ecology.

Mazrui seems to know only the 'negative' tribalism against which Mboya warned, but nothing of the 'positive' aspects, which Mboya had praised. In the following chapter of his book, *The Clash of Cultures*,[71] Mazrui devotes the whole chapter to an analysis of the manner in which Africans adapt to the impact of western and Muslim culture, with only a brief opening reference to tribalism, this in the context of an anecdote about a harmful infanticidal tribal practice to which a friend of his was almost subjected as a child, before being saved at the last moment from being killed as a child suffering from polio; the personal history of his friend 'now a learned scholar in both French and English ... is part of the history of medical science in Africa. His family has learned a lot during his single lifetime.'[72]

I cannot attest as to the education of the friend's family, but one of the aspects of life which many western medical doctors have learned in Africa, is the need to work together with traditional healing practices in order to be most effective.[73] Be that as it may, it is not the biological basis to tribe that concerns us, but the cultural manifestations, the specific area which Mazrui totally ignored in dealing with the 'African Condition'.[74]

But there are other writers who argue that an understanding of tribe is central to an understanding of modern Africa, just as perhaps an understanding of Christianity is essential to understanding modern western secular civilization,[75] or Buddhism and Confucianism to understand China, even modern Communist China.[76]

It is these factors that we shall attempt to probe in this work, inasmuch as modern states – whether settler countries faced with indigenous peoples, clamoring for their lost rights, or modern recently independent states, subdivided into different language and ethnic groups (also known as tribes) – are obliged to decide what degree of tolerance to display to the separatist practices of these groups. Drawing on Mazrui's example and using Mboya's perspective, basically the issue is now to differentiate between the negative aspects, such as of a proposed infanticide because of serious illness, and the host of other cultural expressions that are rich in the vitality of tribal life, are meaningful to the people involved, and are relevant to the developing mosaic of the modern world.

But first we must examine if the tribe still exists, not in substance, but in name – as an accepted term to describe a particular social phenomenon.

NOTES

1. On the borders of Africa, see Ian Brownlie, *African Boundaries: A Legal and Diplomatic Encyclopedia* (London: C. Hurst, 1979).
2. On pluralism see Leo Kuper and M.G. Smith (eds), *Pluralism in Africa* (Berkeley: University of California Press, 1971); John Rex, 'The Plural Society in Sociological Theory', *British Journal of Sociology* 10 (1959), p. 114.
3. A recent book argues that the three monotheistic religions, Christianity, Islam and Judaism should be considered as one religion. See Allan H. Cutler and Helen E. Cutler, *The Jew as Ally of the Muslim: Medieval Roots of Anti-Semitism* (South Bend, IN: University of Notre Dame, 1986). The opening sentence is 'Judaism, Christianity and Islam are not three separate religions, but *three branches of the same religion,* the religion of Abraham.'
4. See Mala Tabory, 'Language Rights as Human Rights', *Israel Yearbook on Human Rights* 10 (1980), p. 167, especially at pp. 188–9 for the discussion of distinction between language and dialect. See also Stanley Rundle, *Language as a Social and Political Factor in Europe* (London: Faber & Faber, 1946).
5. See, for instance, G.A. Ghurye, *The Scheduled Tribes* (Bombay: Bhaktal, 1963).
6. The term 'ethnicity' was used originally partly in order to avoid using the term 'race', which was coming into disfavor.
7. Ferdinand Tönnies, *Community and Society* (East Lansing: Michigan State University Press, 1957).
8. One of the best expositions of this approach is in Ian Taylor, Paul Walton and Jock Young, *The New Criminology: For a Social Theory of Deviance* (New York: Harper Torchbooks, 1976).
9. See Natan Lerner, *Group Rights and Discrimination in International Law* (Dordrecht: Martinus Nijhoff, 1991). See also collection of articles in *Israel Yearbook on Human Rights,* Vol. 21 (1991).
10. See discussion below in Chapter 8, 'The Right to Group Rights'.
11. This is a theoretical example; until now there has been no such case.
12. This description is based on a specific case (which will be discussed in more detail in Chapter 9), in which a Canadian lodged a petition with the United States Commission on Human Rights (*Lovelace v. Canada*, (R.6/24) HRC 36, 166).
13. See J.B. Ojwang and J.N.K. Mugambi (eds), *The S.M. Otieno Case: Death and Burial in Modern Kenya* (Nairobi: Nairobi University Press, 1989). This too is discussed in Chapter 9.
14. These problems are even applicable to corporations, and not just to individuals for instance in respect of laws relating to trading with the enemy The plight of Japanese-Americans during the Second World War is a good example of the complexities, and injustice that might result – see Peter Irons, *Justice at War* (Berkeley: University of California Press, 1993).
15. Several important court cases have been held on this issue, where the courts use basically secular criteria to determine who is a Jew. There have been government crises on occasions in response to decisions, which are not regarded favorably by small, but powerful, religious parties. In general, see S. Zalman Abramov, *Perpetual Dilemma: Jewish Religion in the Jewish State* (Rutherford, NJ: Farleigh Dickinson University Press, 1976).
16. The decision was to deny the petition, although one judge did note that had a religious criterion been used, the petitioner might well still be considered a Jew, as in religious terms, birth is normally the decisive factor. See H.C.J. 72/62 *Rufeisen v. Minister of Interior,* 16 P.D. 2428 (1962). See English translation in *Selected Judgments of the Supreme Court of Israel,* 1 (1971). In general, see Izhak Englard, 'Law and Religion in Israel', *American Journal of Comparative Law* 35 (1987), p. 185, especially at pp. 193–6, subtitled 'Who is a Jew?'
17. John Austin, *Lectures on Jurisprudence, or The Philosophy of Positive Law* (London: J. Murray, 1920).
18. H.L.A. Hart, *The Concept of Law* (Oxford: Clarendon Press, 1961).
19. Karl von Savigny, *On the Vocation of Our Age for Legislation and Jurisprudence* (New York: Arno Press, 1975).
20. Roscoe Pound, *The Spirit of the Common Law* (Boston: Beacon Press, 1963).
21. Eugen Ehrlich, *Fundamental Principles of the Sociology of Law* (Cambridge, MA: Harvard University Press, 1936).
22. See W. Fisher, M. Horwitz and T. Reed (eds), *American Legal Realism* (New York: Oxford University Press, 1993).

23. See J. van Velsen, 'Procedural Informality, Reconciliation, and False Comparisons', in Max Gluckman (ed.), *Ideas and Procedures in African Customary Laws* (London: Oxford University Press, 1969), p. 137.
24. In many cases in Africa, White commissioners were appointed to adjudicate on issues of customary law.
25. For various approaches, see the issue of the *Journal of Legal Pluralism and Unofficial Law* devoted to the topic of 'The New Relevance of Traditional Authorities to Africa's Future' Nos. 37 and 38 (1996).
26. On indirect rule, see, for example H.F. Morris and James S. Read, *Indirect Rule and the Search for Justice: Essays in East African Legal History* (Oxford: Clarendon Press, 1972).
27. See Symposium in *Indiana Law Journal* 34 (1961) on judicial law-making. See also E. Veitch, 'Some Examples of Judicial Law Making in African Legal Systems', *Modern Law Review* 34 (1971), p. 42.
28. James Zion, 'Searching for Indian Common Law', in Bradford Morse and Gordon Woodman (eds), *Indigenous Law and the State* (Dordrecht: Foris Publications, 1988).
29. Ibid., pp. 123–4.
30. Tom W. Bennett, *Application of Customary Law in Southern Africa* (Cape Town: Juta, 1985).
31. Ibid., p. 16.
32. Ibid., p. 1. The reference is in Schrieke (ed.), *The Effect of Western Influence on Native Civilization in the Malay Archipelago.*
33. Ibid., p. 1.
34. Ibid., p.1. The reference is to A. Allott, *New Essays in African Law* (London: Butterworths, 1970).
35. The problems of conflict of laws between different regional states within one country, or between federal and state governments are often no less complex than other conflict of law situations, within a state, such as for customary law, or between states.
36. Ian Macduff, 'Biculturalism, Partnership and Parallel Systems: The Context of Maori Rights', in William Twining (ed.), *Issues of Self-Determination* (Aberdeen: Aberdeen University Press, 1991), p. 102 – publication based on 14th World Congress in Philosophy of Law and Social Philosophy (Edinburgh, 1989).
37. Ibid., p. 103.
38. See Claudia Orange, *The Treaty of Waitangi* (Wellington: Allen & Unwin, 1987).
39. The various issues of the *Journal of Legal Pluralism and Folk Law* contain many good examples of legal pluralism in action.
40. Maori Language Act of 1987.
41. See discussion below in Chapter 7, 'Between Recognition and Repugnancy'.
42. See, for instance, L. Neville Brown, *The Court of Justice of the European Communities* (London: Sweet & Maxwell, 1989, 3rd edn.). He writes: 'an essential role in the application of Community law is played by the whole range of national courts and tribunals … these courts may have to apply community law, and they too are therefore, in a very real sense, Community courts. In this capacity they are to be guided and assisted by the Court of Justice, and, to adopt the principles of interpretation developed by the Court' (p. 11).
43. See, for instance, Anthony Babington, *The Rule of Law in Britain from the Roman Occupation to the Present Day* (Chichester: Barry Rose, 1995), at pp. 232–4.
44. See Article 3, Sec. 2 of the US Constitution: 'The judicial power shall extend to all cases, in law and equity'.
45. Ralph Newman, *Equity and Law: A Comparative Study* (New York: Oceana, 1961).
46. See, for instance, J.A. Crook, *Law and Life of Rome* (London: Thames & Hudson, 1967). At p. 24, he writes that the Praetors built up 'alongside the primitive system [of law] more flexible institutions, enabling the law of the Republic to keep pace with its economic and social development and its increasing contact with foreign peoples. This was the *ius honorarium,* the "Roman Equity".'
47. In general, see Leon Sheleff, *Generations Apart: Adult Hostility to Youth* (New York: McGraw-Hill, 1982).
48. See, for instance, Milton Gordon, *Assimilation in American Life: The Role of Race, Religion and National Origins* (New York: Oxford University Press, 1964).
49. Tom Mboya, *Freedom and After* (London: André Deutsch, 1963).

50. Ibid., pp. 67–8.
51. Leopold Senghor, *Négritude et Humanisme* (Paris: Editions du Seuil, 1964); see also Maulana Karenga, *Introduction to Black Studies* (Los Angeles: Kawaida Publications, 1982).
52. Leopold Senghor, *On African Socialism* (New York: Praeger, 1964).
53. See below, Chapter 10, 'The Local Tribe in the Global Village'.
54. See Abner Cohen, *Custom and Politics in Urban Africa* (London: Routledge & Kegan Paul, 1969).
55. On Tammany Hall politics, see Martin Sheffer, 'The Electoral Foundations of the Political Machine: New York City, 1884–1897' in J. Silbey, A. Boque and W. Flanigan (eds), *The History of American Electoral Behavior* (Princeton, NJ: Princeton University Press, 1978), p. 263.
56. On ethnic voting in the United States, see Robert Lane, 'The Way of the Ethnic in Politics', in H. Bailey and E. Katz (eds), *Ethnic Group Politics* (Columbus, OH: Charles Merrill Publishing, 1969), p. 85.
57. See discussion below, in Chapter 7, 'Between Recognition and Repugnancy'.
58. See discussion below, in Chapter 8, 'The Right to Group Rights'.
59. One of the few exceptions is the more limited convention, No. 107 of the International Labor Organization, in their Convention on the Protection and Integration of Indigenous and Other Tribal and Semi-Tribal Populations of 1957.
60. See especially the work – and the publications – of Survival International and Cultural Survival. See also work of the World Council of Indigenous People, Inuit Circumpolar Conference, Indian Council of South America, Four Directions Council and Indigenous World Association.
61. See discussion below, in Chapter 6, 'The Invention of Discovery', and in Chapter 12, 'Land is Forever'.
62. Citizenship was only granted to all Amerindians in the United States in 1924. See 8 USCA, Sec. 1401(a)(2). Prior to this, citizenship was granted only on an individual basis to those who had left their tribal life.
63. *Cherokee Nation v Georgia*, 30 US (5 Pet.) 1 (1831).
64. See discussion in Chapter 4, 'Whither the State?'
65. For example, in Papua New Guinea, the term used is village courts; in Zimbabwe, the term used is local courts; in the United States, the term used is tribal courts.
66. Ali Mazrui, *The African Condition: A Political Diagnosis* (London: Heinemann, 1980).
67. Ibid., Lecture 2, 'The Cross of Humiliation', pp. 23–45.
68. Ibid., p. 42.
69. Ibid., p. 43
70. Ibid., p. 44
71. Ibid., Lecture 3, 'A Clash of Cultures' pp. 46–69.
72. Ibid., p. 46.
73. See, for example, Charles M. Good (ed.), *Ethnomedical Systems in Africa: Patterns of Traditional Medicine in Rural and Urban Kenya* (New York: The Guilford Press, 1987).
74. It is of some interest to note that Mazrui himself, in a book with Michael Tudy, has been critical of African intellectuals (University teachers and graduates), who have not been 'among the major cultural revivalists, nor have they as a rule shown either respect for indigenous political institutions or sympathy with indigenous belief systems and modes of entertainment and aesthetic experience. University graduates in Africa, precisely by being the most deeply Westernized, were the most culturally dependent. The very educational institutions which produced nationalists eager to end colonial rule were insensitive to the indigenous cultural heritage.' See in *Nationalism and New States in Africa – from about 1935 to the present* (Nairobi: Heinemann, 1984), in Chapter 17, 'Reviving African Culture', pp. 298–325, at p. 313. Mazrui also makes positive references to tribal customs in a keynote address delivered at a plenary session of an international conference on the philosophy of law, held in Edinburgh in 1989. It is possible that his ideas have undergone a transformation over the years, but there is no such specific acknowledgment in his later work, where he is more positive towards African culture, which includes, of course, tribal traditions. See Mazrui, 'Post-Colonial Society and Africa's Triple Heritage of Law: Indigenous, Islamic and Western Tendencies', in N. MacCormick and Z. Bankowski (eds), *Enlightenment, Rights and Revolution: Essays in Legal and Social Philosophy* (Aberdeen: Aberdeen University Press, 1989), p. 252.
75. See, for instance, Max Weber, *The Protestant Ethic and the Spirit of Capitalism* (New York: Scribner's, 1958).
76. At a recent conference of Asian sociologists, several papers were presented dealing with the residual impact of Confucianism in several countries of Asia, including China. See Proceedings of 7th Conference of Asian Sociologists, held in Beijing, November, 1995.

Tribalism – Vague but Valid

The concept of tribe is undoubtedly a problematic one – vague in its initial formulation, overextended in the kind of groupings included within its orbit, exploited by those, colonialists and others, who wish to stress the alleged primitiveness of local peoples and the divisions among them, and critically and negatively analyzed by many political activists and social scientists, who claim that its continued use will serve only to foster the negative trends they wish to counter.

Yet, much of the criticism is based on certain assumptions, which are as dubious and debatable as the concept itself is problematical – namely, that there are no similar problems as to most of the alternative concepts being suggested, such as indigenous or ethnic groups (both of them in any case entirely different in their compass, the former narrower, the latter broader), or ancillary concepts with which it is contrasted, such as state or nation, or, for that matter, a whole host of other social science concepts, which are vague, unclear, have been inaccurately or unfairly used, and whose validity has been challenged, such as class or caste.[1]

As an opening gambit, it should be made clear that the issue of adequate and acceptable terminology in the social sciences is often encountered – and there are few concepts that are universally and unequivocally recognized. Within this context, the problematics of tribe are not unique; the term is not being used as some sort of diabolical trap set by those who wish to retain its use as a guarantee for continued tribal strife, or for prolonged backwardness. On the contrary, the concept of tribe may well speak to the uniqueness of aspects of culture and living that are not easily encompassed within other rubrics. While this factor may be of only minor relevance when dealing with artistic aspects of a culture ('tribal art', 'tribal dance', 'tribal music' – it would make little difference to the aesthetic value or social impact, if they were to be referred to as 'ethnic' music, dance and art) yet it may be of major import where some of the material aspects of life are concerned, including those that have legal implications – the legal claim to territory, the legal significance of ritual acts, or even (and this may be, as we shall see in subsequent chapters, crucial) issues such as the meaning of sovereignty, the basic rights of minority groups, and the recognized limits of state power.

For in this work, we shall focus primarily on the legal aspects of tribal culture – to what extent recognition is, can be, should be, accorded to tribal customs, or to what extent, tribal groups are entitled *qua* group, *qua* tribe, to rights or even privileges *vis-à-vis* the rest of society, or non-members of their group. Many of these problems are similar, sometimes even identical, to issues that arise in other contexts – of religion, ethnicity or language – but there are also issues of substantive import and of practical impact, that can best be resolved in the context of tribal conceptualization. The issue is to what extent customary law may be recognized as the 'living law' of a community, as part of a commitment to a pluralistic society, including the acutely difficult manifestation of legal pluralism.

While I am not bound by any overwhelming commitment to placing tribalism above and beyond any other concept, the term itself will be used where appropriate, and also intermingled with other similar terms. In the title of this work I have used the term customary law, and this terminology will, of course, be repeated throughout – but reference will also be made to tribe, sometimes only in the course of quotations from others – but, for this reason, and in order to allay any objections, it is necessary to present some of the rationale for the use of the term tribe. One of the key reasons is certainly that there are some rights, perhaps even privileges, that are best, sometimes perhaps only, guaranteed within the conceptualization of tribe. The issue then is not just semantic, but substantive, not just of a definition of a social group, but of an assertion of legal rights.

Let me stress that I am fully aware of the reluctance to use the term by those eager to ensure the progress of the so-called 'Third World' countries and also fully aware of the exploitation of the term in the past by those intent on divide and rule, on control through indirect rule,[2] on the co-operation of lackey chiefs, and the host of other defects that were associated with tribe in colonial times; and also aware of the term's possible negative implications today – as a divisive or regressive factor.

But to deny its use is also to denigrate much that is of value in the community or group being discussed. More than that, recognition of tribe is important as being one of the internal groups within the modern state that is both entitled to recognition in its own right and may also serve as a focus of allegiance and social identity for many for whom the state fails to evoke the necessary sentiments. In the understandable and justifiable striving for national independence and unity in new nations, there is no need to ride roughshod over the feelings that ordinary citizens have for smaller and more immediate groupings, especially those among the citizenry who lack the easy universalism and cosmopolitanism of the political and intellectual elite.[3]

This need not lead to the fission often feared; on the contrary, it might well be that recognition of intervening groups – between the individual and the state – might be an essential intervening agent for a healthy political community and fruitful social interaction. Properly perceived, responsibly presented, the tribe (no less than the ethnic, language or religious group) may be seen as a positive and constructive mediating factor between the individual and larger social aggregates, such as the state. One may even argue that resentment at the denial of such recognition may lead to alienation from the larger aggregate.

In the context of American society, Will Herberg has suggested that in a large continental state such as the United States, smaller affiliations are needed in order to provide a social mooring for personal identification.[4] He specifically suggests the three major religious trends of Protestantism, Catholicism and Judaism, but, given demographic changes since the 1950s when he wrote, it would today seem necessary to add Orthodox Christianity and Islam, of the monotheistic religions, and perhaps some of the Eastern religions that have made some impact in recent years, as well as, of course, the indigenous American Indian religions; all this incidentally, in a country ideologically and constitutionally committed to a separation of state and religion.

Of course, in other contexts, religious divisions have led to strife, irrespective of whether differentiation was made between state and religion. Similarly, it is not completely clear what the subtle accompanying variables are that vouchsafe for a seemingly tranquil multilinguistic society in Switzerland, in contrast to intermittent eruptions of strife in Belgium; or how Japan copes with a tolerant attitude to religion that allows for dual membership of Shinto (the former state religion) and Buddhism (in its Japanese form of Zen), while the Indian subcontinent, more or less ethnically (but not linguistically) homogeneous, is divided partly on a religious basis of Hindu/India and Muslim/Pakistan, with additional divisions, some of them with nationalistic overtones, such as the Sikhs. Or how much of Northern Ireland's problems are related to religion, and how much to class differences or nationalistic or ethnic aspirations.

Inasmuch as Africa, for instance, seeks unity, either regional or continental, it is by no means clear that it is tribalism that is the major divisive force – it may well be that an identification with tribe might be the very factor that could facilitate the larger striving for unity, whether or not at the expense of the newer states, some of them with their inner controls, often repressive, all of them with their outer symbols of flags, anthems and all the other paraphernalia of statehood. In this context it is of interest to note the developments of regional unity in Europe (whence comes the model of the modern state, however much earlier empires in Africa may serve as present inspirations). These developments toward unity, according to many astute observers of the European scene, may actually facilitate the recognition of smaller local ethnic and national groups. The larger and looser conglomeration of states may make smaller groupings more viable than they previously were, when within the confines of the hermetically sealed boundaries of individual states. The converse pattern may well be true, where a recognition of narrower loyalties, by whatever name, including tribe, may render the establishment of larger, regional groupings more likely.

These are very real possibilities, perhaps only partly sensed at this stage, but before the political and academic worlds cry 'finis' to the idea and the very existence of tribe, they may wish to consider it not merely as an unfortunate and anachronistic reminder of the past, but as a potential valuable resource for the future, a new future that is still being forged, and that offers new prospects for minority groups of various types that until recently were considered to be of only marginal significance in a world of precisely drawn state boundaries. Indeed, the state may be a far greater hindrance to continental or regional unity than tribe.

Yet for many, tribes are really a relic of the colonial age; they originated as no more than the figments of imperial imaginings and designs and so there is a need for revisionist understanding of historical processes, and for a radical understanding of present-day reality.[5] In a thought-provoking book, Martin Chanock[6] has shown how the British policies for Africa included, among other prerequisites for indirect rule, the designation of chiefs and headmen, through whom it would be possible to maintain control over the 'lesser' members of their 'tribes'. It was in the interests of the British colonial administration to recognize the existence of tribes in order to consolidate the power of the chiefs, who, in turn, benefited from the extra authority, power and honor that the European conquerors bestowed upon them. Anthropologists of the time (together with other key figures such as missionaries) fostered such tendencies by similarly using the concept of tribe as the basis of their unit of research. To recognize tribes today is to perpetuate the colonial sin, and to hinder national unity.

However, it is not clear that it is the recognition of tribes that causes the problems in new nation-states, or that other appellations, such as ethnic group or community, would make it easier for these states to coalesce. If differences exist, they do so whatever the name given to the groups. In fact, some of the heightened tensions among different 'tribal' groups are likely to be a direct result of the fact that the states of Africa originally were carved out by the European states without consideration for local needs. Yet, in modern independent Africa, there is a wide consensus not to make any changes in this imposed settlement.[7]

Nevertheless, the war over Biafra, one of Africa's most serious conflicts, was not a consequence of the fact that the Ibos were called a tribe by many – but because there were inter-group tensions.[8] Whether the Ibo were to be known as a tribe, a nation, or an ethnic group was hardly significant in the escalation of the conflict. In fact, elements of the tension may be related to typical so-called 'western' factors – such as religion (the Ibos are mainly Christian, compared to Muslims in the North), or class and power (the dominant role of the Ibos in the capital city of Lagos). In a word, the term 'tribe' as such had little to do with the Biafran war.

One of Africa's leading academic lawyers, B.O. Nwabueze, himself a Nigerian, devotes several chapters in his book *Constitutionalism in the Emergent States,*[9] to the problem of attaining true unity in Nigeria. While aware of the background of tribalism ('Nigeria is perhaps one of the most conspicuously tribalised societies in Africa,' he writes),[10] he points out the many other factors that undermine the sense of national unity, from the very fact of colonialism itself ('Colonialism is intrinsically inimical to the fostering of a sense of national identity')[11] to the ineffective manner which federalism (presumably to make allowance for regional, including tribal, interests), was set up ('The boundaries of the North were the result partly of the accident of its origin and partly of sheer gerrymandering by the British').[12]

Similarly with other internecine wars in Africa, the issue is not the so-called divisive quality of tribalism, but perhaps the lack of an ideological concept of pluralism,[13] that might allow respect for diversity. What many heterogeneous states need in order to achieve a viable, stable environment is recognition and appreciation of the cultural differences among the different groups, linked to adequate political expression. This seems to me to be the major issue and not the question of what the groups are to be called. In fact, many European and Asian countries that do not use the terminology of tribes to differentiate population groups often find themselves with divisive problems no less than, and sometimes greater than, those in Africa – based on language (Belgium), ethnicity (Spain, Yugoslavia), or religion (India, Sri Lanka, Northern Ireland). In Africa one of the most disturbing and long-lasting conflicts, with over a million deaths in several decades of fighting, has nothing whatsoever to do with tribalism – the conflict in Sudan between north and south is based on a combination of ethnicity, nationhood, religion, class and regionalism.[14]

Recent years have seen several attempts to seek alternative appellations for tribe – the most notable being those of 'indigenous people' or of 'fourth world people,' the former term being more official and academic, the latter having ideological overtones; but these do not even resolve the semantic problems; on the contrary, they often create new ones, including that of an awkward terminology.

In fact, there are countries such as India, where the law actually officially recognizes certain tribes – mainly of economically less advanced groups and often from outlying, generally mountainous regions – and by including them in the list of Scheduled Tribes,[15] allows their members to benefit from a whole host of affirmative action policies.[16] The idea of classifying them as 'indigenous' is as confusing as calling the original North American inhabitants 'Indians' – as the 'non-tribal' Indians (in India) are no less indigenous. In fact, the idea of using the term 'indigenous' seems a relic of colonial thinking, raising suppositions that it is only in formerly colonial countries, such as Canada, Australia and New Zealand, that there is a problem, while ignoring the similar needs of similar groupings in other countries, where no settler colonialization took place.

The term 'fourth world' people also raises issues – including the acceptance of a world already divided into three worlds,[17] and the clear gradation, with the connotations of superiority and inferiority, third world being inferior, and fourth world even more so – precisely one of the reasons why many people have sought alternatives to the term tribe.[18] In any event, in terms of ordinal numbers 'first' might be far more appropriate, as used in Canada where the indigenous people are known as 'First Nations'. However, in Canada, there is also extensive use of the term, 'native,' as also increasingly in Australia, a term that in South Africa is – and was – totally taboo by those struggling against the inequities of segregation and apartheid.

But the real problem of the concept of tribe, or any alternative term, is that the issue of satisfactory definitions for population groups is a perennial one for the social sciences. Tribe is not the only definitional categorization that poses problems, especially as to the diversity of the types involved, as to demarcation in the marginal cases, and as to the possibility of incorrect, often negative, characteristics attributed to such entities.

Other widely-used terms are problematical – some of them, such as class or race are already, in fact, far more controversial than tribe; others such as state and religion seem almost beyond dispute, yet they too have their problematic aspects.

Although few concepts in the social sciences seem to be as clear as a reference to a 'state', since states have sovereignty, borders, and enter into relations with other similarly recognized entities, yet the variety in the size, composition and nature of the 190-odd states in the world community today is so great that their diversity is probably more extensive than that of tribes. On the one hand, there are the massive continental states – China, Russia, USA, and India with large and heterogeneous populations; on the other hand, there are the city-states of Monaco, San Marino and the Vatican City, the island state of Nauru (population slightly over 10,000, yet once considered *per capita* the richest country in the world), and small, isolated mountain states such as Andorra and Bhutan.

From another perspective, it is not clear what the ultimate meaning of emerging regional groupings are, with the European Union as the clear pace-setter. Even without entering into the intricacies of whether a new kind of superstate is emerging, or whether the groundwork is being laid for a United States of Europe, the constituent states of the Union already have voluntarily agreed to forgo some of their sovereignty, by making their law in certain specified areas subservient to the provisions of treaties and of judicial norms of the European Court of Justice. Even the much-vaunted sovereignty of the British Parliament has had to succumb to this new wave of change in Europe.

There is one particular term that is receiving increasing support as a useful alternative to tribalism – that of ethnicity; yet whatever advantages it might have, there is little doubt that it is even far more a product of western reality than is the asserted western imposition of the term 'tribalism' in the areas of its imperialistic conquest. For the awareness of a person's ethnicity in North America is generally a consequence of immigration from a home base to the creation of some kind of community on behalf of immigrants. In its original use the immigrant community was of European origin trying to carve out a viable existence for itself in the so-called 'new world'. Later, of course, as migration patterns changed, the number of groups qualifying for ethnic status vastly increased – so now there are ethnic Chinese, ethnic Japanese, ethnic Indian and ethnic African, but not, interestingly, ethnic Nigerian, Ghanaian or other separate national African identities. In fact, the term 'Afro-American' has, in recent years, been replacing Black (which itself replaced Negro) as the term of normal parlance in academic writings and the media – and with it, apparently an acceptance of the term 'people of color', which is being increasingly used, despite the general rejection of the term 'colored people', even though one of the leading civil rights organizations in the United States uses that term in its name – the NAACP, the National Association for the Advancement of Colored People.

In general, then, people from Italy or Greece become ethnic Italian or ethnic Greek only on leaving Italy or Greece, or being children, or perhaps even later descendants, of immigrants. Ethnicity basically replaces lost national or citizenship affiliation. In the United Kingdom, for instance, the Irish or the Scottish are never looked upon as being ethnic groups – only when they leave does their ethnicity become relevant. If anything, in Britain itself, they are seen as 'people' or even as a nation. As for the English who immigrate to other lands, there is, to the best of my knowledge, no use whatsoever of the term 'ethnicity', either in academic jargon, or in popular parlance. In the United Kingdom, then, the real ethnic groups are the immigrant Black or Asian groups, almost irrespective of which 'tribe' or 'nation' they belong to. Conversely White immigrant groups living in the United Kingdom, from Australia or South Africa, for instance, are never referred to as an ethnic group.

So, while ethnicity may have some uses, it seems to be used often in a sort of catch-all manner, and certainly has no clear-cut line, neither of total definition as against other forms of groups, or of any clear-cut demarcation as between the different groups that are considered ethnic.

In fact, Nathan Glazer and Daniel Moynihan, formulating the concept of ethnicity specifically within an American context, have no illusions as to its problematics and its divisiveness and specifically refer to the dangers of 'political realities ... [which] seem to provide a good number of the ingredients for a greater degree of ethnic conflict'.[19] In many instances the presumed divisiveness of different 'tribes' is no greater than the divisiveness of 'ethnic groups'. It is wishful thinking to believe that the change in name – from 'tribalism' to 'ethnicity' for example – will resolve existing tensions, without coming to terms with the underlying reasons for the tensions. Thus, the terms ethnicity and group, largely used in order, at least partly, to forestall use of the more threatening (to the state) term of nation, failed to prevent the disintegration of Yugoslavia and Czechoslovakia.

Further warnings as to the inability of ethnicity as a concept to avoid real-life problems is to be seen in other articles in the anthology edited by Glazer and Moynihan. Talcott Parsons argues that ethnicity is 'an extraordinarily elusive concept and very difficult to define in any precise way',[20] while William Petersen notes that the concept of ethnic groups would be 'unobjectionable except that it is used precisely to designate a variety of entities: some would include a religious denomination under the rubric, others not; some would identify a race as an ethnic group, while for others the latter is a smaller subdivision of races; and so on'.[21]

Petersen's own suggestion is to use the term 'subnation' – which would include 'relatively unchanging groups in the same societies',[22] such as, for example, based on 'race', 'origin', 'language', 'religion'. There are obvious difficulties with the term 'subnation', and in fact it has received almost no support among social scientists. The very use of the prefix, 'sub' with its subordination, is clearly not capable of satisfying those national groups that demand recognition of their national identity (as for many groups in Europe and Asia), while for those ethnic groups that have no such aspirations (for instance in the United States), the appellation 'nation' is far more than they require or desire. In fact Petersen himself refers disparagingly to two small groups in Europe that have actually been accorded a 'national' status by the states where they are – the Romanish-speaking people in Switzerland (1 per cent of the population, yet their language has official recognition) and the Frisian-speaking group in the Netherlands (an ancient German language spoken by very few) – and so Petersen refers to the 'preposterous demands of self-appointed spokesmen for minuscule groups'.[23]

In any event what is of particular interest in Petersen's analysis is the 'language-ethnic' issue in Belgium, where Flemish speakers co-operate closely with their Dutch counterparts, and Walloons with their counterparts across the border in France, thereby contradicting, according to Petersen, 'the conventional wisdom about what determines ethnic identity. Subnations, we are told, are a manifestation of backwardness: they look to the past, thrive on folklore and folk history, maintain themselves best in a village-based culture.' Yet, in Belgium, the 'very movement of more Flemish into upper levels of a fully urban society with an accompanying partial secularization of some important institutions, seemingly resulted in a sharp rise of subnational sentiment'.[24] Petersen notes the need to consider this and similar examples of 'parochial' feelings in studying ethnic relations. The fact is that ethnicity in America has largely different connotations (as applied to immigrant groups) than it does in Europe or Asia.

In fact, there is every prospect today of a greater increase in such sentiments, partly as a result of the capacity of smaller groups to find greater self-expression within a larger community of nations, such as is emerging in western Europe, than they could achieve in the smaller framework of a nation-state. Conversely, of course, a group such as the 50,000 people living in Greenland, requested to stay out of the European Community, of which Denmark (of which they are a part as an autonomous unit) is a member, since the Greenlanders prefer *inter alia* to retain the option to strengthen their traditional 'ethnic relations' with the Inuit people of North America.

Possibly the most devastating criticism of ethnicity is that by Colin Tatz, who examines its meaning in its historical-philological context. He writes:

> 'Ethnic' is overused and misused without the faintest regard for its meaning. It comes from the ecclesiastical Latin *ethnicus,* which means heathen; it also derives from the Greek word for nation, but specifically for the non-Israelitish nations, the Gentiles. Since 1470 it has meant gentile, heathen and pagan. It is time to stop misusing this term in the vocabulary of multiculturalism; it is not a soft synonym for migrants, nor non-English speakers, nor blacks in particular.[25]

In sum, the stuff of science, the stuff of law, the stuff of social reality is the problem of definitions with the accompanying inevitable and intricate problems at the margins.

Three points emerge and must be strongly stressed:

1. tribe is not the most problematical term in social science or in social and political reality;
2. alternative suggested concepts, such as ethnicity, are no less problematic;
3. the use of terms has importance – social, political, legal. Thus to refuse to recognize nationhood means almost inevitably to deny the right to statehood; conversely, where there is a recognition of nationhood, there

is certainly room for according statehood.[26] Similarly, no recognition of a religion may mean no right to practice rituals or to protect sacred sites, whereas recognition opens up all sorts of legal possibilities.

The question, then, is: do similar considerations apply to tribes? Does the recognition of a group of people as a tribe guarantee them any rights (both as individuals and as a collective) which would be denied them if they were to lack such recognition? Would the denial of tribal status lead to the possible denial of certain group rights? Are the possible dangers of recognizing tribalism (such as factionalism in new countries) of greater danger than the potential benefits of tribal rights, rights to land, to legal recognition of customary practices, to the existence of valid alternative legal systems? Would the use of other terms – for example, definitions attuned to language or ethnic group differences – in any way minimize the dangers where friction between groups already exists: or, alternatively, would it provide a greater or lesser prospect to assure group rights?

I wish to argue that there are some rights that can best be protected by a clear recognition of the existence of a tribe, as distinct from other types of groups such as language, ethnicity, or religion. Yet, for as long as the word 'tribe' is presented in negative terms, there will be no prospects of a proper discourse on this issue. Examples of negative approaches need to be examined.

In 1975, Morton Fried, a leading anthropologist, attacked the concept of tribe and argued that there were no 'highly discrete political units in pre-state society'.[27] He notes that the word tribe is of ancient origin, based on the Latin 'tribus', used in differentiating population groupings in ancient Rome, as had been done in earlier large cities, such as in the city-states of Ancient Greece.[28] However, Fried suggests that there are far-reaching implications for the difference between tribe in the ancient and modern worlds. Today, for instance, the word tribe has taken on negative connotations, and it is generally associated with primitive social groups. (In a sense this is really begging the question, since there are a number of leading anthropologists who have argued that the concept of primitive should be seen as positive, a description of a society with many desirable qualities, from which much may be learned, as will be discussed later). Thus Fried goes on to state that

> The nature of the concept of tribe has been a confused and ambiguous one from its earliest period of utterance. Scrutiny of the Greek materials, for example, shows variations in the significance of kinship, as opposed to non-kin relationship, in the composition of 'tribal' membership … Similarly, variations exist in the degree and type of political cohesion in such units insofar as they represent populations integrated for the achievement of diverse internal or external goals, management of the community or warfare.[29]

Fried focuses on the Greek city-states in order to contrast them with what he sees as the negative role of tribes in undermining national unity in new nation-states of the modern world. Thus he claims that it was not because of tribalism that there was an 'absence of centralized government as a characteristic of classical Greek policy' and then adds 'This point is important because analyses of third world political developments, particularly those relating to Africa, are often couched in the most pessimistic terms, with tribalism being described as an unavoidable obstacle to political modernization.'[30]

He also notes that the original use of the term tribe in English as taken from the Latin, was in the translation of the Hebrew word, *shevet*, denoting the biblical tribes. These were perhaps the epitome of what tribe connotes, based on a common ancestral lineage. This point is then used by Fried to argue that many groups known as tribes do not fulfill the essential characteristics of tribe, and should really be considered to be nations or ethnic groups.

Fried also seems to exhibit a great degree of sensitivity to the categorization of tribes as primitive (a concern shared by many others). Yet the truth of the matter is that there is a vigorous, ongoing debate in the social sciences, particularly in anthropology, as to the essential nature and meaning of primitivity. Stanley Diamond has argued very forcefully that the very idea of primitive should be seen in positive terms, and that the characteristics associated with it have significance both for understanding social reality and for clarification in the social sciences.[31] Thus Diamond writes:

> The search for the primitive is the attempt to define a primary human nature. Without such a model, or ... without such a vision, it becomes increasingly difficult to evaluate, or even to understand, our contemporary pathology and possibilities.[32]

After analyzing the importance of such an approach for understanding different areas of human conduct and behaviour (such as medicine, for example), Diamond concludes that in certain 'basic and essential respects ... primitive societies illuminate, by contrast, the dark side of a world civilization which is in chronic crisis'.[33]

In a similar vein, Robin Clarke and Geoffrey Hindley state categorically that the theme of their book, *The Challenge of the Primitive,*

> is that Western man is lost in a search for happiness, and may begin to find his way again only if he is prepared to look into the world of the primitives, a world that he is fast destroying. The objectives of that primitive world have been different from ours. Our quest for progress has led us to dedicate the energies of our society to maintaining imbalance and tension as a motive force. The primitive

> society on the other hand, devotes its resources to the maintenance and nurturing of a social equilibrium, inherited from the past but always adaptable to the present.[34]

Ashley Montagu pinpoints the key issue with direct relevance for the issue of the term tribe. He writes:

> There is a perfectly sound sense in which the term 'primitive' and the concept for which it stands may be used, but not until we have disembarrassed ourselves of the unsound ways in which the word is employed shall we usefully be able to employ it at all.[35]

In contrast to debates of this nature among anthropologists, sociology has almost totally ignored the framework of a tribe. Most basic textbooks make no reference whatsoever to tribe – or when they do, they do so only in order to refer to anthropological research. Yet, the essence of a tribe is almost the epitome of the *gemeinschaft* that Ferdinand Tönnies[36] spoke about so favorably. The distinction between a *gesellschaft* and a *gemeinschaft* is one of the classic characterizations of sociology, but very rarely is the tribe used as an example of *gemeinschaft* properties. Yet tribes focus around the relevant variables of kinship and neighborhood. Further, in both sociology and law there is an increasing search for the essence of community (in sociology)[37] and communitarianism (in law).[38] Both disciplines might find in the qualities possessed by tribes a useful model for the kind of social living that is being theoretically expounded.

Fried himself seems to concede this much. In a final three page chapter, in which he notes the calls of other writers for the preservation of tribalism, he accepts that 'a distinction between destructive nationalism and a more pacific tribalism … is in my opinion a sound idea'.[39] Admittedly Fried seems to be referring mainly to smaller groupings. He may indeed be correct that there is a need to reconsider some of the categorizations that have been made in the past as to tribe, perhaps especially when dealing with particularly large groups numbering in the millions, but then other characterizations also carry their marginal examples that suggest the possibility of endless redefinition.

Another negative critique of the term tribe is to be found in Marshall Sahlins's book, *Tribesmen*.[40] This is a wide-ranging analysis, which also focuses to some extent on the genetic basis, similar to Fried's original critique. Even more noted is the evolutionary framework of his approach – 'Tribes occupy a position in cultural evolution. They took over from simple hunters; they gave way to the more advanced cultures we call civilizations. But civilization is not an advance over tribal society simply by reason of its dominance-power. Civilization is an advance in organization, a qualitative transformation of the culture type.'[41] But the contrast between these two forms of society is even more starkly presented as Sahlins immediately elaborates on his theme:

> In its broadest terms the contrast between tribe and civilization is between War and Peace. A civilization is a society specially constituted to maintain 'law and order'; the social complexity and cultural richness of civilizations depend on institutional guarantees of Peace. Lacking these institutional means and guarantees, tribesmen live in a condition of War, and War limits the scale, complexity, and all-round richness of their culture, and accounts for some of their more 'curious' customs.[42]

Admittedly, Sahlins does indicate that he uses the terms 'War' and 'Peace' in a special sense, which may be why he uses capital letters – in fact, in writing of war he suggests that Hobbes's use of 'Warre' is his actual intention, namely, not so much of external battle, but rather of internal strife – in Sahlins's words, 'a general disposition and right to fight, if necessary'.[43] According to him, then, while there 'need not be violence', the social conditions are such that 'force is a resort legitimately available to all men'.[44]

Nevertheless, there is a certain unavoidable inconsistency in the approach, which Sahlins himself is quick to note – thus, for instance, while 'the Hopi pueblo is as non belligerent a community as one may find' (and thus in essence an exception to the situation of 'Warre' which normally, according to Sahlins, characterizes such communities), on the other hand 'the everyday internal violence of the United States of America has few parallels in history or ethnography'.[45] This manifest contradiction to Sahlins's thesis then leads him to explain that

> politically the American citizenry differ from the Hopi in this: they have a 'Common Power to keep them all in awe'; a Government which precludes that anyone take the law in his own hands, thus keeps the Peace. Tribes such as the Hopi lack a sovereign political and moral authority; the right to use force ... if not the inclination, is instead held by the people in severalty. Technically, this is an internal social condition of Warre. Expressed another way, in the language of older philosophy, the United States is a state, the tribe a state of nature. Or, the United States is a *civilization*, the tribe a *primitive* society.[46]

Continuing in this vein, Sahlins sees the state as the key dividing line in history, more important than any technological or cultural difference, such as the invention of writing, or the establishment of cities. For him, 'The state differentiates civilization from tribal society. The development of civilization was nothing less than a transformation in quality of the social system.'[47] Specifically because of its size, heterogeneity and internal divisions, there is a need for 'special means of control and integration. ... The cultural richness that we call civilization has to be instituted in state form.'[48]

Finally, extending the evolutionary perspective to the limit, returning anthropology to its professional antecedents in organic models, and re-echoing past Darwinian themes that once so characterized the social sciences in the formative stages, Sahlins writes, 'Government is to the social organism as the central nervous system is to the biological organism. Just as in biological evolution, only a certain minimum of cultural complexity was possible prior to the development of a central, sovereign mechanism ... (to complete the analogy, a tribe is an animal without a central regulative system).'[49] In response to these assertions, I do not intend to detail, at this stage, the fullness of social order within tribal systems. Suffice it to note Antony Allott's comment that 'Traditional customary laws on the whole achieved much fuller compliance than modern western laws. ... If there is to be a comparison, modern systems of law come worse out of it. The case against customary Laws and against the existence or efficacy of legal norms in small societies is not made out.'[50]

Having relied on Hobbes for his model of primitive society, Sahlins is then quick to dissociate himself from some of Hobbes's more extreme statements, such as the oft-quoted remark on life in primitive societies being 'nasty, brutish and short' – but in backtracking he seems to undo the very theoretical framework of law, order and stability in states as opposed to an anarchical tendency to violence and strife in tribes that he has so painstakingly built up.

So, on the one hand, Sahlins explains his theme in pithy form; '...where force is held in severalty, the society is inadequately organized to bear an elaborate cultural development. Here is a key to the comparative limitations of tribal society, and to the evolutionary significance of the State'[51] – but, on the other hand, he has to acknowledge that the Hobbesian 'war of every man against every man *has never happened*' (italics in original), and thus concedes also as an explanation that 'tribesmen live in kin groupings and communities within which feuding is usually suppressed, and they have benefit too of economic, ritual and social institutions conducive to good order'.[52] If all this is true, then what is Sahlins's basis for the sharp distinction he draws between tribes and states or civilizations?

Here psychology, basically Freudian, comes to his aid, for we must, according to Sahlins look beyond the outer and superficial picture of order at the unconscious elements. Thus, while 'Primitive anarchy is not the appearance of things [it] is the unconscious of the system. Yet as the outward behavior of a person may not be intelligible except as the transfiguration of unconscious desires, so the objective organization of tribal society may only be understood as the repressive transformation of an underlying anarchy. Many of the special patterns of tribal culture become meaningful precisely as defense mechanisms, as *negations of Warre.*'[53]

And then the *pièce de résistance* – 'For in a situation of Warre where every man is empowered to proceed against every man, peacemaking cannot be an occasional inter-tribal event. It becomes a continuous process, going on within society itself.'[54]

Now, with all due respect, this is close to double-talk. Mechanisms that are moderate and mediative, which tribes all over the world have developed to maintain order, to resolve conflicts and to dispense justice, generally to the satisfaction of all, often through consensual processes, become for Sahlins, some desperate attempt to control the hidden passions and the egoistic urges that drive the tribesmen; implying in contrast, that in modern states, there are no similar urges and passions, and as though the aforementioned large, heterogeneous, and internally divided people in a civilized state just willingly go ahead casually handing control to a benevolent and all-powerful sovereign; as though, then, the outward semblance of order in a state does not hide the power which resides in the central authority, in fact, sometimes even naked power repressively and secretly implemented.

To give two random examples chosen from different types of large modern states: The Soviet Union had several decades of relative quiet, while the kulaks were killed for opposing collectivization in agriculture, opponents were dispatched to Siberia, and dissidents hospitalized in psychiatric hospitals. Finally the 1980s and 1990s brought out the seething sectarian tensions, which had only been kept in check by the governmental institutions of a powerful and repressive sovereign state.

Or the manner in which the tranquil 1950s in the United States erupted in the social unrest of the 1960s as the underprivileged and the dispossessed acted out their anger and frustrations on the streets and ghettos of the state. Was the seeming tranquillity and complacency of the Continental United States in the decade of the 1950s merely an 'appearance of things', to use Sahlins's terminology, hiding an anarchy ('advanced' and not 'primitive'?), as the 'unconscious of the system', or were the ensuing riots of the 1960s any less an example of Hobbes's 'Warre' that Sahlins so eagerly imposes so exclusively on tribal societies. Or what of the violence in Los Angeles as a reaction to the acquittal of several policemen of an attack on an arrested citizen, filmed on video? Was it a temporary breakdown of outer law and order, or was it an expression of widespread resentment, much of it bottled up because of fear?

Sahlins presents tribal societies as lacking orderly government, as though all modern states have succeeded in truly representing their subjects, as though they too are not involved in continuous efforts at peace-making, as though 'law and order' is not a captivating political catch phrase that is often electorally successful precisely because of perceptions and apprehensions of its actual or imminent breakdown.

Even the intricate manner, so lauded by many anthropologists, by which economic relations often are not limited to mere utilitarian considerations but are oriented to the cementing of social relations, is denigrated by Sahlins, who sees this not as being a positive contribution to desirable social harmony, but, in the negative sense, of being no more than an effort to avoid strife. The relations are done 'in the interest of peace. The issue is peace'[55] – itself, of course, perfectly reasonable, but for Sahlins negatively represented as the conscious and desperate effort to control the inevitable tendency to strife. They seek peace not for its intrinsic value, but so as to avoid the 'Warre' always lurking threateningly around the corner. And all this one must presume (even though Sahlins does not himself specify it) in contrast to citizens of modern states who apparently eagerly pay their taxes, so that the dedicated police may carefully perform their tasks at the behest of respected politicians loyally serving their satisfied constituents. Sahlins does not write in this vein, but this is the succinct essence of the implications of his negative appraisal of tribal society. If state grows out of tribe, then, of course it does so, *inter alia*, to avoid its unfortunate qualities, as described by Sahlins.

Thus Sahlins also explains that in contrast to the 'Peace' of modern states 'In Warre, the strategic alternative is to be nice or be prepared to fight.'[56] And so Sahlins also presents reciprocal economic exchanges, sophisticated kinship relations, religious rituals, as oriented to keeping the Peace in the face of the ever-present danger of Warre – peace, then, not as an expression of ultimate harmony, but as a desperate attempt to avoid the Warre, always lying close to the surface, always threatening to erupt. To sum up in Sahlins's own words:

> But enough said. The meaning is clear and needs no more repetition.
>
> I have tried to show you that civilizations differ from tribes by virtue of their specialized political institutions, their government, which sovereign, assume the power and right to protect the citizenry and maintain peace within the state. In tribal societies control of force is not withheld from the people, they are in that condition Hobbes called Warre, which is a fatal condition if not checked. Lacking specialized institutions of law and order, tribes must mobilize the generalized institutions they do have to meet the threat of Warre. Economics, kinship, ritual and the rest are so enlisted. In the process, by undertaking this political function, tribal institutions develop particular forms and particular expressions, different and curious perhaps, but each and all understandable as diplomatic arrangements

> for keeping a modicum of peace. Such is the wisdom of tribal institutions.[57]

I have devoted quite some space to Sahlins's analysis, even though it is not part of any major work; its importance lies precisely in it being a summary statement of conventional wisdom of a profession, set out in a series entitled the 'Foundations of Modern Anthropology', of which he himself is the editor. The series is in the mold of evolutionary thought, which in itself is reasonable, except when it becomes all-embracing, with all the defects that such a theoretical framework evokes. In an earlier work I have tried to deal critically with just such similar errors on the part of Durkheim, Weber and Marx, who, whatever their differences, and whatever their individual achievements, are all hidebound by the evolutionary framework within which they worked.[58] Thus I have suggested that Durkheim erred in seeing modern law as being restitutive and ignoring its repressive elements, that Weber erred in his stress on the unique rational quality of modern society and modern law, and that Marx was, for all his critique of modern capitalism, nevertheless attracted by its historical function of serving as the transitory stage to communistic society, and therefore deprecating of simpler societies.

Yet the problem with Sahlins's work goes even deeper, for while intent on describing the desperate striving for Peace so characteristic of the tribal societies that he describes, he makes no reference to the growing accumulation of anthropological research in the anthropology of law, which describes the manner in which it is not the fear of violence, but the search for harmony, that so characterizes primitive societies. Further, that though technologically simple, they possess far more than the rudimentary structure of government; on the contrary they have well-recognized and widely respected institutions. It is this kind of evidence that presents a vastly different picture of 'primitive' traditional societies than that portrayed by the founding theorists of sociology, or those still writing in a narrow evolutionary spirit.

Indeed, if this is the negative, condescending manner in which tribal society is to be presented, then it is no wonder that those eager to further the interests of their members are so reluctant to use its terminology. But in doing so they may well be doing a serious disservice to the very cause they wish to advance. For in rejecting the term because of the negative way it has been used by politicians and administrators, and because of the negative connotations that flow from some of the academic and theoretical descriptions, they are creating a real danger that what will remain is the negative image, partly because of the fact that not sufficient attempt is made to remove it, since the term itself is in any case considered undesirable. And so the negative attributes then become attached to the new term that is used, inasmuch as it deals with what were formerly called tribes. Only if there is continual use of the original term is it likely that there will be a concerted effort made to remove the negative images that attach to it, and to present it in its positive aspects. Changing the concept does not necessarily change the stigma. Indeed the new term often soon takes on the stigma of the former term. Those who proudly use the term 'Third World' as an indication of just struggle against the 'First World', and who believe it is so superior to a former term such as the developing world, should note the extensive use in that very First World of the term Third World in a demeaning manner to connote backwardness, stagnation, economic disaster and political anarchy.

More than that, they might also ponder the term's recent popularity in the light of the comments by Peter Calvocoressi that by 1980

> the concept of a Third World was becoming obsolete. A new group of countries had come into being whose wealth distinguished them dramatically from the world's poor and whose solidarity enabled them to play a forceful role in international affairs. This was the Fourth World of Opec. ... They were developing countries which were rich in cash.[59]

Having posited tribe in contrast to state, I should stress that my intention is not to dismiss the state; I certainly sense no anarchist future in which the state will disappear. What I wish to argue is the need to present the state in proper perspective, including especially its limitations, for only thereby will it be possible, I believe, to fully understand the nature and the role of tribes in the modern world, irrespective of whatever appellation is applied to them; or for that matter also for other constituent social categories found within the modern state. The problematics of the term 'tribe' can only be partly resolved when the problematics of the term 'state' are fully perceived.

In terms of Sahlins's presentation – any attempt to present 'tribesmen' as seeking peace only as a makeshift solution to the constant presence of 'Warre', while conversely hinting that 'modern civilized men' tranquilly go about their lives protected by the unseen, but ever-present, hand of benevolent state power – which is the essence of Sahlins's message – is a parody of reality; not just of tribe as noted but also of civilized society, with its obsession, of how to cope with what Sahlins, quoting Hobbes, calls 'Warre' – with its private security services, with its bodyguards for politicians and business executives, with sophisticated alarm systems protecting homes and businesses, with its market in small weaponry for personal safety, with its insurance policies against personal victimization, with its innovative measures such as neighborhood watches, with its dilemmas about desirable bystander behavior in the face of crime.[60] The injustice done to tribal society seems in fact far less than the excessive partiality that Sahlins, by implication, displays to 'civilized' society, with its presumed orderly government institutions.

Only if we come to terms with the inaccurate descriptions, only if we can see beyond the ensuing reluctance to recognize tribe that these inaccuracies engender, only then can we begin to confront realistically and meaningfully the prospects for tribal life (under whatever name) in the modern world.

Two of the most significant efforts in this regard are the broad range of opinions with contrasting viewpoints, carefully worked out, in the anthology edited by Peter Gutkind,[61] and the thoughtful and penetrating presentation by Marxist anthropologist, Maurice Godelier.[62] The latter, indeed, while not at all enamored of the concept of tribe, does note the shortcomings of many of the critiques of tribe, especially those that are conceived within an evolutionary framework. Thus he briefly and critically mentions a number of the protagonists in the debate:

> It is not enough, like Swart or Turner, to ignore the concept of tribe by referring no longer to it; to appeal to prudence, like Steward; or to criticize its scandalous imprecision (Neiva), its theoretical sterility and fallacies (Fried), its ideological manipulation as a tool in the hands of colonial powers.[63]

Then mentioning specifically the work of Sahlins, Godelier suggests that there are both theoretical and empirical deficiencies in his work and so '... add the limitations of the one to the weakness of the other'.[64] Godelier suggests that the exploitation of a concept for ideological ends cannot lead to its demise, even if as a result it becomes 'a concept which fails to recognize the reality it expresses. The concept itself is quite innocent of its own effects ...'.[65] Further he notes that

> 'difficulties' in concepts of 'tribe' and 'tribal society' are not isolated or unique. They are found in other guises as adjacent or like concepts are made clear: concepts of 'band,' of 'stateless society,' concepts designating other forms under which the social relations of other societies appear and around which people build general schemes of the social evolution of mankind. For this reason we cannot hope to improve on the concept of tribe, cure it of all of its ills in isolation: we must consider other concepts and improve them all in turn.[66]

Finally he concludes that

> we shall not be able to get rid of the difficulties involved in the content of the concept of tribe; we cannot silently bury it with a mere death sentence, or stigmatize those who continue to use it with the epithet 'infamous' empiricism. In so far as new concepts will not appear to resolve our problem, this concept of the 'tribe' will continue

> to be used in more or less refined forms and will deliver the same goods and the same kind of bad service. Until *it loses its* object it will not lose its *place*.[67]

Parallel with the effort to improve the scientific enquiry, in fact as a direct consequence of such activity, he argues that:

> We must continually attack the political and ideological manipulations by which the concepts of 'tribe' and 'tribalism' are used as a tool by the powers who dominate and oppress the young nations of the Third World. These powers often make it seem that tribal conflicts are modern contradictions which have their origins in the functioning of pre-colonial structures, in fact, these conflicts are explainable primarily by reference to colonial domination. While we must not fall into this trap and, in the name of anthropology, become accomplices of such arrant nonsense let us not forget that their value as evidence and political practicality derives from the structural characteristics of former societies of the Third World and from their development. A scientific analysis of these structural characteristics is therefore not a disinterested exercise of pure thought, it is an urgent task involving thought and practical reasoning.[68]

I would suggest that the prospects of doing so are far more likely after examination and evaluation of the nature of tribe *per se* and of the manner in which the term is now being used, than as a result of any outright rejection and wholesale denunciation In fact, Godelier himself, in later chapters of the book, carefully analyzes Marxian approaches to primitive society; and this section of the book is entitled 'Dead and Living Ideas in Marx's Thinking on Primitive Society.'[69]

In the book edited by Gutkind there is a balanced debate, in which the majority of the participants adopt a stance critical of the term 'tribe', with varying degrees of intensity, while a minority of the writers argue for its validity. The nature of the debate in general is well presented in the opening sentence of the preface, where Gutkind quotes from one of the participants, Clyde Mitchell: 'The emotions aroused by the topic of 'tribalism' in erstwhile colonial countries has made it a topic outside objective scientific enquiry'[70] – but as Gutkind himself adds, this particular collection of articles avoids, for the most part, the faults that have affected the work of others.

One of the most interesting and revealing contributions is by Herbert Chitepo, a political activist, formerly involved in the political struggle for the independence of Zimbabwe, who explains that definitions of 'tribe' inevitably 'reflect an implicit subjective judgement by the user of the word that people he is talking of are "primitive," that is to say, underdeveloped, backward and even inferior – certainly to himself – for whoever heard anyone call himself primitive.'[71] Perhaps, on this last score, somebody might wish to do so if he were to read the important work on the primitive by those authors,[72] as noted earlier, who expound on the importance of primitivity and its many advantages, particularly in the modern world. But aside from such a critical approach, the definition of tribe does not necessarily correlate with primitive or even backwardness, certainly not with inferior – except by those who twist it for their own ends, or those who, surrendering to these distortions, then relate critically to the term within these narrow confines.

In contrast Aidan Southall, though also critical of the concept, rightly notes some of its ambiguity: 'It is in the political context that tribalism is regarded with particular disfavor and in a number of social and economic contexts also. But those who rightly stigmatize the carryover which is tribalism in these contexts would in others often favor it, especially with respect to certain family values and to aesthetic modes of expression, as for example in music, dancing and plastic arts.'[73] But the issue of tribalism is, of course, not just of arts and culture – it is also of religious beliefs and rituals, of customary practices and law, of philosophical concepts of land and ecology, of kinship patterns and familial relationships, of economic interactions and obligations, and of group loyalty and allegiance. These are some of the real issues of tribes – and they are so real and meaningful that they have survived the years of colonial dispossession, of political subjugation and of personal and group humiliation.

However, Southall concludes that Western anthropologists will have to learn to adapt themselves to the approaches of their non-western colleagues 'whose fathers or grandfathers were members of non-literate societies, to remove "the colonial taint", and to reject the uses of the terms "primitive" and "tribe" in reference to societies in the modern world, and to replace them with the term "ethnic group".'[74]

Yet it is specifically an African anthropologist, Victor Uchendu,[75] in the very next chapter of the anthology, who pleads for the right of tribal people to be heard and respected. And, perhaps most pertinently, he challenges not only western anthropologists but African intellectuals who fail to ask tribespeople about their needs and desires. And so Uchendu argues pointedly that 'the dreams and the frustrations of the African elite must not be misplaced'[76] on to those still living in the tribe. He argues that the tribesperson 'is heir to rich and diverse cultures, [yet] is still pictured as living in an undifferentiated, small-scale, society where social experience and historical processes are assumed to impinge equally on all bearers of tribal cultures'.[77] Important as it is to combat the negative impressions, it is no less essential to ensure the presentation of the 'rich and diverse cultures'.

Indeed, Uchendu cuts through to the heart of the issue of tribalism in modern Africa, claiming that much of the tribal tensions that have arisen have been as the consequence not of inherent circumstances linked to tribal differences, but a consequence (similar to processes that occur in many other plural societies even without tribes) of overlapping inequities and inequalities, where 'Imbalance in development is noted … between one ethnic group or region and the other'.[78] In fact, part of the reason for the resurgence of 'tribal nationalism' is the awareness of inequality in some of the newer states. He also warns against those 'among the elite who denounce "tribalism" though they exploit tribal sentiments in order to establish their tribal base'.[79] Finally Uchendu ends with a plea to allow the tribal people themselves, those still living in their traditional settings, to determine the rate of development, and specifically which of their institutions they wish to change, and which they wish to retain.

In a further contribution to the anthology, Colin Legum, a British journalist, with much knowledge of and experience in Africa, expresses the opinion that 'Tribalism is Africa's natural condition, and is likely to remain so for a long time to come.'[80] The basis for such a prognosis is the fact that similar ethnic groupings in Europe have sustained their identity and cohesion. Of course, Legum could have simplified his analysis by using the term 'ethnic group' as others have done instead of tribe, since these were the groups in Europe who were serving as his model. But Legum prefers retaining the term that has been applied extensively in Africa, and in fact essays a definition for the purpose of his essay – 'Tribalism', he writes, 'is the manifestation of over-riding group loyalties by members of culturally-affiliated society to locally-based interests, which involve tradition, land and opportunities for survival and growth.'[81] He notes a further crucial factor, that 'Tribalism must be distinguished from traditionalism. Traditional systems may pass away while tribal affiliations remain strongly entrenched in defence of ethnocentric interests … the 'tribal' factor cannot simply be abolished from the academic vocabulary … What is badly needed are agreed definitions among academics to fit the modern phenomena of "tribe" and "tribalism".'[82]

In addition, 'tribalism is not inherently anti-modern, even though its internal political system is basically pre-modern. Tribalism in Africa has largely survived in its present strength because of the willingness of traditional societies to meet the challenge of modernization by adaptation.'[83] Indeed, the most notable fact is that 'tribalism has by and large been either an active or at least an acquiescent participant in the process of modernization'.[84]

After carefully considering the pros and cons of different terminology, acknowledging the sensitivity of the debate over the term, and examining some of the empirical evidence, P.H. Gulliver, too, concludes that 'One great importance of tribalism lies in its intrinsic flexibility as a concept, and in its ability to represent a highly flexible social process: the tribe, variously defined according to circumstances and need, can be made the unit of reference, the banner, and the cluster of symbols, for groups of people involved in the manifold upheavals and opportunities in the contemporary world.'[85] And in terms of the legal problems of that world, the issue is how to preserve the living customs of a tribe, how to guarantee its group rights, how to assert the importance of its legal system, and how to protect its individual members from the intrusive, often repressive, power of a modern state, molded on the model of an alien culture.

NOTES

1. In the United States, for instance, there have been endless debates as to whether it is a society based on class or not. There have also been attempts to describe the society as being based on principles of caste, this at a time when there were many legal disadvantages imposed on Blacks. See Oliver Cox, *Class, Caste and Race: A Study in Social Dynamics* (New York: Monthly Review Press, 1959).
2. For a brief historical analysis see H.F. Morris, 'The Framework of Indirect Rule in East Africa', in H.F. Morris and James Read, *Indirect Rule and the Search for Justice: Essays in East African Legal History* (Oxford: Clarendon Press, 1972), p. 3.
3. Almost all radical movements encounter the problem of the relationship between leaders, particularly intellectuals and thinkers in the vanguard of a political struggle, and those on whose behalf they struggle. Socialist and national struggles in many parts of the world have been characterized by such difficulties, but they may take on added pertinence when dealing with indigenous people.
4. Will Herberg, *Protestant, Catholic, Jew: An Essay in American Religious Sociology* (Chicago: Chicago University Press, 1970).
5. For an anthology of articles dealing with such issues, see Leroy Vail (ed.), *The Creation of Tribalism in Southern Africa* (Berkeley: University of California Press, 1989).
6. Martin Chanock, *Law, Custom and Social Order: The Colonial Experience in Malawi and Zambia* (Cambridge: Cambridge University Press, 1985).
7. See David Lamb, *The Africans* (New York: Vintage, 1984).
8. See Frederick Forsyth, *The Biafra Story* (Harmondsworth, Middlesex: Penguin, 1969); for a personal viewpoint see C. Odemegwu Ojukwu, *Biafra: Selected Speeches with Journal of Events* (New York: Harper & Row, 1969).
9. B.O. Nwabueze, *Constitutionalism in the Emergent States* (London: C. Hurst, 1973).
10. Ibid., p. 83.
11. Ibid., p. 89
12. Ibid., p. 118. Because of the many tribes, Nwabueze basically favors federalism, but claims that the framework in Nigeria was badly set up. See also Ugbana Okpu, *Ethnic Minority Problems in Nigerian Politics: 1960–1965* (Uppsala: Studia Historica Upsaliensia, No. 88, 1977).
13. See Leo Kuper and M.G. Smith (eds), *Pluralism in Africa* (Berkeley: Berkeley University of California Press, 1969; and L. Kuper, *Race, Class and Power: Ideology and Revolutionary Change in Plural Societies* (London: Duckworth, 1974).
14. See, for instance, Dunstan Wai (ed.), *The Southern Sudan: The Problem of National Integration* (London: Frank Cass, 1973).
15. See, for instance, G.A. Ghurye, *The Scheduled Tribes* (Bombay: Bhaktal, 1963); Other groups protected are the Backward Classes and the Scheduled Castes. For a good discussion of the historical, legal and constitutional background to this preferential treatment, see G.P. Verna, *Caste Reservation in India: Law and the Constitution* (Allahabad, India: Chugh Publications, 1980). See also Marc Galanter, 'The Problem of Group Membership: Some Reflections on the Judicial View of Indian Society', *Journal of the Indian Law Institute* 4 (1962), p. 331.
16. Sec. 46 of the Constitution reads: 'The State shall promote with special care the educational and economic interests of the weaker sections of the people, and, in particular, of the

Scheduled Castes and the Scheduled Tribes, and shall protect them from social injustice and all forms of exploitation.'

17. See comments by Irving Horowitz in the Preface to the second edition of his book, *Three Worlds of Development: The Theory and Practice of International Stratification* (New York: Oxford University Press, 1966).
18. See N. Dyck (ed.), *Indigenous Peoples and the Nation-State: Fourth World Politics in Canada, Australia and Norway* (St Johns: Memorial University, 1985).
19. Nathan Glazer and Daniel Moynihan (eds), *Ethnicity: Theory and Experience* (Cambridge: Cambridge University Press, 1975), p. 24.
20. Talcott Parsons, 'Some Theoretical Considerations on the Nature and Trends of Change of Ethnicity', in Glazer and Moynihan, *Ethnicity*, p. 53.
21. William Petersen, 'On the Subnations of Western Europe,' in *Ethnicity,* p. 181.
22. Ibid., p. 181.
23. Ibid., p. 187.
24. Ibid., p. 208.
25. Colin Tatz, *Aborigines and Uranium and Other Essays* (Richmond, Victoria: Heinemann, 1982), p. 6; originally published as article, 'Aboriginality as Civilization', *The Australian Quarterly,* March 1981, p. 41.
26. See James Crawford, *The Creation of States in International Law* (Oxford: Clarendon Press, 1979). On the specific issue of the creation of constituent states within a larger federal state, see Eme Ekekwe, *Class and State in Nigeria* (Lagos, Longman, 1986), Part 4, 'The Debate on State Creation', pp. 154–94.
27. Morton Fried, *The Notion of Tribe* (Menlo Park, CA: Cummings, 1975), preface.
28. Ibid., pp. 3–5.
29. Ibid., p. 5
30. Ibid., pp. 5–6
31. Stanley Diamond, *In Search of the Primitive: A Critique of Civilization* (New Brunswick, NJ: Transaction Books, 1974).
32. Ibid., p. 119.
33. Ibid., p. 160.
34. Robin Clarke and Geoffrey Hindley, *The Challenge of the Primitive* (New York: McGraw-Hill, 1975), p. 9. See also Pierre Clastres, *Society Against the State* (New York: Urizen Books, 1977).
35. Ashley Montagu (ed), *The Concept of the Primitive* (New York: Free Press, 1968), p. 1.
36. Ferdinand Tönnies, *Community and Society* (East Lansing: Michigan State University Press, 1957).
37. See Robert Nisbet, *The Quest for Community* (London: Oxford University Press, 1953).
38. See, for instance, Stephen Mulhall and Adam Swift, *Liberals and Communitarianism* (Oxford: Blackwell, 1992).
39. Fried, *The Notion of Tribe,* p. 113.
40. Marshall D. Sahlins, *Tribesmen* (Englewood Cliffs, NJ: Prentice-Hall, 1968).
41. Ibid., p. 4. This is not an isolated quote. Elsewhere Sahlins writes 'having bit deeply into native custom, civilization allows itself the luxury of an intellectual digestion: the primitives are largely anthropologized (so anthropology, as one amateur practitioner cynically observed, becomes an inquest into the corpse of one society presided over by members of another).

    'If the world today belongs to nation-states to do with what they will, in a similar way several thousand years ago it had fallen to tribal peoples. The spread of modern civilization has been likened to an evolutionary success story; the rise, extension, and diversification of an advanced type, spelling the displacement of primitive types.' (pp. 1–2). Lest there be any doubt as to who are the referents, it should be noted that Sahlins speaks of tribesmen being farmers or herders, that is beyond the stage of hunting and gathering herds, and provides a map of those 'tribes' included in his survey. Among the 49 tribes mentioned, from all corners of the globe are Azonde, Bedouin, Cheyenne, Comanche, Creek, Crow, Fijons, Fulani, Hawaiians, Herero, Hopi, Hottentot, Iroquois, Lapps, Maori, Masai, Mongols, Navaho, Nuer, Sioux, Tahitians, Tallensi, Tiv, Tongans, Trobriands, and Zuni.

    Let me stress: my aim is to show that there is worth in the culture of these and other tribes, and to suggest how the legal system may grant recognition to their customs.
42. Ibid., p. 5.

43. Ibid., p. 5.
44. Ibid., p. 5.
45. Ibid., p. 5.
46. Ibid., p. 5 (italics in original).
47. Ibid., p. 5.
48. Ibid., p. 6.
49. Ibid., pp. 6–7.
50. Antony Allott, *The Limits of Law* (London: Butterworths, 1980), pp. 66–7.
51. Sahlins, *Tribesmen*, p. 7.
52. Ibid., p. 7.
53. Ibid., pp. 7–8 (italics in original).
54. Ibid., p. 8.
55. Ibid., p. 9.
56. Ibid., p. 9.
57. Ibid., pp. 12–13.
58. See my *Social Cohesion and Legal Coercion: A Critique of Weber, Durkheim and Marx* (Atlanta, GA, and Amsterdam: Rodopi, 1997). See also Leon Sheleff, 'From Restitutive Law to Repressive Law: Durkheim's Division of Labour Revisited', *European Journal of Sociology* 16 (1975), p. 16; and 'The Illusions of Law: Psychoanalysis and Jurisprudence in Historical Perspective', *International Journal of Law and Psychiatry* 9 (1986), p. 143.
59. Peter Calvocoressi, *World Politics Since 1945* (London: Longman, 1987) (5th edn.). However, it should be noted that Calvocoressi is himself guilty of using loose language, when referring to the rich developing Opec countries as the Fourth World, a term that has been in wide use for some time to refer to indigenous tribal people.
60. See Lillian Rubin, *Quiet Rage: Bernie Goetz in a Time of Madness* (New York: Farrar, Straws and Giroux, 1988). On bystander behaviour and community protection, see Leon Sheleff, *The Bystander: Behaviour, Law, Ethics* (Lexington, MA: Lexington Press, 1978).
61. Peter Gutkind (ed.), *The Passing of Tribal Man in Africa* (Leiden: E.J. Brill, 1970). The book is a reprint of *Journal of Asian and African Studies* (1970) vol. 5, nos. 1 and 2.
62. Maurice Godelier, *Perspectives in Marxist Anthropology* (Cambridge: Cambridge University Press, 1977), Chapter 3: 'The Concept of the "Tribe": A Crisis Involving Merely a Concept or the Empirical Foundations of Anthropology Itself,' pp. 70-98. In general, see also his *Marxism and Anthropology: The History of a Relationship* (Oxford: Clarendon Press, 1983).
63. Godelier, *Perspectives in Marxist Anthropology*, p. 90.
64. Ibid., p. 90. Godelier also argues, in direct contrast to Sahlins, that, 'there is no evolution 'in general'; nor is there a "general evolution" of mankind … History is not the story of how a term or organism develops'.
65. Ibid., p. 95.
66. Ibid., p. 95.
67. Ibid., pp. 95–6 (italics in original).
68. Ibid., p. 96.
69. Ibid., p. 99.
70. Gutkind, *Passing of Tribal Man* at ft. 32, p. 1, quoting from article by Clyde Mitchell, 'Tribe and Social Change in South Central Africa: A Rational Approach', p. 83. See also his lecture, *Tribalism and the Plural Society* (London: Oxford University Press, 1960).
71. Herbert Chitepo, 'The Passing of Tribal Man: A Rhodesian View', in Gutkind, *Passing of Tribal Man*, p. 10.
72. See notes 32–35.
73. Aidan W. Southall, 'The Illusion of Tribe', in Gutkind, *Passing of Tribal Man*, p. 30.
74. Ibid., pp. 47–8. He adds that 'This may be a case in which human feelings have to prevail over strict logic.'
75. Victor C. Uchendu, 'The Passing of Tribal Man: A West African Experience,' in Gutkind, *Passing of Tribal Man*, p. 63.
76. Ibid., p. 63.
77. Ibid., p. 63.
78. Ibid., p. 64.
79. Ibid., p. 57. He also notes the arguments by some that anthropologists 'should not explore

those issues which divide modern Africa' (p. 57).

80. Colin Legum, 'Tribal Survival in the Modern African Political System' in Gutkind, *Passing of Tribal Man*, p. 102.
81. Ibid., p. 103.
82. Ibid., p. 103.
83. Ibid., p. 103.
84. Ibid., p. 103.
85. P. H. Gulliver (ed.), *Tradition and Transition in East Africa: Studies of the Tribal Element in the Modern Era* (London: Routledge & Kegan Paul, 1969), p. 35. See also some of the articles included in this anthology: W.J. Argyle, 'European Nationalism and African Tribalism,' pp. 41–58; G. Bennett, 'Tribalism in Politics', pp. 59–88; E. Cotran, 'Tribal Factors in the Establishment of the East African Legal Systems', pp. 127–46. For a good overview of the subject at the textbook level, see Roger M. Keesing, *Cultural Anthropology: A Contemporary Perspective* (New York: Holt, Rinehart and Winston, 1981) (2nd edn.), Part 3, 'Tribal Peoples: Towards a Systematic View' pp. 109–74: and Part 4, 'The Tribal World: The Legacy of Human Diversity', pp. 175–376.

4

Whither the State?

The problem associated with groups of people seeking pluralistic forms is not limited to the semantics of confused terminology, inaccurate presentations and overlapping concepts. While it is important to clarify the manner in which terms are used, the real issue is a substantive one, and it is this issue that we must now address in this chapter.

Whatever the nature and the variety of states, and whatever the appellation to be applied to those groups that have traditionally been known as tribes, the key issue that needs examination is whether these two forms of framework are compatible with each other, and how – if there is the will to do so – the state can accommodate itself to the demands and the needs of tribal groupings existing within its borders. There should, however be no illusions on this score; more than any other human groupings – language, religion – tribe poses a threat to the state. It is theoretically at least, far more comprehensive and more embracing than other conceptual groupings, and far more than them it offers an alternative source of authority and of allegiance, one which is not focused on only one particular aspect of social life, such as belief system as for religion or means of communication as for language, but which touches on both religion and language, and in addition on obligatory customs dealing with family life, economic arrangements, social control, concepts of property ownership, rights to land and environmental consciousness.

It is specifically this that differentiates tribe, by whatever name, and ethnicity, again by any name. Whatever the overlap and similarities, tribe, both in its historical context and in its present potentialities, offers an alternative means of providing those qualities and properties that are characteristic of a state, and, in particular for the purposes of this essay, its legal system.

It is true that in many respects, ethnicity, too, may be considered to be all-embracing, to pose a threat to the state and to deal with the nature of customs. At the lowest level, it may involve the need to determine judicially which customs to recognize or not – and in England, for instance, the influence of many immigrants, or even visitors, has often led to litigation in the courts, as set out so well by Sebastian Poulter.[1]

More significantly, ethnic groups, when they are really nations, or claim to be such, may strive for self-determination and independence, or autonomy of various degrees. In these cases, the problem is usually resolved (not always entirely to everybody's satisfaction) in a formal dispensation, carefully spelled out in legal terms. Beyond this, it could, of course, lead to a dissolution of the state where the ethnic group defines itself as a nation, claims the right to self-determination, and translates this into a declaration of independence.[2]

But going beyond this, there are ideological and theoretical implications that make the nature of interaction between tribe and state vastly different. Firstly, in historical terms, it is widely held, especially by those who see historical development as being an evolution in stages, that the tribe was a precursor to the state,[3] a stage in the onward march of human history, which, in a world of nation-states, has fulfilled its historical role, except for a number of basically irrelevant groupings, living on the margins of society, scattered in various places all over the world, and numbering *in toto* no more than a few tens of millions, with many of them in any event being drawn inexorably into the vortex of modern industrial and technological life.[4]

It is partly on this basis that there is such a great insistence on the choice of ethnicity over tribe. The latter seem to indicate some sort of atavistic regression into a dwindling past. What I wish to suggest is that the concept of tribe, the existence of tribe, is perfectly compatible with the needs of a state. Tribe and state may coexist in the modern world. The 'threat', if so be it, is not to the existence of the state *per se*, but to the nature of the state. True pluralism must come to terms with this fact. In the earlier chapters I suggested that in the clash of custom and law, it was law that might well be more problematical than custom; similarly, it may well be that it is state that is more problematical than tribe. To probe this issue, it is necessary to examine the essence of what is a state – its sovereignty. However, it is specifically on this issue that there are differing conceptions, some of which are antagonistic to the idea of a shared control and authority, others of which are compatible. This, it seems to me, is the crux of the issue over the place and role of tribal customs in the legal systems of the modern world.

We have noted already how some states are shedding some of their sovereignty in terms of their external powers – by voluntarily submitting themselves to the surveillance of larger supranational authorities. Can the state similarly divest itself of some of its internal sovereignty – as is basically the case in federal systems? Can such concessions be made by a state not on the basis of geographical entities, precisely mapped out, as in a federal system, but in respect of looser amorphous groupings, as in a true pluralistic framework?

There are varying definitions of sovereignty, but the two dominant ones refer, on the one hand, to the source of authority stemming from the state as such, focused on its central organs of government, and, on the other hand, of an attribution of sovereignty to the people who make up the state, who are considered to be the font of whatever power and authority is granted to those in temporary charge of its daily running and its fortunes.

These two conceptions are deeply embedded in philosophical discourse as to the ultimate legitimacy of the state and those who wield power within its framework. They emerged as a result of a centuries-old battle between various groups within society, for instance the church and monarchy, or the aristocracy and the common people, or between a territorial entity and those on the periphery. In recent years the issue of sovereignty has centered around where, within the state, it truly resides, with the people or the organs of government.

This is well brought out in an article by Xavier Arlos[5] who discusses the role of Leon Duguit[6] in outlining the nature of the dilemma. Duguit presented the First World War as being a struggle between 'two forms of social life'[7] – that represented by Germany in which sovereignty belongs to the state, and the nation is but an organ of the state, and that represented by France in which sovereignty resides with the nation, and the government is subject to its will.

Duguit's own approach to the issue of sovereignty was influenced by the increasing role of the government in the lives of its citizens. This process, according to him, must perforce, and paradoxically perhaps, involve a diminution of the state's sovereignty. It is specifically the state's increasing intervention in social life, and its expansion of services – education, public works and transport, central communications, social welfare – that must make it increasingly subject to legal restraint. The old form of sovereignty residing in the state was valid only for as long as its powers were limited to police, military and judicial functions. Since these interventions by the state have to be 'regulated and ordered by a system of public law … this system can no longer be based on the theory of sovereignty. Modern institutions … take their origin not from the theory of sovereignty, but from the notion of public service'.[8]

Arlos draws a distinction between the nation-state and the state-nation – the former emerging as a personification of the nation which was pre-existing, by virtue of its homogeneity in terms of culture, language, history, and the latter as an artificial construct, in which the idea of a nation only takes on substance in the wake of the creation of a state, the example he provides being that of Yugoslavia.

Bernard Susser and Eliezer Don-Yehiya[9] analyze the nation-state in its original form, emerging most conspicuously out of the French Revolution as an amalgam of the expression both of nationalistic fervor and commitment to democratic ideals. They argue that, in the modern world, there are few and dwindling examples of such dualistic structures – most democratic nations have become pluralistic; in essence, reneging on the nationalist base by allowing minority groups a degree of recognition. Leading off from this is the inverse situation where the attempt to make the people into one nation is done at the expense of democratic principles.

In an article which has had much impact, Walter Connor has argued that those intent on nation-building, especially in new states, have often ignored the power and the impact of ethnicity.[10] Inaccurate use of terminology, according to him, has led to an incapacity to even understand the nature of the phenomenon being discussed, and the power and the impact associated with it.

By calling such groups ethnic, and by defining states (at least initially) as nation-states, the term nationalism has been pre-empted for the latter and denied for the former. Yet it is nationalism that evokes an emotional response; indeed there is no parallel term of 'ethnocism' to signify the sentiments and feelings bound up with ethnic identity (which, it might be added parenthetically, may well be why the term has attained such widespread approval).[11] But, according to Connor, words have been used to create a façade that hides reality – until it erupts in factional struggle, as for instance in former Yugoslavia. For the linguistic logic would have long ago suggested a word such as statism to refer to the patriotism linked to citizenship, and reserving nationalism for true 'national groups', generally known as no more than ethnic.

Connor argues that scholars felt

> compelled to offer a substitute to describe loyalty to the nation. Regionalism, parochialism, primordialism, communalism, ethnic complementarity, and tribalism are among those that have been advanced. Unfortunately, however, the perpetuation of the improper use of the word nationalism to refer to devotion to the state, while using other terms with different roots, and with fundamentally different connotations to denote devotion to the nation, is hardly conducive to resolving the confusion surrounding the two loyalties. On the contrary, it is conducive to dangerously misunderstanding the magnetism and the staying power of ethnic viability, for those terms simply do not convey the aura of deeply felt, emotional commitment that nationalism does.[12]

Beyond that, one should note that some, at least, of the terms quoted have clear negative connotations, such as parochialism or primordialism.

Connor suggests that the fact of ethnicity is often ignored because it seems to threaten the process of nation-building. In other words, that the lack of a nation as the basis of a state, is part of the reason why efforts are made to ignore this reality, and by denying the existence of ethnic groups to avoid facing the reality that it is not a true nation-state. Indeed, in a passing statement, he notes that two of the few nation-states in the world are Germany and Japan, where state, nation, and ethnicity overlap (hinting also at possible unfortunate consequences that may emerge).

For Connor, ethnicity is not a mere impediment to nation-building, to be easily overcome by the force of communications and contact or by the pride of sentimental patriotism and progress; it is an ongoing reality, which may, if ignored, wreak havoc on the rhetoric of politicians and the supporting research of academics. He draws widely upon ethnic formation in different parts of the world to suggest that nation-building is inherently far more complicated than is often admitted – and some of his examples have taken on an added pertinence in recent years. He is particularly critical of those who have been in the forefront of the analysis of nation-building as it relates to newly independent countries.

He quotes from Karl Deutsch,[13] one of the foremost writers in this area (during the period of focus on development for new nations), to suggest that there is an implicit supposition of adaptation by ethnic groups to changing circumstances. Connor quotes from Deutsch in terms of the latter's specific reference to tribes as possessed of a critical capacity to change, this in an effort to suggest also their ability to be molded into a larger entity. Deutsch may indeed be correct in his assertion of a capacity to change, but the implications are not necessarily of total submergence in the new and larger reality of a state; this is indeed what is at issue – whether a tribe will submerge itself in the state, retaining no more than a loose identity as an ethnic group (for example, possessing, for instance, its own language, that differentiates it, posing no real problem when the official language of the country may well be that of the former colonial rulers), or whether it will seek to forge for itself a particularistic role, not necessarily in conflict with the state, or in submergence to it, but in harmonious partnership with it.

Deutsch's own model for the future is based on the historical parallel and precedent of tribes in Europe that were absorbed into larger groupings. He writes, and is fully quoted by Connor in this regard; 'Tribes, as we know from European history, can change their language and culture; they can absorb other tribes; and larger tribes came into federation or mergers of smaller tribes or through their conquest or absorption by a larger one.'[14]

In contrast to the picture of plasticity and change, Deutsch argues that many writings on African and Asian politics still seem to treat tribes as fixed and unlikely to change in any significant way in the near future. The implication here is that the nature of the change will be in the same direction as the tribes of Europe – that basically disappeared as close-knit entities, and became instead mere amorphous, ethnic groups.

Yet, it is possible for tribes to change, to become part of larger entities such as states, to adapt their way of life, and yet to retain the uniqueness of their tribal identity, without endangering the state, without having a divisive impact, without being involved in conflict with other tribal groupings, without the insistence on endogenous marriage patterns and exclusive membership rules, and without elevating the biological nexus to a supreme or sacred rule.[15] To succeed in avoiding all these pitfalls will indeed require the plasticity and capacity for change that Deutsch talks of, but – and this is what is lacking in the analysis – will require also a simultaneous and parallel ability on the part of states to adapt to a tribal reality. A mutual reassessment and an interactive remolding of the nature of both entities, raises prospects, serious and meaningful, of a new style of political settlement.

The fact that, in Europe, tribes were absorbed and disappeared is not necessarily a deterministic historical precedent for a repetition in Africa and Asia – or for that matter in America or Oceania. The state that absorbed was often indeed an empire, crumbling at that, and based often on a fragile concept of divine right. Whatever model of state is used today, that of a centralized state sovereignty, as in Duguit's model of Germany from the earlier part of this century, or that of popular sovereignty, à la France, according to Duguit, neither emerged out of a struggle against tribes, whatever their inroads as states into local communities. The struggle over tribes was determined many centuries before; and standard history records the process of the struggle of the 'barbarian hordes' threatening the civilized remnants of Greek and Roman civilization.

Yet it is not clear what a revisionist history may not deduce as to the way of life, and the value-system of the so-called 'barbarians',[16] or to what extent the remnant of the empire was a true guardian of the values and culture of the earlier civilizations. While the military struggle had diverse and conflicting results, the cultural outcome was largely the demise of tribal culture. There is no historical necessity that obligates a similar process of absorption and destruction in the modern world.

I have chosen to probe this issue in several different areas, basing myself on little-known articles that have appeared in local journals. Their importance lies in the persuasive power and logic of their analysis, and the attempt at general theorizing based on the empirical facts of localized circumstances. In addition, it seems to me that their importance lies also in their very marginality to the overall academic discourse. Their unique approaches, based partly on personal perceptions, deal with the dilemmas of those intimately involved in struggles and frustrations in crucial existential questions of identity and belonging.

The possibilities ensconced in such an approach – for both historical understanding and present-day politics – are ably brought out by the work of Peter Skalnik, which tentatively raises such issues to meaningful intellectual debate.[17] Based on one particular ethnic or tribal conflict in Ghana, Skalnik suggests that there is a deeper truth embedded in the conflict that he carefully describes.

From a theoretical point of view he draws a distinction between authority and state power. He describes the unfortunate consequences that are liable to flow from an injudicious and inequitable application of the latter, particularly in situations where the state itself lacks full legitimacy – not because of tribal loyalties, but because of its failure to function effectively in the daily lives of its citizens.

Skalnik openly challenges many of the truths abounding in Africa today with its state boundaries and state power. More importantly, though, he hints at an alternative model, which though it admittedly draws on only one case-study, may, as he suggests, be a symptom of similar processes existing elsewhere – as a result of which he suggests that there is an 'ultimate inadequacy of the concept of the "state" in indigenous Africa'.[18]

Discussing the nature of authority in the tribe under discussion, the Nanumba, he argues that, for them, the chief was not the source of power, but the embodiment of consensual authority – in terms of modern sovereignty, this could be presented as sovereignty residing not with the centralized power of the dominant figure, the chief, but with the people. Indeed, the very longevity of the situation – from pre-colonial times and into the post-independent state – was the result of it being a 'powerless authority of naam'.[19] He then goes on to describe the naam in the context of its continued survival within a larger political entity – whether under a foreign colonial power or in a modern independent state. 'Naam is not an opponent of imported state power, colonial or post-colonial, rather it is its virtual alternative. The two systems communicate with the people in their spheres in quite different languages. Power, seen as "illegitimate" and "violent", is an attribute of the state, and is alien to the authority of naam and its incumbents in Nanum and perhaps many polities of the "archaic" world seem to suggest examples of a social order more stable and a *sub specie aeternitatis* more acceptable and useful to all members than any historical form of the state. Therefore Nanum is not a state in the conventional Western understanding of the concept, whether we try to call it early, specific African or primitive.'[20]

Giving an example of how a state may disregard latent problems by ignoring the existence of social reality, Skalnik describes the move of many members of the Konkumba tribe into the area settled by the Nanumba. This in itself need not have led to problems, but a lack of sensitivity in recognizing differences in certain customs (involving *inter alia* procedures for the resolution of conflicts between neighbors) led to fighting, 'tribal fighting', in which the newcomers were basically victorious. Skalnik sees the violence as being an unnecessary escalation of problems that could easily have been peacefully and satisfactorily resolved, by judicious intervention based on proper understanding.[21]

But the essence of his message is far deeper and it deals with the nature of authority, and the role of typical political patterns in a modern state that has failed to function to the satisfaction of its citizens. He sums up the local situation as follows: 'the old conflicts were revived and new ones added. This happened proportionally with the extent that the "traditional" precolonial structures were destroyed and replaced by "modern" shortcut solutions introduced by the state ... local competing ethnic feelings won over the almost defunct state nationalism.'[22]

However this is more than a recipe for conflict resolution. Skalnik poses painful and penetrating questions for the existing and static political structure of Africa. He suggests a new approach to an understanding of the political failures that have so characterized Africa in the years of post-colonial independence. He writes: 'The explanation for the so often lamented instability of modern states in Africa and elsewhere in the underdeveloping world is to be sought in the struggle between their West-imposed state systems and the tenacious indigenous social and political institutions. I suggest that these African indigenous institutions show the world that without the state a society could function quite well, even better than with it.'[23]

Part of the tragedy of the present political situation in Africa is that 'the alien state model was imposed on the indigenous systems of authority with such a vigor that in many parts of the continent whole nations lost their identity and orientation'.[24]

Skalnik explains that his example forms one particular instance of an escalation of conflict into a violent struggle between two opposing and intermingling tribal groups; the research was carried out in order to 'investigate indigenous African alternatives to violent power',[25] so as to 'explain why modern Africa is so ridden with coups, tyrannies and atrocities'. He claims that 'The whole world can learn from African alternatives to violent power. The institutions of the authority of chiefs and elders, and the various institutionalized checks on these incumbents of authority, which spontaneously and independently developed in Africa and elsewhere, could serve as an inspiration to all.'[26]

Then, while not saying so specifically, Skalnik directly challenges those who see the tribe as an artificial construct, created to serve the needs of the colonial powers. Having already described how the chief's authority was basically an embodiment of social consensus, he then turns upside-down the contention of those who see the tribe as a colonial imposition by stating categorically that

> The purpose of the article has been to show that the State as a specific social and political phenomenon was 'invented' in Africa by outsiders

> because they were looking at African institutions like the Naam of the Nanumba through Eurocentrist eyes ... By labelling ... a certain kind of African political organization a 'state' one does disservice to African history and the Africans themselves because not only is African originality forced into a Eurocentrist strait-jacket but worst of all this bias denies the possibility that, in Africa, viable alternatives to the state, as it evolved in the West, may have developed. The state is by and large a Euro-Asian invention, whereas the Africans gave the world their systems of chieftainship or their ingenious systems of kinship-based organization.[27]

Skalnik's presentation opens up new possibilities for both academic theorizing and practical politics – but it raises perhaps more questions than it resolves. Going beyond the question as to whether his empirical data justify his conclusion, or whether one case-study provides a model for a total continent, the basic question is whether in Africa, the state is to be abandoned, as an irrelevant western invention, so that the ethnic group, known also as tribe, may reclaim its position of grandeur as the basic unit of social and political life; or whether the tribe, with its primordial tendencies and the pressures that they create for parochial concerns, should not be abandoned in favor of the state, even if it is a transplanted and alien invention; or whether an accommodation must be sought between the tribe representing the old traditions, and the state representing the basic unit of the modern world.

And what of the prospects of regional or continental unity? Will not an emphasis on the tribe undermine these strivings, as so articulately presented by some of the dominant figures – intellectual and political – of the first decades of African independence – including cultural concepts of negritude, philosophical manifestations of a special African road to socialism, and political yearnings for pan-African unity?[28]

Indeed, it is of no small interest to note that, while in Africa, the prospects of some overriding unity are receding (and the few attempts at partial, regional arrangements have generally broken down), the states of Europe have moved to closer unity, whether in the European Union or the larger culturally oriented Council of Europe, or even the pan-continental security organization. All this took place with little ideological trumpeting of a vaunted shared purpose,[29] that so characterized Africa in the 1960s and 1970s as hopes that the Organization of African Unity would move beyond a mere state-bound organization into a real union that was embodied and emblazoned in its name. As already pointed out, there is a paradox here of African states proudly guarding their new-found sovereignty, while their ex-colonial overlords move fairly rapidly into a newer and tighter association of states.

The point must be made crystal clear – it is not narrow parochial tribalism that is hindering Africa from reaching out into common markets, transnational courts of human rights, continental conventions on environmental protections, free passage between states; it is the existence of states, and the political leaders desperately trying to build up a loyalty among the citizens, often through one-party states, that, at this moment in history, might constitute the main stumbling-block to larger unity.[30]

From a sociological point of view, one could argue for layers of social reality – at the immediate personal level of the need to assure the individual of his human rights of free and unfettered expression of his autonomous self; then the need for expression of affinity and affection within an intimate familial setting, whether nuclear or extended; beyond that the need for membership as citizen in a state that will guarantee protection of rights and provision of basic social and economic needs; and ultimately the need for a larger striving at the continental and world level for a common recognition of shared humanity, the basis of those human rights that then revert back to the individual and his own individual rights.

In addition, there may be a need for a further layer, between family and state, that will answer to the needs of belonging;[31] this may be found in the form of membership of a religious or ethnic group, or even of an ideological or cultural entity – or of membership of a tribe, inasmuch as a distinction may be drawn, as I have argued, between ethnic group and tribe. To deny the support and vitality that such membership may provide is to negate one of the needs that are an essential of full social life.

For those without tribe, it is clear that religion or ethnicity or even language or ideological connections, provide adequate groupings[32] – but that is no reason why for those who have tribe as a membership category, they should be deprived of it merely because historically tribes seem to be doomed, as occurred in Europe, or because they seem to threaten the unity of a state, or because they conjure up pictures of primitivity.

The problem is not unique to Africa, though it certainly takes on different, if more acute, dimensions there, because of the nature of its pre-state society. The problem of belonging, the underlying tensions of artificially created states, lacking the attributes of nationhood, lacking a common language or a common belief-system, is rife throughout America, Asia and Oceania.

One of the outstanding examples is the Philippines, one of the only countries which is part of the Common Law system without ever having been under direct British control. It was during five decades of American control that the principles of the Common Law were introduced to the Philippines, but it was over the preceding three centuries of Spanish rule that the concept of a Philippine nation was forged.[33] Yet almost four hundred years of imposed unity has possibly not succeeded in creating the nation that is at the basis of the state – and the problem consists of fissions in terms of language, ethnicity, religion (a concentrated Muslim minority) and of tribe, in terms of the seven million people (about 15 per cent of the population) that are considered to be members of various tribes, mainly in some of the outlying islands of this archipelago state.

Fernando Zialcita makes a comparison between the Filipino nation and France, noting both the differences between them in their historical antecedents and in their present composition, and the problematics involved in the concept of the French nation as some sort of distinguishable entity.[34] Thus he notes that, on the one hand, French was spoken as a language in the neighboring states, Belgium and Switzerland, while, on the other hand, there are minorities in France itself which do not have French as their mother-tongue, such as the Basque, Breton and Provençal groups. The point he is trying to make is that the prototype western model of a nation-state, is not a pure one.

For the Philippines there is the further problem that, inasmuch as there is a common culture, it is one which is not limited to the boundaries of the state, but is shared with other members of what he terms Austronesian culture, such as Malaysia, Indonesia, Madagascar, Micronesia and Polynesia.[35] He stresses the differences between a nation and an ethnic group (for which he uses the term, ethnie). An ethnie (which itself may comprise several small ethnies) 'exists when people are aware of sharing a common fund of "myths, memories, values and symbols".'[36] However, according to Zialcita, the solidarity of a nation goes much deeper, partly because it is also sustained by a legal framework: 'A community of laws and legal institutions takes hold, applying to all without exception, regardless of creed, class or ethnic affiliation.'[37]

Since many consider France to be the epitome of the nation-state, the state in this case emerging from the nation, it is of some interest to note Zialcita's alternative explanation, itself presented specifically for its relevance to the present-day problem of Filipino nationalism, which is by no means a unique case. According to him, French nationhood was artificially created, based on Paris. He argues that 'The consciousness of being French was the child of an expanding central authority rather than its parent. To make newly incorporated subjects more pliant, the monarchy propagated symbols that made them feel more French, that is Parisian,. One such symbol was the French language, which was originally merely the dialect of the capital region. During the twelfth century, a formidable rival in the south was Provençal.'[38]

Relying on the work of the French historian, Fernand Braudel, he continues in this vein, stressing that, 'prior to the French Revolution, France was a collection of ethnies over which a favored ethnie, Parisian culture, was steadily gaining dominance. The French kings used other symbols in this ethnie to extend their prestige over newly incorporated realms.'[39]

The French revolution itself only partially changed this situation – the king was removed, the people were given power, but the process of incorporation and centralization continued. 'Thus the boundaries that the kings had acquired for their own selfish reasons were retained as factual givens. Moreover the revolutionary government continued the centralizing programs of the French Kings – through conscription, compulsory education, standardized weights and measures. 'The nation, as an imagined landscape that stretched back into the misty past and contained all who had lived and died in it, began to be universally accepted as a natural condition.'[40] So, according to this approach, French identity seems to have arisen historically from mythical and biological circumstances not different from what is often – negatively – ascribed to tribal peoples. Similar sentiments are expressed by J. Hayward in a perceptive analysis of the French political culture. He categorically states that

> France is a state-nation rather than a nation-state. The nation is an artifact of the state … . France is a unitary state superimposed upon a multinational society, the authority of Paris having been established under the monarchy, expanded by Napoleonic Empires and reinforced by the Republics over Alsacians, Basques, Bretons, Catalans, etc.[41]

Zialcita argues that similar processes of incorporation and centralization are at the core of the Filipino people – in this case, of course, originally artificially carved out by the Spanish, later embellished and entrenched by central political power from Manila. This itself led to further problems in the very capacity of the Filipino nation to emerge with a defined consciousness. 'The islandwide ethnie,' he writes, 'that first brought together hispanized Filipinos centered originally around loyalty to the Church and the Spanish monarchy. It excluded pagans and Muslims.' Later, however, 'the religious-based ethnie became a secular, Filipino nation'.[42] However the nation (like so many other newer nations) lacks many of the unifying symbols that characterized France and other European nations – a national language has not come about; the attempts to make Filipino/Tagalog the national language is a manifestation of centralized pressures, as it is the language spoken mainly in the Manila area – and so, 'It is not surprising that a Cebuano sense of nation, not necessarily separatist, is emerging in response to actions by the Philippine state.'[43]

In fact, he quotes from an interviewer who stated that there are many Cebuanos who take a pride in not speaking Tagalog (and, of course, English is still widely spoken, at least in the urban areas). It might be noted in this respect that while it is often considered that the mass media, in particular television and radio, may help bridge these differences (if it helps for a 'global village', why not for a 'national archipelago village?'),[44] the truth is that, specifically because these media are often state-owned, they can become counterproductive to creating a sense of nation, since the state is generally obliged to provide programming for the various languages, thereby from its powerful center, contributing to the babble of tongues.

Finally, just as in the case of Skalnik, Zialcita offers some generalized ideas that flow from his thought-provoking thesis: 'Because the nation is ultimately an artifact, continuing dialogue should be normative within it. There are no prior genetic or metaphysical bonds that can be appealed to. Commitment to the imagined community has to be renewed constantly.'[45]

This commitment will have, he claims, more chance of success if there is an understanding of those at the periphery of the nation, if there is an awareness of the differences among them and if there is a rejection of the myth held by some of an original Filipino nation that was only divided by colonialism.

In a summation that is relevant to many other new states, he asserts that 'Perhaps it is time to scrap the French model of national unity in all domains, starting with language, for it seems not to be workable in our context. Indeed it may not have worked well in France either. The famous instability of France over the past two hundred years has been aggravated by Paris' insistence on an abstract unity that ignores conflicting regional interests.'[46] He suggests an alternate model for meaningful nation-building, based on decentralized and local groupings.

Zialcita is not alone in his appraisal of the situation in the Philippines. Eric San Juan also proposes a re-examination of crucial terms since 'the nation itself is a social construct'.[47] In the Philippines 'The authority of the Philippines republic – the public good – remains to be legitimated in its local constituencies. The crux of the Filipino national problem here is state formation … not traditional kinship.'[48] It should be remembered that part of the specific problem of the Philippines is that it has no history of prior pre-colonial statehood, but this does not detract from the larger implications of the arguments being made in that context. It is possible that it is the uniqueness that helps to clarify factors and processes that may go unnoticed elsewhere.

In any event these arguments relate not only to the larger question of nationhood and its relation with local groupings (which is no more than the background for this book) but also have direct relevance for the legal situation and for the role of tribes, as is brought out vividly in Sidney Silliman's analysis of what he terms the 'Folk Legal Culture of the Cebuano Filipino'.[49] He notes the basic alienation of peasants in the outlying rural areas of the Philippines from the central norms, concerns and structures, of the state.

Whereas the other two writers quoted dealt with the overall problems of Filipino nationalism, Silliman focuses on the legal system as such, opening his article with the assessment that 'the roots of the Philippine national legal system do not run deep. Much of the rural population in the Philippines ... does not share in the emphasis of the national legal culture on procedural justice. In addition, the Western-style courts are only one among a variety of mechanisms – ranging from self-help to informal mediation by community leaders – by which people in the lowland Philippines process their disputes.'[50] This seems to be based not merely on the convenience and familiarity of the local customs but also on an alienation from, indeed an antagonism to, the national legal structure in which, so it is widely believed, 'The elite classes have a distinct advantage'.[51]

He notes the many reservations that ordinary Filipinos have as to the legitimacy of the national legal system – and, no less important, of the lack of research that is able to elucidate the sentiments that they have as to the preferable manner in which disputes should be resolved. There is, he argues, 'no significant investigation of what lowland Filipinos perceive as unjust or injurious circumstances; what they think is required to alleviate such wrongs; and what they understand as an acceptable method for righting a wrong. In other words, a major gap in our knowledge of the rule of law in Philippine society is what lowland Filipinos comprehend on justice.'[52]

His own research was aimed at eliciting such information from his interviewees; it could serve as a model for those who wish to understand how people in the margins of society relate to concepts of justice – it seems clear that what they actually prefer as a means for resolution of conflict are local processes aimed at the return to an amicable relationship.[53]

Silliman's work does not relate to tribes as such, and it is not clear whether the peasants interviewed could be defined as tribespeople or not – but there is no doubt that his research provides valuable insights into the possibilities of, and even need for, pluralism in the administration of justice.

This aspect of tribal life in the Philippines is well brought out in a detailed analysis by Lourdes Aranet-Sereno and Roan Libarios, of the struggle for land rights against the intrusiveness, and often the injustice, of the national legal system.[54] The impetus for the struggle was, according to the authors, 'the government's failure to understand and recognize indigenous systems of land ownership';[55] their summary appraisal is that the struggle over land rights has 'dramatized the inherent antagonism between the national and indigenous systems and concepts of land ownership'.[56]

Finally, an American jurist, Owen Lynch, who has carried out research in the Philippines, addresses the question of how to give specific recognition to indigenous legal systems.[57] He explains that:

> A small but growing sector of the Philippines legal community recognizes the need to reorient the national legal system and make it more reflective of indigenous juristic elements. This development emanates from an awakening pride in the beauty and practicality of indigenous Philippine culture, and a yearning for genuine national independence and self-determination. It reflects the increasingly clear perception that in most respects the present national legal system is not adequately founded on dominant native values. This, in turn, causes the national system to be culturally disruptive, and oftentimes even an accessory to the systematic destruction of indigenous legal systems and culture.[58]

Lynch's work is penetrating and original, the work of an outsider who laments the paucity of material by local writers, and the reluctance of local lawyers and anthropologists to probe deeply the nature of the indigenous local culture. He describes a dual process, where, on the one hand, 'subjugated Filipinos learned to disdain their cultural heritage and … national traditions and legal systems slowly withered',[59] while, on the other hand, at least in the rural areas, the indigenous legal systems endure in varying degrees.

The political impact of the legal situation, the perceived 'threat' to the state, and the need for a re-evaluation is brought out neatly in Robert Benedicto's contention that while the state is disregarding indigenous legal systems, the struggle over their validity as an accepted alternative to the dominant but inappropriate western legal model goes 'to the very core of our struggle for self-determination and nationhood'.[60] This struggle is by no means unique to the Philippines, despite its own special history, and its original imposed nationality, the product of foreign conquest and long-term domination.

The attempt to reorient legal thinking is taking place in many other parts of the world. For the most part there is a combination of political activism and academic theorizing. Thus, Ian Macduff's appraisal of bicultural jurisprudence[61] was originally presented shortly before the commemoration of 150 years to the Treaty of Waitangi, and contained a warning of the need to conduct a reassessment of its meaning and its modern applicability so as to satisfy the demands of the Maori people, some of whom saw the Treaty as being the source of their dispossession from their lands, particularly because of a distorted interpretation.

The last decade has seen a concerted effort to redress some of the wrongs, much of it within the framework of an emerging concept of bicultural jurisprudence, which involves also a need to expound on Maori jurisprudence, still, at least theoretically, in a partly inchoate form, the inroads of the state legal system having undermined much of traditional custom. A true bicultural jurisprudence will only be established when there is a full rejuvenation of the culture on which it is based. For some Maoris in New Zealand, this is very high on their political agenda.[62]

In Papua New Guinea, in an entirely different situation, attempts have also been made to give deeper recognition not merely to any specific rules and customs, but to give expression to the bedrock of a special Melanesian jurisprudence. In the constitution itself, provision is made for referring to the 'underlying law' where neither enacted law nor judicial precedent provide solutions to legal problems.[63] This is a broad concept which still requires much elucidation, but one of the country's leading jurists, Bernard Narakobi, has, on many occasions given expression to the value that he sees ensconced in this phrase, and the potentialities it holds for creative adjudication.[64]

Specifically in terms of legal systems M. Hooker has summarized the situation, based on a broad comparative study of legal pluralism in operation in many countries throughout the world.[65] He writes:

> The form of political organization within which plural legal systems exist today is the nation-state. It is fundamental to the idea of the state that its institutions alone can be the source of law. Laws are valid only in so far as they are acknowledged in some way by the organs of the state. The law is defined, in other words, as a set of consistent principles, valid for and binding upon the whole population and emanating from a single source. The written, national state system is the only one which is 'properly law.' This may be a proper view in a culturally and economically homogeneous society, but such societies are the exception rather than the rule. An undue emphasis on this view of law is often a distortion of reality and not uncommonly a downright misrepresentation in many states. The official or state legal system may not in fact be effective for a number of reasons. The reality of the law might be quite different from its formulation in code or statute. This occurs where there are multiple systems of legal obligation existing within the confines of the state.[66]

These attempts at a flexible jurisprudence focused on legal pluralism run counter not only to the positivism of the dominant schools of the philosophy of law, but also to the leading theories in political science as to the twin ideas of state and sovereignty. Jean Bodin, considered the earliest modern exponent of the concept of sovereignty, emphasized the need for only one source of authority in the state.[67] Bodin, of course, did not write in a political vacuum, and his theory was clearly oriented to enhancing the power of the monarchy at the expense of its rivals, the aristocracy, the church, and the rising bourgeoisie.

The initial support for these ideas was subsequently eroded as liberal ideas of the rights of the individual and the sovereignty of the people began to attract attention. But for the most part these amendments and embellishments to Bodin's ideas revolved around the idea of the nation as a basically homogeneous people. There was little attempt to seek a modification based on some intervening group between the people as such and the state as such. And as between the state and the people, there were also no attempts at a shared sovereignty. Where sovereignty was claimed to reside in the people, the ruler was in power at their will, and could be removed, including by the right to revolt[68] – but there was little development in the direction of shared sovereignty, for instance where some legislation could be enacted by referendum, so that the people could share in the legislative process.

The idea of shared sovereignty has been developed by a group of Dutch jurists and philosophers, and has aroused little interest or even notice outside of the Netherlands. The term that they suggest is 'sphere sovereignty', that is an acknowledgment of the fact that there might well be spheres within a state for which limited sovereignty could be granted, relative to the concerns of that sphere of social activity. J. van der Vyver explains that 'The doctrine of sphere sovereignty ... developed under the auspices of neo-Calvinistic sociological thought', and 'denotes an enclave of competence belonging to a social entity of its own accord – without that social entity depending on any other person or institution for the possession or exercise of those powers'.[69]

The leading exponent in recent times of the idea is Herman Dooyeweerd, who describes a situation where, within one society, there would be different social structures, each entitled to make its own rules.[70] A succinct presentation of his ideas is given by van der Vyver, who denotes its three key qualities:

a) the state is not the only structure within human society that exercises a judicial function
b) social entities do not derive their internal authority from any other social entity of a radically different kind
c) the juridical competence of the repositories of state authority to enact laws is not absolute.[71]

Sphere sovereignty then opens up possibilities of shared sovereignty, allocated according to the functions that any institution or corporate body exercises. Included in the possibilities are a family unit, an ecclesiastical denomination, business corporations and other voluntary associations. Each is presumed to be sovereign within its own sphere, but also subject to the state's courts of law, which are presumed to act from a cognizance of shared sphere sovereignty.

The idea of sphere sovereignty opens up many possibilities, but it also poses many problems. It is deeply embedded in religious thought,[72] to the extent that it occasionally seems that its major aim is to reconstruct religious power as a counterweight to the state.

This fits in well with Harold Berman's thesis as to how secular legal systems developed: initially there had been clear power-sharing between the secular and the ecclesiastical authorities, each recognizing the sphere of influence and jurisdiction of the other – both the secular state and the ecclesiastical authorities '... would introduce and maintain their own legal systems, that is would regularly enact laws, establish judicial systems, that is government departments, and, in general, rule by law. If the church was to have inviolable legal rights, the state had to accept those rights as a lawful limitation upon its own supremacy of the church. The two powers could only coexist peacefully through a shared recognition of the rule of law, its supremacy over each.'[73]

It is this kind of model that Dooyeweerd seems to have in mind, but it is doubtful if this historical situation can be re-created. More likely are various federal ideas for shared power and sovereignty, but this is clearly not Dooyeweerd's main intent as his model basically links regional civil authorities (municipalities and local governments) to the state itself, since this is where local authority derives its power.

Finally, it also sees tribes (whether in history or the present day) as being too all-encompassing to partake of sphere sovereignty, of being hide-bound by the force of tradition and of being hermetically sealed from outside influence.[74] However, this seems to be an incorrect, almost stereotyped, perception, as pointed out in earlier chapters. In fact, the contrary may be true; that a different and more realistic, understanding of tribe – as flexible in its own framework, and as interactive with the outside world – would suggest it as being well suited to the benefits of a sphere sovereignty.

Sphere sovereignty presents no simplistic solutions, but involves a sophisticated presentation of socio-legal reality. It leaves the ultimate task of determining the juridical validity of any act in the hands of the state courts. This is precisely what state courts have done in profusion over the years for tribes. But what they lacked was a theoretical framework which would clarify the nature of this judicial activity, allowing them to recognize the full extent of the autonomous source of authority from which the customs at issue derived their obligatory power.

Given the many gropings in Europe for a new understanding of political structures – from the European Union moving toward greater integration, to the attempt at a Commonwealth of countries formerly part of the Soviet Union – it would seem that the idea of sphere sovereignty contains many penetrating and fruitful insights. They may well serve to help elucidate also the nature of tribal authority in new (and not so new) states.

Furthermore, a parallel model exists in practical terms that is evoking much interest – namely that of consociational democracy as practiced in such a special manner in Switzerland.[75] Linked also to this idea, is that of a civil society, also being increasingly touted in many places; though largely parallel to the state, it preserves some distance from it.[76] Ideas of this nature are also of great import in evaluating the nature and role of tribal communities and their legal systems in the modern state.

In fact, it is rigid, and possibly antiquated, ideas of the citizenship that is associated with state, that is preventing the creative development of a synthesis between the state and tribe as one of its constituent elements. More than this, the very prospect of compatible shared loyalties may be based on tribal models from the past. An interesting and important article dealing with the status of women – as citizens and members of tribe – in Zimbabwe provides a fascinating insight into the reality of status determination in heterogeneous states. A.P. Chester and R.B. Gaidzanwa[77] describe a legal situation in Zimbabwe, as in other southern African states, that insists on exclusive citizenship, based on a denial of the possibility of shared loyalties and allegiances (many western societies also adopt similar approaches, although a recent trend is noticeable, allowing for greater flexibility). They are critical of the approach, and explain that the model for allowing dual loyalty may be found in the manner in which some tribes accommodated their members who had married someone from another tribe. In patrilineal and patrilocal societies, this approach has particular significance for women, as it enables them to retain close contact with their family of origin. Chester and Gaidzanwa argue that a denial of the possibility of dual citizenship ignores the

> reality that the exogamous patrilineal systems characteristic of Southern Africa never expected married women to abandon all links to their natal families, even when they were normally required to live with their husbands. Indeed, in patrilineal systems, their families were and are expected to provide significant protection for married women against abusive husbands; and women have routinely to juggle simultaneous loyalties to their natural kin and affines in ways not required of men. As daughters, aunts and sisters, women married exogamously continue to play important roles in their own patrilineages, to which they are required to maintain loyalties and in return receive potential protection against affinal abuse … . Women's [precolonial] 'citizenship' in patrilineal societies has thus been fundamentally different from that of men … men in agnatic societies … never experience the female process of balancing and juggling two sets of loyalties simultaneously, in a way that is standard for women in these systems. This deficit presumably is, at least in part, the ideological failure by men of the ruling class … to comprehend the

> realities of simultaneous loyalties to more than one identity and community ... .[78]

They claim also that the unwillingness of the states in the region of southern Africa to allow this shared loyalty, because of their insistence on exclusive citizenship, is detrimental to the interests of women, especially given their greater mobility, including across borders (as traders or workers). Their conclusion is that this

> narrowing down and removal of women's rights as citizens is a very deliberate post-colonial phenomenon, pushed through legislative assemblies against public female political resistance ... in the name of 'tradition'. In many cases, these post-colonial changes have left black female citizens worse off than they were under colonial law.[79]

I draw attention to this rather unusual insight into patrilineal structures (at least in the region under study) to suggest that there may be unnoticed subtleties which may help to clarify certain phenomena in modern states, including the touted possibility of shared sovereignty. In another context, also in Zimbabwe, the law in relation to the rights of widows is also shown to be a consequence of judicial precedent, based on western concepts of rigid law (becoming increasingly outdated in the west itself), whereas a proper understanding of customary law as a living system, would allow for needed change. Drawing on examples of research carried out in Zimbabwe by women in terms of women's needs and interests, Anne Hellum explains how to ensure creative molding of existing customs.[80] She argues that:

> Women's law research has demonstrated the need for legal science which through empirical descriptions of people's living customs lays the foundation for the application of a more contextual, dynamic and flexible customary law by the courts than is the case today.[81]

Hellum suggests that such an approach has 'challenged established theories about what valid customary law is and should be'.[82] Underlying her analysis, it seems, is not just the specific rule being applied, but the affirmation of parallel legal systems, existing side by side – thus, she criticizes anthropological approaches based on cultural relativism, which leads to a narrow legal pluralism both passive and past-oriented.

Dealing with the refusal to recognize the right of a widow in customary law to be appointed an heir to her deceased husband's estate, Hellum argues that the Supreme Court in Zimbabwe uses a 'static and precedent oriented approach', which is 'in line with the dominant rule and precedent-oriented tradition within customary law theory, made on the basis of written sources of customary law which originated from the colonial period'.[83] She concludes that there is a need to reject the narrow reliance on judicial precedent, the limited descriptive work of anthropologists and the remaining misconceptions of colonial times, in order to reach an appreciation of customary law as (in the words of Julie Stewart, a Zimbabwean legal scholar) 'a living system, defined and modified by constant use'.[84] This kind of understanding will allow for full expression of concepts such as legal pluralism, or shared sovereignty, concepts that provide a framework for the continuation of customary law in a modern state.

NOTES

1. Sebastian Poulter, *English Law and Ethnic Minority Customs* (London: Butterworths, 1986).
2. Those who believe that the term ethnicity is a guarantee against fission, whereas tribe seems to be divisive, should note the recent history of a number of states whose 'ethnic groups' began to make political demands as a nation.
3. See, for instance Elmer Service, *Primitive Social Organization: An Evolutionary Perspective* (New York: Random House, 1962). For a critique of this approach, see Morton Fried, *The Evolution of Political Society: An Essay in Political Anthropology* (New York: Random House, 1967).
4. The numbers of Fourth World peoples are estimated at about 50 million throughout the world – but of course there can be no certainty in this regard, either as to what groups to count, or as to an accurate estimate of their numbers.
5. Xavier Arlos, 'Nation-State: The Range and Future of a Concept', *Canadian Review of Studies in Nationalism* 17 (1990), p. 61.
6. Arlos, ibid., refers to a series of lectures given by Leon Duguit, *Souveraineté et Liberte* (1920–21).
7. Arbos, ibid., p. 61.
8. Leon Duguit, *Law in the Modern State* (London: George Allen & Unwin, 1921), p. 31.
9. Bernard Susser and Eliezer Don-Yehiya, 'The Decline of the Nation State in the West: Israel as a Deviant Case' (unpublished paper).
10. Walter Connor, 'Nation-Building or Nation Destroying', *World Politics* 24 (1972), 321.
11. While there is no term ethnicism to describe the emotional force that a group may possess, this does not necessarily mean that the emotional aspect will not find an outlet, including by a change of name, as when an ethnic group becomes defined as a nation.
12. Connor, 'Nation-Building', p. 334.
13. See Karl Deutsch, *Nationalism and Social Communication: An Inquiry into the Foundations of Nationality* (Cambridge, MA: MIT Press, 1953). See also K. Deutsch and W. Foltz (eds), *Nation-Building* (New York: Atherton Press, 1963).
14. Connor, 'Nation-Building', p. 322, quote from Deutsch, *Nationalism and Social Communication*.
15. For example of change in tribal structure, and intermingling among tribes, see Ronald Cohen and John Middleton (eds), *From Tribe to Nation in Africa: Studies in Incorporation Processes* (Scranton, Penn: Chandler Publishing, 1970).
16. This would be of most interest in the realm of law, where many procedures were practiced that might by hindsight be seen as superior to that of the Roman Law.
17. Peter Skalnik, 'Questioning the Concept of State in Southern Ghana', *Social Dynamics* 9 (1983), p. 11.
18. Ibid., p. 11.
19. Ibid., p. 17.
20. Ibid., p. 17
21. Skalnik (ibid.) writes that 'The modern state with its nationalist ideology failed to live up to the expectations of ordinary people .... The Ghanaian state seems to have taken upon itself, through its colonial masters and their post-colonial apprentices from among Ghanaian literates a heavier load than it can carry. In the absence of a well-functioning modern nation, the values and organizational principles which the Nanumba or the Konkomba have evolved as a result of their centuries long historical experience re-emerge as the dominant logic. Dormant ethnicity has been awakened and has taken over the tasks which the modern state has failed to solve' (p. 23).
22. Ibid., p. 23.
23. Ibid., p. 25.

24. Ibid., p. 26
25. Ibid., p. 26
26. Ibid., p. 26
27. Ibid., p. 26
28. For a succinct, contemporaneous analysis, from a Ghanaian perspective (Ghana's first prime minister, Kwame Nkrumah, being one of the foremost proponents of Pan-African unity), see William Burnett Harvey, *Law and Social Change in Ghana*, Chapter 3, 'The Option for Unity', (Princeton: Princeton University Press, 1966), pp. 123–70.
29. It should, however, be noted that since the end of the Second World War, voices have been raised in favor of a United States of Europe.
30. On one-party states in Africa, see G. Carter (ed.), *African One-Party States* (Ithaca: Cornell University Press, 1964).
31. On the sense of belonging and membership in intra-state groups, see Chapter 9.
32. For a good discussion of the problematics of state, and of the possible alternatives to it, see John Hoffman, *Beyond the State: An Introductory Critique* (Cambridge: Polity Press, 1995).
33. On the Philippines, see Renato Constantino, *Identity and Consciousness: The Philippine Experience* (Quezon City, Phil.: Malaya Books, 1974).
34. Fernando Zialcita, 'Nations as Artifact', *Philippine Quarterly of Culture and Society* 18 (1990), p. 227.
35. Austronesian culture refers mainly to the island states in the Pacific.
36. Zialcita, 'Nations as Artifact', p. 230.
37. Ibid., p. 230.
38. Ibid., p. 234.
39. Ibid., p. 234; for Braudel's work see Fernand Braudel, *The Identity of France* (London: Fontana, 1988). Braudel writes that 'unity was created ... in the area centred on Paris ... There can be no doubt that it was from this nuclear, this centre, that everything began. French unity was created outwards from a central point' (p. 301).
40. Ibid., p. 234.
41. J.E.S. Hayward, *Governing France: The One and Indivisible Republic* (London: Weidenfeld & Nicolson, 1983) (2nd edn.), p. 21.
42. Zialcita, 'Nations as Artifact', p. 234.
43. Ibid., p. 248.
44. See Marshall McLuhan and Quentin Fiore, *The Medium is the Message* (New York: Bantam Books, 1967).
45. Zialcita, 'Nations as Artifact', p. 249.
46. Ibid., p. 250.
47. Eric San Juan, 'Making Filipino History in a "Damaged Culture",' *Philippines Sociological Review* 37 (1989), p. 1.
48. Ibid., p. 2.
49. G. Sidney Silliman, 'The Folk Legal Culture of the Cebuano Filipino', *Philippines Quarterly of Culture and Society* (1982), 10, p. 225.
50. Ibid., p. 225.
51. Ibid., p. 225.
52. Ibid., p. 226.
53. Ibid., p. 242.
54. Lourdes Aranet-Sereno and Roan Libarios, 'The Interface Between National Land Law and Kalanga Land Law', *Philippines Law Journal* (1983), 58, p. 420.
55. Ibid., p. 420.
56. Ibid.
57. Owen Lynch, 'The Philippine Indigenous Law Collection: An Introduction and Preliminary Bibliography'. *Philippines Law Journal* 58 (1983), p. 457.
58. Ibid., p. 457.
59. Ibid., p. 458.
60. Roberto Benedito, 'Law and Nationhood: The Cracks in the Parchment Curtain', *Philippines Law Journal* 59 (1984), p. 415.
61. Ian MacDuff, 'Biculturalism, Partnership and Parallel Systems: The Context of Maori Rights', in William Twining (ed.), *Issues of Self-Determination* (Aberdeen: Aberdeen University Press,

1991), p. 102 – based on a paper given at 14th World Congress of the International Association for Philosophy of Law and Social Philosophy, Edinburgh, August 1989).
62. See, for instance, Moana Jackson, *The Maori and the Criminal Justice System* (Wellington: Department of Justice, 1988).
63. For a good discussion of the background to the idea of using the 'underlying law', see D.R.C. Chalmers and A.H. Paliwala, *An Introduction to the Law in Papua New Guinea* (Sydney: Law Book Co., 1984), pp. 61–5.
64. Bernard Narakobi, *Lo Bilong Yumi Yet – Law and Custom in Melanesia* (Suva, Fiji: Melanesian Institute for Pastoral and Socio-Economic Service and University of South Pacific, 1989).
65. M. Hooker, *Legal Pluralism: An Introduction to Colonial and Neo-Colonial Laws* (Oxford: Clarendon Press, 1975).
66. Ibid., pp. 1–2.
67. See Jean Bodin, *On Sovereignty: Four Chapters from 'The Six Books of the Commonwealth'* – edited and translated by Julian Franklin (Cambridge: Cambridge University Press, 1992).
68. See Haim Cohn, 'The Right and Duty of Resistance', *Revue de l'homme* 1 (1968), p. 491.
69. J.O. van der Vyver, 'The Concept of Political Sovereignty', in C. Visser (ed.), *Essays in Honour of Ellison Kahn* (Cape Town: Juta, 1989), p. 303.
70. See Herman Dooyeweerd, *A New Critique of Theoretical Thought* (Amsterdam: H.J. Paris, 1953).
71. Van der Vyver, 'Concept of Political Sovereignty', p. 309.
72. See, for instance, Herman Dooyeweerd, *Roots of Western Culture: Pagan, Secular, and Christian Options* (Toronto: Wedge Publishing, 1979), pp. 40–60. These are a series of articles written after the Second World War. The thrust of his thesis is well summarized by the translator, John Kroy, who explains the author's warnings against an artificial unity of the nation (stemming from the common struggle against the enemy during the war), and how those who were striving for an all-encompassing national unity as having been

> uprooted by the crisis of the western world in the twentieth century, an uprootedness, which had become the more existential because of the horror and atrocities of that terrible war. Consequently they were unable to really come to grips with the question as to the direction postwar renewal would have to take. Dooyeweerd was convinced that this question would be answered only against the background of a fundamental reflection on, and reappropriation of, one's roots .... To be radical one must go back to the roots of one's culture, to the sources of the communal ways of life in which individuals, institutions, and organizations live and move and have their being (p. ix).

73. Harold J. Berman, *Toward Revolution: The Formation of the Western Legal Tradition* (Cambridge, MA: Harvard University Press, 1983), p. 292. It should be noted that Berman also argues that the modern state was originally established by the church.
74. Dooyeweerd, *A New Critique of Theoretical Thought*, p. 75.
75. See K. McRae (ed.), *Consociational Democracy: Political Accommodation in Segmented Societies* (Toronto: McClelland and Stewart, 1974); and Arend Lijphart, 'Consociational Democracy', *World Politics* 21 (1969), p. 221.
76. See, for instance, John Keane (ed.), *Civil Society and the State* (London: Verso, 1988). For an interesting analysis of the overlap with civil society and religion, which also has much relevance for Dooyeweerd's work (though he is not mentioned in the book), see Andrew Shanks, *Civil Society, Civil Religion* (Oxford: Blackwell, 1995).
77. A.P. Chester and R.B. Gaidzanwa, 'Citizenship in Neo-Patrilineal States: Gender and Mobility in Southern Africa', *Journal of Southern African Studies* 2 (1996), p. 189. See also an interesting article that deals, *inter alia*, with the difference between 'citizenship as a legal status' and 'citizenship as participation and membership within a democratic community' – Kim Rubenstein, 'Citizenship in Australia – Unscrambling its Meaning,' *Melbourne University Law Review* 20 (1995), p. 503.
78. Chester and Gaidzanwa, p. 194.
79. Ibid., p. 194.
80. Anne Hellum, 'Actor Perspectives on Gender and Legal Pluralism in Africa', in H. Petersen and H. Zahle (eds), *Legal Polycentricity: Consequences of Pluralism in Law* (Aldershot: Dartmouth, 1995), p. 13.
81. Ibid., p. 25.
82. Ibid., p. 25.

83. Ibid., p. 25.
84. Julie Stewart, 'Untying the Gordian Knot! Murisa v. Murisa S-41-92. A Little More Than a Case Note', *Legal Forum* 4 (1992), p. 13.

Customary Law as Common Law

The role of custom is basic to an understanding of the development of the common law; it also lies, paradoxically perhaps, at the heart of the problematics in according recognition to the customary practices of tribal communities that came into contact with the representative authorities of the common law in the furthest reaches of the British Empire.

Both major European legal systems, the common law and the European civil law, have spread widely throughout the world, partly through imposed law as a result of conquest and annexation, partly as a result of deliberate reception of the law. The latter aspect is particularly noticeable in the case of the civil law system, since a number of countries, outside of Europe, and which had not been subject to colonial rule, voluntarily adopted certain aspects of the legal system of dominant European countries. Countries such as Japan, Thailand, Ethiopia and Turkey drew extensively upon the codes of European countries, mainly France and Germany, as an anticipated means of accelerating their economic and technological development.[1] The existence of codes in civil law countries certainly facilitated the process of reception of a foreign legal system. It is much easier to attempt reception of a legal system, when its central factor is a code; far more difficult when it is based on custom.

A central factor in a Civil Law system is the dominant role of a written code, which is presumed to provide certainty and comprehensiveness, with the role of the judge being to apply the law, while having little discretion for the judicial law-making that so characterizes the common law system.[2]

Indeed, one of the main differentiating factors between the two major legal systems is the role of judges, and the degree of activism that each system assigns to them. In the common law, the judge is a meaningful partner in the creation of legal norms.[3] Judicial precedent is a recognized component of the legal system; and an essential factor in this aspect is the role of custom, with judges examining and evaluating the customary practices of the inhabitants of the realm, in order to decide whether or not to grant them the primatur of legal recognition. Historically, the origins of the common law were in the pronouncement of those customs that the king's courts held to be of general validity – that is, customs that were common to all of the realm, in contrast to the local customs of a particular area, that were slowly superseded.

In its initial stages, it was the customary law that formed the basis of the emerging common law system, and it was only gradually that statutes of Parliament came to be recognized as an important part of the law; in fact the original role of Parliament was as an advisory body (similar to the European Parliament of today); it even had a judicial function that was almost of parallel significance to its legislative capacity (still noted in the leading role of the House of Lords at the apex of the judicial hierarchy). Thus, for instance, Charles McIlwain, in his study of the British Parliament, notes that, until the end of the seventeenth century, the legislative function of Parliament was of negligible import: its major role was not to make law but to declare law, a role more judicial than legislative.[4]

But .even so, as the Parliament increasingly took over the task of legislation, the traditional structure and culture of the legal system remained, for the most part, as it had been – with the court continuing to play an important role in the formation of the law through their role in interpretation.

In fulfilling such a role, judges are not presumed to be acting in an arbitrary or idiosyncratic manner, neither laying down the law as an oracle, nor furthering their own individual beliefs or interests; rather they are considered as giving expression to the sentiments of the people, seeking to dispense justice in terms of standards and criteria that are acceptable to the community.[5]

It is specifically this reasoning that is at the heart of the reluctance to set out codes, which tend to minimize the impact of evolving beliefs and practices. Indeed, as Guido Calabresi has pointed out, the increased role of statutory law in common-law countries, poses serious problems for the capacity of the law to reflect changing social and cultural conditions, or even to fulfill its traditional role of judicial law-making; and he suggests means by which the role of the courts could be revived – for instance in declaring laws to be in disuse.[6]

It was the constrictive impact of codes on the possibility of continued natural evolution that led Karl von Savigny to battle so vigorously (yet in the final analysis, so unsuccessfully) against the movement to adopt a code for Germany.[7] His historical approach to the law was much more in line with the reality of the English common law than it was with the more rigid pattern of law in the civil law countries.

Paradoxically, the converse was also true; the positivistic approach to jurisprudence, so characteristic of English jurisprudence, was far more apt and relevant for the continental civil law system than it was for the English legal system, upon which it was ostensibly based. Indeed, given the problematics of judge-made law for a positivistic position, John Austin and others provided a basically false and fictitious picture of the role of the judge as only pronouncing the law, and not actually helping to make the law.[8] In fact, Max Weber referred to the difficulties that he had with the English legal system as it did not quite fit into his own model of a 'rational' modern law.[9]

A leading English historian of the law, Brian Simpson, has strongly criticized the Austinian approach, and pointed out the inevitable inconsistencies that flow therefrom.[10] He suggests that the positivistic approach describes the judicial function in terms that have very little connection with the manner in which judges operate, and with the essential framework within which the law is interpreted. Thus Simpson raises a query: 'If, however, we abandon the positivist conception of the common law, in terms of what other conception can the institution be more realistically depicted?' According to him, 'Positivists take as their basic model of law an enacted code, but a better starting-point, if we are concerned with the common law, is the traditional notion of the common law as custom which was standard form in the older writers'.[11] Simpson refers here to significant figures in the history of the common law, such as Hale and Blackstone, and he claims that their presentation of the law was in essence far more accurate than the rationalizations of later writers, such as Jeremy Bentham. And so he concludes; 'We need … to conceive of the common law as a system of customary law and recognize that such systems may embrace complex theoretical notions which both serve to explain and justify past practice … and provide a guide to future conduct.'[12]

Such an approach to the common law would certainly allow for greater sensitivity to the fluid nature of customs, and so there would be more consciousness of change in the law, and of the development of newer doctrines, instead of the routinized perception and rote pronouncement of custom as being of immemorial usage.

In this context, William Sumner, in his classic work, *Folkways,* explains how law emerges out of the mores; in fact, 'Legislation, to be strong, must be consistent with the *mores.*'[13] Geoffrey Sawyer notes, in a chapter devoted to a comparison of 'Folkways, Law-Ways, and State-Ways', that 'there is … a recurrent theory, attitude or assumption, manifested in both popular speech and in academic speculation, which attributes a secondary role to Law and a primary role to social behaviour conceived of as existing independently of Law'.[14] In similar vein, A.S. Diamond states that law is 'the distilled essence of the civilization of a people',[15] a factor that leads to constant change in response to societal advances.

It is true that, over the years, statute has played an increasingly important role in common law countries; further, that certain aspects of the law have been comprehensively presented in the form of codes or consolidating acts; indeed, model codes have been drawn up in the United

States in order to encourage consistency among the states, especially noted in the key areas, for a federal state, of commercial and criminal law, but while the term code is used, these are not in essence true codes in the full sense of the word as used in civil law countries, as being a unified and single document, covering all, or almost all, areas of the law in an integrative and interrelated manner.[16] This, the common law countries have failed to do, and so continue to work within a legal culture that is still basically oriented to the flexible development of the law in which judges help make the law, and do so in terms of their understanding of an evolving society.

In fact, it was not only the judges who contributed to this development, but the common people, in their role as members of the jury, as Marianne Constable so ably reminds us in her fascinating book, *The Law of the Other.*[17] She describes a little-noticed aspect of the jury system, the mixed jury, in which every effort was made to ensure full representation to the different communities in the society, when the litigants were members of such different communities. She writes that 'References to the use of early mixed juries – in local courts and in cases of Jews and merchants in central courts – must be considered against the background of the plurality of communities, customs and courts'[18] (which she describes in some detail).

> When persons from the two communities were involved in a dispute, both communities would be represented. Local courts treated as 'others' not only members of distant areas, but also local residents, who belonged to 'other' communities.[19]

Most significantly, for the purposes of understanding the inherent, pluralistic nature of common law from its inception and through its development, Constable states that

> The mixed jury epitomizes the principle accompanying the multitude of customs and courts in England in the Middle Ages, of personal law: the judgment of a person must be according to the law or customs of that person's community; such judgment must be made by those with knowledge of those customs or ... by those who share in those customs and belong to the same community.[20]

On this basis, it is clear that custom lies at the heart of the common law system – and it is this historical tradition, still pertinent today, that facilitates a meaningful appreciation of customary law, as it is practiced by various population groups, such as tribes, struggling to maintain their integrity in their contacts with the larger culture, sometimes an alien culture.

We have already noted, in an earlier chapter, the suggestion by James Zion that the best way to present the law of the American Indians is as

Common Law – as a law, that is, that, in its structure, bears much resemblance to the framework within which the common law itself developed.[21]

In this context, the historical debate as to whether or not the tribes, in various parts of the far-flung British empire, had a legal system, or whether they were controlled 'merely' by custom, is indicative of myopic thinking of the worst order, or a lack of knowledge of the historical development of the law, or of a deliberate denigration of the societies – or a combination of these factors.

For, if it was true that 'custom was king', as many were wont to state, why should that, in any way, detract from its role as law, as many were wont to argue, or raise questions as to whether or not there was a stable political order.[22] It was only after pioneering work by legal anthropologists such as Malinowski, Hoebel and Gluckman,[23] that grudging recognition was given to the fact that custom was not so-called 'king', but was, in fact, 'law' – a theoretical concession that was made easier by the desire to grant recognition of a minimum degree of order, as understood by the West, so as to allow for indirect rule, which in some places (particularly where there were large population groups under the control of minimum colonial forces, as in Africa) was crucial for the purposes of effective control.[24]

The fact is that there was no need to show, as Hoebel tried to do,[25] that the customs of the tribes that he examined, could be explained within a sophisticated jurisprudential system, as set out by Hohfeld.[26] The legitimacy of customary law did not require such a static explanation; its legitimacy, as the basis for law – was a natural outcome of the very development of the English Common Law. The parallels were not, then, just in the ultimate framework of the law *à la* Hohfeld, but in the manner in which the law was formed, accepted and respected.

In this sense, customary law was akin to the common law and the validity of custom could only be denied by ignoring the very nature of the Common Law itself. Part of the reason for this may lie not just in an ethnocentric approach to the habits of tribal, and presumably less civilized, people, but to the fallacies as to law being propagated by a narrow positivistic doctrine of jurisprudence, one which was itself out of touch with its own legal system.[27]

But some of the frictions of positivistic jurisprudence continued to affect the manner in which custom was perceived, even after it had been given a certain amount of legitimacy. The customs of indigenous peoples in various parts of the British empire were accepted not on their own terms, but within the context of custom as perceived within a positivistic spectrum – thus the qualities that were attributed to custom, in terms of the Common Law, were now also associated with the custom of tribes, namely of being of immemorial usage, a static approach to custom that had been adopted by the Common Law judges (partly perhaps in answer to the logic of positivism). A custom could only be accepted as law, if its origins were unknown, and so a date in the twelfth century, 1189, was declared as being the presumptive moment in time when all recognized customs were in effect.[28] This was a legal fiction that worked quite well for the English Common Law (and even then not always, as the parallel system of equity to rectify faults in the law proves) but was to have a stultifying impact on the tribal common law – at least as perceived by those governmental authorities that were prepared to concede legitimacy. For it led almost inevitably to the tribal customs being regarded as of long usage, and indeed of tribal society being seen as static, not susceptible to change: and those changes that were noted were often attributed to the influence of western society, ignoring the fact that change and progress were inherent in tribal society, and were of the essence of custom itself, as well as ignoring the fact that tribal societies nearly always maintained some degree of contact with other local societies, whose influence could also often lead to change. The predominant view of custom as static was to have far-reaching implications on the attitudes to custom in a modern world dedicated to change and progress.

Any attempt to relate to customary law must, it seems to me, come to terms with the impact of jurisprudential thinking on the manner in which custom is incorporated into a legal system – whether as being of immemorial use and therefore static, or whether as being part of a living group, reflecting changing mores, responding to changing circumstances, flexible enough to adopt to changing needs.

The manner in which customary law is perceived is of vital import for the possibility of creating a framework of legal pluralism. A perception of custom as some formalized relic of a backward people, will lead to certain inescapable consequences, that customs can only be recognized if they are of long-standing usage, and once recognized, cannot be changed; or alternatively that they are not acceptable by the standards of the dominant culture and thus must be totally eradicated; or where several such customs exist, that the whole system must be rejected, without any opportunity for the customs to respond dynamically to the changing environment, including those changes which are triggered by the impact of another culture, which may also well be the dominant culture.

Those kinds of issues are not unique to customary law. One of the classic legal debates in the United States relates to the manner in which the constitution should be interpreted – whether in terms of a strict constructionist approach that hues close to the presumed intent of the framers, or whether in terms of a living document that is easily adaptable to the continuous development of a vibrant society.[29]

Thus, for instance, a leading constitutional scholar, Raoul Berger[30] has argued forcefully in favor of the retention of capital punishment, without reference even to the substantive current criminological and philosophical debate, as the death penalty was in effect at the time of the constitutional convention. In direct contrast is the approach that examines penal policy in the light of what the Supreme Court defined as the 'evolving standards of decency',[31] a theoretical framework initially applied to punishment in general, and then activated specifically in terms of the death penalty.

It is clear that, in the modern world, any approach that sees custom – particularly of another culture – in static terms, dooms that very culture to stagnation, and ultimately rejection, by imposing on it a rigidity which is generally by no means inherent in its nature. It also makes for a reluctance to grant recognition *ab initio,* or where recognition is granted, to impose other norms upon it, instead of allowing for a natural and gradual growth.

It is quite possible that tribal customs that seem to be incongruous in the modern age will gradually be eased out by the members of the tribe themselves, as their contacts with other cultures make them aware of alternative modes, or even where changing economic and social conditions make it increasingly difficult to practice the old customs. Polygamy becomes difficult to maintain in the light of pressures on the availability of land, bride-price becomes difficult to pay in a cash economy, and in any case takes on the appearance more and more of dowry, witchcraft loses some of its influence as medical knowledge is extended. On the other hand, respect for nature, originally the result possibly of fear for its overpowering might, takes on enduring qualities that not only survive outer pressures, but may present an intrinsic attraction to others, desperately trying to redefine their own attitudes to the environment, and searching for a viable ecological ethic. But, one way or the other, it is the people themselves who must contend with the issues of how to maintain their customs in a living culture.

Custom is an important source of law for all legal systems, and, of the modern systems, particularly for the common law system. An awareness of its flexible nature is essential for its vitality and for the continuing viability of the culture.

It is possible that anthropologists are partly to blame for the inaccuracies that often attach to the customary law. Often even when stressing the nature of custom as law, they would tend to describe it as an inflexible framework, basically as it was at the time of the research. Very few anthropologists probed to determine how the customs have developed over time. Often where changes are noticed, particularly as a result of a return to the tribal community after the passage of time, these changes will be attributed to the influence of the dominant culture, part of a process of acculturation, instead of noting how much of the change is self-engendered, part of the ongoing history of the particular tribe, part of its essential resilience and capacity to adapt according to changing circumstances and changing needs.

For a full appreciation of the nature of customary law, it is advisable to note the role of custom in general in any legal system, including those that are recorded in writing and considered as sophisticated and complex. Thus leading textbooks in jurisprudence refer to custom in terms that make it not just perfectly compatible with the needs of a modern legal system, but also of manifest positive benefit. Thus George Paton writes of custom being 'useful to the lawyers and codifier', as it 'provides the material out of which law can be fashioned' and 'psychologically, it is easier to secure observance for a code if it claims to be based on customs immemorially observed and this is true even though historically the claim cannot be substantiated'.[32] He goes on to argue that custom having the force of law is based on 'the recognition that there is authority behind it'.[33]

However, a more acute sensitivity to the role of custom in legal systems will emerge not only from such formal definitions, or even from a reminder of the historical development of the common law itself, but also from a jurisprudential perspective that takes due accord of the manner in which law is used in the real world, that allows for the obligatory nature of rules, that have been neither enacted by statute nor pronounced as precedent by the judiciary.

Sociological jurisprudence has always argued for the need for law to be attuned to social reality and to develop in terms of relevant social policy. But going beyond this approach, are schools of thought that place special emphasis on the law in its extra-legal and extrajudicial manifestations.

There are several theoretical perspectives in jurisprudence that place the emphasis in law not on the statute book or judicial precedent, but on the rules and norms that people lay down in the course of their everyday lives. It is these rules that determine, for so many people, the nature of the rights and obligations *vis-à-vis* their neighbors. Most people do not examine the minutiae of the law, or seek the aid of a legal expert to resolve a particular issue. They rely on the prevailing norms that exist in their community, or their profession, or in a particular field of endeavor. Basically, they seek to enforce their rights in terms of those customary practices and patterns of behavior that have developed in response to similar kinds of problems in the past. Eugen Ehrlich has referred to this aspect of legal and social life as the living law.[34] Similarly, the theorists of the Scandinavian school of legal realism have suggested that legal rules are no more than a particular form of general social norms, and should be understood in that light.[35]

From the perspective of historical jurisprudence, it is here that the key norms of a society are being forged, and in an ideal situation law will, in the long run, give formal recognition to such practices, and in essence, a recognition to the customs of the people. Savigny writes: 'in the general consciousness of a people lives positive law and hence we have to call it people's law ... it is the spirit of a people living and working in common in all the individuals, which gives birth to positive law'.[36]

There are also advanced cultures, such as in China and Japan, where every effort is made to avoid litigation and legalistic solutions for what are generally considered to be social and human problems. Slowly, overall normative systems emerge, such as the *giri* in Japan to describe how individuals resolve their differences without recourse to the formal legal system.[37]

In recent years many efforts have been made to emphasize the positive role of alternative dispute resolution in the modern world; indeed, part of the attraction of this phenomenon is as a reaction to the frustrations of the expense, the procrastination, the uncertainties and the tension associated with the formal legal system. In this kind of context customary law becomes merely one aspect of a larger movement that seeks flexibility in both the procedural and substantive aspects of the law.

The truth is that the common law was originally of this type. Its origins were through processes very similar to that being described in some of the less dominant, yet nonetheless extremely important, theories in jurisprudence. In reality, this is still an aspect of the common law, a factor that makes for a greater understanding of a customary law system.

Customary law, then, should be seen as part of a larger jurisprudential reality, as similar in many respects to the common law itself, as an expression of law-making that seeks to retain a close link between obligatory norms and popular sentiment, that makes for a fluid normative system, that is attuned to changing circumstances, and that allows for particularistic considerations within a pluralistic legal base.

Custom, then, far from being a problematic aspect of tribal life in the context of the modern world, becomes an integral aspect of a legal system, not an artificial addition reluctantly conceded, but an essential component of a meaningful law that is willingly accepted by the citizenry, because it is deeply embedded in their consciousness as a living part of their culture.

Furthermore, it is not inherently inferior to law. Peter Goodrich, in stressing the importance of custom, takes issue with Hart's somewhat condescending attitude to custom; an attitude in which custom is seen as the precursor of the later and more perfect law. Goodrich suggests, on the contrary, that far from law being the 'inheritor of custom', as claimed by Hart, or the pinnacle of legal development replacing 'non-legal or customary order',[38] it is destructive of those orders. Focusing specifically on the consequences of imperial expansion, Goodrich writes:

> Colonization of territories invariably brought with it a ... degree of Western legal order: centralized courts and enforcement agencies, rules and formal methods of adjudication were imposed upon non-

> legal cultures in the interests of domination, exploitation and administrative expediency. It is salutary ... to recall that the Western tradition of law is the product of a very specific, localized yet imperialistic culture and that it has never been the indigenous tradition of more then one small but highly expansionist group of European cultures.[39]

Goodrich goes on to argue that

> To the cultural relativity of legal order should be added its historical and social limitations … . Law is an essential aspect of the modern Western political tradition and of the ideology of government; it justifies authority and makes it appear natural, but as it is studied and reported it is of limited practical significance. Custom surrounds the law and lives within it; corporate self-regulation, shared expectations and specific local and ethnic practices, are as likely if not more likely to prevent or resolve disputes or disorder than the centralized, bureaucratic and highly expensive legal administration.[40]

However, Goodrich also suggests that the meaning of custom has been transformed, referring in the common law system not so much to the customary practices of the people, but specific types of habitual activity of specialized groups (for example, professions), as 'selected, interpreted and applied by the privileged class of experts in the law'.[41]

It is this development that has tended to undermine the more general law of custom, which is the essence of customary law. However, as ideas of legal pluralism spread and as customary law gains greater respect and recognition, so it is possible that there may be a reassessment of the common law itself, and a renewed appreciation of the role of custom both in its historical development, and in its natural potentialities as an integral part of the legal system.

An argument of this nature has been put forward by Richard Bartlett who argues, in the words of the title to his article, that the recent, important *Mabo* decision in Australia is 'Another Triumph for the Common Law'.[42] As others have pointed out (and as I shall explain in the next chapter), the historic *Mabo* decision has its limitations in terms of its general jurisprudential value, but there can be little doubt that its major contributions (especially the negation of the *terra nullius* doctrine) are an excellent example of the manner in which the common law may be utilized in a creative, humanistic and progressive manner.

NOTES

1. See, for example, Alan Watson, *Legal Transplants: An Approach to Comparative Law* (Edinburgh: Scottish Academic Press, 1974).
2. For a good description of the civil law, see J.H. Merryman, *The Civil Law Tradition: An Introduction to the Legal System of Western Europe and Latin America* (Stanford: Stanford University Press, 1969). For a comparison of the civil law and common law systems, see Rene David and J.E.C. Brierley, *Major Legal Systems in the World Today: An Introduction to the Comparative Study of Law,* 3rd edition (London: Stevens, 1985).
3. See, for instance, John Brigham, *The Cult of the Court* (Philadelphia, PA: Temple University Press, 1987).
4. Charles McIlwain, *The High Court of Parliament and Its Supremacy: A Historical Essay on the Boundaries between Legislation and Adjudication in England* (New Haven, CT: Yale University Press, 1934).
5. See, for instance, Peter Karsten, *Head v. Heart: Judge-made Law in Nineteenth Century America* (Chapel Hill: University of North Carolina Press, 1997).
6. Guido Calabresi, *A Common Law for the Age of Statutes* (Cambridge, MA: Harvard University Press, 1982).
7. Karl von Savigny, *On the Vocation of Our Age for Legislation and Jurisprudence* (New York: Arno Press, 1975).
8. John Austin, *Lectures on Jurisprudence, or the Philosophy of Positive Law* (London: J. Murray, 1920).
9. See my discussion of this issue in *Social Cohesion and Legal Coercion: A Critique of Weber, Durkheim, and Marx* (Atlanta, GA, and Amsterdam: Rodopi, 1997), Part 1, 'Weber Revisited'.
10. Brian Simpson, 'The Common Law and Legal Theory', in William Twining (ed.), *Legal Theory and Common Law* (Oxford: Blackwells, 1986), p. 8.
11. Ibid., p. 18
12. Ibid., p. 18.
13. William G. Sumner, *Folkways* (1906), p. 55.
14. Geoffrey Sawyer, *Law in Society* (Oxford: Clarendon Press, 1965), p. 170.
15. A.S. Diamond, *The Evolution of Law and Order* (London: Watts, 1951), p. 303.
16. For a discussion of codification, as developed originally in France, see A. West *et al., The French Legal System: An Introduction* (London: Fourmat Publishing, 1992), at pp. 24–7. See also Csaba Varga, *Codification as a Socio-Historical Phenomenon* (Budapest: Akademiai Kiado, 1991), who writes: 'The transition through codification of customary law appears to be a necessary phase ... . African states almost unanimously accept the consolidation of customary laws; nevertheless, their attitude is characterized by hesitance' (pp. 184–5).
17. Marianne Constable, *The Law of the Other: The Mixed Jury and Changing Conceptions of Citizenship, Law and Knowledge* (Chicago: University of Chicago Press, 1994).
18. Ibid., p. 16.
19. Ibid., p. 16.
20. Ibid., p. 25.
21. James Zion, 'Searching for Indian Common Law', in Bradford Morse and Gordon Woodman, (eds.), *Indigenous Law and the State* (Dordrecht: Foris Publications, 1988); see my discussion of this work above in Chapter 2, 'Pluralism in the Modern World'.
22. For a recent, interesting analysis of custom, see H. Patrick Glenn, 'The Capture, Reconstruction and Marginalization of "Custom",' *The American Journal of Comparative Law* 45 (1997), p. 613.
23. For representative examples of the work of these anthropologists, see Bronislaw Malinowski, *Crime and Custom in Savage Society* (London: Routledge & Kegan Paul, 1970); E. Adamson Hoebel, *The Law of Primitive Man: A Study in Comparative Legal Dynamics* (Cambridge, MA: Harvard University Press, 1954); Max Gluckman, *The Judicial Process among the Barotse of Northern Rhodesia (Zambia)*, 2nd edn (Manchester: Manchester University Press, 1973). See also comment on their work below in Chapter 15, 'From Harm to Harmony'.
24. See H.F. Morris and James S. Reed, *Indirect Rule and the Search for Justice: Essays in East African Legal History* (Oxford: Clarendon Press, 1972).
25. See also Hoebel's joint work with the jurist Karl Llewellyn, *The Cheyenne Way – Conflict and Case Law in Primitive Jurisprudence* (Norman: University of Oklahoma Press, 1967).

26. W.N. Hohfeld, *Fundamental Legal Conceptions as Applied in Judicial Reasoning and Other Essays* (New Haven, CT: Yale University Press, 1923).
27. See, for instance, Jerome Frank, *Law and the Modern Mind* (Garden City, NY: Doubleday, 1963).
28. The year 1189 was partly an arbitrary date – based apparently on an analogy with the 'limitation period fixed by the State of Westminster of 1275, for bringing writs …'. (See Dermit Lyod, *Introduction to Jurisprudence,* Stevens and Sons, 1959), p. 340.
29. For opposing views on the Constitution, see Richard Stevens, *The American Constitution and its Provenance* (New York: Rowman and Littlefield, 1997), especially Part 2: 'The American Constitution', and Part 4: 'On Constitutional Commentators'.
30. Raoul Berger, *Death Penalties: The Supreme Court's Obstacle Course* (Cambridge, MA: Harvard University Press, 1982).
31. See *Trop v. Dulles,* 356 US 86 (1958), For general discussion see my *Ultimate Penalties: Capital Punishment, Life Imprisonment, Physical Torture* (Columbia: Ohio State University Press, 1987).
32. George Paton, *A Textbook of Jurisprudence* (Oxford: Clarendon Press, 1972), p. 192.
33. Ibid., p. 192.
34. Eugen Ehrlich, *Fundamental Principles of the Sociology of Law* (New York: Arno Press, 1975).
35. On Scandinavian realism, see, for instance, Alf Ross, *On Law and Justice* (London: Stevens, 1974).
36. von Savigny, *On the Vocation of Our Age*, p. 342.
37. On the *giri* in Japan, see Yosiyuki Noda, *Introduction to Japanese Law* (Tokyo: University of Tokyo Press, 1976), pp. 159–97.
38. Peter Goodrich, *Reading the Law: A Critical Introduction* (London: Basil Blackwell, 1986) pp. 63–4; the reference is to H.L.A. Hart, *The Concept of Law* (Oxford: Oxford University Press, 1961).
39. Goodrich, *Reading the Law*, p. 64.
40. Ibid., p. 64
41. Ibid., p. 64.
42. Richard Bartlett, 'Mabo: Another Triumph for the Common Law', *Sydney Law Review* 15 (1993), p. 178.

PART II: THE FRAMEWORK

6

The Invention of Discovery

The history of the world is, in many respects, a narrative of population migration and of territorial conquest. Boundaries, artificially carved out by historical events, have often nullified the natural divisions of rivers and mountains created by the force of geography. However, what distinguishes the imperial expansion of the past 400 years, is the physical separation between the home base, the center of political power, and the area that was brought under control. In some instances the land claimed was colonized by settlers, in others it was the trade in raw materials (from the territories) and in finished products (to the territories) that was often the major motivation, linked often to missionary activity and the provision of benefits such as medicine and education, all of which involved only minimal presence by the representatives of the imperial power.

Because of the lack of proximity to the conquered areas, they were generally not annexed (in contrast to the situation where the territory was contiguous to the borders of the victorious party), nor was there normally an immediate large-scale transference of population, and so the inevitable question arose as to the nature of the control being exercised, the right to such control as was established, the political status of the original inhabitants and their residual power – as individuals and as a group – and the recognition to be accorded the various aspects of their way of life.

The British never adopted any uniform clear-cut approach, apart from the pragmatic purposes of protecting their presence and a theoretical desire to reach an agreement, where possible, with the inhabitants (although these two aims were not always compatible).

A number of broad categories may be discerned, the result only partly of deliberate policy decision-making or of an ideologically articulated civilizing mission, but also of a host of chance factors, ranging from the personnel involved (some colonial experts having left an indelible mark, such as Lugard in West Africa, Shepstone in southern Africa, Grey in Australia and New Zealand and Warren Hastings in India),[1] through the unique exigencies of different periods (for example, the transportation of convict labor overseas) to the varying influence of climatic conditions (whether amenable or not to a settler population).

The legal possibilities varied from total non-recognition of any political authority (as was the case in Australia) to some form of formal recognition through treaties (as was the case in New Zealand and North America), with various degrees of partial acknowledgment and underlying understandings (as was the case in Africa and the subcontinent of India).

However, where treaties were signed, these formal aspects often were (or became) no more than ritualistic courtesies (for instance, where no complete meeting of minds emerged, often because of faulty translation or of verbal ambiguity, as in the Treaty of Waitangi in New Zealand) or where their provisions were ignored or violated, sometimes with the acquiescence of legal and judicial authorities, sometimes in defiance of them (and the United States provides ample examples of both situations).[2]

In many instances, the area being put under political control had not even been physically conquered or brought fully within the orbit of a foreign presence (such as the far western and northern reaches of the continent of Australia, much of the South Island in New Zealand, or the territory of Alaska, sold and ceded to the United States by the Russians, who barely maintained a token presence there, and for that reason were more than delighted with the price they received for what was mainly a heavy burden, costly in human losses and national prestige).[3] In some instances, arbitrary lines were drawn on inaccurate maps, such as at the Congress of Berlin in 1885, when Africa was carved up and shared out amongst European powers to provide some semblance of order in the wild 'scramble for Africa',[4] a resonating echo of the earlier papal decree that delineated areas of future conquest for Spain and Portugal.

The variety of these approaches have all been subjected to critical review over the years, reaching a crescendo in the past few years, some of it in terms of revisionist reappraisals of history, as carried out in both academic research and investigative journalism, some of it as official pronouncements of governmental commissions or judicial precedents – and in the last decade, there have been some major developments. Yet even when there are significant breakthroughs, such as the *Mabo* case in Australia,[5] a great deal of ambiguity persists, especially where there are several opinions given in the judgment, or where the ratio decidendi is not fully articulated, or where the specific problem adjudicated allows for a result that may not necessarily serve as a useful precedent for the future.

For instance, the *Mabo* decision dealt with a small group of people (no more than a thousand) on the Murray islands in the Torres Strait, different in many respects from Aborigine groups on the continent, and also dealt with territory originally annexed by a state (Queensland), known for its idiosyncratic approach to such issues relative to some of the other states in Australia.[6] Given the small size of the area in dispute, (about 9 sq km) and given the clear demarcation of its limits (at the sea's edge), it was relatively easy for a judicial pronouncement (categorically made for the first time in

Australia's history) that the Torres Straits Islanders had indeed maintained an independent and recognized political authority, prior to contact with Europeans – and so similar results may not necessarily have been attained if the case had been based on areas in the Australian mainland, over extensive tracts of land, some rich in mineral resources.

To express these reservations, is not to gainsay the tremendous significance of the *Mabo* decision; rather it is to draw attention to the problematics involved in using it as a precedent elsewhere on the Australian continent, for instance, in the limitless expanses of the Northern Territories, or in Western Australia, especially in areas where the Aborigines themselves practiced a nomadic existence (in contrast to the sedentary style of the Islanders), or on land where the prospects of rich sources of mineral wealth beckon, in contrast to the agricultural and horticultural nature of the islands.

Furthermore, Australia has only now embarked on a meaningful legal confrontation with its past, after over two hundred years of rejection of any claims to any form of even limited political authority or sovereignty.[7] Australia, till recently, was seen as having been *terra nullius* – a continent without even the slightest semblance of political rule for its original inhabitants.[8] New Zealand, too, has seen tremendous strides being taken in a reassessment of the rights of its Maori population, with the benchmark Treaty of Waitangi being rescued from the oblivion to which it had once been assigned by a series of judicial decisions asserting that it had no legal validity whatsoever.[9]

Compared to the situation in these two countries (and we shall return to examining their legal framework later on in this chapter),[10] the United States has presented a long string of authoritative judicial pronouncements, dating back to the early years of the nineteenth century, in which the nature of recognition accorded the Native American tribes was constantly being reinterpreted. Central to this ongoing debate was the opening gambit of recognition of their special status, a problematic assertion in itself, since it was linked not to a status of independence, but to a hybrid definition of the tribes being domestic dependent nations with therefore only limited sovereignty, as wards of the more dominant western society. Yet, within that framework, the tribes were allowed a significant degree of autonomy, including the right to have their own political and judicial frameworks. However, the definition of domestic dependent nations was a concept of great ambiguity – which could be used either as the basis for asserting rights (especially *vis-à-vis* the individual states in which the reservations were situated), or which could be used to deny even the preliminary right of access to the court, as happened in recent times, where the 11th Amendment (allowing for interstate judicial dispute) was held to be not applicable to an Indian nation.[11]

Furthermore, much of the adjudication dealing with the rights and status of Native American tribes was determined in cases, to which the Indians themselves were not parties – and crucial decisions as to their fate were made without their voice being heard. Thus, when two non-Indians disputed their property rights – as to land bought from the Indians or appropriated from them – the decision was based on the Court's description of the legal status of the tribe, yet with the tribe having no standing, not even as an *amicus curiae*, a friend of the Court (a position that was not yet recognized at that time) and thus unable to present its perspective and defend its rights, not in respect of the case alone but in general.

In addition, the debate over the status of the tribes can only be understood in the framework of political strife in the United States, especially focusing on the explosive issue of Federal power vs. states' rights. Briefly, it was only the Federal government that had treaty-making power, and so grants of land to be set aside for Indian reservations would be carved out of land within a state by the Federal government, with all the resultant complications of conflict of laws and clashes of authority.[12]

The fact of opposing interests at stake as between the Federal government and the states was a complicating factor in and of itself, but it became even more intensified, because of deep ideological divisions – with the Federalists seeking greater unity for the nation at large, and greater central power for the national government, as opposed to the anti-Federalists seeking to minimize federal control, and to protect states' rights. This rift found even personal expression, with the appointment in 1801 of Chief Justice Marshall to his high rank in the waning days of the last Federal Party government, in which Marshall himself had been a dominant figure as Secretary of State. It is widely accepted that the purpose of his appointment was to seek a strong Supreme Court that could balance the electoral victory of the anti-Federalists, under Thomas Jefferson.[13]

Many years later, echoes of this ideological struggle may be noted in the series of Indian cases, notably the struggle of the Cherokees against their 'host' state, Georgia.[14] In many respects, Marshall is considered to have come to the assistance of the Cherokees, but in essence his aim was to minimize the power of the state of Georgia. In the event, the state of Georgia ignored those aspects of his judgment that held out immediate support for the Indian position, with the connivance of the Federal government, under President Jackson. The Cherokees were eventually dispossessed of their lands – while the larger definitions laid down on behalf of the Indians were not to provide them in the future with the legal framework they had sought in mounting a judicial struggle.

The ostensible sympathy that Chief Justice Marshall may have felt toward the Cherokee is poignantly expressed in the two opening paragraphs of one of his later judgments:

> This bill is brought by the Cherokee nation, praying an injunction to restrain the state of Georgia from the execution of certain laws of that state, which, as is alleged, go directly to annihilate the Cherokee as a political society, and to seize, for the use of Georgia, the lands of the Nation which have been assured to them by the United States in solemn treaties repeatedly made and still in force.
>
> If courts were permitted to indulge their sympathies, a case better calculated to excite them can scarcely be imagined. A people once numerous, powerful and truly independent, found by our ancestors in the quiet and uncontrolled possession of an ample domain, gradually sinking beneath our superior policy, our arts and our arms, have yielded their lands by successive treaties, each of which contains a solemn guarantee of the residue, until they retain no more of their formerly extensive territory than is deemed necessary to their comfortable subsistence. To preserve this remnant, the present application is made.[15]

These opening remarks hint already that the outcome will only add to the tragedy described. Since the Constitution limits the power of the Supreme Court to act in the first instance only in cases between a state and the citizens thereof, or when one of the parties is a foreign state,[16] the Court holds that despite the special status of the tribes, they cannot be considered a 'foreign state', nor are they citizens – and they therefore have no standing in presenting a petition directly to the Supreme Court. The petition itself sought to prevent interference by the state of Georgia in the affairs of the Cherokee people, including attempting to invalidate laws and ordinances duly promulgated by their authoritative bodies pursuant to treaties signed with the Federal government. The tribes are a special type of political unit and, according to the Court, they may 'be denominated domestic dependent nations … They are in a state of privilege. Their relation to the United States resembles that of a ward to his guardian.'[17] As such, the Court comes to the (apparently) reluctant conclusion that 'If it be true that the Cherokee nation have rights, this is not the tribunal in which those rights are to be asserted. If it be true that wrongs have been inflicted, and that still greater are to be apprehended, this is not the tribunal which can redress the past or prevent the future.'[18] The implication, of course, is that the highest judicial authority in the land is incapable of providing the wards of the state with the protection they seek. In passing, it should be noted that, although Justice Marshall's opinion is given as the opinion of the Court, it is really no more than a plurality opinion, a compromise position (supported by only one other justice) between two other justices who wished to recognize the Cherokees as a foreign nation and two more justices, who wished to deny any special status to the subjugated Indian people – a seventh justice took no part in the proceedings.[19]

Within a year of this moral victory yet judicial defeat for the Cherokees, the Supreme Court was once again involved in a dispute involving the nature of the relationships between the state of Georgia and the Cherokee nation. This time, though, the Court had jurisdiction, as the issue was brought before it on appeal – not by the tribe, but by two non-Indians, missionaries who had been convicted of the crime of residing in the territory of the Cherokees (with their approval), but in violation of a Georgia law which made any such residence dependent on the grant of a license by the state governor. Violation of this statute entailed a minimum penalty of hard labor for four years.[20] This time the decision is an indirect judicial victory for the Cherokees with the nullification of the convictions, but the triumph is mainly symbolic, and practically worthless, as Georgia contemptuously defied the Court's directives, a successful defiance that is a prelude to the later illegal expulsion of the Cherokees in the 'Trail of Tears'.[21] The Court's judgment, written again by Chief Justice Marshall, deals at great length with the historical background of the tribes and their relation to the European powers and to the United States, including a treaty (the aptly named, but deceiving, Hopewell Treaty) between the Cherokees and the United States.[22]

The Court concluded that the laws and the acts of Georgia in respect of the Cherokee land are unconstitutional, since 'they interfere forcibly with the relations established between the United States and the Cherokee nation ... [and] they are in direct hostility with treaties, repeated in a succession of years, which mark out the boundary that separates the Cherokee country from Georgia ...'[23] and on this basis declared that the conviction had been in error. The import of this case was to recognize the judicial authority of the Cherokees but not their political sovereignty. Far more important, from Justice Marshall's ideological stance, was the limitation imposed by the decision on the power of the individual states. The decision given, it was now up to the authorities in Georgia to carry it out by releasing the appellants, but this they refused to do, and the standoff between the various authorities – judicial and executive, federal and state – was to last for several months before a compromise was reached in which the two prisoners finally acceded to the suggestion of the authorities in Georgia, and formally submitted a request for a pardon from the governor, which was immediately granted.[24]

Another appellant to the Supreme Court, also a victim of the Cherokee–Georgia struggle, was less fortunate. A Cherokee man had been charged with murder by a criminal court in Georgia. The crime had been committed in the Cherokee reservation, but the man, Corn (George) Tassels, had been abducted by the state authorities, after the Cherokee authorities had arranged a reconciliation ritual (including compensation) with the victim's family. On conviction in a Georgia court[25] he had been sentenced to death, and immediate attempts had been made to have the procedure declared illegal, as being a violation of Cherokee sovereignty – but, although a writ was granted by the Supreme Court to examine the procedures in this case, the officials in Georgia defied it, and pre-emptively carried out the execution a few days before the Supreme Court hearing was to take place.[26]

These cases represent the climax of the three-fold conflict between the federal government, the states and the Native Americans in which both positive judicial sentiments as to the qualities of the Cherokees and partially favorable judicial decisions were to no avail. But the groundwork for them was laid in two earlier cases, both dealing with land deeds in which non-Indians clashed in court over property rights in land that had either been sold by the Indians or expropriated from them. In these cases, *Fletcher v. Peck* and *Johnson v. M'Intosh*,[27] the real foundations were laid for the ideological structure substantiating the rights of the Europeans over those of the indigenous inhabitants, even though such a far-ranging analysis was not strictly speaking required in cases where the Indians themselves were not represented; yet their legal fate was conclusively determined – and to their detriment, despite any lingering doubts some of the justices might have had as to the moral implications of their jurisprudence.

At stake was not just the question of who owned a particular piece of real estate, but who was to be the controlling political authority in the great land mass that had been discovered by intrepid adventurers from Europe. In this contest, the struggle was not only, or even mainly, between the indigenous inhabitants and the initial settlers (and not even between the federal government and the states), but between the rival interests of imperial powers.

Indeed, the underlying assumptions of much of the legal and judicial reasoning echoed the earlier machinations of foreign political and commercial interests – namely, that the civilized people of Europe were to fulfill what became known later as a manifest destiny (or in Africa as the 'White man's burden') in populating and settling the 'New World' as its future rulers; the key issue of legal discourse was then not concern for the indigenous population, but the need to determine the rules by which such mastery was to be attained as and between the European powers.

In this context, the judicial authorities of the new and independent United States were more than willing to adopt convenient philosophies and ideologies of leading European jurists. Yet, even if this jurisprudential approach by the European powers was valid (a most dubious assumption, as will be shown), it did not mean that it would automatically apply in a newly independent country, with its total population in constant and direct contact with the indigenous population, in contrast to the distant and peripheral connections of the European powers with the American continent. Cognizant of the basic factors – the presence of a local population, sometimes hostile, sometimes accommodating, and the dangers of relentless rivalry amongst the Europeans for control of territory – a dual jurisprudential solution evolved; on the one hand, a differentiation between rights of occupancy (for the Indians) and rights of sovereignty (for the Europeans), and on the other hand, a legitimization of the conquest for the European power with priority claims, which came to be known as the discovery doctrine.[28] The co-ordinated solution provided that the first European nation to discover a particular tract of land would have a recognized right to sovereign control over it, whether that control was achieved by military conquest over the local population or by a peaceful agreement with them, generally in the form of a treaty, and whether or not the control was accompanied by colonial settlement.

The most recent extensive description of the discovery doctrine is provided by Robert Williams, who categorically castigates its philosophical and religious underpinnings, its political purposes and its human consequences, concluding that 'The Doctrine of Discovery was nothing more than the reflection of a set of Eurocentric racist beliefs elevated to the status of a universal principle – one culture's argument to support its conquest and colonization of a newly discovered, alien world'; and adding that there is no solution to indigenous right without a rejection of the doctrine, as even today the doctrine 'permits the West to accomplish by law and in good conscience what it accomplished by the sword in earlier eras: The physical and spiritual destruction of indigenous people.'[29]

While the novel idea of a 'domestic dependent nation' expounded by Justice Marshall in the *Cherokee v. Georgia* case became the singular concept around which much later debate took place, and while it seems to recognize a certain degree of sovereignty,[30] the real foundations of the legal structure was laid in the two earlier aforementioned (*Fletcher* and *M'Intosh*) cases – and these were the ones to effectively provide a legal imprimatur, in the context of the discovery doctrine, for imperial conquest of the past and political planning for the future.

It should also be noted that, while all these cases have been subjected to much intensive scrutiny, there is some confusion as to their several influences. Thus, some writers talk of the Marshall trilogy – dealing with three cases (*M'Intosh, Cherokee* and *Fletcher*) in which Marshall wrote the majority opinion.[31] Others refer to the *Cherokee* cases (but for some only the two from the 1830s); thus many writers ignore the first case (over which there has been extensive independent debate) – the case of *Fletcher v. Peck,* from 1810, also known as the Yazoo case; with the opinion also written by Marshall and which also dealt with the Cherokee tribe and Georgia. Finally, a recent article has drawn attention to the fact that, in the final year of Marshall's judgeship, a unanimous decision was handed down, written by one of the associate justices, which, according to the thesis represented, deviated substantively from the earlier decisions, but has been largely ignored.[32]

As to the importance of *Fletcher v. Peck,* Jill Norgren, in her more comprehensive discussion of *The Cherokee Cases* explains – correctly it would seem – that 'US Supreme Court involvement in federal Indian law began with *Fletcher v. Peck*'.[33] She adds that, while the case is regularly discussed because of its contribution to contract law, 'Less often do historians note that *Fletcher* began a series of cases in which the chief justice analyzed who, according to US law, had title to the lands of the continent.'[34] It was, in this case, that, for the first time, Chief Justice Marshall noted the limitations on the sovereignty of the Native Americans in the areas which had been set aside as reservations. Thus, while, on the one hand, Chief Justice Marshall recognized that the Indians had title to the land, the rights attaching to this title were linked only to occupancy, and not to sovereignty.

The issue in the Yazoo case involved a questionable land deal, in which land held by Indians in the state of Georgia had been sold to non-Indians by the state authorities without prior consent. An initial sale had later been cancelled by a Repeal Act, and it was the validity of the Repeal Act that gave rise to the litigation. Behind the case was the question to whom the land had originally belonged before its sale to private parties: to the Indians or to the state of Georgia, or possibly to the federal government.

The fraudulent deal is described in Justice Marshall's decision, and in order to clarify the legal issue he explained that the Indians did indeed have title to the land – an important finding for the protection of Indian rights. At the same time, he added that the title extended only to occupancy and not to ownership or sovereignty. Thus, the land could be alienated by the laws of property and contract to individuals, or even taken over by the state. The rights of the Indians were limited to those of possession alone. The essence of the case is well described by Norgren:

> Marshall invented the category of occupancy title and needed a legal rationalization for his confection. He found it in the concept Western jurists called the doctrine of discovery. In its most basic sense, discovery doctrine was a diplomatic rule initially used by European nations to govern their relations with one another in North and South America. To avoid the possibility of overlapping European colonial settlements, this policy dictated that the first European explorer of an area obtained the pre-emptive right with respect to later arrivals to acquire land from a willing Indian nation. Discovery doctrine lacked legitimacy because there had been no genuinely international

> agreement establishing it as a working principle of Native American–European relations ... At a minimum, the doctrine attempted to limit a tribe's right to negotiate freely with the government of its choosing. Over time, the doctrine came to express the view that by their very arrival Europeans had gained certain land rights despite the presence of the original Indian inhabitants.[35]

Norgen explains the various advantages that accrued to the United States by virtue of its adopting the discovery doctrine. Because of its European bias, it catered to the legitimacy sought by the United States, while at the same time facilitating the extension of further control over Indians in the western territories, still beyond the borders of the new country.

Although *Fletcher v. Peck* has attracted little attention in the literature on Indian rights, it should be noted that a strong dissenting opinion was recorded by Justice Johnson, who argued cogently for a recognition of the Indians' absolute ownership, especially since many treaties with the Indians were based on their recognition as an 'independent people'.[36] The Indian aspect of the decision, however, was overshadowed by the fraudulent activity that characterized the case.

This lacuna was remedied in 1823 with the case of *Johnson v. M'Intosh*,[37] where the Court confronted the dilemma of two ostensibly legal transfers of the same property, the first time by the Indians a few years before independence, the second time after independence, when the same tract of land was granted to non-Indians by the federal government, after it had taken possession of land that was presumed to be held by the Indians. The question before the Court was which grant of land was to be declared the binding agreement?

Once again, the opinion by Chief Justice Marshall relied heavily on the doctrine of discovery. This time he even extended its implications, adding several factors, including the wide gap that differentiated between the civilization of the conquerors and the backward state of the indigenous inhabitants; he holds that:

> the tribes of Indians inhabiting this country were fierce savages whose occupation was war, and whose subsistence was drawn chiefly from the forest. To leave them in possession of their country, was to leave the country a wilderness; to govern them as a distinct people was impossible because they were as brave and high-spirited as they were fierce, and were ready to repel by arms every attempt on their independence.
>
> That law which regulates, and ought to regulate in general, the relations between the conqueror and the conquered, was incapable of application to a people under such circumstances. The resort to some new and different rule, better adapted to the actual state of things, was unavoidable.[38]

With this kind of differentiation between the civilized people of Europe (of whom the settlers in America, now the citizens of the United States, were an extension), and the savage indigenous inhabitants of America, it needed only the formal application of facile logic to incorporate the doctrine of discovery into the American legal system, with all of its far-reaching implications. Marshall explains in his opinion that:

> On the discovery of this immense continent, the great nations of Europe were eager to appropriate to themselves so much of it as they could respectively acquire … But, as they were all in pursuit of nearly the same object, it was necessary, in order to avoid conflicting settlements … to establish a principle which all should acknowledge as the law by which the right of acquisition, which they all asserted, should be regulated as between themselves. The principle was that discovery gave title to the government by whose subjects, or by whose authority, it was made, against all other European governments, which title might be consummated by possession.[39]

As a consequence, all European states recognized the exclusivity of rights flowing from initial discovery. The key question for the Court then becomes: 'Have the American states rejected or adopted this principle?'[40] The answer is categorical, though the consequences may be ambivalent:

> The United States … have unequivocally acceded to that great and broad rule by which its civilized inhabitants now hold this country. They hold, and assert in themselves, the title by which it was acquired. They maintain, as all others have maintained, that discovery gave an exclusive right to extinguish the Indian title of occupancy, either by purchase or by conquest; and gave also a right to such a degree of sovereignty, as the circumstances of the people would allow them to exercise.[41]

The consequences are then spelled out in more detail, but not necessarily with full clarity, and it was specifically the veiled language that led later to the litigation of the early 1830s. The Court explains that

> the rights of the original inhabitants were, in no instance, entirely disregarded; but were necessarily, to a considerable extent, impaired. They were admitted to be the rightful occupants of the soil, with a legal as well as just claim to retain possession of it, and to use it according to their own discretion; but their rights to complete sovereignty, as independent nations, were necessarily diminished … .[42]

The doctrine of discovery thus took on additional meaning when applied, not by different colonial powers to avoid continued friction overseas and perhaps even an embroilment in Europe arising out of such friction, but a new nation, recently established by settlers, who had themselves sought – and succeeded – in escaping the yoke of domination. For this new nation, the key factor confronting it in its relations with the indigenous inhabitants was not how to allocate land as between rival foreign nations, but how to come to a viable *modus vivendi* with those indigenous inhabitants. In this respect, the discovery doctrine was a red herring, perhaps of some historical import, but not strictly relevant to the reality of a new nation in the recently 'discovered' continent. More important, beyond the borders of the United States, as then constituted, were extensive unexplored areas and many more as yet 'undiscovered' tribes.

Whatever the weight of historical facts and theories, the Cherokee cases presented an ideal opportunity to elucidate a new pattern of interaction between the settlers (now citizens of a new country) and the Indians. One of the possibilities was to create a mosaic of shared land, some of it under control of the settler-citizens, moving west, some of it under control of the Indian tribes with each group possessing equal status; the possible solution was not a federal grant of a reservation to Indians on state land (with all the complications that ensued), but a clear-cut demarcation between them; with the Cherokees (or any other tribe) not a domestic nation, but a fully-fledged state. In fact, the Cherokees had made every effort to adapt their political and legal structures to the model of the new country that had arisen in their midst, including a tripartite separation of powers and a written constitution guaranteeing civil rights.[43] If there was any truth in the oft-quoted assertion of a 'civilizing mission' in the Americas for the Europeans, the Cherokee people were an outstanding example of the success of that aim.

Among the many positive descriptions that exist of Cherokee achievements, is this nineteenth century explanation by Helen Jackson:

> In the whole history of our governments dealings with the Indian tribes, there is no record so black as the record of its perfidy to this nation … . From the beginning of the century they had been steadily advancing in civilization … . Every family had its farm under cultivation. The territory was laid off into districts, with a council-house, a judge and a marshal in each district. A national committee and council were the supreme authority in the nation. Schools were flourishing in all the villages. Printing-presses were at work.
>
> Their territory was larger than the three states of Massachusetts, Rhode Island, and Connecticut combined… they were enthusiastic in their efforts to establish and perfect their own system of jurisprudence. Missions of several sects were established in their country, and a large number of them had professed Christianity, and were living exemplary lives.

> There is no instance in all history of a race of people passing in so short a space of time from the barbarous stage to the agricultural and civilized.[44]

Here were special circumstances, which would have enabled the creation of a truly new form of shared government, linked to legal pluralism. But it was precisely these achievements that aroused the authorities in Georgia to action – in the realization that such an organized community would be reluctant to allow further inroads into its territory, its authority, and its way of life. Thus, the urgency of imposing political and judicial control over them, of continuing the purchase of their territory – and later, of forcible population transfer. Thus, far from the idea of a domestic dependent nation providing a positive solution it was a failed alternative to the possibility of full recognition. Of course, at the time, the Indians were not citizens of the United States, but in the course of several lengthy judgments, the Supreme Court had ample opportunity to ponder over such possibilities (as they had gratuitously posed other speculative ideas). Thus Marshall had noted the very 'extravagance' of the claim to discovery of an inhabited nation by conquest – yet had accepted its validity, despite the fact that much of the land had not been 'conquered' as such but attained through purchase. Furthermore, Marshall had not hesitated to be creative in determining the right of judicial review.[45] What was to hinder him in displaying similar creativity *vis-à-vis* Indian rights? The idea itself had even been raised during the discussions on confederation as the young nation sought support for its cause among the Indians, while the Treaty of Hopewell with the Cherokees had specifically envisaged the possibility of representation for the Cherokee tribe in Congress.[46]

Yet the ultimate paradox is that, a few years after the *Cherokee* case, the Supreme Court pronounced a judgment which seemed to be a *volte face* to its earlier decision. This decision has gone almost totally unnoticed, and efforts to revive its impact have yet to gain wide acceptance. In 1835, the Supreme Court in a unanimous judgment, set out a new understanding and definition of Indian rights.[47] David Wilkins has forcefully argued that the decision in *Mitchel v. United States* is of major importance, especially since it '... fundamentally contradicts the doctrines enunciated in *M'Intosh*. A critical review of *Mitchel* will reveal that ... the doctrine of discovery elaborated by Marshall in *M'Intosh* and used to diminish tribal sovereignty is without credibility as a legal principle.'[48]

Wilkins notes the 'scant attention' given this case, and suggests several reasons for it. While it also dealt with complicated land issues, some leading writers, such as the recognized authority, Felix Cohen, had downgraded its importance, because the 'Indian sale to whites had been made with the consent of the sovereign'.[49] Furthermore, the opinion, albeit a unanimous one, had been written by Justice Baldwin – 'one of the least liked and most bizarre justices and not the vaunted Chief Justice John Marshall ...'[50] Wilkins argues that the unanimous decision '...shows that the key concepts of "discovery" and "conquest" were actually terms designed more to limit competition between European nations; they were not, strictly speaking, created to diminish indigenous rights.'[51] Wilkins even suggests that the very radical nature of the opinion may have discouraged interest, as it tends to undermine standard thinking about aboriginal rights.

The case dealt with the sale of land by Indians (the Seminole tribe) to non-Indians in the state of Florida, when that territory had been under Spanish rule. Since the Spanish monarch had given his assent to the sale, its validity would be recognized even after the transfer of the territory to the United States. The case itself, from this perspective, seems quite straightforward, but the Court (through Justice Baldwin) took the opportunity to describe once again the nature of Indian title. The Court note that 'Friendly Indians were protected in the possession of the lands they occupied, and were considered as owning them by a perpetual right of possession in the tribe or nation inhabiting them as their common property from generation to generation.'[52] In addition, legal recognition was given to property held even in a different manner from that of western standards – thus, 'Indian possession or occupation was considered with reference to their habits and modes of life; their hunting-grounds were as much in their actual possession as the cleared fields of the whites...'.[53]

Specifically in terms of the impact of discovery, and the rights of the United States as a successor state to the European countries, the Court explains that the United States could not assume any '... right of conquest which may at any time have vested in Great Britain or Spain, for they had been solemnly renounced, and new relations established between them by solemn treaties'.[54] While the unique aspects of this case may have affected the reasoning of the justices, Wilkins argues that

> Whereas *M'intosh* stressed the discovery principle as the prime diminishing element to tribal political and proprietary rights, *Mitchel* never broached the doctrine ... Whereas *M'Intosh* relied on ethnocentric arguments of alleged tribal cultural inferiority as a significant factor that reduced Indian rights, *Mitchel* stated that even the hunting territory of tribes was entitled to protection and was equally as valid as the 'improved' farm fields of Anglo farmers.[55]

Wilkins concludes that

> Based on the historical, political and legal record examined, it is clear that the *Mitchel* decision is a far more accurate inquiry into the recognized rights unaffected by either the doctrine of discovery or the doctrine of conquest. In *M'Intosh*, history was 'discarded' and Marshall meticulously established the legal fiction of discovery and

> conquest to rationalize the diminution of tribal sovereignty and tribal property rights. But in *Mitchel*, Baldwin drew from and relied upon the historical record and the fact of tribal independence. The fact that the decision was unanimous, that it was written by Henry Baldwin [who in earlier cases had been one of the justices denying any rights whatsoever to Indians – L.S.][56] and that it was rendered a dozen years after *M'Intosh* should give legal, historical and political scholars pause to reconsider this powerful case ... .[57]

The possibility of undertaking a rewriting of the legal history of the past two hundred years seems a forlorn hope, yet that is precisely what the Australian Courts have consciously and deliberately done, in an attempt to revamp accepted axioms, and to partially redress past wrongs. But the issue in Australia was far more extreme – not a partial recognition of limited sovereignty, but a total denial of any rights, in an unfounded assumption that the Aborigines were devoid of any political authority. To the dubious legal doctrine of discovery, was added the recognized doctrine of *terra nullius*, but applied to a totally irrelevant situation. *Terra nullius* provided greater power even than discovery – it allowed absolute control to the discoverer of land lacking any recognized political authority. A land belonging to no one could be claimed in its entirety. Small uninhabited islands were the most obvious example of such a situation – but the doctrine was used for the land-mass of the entire continent of Australia – to its furthest reaches, where no settler had yet set foot, in desert or mountainous areas, where the Aborigines, in hundreds of small groups, maintained a degree of recognized authority. In Australia, thus, there were no treaties, nor semi-autonomous reservations set aside for dependent nations, no recognized tribal courts, nor title to the land. The denial of political power and of civil rights was absolute – but so was the denial of the social reality. It is only in recent years that attempts have been made to come to terms with this distorted picture, in which the *Mabo* decision is the most fundamental breakthrough, although some at least of the factual data and the changed social and political climate had been created earlier by academic research and a government commission on Aborigines.[58]

Within the spectrum of possibilities outlined in the opening paragraphs of this chapter, the Australian situation is at the opposite end to the American situation, not only in the rejection by the Australians of any need to grant any recognition to the indigenous peoples in contrast with the willingness of the Americans (and the British before them) to enter into treaties, but also in such additional matters as the fact that initially the legal determination of rights and status of Aborigines was largely a state matter, and not a federal concern, as in the United States.[59] Furthermore, the Australian approach has been transformed from one generally seen as being the most backward to a sea-change situation of being among the most progressive in its willingness to contemplate the adverse implications of the past and to countenance the introduction of new normative principles that are simultaneously deeply embedded in the age-old values of the common law.

Just a little over a hundred years after the Murray Islands (in the Torres Straits) had been annexed by the then colony of Queensland, in terms of official documents authorized by Queen Victoria, a group of islanders challenged the legal consequences of this action, which deprived them of ownership of the land. The petition for the recognition of native title was submitted to the court in 1982, and, after a lengthy process (in several court jurisdictions) the High Court of Australia (the highest court in the land) in a Full Bench decision handed down, a decade later, in 1992, declared that by the ordinary principles of the common law, native title remained intact.

There are many paradoxes to this case. The radical nature of the judgment is to be seen not in its consequences, which are minimal compared to the legal situation in other countries, but with its reasoning, and its utter rejection of earlier precedents. The issue at stake was after all neither sovereignty, nor the authority of courts, nor of political power, but merely of ownership rights. Also, the case is widely known by the name of the first applicant, a long-time political activist; but he had died shortly before the final judgment, although by then he had been secure in the knowledge (as indicated in his diary), that the ultimate legal victory was at hand.[60] Furthermore, the area involved was annexed in a separate act of the Crown in 1879 and was not incorporated as part of the wholesale declaration by which all of Australia was brought under British control[61] and there is a hundred years between these two acts, yet the court unhesitatingly and unnecessarily spread the ambit of its discussion into the earlier act, and it is this which gives major importance to its findings. In addition, the islanders themselves recognized individual or family ownership of land, whereas part of the legal problems associated with Aboriginal rights was their communal attitude to the land.[62] Indeed, in many respects, the specific issue at stake was so simple and clear-cut that one can only wonder at the inordinate amount of time it took for the petitioners to be accorded the justice of their claim.

Finally, the rights recognized by the Court are clearly of a conditional nature, since the judgment concedes that even the ownership that was acknowledged could be terminated by legislative expropriation, under similar conditions, for instance, of fair compensation as could be applied to other property owners. Parenthetically, it might also be noted that, subsequent to the decision, which laid much stress on the continuity of traditions in the Torres Strait Islands, a research report described how much change had actually been induced by the impact on the islands not of Europeans, but migrant Pacific Islanders. Anna Shnukal writes that

> Traditional institutions and relationships were constantly manipulated by the Pacific Islanders...[who] became the primary reference group for Torres Strait Islanders until the middle of this century.
>
> Torres Strait Islanders' perceptions of Pacific Islander 'custom' influenced almost every aspect of their traditional life for the first two contact generations.[63]

Because of these and other factors, the reaction to the judgment, while mainly positive, has also evoked a certain amount of criticism and skepticism.[64]

The basic transformation in the law – not strictly relevant for the specific legal issue under review – was the total negation of the doctrine of *terra nullius,* of the underlying assumption that the British had taken under their control a tract of land – a whole continent – that was devoid of any recognized political structure.

The idea of a legal situation of *terra nullius* in Australia had a long pedigree in its jurisprudence with several decisions in the nineteenth century, one as early as 1847, and later including affirmation of that stance in a Privy Council decision of 1889[65] and in the Australian High Court in two celebrated cases, as recently as the 1970s.[66] In the first case, an area reserved for Aborigines in the northern part of the country was handed over to a mining company for commercial exploitation. The lower court decision in favor of the company, denying any native title, was not appealed. The second case led to a High Court decision, which also reaffirmed that the doctrine of *terra nullius* was fundamental to the political and legal structure of Australia. Shortly thereafter, in a little-known case, which came to have some chance historical significance, the Court rejected a claim that a particular island in the Torres Straits was not part of Australia as it lay beyond the 60-mile limit of the borders of the state of Queensland.[67] Although the Court did concede that an error had been made in the demarcation of the border, this was interpreted as being merely technical. The following year, 1982, the Murray Islanders embarked on their lengthy quest for justice, which led ten years later to the *Mabo* decision.

The limitations of the doctrine of *terra nullius* had been amply expounded a few years earlier by the International Court of Justice in the important *Western Sahara* case, where it stated that in general practice current among the nations in the past 'territories inhabited by tribes or peoples having a social and political organization were not regarded as *terra nullius*...In the case of such territories the acquisition of sovereignty was not generally considered as affected unilaterally through "occupation" of "*terra nullius*" by original title but through agreements concluded with local rulers.'[68]

Similarly, in much of the common law world, several decisions in other countries had stressed the inherent nature of native title – most particularly three of seven justices in the 1973 Canadian decision of *Calder v. Attorney-General of British Columbia*.[69] In the absence of treaties in Australia, it is of particular significance to note that even though in Canada, official documents had been signed, recognizing indigenous rights, the Court spelled out the fact that, beyond any treaties or even special laws, it was the basic principles of the common law that provided the juridical recognition of native title.[70]

Within this emerging legal framework, the Australian High Court finally set aside the *terra nullius* doctrine. Perhaps more than the decision itself is what may be termed the meta-jurisprudence, the underlying themes that enabled the Court to overthrow long-standing precedents in a case with strong political overtones. Jeremy Webber, a Canadian jurist, has essayed a fascinating attempt to interpret the meaning of this approach and to supply the inner, hidden background to the decision – and, it seems, his thesis not only presents an accurate picture of the underlying factors in Australia, but also has a great deal of relevance for other troublesome legal situations.[71]

Drawing on the work of Gerald Postema,[72] Webber describes how a 'jurisprudence of regret' finds its expression in special situations, where the Court fulfills a unique role in exposing historical mistakes, and articulating the regret sensed at the injustices perpetrated in the past. Webber argues that without such sensitive willingness on the part of the Court, the legal factors on their own would not necessarily be sufficient to effect the radical change. Webber quotes from Postema's work to explain the

> way in which the past is crucial to our moral reasoning, one in which the past does not furnish positive models but instead gives rise to regret – in which we reflect on our actions in the past, we even acknowledge that they were a part of ourselves, but we believe that they pointed in a direction that we now judge to be wrong. We therefore seek to act in the present in a way that gets us back on the right track, coming to terms with our past, rectifying its effects on the present (to the extent we can), and charting a future course that accords better with what we take to be good in our community's experience. That ... is the nature of the moral enquiry underlying the recognition of indigenous title in Australia. The jurisprudence in *Mabo* is, above all, a jurisprudence of regret.[73]

Webber quotes from the several opinions in this case to show how the justices were indicating in one way or another, their sense of regret:

> The role of regret is patent in the judgment of Deane and Gaudron JJ. Their reasons refer to the 'conflagration of oppression and conflict'

> which was to 'dispossess, degrade and devastate the Aboriginal peoples and leave a national legacy of unutterable shame.' The acts and events of dispossession constituted, according to them, 'the darkest aspect of the history of this nation.' In those circumstances, the Court was under a duty to reconsider the legal doctrines that had ratified that dispossession, despite their long acceptance. 'The nation as a whole must remain diminished unless and until there is an acknowledgment of, and retreat from, those past injustices ...'[74]

He notes that even when such visible expressions of regret are absent, they may be subsumed within the rationale of the opinion. As an example, the opinion written by Justice Brennan, discusses equality but not, according to Webber, in a formal sense, but as a rejection of the 'discriminatory denigration' of the past. Brennan's language is more restrained and 'focuses on setting the Australian common law on a course free from the discriminatory attitudes of the past, not on roundly denouncing that past. But, in its way, it too is concerned with coming to terms with Australia's history, ridding the law of the legacy of discrimination and its complicity in the rationalisation of dispossession.'[75] Webber concludes this aspect of his analysis by asserting that the rejection of the earlier cases 'was an essential step in freeing the law of its discriminatory foundations and of welcoming Aborigines and Torres Strait Islanders to full membership in the Australian moral community'.[76]

In his final comments Webber stresses the role of judges in coping, on behalf of the nation, with the burdens of the past, and of elucidating its present concerns within the context of creating and expressing the new moral standards of the total community. Judges cannot escape the dilemmas of the past, when litigants raise these issues in their courts – in those circumstances, the courts are 'faced with the continuing presence of (the) legacy in the law' and are then forced 'to perpetuate or renounce it'.[77]

Indeed, arising out of the *Mabo* case, there have been further developments in the spirit of its decision. Legislation was enacted as a direct response to the Court's findings. At the Federal level, the Native Title Act of 1993 defined title as 'the communal group or individual rights and interests of Aboriginal peoples or Torres Straits Islanders in relation to land or waters, where (a) the rights and interests are possessed under the traditional laws acknowledged and the traditional customs observed, by the Aboriginal peoples or Torres Straits Islanders; (b) ... [they] by those laws and customs, have a connection with the land or waters; and the rights and interests are recognized by the common law of Australia'.[78] A Native Title Tribunal has been established to oversee the determination of title holding. Some of the land is in rich mining territory, and this involves examining the manner in which the state governments negotiate with mining groups for the right to lease land for mining purposes. There is an obligation to negotiate in good faith, and early decisions of the Tribunal indicate its intention to be activistic and sensitive to the claims of the Aborigines; where the Tribunal is not satisfied that the state government has fulfilled its fiduciary duty, it will intervene to protect the interests of Aborigines, even against the pressures of powerful mining and financial groups. However, as of this writing, the whole situation is in a state of flux and uncertainty, in the wake of the *Wik* decision,[79] in which the High Court extended its reasoning in *Mabo*, to recognize aboriginal rights in property considered to have been expropriated from them – a judicial decision, which touched off a heated political debate, leading eventually to an election in which opposing approaches to the rights of the Aborigines was one of the key issues.

In New Zealand, too, recent years have seen a reassessment of past policies toward the Maoris and former judicial precedents. In this instance, there is a treaty - in contrast with Australia, where there is none; but also, in contrast with the United States with its host of treaties, there is only one treaty – the Treaty of Waitangi of 1840.

Here was an attempt to ensure an organized and recognized transfer of authority from the original inhabitants to the representatives of the foreign power. Several hundred Maori chiefs from all over the land that was then known as (and is still called) Aotearoa, met with a delegation representing the British government, and after several days of intensive negotiations at Waitangi, in the north of the country, signed a short document, purporting to hand over authority to the British. Yet, ever since, the document has been a source of debate, as to the intent of the signatories and the meaning of the words, including contentions that the translation does not faithfuly convey the same message in the two versions, English and Maori; furthermore arguments have been advanced that not all the chiefs were party to the negotiations, and despite efforts to attain their subsequent consent, there were many, especially in the South Island, who refused to append their signatures. In any event, the treaty did not prevent a series of local wars between Maoris and settlers, and has been the object of diverse interpretations, ranging through a variety of approaches – from lacking all legal validity or, at the other end of the spectrum, a formalistic ruse to annex the country without bloodshed, to a constitutional document at the basis of New Zealand's political structure, and reaching a positive appraisal that sees it as the equivalent of a Magna Carta of rights.[80]

The treaty itself is short and simple, there is no reference to a transfer of land, nor is there even any direct reference to the British government. It is the Queen of England who is given 'all the rights and powers of sovereignty' and in return guarantees to the Maoris the 'full, exclusive and undisturbed possession of their Lands, Estates, Forests, Fisheries and other Properties', as well as the rights and privileges of British subjects (but not as citizens).[81]

One of the major problems of the treaty relates to the word 'sovereignty' – which, according to some Maori representatives, is not the meaning conveyed in the Maori version – which refers to no more than authority.[82] In fact, it would seem that the Maori chiefs were seeking, from their perspective, some form of protection or suzerainity mainly in order to pre-empt any efforts on the part of other European powers to take control. They preferred what they sensed was the more benign role of the British, or to be more exact, of the Queen. It was the authority of the British Sovereign that they sought, and not the sovereignty of the British government.

In any event, the dominant judicial approach in New Zealand was to denigrate the value of the treaty. Chief Justice Pendergast, in an 1877 judgment,[83] referred to the treaty as 'a simple nullity', since 'No body politic existed capable of making cession of sovereignty nor could the thing itself exist.' For, after all, the Maori were, in the words of the judgment, no more than 'primitive barbarians'. However, this decision was actually in conflict with an earlier decision, which basically recognized native title of ownership as such.[84]

More recently, the treaty has been rejuvenated – in judicial decisions, in academic research and in polemic debate. Increasingly it is seen as being a document with properties of a grundnorm[85] – of a foundational document; however, not so much for the recognition of sovereignty, but as providing wide-ranging protection for the group rights of the Maori and for their many cultural manifestations. On this basis, the Waitangi Tribunal, set up in the 1970s, has been active in helping to reconstruct historical demands for Maori rights in land and water, hunting and fishing, and in respect for the culture. More particularly, the 'nullity' doctrine was specifically nullified in the leading 1987 case, *New Zealand Maori Council v. Attorney-General*, which unhesitatingly underlined the deep moral obligations to protect Maori rights and preserve Maori culture, which flow from the treaty.[86]

However, there is not yet consensus as to its meaning and impact, as is borne out, in a brief, but pointed, manner, in a recent debate in the *New Zealand Law Journal.* Guy Chapman sees the treaty as being, no more than a 'fertile ground for judicial (and academic) myth making'.[87] According to him, the treaty 'is not, and never will be, a Bill of Rights or a constitutional document of any kind. Its modesty, its purposes and its non-legal character, preclude this.'[88] Beyond this, Chapman argues that neither the British representatives nor the Maori chiefs had the necessary authority to sign 'a treaty of cession'. On the contrary, it is no more than 'a legitimising pact of affirmation and allegiance',[89] and to substantiate this argument, he returns to Chief Justice Pendergast's 1871 decision, which he praises as having 'stood the test of time' with … its clarity of exposition, and basic soundness of judgment'.[90]

This article elicited immediate responses; thus Joe Williams[91] points out that lack of recognition of the treaty would put the whole British acquisition in jeopardy, for while it provides the Maoris as a group with certain selective advantages (which Chapman had criticized as being discriminatory),[92] it also provides the only basis by which British control of the islands could be recognized – since the *terra nullius* doctrine is clearly not applicable, nor was there at that stage, any military confrontation, which could have provided annexation by conquest. But beyond these technical arguments, Williams emphasizes the social and moral meaning of the treaty, stating that 'The court of Appeal in the *Maori Council* case took the view unanimously that the central principle of the treaty was the principle of partnership. The two important elements of that principle were, in that case, the duty of utmost good faith and the presence of responsibilities akin to fiduciary duties.'[93] He concludes that, whatever defects may be found in the treaty, there can be no return 'to the racist doctrines of the latter half of the nineteenth century … the Treaty of Waitangi is now firmly embedded in our legal and constitutional firmament'.[94]

With or without treaties, with or without dubious doctrines of discovery or of *terra nullius,* with or without Reservations set aside for the indigenous population, it is clear that the nature of the title that indigenous groups hold (in various parts of the world) is in dire need of intense scrutiny and overall reassessment, including willingness to examine historical evidence, criticize mythical conceptions, nullify legal errors – and search for practical means of expressing positive partnership, shorn of the biased assumptions of the past, and oriented to redressing the grievances that resulted, within an ideological framework of recognition of their basic rights, which were for so long denied, ignored or downgraded. It was faulty or biased judicial interpretation, no less than commercial interests or political intrigues, that contributed to the harm inflicted; it is through judicious judicial intervention that some of this hurt may be assuaged.

NOTES

1. See, for instance, Frederick Lugard, *The Dual Mandate in British Tropical Africa* (London: Frank Cass, 1965); Runcajit Guha, *A Rule of Property for Bengal: An Essay in the Idea of Permanent Settlement* (Durham, NC: Duke University Press, 1996 – first published 1963).
2. On the Treaty of Waitangi, see Claudia Orange, *The Treaty of Waitangi*, (Wellington: Allen and Unwin, 1987). On the position in the United States, see for instance, Francis Paul Purcha, *The Great Father: The United States Government and the American Indian* (Lincoln: University of Nebraska, 1984); Wilcombe Washburn, *Red Man's Land/White Man's Law: The Past and Present Status of the American Indian* (Norman: University of Oklahoma Press, 1995, 2nd edn); Petra Shattuck and Jill Norgren, *Partial Justice: Federal Indian Law in a Liberal Constitutional System* (New York: Berg, 1991).

3 See, for instance, Hector Chevigny, *Russian America* (New York: Viking, 1965); and S.F. Starr (ed.), *Russia's American Colony* (Durham, NC: Duke University Press, 1987). See also Sidney Harring, 'The Incorporation of Alaskan Natives under American Law: United States and Tlingit Sovereignty, 1867–1900', *Arizona Law Review*, 31 (1989), p. 279.
4. See Thomas Packenham, *The Scramble for Africa* (Johannesburg: Jonathan Ball Publishers, 1991). See also Ian Brownlie, *African Boundaries: A Legal and Diplomatic Encyclopedia* (London: C. Hurst, 1979).
5. *Mabo v. Queensland*, (1992) 175 CLR 1; 66 ALJR 408; (1992) 107 ALR 1. See discussion of this case in latter part of this chapter.
6. On Queensland, see, for instance, Garth Nettheim, *Victims of the Law: Black Queenslanders Today* (Sydney: George Allen & Unwin, 1981). It should also be noted that there were special legal circumstances related to the incorporation of the islands into Australia.
7. See, for instance, Chava Shachor-Landau, 'Protection of the Aborigines in Australia: Law and Practice', *Israel Yearbook on Human Rights* 21 (1992), p. 87.
8. For a recent case prior to *Mabo*, see *Milirrpum v. Nabalco Pty. Ltd. and the Commonwealth of Australia*, (1971) FLR 141.
9. See, for instance, special issue of *New Zealand Universities Law Review* (1990) on the Treaty of Waitangi; see also I.H. Kawharu (ed.), *Waitangi: Maori and Pakeha Perspectives of the Treaty of Waitangi* (Auckland: Oxford University Press, 1989). And see below in this chapter.
10. For a recent general, comparative discussion, see Richard Bartlett, 'Native Title: From Pragmatism to Equality before the Law,' *Melbourne University Law Review* 20 (1995), p. 282. As explained in the headnote, 'This article presents an overview of the law and practice of native land in The United States, Canada, New Zealand and Australia'. He argues convincingly that 'The concept of native title raises fundamental questions as to the nature and evolution of law' (p. 283).
11. See *Blatchford v. Native Village of Noatak*, 111 S.Ct. 2578 (1991).
12. See David Currie, 'The Constitution in the Supreme Court: the Power of the Federal Courts, 1801–1835', *University of Chicago Law Review* 49 (1982), p. 654.
13. See, for instance, the biography by Leonard Baker, *John Marshall: A Life in Law* (New York: Macmillan, 1974); he writes (p. 350): 'Adams knew he himself would not have another term in office; Jefferson would most likely be the next President. The Federalists also were in trouble in Congress. Only the appointment of a strong Federalist to the chief Justiceship offered the prospect of securing the remaining branch of government to the Federalists.'
14. In general, see Jill Norgren, *The Cherokee Cases: The Confrontation of Law and Politics* (New York: McGraw-Hill, 1996); and Joseph Burke, 'The Cherokee Cases: A Study in Law, Politics and Morality', *Stanford Law Review* 21(1969), p. 500.
15. *Cherokee Nation v. Georgia*, 30 US (5 Pet.) 1 (1831), pp. 10–11.
16. This was a key factor in the major decision of *Marbury v. Madison*, widely assumed to be the basis of judicial review. However, there are arguments that it was wrongly decided, as Congress has the power, by virtue of the exception clause in Article 3 of the Constitution, to add to circumstances in which the Supreme Court may sit as a court of first instance, beyond the two examples given in Article 3. For arguments to this effect, see William Van Alstyne, 'A Critical Guide to *Marbury v. Madison*', *Duke Law Journal* 1 (1969), p. 15. For a differing viewpoint, see Robert Clinton, *Marbury v. Madison and Judicial Review* (University Press of Kansas, 1989) at pp. 94–7.
17. *Cherokee Nation v. Georgia*, p. 12.
18. Ibid., p. 14.
19. The dissenting justices were Storey and Thompson, who argued that 'the Cherokees compose a foreign state within the sense and meaning of the Constitution, and constitute a competent party to maintain a suit against the state of Georgia' (p. 80).
20. *Worcester v. Georgia*, 31 US (6 Pet.) 515 (1832).
21. See, for instance, John Ehle, *Trail of Tears: The Rise and Fall of the Cherokee Nation* (New York: Doubleday, 1988), and W.L. Anderson (ed.), *Cherokee Removal: Before and After* (Athens: University of Georgia Press, 1992).
22. Treaty of Hopewell, 28 November 1785, United States–Cherokee Indians, 7 Stat. 18.
23. *Worcester v. Georgia*, p. 560.
24. See Norgren, *The Cherokee Cases*, at pp. 126–8.

25. *State v. George Tassels*, 1 Dud. 229 (1830).
26. For description of this case, see Norgren, *The Cherokee Cases*, pp. 95–8, sub-titled, 'The *Tassels* Case: Failure of a Legal Test of Cherokee Rights'.
27. See *Fletcher v. Peck,* 10 US (6 Branch) 87 (1810); and *Johnson v. M'Intosh,* 21 US (8 Wheat) 543 (1823).
28. The two leading European authorities as to the international law situation were the Spaniard, Francisco de Victoria, who strongly supported Indian rights ('On the Indians Recently Discovered') and the Swiss, Emmerich von Vattel ('The Law of Nations or the Principles of Natural Law'). However, despite support for aboriginal rights Van Vattel also argues, that when 'the Nations of Europe, which are too confined at home, come upon lands which the savages have no special need of and are making no present and continuous use of, they may lawfully take possession of them and establish colonies in them.' But even such possession is premised on prior consideration of aboriginal needs and usage.
29. Robert Williams, Jr., *The American Indian in Western Legal Thought: Discourses of Conquest* (New York: Oxford University Press, 1990), p. 326. Williams ends his book with a final lengthy footnote, which culminates in the claim that the 'Doctrine of Discovery … is fundamentally at odds with the universal principles of the equality and human dignity of all peoples reflected in contemporary human-rights law and standards' (p. 333). See also his more recent book, in which he 'examines the response of North American Indian peoples to the West's "will to empire" over them' – Williams, *Linking Arms Together: American Indian Treaty Visions of Law and Peace, 1600–1800* (New York: Oxford University Press, 1997), p. 3.
30. The degree to which the concept of 'domestic dependent nation' was intended not merely to assure Federal control over the Indians and pre-emptive rights *vis-à-vis* the states, but also to assert claims against European countries, may be seen in Chief Justice Marshall's comments immediately after using that term – he writes, in *Cherokee v. Georgia*:

    > They [the Indians] look to our government for protection; rely upon its kindness and its power; appeal to it for relief to their wants; and address the president as their great father. They and their country are considered by foreign nations, as well as by ourselves, as being so completely under the sovereignty and dominion of the United States, that any attempt to acquire their lands, or to form a political connection with them, would be considered by all as an invasion of our territory, and an act of hostility (p. 12).

    Of course, inasmuch as the Court itself was part of this government to which the Indians looked for protection, it was not forthcoming in this case, the *Cherokee Nation v. the State of Georgia.* In fact, in the very next paragraph, the crucial decision not to accept jurisdiction, is explained: 'The considerations go far to support the opinion, that the framers of our Constitution opened the courts of the union to our controversies between a state or the citizens thereof, and foreign states' (p. 12) (and thus, by implication, not to domestic, dependent nations). Finally, in order to provide some local flavor to his argument, Marshall adds:

    > In considering this subject, the habits and usages of the Indians, in their intercourse with their white neighbours, ought not to be entirely disregarded. At the time the Constitution was framed, the idea of appealing to an American court of justice for an assertion of right or a redress of wrong, had perhaps never entered the mind of an Indian or of his tribe. Their appeal was to the tomahawk or to the government. This was well understood by the statesmen who framed the Constitution of the United States, and might furnish some reason for omitting to enumerate them among the parties who might sue in the courts of the Union (p. 12).

    Of course, even here Marshall was in clear factual error, as the constitution referred not to the Courts, which were not yet in existence at the Federal level, but to the Supreme Court. Furthermore, the reference to 'controversies between a state or the citizens thereof, and foreign states' seems to be a reference to the Supreme Court alone – referring to cases where it could be a court of first instance. Had it not been for this error, he might well have suggested to the petitioner that they submit their plea in the first instance to a lower court, with the hint even that the Supreme Court would be sympathetic to their petition if the matter should come to it on appeal.

31. See, for instance, Philip Frickey, 'Marshalling Past and Present: Colonialism, Constitutionalism, and Interpretation in Federal Indian Law', *Harvard Law Review* 107 (1993), p. 381. Frickey's approach is most positive toward Marshall's decisions, and argues for the need to revive his ideas, in particular the legal importance of Indian cases. Noting the disdainful attitude adopted by many justices to Indian cases, he writes: 'Federal Indian law does not deserve its image as a tiny backwater of law inhabited by impenetrably complex and dull issues. From the standpoint of scholarly interest, few areas, if any, are more fundamental to an assessment of the normative and constitutional components of American law' (p. 383). Then arguing for a return to the legacy of Marshall, Frickey claims that 'The history of federal Indian law since Chief Justice Marshall has been filled with tragedy, a story in which the rule of law has become a vehicle to rationalize what can only be understood as crimes against humanity' (p. 427). For an interesting survey of the Marshall legacy (based on the two cases from the 1830s) in comparison to a more recent decision, written by Justice Thurgood Marshall, see Rennard Strickland and William Strickland, 'A Tale of Two Marshalls: Reflections on Indian Law and Policy, the Cherokee Cases, and the Cruel Irony of Supreme Court Victories', *Oklahoma Law Review* 47 (1994), p. 111. The later case is *Choctaw Nation v. Oklahoma,* 397 US 620 (1970), (while the authors focus mainly on the Worcester decision, in which, of course, the Cherokees were not parties). They write: 'A uniting thread between these two Indian law cases, authored by two different Justice Marshalls, is that while the tribe prevailed in each, the victory was cruelly ironic. In each case, national policy ultimately trumped the Supreme Court's legal judgment' (p. 111).
32. David Wilkins, '*Johnson v. M'Intosh* Revisited: Through the Eyes of *Mitchel v. United States*' *American Indian Law Review* 19 (1994), p. 159. The case is *Mitchel v. United States*, 34 US (9 Pet.) 711 (1835).
33. Wilkins, '*Johnson v. M'Intosh Revisited*', p. 87.
34. Ibid., p. 88. The case is described in full detail in C. Peter Magrath, *Yazoo: Law and Politics in the New Republic – The Case of Fletcher v. Peck* (Providence: Brown University Press, 1966). Despite its detail, the book makes only some half-a-dozen references to the Indians. Magrath explains how the first Yazoo sale eventually fell apart. The land lay deep in Indian territory controlled by a powerful confederation of Cherokee, Creek, Choctaw, and Chickasaw tribes. Spain, which claimed the territory south of the Yazoo River, encouraged the Indians to attack the frontier settlements in this vast region. Not surprisingly, the land companies found it difficult to promote colonization schemes. They suffered another setback in 1790, when President Washington warned them not to interfere with the treaty rights of the Indian tribes; under the new federal Constitution the power to negotiate treaties with the Indians belonged exclusively to the national government (pp. 4–5).

    Later Magrath explains:

    > It is true that the land companies had bribed many ... members [of the legislature], but the terms of the sale were not unreasonable. If it was a corrupt bargain, it was not necessarily a bad one. The Georgia treasury was empty, and the state needed cash with which to pay her militia. Was it really such bad trade for Georgia to sell land whose title was in many places clouded by three sets of conflicting claims – those of Spain, the federal government, and the Indian tribes? As a matter of fact, the sale act protected the state of Georgia in case her title should prove defective. It declared that the grantees of the land were to assume all the expenses of extinguishing the Indian claims and it wisely provided that the state was to be free of suits if any of the competing claims prevailed over those of Georgia ... it is well to remember that the Yazoo territory was a remote wilderness in the late eighteenth century (pp. 14–15).

35. Norgren, *The Cherokee Cases*, p. 89.
36. *Fletcher v. Peck*. Justice Johnson was to adopt a contrary position in some of the later decisions.
37. *Johnson v. M'Intosh*.
38. Ibid., p. 590.
39. Ibid., p. 572.
40. Ibid., p. 583.
41. Ibid., p. 586.
42. Ibid., p. 572. There is an interesting consequence to the legal denial of rights of sovereignty –

in terms of the status of Amerindians captured in the course of violent battles between them and the official soldiers of the United States or one of the states. Was the conflict a war, in which case, they were to be treated as prisoners of war – or was it an insurrection for which the participants could be punished? For the trial in 1862 in a Military Commission, of nearly 400 Dakotans (part of the Sioux people), most of whom were convicted, and sentenced to death (with the majority being pardoned by President Lincoln, and 38 being executed), see Carol Chomsky, 'The United States–Dakota War Trials: A Study in Military Injustice', *Stanford Law Review* 43 (1990), especially at pp. 76–81, referring, *inter alia*, to some of the Cherokee cases. She opens the discussion of this issue: 'The first question is whether the Dakota were a sovereign people capable of declaring war on the United States. The Dakota had no doubt about their own sovereign status and their consequent right to declare and fight a war.'

43. For a good description of the Cherokee political and legal structure, see John Reid, *A Law of Blood: The Primitive Law of the Cherokee Nation* (New York: New York University Press, 1970).
44. Helen Jackson, *A Century of Dishonor: A Sketch of the United States Government's Dealings with some of the Indian Tribes* (Michigan: Scholarly Press, 1974 [1880]), pp. 270–1. This book has some historical importance as one of the first comprehensive and critical studies of the status of the Indian tribes, with separate chapters on the Delaware, Cheyenne, Nez Percés, Sioux, Poncas, Winnebagoes, and the Cherokee tribes, and a separate section dealing with three massacres of Indians by Whites. For good descriptions of other organized tribes, especially in the pre-colonial period, see Dorothy Jones, *License for Empire: Colonialism by Treaty in Early America* (Chicago: University of Chicago Press, 1982), especially Chapter 2, 'Iriquois Mystique', p. 21. She writes that: 'The organizational skill of the Iriquois is evident in the structure and longevity of their confederacy. Confederation was a common political form throughout eastern North America ... Long before the coming of the Europeans, the Indians of the area were forming themselves into confederacies of varying size, strength, cohesion, and formality in a constantly shifting pattern of alliances and conquests' (p. 23). For a further example of the special attitude of respect held toward the Iriquois, see an unusual document – Extra Census Bulletin – Indians – The Six Nations of New York (1892) – recently reprinted by Cornell University Press, 1995. In his introduction to the Reprint edition, Robert Venables explains that at the time of the 1890 census, the US Government was attempting to break up tribal land into individual allotments, in terms of the Dawes Act of 1887. However, 'Because the legal status of the Six Nations was complex, the Iroquois Confederacy had been exempted from the act. The Six Nations is in part an attempt to see if and how the principles of the Dawes Act could be applied to the Iroquois' (p. viii). The book provides details of these six tribes showing how advanced they were. 'Such facts permitted officials to calculate whether the Six Nations were ready to join the American mainstream' (p. viii) – but the very treaties signed with such an organized group, posed problems in their assimilation on an individual basis. It does not seem to have occurred to the authorities that they could have been incorporated as a group into the country's federal structure.
45. This is based on his decision in *Marbury v. Madison,* but see my earlier critical comments at n. 16. I have discussed this case critically in my Hebrew book, *The Rule of Law and the Nature of Politics* (Tel Aviv: Papyrus Publishers, Tel Aviv University, 1996).
46. Before the American Constitution was adopted, the idea of Indians joining the Confederation had been raised, for instance in the Treaty of Ft. Pitt, signed with the Delawares on 17 September 1778. A similar offer was made in 1785 in the Treaty of Hopewell with the Cherokees, where it was suggested that they send a deputy to Congress. See Arnon Gutfield, 'The Deprivation of Indian Sovereignty, 1776–1871' (unpublished manuscript) – for documents see Charles Kappler (ed.), *Indian Affairs, Laws, and Treaties*, 5 vols (Washington, DC: (1903–41). There is also much evidence of lobbying activities by representatives of the Indians in Washington. Furthermore, three years before the Declaration of Independence, a 1773 Privy Council decision (*Mohegan Indians v. Connecticut*) had drawn a parallel between the legal status of the tribes and the then colonies. The very language of the Declaration of Independence could well have been used – if not by politicians, then by the judiciary – to accord the same right to independence for the tribes that had been so eloquently asserted for the colonists. Nearly all American jurists ignore the *Mohegan Indians v. Connecticut* case in their analyses, but it is reported in J.H. Smith, *Appeals to the Privy Council from the American Plantations* (New York: Columbia University Press, 1950). Interestingly, it is mentioned by a Canadian jurist; see

Bruce Clark, *Native Liberty, Crown Sovereignty: The Existing Aboriginal Right of Self-Government in Canada* (Montreal: McGill–Queens University Press, 1990). Clark makes reference to this case because he argues that, having been decided before the American Revolution, it is a binding precedent in Canadian law, without reference to its status in the United States. It should however be noted that, in terms of land rights, the Indians lost.

47. *Mitchel v. United States.*
48. Wilkins, '*Johnson v. M'Intosh Revisited*', p. 160.
49. Felix Cohen, *Handbook of Federal Indian Law* (Washington: Government Printing Office, 1942), p. 160, at n. 7.
50. Wilkins, '*Johnson v. M'Intosh Revisited*', p. 161. It may be noted that this was the last decision in which Marshall participated.
51. Ibid., p. 161.
52. *Mitchel v. United States*, p. 758.
53. Ibid., p. 758.
54. Ibid., p. 754.
55. Wilkins, '*Johnson v. M'Intosh Revisited*', p. 179.
56. See, for instance, Justice Baldwin's concurring opinion in *Cherokee Nation v. Georgia,* where in denying the petition, he also disagreed with Marshall's concept of 'domestic dependent nation'. Thus, Baldwin writes of Georgia's control over Indian territory as being 'as supreme as that of Congress over what the nation has acquired by cession from the states or treaties with foreign powers ... Within [Georgia's] boundaries there can be no other nation, community, or foreign power ...' (p. 31).
57. Wilkins, '*Johnson v. M'Intosh Revisited*', p. 181.
58. The Commission's Report was published in 1990, shortly before the High Court decision in *Mabo v. Queensland*, (1992) 175 CLR1 was handed down in 1992. See *The Recognition of Aboriginal Customary Laws* (Canberra: Government Publishing Service, 1986).
59. However, it should be noted, that the Northern Territory, where there is a large concentration of Aborigines (though not a majority of the population) in a sparsely populated area, is not a state, but is under some partial federal control – for instance, legislation passed by the legislature of the Territory may be overruled by the Federal Parliament.
60. See fascinating account of his life, with extracts from his diary, in Noel Loos and Koiki Mabo, *Edward Koiki Mabo: His Life and Struggle for Land Rights* (St Lucia: University of Queensland Press, 1996).
61. Some legal argument has related to the fact that Captain Cook, in his proclamation, exceeded the authority given him, as he had been mandated to first check if the land was uninhabited in order to claim it by discovery, but if inhabited, to take possession only 'with the consent of the native peoples.' This point was cited in an unreported 1989 case. See *Aboriginal Law Bulletin* 2 (April, 1989), p. 14, for discussion of *Rex v. Walker.* It should also not be forgotten that part of the motivation for seeking possession was to have a place to send convicts to. While Cook landed in 1770, the formal ceremony of acquisition took place in 1788, although the western area was populated only some 50 years later.
62. See also a different perspective (also describing 'substantial factual differences' between the islanders and '... the Aboriginal inhabitants of the remote areas of mainland Australia' – at p. 164) in Michael Hunt, 'Mineral Development and Indigenous People – the Implication of the Mabo Case', *Journal of Energy and Natural Resources Law* 11 (1993), p. 155.
63. Anna Shnukal, 'Contact and Cultural Creolisation in Torres Strait,' *Australian Aboriginal Studies* 2, (1995), p. 52.
64. For general discussion, see M. Stephenson and S. Ratnapala (eds), *Mabo: A Judicial Revolution* (Brisbane: University of Queensland Press, 1993). See also Melissa Manwaring. 'A Small Step or a Giant Leap: the Implications of Australia's First Judicial Recognition of Indigenous Land Rights: *Mabo and Others v. State of Queensland*, 107 A.L.R. 1 (1992) Aust', *Harvard International Law Journal* 34 (1993), p. 177.
65. See *Attorney-General v. Brown* (1847) 1 Legge 312i; and for the Privy Council decision, *Cooper and Stuart*, 14 App. Cas. 286 (1889).
66. See *Milirrpum v. Nabalco* (also referred to as Cove Land Rights Case), and *Coe v. The Commonwealth of Australia,* 53 A.L.R. 403 (1979).
67. *Wacando v. The Commonwealth and the State of Queensland*, 148 C.L.R. 1 (1981). The case is

discussed in Nii Lante Wallace-Bruce, 'Two Hundred Years On: A Reexamination of the Acquisition of Australia', *Georgia Journal of International and Comparative Law* 19 (1989), p. 87.

68. Advisory Opinion on Western Sahara [1975] ICJR 12, p. 39.
69. *Calder v. Attorney-General of British Columbia*, (1973) 34 DLR (3d) 145.
70. For a comprehensive argument as to the common law's approach to native title, see K. McNeil, *Common Law Native Title* (Oxford: Clarendon Press, 1989).

    See also his article 'A Question of Title: Has the Common Law been Misapplied to Dispossess the Aboriginals?', *Monash Law Review* 16 (1990), p. 91. For discussion of his work, and that of other Canadian jurists, see below, Chapter 12, 'Land is Forever'. Despite their references to sovereignty and authority, the key judicial issue in Canada is of land rights. Some of the specific land aspects that have emerged in Australia since the *Mabo* decision, and as a direct result of it, will also be discussed below in Chapter 12, including ensuing legislation, such as the Federal Native Title of 1993, aiming to support the thrust of the *Mabo* decision and some state legislation aimed at frustrating it.
71. Jeremy Webber, 'The Jurisprudence of Regret: The Search for Standards of Justice in Mabo', *Sydney Law Review* 17 (1995), p. 5.
72. Gerald Postema, 'On the Moral Presence of our Past', *McGill Law Journal* 36 (1991), p. 1153.
73. Webber, 'The Jurisprudence of Regret', p. 10.
74. Ibid., p. 16.
75. Ibid., p. 16.
76. Ibid., p. 17.
77. Ibid., p. 28.
78. Sec. 223(1) of Native Title Act 1993. See special edition, published in 1994 with Commentary by the Attorney-General's Legal Practice. See also Collection of articles in M.A. Stephenson, *Mabo: The Native Title Legislation: A Legislative Response to the High Courts Decision* (St Lucia: University of Queensland Press, 1995), (Special issue of *University of Queensland Law Journal*).
79 Wik (1996) 187 CLR 1.
80. See, for example, Paul MacHugh, *The Maori Magna Carta* (Auckland: Auckland University Press, 1991).
81. See discussion by Ian MacDuff, 'Biculturalism, Partnership and Parallel Systems: The Context of Maori Rights' in William Twining (ed.), *Issues of Self-Determination* (Aberdeen: Aberdeen University Press, 1991), p. 102.
82. The Maori term used is 'rangatiratanga', which does not convey the idea of sovereignty. See MacDuff, 'Biculturalism, Partnership and Parallel Systems', pp. 107–12.
83. *Wi Parato v. Bishop of Wellington*, (1877) 3 N.Z. Jur. (NS) 72, S.Ct.
84. See discussion of relevant cases in Frederick Hackshaw, 'Nineteenth Century Notions of Aboriginal Title and Their Influence on the Interpretation of the Treaty of Waitangi', in Kawharu (ed.), *Waitangi*, p. 92, especially referring to *R. v. Symonds* (1847) NZ PCC (1840–1939) 387.
85. See Hans Kelsen, *General Theory of Law and State* (Cambridge, MA: Harvard University Press, 1949).
86. *New Zealand Maori Council v. Attorney-General* [1987], NZLR 641. This is only one of several cases in which the petitioner was the Council; see also, for example, *New Zealand Maori Council v. Attorney General* [1989] 2 NZLR 142 (CA).
87. Guy Chapman, 'The Treaty of Waitangi–Fertile Ground for Judicial (and Academic) Myth-making', *New Zealand Law Journal* (July 1991), p. 228.
88. Ibid., p. 235.
89. Ibid., p. 231.
90. Ibid., p. 231.
91. Joe Williams, 'Chapman is Wrong', *New Zealand Law Journal* (October 1991), p. 373.
92. For instance Chapman, 'The Treaty of Waitangi', writes (at p. 233), that the myth expresses 'the apparent wishful desire of some of our judges for a 'higher law' Constitution, which, fortunately for the rest of us, does not exist and, with continuing good political management, will never be imposed upon us.'
93. Williams, 'Chapman is Wrong', p. 375.
94. Ibid., p. 375.

—7—

Between Recognition and Repugnancy

The extent to which recognition is accorded to customary law and to the basic rights of tribal communities is a consequence of a multiplicity of factors, none of which is determinative, and all of which have an effect to some degree or another. The most pronounced factor is formal acknowledgment in a legal document – such as where a treaty is entered into or a law legislated, laying down in uniform manner the parameters within which customs may continue to be practiced, or alternatively stating their subordination to the state legal system, or even their abolition.

However, there are few spheres in which social reality so insistently takes precedence over legal dictate as the tenacity with which people adhere to their way of life as forged in the crucible of everyday living; and so, whatever the declared legal situation, cognizance must always be given to the 'living law' of the community. This is indeed true of any community, and becomes all the more pertinent when that community, by whatever name known, has some sort of consciousness of its own separate identity.

Linked to these factors – of law and of reality – is the ideological background within which people perceive of the surrounding social environment, and in particular – in the context of culture contact – the manner in which they relate to their own culture (proud of its dominance or humbly aware of its limitations, or alternatively, disheartened by its subjugation or defiant at its conquest) or to other cultures (exotic, quaint, abhorrent, attractive, irrelevant).

A further possibility is whether the more powerful entity ignores or denies the very existence of any organized social order, thus refraining from making any specific dispensation, on the general assumption that there will only be one organized and unified legal structure, that of the dominant group.

Finally, there is the legal doctrine which is applied, itself partly based on the presumed nature of reality. In the common law, distinctions were traditionally made between territories that were conquered by force, those ceded by agreement, and those occupied in the presumed absence of any claim by the original inhabitants to effective control. Different consequences arose from such distinctions in terms of how much tolerance would be displayed to the changing life of the indigenous population.

Within these broad frameworks there are a host of possibilities and, as we shall see, it was various combinations of factors that led to differing approaches in the various reaches of the British empire. Indeed, critical decisions made in earlier centuries of British conquest still continue to influence the legal structure of countries that have themselves undergone vast transformation, including gaining their own independence from Britain.

In Australia, in the absence of a treaty, and in the light of obliviousness as to any ordered life among the indigenous inhabitants, no formal decision was ever made as to what was to be the status of customary practices – and, over the years, where problems of conflict arose, it was left to the judges to struggle over the degree of recognition that they would accord the inhabitants whenever issues of customary law arose.[1] Very little of this litigation reached the higher levels of the judicial hierarchy, so that it remained, for the most part, localized, preventing a proper examination of the full meaning and ultimate consequences of cultural contact. Part of the reason may attach to the fact that much of the legal disputation took place in the Northern Territory which, to this day, has not yet been accorded the status of State in the Commonwealth of Australia, and so attracted little central concern.

In the United States, on the other hand, in line with the internal control conceded to many of the Amerindian tribes, they were for the most part able to adjudicate in terms of tribal customs, even though occasional frictions arose.[2]

But the most significant approach was that adopted in Africa – where a constant pattern developed of legislation or proclamation that accorded recognition to tribal customs subject to the provision that the custom itself would not be 'repugnant' to certain standards considered to be widely, if not universally, valid and applicable. The word 'repugnant' was the term used almost exclusively to indicate the standard for determining non-compliance, with the values of western culture being used as the yardstick, and so the provision is referred to in the literature as the repugnancy clause. The standards by which the customs were to be judged were of their compatibility with public policy, natural justice, equity, morality and good conscience in different combinations of formula. If a custom was deemed to be repugnant in accordance with any of the designated criteria, it would be refused recognition unless, in terms of a further clarification, or perhaps qualification, it would be allowed recognition despite its repugnance. The repugnancy clause became a standard provision in most African territories, and forms an integral part of the manner in which the legal framework of British control was established and developed, and is still in use in some independent countries.

Much litigation revolved around the issue as to what constituted repugnancy. It must be noted that those responsible for the legislation did not present it merely, or even mainly, as being some sort of compromise between conflicting value-systems and their normative rulings, but as being an expression of minimum standards being applied as a qualification to the toleration being accorded (by recognition) to the basically unacceptable norms of 'backward' communities.

Recognition also involved part of a dubious *quid pro quo,* in which it was presumed that the granting of recognition of a custom would provide a guarantee of the preservation of order in the subject territories; there certainly seems to have been very little expression of any real awareness of intrinsic value to the practices themselves. It was a recognition sometimes only reluctantly given, and frequently restrictively interpreted. But once the formula had been established, it became a widespread pattern throughout the continent, differing only in its specific formula. In a sense, the repugnancy clause becomes a litmus test for the value-system of both foreign rulers and the local conquered population. At stake are perceptions of morality – indeed, this is almost the acme of the connection between law and morality, and it is of no small significance that in the wide-ranging debate over law and morality, almost no mention has been made of this aspect of the problem, and almost no precedents from its judicial framework have been quoted. For, as we shall discuss in later chapters, here are examples that touch on the manner in which law may be used, if so wished, to carve out the contours of either minimum morality or of maximum morality (depending on one's stance on the law and morality issue) that a state may or should insist upon.

From polygamy in marriage and drugs in religious ritual, to the problems of paternalistic protection for dependent groups, such as the aged, the young, or the handicapped, the repugnancy clause provided a useful, potential framework for deep moral and intellectual consideration. Yet when Hart,[3] in his influential book presenting a liberal approach to the issue of law and morality, uses polygamy as an example, he makes no mention whatsoever of the attempt, basically unsuccessful, to impose a western morality of monogamy on a polygamous social system (an attempt which would, of course, have undermined his theoretical premise, as will be discussed later).

In any event, the recognition of customs and the repugnancy clause can perhaps best be understood in terms of a utilitarian or consequential morality – an inescapable coming to terms with the prevalence of custom and its compelling force. Unable to rapidly eradicate the customary practices, the authorities chose to make a minimum accommodation with reality, given their need to assume effective control over the inhabitants of their newly acquired territories.

Exactly how much consideration of both social control and inculcation of new moral systems was uppermost in the minds of some of the administrators, and exactly how much relative conceptions (and not necessarily universalistic ones) were at stake, may be noted in the revealing explanation by Edgar Brookes of how the apparently perfectly acceptable punishment of the death penalty for murder was 'skillfully introduced' in Natal to tribes that worked in a totally different framework of compensation for killing.[4]

'Let us take, for example', Brookes writes, 'the grafting into Native legal conceptions of the imposition of the death-penalty for murder. That a murderer should necessarily suffer death was a conception foreign to the Native mind which was still in the *weregild* stage.' The renowned administrator, Shepstone, a key figure in the process, 'introduced the European ideas on the subject by the argument that a man's life was the property of the Supreme Chief, that the Lieutenant-Governor was Supreme Chief, and that he could not, in future, be satisfied with cattle compensation for property lost by murder. Thus, by a series of typically Bantu ideas, he gave to the Native mind the conception, now well understood, that the appropriate punishment for murder is death, unless the Supreme Chief is prepared to remit it.'[5]

Brookes, writing in 1924, was expounding on what he took to be some of the virtues of a western civilization that knew how to apply relevant responses to extreme criminal behavior. At the time, capital punishment was a widely practiced punishment in the western world for the crime of murder (and indeed for other serious crimes). In England, much progress had by then been made in reducing the number of crimes for which the death penalty might be imposed, but the century-old struggle for its total abolition was then only at the half-way mark.[6] In the United States, a few probing attempts to have capital punishment declared, even if only partially, in violation of the 8th amendment prohibiting cruel and unusual punishment,[7] had failed – it was to take another half-century before the *Furman* decision of 1974[8] was to (temporarily) abolish the death penalty, or before it was to be limited solely to cases of murder, because of considerations of proportionality.[9] Furthermore, international and regional conventions had not yet been formulated placing restrictions on the use of the death penalty.[10]

Yet the fact is that, at that stage, it was a penalty considered compatible with universal values – while also regarding the African alternative to be somehow seriously in default. This is not to suggest that compensation for murder was necessarily the preferred alternative – the issue of ultimate penalties and their alternatives is still a major challenge for the modern world;[11] but what is clear is the ethnocentric manner in which a particular legal rule of western society is presented as having overwhelming qualities of rectitude, whereas the African traditional approach is seen as being in obvious need of reform. Part of the tragedy of this approach is the present widespread use of capital punishment in many African countries, as a relic of colonial rule – and not just for murder – which is sometimes carried out in public,[12] this at a time when Britain itself has abolished the penalty, as also have all the ex-colonial powers in Europe.

The quotation from Brookes, himself a well-known liberal, is an extreme example perhaps, but it is indicative of an overall value system oriented to its own world-outlook, and to the disparagement of others. It is from this perspective that the issue of repugnancy must be examined. For, truth to tell, it is most likely that many Africans looked upon the ultimate penalty of death as abhorrent and a gross violation of their own normative values as expressed through compensatory procedures to resolve violent disputes. Which is the better of the two alternatives is debatable – but, and this is the important point, it is at least debatable.

Of course, the issue of the death penalty itself was not itself decided in terms of the repugnancy clause (it was after all the death penalty that was, if anything, repugnant to the Africans), but, specifically for that reason, it provides an illuminating insight into the kind of thinking that often lay behind intricacies of legal reasoning in interpreting the repugnancy clause.[13]

A further factor that should be noted is that in many cases of contact between different cultures, there is an inevitable interplay of influence. Traditionally, the term that has been used to indicate such influence in the legal sphere is 'reception' of another legal system, and generally it was held that the English common law had indeed been received into the particular geopolitical entity over which the British laid claim.[14] This law was, in the first instance, for the use of all those – traders, missionaries, officials, settlers – who came as representatives of the colonial power, but it was also used for those many situations where inter-tribal contacts took place, that is, where litigation involved people from different tribes, with possibly different customs.

But the term 'reception' does not convey a proper connotation of the process – for in the reference to the 'receiving' of the law, the intention is to indicate that it was those receiving the law who would determine the nature of that reception. Such was the situation for the reception of Roman Law in Continental Europe in the eleventh and twelfth centuries; such was the situation for the reception of Continental civil law codes in Japan and Turkey in modern times.[15]

But such was not the situation in African law in those places where colonial powers 'transplanted' (the term is being increasingly used)[16] their own law into their colonial possessions. The term that is more apt to indicate the true nature of the process is 'imposed law', the law of the conquering power, applied without the consent of those who are to be subject to it.[17] Indeed, it is specifically because the legal regimes of almost all the colonial territories were based on imposed law that there was a necessity for special recognition of the local, customary law, with the inevitable repugnancy clause as a means of monitoring and controlling those aspects of the indigenous culture that were considered unacceptable – and therefore from which recognition would be withheld.

But the idea of reception, in and of itself, and even under the most ideal conditions, creates a great deal of legal problems, for it is never entirely clear how much of the foreign law is actually received, whether the date of reception becomes a bench-mark base, after which the receiving country then proceeds to develop its own interpretation of what has been received, or whether it continues to absorb later decisions made in the country from whence the law was received. In the latter case, the question then becomes whether the juridical decisions of the original jurisdiction of the imposed law are binding or only of persuasive value. In the former case, there is an inverse problem, where there is a very real possibility that laws or rules that have been repealed or overruled in England will continue to subsist in the receiving country.

In the case of an imposed law, with the judges often representatives of the dominant culture, or even where local people are probably trained in its legal institutions, and attuned to its legal system, the tendency is to retain a continual link with that system. In the case of the British empire, that tendency was institutionally reinforced by the role of the Privy Council as an overriding influence, through it being designated as the final court of appeal for the empire, and subsequently also, for many of the independent states of the commonwealth. Although it deals with very few cases, it has an impact in ensuring an entrenchment of the imposed law. At one stage, in fact, serious consideration was given to revamping it as a court for all commonwealth countries, including Britain, which would focus specifically on broad universal issues, such as human rights, but the proposed project was abandoned. Had it succeeded, it could indeed have developed into a legal tribunal well suited to deal with the interplay of law and morality on a transcultural basis.

A further aspect of the nature of the law that was received, is the fact that over the years the law of England developed in two parallel, not always harmonious streams, that of the common law, and that of equity, the latter allowing for a greater flexibility that was not always possible in the former; it is specifically considerations of equity, sensitively and sensibly applied, that was frequently required in the often difficult situation of trying to adapt the rules laid down in England, to a different culture. Indeed, the success of applying the repugnancy clause in a fair and effective manner was often a reflection of the same judicious use of equitable considerations that so characterized the system of equity. Thus it could be argued that the application of the repugnancy rule can also be seen – shorn of its imposed aspect – in more everyday terms as part of the complex legal situations that continually arise, irrespective of reception and irrespective of reference to customary law.

In an earlier chapter, the work of Tom Bennett was quoted to indicate that many of the legal problems could be resolved in terms of typical conflict of law reasoning.[18] Developing this theme and applying it specifically to the repugnancy clause, Robert Leslie has suggested that the reasoning process is not much different from that generally used when dealing with foreign legal systems.[19] Courts apply a legal approach of public policy considerations in a conflict of law situation. Included as guidelines is the equitable nature of the outcome. In his words, 'some of the problems raised by the operation of the repugnancy rule are similar to those raised by the application of the external public policy rule in conflict of laws ...'.[20]

Leslie's approach provides a useful framework for examining the manner in which recognition for particular customs is withheld because of the repugnancy rule. For, while on the one hand indicating the sheer normalcy of the procedure, on the other hand it also indicates the failure of many courts to restrain their interventionist tendencies; there are a fair amount of cases in which repugnancy was declared for a custom that was no more than different from the legal position in England, that is, a standard of inconsistency with the law was applied instead of repugnancy to moral standards. Leslie suggests that some of the error, at least, could have been avoided had there been more awareness of the normalcy of the process and, therefore, the need also to minimize intervention. But, of course, as already noted, it was clearly not just neat legal rules that were being processed – there was also a large amount of ideological factors that were having an impact on the perceptions of judges. The key issue then becomes what criterion they used to determine whether a particular custom was repugnant – would they be more oriented to real universalistic values, or would they be influenced by their own value-system or that of their society?

Two Nigerian jurists have addressed this issue. T.O. Elias writes that 'a constant judicial dilemma is to strike a nice balance between what is reasonably tolerable and what is essentially below the minimum standard of civilized values in the contemporary world.'[21] Akintunde Olusegun Obilade claims that the dilemma has never been satisfactorily resolved;[22] thus, noting that 'the courts have never attempted to explain in detail the meaning of the clause,' he quotes from two Privy Council cases[23] which 'appear to hold the view that a custom is repugnant to natural justice, equity, and good conscience if it is uncivilized'.[24] Then, relying on several other cases, he stresses that 'this does not mean that a custom fails the repugnancy test if it does not conform to the standard of behavior acceptable in communities which have reached an advanced stage in social development, for instance, the English community'.[25]

Nicola Peart goes beyond this in claiming that slowly over the years, the courts have worked out an acceptable framework, reflecting their striving for universalistic standards –

> From a reading of the cases, it can be concluded that the majority of the decisions were based on principles of natural justice. By eradicating those rules of customary law which were in conflict with basic human rights, the courts have attempted to bring customary law into line with a universal standard. In so far as the repugnancy clause has been used to protect human rights, one cannot object to its application. No cultural bias is shown here, in that the criterion used is notionally universal.[26]

Yet, some of the very cases that she quotes and relies on, belie the theme of universality as the major criterion. Thus, in a 1938 case, the court held that the 'only standard of justice and morality which a British court in Africa can apply is its own British standard',[27] while in an earlier case, the court had applied the repugnancy rule in terms of inconsistency merely with the law in England.[28] In a South African case, the judges stated clearly that 'Native customs must be evolved in conformity with our concepts of what is right and just.'[29]

William Harvey has summarized five major areas where the repugnancy clause has been most often activated – in procedural matters where there has been a deficiency in the manner in which a trial had been adjudicated (for example, not hearing both sides); in denying slavery or even a customary set-up reminiscent of slavery; in property claims where too long a period had elapsed to justify a claim against another's possession; in various matters relating to marriage; and in actions dealing with various aspects of witchcraft.[30] He suggests that in independent African countries there might well be a need to abolish the repugnancy clause:

> Since the repugnancy clauses served as the vehicles by which the dominant culture condemned and rejected customary African norms, it would not have been surprising if they had been repealed promptly when new, independent African governments succeeded to power.[31]

Yet, there is also the distinct possibility that 'the independent African governments may have policy orientations and objectives that would not be well-served by an uncritical acceptance and implementation of the wide variety of customary practices and norms existing within their territories'.[32] Thus, whereas some countries have rejected the repugnancy clause, others have retained it, while yet others have tried to minimize the role of customary law altogether.

Here it should be emphasized that the repugnancy clause, without the overtones of the value-system of a dominant culture, may actually be implemented within a far more neutral framework, one that is regularly used by judges in creatively interpreting the law. Often, for instance, the problem is not of the violation of standards of justice and good conscience in general, but of such a consequence in a specific case. Obilade[33] is of the opinion that any one case which failed the repugnancy test would be indicative of the failure of the particular rule as a whole, that is that the court would not be entitled to declare the rule inapplicable in the instance under scrutiny, while declaring that the rule as such could be retained and used in a later case. Any one failure in a specific case would inexorably lead to the rejection of the rule *in toto*.

More than that, he argues that even if the results are thought to be satisfactory in general, the court is still obliged to consider other possibilities, and if the rule is found wanting in such a potential case in the future, then the rule as such should be declared void by the repugnancy standard. He writes, 'a case which is invalid for any particular purpose is invalid for all other purposes'.[34] To emphasize his point, Obilade critically discusses a case which failed to apply the repugnancy rule and to reject the custom as such even though, on the facts of the particular case being decided, the court held that the consequences would be repugnant. The court explained in that case that 'we must not be understood to condemn this native law and custom in its general application. We appreciate that it is basically sound and would in almost every case be fair and just in its results.'[35]

It would seem that Obilade is placing too restrictive an interpretation on the repugnancy clause, and that the court judgment quoted (of which he is critical) might actually provide a better application of the rule. Harvey, for instance, sees no reason why the normal, creative processes of judges actively participating 'in shaping and modifying the law,' should not be allowed, and suggests that the whole issue of repugnancy considerations in a modern state should be resolved within the terms of 'the very nature of the judicial process'.[36] There does indeed seem to be no reason why equity-like principles should not be adduced to solve problems arising from undesired consequences of applying customary law, without the necessity of relying specifically on a repugnancy clause. In other words, the thrust of the law should be to allow the use of equity to avoid any decision that would seem to be unjust or unfair, whether its origins are in a customary rule or in a legislative rule.

Leslie's work in this connection seems to contain useful insights and to provide a model that could be used in a practical manner, as he notes the strong resemblance between applying the repugnancy rule in terms of customary law and applying the widely accepted legal principle of public policy in ordinary judicial situations. Indeed, Peart, despite her stress on universal values, concedes that there were cases which dealt not with human rights, but merely with public policy, a policy geared not mainly to adopt African institutions to the impact of a changing modern world, but 'to abandon them in favor of European institutions'.[37]

Leslie's approach seems to provide a solution for this kind of dilemma, particularly in the context of independent countries struggling for a legal identity that will adequately reflect the pluralistic nature of their societies. In fact, Leslie describes a possible legal framework for understanding and for action, an underlying philosophy which will guide those entrusted with interpreting the law, evaluating the custom, and doing justice in a way that will satisfy community aspirations.

The legal framework, then, is that which is applied in any normal conflict of law situation where a court, having decided that a foreign legal system is applicable to the issue in dispute, then refuses to enforce a particular rule of that system which violates, in the language of Justice Cardozo in a United States case, 'some fundamental principle of justice, some prevalent concept of good morals, some deep-rooted tradition of the common weal'.[38]

Leslie describes some of the problems involved in activating the external public policy rule, and the danger that, instead of applying larger, universalistic standards, courts will be tempted to measure the foreign rule in terms of narrow parochial considerations. The connection between the external public policy rule and the repugnancy rule is well brought out as Leslie expounds on his theme that the court may fail to appreciate '... the real role of the foreign rule in its own system and community. This too has been the experience with the repugnancy rule.'[39]

Leslie effectively joins the two rules by an example where a particular custom was declared to be repugnant by a British court in Africa, only to have a similar legal provision, in a later case, declared compatible with common law principles. At issue was the right of a husband to claim damages for the tort of seduction of a wife when the adulterous behavior had subsequently been condoned by him. When the issue arose in a Rhodesian court, the judge held the custom of allowing damages in such a situation to be repugnant, but later, in a South African case, 'it was held that the common law also permitted an action in these circumstances'.[40]

Finally, Leslie's attempt to draw a parallel between the two rules, leads him to suggest a broader role for the 'repugnancy' rule, one which would not be limited to '...merely excising from the body of customary law abhorrent rules of law'.[41] He thus suggests the use of the rule as an 'equitable jurisdiction', where the court could 'depart from a rule of customary law, not because the rule itself is repugnant to natural justice or morality, but because its enforcement in the particular circumstances of the case then before it would have results considered by the court to be repugnant to natural justice or morality'.[42]

Thus Leslie uses the basic rationale of the external public policy rule to give new meaning and enforced vigor to the repugnancy rule, to make it not merely an unfortunate and even embarrassing relic of colonial times, but to reflect the vitality of an activist judicial system in changed circumstances. His suggestion of applying the rule to deny enforcing a custom in the specific circumstances of a particular case where the result would be inequitable, while leaving untouched the general validity of the custom itself, is contrary to the approach of Obilade. But it may well provide a broad solution to the very dilemma that Obilade and others such as Elias and Harvey have referred to – how to recognize custom in general, while still retaining the right to selectively reject aspects of the body of custom, and how modern independent states can deal with these dilemmas without being overly hidebound by the terminology, the perceptions and the precedents of the colonial era.

But much more may be at stake than mere satisfactory legal formulae for resolving disputes. Whereas formerly there was a reluctant acquiescence in a deplored, but unavoidable, social reality by a foreign colonial power, the possibility now exists of a positive affirmation of an indigenous culture that requires constant and careful adaptation to the needs of a changing society, exposed not just to the pressures of a world economy and western technology, but also to the emerging consensus of universalistic values oriented to basic human rights and enshrined in international conventions.

As Harvey points out, the very idea of a 'repugnancy rule' is incongruent in an independent country, for though the repugnancy rule was couched in general and universalistic terms, there can be little doubt that it was a reflection and an expression of a dominant culture imposing its rule, will and values over a subjugated people, whose culture was forcibly made subordinate. However, in a situation of independence, while there may well be respect for that culture as a living body of meaningful rules, the problems of legal pluralism will still arise, as well as the problem of customs that are antiquated in terms of changing social life, or inconsistent with broader values. It is here that Leslie's approach becomes so pertinent – but it requires a special conceptualization – for, after all, while the rationale of the external public policy rule is relevant, the reality is of a custom or rule of law that is *internal* to the judicial body applying the rule.

In other words, the dilemma caused by the respect for traditional customs, on the one hand, and the exigencies of social life in a modern state, on the other hand, may be resolved by empowering the judges to activate and enforce the customs within an overall framework of equitable considerations. Since the legal system is based on common law principles, the solution would be similar to the manner in which the common law itself was developed to meet changing social reality. Further, this is specifically the manner in which custom itself, in the traditional tribal environment, was adapted and developed. In any event, within legal systems, it is an accepted rule that judges may take account of public policy factors. In other words, the judges would not be examining a rule alien to them, but contributing to the very development of the customary law.

Such an approach would, however, only be feasible if all its premises were fully recognized – including that of the aforementioned respect for traditional customs. It is not clear that all those entrusted with judicial capacity – often trained in foreign universities, certainly far more exposed, in terms of professional training and experience, to its rules and operations – are personally geared to such an undertaking.[43] Without a commitment to the culture *per se*, the consequences of judicial intervention could be disastrous for the customary law. But with a sense of its intrinsic value, with a sensitivity to its relevance and applicability, it could be molded to answer, within an overall context of equity, to the specific problems that arise. In contrast with the original, historical equity jurisdiction (and freed from its political context of competing rivals jockeying for influence),[44] the courts could play a significant monitoring role – of simultaneously validating and moderating custom. This would not be a mere semantic change – from repugnancy to equity – but would have substantive implications. This would also constitute a challenge – on the line of judicial law-making in common law countries, or in terms of judicial review of written constitutions. These do not take place in a social and cultural vacuum. On the contrary, they are deeply attuned to (often unfortunately also far too much involved in) the changing ideological struggles of the day. But it is a challenge which would match the validity of a common law system with the values of the culture.

John Bell,[45] in discussing the necessity for judges to be aware of the larger social implications of their decisions, suggests representation of public interests, particularly in what are known as hard cases – that is, where a difficult legal issue is placed before the courts, the result of which may have far-reaching consequences for the society at large. Dealing specifically with the British legal system, he notes the problems of ensuring, in a plural society, that all sectors of the population are represented. He accordingly contends that:

> the judicial process must … be opened to a wider range of inputs, so that a greater variety of social views can be brought to bear on a decision. The adversarial nature of present English procedure means that the issues raised before the court are limited to those which are to the advantage of the litigants, and this may often cause other

> important issues and perspectives to be ignored when the judges devise a new rule.[46]

These observations take on added import when applied to judicial considerations of the validity and applicability of customary law. Certainly higher courts of a state system need to be fully apprised not just of the impact of a custom on the fate of the litigants, but of the manner in which such customs affect the life of the community. His suggested solutions are to allow for the widening of the judicial debate by the inclusion of a public representative, as is the role of the French *Ministère Public,* whose task it is to put before the court the larger public effects of a decision in a case,[47] or alternatively, and preferably according to him, to allow and to encourage the presentation of 'Brandeis briefs' to be presented by public interest groups.[48] In the context of state adjudication as to customary law, it would seem advisable for a legal representative of the tribal group to explain the interest of the tribe in the maintenance of the custom in dispute – that is, not to explain the custom (a separate problem in and of itself)[49] but to clarify the role it still plays in the life of the community, or alternatively, to suggest how it might best be amended to allow for its responsive adaptation to changing social reality. But this can only become a meaningful process if both judges and the legal fraternity work within a political climate and a legal culture that recognizes and respects the particularistic customs of local communities.

This does not necessarily mean capitulation of a state to tribal dictate. On the contrary, the judicial organs can play a key role in the constant development of customs – not least in trying, by creative and sensitive interpretation, to make them compatible not just with state law, but with larger universalistic principles – not in terms of negative denial by virtue of the repugnancy rule, but in terms of positive application of human rights principles, especially those that have been incorporated formally into international and regional conventions.[50] These now provide a standard by which, in the midst of the diversity of localized tribal and other particularistic groupings, common humanity may be expressed through acceptance of universalistic norms. For, while the customary law will continue to be applied at the local level by customary-oriented courts, as is provided for in so many countries, there will always arise a particularly hard case which will reach the higher echelons of the judicial framework and serve as a trigger for overall assessment and evaluation, and a catalyst for change and updating. Not repugnancy leading to rejection, but respect leading to rejuvenation is what is required.

NOTES

1. One particular judge whose judgments have been noted is Justice Kriewalt, who was a judge in the Northern Territory, whose opinions have been widely referred to. See discussion of some of his decisions in Chapter 14, 'A Reasonable "Cultural" Defense'.
2. See, for instance, Felix Cohen, *Handbook of Federal Indian Law* (Buffalo, CO: William S. Hein, 1980 [1942]).
3. See H.L.A. Hart, *Law, Liberty and Morality* (London: Oxford University Press, 1968).
4. Edgar Brookes, *The History of Native Policy in South Africa* (Cape Town: Nasionale Press, 1924).
5. Ibid., pp. 51–2.
6. See, for instance, James Christoph, *Capital Punishment and British Politics: The British Movement to Abolish the Death Penalty, 1945–57* (Chicago: University of Chicago Press, 1962).
7. See, for example, *In re: Kemmler,* 136 US 436 (1890), which unsuccessfully challenged the use of electrocution in executions.
8. See *Furman v. Georgia*, 408 US 23 (1972).
9. See *Coker v. Georgia*, 433 US 584 (1977). The case dealt with the crime of rape.
10. See, for example, 'Protocol to the Convention for the Protection of Human Rights and Fundamental Freedom Concerning the Abolition of the Death Penalty', European Convention on Human Rights, Additional Protocol, No. 6, 1983, in *International Legal Materials* (1984), p. 539.
11. See my *Ultimate Penalties: Capital Punishment, Life Imprisonment, Physical Torture* (Columbus: Ohio State University Press, 1987).
12. See ibid., pp. 171–2.
13. One of the first judgments of the new constitutional court in South Africa was to declare the death penalty unconstitutional; *S. v. Makwanyane*, (1995) 6 BCLR 665 (CC).
14. See, for instance, Robert Seidman, 'The Reception of English Law in Colonial Africa Revisited', *Eastern African Law Review* 2 (1969), p. 47.
15. On Japan, see, for instance, Robert J. Smith, 'The Sources and Proponents of "Tradition" and "Modernity" in Japanese Law', *Journal of Legal Pluralism and Unofficial Law* 33 (1993), p. 231. His opening sentence is: 'Japan's legal system, based largely on adaptations of Chinese codes throughout most of its history, took on a new complexity following the Meiji Restoration of 1868 and the attendant desperate search for Western models for the new Japanese Law and constitution.'
16. See Alan Watson, *Legal Transplants: An Approach to Comparative Law* (Edinburgh: Scottish Academic Press, 1974).
17. See Sandra Burman and Barbara Harrell-Bond (eds), *The Imposition of Law* (New York: Academic Press, 1979).
18. Tom W. Bennett, *Application of Customary Law in Southern Africa* (Cape Town: Juta, 1985).
19. Robert Leslie, 'The Repugnancy Rule in African Law and the Public Policy Rule in Conflict of Laws', *Acta Juridica* (1977), p. 117.
20. Ibid., p. 117.
21. T.O. Elias, *British Colonial Law: A Comparative Study of the Interaction between English and Local Laws in British Dependencies* (London: Stevens, 1962), p. 104.
22. Akintunde Olusegun Obilade, *The Nigerian Legal System* (London: Sweet & Maxwell, 1979).
23. The cases are *Laoye v. Oyetunde* [1944] A.C. 170; and *Eshugbayi Eleko v. Officer Administering the Government of Nigeria* [1931] A.C. 662.
24. Obilade, *Nigerian Legal System*, pp. 100–1.
25. Ibid., p. 101.
26. Nicola Peart, 'A Consideration of Certain Aspects of African Customary Law' (LLM Thesis, University of Cape Town, 1981), p. 32.
27. *Gwao bin Kilimo v. Kisunda bin Ifuti*, (1938) TLR 403 at 405.
28. See *Lewis v. Bankole*, (1908) NLR 81.
29. *Phiri v. Nkosi*, 1941 NAC (N & T), 94 at 98.
30. William Burnett Harvey, *Introduction to the Legal System in East Africa* (Kampala: East African Literature Bureau, 1975), p. 524.
31. Ibid., p. 524.
32. Ibid., p. 524. See also W. Maqutu and A. Sanders, 'The Internal Conflict of Laws in Lesotho',

Comparative and International Law Review of South Africa 20 (1987), p. 377.
33. See Obilade, 'Internal Conflict of Laws', at n. 25, p. 103.
34. Ibid., p. 103.
35. *Mariyama v. Sadiku Ejo,* 1961 N.R.N.L.R. 81.
36. Harvey, *Introduction to Legal System in E. Africa*, at n. 31, p. 525.
37. Peart, 'A Consideration of Certain Aspects' at n. 27, p. 33.
38. *Loucks v. Standard Oil Co.*, 224 NY 99 at 111; 120 N.E. 198 at 202.
39. Leslie, 'Repugnancy Rule', p. 118.
40. Ibid., p. 118. The case discussed in what was then Rhodesia, is *R. v. Mchenji and Chargwi*, 1917 SR 69; the later South African case referred to is *Viviers v. Klein*, 1927 AD 449.
41. Leslie, 'Repugnancy Rule', at n. 22, p. 119.
42. Ibid., p. 119.
43. For general discussion of the legal profession in Africa, see L.C.B. Gower, *Independent Africa – The Challenge to the Legal Profession* (Cambridge, MA: Harvard University Press, 1967). He is most critical of the failure of the English legal profession to contribute to an adequate preparation for those many overseas students who studied law in London, more particularly at the Inns of Court. Referring to the situation in the first decade of independence, he writes:

> The failure of the English legal profession to do more for African students constitutes, to my mind, one of the gravest indictments that can be levelled against us. Ever since the war, African bar students in England have outnumbered English students by about four to one. At any one time there have been in London about 2,000 African Law students, some of whom would undoubtedly be the future leaders of their countries. Had the Inns of Court faced up to this challenge, instituted courses suitable for future practitioners in Africa ... not only might the Inns of Court have become again the great educational institutions that they were in the Middle Ages, but bonds of goodwill might have been forged which could have affected the whole history of the Commonwealth and of the Common Law. Instead, they did nothing until it was too late. All too many of the overseas students returned disgruntled and bearing ill-will. All returned inadequately equipped for their future roles.

Gower is not here dealing specifically with the problem of customary law, but his comments and criticism have relevance for this issue too – and have not necessarily become less relevant now. There is still not sufficient attention given to customary law and its interaction with state law in legal education.
44. The Courts of Chancery were set up originally not merely to advance the cause of justice, but also to provide the King, through his Chancellor, acting as the 'King's conscience', with a counterweight to the growing independence and influence of the common law courts. See Margaret Judson, *The Crisis of the Constitution: An Essay in Constitutional and Political Thought in England, 1603–1645* (New Brunswick: Rutgers University Press, 1949), especially discussion of the case of the *Earl of Oxford* at pp. 96–9.
45. John Bell, *Policy Arguments in Judicial Decisions* (Oxford: Clarendon Press, 1983).
46. Ibid., p. 264. Although dealing with the British judicial system, many of his comments have particular pertinence for a multitribal society. Judges, he states, 'profess to be giving effect to the values of the community' but 'in a pluralistic society, the judge has competing value-systems on which he can draw, which makes the performance of his task more difficult' (p. 254).
47. See discussion of the French approach in John Henry Merryman, *The Civil Law Tradition: An Introduction to the Legal System of Western Europe and Latin America* (Stanford: Stanford University, 1969).
48. The idea of the 'Brandeis brief' is based on the pioneering efforts of Justice Louis Brandeis, when still a lawyer, to present a documented file to the court on the social factors forming a background to a particular case.
49. See discussion below in Chapter 19, 'Proving the Customary Rule'.
50. See discussion in next chapter on 'The Right to Group Rights'.

The Right to Group Rights

The liberalism of the modern age has provided much of the impetus for the formulation and consolidation of human rights as an integral part of modern legal systems, often expressed through constitutional bills of rights or international conventions, and as an underlying aspect of its legal culture, generally expounded in academic treatises or in philosophical debate. Central to this liberalism is the human being as an autonomous person capable of creating life's own opportunities, each entitled to the protective mechanisms of the state, each carving out a personal pattern that is unique by virtue of the idiosyncrasies of every individual. Thus, the freedoms of speech, expression and religion and the protection from arbitrary arrest or harsh punishment.

It is liberalism which has placed the individual at the forefront of social, legal and moral thought. Major legal and political developments at the onset of the modern age found their inspiration from thinkers such as John Locke or Jean-Jacques Rousseau.[1] Echoes of their innovative ideas may be found in such legal documents as the United States Constitution or the Declaration of the Rights of Man of the French Revolution, where assurances were given as to the means required to allow the individual full control of his conduct and inner beliefs.

On the international stage, this pre-eminence (at least in the western world) has been challenged, in recent decades, both by communist states and newly independent states, all searching for the elixir of meaningful economic development for the nation which would guarantee to all the rights to food, clothing and shelter, while forgoing what they considered the luxury of liberalism's amorphous and abstract human rights. These newer rights are known as the second generation of rights and the controversy over their validity and necessity had not yet abated, when the first inklings were given of a further group of rights, the third generation of rights, amongst which the idea of group rights was pre-eminent.[2]

Most of the attention of such group rights focuses on the need to recognize and protect the special needs of minorities *qua* minorities in the polymorphous 'nation-state'. The typical examples given are of linguistic, religious and ethnic minorities. In these circumstances, it is not the right of individuals to practice their religion or speak their language that is the key issue, but the overall consideration that must be accorded to these factors within a community. An example of the difference would be the right of an individual as part of a minority religion not to work on a day of rest, which is a working day for the population at large (for instance Seventh-Day Adventists or Jews, where Saturday is a working day and Sunday is the day of rest),[3] in contrast to a situation where both days are declared to be optional days of rest, because account is taken of both the majority and the minority religions in determining the day of rest. Similarly for language, where the difference would be in terms of facilities offered for studying a minority language in the educational system as a second language, in contrast to the right of a minority group to have its language recognized as an optional medium of instruction in public schools for all subjects, as well as the language of public signposting and official forms. The problems of linguistic rights may vary from a prohibition to use the language in public (which the British imposed on the Dutch-speaking white settlers in Cape Colony after its conquest at the beginning of the nineteenth century, or as applied to English on private signs in public places in Quebec) to the kinds of issues that were placed before the European Court of Human Rights in the well-known Belgian linguistic case, dealing with choice of language instruction in schools.[4]

The first, and still most definitive, statement in an international document in regard to group rights is contained in Article 27 of the International Covenant on Civil and Political Rights of 1966 which states: 'In those states in which ethnic, religious or linguistic minorities exist, persons belonging to such groups shall not be denied the right, in community with the other members of their group, to enjoy their own culture, to profess and practice their own religion, or to use their own language.'[5] Lacking in the broad sweep of this clause is any specific reference to tribe. The key question is whether this is a lacuna, an inadvertent omission on the part of the signatories; or a deliberate exclusion, an indication of the irrelevance of tribe for the purposes of the covenant; or a conscious inclusion of tribe within the rubric of ethnic group, a value judgment as to its limited uniqueness not requiring special reference; or an embarrassed silence, an admission of the additional and special complications associated with the existence of tribes. For tribes not only often have their own language and religion, but their culture is all-embracing in a manner which is not true of ethnic groups, and may well involve obligatory customs, judicial frameworks and defined rules as to membership and participation, making in all for a separate legal system, as pointed out in earlier chapters.

But, whatever the reason for the omission of any reference to tribe (or any of the accepted alternatives, such as indigenous population) the developments of the last 30 years indicate clearly the inadequacy of only a tri-partite reference to groups.

In the years since then, there have been major judicial precedents (*Mabo* in Australia, *Calder* in Canada, the *Maori Council* cases in New Zealand, *Otieno* in Kenya),[6] national legislation (such as the Canadian Charter and Bills of Rights in some new African countries),[7] increased activities of non-governmental organizations dedicated to the cause of tribal communities (both of interested outsiders and of involved tribespeople),[8] and an updating of the only international document that had in the past, shown any concern for tribal people (the convention formulated by the International Labor Organization – concerning Indigenous and Tribal Peoples in Independent Countries).[9] This latter document is of major importance, both as a pioneering statement on behalf of tribal people, and as a reflection of the changing conditions.

From its inception in the 1920s, the ILO had shown a great deal of awareness of the specific needs of tribal people, exposed as they were to exploitation by powerful economic and political forces, both state and private; and had finally, in 1957, given formal expression to its concerns with the aforementioned convention. In 1989, the updated version in its preamble makes passing reference to the influence of other international statements, such as the key international covenants dealing with economic, social and cultural rights,[10] and civil and political rights, and then proclaims: 'Considering that the developments which have taken place in international law since 1957, as well as developments in the situation of indigenous and tribal peoples in all regions of the world, have made it appropriate to adopt new international standards on the subject with a view to removing the assimilationist orientation of the earlier standards ...'. It further notes such factors as 'aspiration of these peoples to exercise control over their own institutions, ways of life and economic development and to maintain and develop their identities, languages and religions' and the fact that 'their laws, values, customs and perspectives have often been eroded' as well as remarking upon 'the distinctive contributions of indigenous and tribal peoples to the cultural diversity and social and ecological harmony of humankind'.[11] The operative part of the document deals extensively with a wide range of special considerations that should be vouschafed to tribal people that actually exceeds by far the focused mandate of the ILO to deal with labor issues and embraces areas such as land, health and education. Article 30 is of particular pertinence for its general statement that 'Governments shall adopt measures appropriate to the traditions and cultures of the people concerned to make known to them their rights and duties, especially in regard to labor, economic opportunities, education and health matters, social welfare and their rights deriving from this convention.' Such considerations do not apply in their entirety to religious and linguistic minorities, and only occasionally and then partially and peripherally to most ethnic minorities.

Even so, the impact of this convention has been minimal, and it has also evoked a certain amount of critical response. For instance, Lee Swepston has argued that not only does the convention not really remedy the denigrated status of tribal groups, but has, in some respects, even deepened the problem.[12] According to Swepston, 'the convention contains a fundamental flaw. It takes a patronizing attitude towards these population groups – referring to them as "less advanced", for instance – and promotes eventual integration as the way to resolve the problems caused to states by their continued existence. It presumes that they will disappear as separate groups once they have the opportunity to participate fully in the national society and attempts to ease the transitional period.'[13]

Swepston's critique may be overly and unjustifiably pessimistic. For recent years have seen a growing awareness of the special needs of tribal communities, and of the real possibilities that they will, despite strong outside influences, manage to resist the assimilationist forces and to retain – and enhance and adapt – their culture. Even the ILO Convention will not 'remain unique' (Swepston's words),[14] as efforts are now under way to formulate a comprehensive document, on the rights of indigenous people, efforts which were given added impetus in 1993, during the Year of the Indigenous People. In fact, it is not mere eurocentrism with its disparaging attitude to non-western culture that constitutes a major stumbling-block to more explicit expressions of tribal rights, but the confusion that still exists as to the parameters of group rights – on the one hand, their differentiation from human rights at the individual level, (a third-generation right, which still lacks broad acceptance in the western world); on the other hand, the constant growing uncertainty as to the ultimate consequences of recognizing the rights of groups in general, with the possibility of demands being raised for self-determination – including the right to autonomy, and beyond that, to independence. As Anna Michalska comments, 'The analysis of rights of peoples would appear to be a much more complex and difficult task than the study of human rights ... because the notion "people" is ambiguous and used in different contexts'.[15]

In any event, the very uniqueness of tribal communities has elicited special responses, in terms of human rights, at the national and regional level, ranging from special constitutional documents dealing solely with tribes, or the incorporation of references to tribes into more comprehensive Bills of Rights.[16] At the regional level, while no specific reference is made to tribes as such, the African Charter on Human and Peoples' Rights states, in Article 17, that 'Every individual may freely take part in the cultural life of his community' and that 'the promotion and protection of morals and traditional values recognized by the community shall be the duty of the State'.[17] However, even such positive statements with their strong hints as to tribal rights are only general pronouncements, the worth of which can only be measured in the crucible of everyday activities, policy directives and judicial rulings. Here, all the problematics of tribal life within a modern state become even more involved because of the problematics in general of according recognition to group life within a legal and ideological framework created and sustained by the ideas of individualistic liberalism.

Even without any specific reference to tribe, a legal debate has evolved, particularly in the United States, as to the limits of liberalism, and of the need to temper its ultimate implications with a communitarian vision, one which will take account of social factors;[18] a perspective which sees the individual not only as an autonomous being entitled to a full measure of rights restricted only by the need not to interfere with or undermine similar rights of others, but also, no less, as a social being, linked to and dependent upon a community, within which – and perhaps only within which – it is possible to attain a full expression of self. In this sense, liberalism will find its most extensive expression when the minimum demands of communitarianism are fulfilled.

However, what must be made clear is that the community being referred to in most cases is not equivalent to the state, but something much less, a group that is embodied within a state – although there may also be situations where the group transverses two or even more states. James Crawford, in his summation of an edited book dealing specifically – and for the most part positively – with group rights found it wise to warn of some of the dangers involved in group rights. He explains that 'the excessive generality and the disregard for content demonstrated in some of the elaborations of new rights not only raise questions about individual proposals, but reflect badly on the notion of a "third generation" of rights as such'.[19] Most pertinently, he is concerned that an extension of group rights might be attained by a contraction of existing individual human rights. He argues that 'if the various peoples' rights elaborated in the African Charter of Human and Peoples' Rights are more likely to be relied on as modifying other rights or rules than as creating new autonomous rights, then peoples' rights would seem to be rather a new range of excuses for reducing the scope of other rights – in effect, a new range of State rights in disguise.'[20] Having said that, Crawford suggests that avoidance of 'the more exaggerated claims' in respect of group and other 'third generation' rights, will facilitate the gradual acceptance of these newer rights, '... in particular the right to existence of groups and to certain minimum rights of subsistence and, perhaps, sociality involved in the existence of human groups'.[21]

The difficulties involved in creating a synthesis between personal and group rights, between liberalism and communitarianism, between recognized first-generation individual rights and innovative third-generation group rights, between the traditional concerns of the western world and the concerns for tradition of the tribal world, are well brought out in Aviam Soifer's work that is oriented to the sociological need for legal recognition of groups.[22] In the opening sentences of his book (and indeed in the title, 'Law and the Company We Keep'), Soifer cuts right through to the heart of the issue:

> Our collective problem lies not in any one word, but in ourselves. As individuals, we are largely defined by our groups. Associations – whether voluntary or imposed – constitute inescapable elements of identity. Yet the American legal system lacks any theory to handle groups. The dominant legal paradigm in American Law is the relationship between individual and state. The company we keep is presumed to be each person's own business, beyond the notice of the law.
>
> This book directly faces the 'smudginess' of collectivity. It is a sustained account of the presence and importance of groups throughout our legal culture.[23]

Soifer explains how essential it is for legal discourse to take account of culture, pluralistic values and the contribution of various social sciences that deal with community and the role of groups. In fact, by Soifer's account, the only group that the present-day Supreme Court in the United States is prepared to relate to is the nuclear family, an assertion that he makes as he critically and caustically notes the inability of the Court to protect an abused child within a family context.[24]

While Soifer, in line with other jurists searching for community or communitarianism, focuses on judicial decisions, social science has indeed clarified the importance of a community base for social life – ranging from the *gemeinschaft* of Tönnies, as discussed earlier, and Durkheim's stress on the collective conscience and social solidarity,[25] to the more recent work of Robert Nisbet with his description of the important role of the concept of community in social analysis.[26] In recent years, there has also been discussion, particularly in political science, of the importance of recognizing a 'civil society', which may or may not be coterminous with the state,[27] but is in any case the source of norms, values, culture, which emerge and exist apart from the authoritative and obligatory laws of the state. The American Supreme Court, however, seems to be blissfully unaware of such thinking, or perhaps, as Soifer suggests, desperately determined to avoid any recognition of group association or the historical context in which groups functioned;[28] and, in fact, the Court specifically fails 'to concede constitutional weight to tribal entities'.[29] Referring to several Supreme Court decisions in 1988, Soifer notes that 'The Court … confronted several cases involving Native American tribes, social groupings so anomalous that their stories generally are omitted from American constitutional law accounts. The deeply paradoxical approaches the Court took in its decisions about familes and tribes illustrate the importance of thinking more clearly about involuntary groups.'[30]

It thus seems clear that recognition of tribal rights is one aspect of a larger problem, namely that of group rights – but also in more intensified form, both because tribes are not always included as examples of groups and because of the all-encompassing nature of tribal culture and customary law.

What emerges from the complex issue of clashes between individual and group rights is that the solution in any particular instance may be purely fortuitous, a consequence not necessarily of deep principle, but of chance factors that may lend weight in either direction. In subsequent chapters, a number of examples will be given; for instance, in terms of belonging, should this be determined by the free desire of the individual or the overriding rules of the tribe;[31] or in terms of cultural practices, what should be the attitude to female circumcision, the traditional rights of the tribe or the protective needs of the young girl?[32] Occasionally, the clash may be between two different rights, which are both part of the third generation of rights, for instance, traditional patterns of hunting or trapping, which clash with specific imperatives of environmental concern.[33]

In this context, it must, nevertheless, be remembered that it is not only clashes between group and individual or tribe and member, that create problems in the enforcement of human rights. Within any constitutional document there are liable to be potential contradictions, for instance, the right to privacy as against the right to know, or the rights of the accused in a criminal trial *vis-à-vis* the rights of the victim, and some rights even have built-in reservations and limitations. Whatever the outcome in a particular case, the major development in recent years has been the willingness to incorporate aboriginal rights into the culture and customs of state-wide constitutional documents, noted both in new countries in Africa, Asia and the Pacific, and in the recent legislative and constitutional acts of older countries. Of the latter, for instance, the United States has enacted a special law guaranteeing freedom of religion for the Native American Church, while Canada has a special clause in its recent Charter of Rights and Freedoms dealing with aboriginal issues.[34] These developments do not guarantee that desirable judicial consequences will follow (and there have already been some disappointing decisions),[35] but at least a more firm constitutional arrangement is operative than existed formerly.

One of the major problems that emerges from such constitutional or quasi-constitutional documents, is whether special consideration being given to specified groups within the society is compatible with such concepts as the rule of law or equal protection before the law. Can compensatory mechanisms be activated on behalf of formerly deprived groups to redress past wrongs without inflicting new wrongs on others, can affirmative action be undertaken without undermining some of the basic structure of true liberalism, can protective paternalism be applied without arousing side-effects of subtle denigration of those being helped and smoldering anger of other groups that are being ignored or denied? As Darlene Johnsson explains,

> Reaction to the idea of collective rights is strongly negative in some quarters. Collective rights are seen as inherently dangerous and oppressive. Their reaction stems from a perceived clash between individual rights and group rights. Collective and individual interests, however, are not inevitably antagonistic. The supposed antithesis seems to be based on a particular and intolerant conception of the nature of group rights.[36]

The Canadian situation is of particular interest both because of the relatively recent enactment of its Charter of Rights and because of the general constitutional crisis which Canada has undergone in the past few years in which the aboriginal issue is generally considered secondary to the struggle for independence for Quebec and the rejections of the controversial Meech Lake Accord.[37] In fact, the model of multiculturalism affects the French-speaking population as a minority in Canada, but a majority in Quebec, probably no less and possibly more than the native Canadians. Furthermore, any secession of Quebec in the future would raise serious questions as to the fate of those areas in Quebec where native Canadians live on land that was once transferred, without consultation with them, from the Federal government to Quebec.[38] Should they not, in the future, be entitled to a referendum of their own – with a choice of staying in Quebec, staying in Canada, or independence for themselves? In fact, outside of Quebec, what is the impact of Quebec's quest for withdrawing from Canada on other distinctive groups? In any event, section 25 of the Charter clarifies that, whatever the nature of the rights outlined in the charter, they must be interpreted in such a way as to avoid any negative consequences for aboriginal rights. In the words of the Charter, its provisions 'shall not be construed so as to abrogate or derogate from any aboriginal treaty or other rights or freedoms that pertain to the aboriginal peoples of Canada...'. In addition, section 35 proclaims unambiguously that 'the existing aboriginal and treaty rights of the aboriginal peoples of Canada are hereby recognized and affirmed'.[39]

In contrast to the brief and generalized nature of these sections of the Charter, is a declaration made just a year earlier by representatives of the native Canadians with its more detailed affirmation of rights, and with its strong religious overtones. The Declaration begins with the simple statement, yet pregnant with meaning, that 'We, the Original Peoples of this Land, know the Creator put us here.' The Declaration then continues with further clarifications articulated in religious terms:

> 'The Creator gave us laws that govern all our relationships to live in harmony with nature and mankind … . The Creator gave us our spiritual beliefs, our language, our culture and a place on Mother Earth which provided us with all our needs. We have maintained our freedom, our languages, and our traditions from time immemorial …. The Creator has given us the right to govern our-selves and the right to self-determination. The rights and responsibilities given to us by the Creator cannot be altered or taken away by any other Nation.[40]

The Declaration has importance not merely as some sort of unofficial aspiration, but because the official constitutional document – the Charter enacted a year later – will be interpreted and utilized by many native Canadians, as individuals and as groups, in the light of this authoritative statement (even if unofficial and extralegal). The very generalized and abstract nature of section 35 of the constitution lends itself to different interpretations – a further section, section 37, acknowledges this by providing for further consultations by politicians in connection with clarifying the parameters of these rights.[41]

A Canadian anthropologist, Michael Asch, summarizes the situation as follows:

> … the nub of the position of the native organizations is that aboriginal peoples have the right to maintain ways of life that are distinct from those of recent immigrants to Canada. These ways of life are not to be interpreted as ethnic in the sense of a Canadian mosaic, but rather as a composite of autonomous systems that integrates languages, economics, social organizations, political organizations, religions and other values into a total culture. Central to the ongoing viability of these is a land-base and self-government.
>
> The right to preserve and develop such autonomous systems in Canada is perceived to derive, in part, from the manifest failure of the current programs designed to establish viable lifeways for the majority of the aboriginal population. However, at the core, it arises from a vision of Canada as a colonial manifestation and from the perception of aboriginal peoples as 'colonized' nations that, like those indigenous populations on other continents, have an inherent right to assert their self-determination and control over their own affairs. It is a goal that is perceived to be attainable within the context of Confederation.[42]

Asch considers this position a moderate one, since it does not involve secession from an existing state, although he is aware that it is liable to be rejected by both the native Canadians and by other Canadians, both by those who consider his approach too radical and by those who consider it not radical enough. In any event, the one factor that certainly distinguishes Canada from other countries with a majority of non-indigenous people is that amongst this latter group, there is a substantial percentage (the French-speaking) who are considered a separate culture and among whom there is a significant number (at the last referendum on the issue of Quebec indepence, almost half in Quebec),[43] who would prefer independent statehood. Within this kind of situation, Asch considers a consociational solution (a Swiss-style model), which he sees as being moderate and feasible – and 'consistent with liberal-democratic rule'.[44]

In the final analysis, beyond the political questions, are a whole host of rights enumerated and enshrined in the Canadian Charter, that are not intrinsically compatible with fundamental aboriginal rights, because of deep differences in the underlying philosophies and ideologies of modern western society and those of the First Nations of Canada. Menno Boldt and Anthony Long explain, in measured terms and with detailed examples, the many distinctions in concepts and perceptions – in particular the essence of the differing approaches to the individual and the group.[45] They point out persuasively that 'an urbanized industrial-capitalist society with an individualistic emphasis requires a different set of rules to protect its citizens against the arbitrary exercise of power than does a small face-to-face communal society'.[46] Most particularly, the very nature of the political structure differs – 'The tribal community performed all governmental functions in an undifferentiated fashion … . Social order was based on spiritual solidarity derived from the moral integration that came from acquiescence to tribal customs.' It was the force of customary law that enabled the tribal community to avoid coercive political power in the hands of dominant authority. Thus, 'Custom not only offered a well-elaborated system of individual duties and responsibilities, but was designed to protect human dignity. If all members of the tribe obeyed the sacred customs then as a logical outcome each member would be assured of equality, self-worth, personal autonomy, justice, and fraternity, that is, human dignity. Dignity was protected by a system of unwritten, positively stated mutal duties rather than negatively stated individual legal rights'.[47]

The authors concede that their description is not necessarily operative in the daily life of the First Nations, but that it is relevant as what they describe as a 'charter myth' accepted by the aboriginal peoples, 'much as western democratic societies have adopted equality and individual rights as their charter myth and version of the "good society"'.[48]

In the final analysis, Boldt and Long argue that, given the differing approaches of different cultures to the question of rights, it would seem that the desirable consensus should be oriented to the attainment of 'human dignity', allowing each society to determine what emphasis to place on specific aspects of social life – for instance, the role of the individual or the demands of the society – in expressing such dignity. In their words,

> despite divergencies in attitudes toward individualized human rights, virtually all societies have cultural and ideological systems that deem everyone entitled to human dignity … . Why not shift the emphasis from a universal doctrine protecting individualized human rights to a doctrine guaranteeing human dignity? The concept of human dignity … . is more encompassing than that of human rights, and subsumes all of the humane objectives implied in the Universal Declaration … .
>
> The pathway to implementing a universal doctrine of human dignity can be uniquely plotted by each society to fit its cultural history and contemporary situation. Some societies may emphasize the individual, others the collectivity. Some may seek to achieve the goal of human dignity through guarantees of individual rights, others through an emphasis on personal responsibilities.[49]

The idea of human dignity being used as an overall framework for guaranteeing human rights (and also perhaps needs) is an intriguing one, latent with potentiality. Human dignity is a concept which appears in more recent constitutional documents and theoretical writing and contains perhaps the basis of far-reaching implications, which go beyond the specific issues of guaranteeing the traditional liberal rights.[50] For instance, it has been argued that the term may be constructively interpreted when judges are faced with issues at the forefront of innovative and inchoate rights, some of them, the product of modern life, for instance, the question of a right to die in dignity as opposed to the activation of advanced medical technology to sustain life in conditions of pain and/or meaninglessness. Ultimate questions of individual rights ignored in the past, such as the right to privacy or to conscientious disobedience, may also find useful solutions through sensitive understanding of the fuller meaning of human dignity. This term may also be used as an effective comprehensive framework to cover all three generations of human rights – the traditional individual liberties (the right to express oneself, practice one's religion, be free from arbitrary arrest), the newer economic rights (the dignity associated with adequate physical sustenance) and the third generation rights (the dignity associated with the recognition of a person's social identity, for instance as a member of a tribe or the right to use his own language in public discourse).[51]

Inasmuch as the United States Constitution serves as a model for so many later constitutions, it should be remarked that it contains no reference in the Bill of Rights or elsewhere to human dignity.[52] In fact, one of the first dominant documents to proclaim dignity as a fundamental constitutional concern was the post-war constitution of West Germany, in its opening declaratory clause, and several other countries have in recent years followed suit.[53]

The US Constitution and its legal system has other limitations; thus the 1968 Indian Civil Rights Act in the United States is not intended to come to terms with the unique collective rights of Indians, but attempts to incorporate some of the traditional rights of the American Constitution into the court system of Indian tribes.[54] Stephen Revar points out that the Indian Civil Rights Act is actually 'a highly controversial law because it authorizes federal courts to intervene in intratribal disputes, a power they never had before', a development which 'many Indians bitterly resent'.[55]

The approach suggested by Bolt and Young has a great deal of relevance for other countries. Given the heterogenous nature of most modern states (very few are 'classical' nation-states) and given the prevalence of tribes in some of the newer countries (including in countries, such as in Africa, where tribe is downgraded and alternative terminology is preferred), the use of dignity might supply an immediate semantic solution, with far-ranging substantive consequences.

In an important article, a jurist from Malagasy has shown how necessary it is to combine any concern for human rights with full consideration of people's rights – that is, individual rights must be examined in the context of collective rights.[56] Dealing specifically with the situation in Africa, Hughes Andriamihaja explains that 'Africans, who are more attached to groups, having a more highly developed "gregarious instinct" than Westerners, feel secure only when they are together and consequently their individual rights are meaningful only to the extent that they are connected with those of the other members of the clan, the tribe or the community'.[57] For instance, even such a basic right as the right to life must be seen in the context of the collective – a contribution to the perpetuation of the group over the generations; thus, 'every human being, every life, helps to give the community the strength and influence it needs to establish and impose itself for the benefit of all … This fitting of the individual into the collective mould is encouraged by the very way in which traditional African society is organized, being fundamentally and essentially community-oriented.'[58] Andriamihaja adds that, within such a political structure, there was much scope for direct democracy, for the search for consensus, for harmonious coexistence. Indeed, there is a danger that in the modern era – even with its formal constitutional rights – both the individual and the collective will be denied their full rights.

Despite the outward attraction of legally-formulated rights, state power may often be given precedence. Even in modern western societies, the individual has often to forego some of his individuality in response to state demands – the military draft, taxation, and so on. Critical in general of the state, with its basis of power, Andriamihaja warns against any equation of the state with the people, in a style reminiscent of those who argue, as noted, for a civil society, and then claims that the 'problem of the relationship between human rights and people's rights arises acutely in the African context on account of the specific attitude of African politicians to the state and their idea of Africa and Africans … [P]oliticians identify with the state and this identification makes for the privatization and monopolization of the power vested in the state.'[59] Beyond this, the reality of Africa is that 'African states, demographically and culturally heterogeneous, cannot constitute a well-integrated "spiritual family", ethnic allegiance nearly always taking precedence over national consciousness and, inevitably, in the event of conflict, the state representing and protecting the ethnic group in power. In such distressing situations, the state claims, with the use of force, to be defending national unity made into a dogma and enshrined in international texts. Cultural, ethnic and religious differences are considered as threats to national unity.'[60] Thus, in the name of state unity, peoples' rights are denied – but an unwillingness to recognize the diversity that exists may paradoxically lead to greater divisions, based on the resentment and frustrations of minority groups.

While acknowledging the significant achievement of the African Charter on Human Rights and Peoples' Rights, Andriamihaja concludes that '… even though it attempts in all its articles to have the relationship between the individual and the people recognized as being indissoluble and interdependent, the lack of precise definitions regarding the concept of people and the individual provides African political leaders with a way out in that it enables them to take advantage of ambiguities and omissions in the text'.[61]

But, of course, some of these ambiguities relate to the very use of the word tribe – a word that Andriamihaja carefully refrains from using, until right near the end and then only in the course of expressing a hope that 'tribal and ethnic division' will be overcome to allow Africa to fulfil its potential – 'the African people … must be reborn'.[62]

Inasmuch as there is a uniqueness to the social structure of African society, much of it relates to its heterogeneous nature for the vast majority of the states in sub-Saharan Africa. While the structure of most of these groups are different from most of the 'tribes' in North America or Australia, being much larger in size as one example, these African groups are also no less different from ethnic groups in Europe or various parts of Asia, or what goes by the name of ethnic groups in North America. What differentiates the African groups from most of the ethnic groups in the northern hemisphere and what links them to so many of the 'tribes' in

America and Australia is specifically the existence of customary law and the precedence given to the collective. A recognition of this commonality may help to clarify then the special nature of collective rights – the rights of peoples, as distinct from but not in opposition to individual human rights, but differentiated also from ethnicity, while also partly different from the indigenous people, which has been the concern of the ILO, and which alone were celebrated in the Year of the Indigenous People. The challenge for international law is to recognize – beyond religion, language, ethnicity and indigenous groups – also tribes.

NOTES

1. John Locke, *Second Treatise of Government: Of Civil Government* (Hackett Publishing Co., 1980 [1681]); and Jean-Jacques Rousseau, *The Social Contract* (Reading, MA: Addison-Wesley, 1997 [1762]).
2. See, for instance, Natan Lerner, *Group Rights and Discrimination in International Law* (Dordrecht: Martinus Nijhoff, 1991). Lerner deals at various points with tribal populations, referring *inter alia* to the work of Jose Martinez Cobo, special rapporteur of the UN Sub-Commission on Prevention of Discrimination and Protection of Minorities, who includes indigenous groups among his comments. But, for a more critical approach, see Jack Donnelly, 'Third Generation Rights', in C. Brölman, R. Lefeber and M. Zieck (eds), *Peoples and Minorities in International Law* (Dordrecht: Martinus Nijhoff, 1993), p. 119.
3. For examples in the United States of cases dealing with sabbath observance, see *Gallagher v. Crown Kosher Meat Market*, 366 US 617 (1961); and *Braunfield v. Brown*, 366 US 599 (1961). For a Canadian case, see *R. v. Big M Drug Mart,* (1985) I.S.C.R.295
4. *Belgium linguistics case*, European Court of Human Rights, Ser. A No. 6 (1968); see also an earlier case in 1935 dealing with the Greek minority in Albania, adjudicated in the Permanent Court of International Justice – *Minority Schools in Albania,* PCIJ, Ser. A/B, No. 64, 1935.
5. International Covenant on Civil and Political Rights, U.N. General Assembly Resolution 2200A (XXI), 10 December 1966.
6. *Mabo v. Queensland*, (1992) 175 CLR 1; 66 ALJR 408; (1992) 107 ALC; *Calder v. Attorney-General of British Columbia*, (1970) 8 DLR (3d) 59; (1970) 13 DLR 64; (1973) 34 DLR (3d) 145; *New Zealand Maori Council v. Attorney-General*, [1987] NZLR 641; *Otieno v. Ougo and Siranga* H.C.C. No. 4872 (1986) (Kenya).
7. For Canada, see, in general, E. Belobaba and E. Gertner (eds), *The New Constitution and the Charter of Rights* (Toronto: Butterworths, 1983); for Africa, see Issa Shivji, *The Concept of Human Rights in Africa* (London: Codesria Book Series, 1989).
8. See discussion in Chapter 10, below, 'The Local Tribe in the Global Village'.
9. The International Labor Organization Convention Concerning Indigenous and Tribal Peoples in Independent Countries (Convention 169), 27 June 1989; revising Indigenous and Tribal Populations Convention, 1957 (No. 107).
10. International Covenant on Economic, Social and Cultural Rights, UN General Assembly Resolution 2200A (XX), 16 December 1966.
11. The covenants and conventions mentioned and quoted in this chapter may be found in a publication from 1994 of the Center for the Study of Human Rights at Columbia University, *Twenty-Five Human Rights Documents* (New York: Center for the Study of Human Rights, Columbia University, 1994).
12. Lee Swepston, 'The Adoption of the Indigenous and Tribal Peoples' Convention, 1989 (No. 169)', *Law and Anthropology* 5 (1990), p. 221.
13. Ibid., p. 222.
14. Ibid., p. 222. For general discussion of the changes to the Convention, see R. Barsh, 'Revision of the ILO Convention No. 107', *American Journal of International Law*, 81 (1987), p. 756.

15. Anna Michalska, 'Rights of Peoples and Human Rights in International Law' in Georges Kutukdjian and Antonio Papisca (eds), *Rights of Peoples* (Padova: CEDAM, 1991), p. 33. She notes that the 'notion "people" has been used in international instruments in many contexts. Yet, at the same time, no definition of that notion is provided by international law …' (p. 33).
16. See discussion later in this chapter on legislation in the United States and Canada.
17. African Charter on Human and Peoples' Rights, 17 June 1981; entered into force on 21 October 1986.
18. On communitarianism, see Michael Sandel, *Liberalism and the Limits of Justice* (Cambridge: Cambridge University Press, 1982).
19. James Crawford, 'Some Conclusions', in Crawford (ed.), *The Rights of Peoples* (Oxford: Clarendon Press, 1988), p. 159.
20. Ibid., p. 159.
21. Ibid., p. 174.
22. Aviam Soifer, *Law and the Company We Keep* (Cambridge, MA: Harvard University Press, 1995).
23. Ibid., p. 1.
24. In this context, Soifer discusses the case of *DeShaney v. Winnebago County Social Services Department*, 489 US 189 (1989). The young 4-year-old Joshua DeShaney had suffered beatings by his father of which the Social Services had had knowledge for about two years, but had failed to intervene adequately to protect him. The Supreme Court found no direct fault in this omission. Soifer concludes his discussion of this case with the comment, 'According to the *DeShaney* decision, a family with custody of a child is the only source of protection for that child as a matter of constitutional law, unless and until the state formally takes or reassigns custody' (p. 141).
25. Ferdinand Tönnies, *Community and Society (*East Lansing: Michigan State University Press, 1957); on Durkheim, see my critique of his work in *Social Cohesion and Legal Coercion: A Critique of Weber, Durkheim and Marx* (Atlanta, GA, and Amsterdam: Rodopi, 1997).
26. Robert Nisbet, *The Quest for Community* (London: Oxford University Press, 1969); see also his discussion of the idea of community as a basic concept in sociology in his book *The Sociological Tradition* (London: Heinemann, 1966).
27. For an excellent and comprehensive discussion, see Jean Cohen and Andrew Arato, *Civil Society and Political Theory* (Cambridge, MA: Massachusetts Institute of Technology Press, 1992).
28. See especially the discussion in Chapter 7 of Soifer, *Law and the Company We Keep*: 'Involuntary groups and the Role of History in American Law'. Soifer states in the opening sentence, 'History is crucial in identifying the groups that warrant particular legal protection … In the United States we are notorious for assuming that the past has emphatically passed. Still, it is worthy of notice when even the Justices of the United Supreme Court are wilfully blind to the burdens of the past. Judges today evince a profoundly ahistorical approach to groups that most obviously warrant special judicial concern on the basis of past wrongs' (p. 127). See also Frances Svensson, 'Liberal Democracy and Group Rights: The Legacy of Individualism and its Impact on American Indian Tribes,' *Political Studies*, 27 (1979), p. 421.
29. Soifer, *Law and the Company We Keep*, p. 141
30. Ibid., p. 140.
31. See Chapter 9, 'Belonging and Identity'.
32. See Chapter 18, 'Women and Children First'.
33. See discussion in Chapter 12, 'Land is Forever'; and see particularly Harriet Ketley, 'Cultural Diversity versus Biodiversity', *Adelaide Law Review* 16 (1994), p. 99.
34. American Indian Religious Freedom Act (AIRFA), Pub. L. No. 95–341, 92 Stat. 469; codified in part – 42 USC. Sec. 1996; and sec. 35 of Canadian Charter. For a good discussion and presentation of the constitutional recognition of constitutional rights in a number of Latin American countries, see Marie Leger (ed.), *Aboriginal Peoples: Toward Self-Government* (Montreal: Black Race Books, 1994).
35. For a critical view in general of the United States Supreme Court to issues of freedom of religion, see Leon Sheleff, '"Thou Shalt Not Be Too Different": Civil Rights, Social Control and Deviant Religious Practices in the United States', *Israel Yearbook on Human Rights* 23 (1994), p. 193; included is a discussion of judicial attitudes to the peyote case.

36 Darlene Johnston, 'Native Rights as Collective Rights: A Question of Group Self-Preservation', *Canadian Journal of Law and Jurisprudence* 2 (1989), p. 19.

37. See M. Behiels (ed.), *The Meech Lake Primer: Conflicting Views of the 1987 Constitutional Accord* (Ottawa: University of Ottawa Press, 1989). For a perceptive discussion of the similarity of ethnic or national minorities in their struggles for autonomy or independence, seen in the context of 'tribal' sentiments, see Tom Franck, 'Postmodern Tribalism and the Right to Secession', in Brölman *et al.*, *Peoples and Minorities in International Law*, p. 3. He writes: 'Tribalism, in its postmodern form, is not – as it was once perceived – the exclusive property of so-called backward peoples ... It manifests itself in efforts to break up, equally, the old nations of Europe (such as the Union of Scotland with England and Wales), the nineteenth century nations of the Americas (such as Quebec's pursuit of secession from Canada) and the newest nations of the third world (such as the Karen effort to secede from Myanmar)' (pp. 3–4).

38. See, in general, Christopher Manfred, *Judicial Power and the Charter: Canada and the Paradox of Liberal Constitutionalism* (Norman: University of Oklahoma Press, 1993), Chapter 5, 'Equality Rights', p. 120, especially at pp. 128–31.

39. Canada Constitution Act, 1982.

40. See 'Declaration of the First Nations – 1981', in Menno Boldt and J. Anthony Long with Leroy Little Bear (eds.), *The Quest for Justice: Aboriginal Peoples and Aboriginal Rights* (Toronto: University of Toronto Press, 1985), p. 359.

41. Sec. 37(1) of Constitution Act, 1982, reads: 'A Constitutional Conference composed of the Prime Minister of Canada and the first Ministers of the provinces shall be convened by the Prime Minister of Canada within one year ...'. Subsection (2) provides for invitations to be submitted to representatives of the aboriginal peoples in respect of 'constitutional matters that directly affect the aboriginal peoples of Canada'. The first such meeting was held in 1983.

42. Michael Asch, *Home and Native Land: Aboriginal Rights and the Canadian Constitution* (Toronto: Methuen, 1984).

43. The last referendum in Quebec was held in 1995, and the proposal for independence was only narrowly defeated. The constitutional status of this vote is not clear – for instance, it is not known what would have been the immediate impact of a positive vote for independence. It would seem there is no binding power to the vote.

44. Asch, *Home and Native Land*, p. 104. Asch presents a political program set forth for the Northwestern Territories by aboriginal groups, the Dene people, who live there – see Dene Declaration of 1975, Appendix G, p. 127 in Asch's book.

45. Boldt and Long in their edited book, *The Quest for Justice*, 'Tribal Philosophies and the Canadian Charter of Rights and Freedoms,' pp. 165.

46. Ibid., pp. 167–8.

47. Ibid., p. 169.

48. Ibid., p. 169.

49. Ibid., p. 178.

50. On human dignity, see Haim Cohn, 'On the Meaning of Human Dignity', *Israel Yearbook on Human Rights*, 13 (1983), p. 226. See also collection of essays based on Aspen Institute Workshop, *Human Dignity: The Internationalization of Human Rights* (Dobbs Ferry, NY: Oceana Publications, 1979). See also several articles in vol. 53 of *Southern California Law Review* (1980) – W. Murphy, 'An Ordering of Constitutional Values', p. 703; P. Brest, 'Accommodation of Majoritarianism and Rights of Human Dignity', p. 761; D. Fellman, 'Principles Other Than Human Dignity in Constitutional Analysis', p. 765.

51. See especially Jack Donnelly, 'Human Rights and Human Dignity: An Analytic Critique of Non-Western Conceptions of Human Rights', *American Political Science Review* 4 (1982), p. 303; see also Adamantia Pollis and Peter Schwab, 'Human Rights: A Western Construct with Limited Applicability', in Pollis and Schwab (eds), *Human Rights: Cultural and Ideological Perspectives* (New York: Praeger, 1979), p. 1.

52. I have raised these issues in a series of articles in Hebrew based on the 1992 Israeli Basic Law: Human Dignity and Liberty. See for instance, my article, 'Human Dignity: Legislation and Litigation' in *Mechkarei Mishpat – Bar Ilan University Law Review* (1996) (in Hebrew).

53. Article 1 of German Constitution reads: 'Human Dignity is Inviolable'. This declaration obviously reflects the desire to make a break with the Third Reich, and to provide a

comprehensive constitutional protection against a repetition of the Nazi regime's practices.

54. Indian Civil Rights Act (ICRA), 1968, 25 USC.
55. Stephan Pevar, *The Rights of Indians and Tribes: The Basic ACLU Guide to Indian and Tribal Rights* (Carbondale: Southern Illinois University Press, 1992), p. 240.
56. Hughes Andriamihaja, 'The Relationship Between Peoples' Rights and Human Rights in the Context of the Countries of Africa', in Kutukdjian and Papisca (eds), *Rights of Peoples*, 107.
57. Ibid., p. 107.
58. Ibid., p. 108.
59. Ibid., p. 109.
60. Ibid., p. 109. In this context, see Jan Klabbers and René Lefeber, 'Africa: Lost Between Self-Determination and *Uti Possidetis*', in Brölman *et al.* (eds), *Peoples and Minorities in International Law*, p. 37. The rule referred to – of *uti possidetis* – is a 'rule of continuity *ipso iure* of boundary and territorial treaties' – quoted, p. 66, from a 1982 case in the International Court of Justice (*Tunisia v. Libyan Arab Jamahirija,* IJC Rep. 1982, 18).
61. Ibid., p. 110.
62. Ibid., p. 111.

Belonging and Identity

The futility of denying the reality of tribal existence is rarely so graphically and emotionally exposed as in the Otieno Affair in Kenya[1] – a 6-month legal struggle to determine the place of burial of Silvanus Otieno, waged between the members of his immediate family (his wife and children) and his tribal relatives (mainly a brother). The affair riveted the attention of the people of Kenya as argument and counter-argument, facts and opinions and their countervailing facts and opinions, were placed before the judges in a number of courts. The local media[2] extended full coverage to a story pregnant with social meaning and perhaps even personal relevance to many and fraught with emotional human tension, as days, then weeks and months, passed, while the deceased's nuclear family struggled against his extended tribal family, for the legal right to determine where he would find his eternal rest – in a cemetery near where he had lived and worked, had married and raised his children, or in the ancestral tribal lands, in the area where he had been born and bred. Otieno, a successful Nairobi lawyer, a member of the Luo Tribe, had married a wife from another tribe, and their children had been brought up in an urban environment (including some schooling in England), with only minimum ties to either of the tribes of their parents.

The degree to which Otieno himself retained physical contact was one of the matters of contention in the litigation, and similarly there was no consensus as to the nature and extent of his own deeper emotional attachment to his ancestral connections.

While the legal contest was in process, his corpse was kept in cold storage and the burial took place only after a half-year of complicated and agonizing judicial involvement – with the final decision in favor of the tribe.[3] His widow had made it clear that she would not participate in those tribal tasks assigned to her as a widow, not just because of their strangeness to her as a member of another tribe, but also because of her distaste for some aspects of these customs (for instance, being together with the corpse throughout the night prior to the day of burial). She has since also indicated, on occasion, that she has not reconciled herself to the adverse decision and intends making further attempts to re-bury the body in a cemetery near to where she lives.

The case aroused a great deal of interest – not only among the public and in Kenya. It has been extensively analyzed in academic research – law, sociology, anthropology and history and elicited much overseas interest, both general media coverage and academic analysis.[4]

As far as the factual aspects of the case were concerned, the various judgments tended to favor the evidence that indicated a desire on the part of the deceased to be buried in accordance with tribal custom – in practical terms near his father's grave, as he himself had not established a home, as so understood by Luo custom. The two dwelling-places in which he lived with his family (one in Nairobi, and one on a nearby farm) were to be considered only as houses in which he resided, and not as a 'home', which would indicate the severance of his ties with his father, and thus the right to be buried elsewhere. The evidence indicating this intention on his part was, according to some critics of the judicial decision, most suspect, as it was based largely on that of the tribal gravedigger, who recounted conversations of this nature with the deceased – but who also added comments, which indicated his fear of the dire consequences that might ensue if tribal custom were violated.

However, the major factor in this case was not so much the determination of the facts, but the determination of the status of customary law. In effect the outcome of the litigation was a recognition of its pre-eminence. Thus, the Court of Appeal, affirming the stance of the lower court on this issue, stated emphatically that 'It matters not that the deceased was ... sophisticated, urbanized and had developed a different life-style' and then added, in general terms, that 'At present there is no way in which an African citizen of Kenya can divest himself of the association with the tribe of his father if customs are patrilineal. It is thus clear that Mr. Otieno having been born and bred a Luo remained a member of the Luo tribe and subject to the customary law of the Luo people.'[5]

M.D. Okech-Owiti is extremely critical of the judgment and claims these statements are 'clearly unsustainable assertions'.[6] However, even more pertinent are his comments on the manner in which customary law should be applied. On the assumption that the customary law of the Luo tribe was relevant, he points out that the rules as to burial procedures were long-standing, and thus in need of revamping. He argues that 'the suggested rigidity' which the judges assumed, 'goes against the philosophical foundation of custom. Custom arises from and relates to concrete practice. And one of the major foundations of customary practice is reconciliation and the effort to maintain the main fabric of social life. Thus, if in the process of this concrete practice novel circumstances arise, they are accommodated by way of appropriate modification of the custom to *solve* the problem.'[7] It was this flexibility that was lacking in the conflict that arose, that might well, according to Okech-Owiti, have been resolved by a group of elders of the tribe 'sitting together and discussing the possible alternatives'.[8] A feasible compromise was at hand since 'the very fact that customs arise out of practice (are a cultural phenomenon) means that they are, like the rest of social phenomena, dynamic'. Thus, 'Any suggestion of a static characteristic is, therefore, unhistorical'.[9] The implication of this approach is not just to acknowledge the existence and applicability of the customary law, but to stress its fluid quality; its relevance for the modern world is thus predicated on its consideration of modern conditions. What is clear is that the customs cannot be ignored, for these are of major import to the tribespeople. As A.B.C. Ocholla-Ayayo, an anthropologist, points out, 'There was cause to fear evil consequences if there was departure from tradition [which] ... would lead to the disintegration of the clan [and] ... to the disappearance of the spiritual and social bond that gave form, durability and hope, to the ... clan.'[10]

However, having said so much, let me clarify two points, as to the Court judgment. First, that the decision was not necessarily a correct one or of overwhelming validity in other jurisdictions; from the perspective of this book, the decision itself is not as important as the process, or the fact that there was a legal issue of major import to be decided in a court of law dealing with tribal membership, tribal custom and tribal rights in a way that would not be possible if the group concerned was clearly no more than an ethnic community – indeed the court might possibly have come to a decision that the Luo were not a tribe at all, but 'only' an ethnic group, but surely not without the same deep legal debate and analysis that accompanied their contrary decision. In the event, of course, the Court did relate to the Luo as a tribe, an essential prerequisite for their ultimate finding as to the burial place, but even if their interpretation of the facts at issue and of the custom in dispute, may be criticized on the merits, their working assumption that the Luo are a tribe is of no mean significance.

Second, the struggle over a burial place was not a consequence of any 'primitivity' that might be attributed to the parties (or some of them) to the dispute. Problems of burial do sometimes arise in other contexts shorn of any tribal overtones – as between, for instance, a widow and her in-laws as to the burial place of the husband/son,[11] especially of a recently married young couple without children, where the bereaved parents, in a modern, western, urban environment, may well surmise that the widow may possibly remarry, and over the years tend to neglect the burial site (or even move to another area), which thus should be nearer to the parents.

Furthermore, it is not only tribal customs that spawn such problems relating to the accident of birth and ensuing forced membership of a group. Religions often do likewise, for instance, Islam assigns membership according to the religion of the father, Judaism according to the mother and it is not easy to forgo such membership subsequently.[12]

But then, states also apply similar arbitrary decision-making processes, often with even more far-reaching inevitable consequences – for instance, automatic citizenship for those born in the country (even when the parents are not citizens themselves), later perhaps compulsory military service; even the act of relinquishing citizenship may be complicated – mere change of residence will not suffice and citizenship may be maintained against the person's wishes, or one may be deprived of citizenship under certain circumstances. Most pertinently a host of problems are associated with questions of dual citizenship or where citizenship is sought based upon kinship principles, for instance receiving citizenship of a country in which one is not resident (or has not even visited, based on the citizenship of parents or even grandparents).[13]

Again, even voluntary decisions to join a group may lead to legal complications, especially in terms of how membership may be terminated or even how the group as a whole may be disbanded. The break-up of a business partnership may create no less problems and anomalies than questions dealing with relinquishing tribal membership, or conversely, the insistence on membership in a particular group, because of advantages that may accrue as a result.

In fact, those who try to artificially create a tribe-like, utopian community, often encounter acute dilemmas in determining who belongs to the group, who is entitled to the advantages and benefits – and perhaps profits – or who is subject to its burdens and obligations, and perhaps even debts. Carol Weisbrod's analysis of four American Utopian Communities describes 'controversies between former members of the societies and the societies themselves and treats in detail a number of lawsuits involving four of the most famous of the nineteenth century American Utopian Communities – the Shakers, the Harmony Society, Oneida and Zoar'.[14] These, of course, are not mainstream groupings, but there is much in the manner of the conflict, in its human ramifications and even tragedies, to bear reminder of partnerships that break down, or past business associates carrying scarred remembrances of mutual recriminations, or political bedfellows of yesteryear now engaged in acrimonious rivalry. However, no less important than the internal problems, is the willingness by the State to give legal (in these cases, contractual) recognition to the 'alternative worlds, represented by the utopian societies',[15] – thus the state allows litigation over the utopian contracts entered into between the group and its members, thereby expressing its toleration – even recognition – of special and unique community arrangements.

These facts should be borne in mind as we probe some of the problems that have arisen in connection with tribal membership – in which it is not the tribe's custom alone, but also sometimes, state law or policy that is decisive. It should also not be forgotten that in some countries, for instance, the United States and Australia, the tribespeople were initially not given citizenship. The full meaning of this position was spelled out by the Supreme Court in the 1884 case of *Elk v. Wilkins* when it was held that 'Indians born within the territorial limits of the United States, members of, and owing immediate allegiance to, one of the Indian tribes (an alien, though dependent power), although in a geographical sense born in the United States, are no more born in the United States and subject to jurisdiction thereof, within the meaning of the first section of the Fourteenth Amendment, than the children of subjects of any foreign government born within the domain of that government, or the children born within the United States, of ambassadors or other public ministers of foreign nations.'[16] The larger consequence of this decision was, of course, to deny the Native Americans the protection of the Bill of Rights, including those key amendments passed in the wake of the civil war, and intended (albeit with only limited immediate effect) to safeguard the interests of the black people of America, recently released from their enslavement.

In any event, at stake in the question of membership is not just some strange foibles of tribal societies, but legal issues that states and religions (but not ethnic groups) are continually confronting. In all these instances, deeper philosophical factors underlie the problem; who should be entitled to make the decision as to membership – the person, the group, or the state, and by what form – law, custom or practice? In recent years, several Canadian cases involving tribal membership have aroused a great deal of interest, even beyond the borders of Canada, partly because an attempt was made to activate outside United Nations humanitarian intervention. The Sandra Lovelace affair[17] involved the right of a woman to retain her tribal status, when she married a non-member of the tribe. In this particular case, she requested her membership back after a divorce, but she was denied the request. The matter was brought before the Human Rights Committee of the United Nations, on the basis of gender discrimination, for a male marrying a non-member of the tribe would not lose his membership.

The Committee held in favor of the petitioner, on the basis of Article 27 of the International Covenant on Civil and Political Rights, which guarantees to members of ethnic, religious or ethnic minorities 'the right in community with the other members of their group to enjoy their own culture, to profess and practice their own religion or to use their own language'.[18] While the facts are clear-cut, the rationale is not conclusive because of the complexity of the facts – the facts of gender discrimination, the fact that the demand was based not on loss of membership (at time of marriage), but request for renewal (at time of divorce), and because the decision was not based purely on tribal rules, but had a statutory basis in Canadian legislation – the Indian Act of 1970, which was no less determinative than the tribal law.[19]

Yet, this case touches on a crucial issue, in Canada and elsewhere; the degree to which customary rules of tribes must be interpreted in terms of human rights principles, whether of international conventions (as in the Lovelace case) or specific constitutional provisions. An earlier case in Canada had dealt with this issue in the only instance where an ordinary law dealing with civil rights had been activated to nullify a law in conflict with its principles.[20] In 1960, Canada had enacted, by ordinary legislation, a Bill of Rights, and its terms, guaranteeing equality, had been the basis for declaring invalid a law, providing for special treatment for Native Americans, namely, prohibiting the sale of alcohol to Native Americans, because of its deleterious effects on them. Since then, Canada has enacted an entrenched Charter of Human Rights as part of its new constitutional structure and the courts have more often resorted to US-style judicial review, but until now, no law dealing with the special status of native Americans has been adjudicated, though a number of writers have drawn attention to possible ramifications of the Charter on customary rules, and practices.[21]

A more recent case dealt with the protections that Canadian law could provide to a person, born an Indian who resented the imposition of tribal membership upon him in a ritual that had been coercively performed, and which included denial of food, physical attacks on his body and humiliating procedures such as a naked walk through a creek. Subsequent to this ritual he sued those responsible, pointing out that as his residence was off the tribal reserve, he was no longer a member and thus should not be subject to its customary practices.[22]

The gender issue (in terms of membership), on a basis similar to the *Lovelace* case, has also been the source of litigation in the United States in *Santa Clara v. Martinez.*[23] Here too, selective and special legislation, the 1968 Indian Civil Rights Act,[24] was a key factor – this was legislation aimed at introducing civil rights factors into the legal structure of tribal life. However, while many authorities presumed that this legislation would contribute to advancing civil rights in general among the Indians, Vine Deloria and Clifford Lytle comment that 'unfortunately, none of the legal scholars anticipated that the act would become embroiled in a very difficult case that involved two explosive contemporary issues: the status of women within the tribe and the right of a tribe to determine its own membership'.[25]

The issue here was almost identical to that which had arisen in the *Lovelace* case in Canada – the right of women to retain their membership in a tribe if they marry outside of the tribe, when male members doing likewise were not deprived of membership. However, while general issues of civil rights were relevant and specific issues of gender discrimination were involved, the key factor in dispute was who had the right to determine tribal membership. The Supreme Court held that it was limited in its ability to intervene because of the special nature of tribal government, the one noted exception stipulated in the act being for a *habeas corpus* petition in the case of unlawful imprisonment. Thus, the leading United States case dealing with membership rules placed this power squarely within the tribe itself – even if some of the consequences might raise general civil rights issues.

In analyzing this case in terms of gender discrimination, it should be borne in mind that the issue of tracing descent can be determined by either patrilineal or matrilineal principles – in other words, what is involved is a 'judgment call', in which a tribe (or a religion or even a state) lays down a generalized rule which determines that the continuation of the ancestral line (for tribal membership, religious affiliation or national citizenship) will be maintained either through the male or the female – this may be true also not only between tribes, but also within tribes, when dealing with clans, or also for minorities. Inasmuch as this involves discrimination against either husband or wife (or their group) it is an inevitable consequence of the reality of marriage, which joins together people from different social groups, and a decision has to be made as to which group will continue the ancestral line.

Thus, in most western states, on marriage a woman takes on the family name of her husband, a decision of momentous input to her self-identity: indeed, the enormity of this traditional practice of modern societies has only recently become apparent, as feminist ideas have induced many women to retain their original family name. Even so, key decisions have to be made as to the family name that the children will bear – and even a hyphenated name is effective only for one generation. A married woman using both names (as is the general custom in Latin America and as is becoming more acceptable in Europe and North America) is still acquiescing in accepting her husband's name; even here there is no equality for as long as the husband does not add her family name to his (which only a small number of people have begun to do). While the issue of a name does not have the same consequences as tribal membership, there are similarities. In any event, there are tribes (admittedly a minority) that are also matrilineal and matrilocal. The major effect of the *Santa Clara Pueblo* decision is to grant to the tribe the right to determine the means by which membership will be determined.

However, the recognition granted the tribe to determine membership is the culmination of a lengthy and erratic process, in which, at various stages, efforts were made to undermine tribal unity and to accelerate the prospects of their demise and the assimilation of individual Indians into American society.

The major early phases in this cumbersome process, never consistently applied, was firstly the removal of tribes from their ancestral lands in the

1830s to facilitate the westward drive, and then the 1887 Dawes Allotment Act to entice the Indians out of their communal framework by providing them with individual plots, with the subsequent surplus being made available to non-Indians.[26] After the First World War (in which many Indians participated), a new variable was introduced with the granting of citizenship in 1924, while several years later, a new policy was undertaken, signified by the Reorganization Act,[27] which heralded the revival of tribal life and tribal institutions. After the Second World War, especially in the 1950s, a renewed effort was made, through a policy of termination, once again to encourage the demise of tribes, whereby agreements would be reached as to their disbandment.[28] This too was short-lived, reaching its peak in the 1950s and some legal problematics have arisen for those tribes which then affirmed their willingness to disappear – but the futility of this policy soon became apparent; and since the 1960s there seems to be a clear revival of tribal awareness, with individual Indians eager to find tangible means of expressing their tribal affiliation. The number of institutions, such as courts, have grown, and an activist stance, to be discussed in the next chapter, has assured even economic advancement.

The vicissitudes and sometimes vagueness of tribal existence were aptly brought out in the case of a tribe in New England, where, in a civil trial dealing with land claims in a semi-urban setting, the key question was not of individual membership, but whether or not the tribe was actually in existence.[29] Historical and anthropological evidence presented to the court, indicated different situations at different periods of time – finally, the jury was asked to focus on several specific time-spans and to decide for each point in time whether the tribe existed or not – and thus, whether it could have a group claim to the land in dispute.

In Australia, a key question arose as to whether a particular individual in a particular situation was to be accorded the status of Aborigine. On the occasion, during the Second World War, the legal issue was whether an 'urbanized' Aborigine was liable for conscription – and the court made reference to the way in which he was dressed as an indication of his break with aboriginal status, and therefore his liability to be drafted – evoking the response as to whether he should perhaps have arrived in court in scanty attire and brandishing a primitive weapon, in order to prove his status as an Aborigine.[30]

More recently, the court displayed greater sensitivity to this issue, when, during the enquiries of a government commission into Aboriginal deaths in custody, the question arose as to whether one of the deceased was indeed an Aborigine, and so should be included in the investigation. The court took cognizance of both subjective factors (whether or not he personally identified himself as an Aborigine) and objective factors (the fact of his descent). Because of the ambivalence he had shown as to his aboriginality, the court held that he should not be considered an Aborigine, but, since the objective factor did indicate biological connections, it is possible that the court did not take account of the psychological problems encountered by many Aborigines, leading to a desire to deny their antecedent background.[31]

However, far more complex issues arise with some of the most delicate matters involved in tribal membership – the issue of adoption, wardship, fostering or guardianship when dealing with young children. Momentous decisions as to the destiny of a young child – generally, in fact, an infant – are made at least in some cases, with totally inadequate respect and consideration for the bonds of kinship and the import of group identity.

In a recent decision of the Oklahoma Supreme Court, Justice Kanger explained how the removal of children from their homes had contributed to the undermining of Indian culture and tribal cohesiveness. She writes that: 'Continuing separation of Indian children from their heritage is one of the most tragic and destructive aspects of contemporary Indian life. State intrusion into native American parent–child relationships impedes the ability of the tribe to perpetuate itself …'.[32] Discussing this case, Edward Thompson claims that 'well-meaning social workers sometimes seek the removal of Indian children from their traditional Indian family home because of what they perceive to be abuse or neglect, when, in fact, none exists. They simply misunderstand traditional lifestyles.'[33] These misconceptions are not idiosyncratic occurrences, but are symptomatic of far more deep-seated phenomena which sometimes take on dimensions that are indicative not of naive misunderstanding, but of deliberate intent. While, in many places, there was an underlying assumption that in the course of time, the indigenous culture would be overwhelmed by the sheer force and attraction of the superior western civilization, often policies were introduced to accelerate this process by focused educational programs, oriented to preparing the young child for life in a modern world, in which traditional practices and customs would be no more than a fading memory or a museum relic. The major thrust of this approach was in the removal of the child from the parents' control, often to the extent of outright, formal adoption.

The most blatant expression of such actions was in Australia, particularly, but not only, in the case of half-caste children. In other situations, wardship was instituted, where the child would stay with, and work for, a whole family. As part of the overall reassessment being made in this country to its past *vis-à-vis* the Aborigines, attempts have been made to document the dimensions and the consequences of these policies. A leading figure in this research is Peter Read, who describes how 'Missionaries, teachers, government officials, have believed that the best way to make black people behave like white was to get hold of the children who had not yet learned Aboriginal lifeways,' all in an attempt 'to "breed out" the Aboriginal race'.[34] The basis of the policy was the euphemistically named Aborigines Protection Act of 1909 (in New South Wales, the state being analyzed, but similar legislation was in force in the other states as well), which allowed the welfare authorities (The Chief Protector, as the person was known) to remove children from their parents, not only to prevent the negative factor of neglect, but also in terms of the assertion that such removal would be in the best interests of the child.

Naturally, the question of what constituted neglect or what would be considered as being in the best interests of the child were highly loaded questions, veiled by prejudicial and ethnocentric perspectives, which included even an inability to understand the child-care procedures in a tribal or extended family situation. Parents might be accused of neglect for using other family members to look after their children. However, the real aim was not individual need, but national goals – thus a 1921 Report of the Aborigines Welfare Board declared unashamedly that 'the continuation of this policy of dissociating the children from camp life must eventually solve the Aboriginal problem'.[35]

Read clarifies this statement: '"The Aboriginal problem" meant Aboriginal people who could not, or chose not, to live as white people wanted them to do. The 1926 Report put the Board's intention even more clearly: when children were placed in a "first class private home", the superior standard of life would "pave the way for the absorption of these people into the general population".'[36] Read also notes that the physical limitations of the institutions led to a policy of private foster homes. The consequences of these policies were devastating; aboriginal children were denied ready access to their own culture, but were never really fully integrated into the white culture, where racial stereotypes and prejudices continued to prevail. As adults, many returned to their aboriginal environment, but social problems continued to haunt them in a malaise of unemployment, alcoholism, violence and crime. Read explains the accumulated effects over almost a century:

> The psychological issues in the institutionalization of children are most complex … few indeed of the ex-institution people have been, in fact, accepted by the whites as equals. No amount of 'white' behavior or attitudes can overcome skin-colour, or restore dignity to one's self-concept … Every one of the five thousand children removed from their parents had, and have, their own private and bitter memories of separation and later problems of adjustment. From the point of view of the Aboriginal race as a whole, we can hardly guess at the cost of wasted talent of those who spent a decade in the service of the white. We can hardly guess at the number of men and women who deny their own birth-right as Aboriginal citizens of Australia … . Perhaps one in six or seven Aboriginal children have

> been taken from their families during this century ... there is not an Aboriginal person in New South Wales who does not know, or is not related to one or more of his/her countrymen who were institutionalized by the whites.[37]

Read, together with Coral Edwards, has also described in detail the fate of 13 'lost children' and their 'struggle to find their natural parents'[38] – Edwards herself was taken from her aboriginal home as an infant, and it was 30 years later before she regained contact with her family, a personal saga that led her to set up an organization, Link-up, dedicated to the task of helping children and parents to reunite. Light-skinned children, generally 'half-castes', were placed in environments, including general welfare homes or even full-scale adoption into a family, which would remove all trace of their aboriginal identity. They claim that the total sum is of a colossal disinheritance – 'In Australia to-day,' they write 'there may be one hundred thousand people of Aboriginal descent who do not know their families or communities, some do not even know they are of Aboriginal descent.'[39]

Included amongst such people would be particularly those of mixed descent, who would often suffer both the rejection of their non-Aboriginal fathers and the legal restrictions placed on their Aboriginal mothers. As described by Tony Austin in his study of 'Half-caste' youth; 'most non-Aboriginal fathers rejected their mixed-descent offspring, and the higher their status within the dominant society, the greater the likelihood that they would deny any relationship with Aboriginal women', while, on the other hand, 'The law prevented Aboriginal women from raising "half-caste" children themselves,' since it was the perception of the Whites that 'Aboriginal motherhood, almost by definition, meant the neglect of children; that judgment was given a sharper edge where children with European ancestry were concerned.'[40]

In his book, Austin explains some of the concerns as to possible detrimental results of miscegenation (almost always an Aboriginal woman with a non-Aboriginal man), based to a large extent on populist concerns arising out of Darwinian explanations of evolution. Thus,

> As the significance of the great revelations about natural selection sank in, social applications of Darwin's biological theory began to influence the complex intellectual ferment of the rest of the nineteenth century and beyond ...
>
> Social Darwinism caused much to be said about race and about the place of Aborigines in a racial hierarchy. The emergence of the eugenics movement resulted in much scientific and psuedo-scientific thought about the effects of miscegenation and the place of people of mixed descent.[41]

Ambivalent attitudes and ambiguous policies characterized the attitude to those of mixed descent, with the constant dilemma of how to define them. Austin describes how

> Authorities, experiencing a dull awareness of the stigma attaching to the term 'half-caste' began to replace it with 'part-Aboriginal' and even, for a time, 'part-European'. They also sometimes managed to acknowledge that the 'problem' was more a function of white racism than 'half-caste' inferiority, and exemptions were granted a little more willingly until in 1953, adults of mixed descent were granted unqualified citizenship. This followed agitation by the Australian-Half Caste Progressive Association and others.[42]

(Parenthetically, it might be noted that in Canada, a similar situation was resolved by declaring those of mixed descent as a separate category, the Metis, who, in subsequent developments, were both to suffer from diminished status and then to be accorded many of the benefits later given to the indigenous people).[43]

In recent years, these personal reports, official pronouncements, and academic analyses have found an echo in the court system, with some of the key cases still awaiting final adjudication, including complicated procedural matters as to whether claims for compensation for governmental violation of rights and breach of fiduciary duty are not barred because of the time that has elapsed since the events occurred. In one case, the petitioner, Joy Williams,[44] claimed that she was removed from her Aborigine mother shortly after birth, and made a ward of the Aborigines Welfare Board, in terms of the wide powers given to that statutory body. Several years later, she was removed from the orphanage for Aborigine children, where she had been placed, and transferred to an orphanage for white children. Documentation from that time records the following comment: 'To take the child from association of Aborigines as she is a fair skinned child.'[45] Although brought up to believe that she was white, there is evidence to suggest that she was not accorded the same treatment as the other children in the institution; her unhappiness led her to run away unsuccessfully several times, and on being brought back on one occasion she was told that she was an Aborigine. After release from the home at the age of 18, she encountered both social and psychological problems, being imprisoned for vagrancy, and being hospitalized several times in psychiatric hospitals. In her early thirties, she established contact with her mother, and some years later, with other members of her family. In her late forties, Williams began university education, and during this period, while undergoing psychiatric treatment, became aware of how much of her problems in adult life were a consequence of her childhood institutionalization. On this basis, she sued the state authorities for negligence, breach of fiduciary duty and wrongful imprisonment. Her petition was rejected for procedural reasons, but on appeal, her right to pursue part of her claim was recognized.

The contrasting views of the lower court and appeal judges are almost symbolic of the opposing approaches – of judges and others – in relating to the problems of Aborigines within a historical context. The court of first instance seems to be a mere echo of pre-Mabo attitudes, in its unwillingness to use judicial capacity effectively in order to help redress past wrongs. The judge writes: 'The history of the plaintiff's childhood is a very strange one and nobody could reflect upon it without the stirring of much sympathy. However I cannot allow my decision to be dictated by emotion.'[46] If the judge is using the term 'strange' to indicate an unusual experience, it would seem that he is unaware of how prevalent this kind of experience was for Aborigines, and particularly, half-caste children.

However, the Court of Appeal (in a majority opinion) was to match its emotional sympathy with some practical directives. The President of the Court, reflecting post-*Mabo* jurisprudence, averred that

> The law which has often been an instrument of injustice to Aboriginal Australians can also, in proper cases, be an instrument of justice in the vindication of their legal rights. It is not just and reasonable in this case to close the doors of the Court in Ms. Williams' face. She should have her chance to prove her case. She might succeed. She might fail. But her case will have been heard in full. It will then have been determined as our system of law provides to all Australians – Aboriginal and non-Aboriginal – according to law, in open court and on its merits.[47]

The use of courts to intervene on behalf of Aborigines seeking redress for past grievances, reached a peak in 1995, when a group of Aborigines sued governmental authorities for the harm done to both children and parents as a result of removal for purposes of legal adoption. In this case,[48] claims similar to those in the Williams case were pursued. These cases have far-reaching implications not only for the rights of Aborigines, but for the overall impact of underlying constitutional principles. As noted by Lachlan Kennedy and Deborah Nance, 'The recognition of any of the suggested implied rights would be a significant matter for Commonwealth and State Governments.'[49] But for the Aborigines themselves, and for all other Australians, judicial support for their claims would be part of the struggle for a true reconciliation between the different population groups – one that would recognize the errors of the past and attempt to provide some redress. It would also be an affirmation that the separate identity of the Aborigines is a cultural fact that is deserving of recognition. If such judicial recognition is not forthcoming (because of procedural factors, such as the statute of limitations), then other means will no doubt be sought to provide an accounting for past actions. Thus, for instance, parallel with the litigation, an inquiry into the issue is being conducted by the Human Rights and Equal Opportunity Commission.

Beyond that, arguments are being made for the need to set up a special body to examine specific cases and seek equitable solutions at the personal level. Thus Ron Morkel argues that 'it is neither foolhardy or fantasy to expect or even demand that Reparations Tribunals be established to compensate Aborigine children and their parents for the tragic deprivation which they have suffered as a result of one of the most misconceived and misguided policies pursued against the Aborigine people in recent Australian history … .'[50]

Indeed, the desire for belonging and for a proud recognition of tribal identity is partly an answer not only to the politicians and policy-makers of the past, who attempted through legal and administrative means to make tribalism wither away, but also to those academic theorists who have attempted to achieve the same aim at the intellectual level.

Indeed, in Australia, this debate has taken on renewed intensity in recent years, as anthropologists particularly have presented contrasting views as to whether or not there is any meaning to Aboriginality, if so what is its basis, if such generalized definition does not detract from the individual existence of separate groups, and whether, in any event, other terminology should not be used, especially terms which are themselves indigenous, and not a reflection – as is the case with the term 'Aborigine' – of settler domination.

The pages of a leading Australian journal in anthropology gave focused expression to the parameters of the debate, particularly in regard to two key factors – the identity of Aborigines living outside of their traditional tribal area, and the potent issue of who should be entitled to make these determinations as to nomenclature and as to existence of separate identities. David Hollinsworth suggests that two of the main criteria for declaring identity – through genetic inheritance or cultural persistence – are 'limited analytically and politically. Their strategic inadequacies are particularly apparent in reference to urban Aboriginal people with "mixed" ancestry and "non-traditional" life-styles.'[51] Hollinsworth suggests an alternative approach (which has also been proposed by others), which would be based on an ideological affirmation of Aboriginality-as-resistance. Noting particularly the 'inadequacies' of biological and cultural definitions for 'urban Aboriginal people with "mixed" ancestry and "non-traditional" lifestyles,' he argues that

> the resistance discourse is preferable because it is the most inclusive, dynamic and least readily domesticated by state co-option. That is, the discourse of Aboriginality-as-resistance is better able to incorporate all

> those who identify as Aborigines and to challenge those dominant, racist ideologies on which the category 'Aboriginal' has been historically constructed ... In contrast to the constraining unity of shared 'blood' or common cultural characteristics, resistance is a collective but not uniform enterprise. Its forms, issues, targets, participants and allies are almost infinite in their variety, yet can use powerfully unifying language and symbols.[52]

A number of responses to Hollinsworth's approach were presented – in one of which the issue of who were entitled to make the definitions and determinations was directly raised. Mudrooroo Nyoongah claims that 'too often in such articles as Hollinsworth's, the Koori, the Nanga, the Nyoongah, the Murri, the Yuba, YamadJi, Wongi and other social groupings are ignored in order to establish an overriding sense of Aboriginal identity ... a Nyoongah is not a Koori, and so it goes for the other regional identifications. But, the mere fact of such a debate does point to a search for an "Aboriginality" of identity, and I believe that such a search and any conclusions reached must come from us, from ourselves.'[53] Nyoongah also notes a 'gap between scientific reality and social reality. People do not determine their identity according to scientific principles; but with social conventions and ideological constructs.'[54] Included in this social reality might well be conservative approaches, not those of resistance, especially with 'the template of the Dreaming ancestor being the guide to the present and future, that is conservation rather than revolution'.[55] Finally, Nyoongah emphasizes the need for the definitions to emanate from the people themselves: 'I feel that to engage in a discussion of "Aborigines" and "Aboriginality", "identity" and so on, without placing the importance on Aboriginal theories of identity (mostly oral, and not worked up into papers and books, but none the less valid, for after all Plato supposedly recorded the oral discourses of Socrates, thus giving a literate legitimacy to his thoughts) is to construct academic theories of debate which have little relevance to us, and perhaps may even be dangerous, in destroying that identity it seeks to explain, or postulate.'[56]

Yet, even in these terms, tribal identity is still problematic, not only for external reasons (governmental policy, academic debate), but also because within the tribe there are many who would prefer to divest themselves totally of their tribal heritage. This is perfectly legitimate for those who wish to do so – and in this sense, it is quite possible that the Otieno decision in Kenya is a regrettable precedent. But the real tragedy of the break with one's past is where it is done on a presumably voluntary basis, but mainly because of external factors – where shame at one's tribal heritage, induced by more universalistic ideas, is the trigger force. These factors find their most pertinent expression in extreme situations, where tribalism is exploited for ulterior ends. Such was the case in South Africa during the apartheid regime, and one of those who sought solace from its repressive environment in a distant shore, has in a poignant eloquence, described the enormity of the personal tragedy, which is also that of his tribe.

Mark Mathabane explains, in the preface to his autobiography, that it is not only a personal account of the struggle against apartheid, but

> ... also about how, in order to escape from the clutches of apartheid, I had to reject the tribal traditions of my ancestors. It was a hard thing to do, for there were many good things in my African heritage, which, had it been left to me to choose freely, I would have preserved and venerated. I, too, had the burning need like human beings everywhere to know where I came from, in order to better understand who I was and where I was going in this world. But apartheid had long adulterated my heritage and traditions, twisted them into tools of oppression and indoctrination. I saw at a young age that apartheid was using tribalism to deny me equal rights, to separate me from my black brothers and sisters, to justify segregation and perpetuate white power and privilege, to render me subservient, docile and, therefore, exploitable. I instinctively understood that in order to forge my own identity, to achieve according to my aspirations and dreams, to see myself the equal of any man, black or white, I had to reject this brand of tribalism, and that in the rejection I ran the risk of losing my heritage.[57]

And so Mathabane 'took the plunge'[58] and made his way to the United States, the recipient of a tennis scholarship to an American university where he was afforded '... the rare opportunity of gaining a proper perspective on my African heritage'.[59]

But, for others, lacking his sporting prowess and intellectual talent, the Africa they know is not in some far distant shore, but in the immediate environment – in its language and arts, its culture and customs, its daily living and traditional rituals. Apartheid is gone, but many of its consequences remain – not least the harm caused to tribal pride. Elsewhere, other forms of racism, often in the name of universalism and civilization, have been no less devastating; but hopefully remedies exist, which can only be applied if there is a ruthless honesty in dealing with the past – not just the consequences of imperialist and colonial rule, but also the values of tribal traditions.

NOTES

1. See J.B. Ojwang and J.N.K. Mugambi (eds), *The S.M. Otieno Case: Death and Burial in Modern Kenya* (Nairobi: Nairobi University Press, 1989). Included are sections dealing with 'The Social and Cultural Dimensions', 'Philosophic and Linguistic Aspects' and 'The Legal Dimension'.
2. The *Nation*, the leading daily newspaper, often gave front-page coverage to the case – and subsequently published an anthology of the articles that had appeared; see Sean Egan (ed.), *S.M. Otieno: Kenya's Unique Burial Saga* (Nairobi: Nation Newspapers Publication, 1987).
3. *Virginia Edith Wambai Otieno v. Joash Ochieng Ougo and Omolo Siranga*, Civil Appeal No. 31 of 1987 (unreported); see also High Court case between the same parties, H.C.C. No. 4872 of 1986 at Nairobi.
4. See 'Kenyan Buried in Village He Hated', *Washington Post*, 25 May 1987.
5. *Otieno v. Ougo and Sinanga*.
6. M.D. Okech-Owiti, 'Some Socio-Legal Issues', in *The S.M. Otieno Case*, p. 20.
7. Ibid., p. 22.
8. Ibid., p. 22.
9. Ibid., p. 22.
10. A.B.C. Ochallo-Ayayo, 'Death and Burial: An Anthropological Perspective' in Ojwang and Mugambi (eds), *The S.M. Otieno Case*, p. 33.
11. Recently in December, 1997, a problem, similar to the Otieno case arose in Israel, where a deceased man, who had converted on two different occasions between Islam and Judaism, became the focus of a struggle between two women, each having been married to him by a different religious ceremony, as they engaged in a struggle as to which religious cemetery he would be buried in.
12. An interesting situation arises when, in an inter-faith marriage, the husband is a Muslim and the wife is Jewish, where both religions would claim the children as belonging to them.
13. In an article discussing the legal status of the Golan Heights in the dispute between Syria and Israel, I have used the fact that Israel did not automatically confer citizenship on the Syrian residents living there at the time it purported to annex the Golan to Israel as one of the factors indicating that, from a legal point of view, the Golan was never annexed by Israel, and that it retains the status only of Israeli-occupied territory of land that still belongs to Syria. See Leon Sheleff, 'The Golan was Not Annexed', *Brooklyn Journal of International Law* 20 (1994), p. 333. See opposing viewpoint in same issue by Asher Maoz, p. 355.
14. Carol Weisbrod, *The Boundaries of Utopia* (New York: Pantheon Books, 1980), in 'Introduction,' p. xi.
15. Ibid.
16. *Elk v. Wilkins*, 112 US 94, (1884), at p. 102. It should be noted that in the United States, citizenship was conferred on Indians by legislation in 1924 and in Australia in 1962. See also *United States v. Rogers*, 45 U.S. 567 (1846), dealing with an opposite situation in which a white American was denied the right to renounce citizenship in order to be accepted into the Cherokee nation as a full member.
17. The *Lovelace* case at the Human Rights Committee of the United Nations – GAOR 36th Less. Supp. (No. 40) (A/36/40), Annex XVIII.
18. Article 27 of International Covenant on Civil and Political Rights, UN General Assembly Resolution 2200A (XXI), 16 December 1966.
19. Canadian Indian Law Act of 1970.
20. *The Queen v. Drybones*, (1970) SCR 282.
21. See discussion in special issue of *Manitoba Law Review* (1991).
22. *Thomas v. Norris*, [1992] 2 C.N.L.R. 139 (B.C.S.C.).
23. *Santa Clara Pueblo v. Martinez*, 436 US 49 (1978).
24. Indian Civil Rights Act, 1968.
25. Vine Deloria, Jr and Clifford Lytle, *American Indians, American Justice* (Austin: University of Texas Press, 1983), p. 193.
26. On the removal policy, see Wilcomb Washburn, *Red Man's Land/White Man's Law: The Past and Present Status of the American Indian* (Norman: Oklahoma University Press, 1995, 2nd edn).
27. See discussion in Vine Deloria, Jr, and Clifford Lytle, *The Nations Within: The Past and Future*

of American Indian Sovereignty (New York: Pantheon Books, 1984), Chapter 10, 'The Indian Reorganization Act of 1934 and the Collier Bill: A Comparison', p. 140. The reference to the Collier Bill is to a prior bill drawn up by John Collier, a lobbyist on behalf of the native American and later Commissioner for Indian Affairs – see also Lawrence Kelly, *The Assault on Assimilation: John Collier and the Origins of Indian Policy Reform* (Albuquerque: University of New Mexico Press, 1983).

28. See Larry Burt, *Tribalism in Crisis: Federal Indian Policy, 1953–1961* (Albuquerque: University of New Mexico, 1982), especially Chapter 3 'The Drive to Terminate Various Tribes', p. 29, and Ch. 8, 'Termination in Action and Under Fire', p. 95.
29. *Mashpee Tribe v. New Sebury Corporation*, 592 F. 2d 575 (1979).
30. Unreported case.
31. *The State of Queensland v. Wyville*, 90 ALR 611. It should be noted that a further issue arose in connection with the work of the commission, namely whether a number of Maoris who had died in custody could be considered among the subjects of the investigation. It was decided not to include them.
32. *In re: Adoption of Baby Boy D.*, 742 P. 2d 1059 (Okla. 1985).
33. Edward Thomson, 'Protecting Abused Children: A Judge's Perspective on Public Law Deprived Child Proceedings and the Impact of the Indian Child Welfare Acts,' *American Indian Law Review* 15 (1990), p. 10. See also David Woodward, 'The Rights of Reservation Parents and Children: Cultural Survival or the Final Termination?', *American Indian Law Review* 3 (1975), p. 21.
34. Peter Read, *The Stolen Generations: The Removal of Aboriginal Children in New South Wales 1883 to 1969* (New South Wales Ministry of Aboriginal Affairs – Occasional Paper, No. 1, n.d.), p. 2. The paper was prepared for the Aboriginal Children's Research Project whose aim is 'to reduce the high numbers of Aboriginal children living in non-Aboriginal care, and prevent Aboriginal children being removed from their families and communities. Part of this process involves reconciling Aboriginal and white perceptions of the situation in New South Wales today ...' (p. 21).
35. See ibid., p. 2. The Aborigines Welfare Board was abolished in 1969.
36. Ibid., p. 2.
37. Ibid., p. 18. For a description of a similar situation in Western Australia, see Len Collard and Dave Palmer 'Aboriginal Young People in the Southwest of Western Australia: Implications for Youth Policy', in R. White and B. Wilson (eds), *For Your Own Good: Young People and State Intervention in Australia* (Bundoora'ha: La Trobe University 1991), p. 78.
38. Coral Edwards and Peter Read, *The Lost Children: Thirteen Australians Taken from Their Aboriginal Families Tell of the Struggle to Find Their Natural Parents* (Sydney: Doubleday, 1989).
39. Ibid., p. ix in 'Introduction'.
40. Tony Austin, *I Can Picture the Old Home So Clearly: The Commonwealth and 'Half-Caste' Youth in the Northern Territory 1911–1939* (Canberra: Aboriginal Studies Press, 1993), p. 3.
41. Ibid., p. 9.
42. Ibid., p. 213.
43. See, for example Clem Chartier, 'Aboriginal Rights and Land Issues: The Metis Perspective' in M. Boldt and J. Anthony Long with Leroy Little Bear (eds), *The Quest for Justice: Aboriginal Peoples and Aboriginal Rights* (Toronto: University of Toronto Press, 1985). See also discussion of the editors in the 'Introduction', at p. 4: 'The 1981 census sets Canada's Metis population at slightly over 98,000.' This figure is disputed by representatives of the Metis, the actual number being considered much higher – and 'Much is at stake in these conflicting accounts; if census figures are used as the basis for negotiating settlements with respect to Metis land claims, housing, economic development, and social services, then the Metis will receive much less in the way of benefits than they feel they are entitled to.' In Canada, there is also a further group, known as non-status Indians. In the United States, the approach was to declare anyone with one-quarter Indian ancestry as an Indian.
44. *Williams v. The Minister, Aboriginal Lands Act, 1983 and the State of New South Wales*, 23 December 1994, in NSW Court of Appeal.
45. See Case Notes, 'Seeking a Civil Remedy for Uncivil Acts', *Aboriginal Law Bulletin* 3 (No. 73), (1995), p. 21.
46. Quote from ibid., p. 22.

47. *Williams v. The Minister, Aboriginal Lands Act, 1983.*
48. *Kruger and Ors. v. the Commonwealth of Australia*, High Court, M 21 of 1995 and *Bray and Ors. v. the Commonwealth of Australia*, D 5 of 1995.
49. Lachlan Kennedy and Deborah Nance, 'Stolen Generations: The Kruger Action', *Aboriginal Law Bulletin* 3 (No. 78) (1996), p. 13; see also Barbara Cummings, Jenny Blokland and Rebecca La Forgia, 'Lessons from the Stolen Generations Litigation', *Adelaide Law Review* 19 (1997), p. 25.
50. Ron Morkel, 'Government Culpability: For the Forced Removal of Aboriginal Children from Their Families', *Aboriginal Law Bulletin* 3 (No. 47) (1993), p. 4. Approaches of this nature, hinting at reconciliation and compensation received, renewed impetus after the publication in 1997, of a Report dealing with Aborigine children, removed from their parental homes.
51. David Hollinsworth, 'Discourses on Aboriginality and the Politics of Identity in Urban Aüstralia', *Oceania* 63 (1992-93), p. 151.
52. Ibid., p. 151.
53. Mudrooroo Nyoongah, 'Comments on Hollinsworth', *Oceania* 63 (1992-93), p. 156.
54. Ibid., p. 156.
55. Ibid., p. 156.
56. Ibid., p. 157; see also Colin Tatz 'Aboriginality as Civilization', *The Australian Quarterly*, March, 1981, p. 41.
57. Mark Mathabane, *Kaffir Boy: Growing Out of Apartheid – an Autobiography* (London: The Bodley Head, 1986). The term 'Kaffir' is a term of abuse in South Africa, the equivalent of 'Nigger' in the United States – as Mathabane explains in an introductory note.
58. Ibid., p. xi.
59. Ibid., p. xi.

The Local Tribe in the Global Village

The rule of law is one of the basic tenets of a democratic system.[1] It brings assurances of equality before the law, certainty in applying it, and judgments based not on the whim of individuals but on the authority of the written word. It also bears undertones of justice, fairness and equity.[2] These two aspects are not always in synchronization. In truth, the rule of law, for all its centrality in democratic systems of law, embodies such a wide range of ideas that the ensuing confusion has led to severe critiques – from both radical and arch-conservative (libertarian) perspectives[3] – and reluctant reservations as to its impact on the part of liberal supporters of the idea.

The reality is that there are at least two different (and even contrary) basic meanings ensconced in the concept. These may be defined as a formal rule of law (focusing more on a rigid, presumably equal, application of the law) and a substantive rule of law (focusing on the consequences of law, in terms of the ultimate justice of its implementation).[4] Some writers, aware of this differentiation, have suggested distinguishing between a 'thin' version and a 'thick' version of the rule of law,[5] others on a change in the terminology – thus Gerald Gordon suggests using 'rule *by* law' to describe the formal aspect, which is basically of obedience to the law, and to retain the rule *of* law only for such situations where substantively it might be claimed that justice was done.[6]

It seems to me that this sort of distinction may well serve for an understanding of the role that law has played in the present status of aboriginal groups. Extensive efforts were made in the initial stages to ensure that the taking of land and the restrictions on tribal sovereignty were done in a formally correct manner – with the agreement of the indigenous population, in terms of legal doctrine, sustained by formal treaties, supported by judicial decree.[7] The rule of law was the framework for the overall process – but this was a formal rule of law, devoid, for the most part of those factors and features that characterize just and equitable decisions and solutions. Inasmuch as the rule of law has substantive meaning, touching on justice and fairness and equity, it was absent from the historical dealings that led to the modern situation.

Yet, the ultimate hope for a redress of past grievances may well lie in the possibility of activating this deeper, more meaningful rule of law. What was taken by an exploitative, formal rule of law may yet be partially requited by a sensitive, substantive rule of law. Indeed, the history of aboriginal struggles in the last few decades has been marked by a judicious use of the legal system, with varying degrees of success. Pleas to the court system have been interwoven with other means of garnering support, and some successful judicial decisions have been the climax of a successful prior political and public campaign. In this chapter, we shall draw attention to a few of the many developments of recent years in which political and public struggles were co-ordinated with legislative and judicial activities.

These legal and political campaigns are being conducted by different groups at different levels and in different frameworks. No longer is it mere isolated incidents involving anonymous persons which lead to judicial disputation, but an orchestrated and planned assertion of legal rights presented by organized groups, some of them composed of people holding official positions in the tribe, others led by radical activists. The outsiders who are involved are not those seeking their own personal advancement (as in some of the classical precedents – for instance, Indian rights in the United States being determined in cases where the disputants are non-Indians with names like Fletcher, Peck, Johnson, McIntosh, Worcester)[8] – but groups of concerned individuals working through organizations such as Survival International or Cultural Survival. The legal fora are not only courts of a national legal system, but universal human rights commissions, although this development is still in its early stages, with its full potential still to be realized. In any event, the awareness of the common problems confronting tribal populations in different parts of the world, has also led to regional, hemispheric and global associations.

Linked to these processes is the additional factor of a greater sensitivity on the part of policy-makers and politicians to the plight and the needs of tribal groups – and a number of governmental commissions have provided fairly hard and relatively honest appraisals of the situation of tribal groups, thereby contributing to a climate more conducive to aboriginal legal claims. Academic research has also taken on a more activist approach and anthropologists, historians and jurists have often provided essential empirical data and theoretical arguments that have been – partially or totally – incorporated into reports of government commissions, statements of political policies or judicial decisions.[9]

The more localized and national aspects of the developments are often mirrored in their regional and international aspects specifically because of the frustrations sometimes engendered by the inability to achieve results within the more limited national framework. General international developments also contributed to this awareness as, from the 1950s onwards, the decolonization, in the wake of the Second World War, accelerated and increasingly involved areas where tribal populations, in one form or another, began to achieve independence – a factor partly recognized in Africa, but even more so in the Pacific, where the very size of micro-states elicited a strong sense of identification.[10] If isolated, island nations of only several tens of thousands of people (in a few instances even less than 10,000)[11] could achieve their independence in the emerging world order, why should similar status be denied larger groups of tribal people? Some of these smaller nations even entered into special arrangements (for external defence or diplomatic representation) with their former colonial or trustee powers.[12]

Why should such or similar status be denied those groups which long before had entered into treaty arrangements with these self-same powers, or had even, as in the case of the United States and the Indian tribes, long ago been recognized judicially as 'nations' even if 'dependent and domestic'.[13] Thus, in a changing world, surely the time had come for a reassessment of the status of the Indians, for a reinterpretation of the meaning of 'domestic, dependent' nation or the potentialities subsumed within this definition in a decolonized world, so different from that in which the United States Supreme Court had once laid down its legal definition. Within a jurisprudence of evolving notions of decency[14] and a potentially activist judiciary, the future possibilities seem to offer innovative and creative solutions. Within a world in which colonial powers were slowly divesting themselves of their overseas colonies, there was room for radical reassessment of tribal status. A succinct summary of the situation is provided by an official Report of an unofficial body – of an international NGO (Non-Governmental Organization). A Report by the Independent Commission on International Humanitarian Issues, explains how

> In the early 1970's, indigenous peoples of the Americas, the Arctic and South Pacific formed networks despite the differences in their colonial and national situations and individual circumstances. Since then, hundreds of indigenous peoples' organizations, representing communities of less than a few dozen households to territories with populations of several million, have been founded. These organizations have stretched out from their local communities and interests to meet and support one another.
>
> The first international initiative arose out of the frustration experienced by the North-American-based American Indian government Movement (AIM) in its attempts to have the Indian treaties with the United States and Canada recognized and the violations redressed. In 1974, AIM called a meeting of grassroots indigenous peoples from all over the Western Hemisphere and the Pacific. Over 5,000 people, representing hundreds of local organizations participated and founded the International Indian

> Treaty Council. The new organization immediately petitioned for non-governmental status in the Economic and Social Council of the United Nations (ECOSOC) and established offices in New York. Consultative status in ECOSOC was granted in early 1977, which set a precedent for other federations of indigenous peoples and organizations to apply for the same status.[15]

In essence, this development reflects a broader phenomenon; of the fact that issues of human rights – at both the individual and group level – are becoming increasingly matters that transcend national boundaries. In some respects, this obviously provides advantages to indigenous people, offering a larger arena in which to present their claims and complaints; on the other hand, as noted in an earlier chapter, much of the international human rights movement is oriented to individual rights and not group rights,[16] and, as will be referred to in subsequent chapters, there are often clashes between what are commonly regarded (often facilely and even falsely) as universalistic rights, and particularistic rights (which characterize aspects of tribal life).[17] Nevertheless, the overall impact of the internationalization of the struggle of tribal groups is largely to their advantage.

This internationalization of the struggle of aboriginal people is sustained by four key props – first, existing, activist movements, national and pan-tribal in scope, as the source of the larger international movement;[18] second, similar NGOs dealing mainly with other issues, that have proved the validity for such transnational interactions, have provided the impetus for others to follow and have themselves on occasions shown concerns for tribal rights when these intersect with their own particular mandate (for instance, Amnesty International, Refugees International, Human Rights Watch, International Commission of Jurists, Anti-Slavery Society and Minority Rights' Group); third, specialized organizations whose sole or major activity focuses on tribal people (Survival International and Cultural Survival being the leading examples); and fourth, recognized organs of the international community, devoted to human rights issues, to whom petitions may be presented.

The fact of concerted action by different tribal groups is a major achievement, an interesting development in itself which, at an earlier stage, might have spared the Indians some of their losses. As Hazel Hertzberg describes some of the earliest contacts between settlers and Indians in the United States, 'The Indians were conquered tribe by tribe, locality by locality. Never was there a continental Indian war or a continental Indian peace. By the time the wave of white settlement had flowed over the Appalachians, for example, the seaboard Indians had been largely conquered, eliminated, removed or had reached some accommodation with the whites. This process was repeated over and over as the whites pushed westward.'[19] In her book, Hertzberg describes the various pan-

Indian groupings that later emerged, with much detailed information, but her book was written at the onset of a process that led to even more radical activism.

In fact, a major change took place in 1968, with the establishment of the American Indian Movement, and a number of other movements which were more ethnic-Indian in their orientation than specifically tribal. Vine Deloria and Clifford Lytle describe a major campaign of this period, when 'fish-ins' in the Pacific Northwest – based to some extent on the 'sit-ins' conducted by young blacks in the South – attracted much attention.[20] The emphasis was on the insistence on rights granted by treaty. They write:

> when news of what was happening reached Indians in other tribes and other parts of the country, a transformation of no small importance began to take place. Other Indians saw the struggle to preserve treaty fishing rights, as simply another example of federal failure to guarantee treaty rights, and conflict in the Pacific Northwest became a personal affront to many other Indians. As incident followed incident, it became increasingly obvious that tribal rights in many parts of the country were being trampled under foot, and these incidents, representative of the general condition under which many tribes had to live, turned the issue of Indian rights in part into the struggle of a domestic American ethnic-racial group.[21]

They explain that 'Indian rights and conditions became an ethnic issue, but specific treaty rights and particular situations involving Indians remained a tribal concern.' Furthermore, they continue that

> the March on Washington during election week 1972 was a major turning point for both ethnic and tribal Indians. Caravans began on the West Coast and worked their way through Indian country on the way east … many tribal peoples, including elders and religious leaders, decided to join the caravans. The presence of these people reminded everyone that Indians shared a great tradition of independence and nationhood, which the years had not erased. Many of the marchers now began to consider the specific traditions of their own tribe in addition to the general issues that affected all Indians.[22]

The importance of this awareness of an Indian identity beyond the tribe, of a social and political situation reflective not only of the particular terms of a specific treaty, but of a larger 'ethnic' entity, was, quite likely, an essential prior stage in the possibility of transnational organization and co-operation. Patrick Macklem also argues that 'the border is alien to indigenous peoples', and in the context of the border between the United States and Canada explains that 'for the indigenous people of North America to truly become equal members in the international community of nations … [a] revolution must occur, one that … [will] cause borders to become bridges reconnecting ancient alliances and ushering in new worlds of intercultural and international understanding'.[23]

And parallel to these happenings in North America, similar initial steps were being taken in other parts of the world, particularly in Australia, which were to reach a peak some years later, in the 1980s as official Australia prepared for the celebration of the Bicentennial of British Settlement. For Aborigines, this was a time not for celebration, but for reflection, and for protest, some of it political, some of it legal. During these years, the *Aboriginal Law Bulletin* provided reviews of many of the key issues being placed before the public and the law courts, while many academics, active in this reappraisal, were later directly involved in the work of the Law Reform Commission on Customary Law of the Aborigines, an excellent example of careful academic research, partly of a comparative nature relating to developments in other countries, with clear-cut policy recommendations, empirically based and articulate in its presentation.[24]

Beyond the legal aspect, a series of publicized political activities – a tent 'embassy' in Canberra, a mock arrival at the coast of Dover in England and a proclaimed 'annexation' of the British Isles – served to bring the issue of Aborigines to world consciousness; while Marcia Langton claims that, in the 1980s, the Australian aboriginal groups, led by the Federation of Aboriginal Land Councils, had achieved much success, by virtue of maintaining 'a very strong office in London, a very large support group … throughout the Northern Hemisphere and a great deal of respect from other indigenous nations and certainly from some nation states'.[25]

On the occasion of the Bicentennial, on 26 January 1988, Kevin Carmody, a leader of the Murrie people (the name he and many others use to designate the indigenous peoples of Australia or at least those living in one particular area), gave vent to some of the tensions that were emerging on the Australian political scene. He spoke, in a radio address, of the paradox of the white settlers as being 'the ultimate global nomads', of being 'a shallow, rootless, hollow people', and 'spiritual paupers'; in contrast he referred to his culture, which has provided 'a pride and a dignity, a sense of awe … at the majesty and vastness, the enormity, diversity and sacredness of all creation'.[26]

Clarifying this aspect, the aforementioned Report states that 'the Aborigines of Australia see their landscape as peopled by the spirit forms of their ancestors and it can cause them physical pain when drilling rigs bore through rock on sacred sites'.[27] It is this Report that attempts to describe the common factors shared by indigenous people which make the trans-national organizations possible:

> being indigenous is not simply something that is externally

> manifested. It is a sense of belonging. It is an awareness of having a distinct culture with special characteristics … . The conviction of being an indigenous person unites people of apparently quite different backgrounds. … What is shared by most indigenous people is a world view which incorporates as its dearest principle a custodial concept of land and natural resources: Mother Earth. Indigenous people regard the land or earth as sacred. It is a living entity.[28]

The Report suggests that the population that may be included within this rubric of indigenous population may number as much as 200 million people – from all of the continents in the world, including the Sami (Lapps) and Inuits (Eskimos) in circumpolar states, with as much as 150 million in Asia alone, referring mainly to tribal and nomadic people, the former in mountainous territory, the latter in desert areas.[29] It will be noted, then, that a number of indigenous people, those in Asia, were not included in the groups involved in the initial effort to set up transnational bodies. Here, we encounter again the problematics of the term 'indigenous' – the Report refers to those in Asia as being tribal or nomadic, and it is fairly clear that their problems are similar to those of the aboriginal people in countries settled by Europeans.

India, in fact, has, perhaps more than any other country, tried by legislation to provide support and special programs for its tribespeople, those officially designated as scheduled tribes;[30] conversely China refers to people with similar backgrounds, as national minorities[31] – and these two countries may well account for 50 per cent of all the 'indigenous people' in the world. Even these total figures are problematical, since there are no precise figures for Africa – the Report merely notes *en passant* that 'In the broader sense of the definition, several million in Africa could be included,'[32] but several million will then be limited to those considered 'indigenous', those small groups living in mountains, deserts or forests. However, if larger groups are included, with more sedentary and agricultural ways, then the numbers would reach into the tens of millions, similar to those for India and China.

For the moment, the indigenous people of the former settler colonies seem to be not at all eager to incorporate Africans – of any type, at any level – into the orbit of their struggles and concerns, and so, all sorts of peripheral tribal groups – pygmies in the forests of West Africa, Koi people in Southern Africa, nomadic groups in East Africa and the Berbers of North Africa – are being excluded,[33] both from full participation in the nation-states in which they live, and also from the larger 'ethnic-indigenous' populations striving for co-operative endeavours. But even that leaves begging the question of larger groups, some of them prominent or even dominant in their own state, others suffering from a minority status and the residual consequences of earlier tribal animosities.

For instance, the descriptions of some of the key characteristics of indigenous populations can easily be applied to various larger groups in Africa. Thus, the Report, in attempting to delineate who are the people involved, states: 'An indigenous population, even when it constitutes the majority in a country, possesses all the characteristics of a national minority subjugated by a dominant society ... . Territorial possession or claims characteristically distinguish indigenous populations.'[34] Further, the Report notes: 'Decisions are taken only after a consensus is reached by the community. In this respect, indigenous communities contrast with most modern states. If the voices of indigenous elders are listened to, it is not because they call upon forces of coercion, but because they represent a shared knowledge passed on from generation to generation of community life'.[35]

These problems of delimiting and delineating who are the tribal people are shared by more official bodies – and it is to them that some of the activism of today, political, moral, legal, is oriented. Thus, for instance, the United Nations Commission on Human Rights established a subcommission on Prevention of Discrimination and Protection of Minorities – and the studies presented by Special Rapporteurs have often struggled with the terms of their mandate.

The first Special Rapporteur for the subcommission, Francesco Capotorti, attempted to define a minority group in the following terms: 'a group which is numerically inferior to the rest of the population of a State and in a non-dominant position, whose members possess ethnic, religious or linguistic characteristics which differ from those of the rest of the population and who, if only implicitly, maintain a sense of solidarity, directed towards preserving their culture, traditions, religion or language'.[36] Such a definition would obviously include the classical indigenous groups – Indians and Inuit in America, Aborigines in Australia, Maoris in New Zealand, Scheduled Tribes in India, national minorities in China – as well, of course, as groups such as the Kurds in Iraq, Iran and Turkey, the Berbers in North Africa, Gypsies (the Romany people all over Europe), but the situation would be much less clear in various parts of Africa and Asia, or in the large and small island states in the Pacific. In any event, in this first report, the issue of tribal groups was not mentioned.

Ten years later, a study by another Special Rapporteur did attempt to deal with this issue. Jose Martinez Cobo states: 'Indigenous communities, peoples and nations are those which, having a historical continuity with pre-invasion and pre-colonial societies that developed on their territories, consider themselves distinct from other sectors of the societies now prevailing in those territories, or parts of them. They form at present non-dominant sectors of society and are determined to preserve, develop and transmit to future generations their ancestral territories and their identity, as the basis of their continued existence as peoples, in accordance with their own cultural patterns, social institutions and legal systems.'[37]

Natan Lerner, in his analysis of group rights, devotes a chapter to 'Indigenous Populations', noting at the outset the lax manner in which international law has generally related to the specific problems of such groups.[38] He states that 'It was only after recognition of the notion of group rights in recent instruments, and after active lobbying by spokesmen for indigenous groups, that steps were taken to introduce the subject into positive legislation albeit not to the extent desired by the interested groups.'[39]

However, whatever overall definitions are made or whatever general reports are submitted, a factor of potentially vital importance is the possibility of seeking a meaningful degree of legal support (as well as moral and political) by effective utilization of the international instruments – both the covenants and proclamations of international law, however amorphous, and more specially, the actual institutions established, however weak. One of the most noted instances was the attempt by Sandra Lovelace to seek a solution to her problem of group membership in a Canadian tribe by applying to the UN Human Rights Commision.[40] However, it was not the interests of the tribe that was at stake, but her own interests *vis-à-vis* those of the tribe (even though affected by national legislation – the Indian Act, which allowed for loss of tribal membership for a woman marrying a non-member of the tribe).

Another example of activating the UN Human Rights Commission is the ongoing struggle over land rights, in which the Navajo and Hopi tribes have challenged the United States Government; a complicating factor in this case is that, while in some respects, the two tribes have acted in concert, in other issues, they have been in conflict, including such factors as relocation of Hopi and Navajo families as a result of redrawing of boundary lines. In fact, in one of the submissions of the United States Government, this fact was exploited to make the point that an executive order of 1882 demarcating the Hopi reservation without the consent of the tribal members, was to the advantage of the Hopi as it was done 'in the face of the tremendous Navajo population growth and pressure for additional land [and] saved the Hopi tribe from being overwhelmed by this neighboring tribe'.[41]

The question arises whether direct applications to international bodies by tribespeople *vis-à-vis* the national state might be effective. This is precisely the position adopted in a booklet encouraging the possibility of such actions, brought out by the Indian Law Resource Center in Washington.[42] It draws attention to some activities used by Indians to bring their complaints before international organizations, describes both potentialities and limitations of international law, and advocates the need for using existing frameworks. It notes that the 'United Nations Work

Group on Indigenous Populations is perhaps the most important international organization to which Indians are bringing general human rights complaints at this time. The Working Group is the first and only United Nations body which is involved exclusively with matters concerning the human rights of Indians and other indigenous peoples'; it was set up in 1982 under the auspices of the already noted Subcommission on Prevention of Discrimination and Protection of Minorities. 'Its purpose is (1) to review developments pertaining to the promotion and protection of the human rights and fundamental freedoms of indigenous populations and (2) to give special attention to the evaluation of standards concerning the rights of indigenous populations.'[43] The Working Group serves as a useful forum for exchange of views and documentation of violations of rights, but it has no operative powers of its own. Specific complaints must be presented directly to the Commission – but even when dealing with individual issues, the petitions must be presented only by an accredited NGO, unless the country, whose position is being challenged, has agreed to respond to individual petitions.

However, while international petitions of the type outlined, or of potential future developments in international law, may allow for even more effective results, the basic politico-legal struggles will continue to be national ones. The pan-national importance will be the interchange of information, the implications of successful campaigns in one country for a precedent in another, the exponential development of innovative ideas and programs arising out of ongoing contacts, and the much-needed moral support that such interconnections elicit.

In this context, the work of two major organizations should be noted – Survival International, with its headquarters in London and the American-based Cultural Survival, which also brings out a quarterly journal of the same name. Both of these organizations work on similar principles to these of other international NGOs – serving as a resource base, lobbying at the governmental and international level, facilitating wide media coverage and presenting petitions in the court system. Both organizations provide a constant source of information about the plight of various tribal groups all over the world through regular newsletters and special publications. The work of these two organizations reflects far larger developments in the arena of international law, namely that NGOs, some with observer status at the United Nations or associated bodies, have become significant factors in affecting the changing norms and practices of internal law and influencing the major actors in the legal system: sovereign states. The future parameters of tribal rights, on behalf of indigenous people far removed from the regular corridors of power in the state within which they reside, will be determined in no small measure by the impact of these and other NGOs.

But, in the final analysis, it is within the state that the results must be achieved. Here, in fact, the international NGOs can serve as a useful conduit, in which legal and political successes can be adequately recorded and disseminated for utilization in other countries. This is particularly true of countries, which share a common legal heritage – in which principles pronounced and precedents laid down may be easily incorporated into other state legal systems.

At the moment of writing, there are indeed several politico-legal campaigns being waged, some of which will no doubt enter into the annals of significant breakthroughs achieved on behalf of tribal people in a changing world of emerging and expanding human rights. In fact, it is possible that initial probes within the judicial system may well lead to political compromises in order to avoid protracted legal struggles. What is important for cross-fertilization of ideas is a comprehensive and accurate documentation of past campaigns, so that others, in the same country or other countries, may also derive future benefits.

A good example of such detailed analysis is Marijane Ambler's book, *Breaking the Bonds*, which focuses on 'Indian Control of Energy Development', and deals mainly with tribal struggles (in which the political often intermingled with the judicial) in a number of western states in the United States.[44] She notes the paradox that: 'The discovery of millions of dollars in energy minerals beneath several Indian reservations in the United States presents one of the great ironies of history. From the pioneer farmers' perspective the sites chosen for Indian reservations in the late nineteenth century were generally wastelands that safely could be promised as "permanent" homelands. No one predicted the extent of the underground wealth or how much it would change the lives of the Indian people living over it'.[45]

Ambler describes how valuable land was often taken from tribes after negotiations but at minimum prices (well below their market value) and how, subsequent to 1903, the land would even be taken by government decree, without even minimal bargaining, and even in violation of prior treaty agreements – this in the wake of the *Lone Wolf* decision,[46] in which a challenge to a Congressional decision to sell over 2 million acres of tribal land, belonging to several tribes (Kiowa, Comanche and Apache), was denied by the Supreme Court which held that the Congress could unilaterally abrogate treaties with Indians.

However, shortly after this judicial decision, a further significant development took place with important legal implications, much to the benefit of the tribes – in 1906, Congress entered into an agreement with the Osage Tribe, which provided for split ownership – with the land being made available for private allotment to non-Indian individuals, but the minerals were retained in the ownership of the tribe.[47]

In this sense, the tribes benefited from an overall policy that attempted to keep partial control of mineral wealth in the public domain and out of the hands of private groups, especially monopolies. Thus, the same policy that was applied to public land, was incorporated into the policy of tribal lands – with, it might be added, the further paradox, that it was the collective nature of tribal ownership which made this particular aspect of the policy possible.

At the same time, some tribes preferred to sell out their mineral rights, apparently under apprehension that they would not be able to trust the authorities to pay fair royalties over the years for mineral extraction. As Ambler explains: 'Behind the Five Civilized Tribes' desire to allot their mineral rights was a deep distrust of the federal administration of their income from minerals and land. They preferred totally liquidating the tribal estate to having the government skim off the tribes' funds.'[48]

Ambler describes how, in the 1970s, the tribes began to be more assertive in their demands for control over energy resources, and in 1975, a Council of Energy Resource Tribes (CERT) was established. Ambler suggests that this could be seen possibly as an Indian OPEC[49] – with similar problems and similar potentialities – with additional problematics of royalty management or tax payments,[50] because of the complicated nature of the relations between the tribes and the Interior Department.

Parallel to the issues of energy were other natural resources, such as water.[51] After a methodical analysis of historical forces and legal, economic and political perspectives, Ambler sums up in an optimistic vein:

> Energy tribes face the turn of the century in a much better position than ever before as the result of tremendous changes in their own capacities and in the legislative and judicial atmosphere in which they operate. No longer must tribes devote their attention to defending their resource ownership and their power of consent. These questions are resolved in almost all cases, with recognition of legitimate water rights the most recent. Settling such basic questions freed tribes in the 1980s to focus upon improving the monetary return from old and new contracts, exercising their government powers and developing minerals themselves. In a string of major court and legislative victories, the federal government has recognized tribes' authority to tax mineral producers, enforce royalty regulations, participate in off-reservation energy siting decisions, impose air and water quality standards, issue tax-free bonds and negotiate with industry to develop their own minerals. Tribes' position of strength makes some state governments more willing to negotiate to find equitable solutions to taxing, water rights and civil jurisdiction disputes.[52]

Ambler sees great potential for the advancement of the Native American people through the effective and wise use of energy policy, including trans-tribal co-operation and the moulding of legal and political struggles. She concludes with the statement – 'Indian tribes must break the iron bonds linking them to dependency, paternalism and exploitation.'[53]

Energy resources are an important factor, since in many areas tribal land is situated on rich veins of mineral ore – in fact, in the past, ignored because, for instance, it was in a desert area offering little attraction for a then agriculturally oriented economy. However, energy resources are not a panacea for tribal problems, nor does wise economic policy with financial benefits, assure tribes of their vitality. Indeed, it may threaten much of their traditional culture – thus, in Australia, the struggles against mining companies, although here too, as Colin Tatz argues, there are potentialities in judicious development of natural resources.[54] However, these potentialities are dependent on the power of Aborigines, particularly in the Northern Territory, where the issue is partly bound up with its present status of lacking statehood.[55]

Further, at least in the United States, gambling has become a significant economic factor for many tribes, particularly for those situated in states that ban certain forms of gambling, especially casinos.[56] (It might be noted that the short-lived Bantustans in South Africa also found a 'solution' to their truncated territories and limited so-called 'sovereignty', by offering gambling facilities denied in South Africa).[57] Here too is a paradox that gambling should provide a service to non-Indians which their puritan sentiments deny them outside of Indian territory; while gambling also often spawns other social problems.[58] In any event, gambling was artificially encouraged with ulterior intentions, not just of enhancing tribal economic welfare, but of justifying the federal desire to be shorn of its burden of responsibility for a population with high rates of social problems.[59]

Mention should also be made, in terms of relevant future potentialities, of one further source of energy that poses far fewer problems and offers much easier advantages, which Ambler barely discusses. Solar energy is of great potential benefit to many tribal groups in the United States and elsewhere, where they are situated in desert areas or with plentiful supply of sunny days through most of the year. This source of energy is also the one that would be most compatible with tribal culture and its attitude to the environment, as well as providing direct advantages at the personal level, and not based on complicated political maneuvering, advanced technology and sophisticated economic management; for solar energy can be easily supplied directly to households.[60] Yet, unfortunately, Ambler's one reference to solar energy is to an ambitious scheme, to provide electricity on a large scale, which she dismisses as being 'showy' and 'grandiose'.[61]

Be that as it may – the essential thrust of her book is to explain the advantages of trans-tribal co-operation within the United States; and this provides a model for greater co-operation on a regional and international level. Further, this is an area where careful political planning has led to major legal victories – some in the courts system, others through legislation, policy decisions, or contractual provisions.

Ambler's analysis serves as a pointer to positive results and an encouragement to other groups in other parts of the world, of potential economic and social advantages to be derived by co-operative endeavours and careful planning.

From the legal perspective, it provides an example of how the law, used so often in the past as a formal cover for dispossession of land and denial of rights, may yet be activated in a positive manner for the benefit of tribal people – how the rule of law may be applied not in a narrow, formalistic manner, but on behalf of a substantive rule of law – to advance the interests of tribes, to seek equitable solutions, and perhaps to redress some of the harm done in the past.

Most important, in breaking the iron bonds of past paternalism and dependency, the tribes must not forgo their unique traditional attitudes to land and the environment. These overall ideological issues must be thoroughly discussed – and can perhaps best be probed in trans-tribal settings, both within nations and internationally.

One particular topic that requires deep consideration – basically within each tribe concerned, but also possibly at the pan-tribal level – is the issue of nuclear waste disposal, which, in recent years, has become, no less than gambling, a potential new source of income, but, perhaps far more than gambling, poses complex and difficult problems for tribes that must be carefully weighed. Nancy Collins and Andrea Hall provide a thoughtful presentation of the key issues,[62] describing how the United States has found a potential solution to its growing problem of nuclear waste by offering financial inducements to those prepared to accept the waste (and potentially dangerous) material.[63] They explain that tribal groups were the main applicants to a governmental tender submitted by the newly-created Office of the Nuclear Waste Negotiator. They note that 'The response of Indian nations to the ... offer was ... overwhelming', and that 'Tribal applications stand in stark contrast to the virtual absence of offers from states and non-Indian communities.'[64] The irony of history emerges, as the Indian land has those qualities of geographical remoteness and agricultural deficiency, which make it ideal as a solution for the government's problem.

However, there are those who see such utilization of the land of politically weak and economically impoverished people as 'environmental racism'.[65] Collins and Hall explain that 'The nuclear waste trade presents a pivotal paradox for Native American peoples: the clash between the nuclear waste trade's potential for destruction of Indian land, harmony, values, even tribal existence. The essence of a tribe's sovereignty is land-based. By contrast, dominant American society is essentially nomadic. If land is destroyed or devalued, or if the economy in an area is weakened, other Americans simply move to greener pastures'.[66] To endanger the restricted land areas still in tribal control would have serious repercussions for the tribe as a social entity.

Such factors raise new perspectives on the connection between law and economics, that few in the school of law and economics have considered. Indeed the connection between economics and law has further aspects in the context of indigenous peoples in the sense that economic factors may well give rise to legal (or political-legal) consequences.[67] Economic self-sufficiency may well be a basic prerequisite for political self-determination – that is for various degrees of legal sovereignty whether as an independent state in the community of nations, or as a state within a larger 'nation-state'. For some, at least, of the newer countries in the Pacific (for instance the previously mentioned Nauru), economic self-sufficiency (in fact economic wealth) provided a counterpoint to the small dimensions of the state. Even in terms of the consequences of gambling, Monaco's capacity to retain independence (for a city-state of some 20,000 people) is, to a large extent, a function of its casino-based wealth.

The growing numbers of micro-states pose a very real problem for the world order and for international law and organizations. But the very fact of a willingness to recognize such states creates a new situation for various tribal communities. Such small states were not within the mental parameters of those jurists (such as Vattel) and judges (such as Marshall) who related to indigenous rights and the doctrine of discovery in the past.

This book deals with legal pluralism, that is the possibility of different legal systems coexisting within one political framework. But, one cannot ignore the possibilities of the right to self-determination as a fundamental fact of international law and reality – emerging as a possible claim. Indeed, as I suggested in the opening chapters, it may be precisely such fears that lead to the total denial of tribal existence and tribal rights. As Russel Barsh correctly notes:

> To say that one culturally distinct group is 'indigenous' and as such does not have the right to self-determination, is a form of racism and discrimination. Collective rights must apply equally to all peoples regardless of culture and regardless of race. They are not restricted regionally to Africa or to Asia, any more than indigenousness is peculiar to the Americas and Australia. The United Nations' 1960 declaration on decolonization ... is clear on this point: all peoples have an *equal* right to self-determination regardless of their race, technological status, industrial structure or culture.[68]

Barsh also notes the irrelevance of earlier legal arguments about aboriginal sovereignty, given the changed situation, legally and politically, of today. However, beyond this – or perhaps less than this – is the possibility of self-determination within a federal structure, of the possibility of broader recognition being accorded aboriginal groups than mere control of a particular geographical area, with their own laws, and even courts. It is the possibility of incorporating these groups more directly into the ongoing political framework; one possibility is as a state or province in its own right, for instance the Northern Territory and/or Torres Straits Islands of Australia; in fact, in the Yukon and other northern extremities in Canada initial developments of this kind have been made;[69] or of creating an authorized assembly to deal with typical and unique tribal matters, for instance, in some African and Pacific countries where a House of Chiefs has been established; or of according special autonomous status, (based on regional considerations and not strictly tribal), which allows for a large degree of control of daily life being retained by indigenous people and assurances of cultural vitality for tribal traditions.[70]

As noted in an earlier chapter, such possibilities were raised in the United States for some of the larger tribes, and Barsh calls attention to a similar approach adopted recently in Canada when a 1983 parliamentary report (The Penner Report) 'advocated permitting Canadian Indians to form permanent governments within the Canadian Federal System, like the existing provinces. According to the report, this is necessary to recognize Canadian Indians' legitimate aspirations in accordance with Canada's obligations under the International Covenant on Civil and Political Rights.[71] Inasmuch as some of the problems in setting up such an expanded federal system relate to lack of contiguity among the Indians (and also, though less so, the Inuit) and the small size of the population (though sometimes with large territories), the possibility may well be pursued of a joint organizational structure.[72] Thus, both in the international and in the national sphere, there is a need for linking together tribal groups. As mentioned earlier, ethnicity would be the link, the ethnicity of aboriginal status, while the concept of tribalism would relate to the particular tribes.

To sum up; geopolitical reality in the 'global village' which is the emerging world order with both its micro-states (especially in the Pacific Ocean) and continental confederal structures (as in Europe) – linked to a sound economic basis, which mineral wealth (and perhaps other factors, such as gambling) assures – provides a flexible framework for heightened recognition of tribal groups, of which legal pluralism is an essential foundational variable.

NOTES

1. See, for instance, Vilhelm Aubert, *In Search of Law: Sociological Approaches to Law* (Oxford : Martin Robertson, 1983), Chapter 1, 'The Rule of Law', p. 34; Franz Neumann, *The Rule of Law: Political Theory and the Legal System in Modern Society* (Boston, MA: Dover, 1986).
2. See Geoffrey Walker, *The Rule of Law: Foundation of Constitutional Democracy* (Melbourne: Melbourne University Press, 1988); A.V. Dicey, *Introduction to the Study of the Law of the Constitution* (London: Macmillan, 1908, 7th edn.).
3. For a radical critique, see R. Wolff (ed.), *The Rule of Law* (New York: Simon & Schuster, 1971); for a conservative critique, see F. Hayek, *The Mirage of Social Justice* (London: Routledge and Kegan Paul, 1976).
4. This differentiation is clearly spelled out in a leading Hebrew textbook on constitutional law, Amnon Rubinstein, *Constitutional Law of the State of Israel* (Jerusalem: Schocken, 1991, 4th edn.), Chapter 9 (Hebrew); the implications of the differentiation are discussed in my Hebrew book, *The Rule of Law and the Nature of Politics* (Tel Aviv: Papyrus, 1996).
5. See Allan Hutchinson and Patrick Monahan (eds), *The Rule of Law: Ideal or Ideology* (Toronto: Casswell, 1987).
6. Gerald Gordon 'Judges and Justice', *South Africa Outlook* (January 1981), p. 11.
7. See, for instance, Philip Frickey, 'Marshalling Past and Present: Colonialism, Constitutionalism and Interpretation in Federal Indian Law', *Harvard Law Review* 107 (1993), p. 381. He writes that: 'it is troubling that Chief Justice Marshall's opinion in *Johnson v. McIntosh* ... ratified the use of the rule of law as the means to acquire the Native American land estate' (p. 384, n. 16).
8. See *Fletcher v. Peck*, 10 US (6 Branch) 87 (1810); *Johnson v. M'Intosh*, 21 US (8 Wheat) 543 (1823); and *Worcester v. Georgia*, 31 US (6 Pet.) 515 (1832). These cases are discussed above in Chapter 6, 'The Invention of Discovery'.
9. For examples of anthropological and historical data presented to Court, see discussion below in Chapter 12, 'Land is Forever', and Chapter 19 'Proving the Customary Rule'.
10. See discussion in Vine Deloria Jr, *Behind the Trail of Broken Treaties: An Indian Declaration of Independence* (New York: Delacorte Press, 1974), at pp. 162–74. Deloria provides tables comparing area and population of Indian tribes with the smaller nations of the world – including 'Forty nations with land areas smaller than the Navajo Reservation' (p. 165).
11. The population of the island state of Nauru is today a little over 10,000 on an area of 8 sq ml. Because of phosphate deposits and judicious use of these resources, it used to be one of the richest countries in the world.
12. The United States has entered into such arrangements with a number of Micronesian States, while New Zealand has some special arrangements with the Cook Islands and Nieue Island.
13. See decision in *Cherokee Nation v. Georgia*, 30 US (5 Pet.) 1 (1831) and discussion of this case in Chapter 6, 'The Invention of Discovery', above.
14. The concept of 'evolving notions of decency' has been used in a penological context by the Supreme Court to convey the flexible nature of constitutional interpretation, sensitive to changing circumstances and ideas.
15. *Indigenous Peoples – A Global Quest for Justice: A Report for the Independent Commission on International Humanitarian Issues*, Foreword by Sadruddin Aga Khan and Hassan bin Talal (London: Zed Books, 1987), p. 32.
16. See above, Chapter 8, 'The Right to Group Rights'.
17. See below, Chapter 18, 'Women and Children First'.
18. As examples of such pan-national organizations: World Council of Indigenous People, Inuit Circumpolar Conference, Four Directions Council, Indigenous World Association, International Indian Treaty Council, Indian Law Resource Center.
19. Hazel Hertzberg, *The Search for an American Indian Identity: Modern Pan-Indian Movements* (Syracuse, NY: Syracuse University Press, 1971), p. 2.
20. Vine Deloria Jr and Clifford Lytle, *The Nations Within: The Past and Future of American Indian Sovereignty* (New York: Pantheon Books, 1984), p. 235.
21. Ibid., pp. 235–6.
22. Ibid., p. 237.
23. Patrick Macklem, 'Distributing Sovereignty: Indian Nations and Equality of Peoples', *Stanford*

Law Review, 45 (1993), p. 1315.

24. See Australian Law Reform Commission, *The Recognition of Aboriginal Customary Laws* (Canberra: Government Publishing Service, 1986).
25. Marcia Langton, 'The United Nations and Indigenous Minorities: A Report on the United Nations Working Group on Indigenous Populations', in B. Hocking (ed.), *International Law and Aboriginal Human Rights* (Sydney: Law Book Co., 1988).
26. Kevin Carmody, Statement made on Australian Broadcasting Corporation, Jan. 26, 1988 – see *Aboriginal Law Bulletin*, 30 (February 1988), p. 4.
27. *Indigenous Peoples*, p. 10.
28. Ibid., p. 10; see also Mary Fleming Mathus, 'Local-Level Competition Between Tribals and Non-Tribals' in S.L. Seaton and H. Claessen (eds), *Political Anthropology: The State of the Art* (The Hague: Mouton), p. 121. She sees this competition as being 'a world-wide problem' (136) as 'more and more tribals are presently attaining the socioeconomic skills of the dominant society'.
29. Ibid., p. 11.
30. See P.K. Gupta, *Commentaries on the Scheduled Castes and the Scheduled Tribes (Prevention of Atrocities) Act, 1989* (Lucknow: Eastern Book Co., 1991).
31. On China, see Colin MacKerras, *China's Minorities: Integration and Modernization in the Twentieth Century* (Oxford: Oxford University Press, 1994).
32. *Indigenous Peoples*, p. 10.
33. For discussions of some of these groups, see the journal *Nomadic Peoples*.
34. *Indigenous Peoples*, p. 9.
35. Ibid., p. 10.
36. *Study on the Rights of Persons Belonging to Ethnic, Religious and Linguistic Minorities*, UN Doc. E/CN, 4/Sub. 2/384/Rev. I (1979), Special Rapporteur, Francesco Capatort. See also in 'Minorities' in 8 *Encyclopedia of Public International Law* (1985).
37. *Study of the Problem of Discrimination against Indigenous Populations*, UN, 1987, UN Doc. E/CN. 4/Sub. 2/1986/7 Add. 4. Special Rapporteur, Jose R. Martinez Cobo.
38. Natan Lerner, *Group Rights and Discrimination in International Law* (Dordrecht: Martinus Nijhoff, 1991), Chapter 5, 'Indigenous Populations', p. 99. A key factor in precipitating the slow overall change in attitudes was an NGO Conference held in Geneva in September, 1981, which discussed four major issues – land and treaty rights; indigenous philosophy; the impact on indigenous life of transnational corporations; and the impact of nuclear arms build-up on the land and life of indigenous people.
39. Ibid., p. 99. For an earlier analysis, see Gordon Bennett, 'The Developing Law of Aboriginal Rights,' *Review of International Commission of Jurists*, 22 (1979), p. 37.
40. *Lovelace case* – Communication No. 24/1977 Sandra Lovelace, 36 UN GAOR Supp. (No. 40) at 166, 177 UN Doc. A/36/40 (1981).
41. See UN Economic and Social Council Document, E/CN, 4/GR. 1987/7 Add. 12, 30 September 1987 – United States Government Replies Nos. 3160–3163. See also Document E/CN. 4/Sub.2/1989/35 (Part II) Add. 1, 24 August 1989 – Re Discrimination against Indigenous Peoples – The Relocation of Hopi and Navajo Families.
42. *Indian Rights – Human Rights: Handbook for Indians on International Human Rights Complaint Procedures* (Washington, DC: Indian Law Resource Center, 1984).
43. Ibid., p. 24.
44. Marijane Ambler, *Breaking the Iron Bonds: Indian Control of Energy Development* (Lawrence: University Press of Kansas, 1990).
45. Ibid.
46. *Lone Wolf v. Hitchcock*, 187 US 553 (1903). See also Blue Clark, *Lone Wolf v. Hitchcock: Treaty Rights and Indians at the End of the Nineteenth Century* (Lincoln: University of Nebraska Press, 1994).
47. Ambler, *Breaking the Iron Bonds*, p. 43. She also describes the debate over the profits that accrued to the tribe amongst claims of spendthrift behavior, which was then used as a reason for denying other tribes access to mineral wealth. However, in sum, their approach and their struggle to retain mineral rights served as a basis for the success of other tribes (pp. 49–51).
48. Ambler, ibid, p. 47.
49. See ibid., Chapter 4, 'Indian OPEC? The Council of Energy Resource Tribes', p. 91.

50. For the rights of tribes to tax for mining energy resources, see *Kerr-McGee Corp. v. Navajo Tribe*, 471 U.S. 195 (1985); and for rights of state to tax non-Indian companies extracting oil and gas on Indian reservations, see *Cotton Petroleum Corporation v. New Mexico*, 490 U.S. 163 (1989).
51. See Ambler, *Breaking the Iron Bonds*, Chapter 8, 'No Reservation is an Island: Water and Off-Reservation Energy Development', p. 204.
52. Ibid., pp. 260–1.
53. Ibid., p. 262. See also Lauren Holland, 'The Use of Litigation in Indian Natural Resource Disputes', *Journal of Energy Law and Policy* 10 (1989), who writes: 'If Indians could realize sovereign rights to the low sulfur, coal, uranium, oil and natural gas currently located on their reservations, the pattern of energy development in this country would be altered dramatically (while ... recognition of Indian sovereignty could force a realignment of economic power in the United States) (p. 33).
54. Colin Tatz, *Aborigines and Uranium and Other Essays* (Richmond, Victoria: Heinemann, 1982), especially Chapters 5 and 6, pp. 118–89.
55. See comment by Tatz, ibid., p. 165; 'Statehood for the Northern Territory will ... come to rest more on the way government accommodates its Aboriginal population than on any initiation of resources and mineral developments.'
56. See, for instance, Gary Sokolow, 'The Future of Gambling in Indian Country', *American Indian Law Review* 15 (1991), p. 151. He notes that 'The tribes, like other governmental entities, use these revenues largely for the economic, educational and health benefit of their membership.' According to a 1986 survey, 108 tribes had gaming facilities.
57. One of these became a world-famous resort, Sun City.
58. For an interesting discussion of the problematics of gambling in the context of impoverished areas (with implications for the Indian situation) see 'America's House of Cards: How the Casino Economy Robs the Poor', *The Nation*, 19 February 1996, p. 11.
59. See, for instance discussion by Augie Fleras and Jean Leonard Elliott, *The 'Nations Within': Aboriginal–State Relations in Canada, the United States and New Zealand* (Toronto: Oxford University Press, 1992). They write:

    > In the 1980s the conservative philosophy of 'privatization' was to be extended to reserve economies. The jewel in the crown of the federal privatization program as applied to Native people was the 1984 Presidential Commission on Indian Reservation Economics, which reported that the major obstacle to economic development on reserve lands was government, both tribal and federal. Its analysis was reminiscent of the rationale behind the 1887 Allotment Act, which sought to break up communal land holdings in favour of private enterprise and individual ownership.
    >
    > Three years later, however, President Reagan supported the federal regulation of tribal gaming operations. While the justification was to protect the tribes from organized crime, it was commonly believed that the Indians were seen as 'too successful' at minor gambling operations like bingo, and posed a threat to competition including charities and churches. Thus, ironically, the market forces worshipped by the conservative economists as the final regulator of economic activity were not permitted to operate when open competition favoured aboriginal peoples.

    See also Patrick Morris, 'Termination by Accountants: The Reagan Indian Policy', *Policy Studies Journal* 16 (1988), p. 731.
60. This issue may well be a typical example of North–South conflict, where the research potentialities of the North are not fully utilized as the benefits of solar energy would obviously redound mainly to the South.
61. Ambler, *Breaking the Iron Bonds*, pp. 114–15.
62. Nancy Collins and Andrea Hall, 'Nuclear Waste in Indian Country: A Paradoxical Trade', *Law and Inequality* 12 (1994), p. 267.
63. This includes also the 'dumping' of goods that violate health and safety standards – see Gunther Handl, 'Environmental Security and Global Change: The Challenge to International Law', *Yearbook of International Environmental Law* 1 (1990), p. 3.
64. Ibid, pp. 299-300. Of the 20 applications, 16 were from tribes.
65. Ibid., p. 303.
66. Ibid., p. 274.

67. See Steve Dietrich, 'Tribal Businesses and the Uncertain Reach of Tribal Sovereign Immunity: A Statutory Solution', *Washington Law Review* 67 (1992), p. 113.
68. Russel Barsh, 'Indigenous People and the Right to Self-Determination in International Law,' in B. Hocking (ed.), *International Law and Aboriginal Human Rights*, p. 73.
69. See, for instance, Marie-Anik Gagne, *A Nation within a Nation: Dependency and the Cree* (Montreal: Black Rose Books, 1994).
70. See Marie Leger (ed.), *Aboriginal Peoples: Toward Self-Government* (Montreal: Black Rose Books, 1994), in which descriptions are provided of the background, political struggles and constitutional and legal arrangements in a number of Latin American countries – Mexico, Nicaragua, Colombia, Panama and Brazil.
71. Barsh, 'Indigenous People', p. 79; for the Penner Report, see *Indian Self-Government in Canada* (Special Committee of the Canadian House of Commons, 1983).
72. See also the discussion of subsequent developments in Augie Fleras and Jean Leonard Elliott, *The 'Nations Within'*. The use of the term 'The Nations Within' is taken from the book by Deloria and Lytle, *The Nations Within*.

11

The Trials of Tribal Courts

The average court system is seen generally as being a rigidly structured, hierarchical framework, with layers of jurisdictions rising in pyramidal fashion to an apex where a highest court in the land surveys the lower rungs of juridical work to ensure a correct and just application of the law. Errors are presumably eradicated by courts of appeal, binding guidelines are set by courts in the higher echelons of the judicial system, and the lower courts conduct their daily legal confrontations in terms of either a clear statement in legislation or an interpreted precedent of litigation.

This is the picture presented in most positivistic descriptions of law – but it is one, which, in recent decades, has come under increasing criticism by jurists, philosophers and social scientists, all attempting to see beyond the formal framework of text and textbook – and to fathom the living reality of law as it affects the lives of disputants – not necessarily those whose names become household words in the annals of legal literature, because their unusual case serves as a touchstone for judicial appeal and legal development, but the many anonymous souls whose resolution of conflict takes place far from the spotlight of media coverage or academic scrutiny.

A diverse group of theories – under the names of legal realism or living law, or existential law, or psychological and psychoanalytical jurisprudence[1] – have pointed out the distorted image of law that flows from an over-emphasis on those 'cases' that form a significant part of upper court litigation. These hard cases are the unusual ones, admittedly often important for breakthroughs, intellectual and practical, but not necessarily symbolic of, or even symptomatic of, the bulk of cases that form the heart of the legal system. Sometimes even hard cases do not make it to the highest level, because of procedural restrictions – such as in the United States, where an appellant must first convince a minority of four justices of the nine-member Supreme Court that the case is worthy of a writ of certiorari,[2] or where, as in England, the House of Lords, as the highest court in the land, deals only with a limited number of cases, with the bulk of appealed cases reaching only to the slightly lower Court of Appeal.

So a basic fact about legal systems is that its essence – certainly in terms of number of cases, but also in terms of much of its vital substance – takes place in the lower courts, where judges may deviate from strict application of the law, and even fail to update their decision with the latest precedents of higher courts. In fact, beyond the more formal courts, is an attempt to set up informal structures – of small claims courts, where the official system allows an informal means of attaining rapid, inexpensive and efficient justice, shorn of the formalities, and often the procrastination and complications, of the more regular courts – and of the strict letter of the law.

Some revolutionary or radical regimes have also encouraged the creation of peoples' courts to provide a similar immediate form of dispensing justice.[3] Furthermore, many administrative disputes are brought before special quasi-judicial bodies.[4] The judicial systems of most modern societies are not as monolithic and homogeneous as seems at first glance – or even from a more detailed perusal of leading legal literature. Most systems contain a minimum of pluralism, with parallel or even competing court-systems – in former times in England, for instance, common law courts and equity courts of chancery,[5] in France, hermetically separated administrative courts and regular courts,[6] with even totally different appeal processes, and with a special Court of Conflict to decide, in marginal cases, where jurisdiction lies. Furthermore, occasionally, courts will insist that all prior possibilities of resolving a conflict have been pursued before it will take a plea under advisement. In the Council of Europe, for instance, until a recent change, an informal investigation by a Commission seeking a friendly settlement of compromise between the parties, preceded any judicial proceedings of the European Court of Human Rights.[7]

Within this framework of varied possibilities, a tribal court system becomes only one more aspect of a diversified court system. The application of tribal law becomes merely a special example of a living law, a law activated and modified not by specialized practitioners but by those who in their daily lives, practice the law, living out their traditional customs in everyday contacts – and occasional confrontations with neighbours, rivals, partners, relatives.

The customary law arises from within the people, and so it is right that adjudication should be linked to the reality of their lives. Today, throughout the world, however debatable the concept of tribe may still be, however uncertain the idea of legal pluralism may be, the fact is that customary law is alive and basically well, and an essential part of many legal systems. In some places, such as the United States, these legal frameworks are known as tribal courts; in other places, especially in Africa, they go under a range of names – local courts, chief's courts, village courts, community courts, popular courts; in yet other places, such as Australia, no recognized system exists, but *sub rosa* processes take place, which the official courts are occasionally forced to take note of. But whatever the nomenclature, whatever the jurisdictional authority, the customary law will most often be adjudicated in specialized frameworks in what are basically tribal courts.

Probably the most authoritative courts were those that were set up in the tribal territories – in Indian country – in the United States.[8] Having set aside reservations for the Native Americans, having conceded a certain amount of autonomy to them, having declared the tribes to be 'domestic nations', the inevitable consequence was a recognition of their customary law – at least within the assigned area, and for those who were acknowledged members of the particular tribe. Outside of the reservation, the Indian was generally not entitled to the activation of his 'personal' law as the member of a tribe, while inside the reservation, non-Indians, or Indians who were not members of the tribe, were not necessarily subject to the laws of the tribe; but these were all only secondary issues – dealing with the extent of the court's authority and related questions, such as justiciability – the primary fact was a recognition of tribal law, even when based on custom.

On the other hand, in a country, where no recognition whatsoever was given to the indigenous local authorities, and so no official recognition was given to customary law, as in Australia, there was clearly no room for a recognized tribal courts system. But this fact, in and of itself, did not prevent the continued survival of tribal norms and the means by which they were enforced. On occasion, these informal procedures were brought to the knowledge of the Court, for instance in mitigation of sentence, when a tribal punishment had been imposed, or was likely to be imposed in the future, so as to avoid too harsh a judicial response.[9]

In other places, particularly in Africa, the exigencies of the situation led to the fullest utilization of existing tribal structures in the judicial realm (even without formal boundaries as were drawn up in the United States). This was an essential aspect of the British policy of 'indirect rule' where the local leaders were given the task of preserving order.[10] Without doubt this was an arrangement to the mutual benefit of the British conqueror and the leading figures among the indigenous people – and, no doubt, this fact has been a cause of much of the criticisms made of tribal customary law – in fact of tribe itself and of the exploitative role that some of the leaders played in the intricate web of relations that were set up.[11] Undoubtedly, there were instances where chiefs in Africa or big men in the Pacific derived much of their enhanced power from the support they received from the colonial authorities.

However, in any event, two general aspects of tribal court systems should be noted. On the one hand is the real impact of tribal law on the members of the tribe, even when the tribe lacked formal adjudicative authority. For them customary law is both just and obligatory, an integral part of their personal normative system. On the other hand, is the alienation sensed by many tribal people from state law, because of its lack of relevance to tribal life, or even its absence in a practical sense from the area – where, for instance, there is little police law enforcement and negligible court presence. In most instances, the tribe, as a group, will prefer their own time-honored judicial practices above the formal court system of the state. Even in extreme circumstances, the commission of a murder, the tribe may prefer their own response, which may be one of mediation, compensation and reconciliation, over the formal arraignment in a court, the conviction and the punishment. In many situations, questions of double jeopardy inevitably arise, and so does the import of double punishment – an unofficial penalty, for instance 'spearing' in Australia, as well as a court-imposed prison sentence.

Kayleen Hazlehurst discusses these kinds of problems in an Australian context. She states that 'Western Law has yet to come to grips with the reality that Aboriginals may face a second punishment from their own people on their release from prison.'[12] On the other hand, she also describes the 'deep distrust which Aboriginal people feel towards the Australian criminal justice system ...'[13] Together with other social problems, such as alcoholism, she notes the urgency of developing alternative community-based programs for 'social control'.[14]

In these kinds of conditions, as the country began to reassess its history, the need for increasingly more understanding of tribal institutions became apparent. Hazlehurst, for instance, refers to a 1982 project which involved 'senior Aboriginal custodians in discussions with a magistrate prior to sentencing of the offender, and close pre-court consultation with the defendant's nuclear and extended family'[15] – a procedure which has been much expanded recently, and also applied in other places.

In Papua New Guinea, which gained its independence in the early 1970s, after being under Australian tutelage, an extensive system of village courts was set up in 1975, and today the network comprises some 1,000 courts, covering almost all parts of this island nation.[16] In fact, given the difficulties of communications and transportation, probably the only real means by which the governmental authorities can guarantee any minimum level of social order is by diffusion of authority, including judicial authority. The village courts are generally more attuned to local customs than centralized legislation. Similarly in Nigeria, Richardson states that 'By far the greater part of the work of the courts in Nigeria is heard in customary courts.'[17]

Nevertheless, in analyzing the work of local courts, of whatever ilk or name, it is not always clear that there is a full recognition or appreciation of legal pluralism – in many instances, particularly (but not only) historical colonial situations, it was not an acceptance of the value of variety in legal enforcement or an appreciation of the substantive rules of customary law, that led to the use of tribal courts, but pragmatic considerations as well as subtle co-optation. Williams warns that a façade of legal pluralism may conceal a reality of monocultural legal domination.[18] This may well be a warning for scholars to be cautious in their analysis of attempts by a modern state legal system to operate in a pluralistic manner. There is always a danger that 'peoples'' law becomes distorted and amenable to manipulation by dominant classes, specifically when it is recognized by a state legal system.

Indeed, there are judicial decisions which seem *prima facie* to be of benefit to the aboriginal parties, but that, on deeper analysis, show indications of ulterior purposes, not necessarily consonant with ultimate justice or a real concern for the special needs and status of aboriginal groups. This may even be a crucial factor in relating to procedural questions, for instance, as to which court had authority – the tribal or the state. While often the judgment may deal extensively with matters of principle, there may be underlying factors that are much more mundane – and sometimes even Machiavellian.

In Australia, for instance, where no recognition was given to tribal courts, the authorities sometimes displayed a tolerance toward internal tribal means of maintaining social control. This might even include a willingness to forgo trial in a major criminal case (including, for murder), while allowing the Aborigines to apply their own normative concepts – both the rigorous blood-revenge and the more tolerant reconciliation procedures. At the beginning of the nineteenth century, the court system vacillated as to its response to major crime. In some early cases, the Supreme Court ruled that the Aborigines were not always automatically to be subject to the law. Castles describes how 'elements of doubt and indecision had continued to mark official relations with Aborigines as far as their amenability to ordinary legal proceedings were concerned. As late as 1826 some colonists had voiced consternation when the Supreme Court had ruled that an Aborigine charged with attempted murder could not be tried under English law. In 1829, two judges of the Supreme Court had determined that it would be unjust to try an Aborigine for murdering one of his fellows.'[19].

Decisions of this kind were taken despite the lack of any formal recognition of customary law. The consequences of these early Australian decisions were however, by default, to indicate recognition of whatever form of response the Aborigines might choose; but neither the courts nor the official governmental authorities went one step further to accord official recognition to the system of customary law. Indeed, it is difficult not to sense that the reluctance to extend the protection of the regular court system to extreme aboriginal crime was a consequence of the fact that in all these cases the victim was an Aborigine.

It was only when there was a growing awareness of potential dangers to the white settler population that a new approach was adopted. Thus Castles refers to the need for regular courts to impose recognized law because of the risks to which the Whites might be exposed.

In 1836 the Supreme Court decided a major case (*Murrell*'s case)[20] in which it held that an Aborigine was subject to state law, rejecting defense objections that the accused had acted (in a killing based on family revenge) within the tribal norms, and was in any event not subject to European law, as the law did not provide protection for him as an Aborigine. Although the *Murrell* case served as a precedent, Castles claims that the decision was not clear-cut, and left room for different decisions in the future. Thus, a case five years later, which was unreported (the *Bonson* case), held that the colonial courts had no authority to decide cases in which only Aborigines were involved, this case also being a murder trial.[21]

Far more clear-cut was a case several decades later in the United States Supreme Court (*Crow Dog* case in 1883),[22] which seems ostensibly to grant full recognition to tribal courts in a decision which deals with matters very similar to the Murrell case (a murder case in which both victim and criminal are members of a tribe). However, it may well have been the categorical nature of the judgment, affording exclusive jurisdiction to tribal courts, that led to a reactive series of subsequent actions to restrict the powers of the tribal courts, as will be discussed.

A recently published book indicates the gap that may well exist between true understanding of the reality of Native American life and what seem like generous gestures made in favor of the tribe. In the opening sentences of his acknowledgements the author, Sidney Harring, explains the need to examine, 'the underlying principles of Indian law, the stories behind the cases. We found them "sovereignty stories". Criminal cases are of special interest because sovereignty was defined, ironically, in the context of so much violence.'[23] Discussing the *Crow Dog* case in this larger context, and in terms of insights gained from discussions with Native Americans, Harring adds, 'The first time that I read the *Crow Dog* "case", the published US Supreme Court opinion, it occurred to me that there must be a great gulf between the case as the Supreme Court saw it and the tragic events of that August day in 1881.'[24]

On that day, the accused, Crow Dog, a member of the Brule Sioux tribe, shot to death a chief of that tribe, Spotted Tail, in circumstances that clearly indicate the possibility of self-defense. The background to the killing was apparently tribal politics – more precisely, rivalry between those like Crow Dog, who adopted an adamant stance against officials of the United States government, who were anxious to undermine tribal authority as they embarked on a larger program of assimilation of Indians into the mainstream of American life, and those like Spotted Tail, who were prepared to come to some accommodation with governmental demands.

Shortly after the killing, two parallel processes began. The governmental authorities (in this case the District Attorney of the Federal Government for the Dakota Territory) arrested Crow Dog with the intention of putting him on trial for murder. Meanwhile, his families and the family of the victim, Spotted Tail, had already undergone negotiations, according to tribal law, which led to a negotiated settlement in which the killer's family paid compensation to the victim's family. However, Crow Dog remained in prison and a year later he was tried in a territorial Court for murder, found guilty and sentenced to death. On appeal to a Federal Court, it was held that the tribal court had exclusive jurisdiction over crimes committed in tribal territory, a decision subsequently affirmed by the US Supreme Court.

This judicial support for tribal sovereignty turned out to be only a pyrrhic victory, as within two years the Major Crimes Act of 1885 was enacted, which declared that seven major felonies committed by Indians against Indians in Indian territory could be tried only in federal courts.[25] Furthermore, Harring claims that the *Crow Dog* case did not cause, as many claim, a strong reaction which led to the Major Crimes Act, but that the decision itself was part of an overall concerted policy that had been pursued for some two decades prior to the case – of undermining not just tribal sovereignty (which included tribal courts) but tribal culture in general.[26] Thus it was not just the quashing of the conviction by the Supreme Court that was important (the victim was an Indian), but the manner in which the Court related to Indian justice, presenting it in a negative manner, which was then exploited by those eager to curtail tribal power. Extending the federal criminal law to Indian territory was precisely the social control that the Bureau of Indian Affairs (BIA) was seeking – this would facilitate the growing efforts at ensuring the demise of Indian culture and the assimilation of the Indians (which was to be even further pursued by the Dawes Allocation Act, passed during this period – in 1887).[27] Harring writes:

> 'Popular outcry' does not explain either the decision to prosecute Crow Dog (under existing law there should have been no prosecution) or the passage of the Major Crimes Act. Rather, the BIA cultivated *Crow Dog* as a test case and tried to create other test cases both before and after to gain precisely the end that was won: federal criminal jurisdiction over the Indian tribes. The Supreme Court in reversing *Crow Dog*'s jurisdiction had adopted this view, mischaracterizing the case as one of 'red men's revenge', a racist and false statement that conjured up the 'blood revenge' image of tribal law and invited federal intervention to 'civilize' the Sioux.
>
> BIA officials had been attempting to acquire such jurisdiction since at least 1874, because they needed the coercive power of the criminal law as one means to force the assimilation of the Indians.[28]

Harring does not limit his comments to broad speculative statements, but argues specifically that 'It is clear that beginning the day after Spotted Tail's killing, the BIA engaged in a systematic distortion of the facts of the case. Officials claimed that a popular outcry among local whites necessitated the arrest, even though the Indian agent … had immediately ordered the arrest, well before the killing was known off the reservation. Likewise, the outrage provoked by the Supreme Court's reversal of the case came primarily from BIA officials and Indian reformers.'[29]

Harring is also critical of the Supreme Court decision, arguing that the opinion showed little 'actual knowledge of Sioux law. Although the Supreme Court understood that Crow Dog's case had been processed under the tribal law, nothing in the Court's decision indicated anything but the most superficial comprehension of that law.'[30]

What is most significant in Harring's account is that *Crow Dog*'s case was not the only murder trial involving Indians, then being tried in state or federal courts. There were at least six other cases, which according to him indicates that 'extension of criminal law to the tribes was a matter of BIA policy, and having been unable to induce the US Congress to extend criminal jurisdiction over the tribes, the BIA was trying to induce state and territorial courts to do so in violation of its legal responsibility to defend the interests of the tribes.'[31]

However, the real 'story' behind the *Crow Dog* decision relates to the possibility that the jurisdictional issue (basically a question of constitutional law) was used by the Supreme Court to avoid the penological consequences (basically a question of criminal law) of the original trial. The death penalty had been imposed in a case where there were strong indications that the shooting had been done in self-defense. Harring writing over a hundred years after the decision, explains that

> Although *Crow Dog* is always understood as a significant decision in Indian law, it may be ironic that the most important set of considerations in the case had nothing at all to do with the status of the Indian tribes. *Crow Dog* was also a capital criminal case. At the federal court level, there was no right of appeal at all of an ordinary federal criminal case until 1879 when a right of appeal to the circuit courts was created. It was 1889 before a criminal appeal could be taken to the US Supreme Court … When the Supreme Court first came to hear criminal appeals, it reversed a great many of them, evidently appalled by the quality of criminal justice in many remote courts. To the Supreme Court, death penalty convictions had to show a level of integrity difficult for frontier justice. Crow Dog's offense, committed with an uncertain mental element under an uncertain legal status, may simply not have warranted the death penalty in the eyes of the justices.[32]

Harring puts forward this argument with some hesitation, but it seems to have much validity. If he is right, the consequences, in a trail of strange causative factors, are far-reaching. Briefly, Harring's careful research of a case over a century old leads to the following set of facts – a killing carried out under circumstances which suggest the possibility of self-defence was resolved by traditional tribal compensatory and conciliatory measures; for political reasons, aimed at undermining tribal life, the governmental agencies (the Indian Bureau and the prosecution) put Crow Dog on trial for murder, which ended with his conviction and a sentence of death; the criminal aspect could not be dealt with on appeal, but the constitutional issue of jurisdiction was presented to the Supreme Court; limited to a discussion only of the jurisdictional issue, the Court annulled the federal trial, basing themselves on earlier cases from the decisions of Chief Justice Marshall in the 1830s,[33] but possibly wishing mainly to avoid a capital punishment, which they found unable to quash in any other manner (this aspect is correct to this day, where the Supreme Court monitors penological issues, including the death penalty, only from a constitutional perspective, and not a substantive penological one);[34] as a result of *Crow Dog*'s case, Congress passed the Major Crimes Act, seriously limiting the jurisdiction of tribal courts – thus, the case acknowledging tribal authority, was subsequently exploited for opposite purposes, as part of a larger policy then being conducted to restrict tribal authority and destroy tribal life.

In many respects then, *Crow Dog* is an historical oddity – a firm decision supportive of tribal authority, which was within a few years to be totally undermined; firstly by the Major Crimes Act two years later, which specifically overruled *Crow Dog* by transferring jurisdiction in seven major crimes, including murder, from the tribal courts where the *Crow Dog* judgment had firmly placed it, to the federal courts; and secondly, a further two years later, by the Dawes Allotment Act of 1887, aimed at the final elimination of a separate communal tribal existence by providing for individual allotments of plots, including of 'surplus' Indian land to non-Indians.

Both Acts were challenged as being unconstitutional – since they constituted a violation of earlier treaties guaranteeing basic tribal authority. However, the Supreme Court, relying on an 1871 law which formally put an end to the treaty-making power,[35] applied these legal provisions retroactively to nullify past treaties, and thus to deny the petitions – in *US v. Kagama* in 1886 the Major Crimes Act was declared a valid law[36] and in 1903 in *Lone Wolf v. Hitchcock*, the Dawes Act was also validated.[37] In Harring's succint summary, '*Kagama* … potentially deprived the tribes of the right to make laws to govern themselves, a critical aspect of their sovereignty and their ability to structure their own lives. *Lone Wolf v. Hitchcock* completed this attack by ensuring that the tribes could be deprived of their lands in the same way'.[38]

These cases of *Crow Dog* and *Lone Wolf* and *Kagama* are used by Charles Wilkinson[39] as the examples (together with a few other cases)[40] at opposite ends of a spectrum indicating maximum consideration of tribal rights (as in the *Crow Dog* case), and maximum nullification of tribal authority (as in the *Kagama* and *Lone Wolf* cases). Jurists, and particularly judges, are faced thus with diametrically opposed judicial approaches – examining court opinions at different levels, Wilkinson sees 'two separate bodies of jurisprudence (which) are irreconcilable … . The first, which denies tribes most powers and which traces to the *Kagama–McBratney–Lone Wolf* line, is premised on modern realities,' which tends to justify creating one legal system, open to all on an equal basis, with 'little or no room … for the exercise of modern governmental powers by primitive societies'.[41]

On the other hand there is a line of decisions, starting with *Worcester* and continuing through *Crow Dog* and on to *Talton*[42] which leads judges

> out of contemporary society back to pre-Columbian times. That process, so jolting to a judiciary that prides itself on being forward-looking and progressive, brought focus to bear on traditional tribal justice systems. By definition they held complete power before contact with European nations – there were no competitors save other tribes. If that original status is legitimized and is accepted as continuing … then the courts must turn away from modern realities as a setting and toward an almost mechanical, linear analysis of whether relevant aspects of pre-Columbian status have been abridged by the United States. If not, the pre-Columbian status continues.[43]

Wilkinson's conclusion is that the overall thrust of Supreme Court precedents is in favor of *Crow Dog* and not *Kagama* and *Lone Wolf*, in favor of the approach of Justice Marshall in *Worcester v. Georgia*; in favor of 'a recognition of Indian tribes as permanent, separate sovereigns …'[44] Included in this governmental structure are tribal courts.

While Wilkinson is well aware of the many erosions to tribal authority – through legislation and judicial decisions – he sees a 1959 Supreme Court case, *Williams v. Lee,* as being a turning point in the revival of tribal law.[45] This judgment not only gave renewed recognition to the authority of tribal courts, but even extended it, in the instant case, to apply to a non-Indian, based on contracts that he had signed with Indians on the Navajo Reservation. Recognizing the right of the Navajo to govern themselves, Justice Black explained that denying the jurisdiction of the tribal court, even when one of the parties was non-Indian, would 'undermine the authority of the tribal courts'.[46]

This decision is seen by Wilkinson as putting an end to the erosion caused by the aforementioned legislation and policies of the nineteenth century, and the subsequent Termination policy in the years immediately after the Second World War.[47] He argues that

> American Indian tribes have made a historic recovery from these sterile years. The reforms of the Indian Reorganization Act of 1934 (IRA) and related policies allowed a revival of tribalism. Tribal councils and courts reorganized or began operating formally for the first time. Tribal progress was stilled by the interlude of the termination era during the 1950s but by the 1960s tribes were in a position to capitalize on the opportunity of self-rule … . Tribes have re-asserted their inherent powers during the modern era and seek to fulfil their prerogative of self-rule almost as though the opening of the reservations had never occurred.[48]

For Wilkinson, it is not only the substantive decision in *Williams v. Lee* that leads to his optimistic approach, but because it 'presaged and may in part have spurred the recent resurgence of tribal activity … . The real question was whether Indian tribal courts had exclusive jurisdiction over such cases. In finding exclusive tribal juridical power, the Court recognized a broad tribal jurisdiction and a contracted state jurisdiction …'[49]

However, as will be noted in dealing with various substantive areas in the third section of this book,[50] the overall picture is much more uncertain, while even in matters of jurisdiction, the Supreme Court continues to vacillate. In fact, in 1978, two important and conflicting decisions were given within two weeks of each other. In *Oliphant v. Suqamish Indian Tribe*[51] the court – in conflict with *Crow Dog* and *Williams v. Lee* – held that the tribal court had no jurisdiction over a non-Indian for crimes (of drinking and fighting) committed on an Indian reservation. On the other hand, in *United States v. Wheeler*[52] the Court held that successive prosecutions of Indians in state and tribal courts did not constitute a violation of double jeopardy.

Wilkinson attaches major importance to the *Wheeler* decision (while downplaying the *Oliphant* case), since it appears that the Court 'resolved a major ambiguity in the field by making it clear that tribal powers trace to inherent sovereignty, not to grants from the United States'.[53] Thus, declares Wilkinson conclusively, 'Tribal powers are both preconstitutional and extraconstitutional'.[54] As a result, '*Wheeler* played the crucial role of reviving the tribal sovereignty doctrine and analyzing it at sufficient length to lay the doctrinal foundation …'[55] for later opinions.

Other writers, however, do not accord to *Wheeler* the same degree of importance – Wunder,[56] for instance, in his comprehensive analysis, ignores the case (as also the *Oliphant* case).

Wilkinson seems to have chosen a very selective reading of the judgment, focusing on a few select phrases to justify his triumphant conclusions. Yet, it is difficult to acquiesce in his appraisal of this case.

While the Court admittedly does acknowledge the unique nature of tribal sovereignty, this is by no means a new or radical finding. Moreover, the very fact of allowing for successive prosecutions, despite the 'double jeopardy' provisions of the constitution,[57] cannot but undermine tribal authority, especially when the tribal trial, as in the *Wheeler* case, precedes the state trial – and this is liable to be the situation in general, since tribal trials are usually more expeditious. Given the fact that tribal punishments are also probably more lenient, the *Wheeler* decision opens up disturbing possibilities of a moderate reconciliatory process in a tribal court followed by a more severe punitive process in a state court, the very opposite of what normally takes place, where criminal trials normally precede any civil claims for compensation. (Parenthetically, it might be noted that in general, American jurisprudence on double jeopardy, allowing for successive prosecutions because of claims of dual sovereignty – for instance, federal and state – is an extremely problematic approach, vastly different from what is considered acceptable in European and other jurisdictions).[58] Yet, Wilkinson uses indirectly the denial of double jeopardy to argue for recognition of tribal sovereignty. However, by allowing two trials – one tribal, the other state or federal – the *Wheeler* decision actually undermines tribal authority.

Most significantly, though, Wilkinson ignores a crucial statement in the judgment, where the Court, after noting the 'unique and *limited* character' [author's emphasis] of tribal sovereignty, immediately adds that 'It exists only at the sufferance of Congress and is subject to complete defeasance.'[59] It is difficult to reconcile such a description with Wilkinson's claim to 'inherent sovereignty' of the tribes or that the Court found that Indian tribes possess a third source of sovereignty in the United States.[60] What they found was nothing new, but merely a reiteration of prior admission of a restricted sovereignty, held at the wishes and the whims of the governmental authorities.

An Indian judge, Frank Pommersheim,[61] has, in fact, come to a diametrically opposite reading of the judgment. Discussing the problem of the '... vast expansion of federal authority in Indian affairs [which] has concomitantly and almost brutally constrained the parameters of tribal sovereignty',[62] he notes the restrictive nature of Justice Stewart's opinion as to the sovereignty of Indian tribes and then argues that

> this bold colonizing language suggests that tribal sovereignty is really non-existent. Within a national jurisprudence that recognizes the primacy of order, limits, and predictability within the legal system, such pronouncements seem especially crabbed and destabilizing. This is particularly true for tribes attempting to build and advance their vision of sovereignty. These unjustifiable constraints pose a constant

and paralyzing threat to the efforts of tribes and tribal courts to move forward.[63]

Nevertheless, Pommersheim does see some glimmer of hope arising out of other cases, quoting specifically Justice Thurgood Marshall in *Iowa Mutual*, a 1987 decision, when he stated that 'Tribal courts play a vital role in tribal self-government …'[64] However, overall Pommersheim states that 'Tribal courts remain threatened by the dark shadow of federal plenary authority and the general incoherence of contemporary federal Indian law.'[65]

In fact, shortly after Wilkinson's book was published, the Supreme Court once again, in a criminal case, interpreted the court jurisdiction of tribal courts in a narrow manner, reminiscent far more of the *Oliphant* precedent than the *Wheeler* case. The Court held, in *Duro v. Reina*, that Indian tribal courts did not have the authority to assert criminal jurisdiction over other Indians who were not members of the tribe. The implications of this decision are set out succintly by Justice Brennan in his dissenting opinion when he explains that '… the Court maintains that tribes *implicitly* surrendered the power to enforce their criminal laws against nonmember Indians when the tribes became dependent on the Federal Government'. Brennan refers critically to such an approach as 'a parsimonious view of the sovereignty retained by Indian tribes'.[66]

Pommersheim relates to Wilkinson's book in general[67] and challenges his faith in the Supreme Court to uphold treaties, noting several recent decisions (including *Oliphant*) that have curtailed the authority of tribal courts. Indeed, Pommersheim, in his guarded hopes for the future of tribal courts, seems to place more reliance on solid analyses of the substantive law, formulated by people with respect for Indian life and culture – such as Felix Cohen's monumental work[68] – while remaining wary of the vagaries and fluctuations of Supreme Court decisions.

In fact, Wilkinson may be correct when he writes glowingly of 'The elevation of tribalism' and describes how the tribes have worked effectively 'to gain a place, new though it be, in the community of governments in the United States'.[69] But this situation is not necessarily the outcome of the assumed protective or innovative judicial activity of the federal and state courts, including the Supreme Court, but because of the daily reality, in which a living law, which is tribal law, is being practiced successfully in hundreds of tribal courts throughout the country, both at the trial and appellate level.[70] If anything, with all this myriad of cases being decided, and with the extensive legal literature on American Indian cases in the Supreme Court and federal courts, there is a dearth of analysis of this burgeoning body of law. Most descriptions of tribal law are still written from an anthropological perspective – and even the prestigious and important *American Indian Law Review* deals largely with constitutional and juridictional issues – for instance there would certainly seem to be room for the addition of a regular column dealing with key substantive issues being decided in the tribal courts.

One interesting development is the existence of a National Judicial College, situated in Nevada, where judges for the Indian courts are trained.[71] Meanwhile, most of the literature on the tribal courts deals with the structure of the courts and not so much with the specific and substantive matters that are adjudicated in them. From this perspective, Pommerheim's book is of much importance – for while it does not deal at any length with the content of cases, it provides an incisive account of the everyday work being carried out in tribal courts.

At the outset, he explains that

> the view of this book ... is more of an inside-out view from the grassroots, reservation level rather than the traditional top-down view that permeates most Indian law writing. According to this inside-out view, a pivotal ingredient in realizing tribal sovereignty within such a national pluralistic republic as the United States is the understanding and implementation of the indigenous vision that develops in its localized institutional settings. For example, in this view we should examine tribal court jurisprudence with reference to the tribal perception of its struggle to render justice and fair play within Indian country. This analysis does not ignore federal constraints but seeks rather to place them in a more limited (albeit forceful) context that achieves a better balance and equilibrium from which to view emerging tribal court development. Without this angle of vision, the field of Indian law becomes relentessly monolithic and self-referential. If tribal courts exist only to mimic the majoritarian legal system, the work of colonization and assimilation is complete. Thus, one important goal of tribal court jurisprudence is to produce a creative body of law that synthesizes the best of the dominant legal system with the legal imperatives of tribal history and culture ... In addition, emerging tribal court jurisprudence provides a valuable perspective on the meaning and use of language, the importance of narrative and story, and the meaning of justice from the indigenous point of view.[72]

Pommersheim suggests that far from the general courts providing the basis for recognition of tribal sovereignty, these courts would do well to 'pay close attention to the articulation of tribal sovereignty as it emanates from tribal court jurisprudence'.[73] He bemoans the narrowness of many analyses of tribal law and tribal courts, where the comparison with federal and state systems seems to be more important than the legal system being creatively carved out in the ongoing work of judges. He also notes the problem arising from the Indian Civil Rights Act of 1968 (ICRA), which guaranteed individual-style rights in the Indian courts, despite the communitarian nature of tribal law. Pommersheim notes the dilemma, but responds not with rejection but with a search to resolve it. He writes: 'Tribal councils and other decision makers are increasingly faced with this dilemma of individual rights. There is a need to fashion remedies in tribal courts that allow for some resolution of individual claims against the tribe, but there is also a need to balance *bona fide* tribal concern that such relief might grind tribal activity to a halt or impoverish a tribal treasury.'[74]

In fact, there is a possibility of a meaningful meeting of the liberal ethos of American philosophical jurisprudence and the communitarian basis of tribal life and customs. *En passant* it might be noted that there is an almost total lack of any reference to American-Indian tribal jurisprudence in the analyses of American liberal writers seeking to incorporate a communitarian vision into American law.[75]

Finally, inasmuch as Wilkinson's own involvement with Indian Law is his major contribution as managing editor of the latest revision of Felix Cohen's treatise on Indian Law,[76] it may be mentioned that Pommersheim, although unstinting in his praise of this work, in particular of its contribution to clarifying the issue of tribal sovereignty, nevertheless comments that 'Cohen's *Handbook* says little about civil jurisdiction, particularly in the context of tribal authority over non-Indians and says almost nothing about tribal courts. This is not surprising given tribal inactivity in these areas at the time Cohen wrote. But today this is where the action is in Indian law, and Cohen's writing is not adequate in these contexts. Therefore, those of us who write in his shadow need to bring light to these widespread areas.'[77]

Such an organized and systematic literature might have importance even outside of the United States, where other countries might derive benefit from American Indian jurisprudence, just as American jurisprudence in general has impact elsewhere in the world. For, in political and cultural terms, it is clear that there are many similarities among indigenous people separated geographically, and as they seek to coalesce in common political struggles,[78] so they may find mutual interest in their tribal 'common law'.

Nearly all of them face problems similar to those described by Vine Deloria and Clifford Lytle:

> The greatest challenge faced by the modern tribal court system is in the harmonizing of past Indian customs and traditions with the dictates of contemporary jurisprudence … . While borrowing some Anglo-American notions about the system of justice, tribal courts are struggling to preserve much of the wisdom of their past experiences … . The desired resolution of an intratribal dispute is one that

> benefits the whole Indian community ... and not one designed to chastise an individual offender. Non-Indian critics may not understand such a concept of justice, but within Indian traditions it is an accepted and expected norm.[79]

Of course, this approach is true not just within Indian traditions, but within the overall jurisprudence of tribal communities – and not just what are termed 'indigenous populations', but also other groupings, that, for the purpose of this work I have chosen to call tribal – this involves, in fact, the bulk of the population in the Pacific Islands and in Sub-Saharan Africa. When Bernard Narakobi, for instance, writes of Melanesian Jurisprudence,[80] he is giving expression to concepts, understandings, norms and values that find an echo in many other widely separated areas.

Similarly, even when dealing with large communities of several millions, their normative patterns of behavior and their customary rules (many of them considered obligatory), are characterized by principles and practices that are easily compared with the indigenous populations. Even without the claims of sovereignty, a recognized legal system may exist; even without the use of the concept, 'tribe', a judicial structure may be in place. Unlike the United States, where the substantive literature on these legal systems and judicial structures is still thin (despite official recognition of hundreds of tribal courts), in Africa (where there is a hesitancy to proclaim outright a tribal court), a fairly extensive literature has developed, setting out both the customary practices and some of the exterior influences of the common law. Like the unique *Handbook of Indian Law* by Felix Cohen, there are even attempts to set out some form of *Restatement of African Law*.[81] Included in this literature are descriptions of the structure from which the rules and the rulings emanate – the court system.

The problematics arising out of a political reality that tries to avoid over-emphasis on tribe is borne out in a fascinating analysis by Andrew Ladley, as he describes the situation in Zimbabwe, with the changing role and function of the courts, the changing legislative directives and the changing nomenclature.[82] Furthermore, he provides also a description of the social reality that underlies the legal forms.

Ladley opens his article with a description of the brief ceremony that precedes a session of a local 'village court' – with rhythmic clapping by the spectators and a chanting by the assessor (the 'magistrate-judge') to ancestral spirits asking for guidance in the upcoming deliberations and decisions. He then states that 'The simple opening ceremony in this Shona village court carries vast symbolism, restating an ancient relationship between Shona ancestors, political/judicial authority and the land. This symbolism weaves through this paper.'[83] And not just the symbolism, but the ambivalence of the Zimbabwean government, dedicated to the policy of forging national unity among the tribes (of which the Shona in the north are a majority and the Ndebele in the south the largest minority) while at the same time cognizant of the role and the power of the tribal customs. The solution initially (after independence in 1980 at the end of the armed struggle) was partly semantic, partly substantive – reducing the power of the chiefs and replacing them with local village or primary courts. In effect, there was a transference of judicial (and other) powers from the chiefs to local political and revolutionary functionaries. Ladley explains that

> By a series of Acts passed early in the 1980s, the independence government had substantially weakened the chiefs as *traditional* rural authorities. But the legislation had in fact followed and consolidated changes on the ground which had already taken place, as party and state structures of authority had displaced the chiefs … . It was oft-stated by politicians and apparently believed on the ground in the euphoria of those early years after independence, that the chiefs would fade into the African sunset. They were to be the rural keepers of *tradition* – something never defined by the politicians. It would appear there were some things that even a revolutionary government didn't want to tamper with … . In the dawn of Africa's youngest state, it seemed that Zimbabwe would build a new *nation-party-tribe*.[84]

Yet, a decade later, the Customary Law and Local Courts Bill of 1990 abolished the village courts of the earlier legislation, and restructured the customary law courts, including what Ladley calls, 'something of a chiefly reincarnation'.[85] Ladley's description is very detailed and involves also a keen understanding of the changing role and needs of women in a rapidly changing society. Ladley claims that there was a growing awareness that the new government had gone too far in its denigration of tradition – or even in its attempts to incorporate traditional symbols and rituals into its own governmental structure. There was a need 'to give back judicial power to the chiefs'.[86] However, Ladley is skeptical of this attempt to bring back the chiefs, mainly because of the many changes in customary law. 'The chiefs cannot preside over a return to the past.' Yet, at the same time 'an enduring Shona tribal framework' persists.[87]

A local newspaper in Zimbabwe reports the governmental explanation for the changes introduced. Referring to the Customary Law and Local Courts Bill, the article quotes from a speech by the Deputy Minister of Justice, Legal and Parliamentary Affairs, Senator George Chinengundu at a study seminar for new magistrates, in which reminders were given of the role of some chiefs and headmen in pre-independence days in propagating 'the interests of the then colonial masters'. The report states that 'It had been partly because of these problems that at independence the Government had found it necesssary to replace the traditional courts with community courts. However, various submissions and recommendations had over the years been made to restructure and streamline the whole system in the country.' Thus, 'The Government had decided to restore the judicial functions of chiefs and headmen, while also incorporating the community courts in the magistrate courts'.[88]

In neighbouring South Africa, similar discussions took place in connection with the ratification of the new South African Constitution. After ratification by the political leaders, its terms were subjected to scrutiny by the Constitutional Court, whose task it was to determine whether they were in accord with the principles adopted at the time of the Interim Constitution. According to newspaper reports,[89] some of its provisions were criticized by a national committee member of The Congress of Traditional Leaders of South Africa (Contralesa), who argued that the proposed Bill of Rights in the Constitution would 'inflict an irreparable harm to the entrenched cultural values of the indigenous people of South Africa. There is absolutely no role for traditional leaders at local government level'. (This reference to indigenous people embraces all of the Black people of South Africa – including the major population groups, Zulu, Xhosa, Sotho, Tswana and others, in contrast to those of European or of Asian origin, or the coloured community, and is not directly connected to the term 'indigenous people' as used in international conventions). In any event, the argument drew a sympathetic response in the course of the hearings as Justice Albie Sachs commented that the Constitution appeared to 'marginalize gratuituously' an important sector of the community.[90] People with traditional titles, such as chiefs, can obviously play a significant role in the expression of customary law – but most successfully if they act not just to preserve the customs, but also to adapt them to changing conditions, and also if they avoid using governmental support to extend their authority, and instead accept that they are no more than the instruments confirming the customs which emanate from the people.

This factor becomes even more significant given the vital role played by the people's courts that sprang up all over South Africa during the apartheid regime, in which justice was sought outside of the tainted formal court system.[91] Renewal of customary tribal law, if it is to come about in the new South Africa, must find a meaningful means of retaining this aspect of its recent past. Its experience in so doing could well serve as a model in other places.

NOTES

1. See Jerome Frank, *Law and the Modern Mind* (Garden City, NY: Doubleday, 1963); Eugen Ehrlich, *Fundamental Principles of the Sociology of Law* (Cambridge, MA: Harvard University Press, 1939); George Cohen, *Existentialism and Legal Science* (Copenhagen, 1952; Hebrew translation, Jerusalem: Sifrei Wahrman, 1966); Leon Petracycki, *Law and Morality* (Cambridge,

MA: Harvard University Press, 1955); A. Ehrenzweig, *Psychoanalytical Jurisprudence* (Dobbs Ferry, NY: Oceana, 1971).

2. The Supreme Court grants a writ of certiorari, agreeing thereby to hear a case, on an average, to only about 10 per cent of all the petitions presented to it.
3. For an interesting development in South Africa – of an attempt to maintain some of the extra-state people's framework set up during the apartheid era – see Wilfred Scharf and Daniel Nina (eds), *The Other Law: Non-state Forms of Ordering in South Africa* (to be published). The editors discuss 'Problematising the notion of law in South Africa in the context of the plurality of domains of ordering. What impact do these domains have on state law in the new democratic order?'
4. See Kenneth Davis, *Discretionary Justice: A Preliminary Inquiry* (Baton Rouge: Louisiana State University Press, 1969).
5. On courts of chancery see Anthony Babington, *The Rule of Law in Britain from the Roman Occupation to the Present Day* (Chichester: Barry Rose, 1995), at pp. 100–1.
6. See A. West *et al.*, *The French Legal System: An Introduction* (London: Fourmat Publishing, 1992).
7. In general, see A.Z. Dremezewski, *European Rights Convention in Domestic Law – A Comparative Study* (Oxford: Oxford University Press, 1983).
8. For further discussion, see below.
9. See discussion in Chapter 14, 'A Reasonable "Cultural" Defence,' below.
10. See Lord Lugard, *The Dual Mandate in British Tropical Africa* (London: Frank Cass, 1965).
11. See especially Martin Chanock, *Law, Custom and Social Order: The Colonial Experience in Malawi and Zambia* (Cambridge: Cambridge University Press, 1985).
12. Kayleen Hazlehurst, 'Australian Aboriginal Experiences of Community Justice', *Law and Anthropology* 6 (1991), p. 46.
13. Ibid., p. 47.
14. Ibid., p. 47.
15. Ibid., p. 55.
16. See George Westermark, 'Village Courts in PNG: A Comparative Perspective', *Law and Anthropology* 6 (1991), p. 67. See also the negative appraisal of these courts by Peter Fitzpatrick, *Law and State in Papua New Guinea* (London: Academic Press, 1980). He writes: 'Like "native" officials of the colonial period and local government councils, village courts provide a means for law and state to penetrate traditional social formations … people … are coming to see the village court as another variant in the succession of governmental organizations of coercion and control' (p. 144).
17. S. Richardson, 'The Courts and the Legal System', in L. Blitz (ed.), *The Politics and Administration of Nigerian Government* (London: Sweet & Maxwell, 1965), p. 185
18. D. Williams, 'The Recognition of Native Custom in Tanganyika and New Zealand – Legal Pluralism or Monoculture', in P. Sack and E. Minchis (eds), *Legal Pluralism* (Canberra: Australian Social Science Institute, 1986), p. 152.
19. A.C. Castles, *An Australian Legal History* (Sydney: Law Book Co., 1982), p. 526
20. *R. v. Jack Murrell*, (1836) 1 Legge 72.
21. See discussion of *Bonjon* case in John Hookey, 'Settlement and Sovereignty', in P. Hanks and B. Keon-Cohen (eds), *Aborigines and the Law: Essays in Memory of Elizabeth Eggleston* (Sydney: George Allen & Unwin, 1984), pp. 4-6.
22. *Ex parte Crow Dog,* 109 US 556 (1883).
23. Sidney Harring, *Crow Dog's Case: American Indian Sovereignty, Tribal Law and United States Law in the Nineteenth Century* (Cambridge: Cambridge University Press, 1994).
24. Ibid., 'Acknowledgments', p. xi.
25. Major Crimes Act, U.S. Statutes at Large. 23 (3 March 1885): 385 – now codified as 18 U.S.C. Sec. 153.
26. See, for instance, Harring's comments at p. 60: 'Beginning in the 1870s, the "lawlessness" of the Indian Territory became a national issue often debated on the floor of Congress and in the press. From that time on, a persistent effort was made – primarily by local white businessmen and western politicians – to restrict the legal sovereignty of the Indian nations, one step at a time. The legal foundation for that encroachment had been laid in John Marshall's ambiguous language in *Worcester*. So long as the Indian nations were domestic dependent nations they were subject to some measure of federal authority …'.

27. General Allotment Act, U.S. Statutes at Large 24 (8 February 1887): 388–91. The Act is also known as the Dawes Act, named after its legislative sponsor, Senator Henry Dawes, a Republican from Massachusetts. For a succinct summary of this legislation, and its consequences of dispossession of Indians, see Wilcomb Washburn, *Red Man's Land/White Man's Law: The Past and Present Status of the American Indian* (Norman: University of Oklahoma Press, 1995), Chapter 6, Part 3, 'Indian Land and its Allotment'.
28. Harring, *Crow Dog's Case*, p. 102. The reference to BIA is to the Bureau of Indian Affairs.
29. Ibid., p. 102.
30. Ibid., p. 103.
31. Ibid., p. 115.
32. Ibid., p. 132.
33. The cases are *Cherokee Nation v. Georgia*, 30 US 1 (1831): and *Worcester v. Georgia*, 31 US (6 Pet.) 515 (1832).
34. See my critique of this approach in general penological terms in *Ultimate Penalties: Capital Punishment, Life Imprisonment, Physical Torture* (Columbia: Ohio State University Press, 1987),
35. See 25 U.S.C. sec. 71. This law, actually a rider attached to an appropriation bill, stated: 'No Indian, nation or tribe within the territory of the United States shall be acknowledged or recognized as an independent nation, tribe, or power with whom the United States may contract by treaty; but no obligation of any treaty lawfully made and ratified with any such Indian or tribe prior to March, 1871, shall be hereby invalidated or impaired.' James Falkowski comments on this law and its consequences: 'Although existing treaty rights were not intended to be impaired and Indians were still supposed to be dealt with on the basis of consent, Congress began passing legislation affecting Indians without the Indians' consent. The US Supreme Court upheld such legislation based on a perversion of the trust concept. Indians were regarded as incompetent wards, and the federal government was presumed to be acting in their best interest.' James Falkowski, *Indian Law/Race Law: A Five-Hundred-Year History* (New York: Praeger, 1992), p. 111. The implication of the Court's interpretation of the law is that while the law did not automatically invalidate treaties, it provided a cover for subsequent legislation specificaly invalidating specific treaties.
36. *United States v. Kagama*, 118 US 375 (1886). In his book on the *Crow Dog* case, Harring devotes a chapter to the *Kagama* decision. See Chapter 5, 'Imposed Law and Forced Assimilation: The Legal Impact of the Major Crimes Act and the *Kagama* decision.' Harring writes of '... the Supreme Court's first statement of the plenary power doctrine, the principle that Congress's power over Indian affairs is unlimited by treaty rights or tribal sovereignty' (p. 142).
37. *Lone Wolf v. Hitchock*, 187 US 553 (1903).
38. Harring, *Crow Dog's Case*, pp. 147–8.
39. Charles Wilkinson, *American Indians, Time, and the Law: Native Societies in a Modern Constitutional Democracy* (New Haven, CT: Yale University Press, 1987).
40. The other cases are *McBratney v. United States*, 104 US 621 (1882) – linked to the *Kagama* and *Lone Wolf* cases, and dealing with grant of state jurisdiction to a crime committed on an Indian reservation in circumstances that indicated that the Major Crimes Act was not applicable; and *Worcester v. Georgia*, 31 US (6 Pet.) 515 (1832) and *Talton v. Mayes*, 163 US 376 (1896), both linked, in their judgments, to the *Crow Dog* case.
41. Wilkinson, *American Indians, Time and the Law*, p. 29.
42. *Talton v. Mayer*, held that there was no necessity for a grand jury hearing prior to a criminal case in a tribal court, since the tribal authority existed before the constitution laid down the provision of a grand jury investigation. Thus tribal authority was not traced to the US government.
43. Wilkinson, *American Indians, Time and the Law*, pp. 29–30.
44. Ibid., p. 31.
45. *Williams v. Lee*, 358 US 217 (1959).
46. Ibid., p. 223.
47. On the Termination policy – in the 1950s – aimed at assimilation of Indians into American society, see discussion, in Chapter 9, 'Belonging and Identity'. See also John Wunder, '*Retained by the People*': *A History of American Indians and the Bill of Rights* (New York: Oxford University Press, 1994), Chapter 6, 'A Cancer Within: Termination and Triumph: Surviving Federal Attempts to Liquidate Native American Culture Through Law, 1947–1967', p. 98.

48. Wilkinson, *American Indians, Time and the Law*, p. 21.
49. Ibid., p.3.
50. See in particular the chapters on religion (Chapter 13, 'Holy Rites and Sacred Sites') and land (Chapter 12, 'Land is Forever').
51. *Oliphant v. Suquamish Indian Tribe*, 435 US 191 (1978).
52. *United States v. Wheeler*, 435 US 313 (1978).
53. Wilkinson, *American Indians, Time and the Law*, pp. 61–2.
54. Ibid., p.62.
55. Ibid., p.62.
56. See Wunder, '*Retained by the People*'.
57. See Amendment 5 – the Bill of Rights.
58. See critical discussion, based on capital punishment case, in the United States: Ronald Allen and John Ratnaswamy, '*Heath v. Alabama:* A Case Study of Doctrine and Rationality in the Supreme Court', *Journal of Criminal Law and Criminology* 76 (1985), p. 823.
59. *United States v. Wheeler*, p. 323.
60. Wilkinson, *American Indians, Time and the Law*. He also writes of the Supreme Court decisions as generally being 'principled, even courageous' (p. 4), of the Court opting to honor 'old laws' rather than 'respecting the force of changed circumstances', and of cutting '... against the normal inclinations of Anglo-American judicial decision making by enforcing laws of another age in the face of compelling pragmatic arguments that tribalism is anachronistic, antiequalitarian, and unworkable in the context of contemporary American Society' (p. 5). For an opposing point of view, claiming that in recent years, the Court has undermined the power of the tribal courts, by making their authority dependent on consent of the disputants and not on inherent power, see L. Scott Gould, 'The Consent Paradigm: Tribal Sovereignty at the Millennium' *Columbia Law Review* 96 (1996), p. 809.
61. Frank Pommersheim, *Braid of Feathers: American Indian Law and Contemporary Tribal Life* (Berkeley: University of California Press, 1995).
62. Ibid., p. 49.
63. Ibid., p. 49.
64. *Iowa Mutual Ins. v. La Plante*, 480 US 9 (1987) at p. 14. See also *National Farmers Union Insurance Co. v. Crow Tribe of Indians,* 471 US 485.
65. Pommersheim, *Braid of Feathers*, p. 50.
66. *Duro v. Reina*, 495 US 676 (1990), at p. 698.
67. Pommersheim, *Braid of Feathers*, p. 55, where Pommersheim refers to Williamson's book as an 'influential work'.
68. Felix Cohen, *Handbook of Federal Indian Law* (Buffalo, CO: William S. Hein, 1980 [1942]).
69. Wilkinson, *American Indians, Time and the Law*, at p. 141; Chapter 3 is entitled 'The Elevation of Tribalism'; see especially, the subsection entitled 'The Permanency of Tribal Existence'.
70. For a good succint account of the tribal courts, within the overall tribal system, see Vine Deloria, Jr and Clifford Lytle, *American Indians, American Justice* (Austin: University of Texas Press, 1983), Chapter 5, 'The Indian Judicial System', pp. 110–38. For an example of a book devoted to describing the law itself (in its criminal law aspect), see William Newell, *Crime and Justice Among the Iroquois Nations* (Montreal: Caughnawaga Historical Society, 1986). However, the book is more anecdotal than legal.
71. Judge Tom Tso, 'The Process of Decision Making in Tribal Courts', *Arizona Law Review* 31 (1989), p. 27.
72. Pommersheim, *Braid of Feathers*, pp. 2-3.
73. Ibid., p. 190.
74. Ibid., p. 73.
75. One of the few exceptions is in the work of Aviam Soifer, who, while not writing in the idiom of many of the communitarian jurists, stresses the importance of group rights, and refers on several occasions to the Native Americans. See discussion, above, in Chapter 8 on 'The Right to Group Rights'. See A. Soifer, *Law and the Company We Keep* (Cambridge, MA: Harvard University Press, 1995).
76. See reference in Cohen, *Handbook of Federal Indian Law*, 'Preface', p. x.
77. Pommersheim, *Braid of Feathers*, p. 54.
78. See discussion in Chapter 10, 'The Local Tribe in the Global Village'.

79. Deloria and Lytle, *American Indians, American Justice*, p. 120.
80. Bernard Narakobi, *Lo Bilong Yumi Yet – Law and Custom in Melanesia* (Suva, Fiji: Melanesian Institute for Pastoral and Socio-Economic Service and University of South Pacific, 1989), Chapter 1, 'The Black Islands – Melanesia: Melanesian Jurisprudence', pp. 3–16.
81. See *Restatement of African Law*. See also *Journal of African Law*, with regular articles on customary law.
82. Andrew Ladley, 'Just Spirits? In Search of Tradition in the Customary Law Courts of Zimbabwe'. Paper presented at the International Symposium on Folk Law and Legal Pluralism, University of Ottawa, August, 1990.
83. Ibid., p. 1.
84. Ibid., p. 2 (emphasis in original – L.S.).
85. Ibid., p. 2.
86. Ibid., p.11.
87. Ibid., p.16.
88. 'Seminar Prepares Presiding Officers for Elevation', *Zimbabwe Herald*, 20 February, 1990, p. 4.
89. 'Traditional Leaders Oppose Charter', *Cape Times*, 5 July 1996, p. 7.
90. Justice Albie Sachs is a member of the South African Constitutional Court, and the author of several books and articles dealing with the political and legal aspects of the struggle against apartheid and the striving for a new South Africa (in both of which he played a prominent role).
91. See Scharf and Nina, *The Other Law*.

PART III: THE ISSUES

12

Land is Forever

The home base of tribes is in the rural area. This is where the collective consciousness is forged, where the rituals of religion and the rhythms of life are acted out, where sustenance is sought in the produce and fruits and livestock of the land and in the fish and fowl and the fauna of the surrounding environment; where a relationship is developed with nature in all its aesthetic beauty, its awesome power, its fertile capacities, and its sacred connotations; where the rules of daily living are worked out and laid down. Urban life is not conducive to the all-embracing cohesion of the tribal scene, yet paradoxically, it is often in the cities, far from home base, that expression of tribal affiliation and affinity take on renewed vigor.[1] The physical absence may arouse greater awareness and strengthening of the emotional ties, a factor which makes for continuity of tribe even in an urbanizing and heterogeneous society.

The modern world is one in which there are decreasing prospects of maintaining traditional agricultural patterns of life. In a recent book, Victor Hanson, a scholar of the Greek language, and an active farmer in California on a fifth-generation family farm, in a moving personal document, *Fields Without Dreams,*[2] bemoans the slow and tragic demise of the family farm, and recounts a crucial decade in the 1980s of failed crops, bankruptcy breakdowns and unavoidable sales to large-scale corporations. Hanson fears not for a shortage of food, but for a diminution in the social spirit of the nation. In a sense this is a re-enactment of the earlier expropriation of Indian lands. These were taken partly through political writ and military power, while Hanson writes of losses arising from climatic circumstances and resultant economic pressures. For him, the family farm, with its values, is not just a source of income, but a constant challenging interaction with the fickle and fluctuating forces of nature.

Elsewhere, in Zimbabwe, one of the greatest projects ever undertaken in Africa, the building of the Kariba dam, led not only to the forced removal of inhabitants and animals,[3] but also to personal tragedies in the deaths of about 100 building workers, most of them local inhabitants, in a constant series of work-related accidents on the site. Many tribespeople saw these deaths as being a sign of divine retribution for the interference with nature – and, at a certain stage, local tribal chiefs volunteered to offer up prayers to calm the fury of nature at the disturbances being created to the natural order because of the diversion of the river from its course and by flooding the banks, where so many people lived, where ancestors were buried, where memories were kept alive.

Land is at the heart of much of the strife between European-based political and commercial interests and Aborigine groups. Attitudes toward it are often at opposite extremes. Nevertheless it behoves all to attempt to understand the crux of the problem – land is more than a measured plot on which to grow a crop or dig for minerals or build a home or a town; it is an integral part of the life of a community. It is in this aspect that many of the initial misunderstandings and friction arose between settlers and indigenous peoples. The struggles over sovereignty and political authority (as discussed in an earlier chapter)[4] were only the external manifestations of a no less critical issue with deep human, religious and social dimensions. In many respects, the real issue was not who controls the territory, but how to look after the land. Thus, in many of the original treaties signed, a willingness was expressed to concede some degree of political authority without the concomitant forfeiture of the land; although, in the long run, the land too was often taken.[5]

The start of colonial expansion took place when the ideological ideas of John Locke in England were in vogue, stressing the absolute importance of private property for the overall well-being of society.[6] Thus, for many years the right to participate in the political arena was made contingent on ownership of landed property.[7] In contrast, most indigenous groups claimed the land to be communal (or at least that ultimate authority as to the land resided in the tribe, whatever the manner in which the land might be used and allocated) as a fundamental expression of tribal unity and cohesion, and as an integral aspect of their close communion with the surrounding environment, linked to religious views as to the beneficence of nature and, no less, its occasional wrath.[8] Whereas Western religions set aside special places for worship and designate certain sites for commemorative purposes, in most tribal thought the social and the sacred, the human and the divine, are closely interrelated. The earth is not given to be ruled over, nature is not there to be conquered, but to be respected – not to be exploited to the hilt, but to be preserved to the utmost. There is an extensive literature of quotations taken from statements and speeches made by chiefs and other representatives of tribes in their confrontations with settler populations, in which the sum of their protestations is an expression of the yawning chasm that separates the different perceptions as to land, nature and the environment.

For some, these expressions are, from a social point of view, an example of primitive communism, with the land being owned collectively, a fact to be either welcomed or denigrated, depending partly on one's ideological stance toward modern Marxism.[9] For others, from an ecological point of view, these expressions are an example of an intrinsic and ancient understanding of interrelationship that was often lacking in the modern era until environmental dangers brought it to the forefront of awareness in the past few decades. Earlier ecological thinkers, such as the Americans Henry Thoreau, in the nineteenth century,[10] and Aldo Leopold, in the first part of the twentieth century,[11] were in their time only marginal voices, only recently being given a wider audience with today's wisdom of hindsight.[12] Many of these dilemmas were crystallized in the seminal article in 1962 by Garrett Hardin on 'The Tragedy of the Commons',[13] the dilemmas and the problems that were spawned in the western world as land held in common was divided up and parceled out for individual use.[14]

The intrinsic awareness of tribal communities to factors only now being placed at the forefront of modern concern and scientific research, found many expressions. In a book dealing with 'The Shocking Story of the World's Endangered Wildlife',[15] Lewis Regenstein quotes from a well-known letter sent by Chief Sealth of the Duwanish Tribe in the State of Washington to President Pierce:

> How can you buy or sell the sky – the warmth of the land? The idea is strange to us. Yet we do not own the freshness of the air or the sparkle of the water. How can you buy them from us? Every part of this earth is sacred to my people. Every shining pine needle, every sandy shore, every mist in the dark woods, every clearing and humming insect is holy in the memory and experience of my people. If I decide to accept your offer to buy our land, I will make one condition. The white man must treat the beasts of this land as his brothers. I am a savage and do not understand any other way. I have seen a thousand rotting buffaloes on the prairies left by the white man who shot them from a passing train. What is man without the beasts? If all the beasts were gone, men would die from great loneliness of the spirit, for whatever happens to the beast also happens to man.
>
> All things are connected. Whatever befalls the earth, befalls the sons of the earth. One thing we know – our God is the same. This earth is precious to Him. Even the white man cannot be exempt from this common destiny.[16]

To these words, Regenstein comments:

> In retrospect, Chief Sealth's words were remarkably insightful. It soon became apparent that no animal, no matter how powerful or abundant, was safe from the white man's destructiveness. The 'winning of the west' involved the destruction of the buffalo, which was so abundant as to be considered inexhaustible.[17]

Regenstein then draws a parallel between what happened a hundred years ago to the buffalo (and other species), with the ecological dangers and potential disasters facing the world today.

I refer to animals, although this chapter deals – in its title – with land, because the issue of land cannot be discussed within a limited one-dimensional framework, but must be seen in its total context. From this perspective, land involves the overall environment; the rivers that flow through it, the minerals beneath it, the forest and mountains upon it, the animals who share it with the people who 'own' it. Only with this understanding can there be a meaningful discussion of the legal position as to land in the tribal setting. Thus, in dealing with land, we must examine also traditional hunting and fishing rights, ongoing protection of sites characterized by the beauty of soaring peaks or the abundance of underground minerals, the free flow of water in rivers and the freshness of air unblemished by pollutants, and the continued existence of age-old forests and wetlands, unaffected by gross human intervention.

Further, it should be noted that many of the cases dealing with questions of property – typical issues of Private Law – are interrelated with larger public law questions of political sovereignty and authority. There are thus clear implications for some of the cases discussed in Chapter 6 ('The Invention of Discovery') for some of the issues that will be dealt with in this chapter. In addition, however different the approaches to property are of customary tribal law and modern state law, there can be no denying the impact that years of contact have had on each system, or how the impact of economic factors may impinge on perceptions of land, and the rules attached to it. In fact, as the pecuniary value of land increases (because of the discovery, for instance, of minerals), so its non-material values may diminish. Alternatively, outside intervention may be a catalyst for reviving forgotten basic concepts. Thus, on the one hand, Peter Sack explains, in regard to the situation in Papua New Guinea, that the formal native land laws are now probably basically the same as in pre-contact days; the attitude towards land, however, is changing and this in turn alters the social application of the formal laws.[18] He writes:

> land is becoming an economic asset, whereas it was rarely, if ever, seen as such before the Europeans came. But being recognized as an economic asset reduces the importance of land in other aspects. Land as one of many economic assets begins to lose its unique position as the direct basis of each individual's life … land ceases to be regarded as living space and turns into property …[19]

On the other hand, it was paradoxically specifically the increase in land values that in some cases led to a reappraisal of the role of land as an integral part of tribal life. Of particular interest is the fact that impending intervention by powerful economic interests may have led to a reassessment of attitudes. What had been countenanced when done by companies working within the framework of the country itself, or even a colonial power, could become problematic when multinational companies, lacking clear identity, became involved. This has been most noteworthy in Australia, where there has been an ongoing four-pronged struggle involving federal government, state government, commercial interests and Aborigine tribes, with a tendency on occasion for the federal government to throw in its lot with the Aborigines, often at the cost of rejecting tempting commercial offers or sometimes even reneging on agreements, and at the risk of incurring the wrath of dominant figures on the world economic scene, with their threats of severing all future ties with Australia.

Writing a few years after Sack and referring to a governmental document (the Woodward Report),[20] C.D. Rowley explains that the report (favorable to Aborigines):

> represents the slowly rising swell of public opinion against the primacy of profits in the formation of government policies and against the colonial-style image of Australian policy-makers in relation to the great overseas interests anxious to make money from Australian resources. The great British landed companies, some of which as absentee owners had been holding for generations many of the cattle stations where Aborigines lived in a squalid peonage, were giving way to the still greater multi-national mining companies, especially anxious to exploit the minerals and get out before they had colonial style problems to deal with … . The minerals lay mainly just where traditional land rights were still paramount in the minds of the Aborigines … and still meaningful.[21]

In fact, on a number of occasions since then the federal government (which still has partial control over the Northern Territory, which does not have statehood) has acceded to demands of Aborigine groups and rejected attractive offers, even in some cases, after heavy initial preliminary investments – in pilot studies, for instance – had been made by the mining companies.

A government report in May 1991, is indicative of changing attitudes, when a Judicial Resource Assessment Commission gave strong support to claims by Aborigine groups (as well as environmental groups), as against mining interests.[22] The Report, submitted by Justice Donald Stewart, stressed the need for maximum consideration of claims by the Aborigines despite even some uncertainty on the part of a few senior members of the Jawoyn tribe as to whether or not the site in question, Coronation Hill, possessed special significance. The Commission had no hesitation in determining that the site was part of the traditional territory of the tribe (over which there had been some dispute, with arguments that only recently had the tribe claimed the site) and that it embodied part of a powerful force which, if disturbed, could lead to a variety of detrimental effects. Furthermore, the Commission gave due regard to the attempts to affect reconciliation with the Aborigine people by giving unequivocal indication of its understanding of and respect for the religion and culture of the Aborigine people. It should be noted that this report was tabled before the final decision in the *Mabo* case[23] – in fact at a stage where the *Mabo* litigation in lower courts was unfavorable to the Aborigine petitioners; it may thus very well be seen as a harbinger of that benchmark decision, and possibly as a catalytic agent in contributing to it.[24] There can also be little doubt that the Commission was not only acting as a path-breaker, but was actually reflecting changes – in public opinion, in academic research, in political understanding – both in Australia itself and elsewhere.

Some of the most interesting developments in terms of the specific background of the Common law have come from a group of Canadian jurists, and it is very possible that some special aspects of the Canadian experience – in contrast to other countries – have facilitated the development of these interesting theoretical presentations. However, while most assert the rights of tribal groups to right of ownership and unfettered usage (for instance for the purposes of fishing and hunting, despite restrictions laid down by state law), their reasoning is varied, and indicative, as much as their shared critique of judicial decisions and policy-making, of the complexity of the land issue.

As is succinctly expressed in the title of his book, *Common Law Aboriginal Title,* Kent McNeil argues cogently that a proper perception of the historical foundations of the Common Law and a precise application of its rules in regard to ownership lead to an inexorable logical conclusion that most of the lands in tribal possession are also under tribal ownership.[25] Drawing on the work of two of his compatriots, Brian Slattery and Geoffrey Lester,[26] while yet developing his own perspective, McNeil claims that there is a parallel between the manner in which the British Crown took control of all the lands in England, without depriving the owners of their ownership, and the manner in which the British took control in what is now Canada. He explains that 'The doctrine of common law aboriginal title is based on the presumptions arising in English Law from occupation of land. A person in factual occupation is first of all presumed to have possession. From this conclusion of law other consequences follow …'[27] which by the logic of historical precedent in England indicate that, absent proof to the contrary (for instance that the possession is wrongful), 'An occupier of land is … presumed to have … a valid title as well.'[28]

This is a conclusion that McNeil reaches after considering the legal consequences for the land of the indigenous population, occasioned by the British acquisition of the total territory which allowed for two conflicting opinions. 'On the one hand, there is said to be a presumption that in the absence of express confiscation or expropriatory legislation, those rights would continue after the change in sovereignty. On the other hand, it is said that only such rights as the Crown deigned to recognize would be enforceable under the new regime.'[29] The first approach, termed the 'doctrine of continuity' by Slattery,[30] is the one which McNeil claims is the historically correct one, whereas the second approach, known as the 'recognition doctrine' is in error 'having arisen from unfortunate misinterpretation of a few isolated decisions'.[31]

The argument, then, despite the various complexities of the law of property, is really quite simple. When the Crown used its prerogative power to acquire new territory, it could also, if it so wished, seize land and declare it to be public property. However, where there was no such specific takeover of property, it would remain in the hands of the current owners. This was the situation in England, and, according to McNeil, is the position for most of the land of the indigenous people of Canada.

In his analysis McNeil bemoans the fact that too often,

> When questions involving indigenous land rights began to come before the courts, the tendency was to look for answers outside the English law. Chief Justice Marshall's early American decisions in particular ignored common law principles and constructed a vague theory of Indian title on the basis of doubtful premises drawn to some extent from his own perceptions of international law. In effect, what Marshall did was invent a body of law which was virtually without precedent.[32]

McNeil notes the confusion in defining aboriginal title, and the contrasting approaches adopted in different countries and suggests that his book 'proposes a return to fundamental common law principles as a way out of this muddle. If applied in this context, these principles are capable of providing a comprehensive legal solution to what has long been an intractable problem.'[33] At the same time, McNeil also recognizes the import of the customary law attitude to land ownership – that is, common-law principles allow for recognition of customary law rules.

The implications of this approach is that the differences between the concepts of ownership in English law and aboriginal rules are irrelevant – whatever the nature of aboriginal ownership, as long as there was clear proof of occupancy, the English law would recognize this as ownership. Specific aspects of the possession – that it was communal, that there was no deeds registry, that the boundaries were not always clearly demarcated – were all irrelevant for the purpose of the legal determination of ownership.

Indeed, one could well add to McNeil's thesis that any lack of certainty as to these additional factors could well be attributed to the omission of the British. After all, part of the legal basis of land in England was delineated, shortly after the Norman Conquest, when a precise accounting of land possession (and other factors) was enumerated by agents of the conquering Normans in the Domesday Book.[34] No such similar process was ever undertaken in North America (or other areas under British authority), partly perhaps because the necessary control was not established. Their hold over the enormous land mass of the subcontinent was far less noticeable than the firm grip that the first Norman kings exerted over the border areas of the island realm they had conquered.[35]

A further factor, of major import, in the Canadian situation was the Royal Proclamation of 1763.[36] Unlike the treaties signed elsewhere – in Africa, New Zealand, other parts of North America – a key aspect of the Canadian situation was this unilateral Proclamation. Because of its indebtedness to some of the tribes in the struggle against the French (just recently defeated),[37] and because of threats against them by hostile tribes, the British made an official statement – presumably having legal implications as an Order-in-Council[38] – which, in its preamble stated that:

> Whereas it was just and reasonable, and essential to our interest, and the security of our colonies, that the several Nations or tribes of Indians with whom we are connected, and who live under our protection, should not be molested or disturbed in the possession of such parts of our Dominion and Territories as, not having been ceded to or purchased by us, are reserved to them or any of them as their hunting grounds.

While McNeil downplays the importance of the Proclamation, for legal reasons, relating to 'the fundamental rule of British colonial law that apart from statute the Crown has no legislative authority in settled colonies,'[39] Richard Bartlett, in sharp contrast, claims that:

> The Royal Proclamation of 1763 is the most significant point of origin of the policy of protection, which demanded that only the Crown could acquire traditional aboriginal lands, and only upon the consent of the aboriginal peoples. It is the foundation of the policy of entering into treaties and agreements with the aboriginal peoples with respect to their traditional lands.[40]

Bruce Clark also holds that the Proclamation is a key factor in the constitutional structure of Canada, and that the powers given to the colonial government – in that Proclamation and other legal enactments, such as the Colonial Laws Validity Act – were all subject to its protective provisions.[41] This he clarifies at the outset of his book:

> Native liberty and crown sovereignty complement each other in Canada. Faced with numerous and warlike tribes, and not being entirely impervious to sentiment of natural justice, the imperial government of Great Britain in the eighteenth century recognized the liberty of the indigenous people not to be molested or disturbed on their unceded territories. This liberty received constitutional protection throughout British North America. The imperial government claimed overall sovereignty. Pursuant to that sovereignty it constituted the power of the colonial governments. The powers delegated by the imperial government to these colonial governments were made to accommodate the previously recognized liberty of the natives. This constitutional pattern was never abrogated and thus, under the umbrella of crown sovereignty, it continues to describe a constitutional status in Canada.[42]

Clark makes no reference to McNeil's book which was published a year before, although he does have two bibliographical references to earlier works by McNeil,[43] but the very problematics of the Canadian legal and constitutional situation may be noted in their totally contradictory approaches to the Proclamation. Thus, McNeil even argues that while the Crown may indeed have intended to lay down the law, there is no legal validity to its legislative-style acts, including the Royal Proclamation. In his words, 'It can make no difference that the Crown may have purported to legislate for such colonies (even if the practice remained unquestioned for many years), for without the assistance of Parliament or a local assembly, its legislative acts would simply be void.'[44] However, these comments are made in the process of arguing that the Proclamation could not have limited or modified, in any way, the existing title, whether by virtue of common law title or title of their own customary law. The argument, then, is made in a critique of an early leading case of the Privy Council, *St Catherine's Milling Company v. The Queen*,[45] from 1888, in which Lord Watson held that the Proclamation shows 'that the tenure of the Indians was a personal and usufructuary right, dependent upon the good will of the Sovereign'.[46] In fact, this decision is probably incorrect, but for reasons different from those set out by McNeil.

These contrasting views as to the Proclamation are almost symbolic of the confused state of the legal situation in Canada (with some of the more recent decisions lacking a clear majority in a divided court).[47] It is not my intention to resolve these dilemmas or even to document them fully, but a number of key points should be noted:

(a) I am discussing the Canadian situation in this chapter, and not in the earlier chapter on sovereignty and political authority[48] because it seems to me that the issues in most of the Canadian litigation relate to land rights and not political rights (here it must be noted that

Clark's contention, from his perspective, is that the real legal situation in Canada, which he acknowledges is ignored by most people – judges, politicians, academicians, and even the Indians themselves – is actually of a constituted constitutional right to self-government).[49] As for the fact that *Mabo* in Australia (discussed in the earlier chapter) is also mainly a land issue, it must be remembered that the judgment is an unequivocal rejection of the politically based legal doctrine of *terra nullius.*

(b) The Proclamation echoes sentiments that had been often expressed in other, similar contexts, but without the same official imprimatur. For instance, the written instructions given to Captain Cook as to his actions in Australia, contained a similar directive as to the manner in which he was to deal with the indigenous inhabitants, though such a directive seems to lack legal force (though an argument of this nature, claiming that by ignoring the Aborigines, he was violating his mandate, has been made – unsuccessfully – in an Australian court).[50]

(c) There seems to be no reason why the views of McNeil and Clark should not be seen as complementary. I have presented them here as being in contradiction, because both deal solely with the particular aspect that they are stressing. However, it may well be argued that the Proclamation (if it does indeed have legal validity) and the common law (if it is indeed relevant in the Canadian situation relative to aboriginal rights) enhance each other. (Indeed, a recent article by Scott Gould suggests an additional factor that is becoming increasingly relevant, namely 'the rise of sovereignty based on consent').[51] The unequivocal statement of the Proclamation (shorn of the dubious restrictions of the 1888 Privy Council case) allows for a full recognition of all those common law rights set out so convincingly by McNeil. For instance, Slattery, on whom McNeil places great reliance, includes the Royal Proclamation (along with the common law and later legislation) among the factors making for indigenous rights.[52] McNeil, in his introduction, notes that 'he … will not deal with this aspect' in his book.[53] But for Slattery the two factors are closely aligned. He writes, 'The Royal Proclamation has a profound significance for modern Canada. Under its terms aboriginal peoples hold continuing rights to their lands except where these rights have been extinguished by voluntary cession.'[54] He then adds 'The same position has been held to obtain in common law.'[55]

(d) As for the situation before 1763, the year both of the Proclamation and of the cession of extensive territory by the French, McNeil and Slattery take totally different approaches. Whereas McNeil claims that 'Since we do not know what real property rights, if any, the Indians had under French Law, we are not in a position to evaluate the impact of the Proclamation in that context',[56] Slattery asserts contrariwise that under the French rule, the Indians had retained full authority over their lands. Slattery writes that when France ceded its territories to Britain, it '... could not give Great Britain what it did not possess, namely authority over the native groups inhabiting the ceded territories. These nations were in many cases trading partners of the French and sometimes military allies. If they were not prepared to accept direct French authority, neither were they willing to accept that France might deposit them in the pocket of the English King.'[57] From this perspective, the Proclamation and the common law lead to the same conclusion.

(e) Given the constitutional crisis confronting Canada in recent years – from the failure to ratify the Meech Lake Accords in the 1980s, after the executive leaders of the Federal government and all state governments had reached agreement on its terms, dealing with the multicultural nature of the country, to the narrow vote on the future of Quebec in 1995 – it is of prime importance that, in the thrust-and-parry of the ongoing debate, seeking to redefine the nature of Canadian nationhood, the clear voice of the tribal groups is heard – and that their claims are made from a firm and recognized legal basis. Clark, for instance, believes that prior acceptance of incorrect legal positions may harm the aboriginal cause. Treaty negotiations must be based on the full rights vouchsafed specifically by the Proclamation and guaranteed implicitly by the common law. Furthermore, it must be noted that reservations in applying the Canadian Charter of Rights and Freedoms are relevant only for actions of the Federal and State governments; but that the guarantee of aboriginal rights is not similarly restricted.[58]

(f) In assessing the meaning of the Proclamation, its original wording, including some ignored phrases, must be constantly reiterated, and its subsequent history (not just controversial judgments) borne in mind. As for the former aspect, the Proclamation relates unabashedly to some of the lamentable factors which served as a background and a motivating force for its promulgation:

> And whereas great Frauds and Abuses have been committed in purchasing Lands of the Indians to the great prejudice of our interests and to the great dissatisfaction of the said Indians; in order therefore to prevent such irregularities for the future, and to the end that the Indians may be convinced of our justice and determined resolution to remove all reasonable cause of discontent, we do, with the advice of our Privy Council ...[59]

prohibit sales to private persons and allow only official purchases provided they are done with the consent of the Indians.[60] It should also be noted that the reference to the Privy Council certainly gives the Proclamation the effect of a statutory instrument, since orders-in-council pertaining to colonial territories, were an accepted form of legislation, without the need for a full Parliamentary vote.

(g) As for the second aspect – the Proclamation's subsequent history – specific reference to the Proclamation is made in section 25 of the Constitution Act of 1982, which spells out that there shall be no abrogation or derogation of any 'rights or freedoms that pertain to the aboriginal peoples of Canada including: (a) any rights or freedoms that have been recognized by the Royal Proclamation of 7 October 1763 …'.[61] On this basis, McNeil's denigration of the Proclamation seems to be an unnecessary diversion, devoid of empirical validity or logical force. His arguments on behalf of the impact of common law can stand on their own, without the gratuitous downgrading of the Proclamation, especially when it is remembered how much extra-legal factors, such as the Magna Carta from the thirteenth century, or the prerogative courts fashioning out the principles of equity, or writings of leading jurists in different ages, contributed to the total accumulation of rules that constitute the common law.

(h) Finally, it might be noted that the impact of all these recent attempts by Canadian writers (whatever the differences between them) to create a new jurisprudential ethos within the undoubted change in general attitudes, has found a responsive echo in a recent 1995 decision, *Apsassin v. Canada,* which, building also on earlier cases, clarified that a fiduciary duty that the Crown has to safeguard the interests of the indigenous populations must also be seen, according to circumstances, as a clear directive for a positive obligation to act on their behalf.[62]

In so many respects, the whole point of the common law, and its real beauty, lies in its flexibility, its responsiveness to changing reality, its commitment to social justice. It seems almost self-defeating to deny the value of a document whose validity is recognized and whose importance is acknowledged by others in the very process of arguing for the relevance of the common law in determining property rights. In particular the reference in the Proclamation specifically to subsidiary rights linked to the land (for instance, the reference to hunting rights) has a special relevance, since so much of the clash over land rights has also to do with the uses to which it is being put. Land used for hunting requires far more space than land used for settled agriculture, and this specific factor was even noted, to the detriment of the indigenous people, in some of the legal debate as to rights over land. Thus John Hookey, in a carefully constructed argument, draws attention to the thesis of Vattel, as used in an early Australian case by Justice

Willis.[63] 'While "nomadic hunters, fishers and food-gatherers" were entitled to a fair store of land, certain factors had to be taken into account when the different civilizations came into contact and clashed over an allocation of limited resources in land.'[64] Thus, in attempting to share what was available, consideration must be given, by judicial reasoning, to the fact that:

> those who pursue an erratic life, and live by hunting rather than cultivate their lands, usurp more extensive territories than with a reasonable share of labour they would have occasion for, and have, therefore, no reason to complain if other nations, more industrious, and too closely confined, come to take possession of a part of those lands.[65]

Indirect affirmation of such a process, with its consequences is also provided in a brief description by Chief Justice Marshall in the leading case of *Johnson v. McIntosh:* 'As the White population advanced, that of the Indians necessarily receded. The country in the immediate neighbourhood of agriculturists became unfit for them. The game fled into thicker and more unbroken forests, and the Indians followed. The soil ... being no longer occupied by its ancient inhabitants, was parcelled out ...'.[66] All this, of course, is a modern re-enactment of the earliest clash, related in Biblical times between nomadic Cain and sedentary Abel, or between the roving hunter Esau and the home-linked Jacob.[67]

In any event, the struggle over land has several dimensions. In a joint article, two jurists, an Australian and a Canadian, Bryan Keon-Cohen and Bradford Morse, note that 'within the phrase "land rights", there are two different, yet related concepts: "rights to land" and "aboriginal rights". While the former deals with "proprietary interests in land",'[68] the second concept of aboriginal rights 'is generally used in a wider sense. It includes property rights in land, but also encompasses rights of usage (for example, hunting, fishing, trapping and gathering rights)'[69] (as well as the larger rights of language, culture and politics, and redress for past inequities). It is to the specific rights of usage that we must now turn.

In respect of most of these aspects, recent years have given rise to an overlap between indigenous rights and environmental rights – sometimes the two are compatible, for instance when the argument is made that transformation of the environment, such as building of dams or diversion of water, will infringe on traditional fishing or hunting areas,[70] sometimes in conflict, for instance when regulatory restrictions based on conservation principles affect the rights of Aborigines to engage in some of their traditional practices. One widely covered example is the clubbing of cub seals in Alaska by indigenous groups, strongly condemned by environmentalists and animal activists. In a larger context Harriet Ketley warns that the 'maintenance of biodiversity (the variety of species and their ecosystem), and cultural diversity (in the context of the Aboriginal hunting and gathering) form potential points of conflict'.[71] In other instances though, there is a broad understanding to allow for exceptions for tribal people. A typical recent example is the Canadian case of *Sparrow v. R.*[72] When legislation placed restrictions on the right to hunt, Sparrow claimed that as a member of a tribe, these restrictions were not applicable to him. The court accepted the argument and acquitted him of the regulatory crime (normally a strict liability crime for which very rarely are exceptions made).

Richard Bartlett[73] discusses three recent agreements in Canada entered into between aboriginal groups and governmental authorities, intent on setting up hydroelectric schemes and other irrigation programs, which would affect the water supply available to aboriginal groups in the vicinity. He argues that earlier agreements were detrimental to aboriginal interests, but that a 1985 Agreement provides a better model with a much more effective aboriginal role in the administration of water resources. For both Canada and the United States, he stresses that aboriginal water rights are derived from different origins from those of non-aboriginal persons. He warns against costly and protracted litigation and favors negotiation in which the aboriginal people are enabled to safeguard their interests.

Similarly, it should be noted that in New Zealand the first case of the newly constituted Waitangi Tribunal (to determine Maori rights in terms of land) dealt with 'a matter relating to fishing rights in the Waitemata Harbor'.[74]

However, no less significant than any specific legal victories is a sea-change in perceptions, articulated by Harvey Feit, who writes of the

> revolution in anthropological thought of the last decade brought about by the 'discovery' that the productive activities of hunting and gathering peoples are relatively reliable, abundant and efficient [which] has stimulated the re-examination of a series of anthropological models and explanations. Among the most important areas of revision are the anthropological models of how hunting and gathering societies change and undergo transformation.[75]

He notes the need, and a discernible trend, not to eliminate their way of life and their form of production – which might result in them ending up as anything from slum dwellers to welfare recipients (and not just farmers or skilled laborers) – but a 'transformation of hunting societies into new and potentially viable forms of hunting societies with diverse productive organizations, consumer goods, complex imported productive technologies and extensive state intervention and relationships. In these societies hunting and/or gathering is no longer the sole productive activity, but hunting and/or gathering still is significant economically, and it is often the key productive activity ...'.[76] Feit argues that their traditional way of life is not doomed, nor are they passive in the face of external changes, but they have striven to 'retain their ties to the natural environment, their subsistence production, their society and community, their languages, and their belief systems'.[77]

These factors cannot be limited to academic discussion, but must be recognized by political and judicial bodies. In fact, some land courts (and also the Waitangi Tribunal in New Zealand) have given indication of their cognizance of the special nature of tribal life and of a growing recognition of the need to bring special considerations to bear in examining aboriginal claims. Graeme Neate has provided a detailed description of this kind of work in the Northern Territory of Australia,[78] based on the Federal Law – Aboriginal Land Rights (Northern Territory Act) of 1976.[79] This law stems from an earlier governmental commission headed by Justice Woodward,[80] which recommended that the aims of recognition of land rights be linked to a series of principles, ranging from the doing of simple justice on behalf of people who had been deprived of their rights and the promotion of social harmony and stability, through the immediate practical considerations of providing land to people who were economically depressed, and the larger pragmatic concern of Australia's standing in the world community, to the preservation, where possible, of the spiritual link with the land, and the maintenance of full consultation with the tribal people whose fate was being decided.

Neate[81] refers to a case in which the court[82] quotes extensively from the work of a leading anthropologist, Stanner, in order to grasp the nature of the special relationship to the land.[83] Stanner had written of the difficulties of both understanding and articulating the aboriginal approach to land:

> No English words are good enough to give a sense of the links between an Aboriginal group and its homeland. Our word 'home', warm and suggestive though it be, does not match the aboriginal word that may mean 'camp', 'hearth', 'country', 'everlasting home', 'totem place', 'life source', 'spirit centre', and much else all in one. Our word 'land' is far too sparse and meagre. We can now scarcely use it, except with economic overtones ... . The Aborigines would speak of 'earth' and used the word in a richly symbolic way to mean his 'shoulder' or his 'side'. I have seen an Aborigine embrace the earth he walked on. To put our words 'home' and 'land' together into 'homeland' is a little better but not much. A different tradition leaves us tongueless and earless toward this other world of meaning and significance. When we took what we call 'land' we took what to them meant hearth, home, the source of life, and everlastingness of spirit. At the same time it left each local band bereft of an essential constant

> that made their plan and code of living intelligible. Particular pieces of territory, each a homeland, formed part of a set of constants without which no affiliation of any person to any other person, no link in the whole network of relationships, no part of the complex structure of social groups, any longer had all its co-ordinates.[84]

Since biblical tradition is so strong in much of the western world, it might be noted that there is a strong philological connection between the Hebrew word for a person – 'Adam',[85] and the word for land – 'Adamah', as well as the word for blood – 'dam'. Among the Aborigines of Australia, the relationship with the land finds further special expression in the mystical idea of the Dreaming, which is also to be found in many of its cultural manifestations – the unique form of Aborigine art and much of its storytelling.[86]

Moreover, the full measure of the attachment to the land is often found in more down-to-earth practical ways. This has been the case in a number of countries where legislation transforming the practice of landholding and aimed at furthering modern agriculture or even at advancing political or ideological conceptions, is ignored by the peasants to whom it is mainly addressed. This is particularly true in countries with minimum European settlement, such as in a number of African countries. The situation in the Cameroon has been well documented, and is probably symptomatic of other countries with similar laws and similar social reality.

In 1974 a land act was passed nationalizing the land and thereby implicitly putting an end to the traditional system of landholding.[87] However, in more than two decades since then, little progress has been made in implementing the law because of bureaucratic procrastination and a reluctance on the part of the farming population to carry out the formalities of registration. It is estimated that very little of the land has been officially and properly registered as part of national ownership. In a perceptive study of the situation, C.N. Nagwasari has explained that, while the land might have been nationalized from a legal point of view with the promulgation of the act, factually the indigenous form of land tenure has not ceased to exist.[88] Nagwasari affirms the approach of E. LeRoy that 'state attempts to monopolize the proprietorship of land in Africa is largely attributable to the importation of European property concepts into the continent during the "colonial" era. However, it is African governments that have pushed these concepts to unconscionable extremes.'[89]

The present position, according to Nagwasari, is that while the law did not abolish indigenous tenure, it nevertheless greatly reduced the value of indigenous land rights,[90] converting the farmers into tenants at sufferance with regard to their surviving land rights because the state can eject them whenever it wants.[91]

Similar problems have arisen in many other areas of Africa, to a large extent because of European-based economic systems and ideologies, both capitalist (individual-oriented with the emphasis on private ownership) and communist (collective-oriented, but with the emphasis not on tribal communities, but on nationalization). In many instances, left-oriented politicians have even failed to appreciate the nature of the communal basis toward land in traditional tribal societies, something which radical thinkers could well have welcomed. Certainly, much socialist and anarchist writing, from Robert Owen[92] and Charles Fourier[93] in the former instance, to Pytor Kropotkin in the latter,[94] fits in well with many tribal concepts as to land ownership.

Even in the United States, for all its problematic relationships with the native Americans, the communal basis of land has been recognized, a factor that is often crucial in terms of claims of compensation for past expropriations, or even for sharing in some of the new-found sources of wealth. In fact, the United States had, at one stage, attempted to destroy the communal basis of land in a legislative attempt to eradicate the very basis of tribal life by a new, individual allotment of land. Initially the Northwest Ordinance, promulgated in 1787, to be ratified two years later by the first Congress, declared that 'The utmost good faith shall always be observed towards Indians; their land and property shall never be taken from them without their consent.'[95] Such statements, or later some protective judicial results, failed to prevent the population transfers of the 1830s and 1840s,[96] until in 1887 the Dawes Act – the General Allotment Act[97] – provided for the abolition of communal land and its allocation on an individual basis to Indians, with any surplus land being made available to Whites, whose presence, together with their individualistic way of life and modern agricultural practices were to be further, direct influences in undermining, or destroying, any residual tribal feelings.

By the time the allotment system was abolished almost a half-century later,[98] the lands under Indian control had diminished considerably, the economic situation of many of the people had worsened, particularly for those whose allotment was in areas of limited agricultural potential, and the social basis of tribal life had been severely damaged. By this time, in fact, the overall situation of the Indians was so bad, having been magnified by the economic depression, that a law was passed, The Indian Reorganization Act,[99] the aim of which was '... to rehabilitate the Indian's economic life and to give him a chance to develop the initiative destroyed by a century of oppression and paternalism'.[100] By this legislation, it was possible to redress some of the injustice by redeeming some of the land and reconstituting the tribal framework, but this could only partially alleviate the accumulated harm.

Similar processes are now under way in various parts of Africa, particularly in southern Africa, the last region to be divested of the vestiges of colonialism or of racist concepts (for instance Zimbabwe, independent only in the early 1980s after more than a decade of illegal white settler rule, Namibia, and most particularly post-apartheid South Africa). In all these countries the land question is a crucial one as the residual effects of past policies linger on. As changes in the law are made to redress some of the past injustices, an interesting development in neighboring Botswana should be noticed. Formerly a British Protectorate, with a certain degree of autonomy which assured it of some immunity from the more pernicious aspects of Colonial rule, its experience clarifies, and even accentuates, some of the problematics associated with ownership rights in land and the clash between individual and collective concepts of landholding, as well as the relevance of the norms of customary law *vis-à-vis* the rules – and the rulings – of state law and judicial judgments.

In 1992, the Botswana Court of Appeal handed down a decision which gave precedence to private ownership over tribal ownership, based in part on the Court's understanding of the changing nature of customary law.[101] At issue was the sale of land on an individual basis by a tribesperson who had inherited the land under tribal law from his father. The Land Board in that region applied to the Court for a restraining order against the individual holding, on the basis that the Tribal Land Act provided for the vesting of tribal land in the Land Board, 'in trust for the benefit and advantage of the tribesmen of that area and for the purpose of promoting the economic and social development of all the peoples of Botswana'.[102] The court of first instance upheld the sale, a decision that in a two-to-one verdict, was upheld on appeal, since 'whatever the customary law might have been in the past … the law had apparently developed to permit of private ownership by tribesmen of tribal lands'.[103] A basic factor in the reasoning of the Court was that customary law was not static and so earlier decisions (including those of the Privy Council) indicating the communal nature of tribal land, could be disregarded. However, the Court also rejected the contentions of the two assessors that had sat with the solitary judge at the trial stage as advisors on tribal customs. In the Court's view the judge was under no obligation to abide by their advice, since their status on the bench was purely advisory.

The dissenting justice in the Court of Appeal relied on academic research and the official Reports of Government commissions, as well as the aforementioned opinions of the two assessors, to argue that customary law could not be ignored since not only had the land been inherited by tribal custom, but the transfer itself had been carried out 'by way of customary rights', and the parties had sought a certificate of grant 'of customary land rights' from the Land Board. The dissenting opinion also made reference to the fact that the majority had placed too great a reliance on 'ambiguous statements' as to customary law in 'hurriedly drawn affidavits by persons who have a pecuniary interest or are closely connected with those who have such interest'.[104]

Two responses to this case by Clement Ng'ong'ola in the *Journal of African Law* are extremely critical of the decision. He supports the dissenting judgment, averring that the trial judge and the majority justices 'arrived at their conclusions through a reasoning process somewhat lacking in intellectual rigor'.[105] Most significantly, he claims that 'the majority in the Court of Appeal proceeded on a narrow evidential basis, ignoring policy considerations and the wider implications for tribal land policy of their preferred result'.[106]

In South Africa, unraveling the segregated and discriminatory patterns of land ownership is one of the major challenges facing it in the post-apartheid era, especially as its basis, the Land Act of 1913, precedes official apartheid by almost half-a-century. Even so, there are historical anomalies that sometimes undercut the official plans and laws to dispossess the Blacks. Aninka Claasens quotes from the findings of a governmental commission in 1916, that indicated that there were occasional instances of evading the restrictive provisions of the Land Act. Complaints were apparently made to the commission that 'African purchasers were squeezing whites out of the property market because they were able to pay higher prices' since, according to the evidence of one government official, 'It is all acquired through tribal or collective effort, but generally through the chief or headman.'[107] However, with time these loopholes in the law were cut off by later legislation which 'did finally make African land purchase all but impossible'.[108] Even so, the resourcefulness of the dispossessed Africans was not exhausted, and a combination of their persistence and the need of white landowners for labor led to further unforeseen consequences. Claasens writes that

> just as many people had adapted to the initial loss of their land by entering into the conquerors' terms and buying it [back], so now Africans adapted to the new restrictions by entering into lease and share-cropping arrangements with the nominal owners of the land. By the beginning of the 20th century there was extensive and profitable African occupation of white lands in terms of such contractual agreements. But the white enjoyers of title were not satisfied that their exclusive ownership secured them half the produce of the Africans who farmed their land.[109]

In fact, complaints were made by the white farmers, legally protected by discriminatory legislation, that 'black tenants and share-croppers were farming so profitably that they refused to become servants and labour for white masters'.[110] Claasens sums up the historical situation:

> The history of the land in South Africa has been one of massive state intervention. The land was taken from the initial inhabitants of the country by force and trickery … . And then as African farmers struggled (often amazingly successful) to re-establish themselves within the new legal restrictions imposed on them as blacks, so political intervention by a white oligarchy was used again and again to prohibit their right to enter into ordinary contractual relations.[111]

Claasens stresses the need for an awareness of the historical developments, since they are essential for an understanding of present realities, and the need to seek a redistribution of land allocation. New legislation from 1994 (one of the first pieces of legislation of the new post-apartheid regime) has laid the basis for far-reaching change.[112] One of the issues to be resolved is that of individual ownership *vis-à-vis* communal ownership (by tribe, or a subgroup within a tribe); and if communal and tribal, how to ensure that, in the future, no gender discrimination will be practiced, and that women will be able to enter into agricultural pursuits without restrictions on ownership, possession and inheritance.

Dennis Davis and Hugh Corder point out the need for both legal and historical analysis, noting that 'lawyers have grossly neglected this area of the legal system',[113] and that 'no land reform policy can be viable if it is not built on the traditions of the land struggles that have been fought in South Africa'.[114] It is quite likely that some of the most significant changes in land policy will take place in South Africa in the near future, but at the same time, this is an area where often the facts of daily life in rural areas are no less significant than the formal dictates of legislation. Two recent works, one from South Africa itself and one from the United States, one a historical biography, the other a socio-legal analysis, serve to remind us of the vitality of 'living law',[115] of customary practices.

The first book is a fascinating biography of an ordinary sharecropper in South Africa – 'a man who did not exist',[116] in the words of his biographer, one of the many forgotten people, who were an integral part of the life and history of the country; a man possessed of a phenomenal memory, linked to notes and slips of paper he had preserved; his biographer reconstructs many of the land issues of the country over decades through his vivid and detailed recollections, and in particular the peculiar symbiotic relationship that existed between landless black share-croppers, possessed of agricultural implements and a capacity to work, and poor property-owning whites, farmers lacking the wherewithal to farm productively on their own, and their reliance on the sharecroppers.

The second book is not of tribe or of customary law. It is of how rich cattle farmers and wealthy homeowners in Northern California struggle with each other to resolve the disputes that arise over cattle trespass on unfenced property of neighbors.[117] With large sums of money and valuable property at stake, with political pressures and personal lobbying to achieve a legislative victory, it is not, according to the author, formal legal provision or rational theoretical claims of the law-and-economics school that determine the result, but informal methods of social control – in sum, 'In many contexts, law is not central to the maintenance of social order', and there are many considerations which lead 'people to ignore law in many situations'.[118] It would be well to pay heed to this conclusion as to western-style land issues, when dealing with non-western societies, and trying to redress some of the injustices of the past as well as to understand some of the ongoing rules pertaining to the land that cannot be encompassed in a deeds registry office.

Some of the confusion relating to tribal land quite possibly has to do with misconceptions – generally the land was not communally held as such, but a prior condition for acquiring an individual plot, on which to farm, was membership of the tribe that held the land. On this basis Tom Bennett explains (in the context of South Africa but with wider ramifications) that 'if restoration of land is claimed in South Africa under a doctrine of aboriginal title, only an indigenous people as a collectivity may invoke the right and then only in respect of their traditional lands'.[119] He also points out some of the benefits that accrue, since general tribal rules allow for an equitable distribution of land among the members of the tribe. It is possible that, in the course of seeking recompense for the tribespeople for the dispossessions and expropriations of the past, these advantages will become more apparent to key people involved in the land issue, and that they may come to appreciate the inherent good ensconced in these aspects of tribal existence. Given the inroads that have been made into traditional family farming in western societies, as noted at the start of this chapter, it may be that it is tribal structures that offer some hope of reconstituting individual and family farming, still the backbone of a sound agriculture – and of a healthy social comity.

NOTES

1. While this chapter deals with the land basis for the constitution of tribes, it is important to remember that urbanization does not necessarily lead to what was once called 'de-tribalization'. Tribal ties may well be retained, as pointed out in earlier chapters. See, for instance, Kenneth Little, *West African Urbanization: A Study of Voluntary Associations in Social Change* (Cambridge: Cambridge University Press, 1965).
2. Victor Davis Hanson, *Fields Without Dreams: Defending the Agrarian Idea* (New York: The Free Press, 1996).
3. For the wild animals, the much-publicized 'Operation Noah's Ark' was set up to save them from drowning.
4. See Chapter 6, 'The Invention of Discovery', above.
5. See, for instance, Helen Jackson, *A Century of Dishonor: A Sketch of the United States Government's Dealings with some of the Indian Tribes* (Michigan: Scholarly Press, 1974 [1880]). For more recent work, see Vine DeLoria, *Behind the Trail of Broken Treaties: An Indian Declaration of Independence*

(New York: Delacorte Press, 1974).

6. See analysis by Crawford B. McPherson, *The Political Theory of Possessive Individualism: Hobbes to Locke* (London: Oxford University Press, 1962).
7. In England, it was only with the Reform Acts, from 1830 onwards, that persons (still males only) without property were given the franchise on a limited basis.
8. See, for instance, C.D. Rowley, *Recovery: The Politics of Aboriginal Reform* (Harmondsworth: Penguin Books, 1986), Chapter 5, 'Land Rights', pp. 68–91. He writes:

   > The traditional Aboriginal view of his 'country' is of a trust left by the creative spirits and the ancestors, who in the first days formed it from some primal chaos or matrix before disappearing into it, or into air or sky, leaving certain features of it with special power which must be respected and propitiated for human life to continue (p. 71).

   Among his many other works dealing with Aboriginal claims and attitudes to their country, see especially his *The Law of the Land* (Harmondsworth: Penguin Books, 1987).
9. For Marxists, there is a circular development – from primitive communism at an early stage in history to the communism that was due to develop out of the breakdown of capitalism.
10. See Henry Thoreau, *Walden and Civil Disobedience* (New York: W.W. Norton, 1966).
11. Aldo Leopold, 'The Conservation Ethic', *Journal of Forestry* 31 (1933), p. 634.
12. See, for instance, Mark Sagoff, *The Economy of the Earth: Philosophy, Law and the Environment* (Cambridge: Cambridge University Press, 1988).
13. Garrett Hardin, 'The Tragedy of the Commons,' *Science* 162 (1968), p. 1243.
14. See discussion by Karl Polanyi, *The Great Transformation: The Political and Economic Origins of Our Time* (Boston, MA: Beacon Press, 1965).
15. Lewis Regenstein, *The Politics of Extinction: The Shocking Story of the World's Endangered Wildlife* (New York: Macmillan, 1975).
16. Ibid., p. xxii.
17. Ibid., p. xxii.
18. Peter Sack, *Land Between Two Laws: Early European Land Acquisitions in New Guinea* (Canberra: Australian National University Press, 1973). For a radical view of the legal situation in Papua New Guinea, see Peter Fitzpatrick, *Law and State in Papua New Guinea* (New York: Academic Press, 1980).
19. Ibid., p. 31.
20. *Woodward Report,* 1974.
21. C.D. Rowley, *A Matter of Justice* (Canberra: Australian National University Press, 1974), p. 72.
22. See articles in *The Australian* (Wednesday, 8 May 1991), especially 'Get the Hint: Don't Mine the Hill', p. 1. On the importance of mining in the lands issue, see Daniel Vachon and Phillip Toyne, 'Mining and the Challenge of Land Rights' in N. Peterson and M. Langton (eds), *Aborigines, Land and Land Rights* (Canberra: Australian Institute of Aboriginal Studies, 1983), p. 307; see also Marcia Langton, 'A National Strategy to Deal with Exploration and Mining on or near Aboriginal Land', ibid., p. 385.
23. See discussion of *Mabo* case above, Chapter 6, 'The Invention of Discovery'.
24. *Mabo v. Queensland*, (1992) 175 CLR 1; 66 ALJR 408, (1992) 107 ALR 1.
25. Kent McNeil, *Common Law Aboriginal Title* (Oxford: Clarendon Press, 1989).
26. Brian Slattery, 'The Land Rights of Indigenous Canadian Peoples, as Affected by the Crown's Acquisition of Their Territories', D. Phil Thesis, Oxford University, 1979; Geoffrey Lester, 'The Territorial Rights of the Inuit of the Canadian Northwest Territories: A Legal Argument', D Jur Dissertation, York University, 1981.
27. McNeil, *Common Law Aboriginal Title*, p. 298.
28. Ibid., p. 298.
29. Ibid., p. 161.
30. Slattery, 'Land Rights of Indigenous Canadian Peoples …'.
31. McNeil, *Common Law Aboriginal Title*, p. 162.
32. Ibid., p. 301.
33. Ibid., p. 304.
34. On Domesday (which lasted several days) a precise accounting was made of the legal position of land in England, some twenty years after the conquest by the Normans.
35. See, for instance, Lord Cross and G. Hand, *Radcliffe and Cross: The English Legal System* (5th ed.)

(London: Butterworths, 1971), Chapter 2, 'The Norman Period, 1066–1154', p. 13.

36. For partial excerpt of key passages, see Menno Boldt and J. Anthony Long with Leroy Little Bear (eds), *The Quest for Justice: Aboriginal People and Aboriginal Rights* (Toronto: University of Toronto Press, 1985), Appendix A, p. 357.
37. *Treaty of Paris,* 10 February 1763.
38. Orders-In-Council were Royal edicts made in consultation with the Privy Council, having the force of law in areas outside of Britain.
39. McNeil, *Common Law Aboriginal Title*, p. 274.
40. Richard Bartlett, *Indian Reserves and Aboriginal Lands in Canada: A Homeland—A Study in Law and History* (Saskatoon: University of Saskatchewan Native Law Centre, 1990), p. 10.
41. Bruce Clark, *Native Liberty, Crown Sovereignty: The Existing Aboriginal Right of Self-Government in Canada* (Montreal: McGill-Queens University Press, 1990). See, for instance, p. 7: 'Under the Royal Proclamation of 1783 and several other imperial legislative instruments constituting the self-government right, the natives were assured that the crown would not unilaterally usurp any part of British North America.' He also refers to a 1774 judgment (*Campbell v. Hall*), by Lord Mansfield, Chief Justice of England, that the Proclamation was binding on the King-in-Council and could only be abolished by a statute of the British Parliament (Clark at p. 206).
42. Ibid., p. 3.
43. See Ibid., p. 236.
44. McNeil, *Common Law Aboriginal Title*, pp. 274–5.
45. *St Catherine's Milling Company v. The Queen*, (1888) 14 App. Cas. 46 (PC).
46. Ibid., p. 55.
47. See, for instance, *Calder v. Attorney-General of British Columbia*, [1973] 34 DLR (3d) 145. It may be noted that at least one writer argues that 'the 3–3 split of the Supreme Court in *Calder* suggested a determination by the Court to encourage the negotiated settlement of aboriginal rights' – Richard Bartlett, *Aboriginal Water Rights in Canada: A Study of Aboriginal Title to Water and Indian Water Rights* (Calgary: The Canadian Institute of Resources Law, The University of Calgary, 1988), p. 230.
48. See above, Chapter 6, 'The Invention of Discovery'.
49. The idea of self-government appears in the subtitle of Clark's book. His intention is apparently not of independence, but of autonomy, or even statehood within a federal system.
50. See report of case, *Rex v. Walker* in *Aboriginal Law Bulletin* 2 (April, 1989), p. 14.
51. L. Scott Gould, 'The Consent Paradigm: Tribal Sovereignty at the Millennium', *Columbia Law Review* 96 (1996), p. 810.
52. See, for instance, Brian Slattery, 'The Hidden Constitution: Aboriginal Rights in Canada', in Boldt *et al.*, *The Quest for Justice,* p. 114, especially subsection entitled 'The Royal Proclamation of 1763', pp. 119–23.
53. McNeil, *Common Law Aboriginal Title*, p. 3, where he writes: 'Slattery concluded that there are three distinct, though interrelated, sources of indigenous land rights in Canada: (1) general principles of British Colonial Law; (2) constitutional structures which evolved in the British American colonies to accommodate the existence of both settlers and indigenous groups; and (3) the Royal Proclamation of 1763. Since our concern is with indigenous land rights in the Crown's overseas dominions generally, it is Slattery's first source that is most relevant here.'
54. Slattery, 'Hidden Constitution', p. 122.
55. Ibid., p. 123.
56. McNeil, *Common Law Aboriginal Title*, p. 217.
57. Slattery, 'Hidden Constitution', p. 119.
58. Clark, *Native Liberty, Crown Sovereignty*, especially at pp. 200–3. Thus Clark writes that whereas 'the Constitution Act, 1982 explicitly adopted a reasonableness test regarding the construction of federal and provincial legislation in relation to the enumerated rights and freedoms identified by the charter, (t)hese rights and freedoms do not include aboriginal and treaty rights, which are dealt with separately in another part' (p. 200). 'The imperial Parliament has declared its unqualified intent to be that existing aboriginal and treaty rights enjoy constitutional paramountcy. Therefore, when in conflict with merely domestic legislation the outcome should be beyond cavil' (p. 201).
59. See Boldt *et al.*, *The Quest for Justice*, at p. 358.
60. In general, see Sharon Kornman, *The Right of Conquest: The Acquisition of Territory by Force in*

International Law and Practice (Oxford: Clarendon Press, 1996), Chapter 2, 'The Right of Conquest in Relations between European States and "Barbarian" Communities', p. 41.

61. Sec. 25 of Constitution Act of 1982.
62. See *Apsassin v. Canada (Dept of Indian Affairs and Northern Development)*, 130 D.L.R. (4th) 193 (1995); see discussion in *Aboriginal Law Bulletin,* vol. 7, No. 78 (1995), p. 7. See also *Guerin v. Rex* (1985) 13 D.LR. (4th) 321 (S.C.C.); and for discussion of this latter case, completed before the *Apsassin* decision, see Leonard Rotman, *Parallel Paths: Fiduciary Doctrine and the Crown – Native Relationship in Canada* (Toronto: University of Toronto Press, 1996); and see also Peter Hutchins and David Schulze, 'When Do Fiduciary Obligations to Aboriginal People Arise?', *Saskatchewan Law Review* 59 (1995), p. 97.
63. See John Hookey, 'Settlement and Sovereignty', in P. Hanks and B. Keon-Cohen (eds), *Aborigines and the Law: Essays in Memory of Elizabeth Eggleston* (Sydney: Allen & Unwin, 1984); the case is *Bonjon* as recorded in 'Papers Relative to the Aborigines, Australian Colonies', 1844 British Parliamentary Papers, pp. 146, Vol. 8, as quoted by Hookey at pp. 4–6, and footnoted at p. 310.
64. Hookey, 'Settlement and Sovereignty', p. 6.
65. Ibid., p. 6.
66. *Johnson v. M'Intosh*, 21 US (8 Wheat) 543 (1823).
67. *Genesis*, Chapters 4 and 25.
68. Bryan Keon-Cohen and Bradford Morse, 'Indigenous Land Rights in Australia and Canada', in *Aborigines and the Law*, p. 75.
69. Ibid., p. 76.
70. See Bradley Nye, 'Where Do the Buffalo Roam? Determining the Scope of American Indian Off-Reservation Hunting Rights in the Pacific Northwest', *Washington Law Review* 67 (1992), p. 175.
71. Harriet Ketley, 'Cultural Diversity Versus Biodiversity', *Adelaide Law Review* 16 (1994), p. 99. The article goes beyond positing the conflict and attempts to offer a solution – on the one hand assessing 'the current impact of indigenous hunting on loss of biodiversity,' and, on the other hand, discovering 'the aspirations of Aboriginal communities with respect to species use' (p. 160).
72. *Sparrow v. R.*, [1987] 2 WWR 577.
73. Bartlett, *Aboriginal Water Rights*, pp. 229–31.
74. Orakei Report, Waitangi Tribunal, 1987 (Wai-9). See further discussion in Chapter 21, 'Accounting for the Past'.
75. Harvey Feit, 'The Future of Hunters Within Nation-States: Anthropology and the James Bay Cree', in E. Leacock and R. Lee (eds), *Politics and History in Band Societies* (Cambridge: Cambridge University Press, 1982), p. 373.
76. Ibid., p. 373.
77. Ibid., p. 403.
78. Graham Neate, *Aboriginal Land Rights Law in the Northern Territory*, Vol. 1 (Chippendale, NSW: Alternative Publishing Co-operative, 1989).
79. The Act is a federal one, as the Federal government had responsibility for the Northern Territories.
80. *Woodward Commission Report.*
81. See Neate, *Aboriginal Land Rights Law*, p. 230.
82. *In re Toohey: ex parte Meneling Station (Pty) Ltd.*, (1982) 44 ALR 63 (High Court of Australia); see also earlier decision which had favorably clarified the rights of the Aborigines and the broad powers of the Commissioner (Judge Toohey) – *R v. Toohey: Ex parte Northern Land Council*, (1981) 56 ALJR 164 (High Court of Australia).
83. W.E.H. Stanner, *White Man Got the Dreaming: Essays 1938–1973* (Canberra: Australian National University Press, 1979).
84. Ibid., p. 230. See also discussion of the attempt by one White Australian to understand Aborigine life; Peter Brady, *Whitefella Dreaming: The Authorised Biography of William Ricketts* (Oinda, Victoria: Preferred Image, 1994). Brady explains that Ricketts 'set himself two tasks; creating a means to introduce "new" Australians to the concept of forming a spiritual, and therefore respectful, relationship with the Earth, and then bringing about a complete change in attitude towards Aborigines themselves' (p. 9).
85. *Genesis,* Chapter 2, verse 7 – the words referring to God forming 'man of the dust of the

ground', reads in the original Hebrew: 'Et Ha-adam 'Afar Min Ha-adamah'.

86. See Stanner, *White Man Got the Dreaming*.
87. Decree No. 76/165 of 27 April 1976.
88. C.N. Ngwasiri, unpublished draft manuscript. I have also benefited from personal discussions with Prof. Ngwasiri, and thank him for allowing me to peruse part of his manuscript.
89. Ibid., Chapter 5, p. 3, referred to work of E. Le Roy, *La Réforme du Droit de la Terre dans certains pays d'Afrique Francophone* (Rome, FAO, 1987).
90. Ngwasiri also notes the need to hire experts in order to comply with the formalities of registration.
91. Ngwasiri claims that social disorganization ensued in other countries, for instance Kenya, as a result of land registration.
92. See Robert Owen, *A New View of Society* (London: J.M. Dent, 1949).
93. Charles Fourier, *Design for Utopia* (New York: Schocken, 1971).
94. Pytor Kropotkin, *Mutual Aid: A Factor of Evolution* (New York: Garland Publishing, 1972), and 'Property and Law', in J.S. Schapiro (ed.), *Movements of Social Dissent in Modern Europe* (Princeton, NJ: Anvil Press, 1962).
95. Act of 7 August 1789, 1 Stat. 50.
96. See brief discussion in K. Hall, *The Oxford Companion to the Supreme Court of the United States* (New York: Oxford University Press, 1992) at p. 580 (by Rennard Strickland): 'In the winter of 1838–1839, sixteen thousand Cherokees were driven at gunpoint from their ancestral homeland over what has come to be known as '"the Trail of Tears". More than four thousand of their number died on the way.'
97. General Allotment Act, 24 Stat. 388. Janet MacDonnell succinctly notes that 'fifty years later, when the policy was changed, the government had allotted 118 out of 213 reservations and brought over three-fourths of the Indians under the provisions of the Dawes Act'. See Janet MacDonnell, *The Dispossession of the American Indian, 1887–1934* (Bloomington, IN: Indiana University Press, 1991), p. 10. See also David Wilkins, *American Indian Sovereignty and the US Supreme Court: The Masking of Justice* (Austin, TX: University of Texas Press, 1997), p. 81.
98. For general discussion of the historical process, see Rennard Strickland, 'Genocide-at-law: An Historic and Contemporary View of the Native American Experience', *University of Kansas Law Review* 34 (1986), p. 713.
99. *Indian Reorganization Act* 48 Stat 984.
100. See discussion in Stephen Pevar, *The Rights of Indians and Tribes: The Basic ACLU Guide to Indian and Tribal Life* (Carbondale: Southern Illinois University Press, 1992), p. 6.
101. *Kweneng Land Board v. Kabelo Matlho and Pheto Motlhabane,* Civil Appeal 10/91, Court of Appeal of Botswana, Lobatse.
102. Tribal Land Act, sec. 10(1), Cap 32.02, Laws of Botswana.
103. *Kweneng Land Board v. Kabelo Matlho*, p. 16 of transcript.
104. Ibid., minority opinion.
105. Clement Ng'ong'ola, 'Ownership of Tribal Land in Botswana', *Journal of African Law* 37 (1993), p. 197. See also his article, 'Land Problems in Some Peri-urban Villages in Botswana and Problems of Conception, Description and Transformation of "Tribal" Land Tenure', *Journal of African Law* 36 (1992), p. 140.
106. Ibid., p. 197.
107. Aninka Claasens, 'For Whites Only – Land Ownership in South Africa', in Michael de Klerk (ed.), *A Harvest of Discontent: The Land Question in South Africa* (Cape Town: Institute for a Democratic Alternative for South Africa, 1991), p. 48.
108. Ibid., p. 48.
109. Ibid., p. 48.
110. Ibid., p. 48.
111. Ibid., p. 111.
112. For a good discussion of recent developments (in a comparative context), see Rajesh Choudree and Gregory McIntyre, 'Restitution of Land in Two Jurisdictions: Australia and South Africa', *The South African Law Journal* 114 (1997), p. 187. The article compares the 1993 Native Title Act of Australia with the South African Restitution of Land Rights Act of 1994. The authors, a South African and an Australian, explain that the South African Restitution

Act 'sets out a procedure for restoring land to people who have been prevented from obtaining or attaining title as a consequence of racially discriminatory laws, but differs from the Native Title Act in the sense that it does not rely on establishing the continuing existence of previously unrecognized proprietary rights. It is dealing with rights which have been acknowledged to have been "taken away" and are being "given back"' (p. 194). In their conclusion, the authors see the South African legislation as being 'among the most enlightened legislation of its kind in dealing with the fundamental rights of the historically dispossessed' (p. 196).

113. Dennis Davis and Hugh Corder, 'Restructuring the Rural Economy: Legal Issues', in de Klerk, *A Harvest of Discontent*, p. 139.
114. Ibid., p. 152.
115. Eugen Ehrlich, *Fundamental Principles of the Sociology of Law* (Cambridge: Harvard University Press, 1936). Ehrlich's important work in the sociology of law dealt with rural life in Central Europe.
116. Charles van Onselen, *The Seed is Mine: The Life of Kas Maine, A South African Sharecropper, 1894–1985* (Cape Town: David Philip, 1996). See also Malete Nkadimeng and Georgina Relly, 'Kas Maine: The Story of a Black South African Agriculturist', in B. Bozzoli (ed.), *Town and Countryside in the Transvaal: Capitalist Penetration and Popular Response* (Johannesburg: Ravan Press, 1983), p. 89. For a good critical analysis of sharecropping, see the article in the same anthology by Tim Keegan, 'The Sharecropping Economy, African Class Formation and the 1913 Native Land Act in the Highveld Maize Belt', p. 108. He writes:

> sharecropping and other forms of independent tenancy obstructed and undermined the capitalisation of agriculture as they 'tied-up' potential supplies of labour. They provided African households with a degree of independence which obviated the necessity for them to alienate their labour power regularly and intensively.
>
> The major provision of the Act ... was that which laid down that the only legal form of rent payment by black tenants to white landlords was to be labor service. A rent in the form of a share of the crop or in cash was illegal ... . The 1913 Land Act was aimed at stifling the independent peasantry ... and shutting off alternatives such as those offered by sharecropping landlords (p. 116).

A similar contention has been made by Steven Webster, 'Postmodernist Theory and the Sublimation of Maori Culture', *Oceania* 63 (1992–93), p. 222. He writes, 'Although it is not widely recognized, colonial policies sought to accumulate capital through the control of Maori labour as well as land. Earliest policies explicitly intended to force most Maori into a landless working class by acquiring all "waste" Native land for the Crown and later ... to commercial interests' (p. 227).

117. Robert C. Ellikson, *Order Without Law: How Neighbors Settle Disputes* (Cambridge, MA: Harvard University Press, 1991).
118. Ibid., p. 280.
119. Tom W. Bennett, *Human Rights and African Customary Law* (Cape Town: Juta, 1995), p. 150.

Holy Rites and Sacred Sites

For all the secularism of the modern world, religious beliefs and rituals still play a significant part in its daily life. The sociologist, Max Weber, argued that it was the very nature of religious belief that was a key trigger factor in the making of the modern world, in which the rationality that characterized Protestantism enabled the critical breakthroughs at the heart of science, politics and economics;[1] more recently sociology has eagerly adopted the concept of 'civil religion' to describe some of the ideological underpinnings of modern society.[2] Further, among the most prominent flag-bearers of western culture in the wake of colonial expansion, were the missionaries, particularly in Africa and the Pacific Islands, where the indigenous religions – generally considered and defined as pagan – were in many places largely replaced. Indeed, their success in converting the local inhabitants was often a reflection of the political backing they could rely on. On the basis of an analysis of a few missionaries, Aidan Southall claims that when they, and other strangers to Africa, 'tried to bring new religions into the smaller African societies, without political protection – whether imposed by their own nation or lent them by local rulers – they failed. But when they worked in the larger African societies, under the political umbrella of the ruler, they achieved spectacular success.'[3]

In this chapter the focus will be on the United States, partly because it is the one country in the 'western world', which makes a constitutional separation of church and state, a separation which is often ignored when dealing with American Indian religion. The United States seems, on the whole, to have been moderately successful, in terms of conversions of Native Americans, whether individually or collectively.[4] Parallel with this activity, governmental authorities often expended intense efforts on rooting out religious rituals of the Indians that were considered offensive or threatening. Thus, in the nineteenth century, strong governmental action was taken against rituals such as the Ghost Dance or the Sun Dance, which were seen also to have strong political overtones.[5] Clashes in these contexts sometimes had disastrous consequences, such as their culmination in the Battle of Wounded Knee, where hundreds of Native Americans were killed.[6]

Later, attempts were made – in terms of the ban on drug use – to put a stop to the use of peyote in religious ceremonies but, over the years, a certain amount of consideration was given to its use, partly as a result of pleas made by anthropologists and others who had lived or worked with Native Americans and sought to explain its special qualities, not as an addictive substance, but as a sacrament. Their success was only partial, and as a result, some of the recent litigation has dealt with residual issues relating to peyote use.[7]

Congress recently gave expression to its awareness of inequities inflicted in the past, and of its intention that future policies should be based on according maximum consideration to the special needs and unique aspects of the religion. The American Indian Religious Freedom Act, originally promulgated in 1978 and shortly thereafter codified in 1982, is really no more than a declaration of intent with no operative mechanism to enforce its generalizations.[8] In fact, were it to have effective powers, it would most likely be in violation of the constitutional separation of church and state; even in its existing form, it quite likely does not pass constitutional muster, but it has not been challenged on these grounds. Its dubious constitutional nature, and even the absence of challenge, indirectly speaks volumes for the sins of the past – and it may well be seen as some sort of symbolic penance for them. Yet, as a clear-cut statement of desired future policy, its impact seems to have been minimal, and judicial notice of its provisions have been, it would seen, no more than polite lip-service.[9]

The major declaration states:

> That henceforth it shall be the policy of the United States to protect and preserve for American Indians their inherent right of freedom to believe, express, and exercise the traditional religions of the American Indian, Eskimo, Aleat, and Native Hawaiians, including but not limited to access to sites, use and possession of sacred objects, and the freedom to worship through ceremonials and traditional rites.

However, a full understanding of this legislation can only be gleaned from a perusal of its preamble, which includes such clarifications of the background to its enactment as:

> … Whereas the religious practices of the American Indian are an integral part of their culture, tradition and heritage, such practices forming the basis of Indian identity and value-systems;
>
> Whereas the lack of a clear, comprehensive, and consistent federal policy has often resulted in the abridgment of religious freedom for traditional American Indians;
>
> Whereas such religious infringements result from the lack of knowledge or the insensitive and inflexible enforcement of Federal policies and regulations premised on a variety of laws;
>
> Whereas such laws and policies often deny American Indians

> access to sacred sites required in their religions, including cemeteries;
>
> Whereas traditional American Indian ceremonies have been intruded upon, interfered with, and in a few instances banned ...[10]

Despite this legislation, it may well be claimed that Native Americans have not achieved the guarantee to full and free exercise of their religion in those aspects of it that come into conflict with the dominant society – its belief system, its economic planning, and its secular legislation. As a background to these clashes, it must be noted that, often, the parameters of religious toleration are determined by the contours of the dominant religion, or to be more exact, with the Protestant and Catholic conceptions of Christianity. Thus, in the United States, Mormons have encountered problems with their acceptance of polygamy,[11] Christian Scientists with their commitment to faith-healing,[12] Seventh-Day Adventists with their observance of Saturday as the sabbath,[13] Jehovah's Witness adherents with their refusal to abide by the standards of the civil religion,[14] as well as Orthodox Jews with their dress code (the wearing of a skull-cap) in certain situations (for instance in the military).[15] Within this nature of the challenged legislation or action, the Court looks not to the consequences as they affect a person's religion, but to the motivations of the authorities. If the harm caused was not intended, the courts will then not intervene.[16] Within this context, it is then not so surprising that Native Americans have also encountered a degree of obtuseness among many judges, called upon to adjudicate in cases where clashes have arisen stemming from the belief-system of the Indians. Despite the official recognition of Federal legislation, certain facets of the religion have been most strictly scrutinized by American judges, including on a few limited occasions, by Supreme Court justices. Some of the judicial decisions have aroused strong criticism, and there seems little doubt that the overall thrust of recent precedents is hardly a reflection of the sentiments expressed in the Congressional legislation.

It should also be noted that in most of the other instances of adverse judicial verdicts in relation to other religions, many of them were later corrected – either by the courts themselves (in the case of Jehovah's Witness, for instance, where school children were first denied, and several years later granted, the right not to take part in an obligatory salute to the national flag);[17] or by subsequent legislative or regulatory activity (in the case of the right to wear a skull-cap where military dress had previously demanded uniform bareheadedness);[18] or by changing patterns of behavior (where although polygamy is not recognized in terms of official marriages, various living patterns have developed that have undermined the strict monogamy of earlier years);[19] or a combination of factors (for Seventh Day Adventists, both litigation and changing patterns of Sunday conduct); or even legal maneuvering, prosecutorial discretion or governmental directives (as occurs sometimes in faith-healing for Christian Scientists).[20]

However, it is not clear that Native Americans will benefit similarly by the passage of time and accompanying changes in behavior. In fact, in some of the key decisions, the erosion of religious principles is immutable, as in the cases where claims as to the sacred nature of certain areas have been rejected, thereby giving judicial sanction for their development as tourist sites, for logging operations, or for the building of mountain passes. In other aspects, the harmful nature is much more limited and may yet possibly be corrected – either by legislation or judicial reversal. Thus, the denial of the right to participate in religious rituals that involve the taking of peyote is easily amenable to change, especially since most of the states in the United States have indeed legislated for exemptions for peyote to the ban on drug-taking, similar to the exemptions granted by nearly all states during the years of prohibition to those religions that required the use of wine for some of their rituals (for instance, the Catholics for communion, and the Jews for the prayer of sanctification on the Sabbath and holidays).[21]

In this chapter the analysis will focus on these two issues in terms of recent judicial decisions in the United States dealing with constitutional protection of the free exercise of religion – at the same time it should be noted that similar problems have arisen elsewhere in terms of claims by Maoris in New Zealand as to the sacred nature of rivers that were being polluted, or sacred areas in Australia being exposed to mining exploitation.

In the last decade the United States Supreme Court has handed down two major decisions adverse to the right of Native Americans to freely exercise their right to religion. The decisions themselves, and most of the ensuing debate (mainly critical), revolved around constitutional issues of the free exercise of religion as guaranteed in the First Amendment to the Constitution – in fact, the opening words of the Bill of Rights: 'Congress shall make no law respecting an establishment of religion, or prohibiting the free exercise thereof … .' However, a closer scrutiny will reveal that part of the underlying considerations had to deal with the fact of tribe – that the petition to the Court dealt with a tribal right, and not only a religious one.

In the one case, the Court (in a 6–3 decision), overruled a lower court decision, and granted governmental authorities the right to complete the building of a road, despite pleas by the Indians as to the devastating effect the presence of a road in close proximity to a sacred area, would have on their religion.[22] In the other case, the Court (in a 5–4 decision) placed the efforts of the state to eliminate drug abuse above the right of Native Americans to use peyote in their religious ceremonies.[23] These cases are among the most recent in a lengthy series of judgments that have been detrimental to the practice of the Native American religion, most of them at lower court levels, including a number of cases that the Supreme Court refused to consider (by denying the *writ of certiorari*).[24] Even the occasional decision that does go in favor of the Native Americans may be subsequently overruled.[25]

In dealing with these Native American cases, a number of interesting – and revealing – patterns may be discerned:

(a) An imbalance exists between cases lost by the Native Americans (for which *certiorari* is rarely given when the case is appealed to the Supreme Court) and those won by them at the lower level (for which there is a far greater willingness by the Supreme Court to grant *certiorari* to their legal opponents).

(b) Decisions in favor of one group of Native Americans are used as a rationale in later cases to deny a plea by another group, because of distinguishing factors between the cases, when the distinction itself is highly debatable.

(c) Decisions that perhaps justifiably rejected the claim by Native Americans are then activated in other cases where a logical connection between the later and earlier cases is most dubious.

(d) Protections sought by Native Americans in pursuit of their right to the 'free exercise of religion' are interpreted by the Courts as attempts to activate governmental intervention in a manner that suggests the 'establishment' of their religion – and, on the basis of such reasoning, the petition is rejected.

(e) New (and often artificial) standards are introduced in the adjudication of Native American cases in order to justify the refusal to follow the Court's own precedent laid down earlier in respect of another religion – for instance, claiming in retrospect that the recognition granted in the precedent dealt with a central issue of the other religion, whereas the Native American claim concerned only peripheral matters.

(f) An overall judicial inability (or unwillingness) to understand and appreciate the distinctive features of Native American religions, based on underlying premises and a world-outlook vastly different from the principles of Western religions.

(g) The gratuitous consideration of future hypothetical cases, which might exploit a positive decision in the matter before the Court, and therefore the refusal to hand down a positive decision.

In the leading case of *Lyng v. Northwest Indian Cemetery Protective Association,* the Supreme Court overturned a lower court decision, enjoining governmental authorities from completing a road, intended mainly for logging purposes, as its proximity to a sacred area would prevent the performance of religious rituals, which were dependent on the quiet and the tranquillity afforded by the pristine beauty of the mountainous terrain, known by the Native Americans as 'the high country'.[26] The importance of this case lies not only in the impact of the adverse Supreme Court decision, but in the carefully reasoned argument of the favorable decision of the lower court, based as it was on an extensive official report supporting the Native American position,[27] in the immediate critical response provided in the dissenting judgment (against which the majority opinion attempts to defend itself – in my humble opinion, quite inadequately),[28] and most significantly, in the unabashed admission by the Court of its full awareness of the detrimental consequences that its decision would have for the future preservation of the religion. Thus the Court explains that 'the Government does not dispute, and we have no reason to doubt, that the logging and road-building projects at issue in this case could have devastating effects on traditional Indian religious practices'.[29] These practices involve the ability to find seclusion for the purpose of quiet meditation, and they are:

> intimately and inextricably bound up with the unique features of the Chimney Rock area … Individual practitioners use this area for personal spiritual development; some of their activities are believed to be critically important in advancing the welfare of the Tribe, and indeed, of mankind itself. The Indians use this area, as they have used it for a very long time, to conduct a wide variety of specific rituals that aim to accomplish their religious goals. According to their beliefs, the rituals would not be efficacious if conducted at other sites than the ones traditionally used, and too much disturbance of the area's natural state would clearly render any meaningful continuation of traditional practices impossible … .[30]

Given the unequivocal acknowledgment of harmful consequences, the Court develops a number of new conceptualizations in order to avoid adopting the sort of protective approach that the Federal Act dealing with the Native American religion enjoins, that the constitution clearly hints at, that precedents clearly suggest, and that the logic of the facts allow for.

The Court argues blandly that the Government had indeed been 'solicitous' toward the needs of the Native Americans. Firstly, it points out that, conscious of the problematic situation, the Government had ordered a comprehensive study, which also happened to be favorable to the Native American's position – but surely the purpose of that report is negated when the Forest Service did not adopt its recommendations! The Court mentions this disparity in passing, but immediately adds that 'many other ameliorative measures were planned',[31] namely, seeking alternative routes, which would avoid sensitive areas where specific rituals were performed. The Court thus contends that 'Except for abandoning its project entirely … it is difficult to see how the Government could have been more solicitous.'[32]

Yet, as the Report indicated, as the lower court held, and as the dissenting judgment in the Supreme Court reiterates, the implications of a decision favorable to the Indians demanded no such drastic step. There was ample room to allow the governmental authority to fulfill the major parts of its plan. In fact, the portion of the road that had been completed, could be easily utilized for logging purposes, even without joining the two ends separated by some six miles.

If anything, the majority opinion is overly solicitous to governmental policy. Thus, it poses a hypothetical case in the future, which might make even stronger demands on governmental activity. Noting that the respondents had not objected to the minimum presence of other people in parts of the disputed area, the Court sees this as inviting problems in the future, where later petitioners 'might seek to exclude all human activity but their own from sacred areas of the public lands'.[33] The Court is also wary lest the very need of the petitioners for immersing themselves in an awareness of the broad vistas of the natural environment, allowing unobstructed viewing of the surroundings, could lead to a future case where 'such beliefs could easily require *de facto* beneficial ownership of some rather spacious tracts of public property'.[34] Further, the Court sees the petition as not so much seeking freedom to practice religion, but the power to obstruct governmental plans.[35]

Finally, the Court rejected outright the possibility, raised in the dissenting opinion, of examining the centrality to the religion of the factor under discussion. Justice Brennan, in dissent, had noted that several decisions at the Court of Appeals level had used this criterion (sometimes approvingly, sometimes for the purpose of rejecting the religious claim).[36] However, the Court in its majority opinion, responded that this would impose an intolerable burden on the Court, in that

> We would accordingly be required to weigh the value of every religious belief and practice that is said to be threatened by any government program. The dissent thus offers us the prospect of this Court's holding that some sincerely held religious beliefs and practices are not 'central' to certain religions, despite protestations to the contrary from the religious objectors who brought the lawsuit. In other words, the dissent's approach would require us to rule that some religious adherents misunderstand their own religious beliefs.[37]

Reluctant to be involved in such theological determinations, the Court preferred outright rejection of the pleas of the religious adherents. May it be suggested that the reason was that any such careful measurement would have led inevitably to a finding that would have affirmed the centrality of the issue at stake for the religious practices of the respondents. Perhaps the Court was reluctant to embark on a course whose conclusions seemed so apparent – after all, it was the majority opinion that stated categorically that the project would have devastating effects.

In fact, the idea of centrality was not a novel one – it had been used on several occasions in the past, both to justify intervention on behalf of the religious objectors, and in order to reject their claim in the absence of such centrality. However, the idea of centrality had not been a factor in decisions favorable to other religious petitioners – what the Court had sought in dealing with Seventh-Day Adventists (the *Sherbert* decision)[38] and the Amish (the *Yoder* decision)[39] was the *sincerity* with which the belief was held, not its centrality for the religion.

Even so, the first time that centrality was used, it was done in a creative way on behalf of the Native American petitioners, quite possibly as a sensitive response to the American Indian Religious Freedom Act, which had been passed a few years earlier. The case itself,[40] tried in Alaska, has had little direct impact on American jurisprudence, and is rarely quoted, but has major significance, both for its sensitive consideration of tribal life, and for its understanding appreciation of the centrality issue. In fact, it may be assumed that the centrality issue was broached specifically because the Alaskan Supreme Court was about to overrule a criminal conviction, handed down in a court of first instance, and affirmed at the first appeal, on the basis of the acceptance of an argument that the violation of the law (which was conceded as the facts were not in dispute) was justified for religious reasons. Without saying so specifically, the court was accepting a cultural defense in order to acquit.[41] The Court was, it would seem, eager to allay any doubts and to counter any opposition, by explaining that its acquittal of a member of the Athabascan tribe for killing a moose for the purpose of partaking of its meat at a funeral potlatch, was justified because the purpose of the illegal killing was in order to fulfill a central religious obligation. Specifically because the case was a criminal one, the centrality of the act took on additional weight. In effect, the court was actually recognizing the cultural defense, for which centrality may be important in assessing whether the terms of 'the lesser evil' had been satisfied.[42] Such considerations have admittedly less relevance where the issue is a pre-emptive injunction against a governmental authority, as was the situation in *Lyng*, but the fact is that the idea of centrality has slowly seeped into Native American cases and should not be ignored where convenient for the court to do so, or selectively activated to justify a rejection of Indian claims. In fact, a concept initially used to strengthen a favorable decision, has now become a hindrance in later cases, which bear little relation to the original decision. In a number of cases at the Court of Appeal level, the claim was rejected because the centrality of the issue was not proven.

The Supreme Court of Alaska showed the kind of perception and sensitivity, which is at the heart of the Federal legislation dealing with

Native American religion. In reversing the judgments of two lower courts, Justice Matthews explained the religious basis of the funeral potlatch and the necessity for eating moose meat. He sums up the evidence of the tribespeople and expert anthropological evidence:

> We think the evidence is inescapable that the utilization of moose meat at a funeral potlatch is a practice deeply rooted in the Athabascan religion. While moose itself is not sacred, it is needed for proper observance of a sacred ritual which must take place soon after death occurs. Moose is the centerpiece of the most important ritual in Athabascan life and is the equivalent of sacred symbols in other religions.[43]

In a favorable reference to this case, Jeff Fish draws attention to the manner in which the judicial process should function. He writes:

> In Indian religion cases it is especially important for a court to understand the many aspects of a religion, including those which may intertwine religion with lifestyle. Giving credence to the sincere belief of religious practitioners means accepting the boundaries of a religion as its adherents see it and accepting the significance given to each facet of religious practice ... Because Indian religions are often drastically different from more commonly practiced religions in American society, non-Indian judges need to consider carefully the religious practices at issue to understand fully their import.
>
> The Supreme Court of Alaska in *Frank* recognized this and expended the necessary time and effort to discover the full impact of a funeral potlatch without moose, while still not judging the values of the religion involved.[44]

In the *Lyng* case, there can be little doubt as to the centrality of the area in dispute for the very preservation of the religion – in fact the United States Supreme Court conceded as much in its description of the issues at stake.

The Court in essence was confirming all the earlier lower court decisions (adverse to the Indian petitioners) at the Court of Appeal level, for which it had, at the time, refused to grant *certiorari.* Yet, surely well before the *Lyng* decision, it should have been obvious that a string of cases was emerging which pitted crass commercial interests of logging companies and tourist agencies against the religious needs of Native Americans – yet it was only a decision favorable to the Native Americans that finally elicited a willingness to deal with such a delicate matter on the part of the Supreme Court.

The earlier cases all deal with similar clashes to those dealt with in *Lyng.* The obtuseness displayed by so many of the judges can only be understood within the ethnocentric framework within which they operated. Many of the critiques of these judgments have drawn attention to this factor. Thus, for instance, Howard Stambor opens his analysis of two of the cases with this preamble:

> The various tribal religions practiced by native peoples in the United States are almost without exception inextricably linked with what non-Indian society regards as *culture.* This unity of culture and religion makes American Indian forms of worship alien and difficult for the non-Indian to understand and poses difficult questions for courts that must decide whether certain arguably religious practices of American Indians lie within the shelter of the free exercise clause of the first amendment. Various courts have responded to this challenge with conflicting conclusions about which American Indian practices are indeed religious and which are merely expressions of culture or personal preference unprotected by the first amendment.[45]

One of the first in the recent series of cases (the *Sequoyah* case) again involves the Cherokee tribe,[46] and given the past unfortunate experience of this tribe with the judicial system – and occasionally with its limited capacity for enforcing its judgments when favorable – it might have been expected that the courts would have been overly solicitous to extend their protection. For at issue was the projected flooding, by the building of a dam, of lands held to be sacred, in which, according to the claim, there would be 'irreversible loss to the culture and history of the plaintiffs'[47] because of the inevitable destruction of sacred sites, medicine gathering areas, holy places, and cemeteries, and 'will disturb the sacred balance of the land'.[48]

After step-by-step examining – and rejecting – each of the petitioner's contentions, the court, in its concluding statement, avers that the affidavits presented 'appear to demonstrate "personal preference" rather than convictions "shared by an organized group"' and adds that 'The overwhelming concern of the affiants appears to be related to the historical beginnings of the Cherokees and their cultural development. It is damage to tribal and family folklore and traditions, more than particular religious observances, which appears to be at stake.'[49]

In emphasizing this cultural aspect, and in noting that earlier complaints about the dam (in previous litigation some 15 years before) focused primarily on culture and not religion, that the present action had been filed less than a month before the impoundment was scheduled to begin,[50] and that another action had dealt with protection for an endangered species, the court was hinting rather broadly at the skepticism with which it related to the petitioners' claims. The court did not even hesitate to mention the fact that 'the land in the Valley was owned by persons other than the plaintiffs or members of the class'[51] – namely, non-Indians, ignoring for the moment some of the sad political and legal history that had caused this situation. Finally, the court rejected a suggestion for remand of the case back to the district court to enable some of the doubtful facts to be more clearly ascertained. It is on this specific point that a dissent is offered by one of the judges on the three-judge bench. Judge Merritt argues for a remand to allow for further proof 'concerning the centrality of their ancestral burial grounds to their religion'.[52] He notes the importance of the issue at stake, and the more recent legal developments that might assist the plaintiffs:

> This is a confusing and essentially uncharted area of law under the free exercise clause. At the time the complaint and various affidavits were filed, the centrality standard had not been clearly articulated. It may have been unclear to the Cherokees precisely what they had to allege and prove in order to make a constitutional claim … . In view of … the protective attitude that federal courts should follow in considering Indian claims, we should reverse and remand the case to the District Court in order to give the Cherokees an opportunity to offer proof concerning the significance and centrality of their ancestral burial grounds in light of the standard we have adopted.[53]

Finally, inasmuch as culture was a determining factor, Stambor correctly points out that the earlier relevant cases, dealing with educational factors among the Amish, were far more clearly linked to their culture, and *not* their religion, and were certainly in no way central to their religion.[54]

One of the more interesting comments of the judges is their rejection of the defendant's argument that the Cherokee held no property interest in the area. Here, in one sentence, is at least a minimum acknowledgment to past history – when the court holds that 'While this is a factor to be considered, we feel it should not be conclusive in view of the history of the Cherokee expulsion from Southern Appalachia, followed by the "Trail of Tears" to Oklahoma … '.[55]

In a parallel case[56] (argued three weeks earlier but decided some nine months later) another circuit court specifically overruled a District Court that had stressed property rights of the government. However, this aspect of the decision had little effect on the outcome of the petition, also against the Indian petitioners. At issue was a plea by a group of Navajo Indians to protect the sacred nature of the Rainbow Bridge National Monument, which is surrounded by the Navajo reservation. The creation of an artificial lake in the area had transformed it from an isolated spot to a tourist attraction, and the overall rise in water levels arising from the lake had led to the drowning of some of the tribe's gods, as well as denying access to prayer spots. On these points the court affirms the district court's denial of petition in blunt form – 'We agree with the trial court that the government's interest in maintaining the capacity of Lake Powell at a level that intrudes into the Monument outweighs plaintiff's religious interest.'[57]

Furthermore, although the plaintiffs encounter difficulties 'in performing solemn religious ceremonies in an area frequented by tourists,' this is negated by the 'unquestionable' fact that '… the government has a strong interest in assuring public access to this natural wonder'.[58] More specifically the court practically scolds the plaintiffs, in claiming that what they 'seek in the name of the Free Exercise Clause is affirmative action by the government which implicates the Establishment Clause of the First Amendment'.[59] On this basis the court does not even see reason to grant a constitutional right to the plaintiffs that will ensure that 'tourists visiting the Bridge act "in a respectful and appreciative manner".'[60] In fact, the court notes that the Park Service has imposed certain controls on behavior (as is done in most parks). This is reasonable apparently, as long as it is not done for the purpose of helping the Navajo preserve the sacred nature of the site!

Several years later, the clash between tourism and religious rights of the Indians was discussed by the Court of Appeals in the 8th Circuit.[61] Two major pleas were presented by the petitioners – that the development of tourist facilities in a State Park was affecting their capacity to carry out their religious ceremonies, and that access to the religious sites within the park was conditional on obtaining a permit (even though it was free for those coming for ceremonial purposes). The arguments relied not only on constitutional rights of freedom of religion, but also international human rights instruments such as the Universal Declaration of Human Rights and the International Covenant on Civil and Political Rights.[62] In a short judgment relying on the aforementioned earlier decisions (dealing with Indians only), the court affirms the District Court's rejection of the petition.

In contrast, *Wilson v. Block*,[63] decided ten days later, is a much more extensive judgment dealing with similar issues of the development of a government-owned ski site clashing with the religious rights of the Navajo and Hopi tribes.

The claim of the two tribes is described by the court as follows:

> The plaintiffs stress that development of the Snow Bowl for a ski resort is grossly inconsistent with their beliefs. The Hopis and the Navajos believe that they owe a duty to the deities to maintain the San Francisco Peaks in their natural state. They believe that breach of that duty will lead to serious adverse consequences for their peoples. Navajo and Hopi religious practitioners are deeply troubled by the development that has already occurred upon the Peaks, and expansion of the Snow Bowl will increase their disquiet.[64]

After a discussion of the American Indian Religious Freedom Act, the court goes into far greater detail in discussing a string of environmental laws. In terms of the religious aspect, the court rejects all the petitioners' claims, determining that 'The plaintiffs simply have not demonstrated that development will prevent them from engaging in any religious practices.'[65] This finding relies, *inter alia,* on affidavits submitted by two experts on Hopi and Navajo religion, giving evidence on behalf of the government.[66] Their explanations of the religions seem to have been conclusive, and to have outweighed the affidavits submitted by Hopi and Navajo religious practitioners. In many respects, this decision is the most problematical, as it rejects outright the contention of the Native Americans as to the meaning and import of their religious practices. In the other cases, the courts did at least, in one degree or another, accept the evidence of the petitioners, but held that the religious factor was not sufficient to deny governmental plans. In this latter case, the court blandly states that they need not even consider whether the governmental plans are of a compelling interest as 'the plaintiffs have not shown that development will burden them in their religious beliefs or practices'.[67] Here, not only was centrality not an issue, but what was apparently determinative (even though the court does not spell it out specifically) was the lack of sincerity. While the legal decision, which claims that there is no burden on religious practices and consequently no need for the second phase of measuring religious needs *vis-à-vis* governmental needs, seems to be the more acceptable one, the social implications are in fact far more troublesome.

Yet, of all the cases in the last two decades dealing with the free exercise of religion for the Native Americans, the one that has evoked the most reaction is that which dealt not with access to, and protection of, sacred sites, but the use of the peyote drug. Here, the evidence of many experts over many years to convince, with a certain amount of success, the need for such use in religious ceremonies, or the non-addictive properties of the drug, were suddenly to no avail. Two Indians, dismissed from their jobs as drug counselors when it became known to their employees that they used peyote in religious ceremonies, were then denied unemployment compensation by the State, since they were held personally responsible for their loss of jobs.[68] Their claim that they were being denied the free exercise of their religion was heard at several levels, and on two occasions, before the Supreme Court. After they were initially successful in the Oregon Court of Appeals[69] and the Oregon Supreme Court,[70] the United States Supreme Court granted a writ of *certiorari* to hear an appeal. On the first occasion,[71] the Court held that since they were 'uncertain about the legality of the religious use of peyote in Oregon',[72] it preferred to remand the cases to examine this issue – specifically the question of the criminality of peyote use. However, in dissent, Justice Brennan opens his opinion with the blunt statement: 'Respondents Smith and Black were fired for practicing their religion.'[73]

When the case was reheard, and then returned to the Supreme Court,[74] the narrow majority of Justices (in a 5–4 decision) gave precedence to the compelling necessity of the state's concerns.[75] The Court's decision is perhaps most disturbing in that it seems far less sensitive to religious freedom (let alone tribal rights) than many legislatures. In fact, the Court's decision seems out of touch with majority thinking, considering the large number of States that, in contrast to Oregon, whose legislation was being challenged, had indeed made concessions in their laws to allow for the exception of the use of peyote for religious purposes. This fact was clearly brought out in a dissenting Judgment.[76] It should be mentioned again that similar concessions were occasionally made to religious groups during Prohibition, to allow them to use wine in their sacraments and rituals.

One of the intriguing aspects of the case is that it dealt with both drugs and religion only indirectly, which may actually increase its significance. At issue was not the religious ceremony *per se*, nor even the violation of the criminal sanction on drug use. The respondent in the case was the Workmen's Compensation Board, challenged because of a ruling, as noted, which deprived the claimants, American Indians who practiced the recognized Native American religion, from receiving unemployment compensation after they had been dismissed from their jobs as drug counselors, when it became known that they had participated in a religious ritual where the peyote drug was used.

The Court held that the compelling State interest of doing away with drug abuse should be allowed to claim precedence over any constitutional protection of the free exercise of religion. The Court adduced evidence of the dangers of drugs and the need to control their use. The Court also placed reliance on an earlier precedent of the *Gobitis* case – of the two Jehovah's Witnesses children who had been forced to leave school for refusing to salute the flag – completely ignoring the fact that the case had been specifically and unequivocally overruled three years later!

More important for our thesis, however, is the complete disregard by the judges in the majority of two crucial facts, noted in the dissenting judgment. The first deals with the positive effect that the drug, peyote, had on those using it in the course of a religious ceremony, facilitating the possibility of entering a state of inspiration and deepened awareness. On this score, evidence had been led as to the positive impact of peyote use in religious ceremonies, and the Court's knowledge of this aspect of the use of peyote is clearly established in the dissenting judgment, which also notes that 'The State … offers … no evidence that the religious use of peyote has ever harmed anyone.'[77] The opinion adds that there is no irresponsible use of drugs, and that the spiritual code of the peyote religion is certainly compatible with the values that Oregon is trying to achieve with its drug laws.

Second, passing mention is also made in the dissenting Judgment of the widely-known fact that there is indeed a very real problem of substance abuse among the American Indians (as among other similar social groups, such as the Aborigines in Australia). This abuse, though, is of alcohol, with utterly devastating effects on the physical well-being of both individuals and the social fabric.[78] If there is a compelling need for intervention, it is to stamp out the exploitation of the American Indians' vulnerability to the temptations of alcohol as an outlet for the malaise and anomie of their life, undermined and destroyed as it has been by the dominant surrounding culture, which, at some point in time, declared its preference for the use of alcohol over that of drugs as a legitimate source of substance use. In fact, it is quite possible that the best antidote to the seductions of alcohol, a foreign 'drug', is the resurgence of Indian culture and its religion, along with its ritual and use of peyote. That the majority opinion judges could be insensitive to, or even unaware of, such considerations is one of the most glaring examples of ethnocentric thinking.

Finally, it should be noted that the *Smith* decision overrides an earlier Court of Appeal judgment (*People v. Woody*) that had held that the use of peyote was so central to the Native American religion that the right to use it as part of the free exercise of religion was guaranteed by the Constitution.[79] Paradoxically, or perhaps revealingly, this particular judgment had been quoted in an earlier decision to reject an Indian petition (in the *Sequoyah* case),[80] since it was held that the particular argument in the latter case did not deal with a central aspect of the religion, and so the case was distinguished from the ruling allowing peyote because of its centrality. The Court in *Sequoyah* summed up the attitude to peyote (based on the *Woody* decision in the Court of Appeal):

> The hallucinogenic drug peyote was found to play a central role in the ceremony and practice of the Native American church … . The 'meeting' ceremony, involving the use of peyote was found to comprise the cornerstone of the religion. Peyote was found to be more than a sacrament; it itself was an object of worship.[81]

Although these decisions – in the *Sequoyah* and *Smith* cases – were given at different court levels, the overall implications are a *reductio ad absurdum,* that can only be understood in the context of judicial indifference to Indian pleas and plight, and obtuseness to the compelling needs, not of the state so often injected into court opinions, but of clear-cut constitutional protections. Simply put – in the *Sequoyah* case, the court emphasized the centrality of peyote use in Native American religion (which was not at issue at all) in order to justify rejecting a plea that had to do with sacred sites, on the basis of these sites not being central to the religion; in *Smith* (which *was* based on peyote) the Court ignored the issue of centrality in order to find against the Indian petitioner and in favor of the state's compelling interest in fighting drug abuse. Thus, apparently, for the courts, when peyote is *not* at issue, it is considered a central factor in the religion, but when it *is* at issue, its centrality disappears or becomes irrelevant. The *non sequitur* reveals, I would submit, not merely faulty logic, but prejudicial attitudes. But the upshot is not merely incorrect judicial interpretation of fact and law, but judicial failure to adequately invoke basic constitutional rights. The immediate victims are the Indian petitioners – but the real loss is of the society at large, with its constitutional protections being whittled away by those who are entrusted with the task of safeguarding and enforcing them.

There may well be some tribal customs – in the United States or elsewhere – which pose a problem for modern societies, even within a pluralistic framework, but the use of peyote as a religious sacrament is surely not an example of such a problem – even without a pluralistic perspective. Judicial confrontation with peyote use seems to have led to a greater negative impact on clear thinking and pertinent reasoning on the part of the justices than any proven or even presumed detrimental conduct by those who actually use the drug as a sacrament in their regular religious ritual.

Indeed, the Court seems to be not only insensitive to constitutional factors, but also removed from social reality and overall political concerns; for in the wake of the *Smith* decision, Congress enacted the Religious Freedom Restoration Act of 1993 (RFRA),[82] the name itself indicating clearly the intent to override *Smith*, and limit the impact of the compelling-interest of the state. However, within four years, the Supreme Court, in a case that had nothing to do with the religion of the American Indians (but involved a building permit for the expansion of a church, and the application of zoning law), declared the RFRA to be unconstitutional.[83] Three justices, in dissent, suggested the urgent need for a re-consideration of the precedent laid down in the *Smith* case – their concerns, however, deal with the issue of freedom of religion in general, and not specifically with the problems encountered by Native Americans. Basically, the situation is that the Supreme Court has activated its power of judicial review to nullify an Act of Congress aimed at rectifying the consequences of the *Smith* decision. The Court thus seems lax in activating the constitutional provisions of the free exercise of religion for Native Americans, yet zealous in preventing Congress from offering legislative protection to them.[84]

NOTES

1. See, for instance, Max Weber, *The Protestant Ethic and the Spirit of Capitalism* (New York: Scribner's, 1958).
   For a critique of Weber's emphasis on rationality in the modern world, see Leon Sheleff, *Social Cohesion and Legal Coercion: A Critique of Weber, Durkheim, and Marx* (Atlanta, GA, and Amsterdam: Rodopi, 1997), Part 1, 'Weber Revisited'.
2. Robert Bellah, 'Civil Religion in America', *Daedalus* 96 (1967), p. 1. See also in Bellah, *Beyond Belief: Essays on Religion in a Post-Traditional World* (New York: Harper & Row, 1970).
3. Aidan Southall, 'White Strangers and Their Religion in East Africa and Madagascar', in W. Shack and E. Skinner (eds), *Strangers in African Societies* (Berkeley: University of California Press, 1979), pp. 235–6.
4. See, for example, Robert Berkhofer, *Salvation and the Savage: An Analysis of Protestant Missions and American Indian Response 1787–1862* (Lexington: University of Kentucky Press, 1985).
5. See, for example, James Mooney, *The Ghost Dance Religion* (Chicago: University of Chicago Press, 1966).
6. See, for instance, J.H. McGregor (ed.), *The Wounded Knee Massacre from the Viewpoint of the Sioux* (Rapid City, SD: Fenwyn Press, 1940).
7. On peyote use in religious ceremonies, see D. Aberle, *The Peyote Religion Among the Navaho People* (Chicago: Aldine, 1966); and Hazel Hertzberg, *The Search for An American Indian Identity: Modern Pan-Indian Movements* (Syracuse, NY: Syracuse University Press, 1971), Part III, Chapter 10, 'The Peyote Cult'; p. 239 and Chapter 11, 'The Native American Church', p. 259. See also James Plotkin, *Menomini Peyotism* (Philadelphia, PA: The American Philosophical Society, 1952).
8. S.J. Res. 102, Aug. 11, 1978, Pub. L. No. 95-341, 92 Stat. 469; codified in part 42 U.S.C. Sec. 1996.
9. The American Indian Religious Freedom Act is known also by its acronym, AIRFA.
10. For broad discussion, see special issue of *Cultural Survival Quarterly* devoted to topic of 'American Indian Religious Freedom', 19 (1996), Winter issue.
11. *Reynolds v. United States*, 98 US 145 (1879); and *Davis v. Beason*, 133 US 333 (1890).
12. *Walker v. Superior Court* (1988), 47 Cal. 3d 112.
13. *Braunfield v. Brown,* 366 US 599 (1961).
14. *Minersville School District v. Gobitis*, 310 U.S. 586 (1940).
15. *Goldman v. Weinberger, Secretary of Defense*, 475 US 503 (1986).
16. For general discussion of the issues involved, see Leon Sheleff, '"Thou Shalt not be too Different": Civil Rights, Social Control and Deviant Religious Practices in the United States', *Israel Yearbook on Human Rights* 23 (1994), p. 193.
17. *West Virginia State Board of Education v. Barnett*, 319 US 624 (1943).
18. Legislation in 1988, shortly after the *Goldman* decision, allowed for slight deviations from the dress code for religious reasons, provided that they were not ostentatiously displayed. This was precisely the situation in the *Goldman* case, yet the Court, at that stage, gave precedence to the army dress code.
19. See the discussion in Chapter 17, 'Family Matters'.
20. See discussion in Alison Dundes Renteln, 'Is the Cultural Defense Detrimental to the Health of Children?' *Law and Anthropology: International Yearbook for Legal Anthropology* 7 (1994), p. 27.
21. National Prohibition Act, Title II, a3, 41 Stat. 308. The act gave practical expression to the constitutional amendment, but allowed a degree of flexibility to the States in implementing its provisions.
22. *Lyng v. Northwest Indian Cemetery Protective Association*, 485 US 439.
23. *Employment Division, State of Oregon v. Smith*, 494 US 872 (1990).
24. See formal notifications of a series of cases, which will be discussed later in the chapter, at nn. 46 to 67. The writ of *certiorari* involves a decision by the Supreme Court as to its willingness to hear the appeal. Refusal to do so means that the decision of the lower court stands.
25. This is the situation in both the *Lyng* and *Smith* cases mentioned in nn. 22 and 23.
26. See *Lyng*, p. 464 (dissent of Brennan who notes that 'the high country is indispensable to the religious lives').
27. The lower court decision is *Northwest Indian Cemetery Protective Association v. Peterson,* 795 F. 2d

688 (9th Cir. 1986).

28. *Lyng v. Northwest Indian Cemetery Protective Association*, pp. 456–8. The Court states that 'Notwithstanding the sympathy that we all must feel for the plight of the Indian respondents, it is plain that the approach taken by the dissent cannot withstand analysis' (p. 456).
29. Ibid., p. 451.
30. Ibid., p. 451.
31. Ibid., p. 454.
32. Ibid., p. 454. The Court then suggests that such solicitude accords with the American Indian Religious Freedom Act.
33. Ibid., pp. 452–3.
34. Ibid., p. 453. The Court adds that in making this statement 'No disrespect for these practices is implied.'
35. Ibid., p. 452.
36. Ibid., pp. 473–4.
37. Ibid., pp. 457–8. In general, see also Anita Clark Pryor and Gypsy Cowherd Bailey, 'An Indian Site-Specific Religious Claim Again Trips Over Judeo-Christian Stumbling Blocks', *Journal of Land Use and Environmental Law* 5 (1989), p. 293.
38. *Sherbert v. Werner,* 374 US 398 (1963), dealing with Sabbath observance.
39. *Wisconsin v. Yoder,* 406 US 205 (1972), dealing with compulsory school attendance.
40. *Frank v. State,* 604 P 2d 1068 (Alaska, 1979).
41. On cultural defense, see discussion in next chapter, 'A Reasonable "Cultural" Defence'.
42. The 'lesser evil' is used as a criterion for accepting the defense of necessity or of self-defense – and could be used as a criterion for a cultural defense.
43. *Frank v. State*, p. 1073.
44. Jeff Fish, 'Sacred Site Free Exercise Claims on Government Land: The Constitutional Slighting of Indian Religions', *New Mexico Law Review* 20 (1990), p. 120.
45. Howard Stambor, 'Manifest Destiny and American Indian Religious Freedom: *Sequoyah, Badoni,* and the Drowned Gods', *American Indian Law Review* 10 (1982), p. 59; see also in the same issue, Dean Suagee, 'American Indian Religious Freedom and Cultural Resources Management: Protecting Mother Earth's Caretakers', p. 1.
46. *Sequoyah v. TVA*, 620 F. 2d 1159 (1980); cert. denied, 449 U.S. 953 (1980).
47. Ibid., p. 1164.
48. Ibid., p. 1160.
49. Ibid., p. 1164.
50. Ibid., p. 1162.
51. Ibid., p. 1163.
52. Ibid., p. 1165 (Merritt, dissenting).
53. Ibid., p. 1165.
54. Stambor, 'Manifest Destiny', at pp. 65, 73, 74.
55. Ibid., p. 1164.
56. *Badani v. Higginson,* 638 F.2d 172 (1980).
57. Ibid., p. 177.
58. Ibid., p. 178.
59. Ibid., p. 178.
60. Ibid., p. 179.
61. *Crow v. Gullet,* 706 F.2d. 856 (1983).
62. Ibid., p. 857.
63. *Wilson v. Block,* 705 F.2d 735 (1983).
64. Ibid., p. 740.
65. Ibid., p. 745.
66. Ibid., p. 744.
67. Ibid., p. 745.
68. *Employment Division, Department of Human Services v. Smith*, 494 US 872 (1990) (Smith II).
69. *Black v. Employment Division,* 75 Or. App. 735; 707 P.2d 1274 (Or. App. 1985); *Smith v. Employment Division,* 75 Or. App. 764; 709 P. 2d 445 (1986).
70. *Smith v. Employment Div., Dept. of Human Resources,* 301 Or 209; 721 P.2d 445 (1986); *Black v. Employment Div., Dept. of Human Resources,* 301 Or. 221; 721 P.2d 451 (1986).

71. *Employment Division v. Smith,* 485 US 660 (1988) (Smith I). It might be noted that this case was argued eight days after the *Lyng* case – 30 November 1987 and 8 December 1987; and the decisions were handed down also eight days apart (19 April 1987 and 27 April, 1987).
72. Ibid., p. 673.
73. Ibid., p. 674.
74. *Employment Division v. Smith* (Smith II).
75. For a recent penetrating analysis of the religion clauses, using the *Smith* decision as an opening gambit, see A. Greene, 'The Political Balance of the Religious Clauses', *Yale Law Journal* 102 (1993), p. 1611. For a further recent article, linking the *Smith* decision with a case still before the Supreme Court (argued in November 1992), dealing with animal sacrifice as part of religious belief, see R.E. Drinan and J.I. Hoffman, 'Religious Freedom and the *Oregon v. Smith* and *Hileah* Cases,' *Journal of Church and State* 35 (1993), p. 19. For a broad discussion of the issues involved in the *Smith* case, see A.E. Beeson, 'Dances with Justice: Peyotism in the Courts: An Anthropological Critique', *Emory Law Journal* (1992), p. 1121. For support of decision, see W.P. Marshall, 'In Defense of *Smith* and Free Exercise Revisionism', *University of Chicago Law Review.* 58 (1991), p. 308; and M.W. McConnell, 'Free Exercise Revisionism and the *Smith* Decision,' *University of Chicago Law Review* 57 (1990), p. 1109.
76. Smith II, above, 913. A dissenting opinion by Justice Blackman notes 23 such states with exemption clauses in their drug laws for religious use of peyote.
77. Ibid., p. 907.
78. See discussion in Chapter 16, 'For Shame', below, and the references – Marcia Langton, 'Rum, Seduction and Death: Aboriginality and Alcohol', *Oceania* 63 (1992-3), p. 203; and Anthony Wallace, *The Long, Bitter Trail: Andrew Jackson and the Indians* (New York: Hill & Wang, 1993).
79. *People v. Woody*, 61 Cal. 22 716; 40 Cal. Rptr. 69; 394 P. 2d 813 (1964).
80. *Sequoyah* case, p. 1164.
81. Ibid., p. 1164.
82. Religious Freedom Restoration Act of 1993 (RFRA), 107 Stat. 1488, 42 USCS, Sec. 2000.
83. *City of Boerne v. Flores*, 521 US; 138 L. Ed. 2d. 624. However, for a decision by the Supreme Court in favor of a marginal religious group, mainly because a local law had been narrowly formulated to focus on a particular religious practice, see *Church of the Lukumi Bobalu Aye, Inc. v. Hialeah,* 508 US 520.
84. For a penetrating discussion of this case, dealing not just with the religious aspect, but larger questions of congressional power (for instance to rectify the legal position in response to Supreme Court decisions), see Michael McConnell, 'Institutions and Interpretation: A Critique of *City of Boerne v. Flores*', *Harvard Law Review* 111 (1997), p. 153.

A Reasonable 'Cultural' Defense

The criminal law serves as a crucible for crystallizing a society's value system, for it is within this framework that a society lays down the parameters of acceptable behavior – and more specifically, issues a categorical statement of what conduct is to be disallowed on pain of punishment. However, not all behavior that is considered undesirable or even deviant, necessarily comes within the purview of the criminal law, for at issue is not just definition as to what is or is not desirable or permissible, but also the extent of a society's tolerance – its capacity or willingness to allow behavior despite the disapproval which it evokes among its members, or the majority of them, or a dominant group among them. This is true not only of the substantive rules laid down in the various sections of a criminal code which spell out the forms of behavior which are banned and which will, if performed, be punished, but also of the manner in which the law is to be adjudicated and interpreted.

Thus, a key aspect of any criminal law system is the defenses which are recognized as constituting a legalistic excuse or justification for the commission of the proscribed act. These defenses form one of the most intellectually intriguing and practically important aspects of criminal law adjudication.[1] Beyond the fate of the particular accused lie subtle undercurrents of societal wisdom, the capacity to see beyond the consensual norms of conformist behavior and to understand, perhaps even forgive, the commission of the act because of the idiosyncratic factors which motivate a particular individual in his aberrant behavior in a particular situation.

Occasionally the individual is exonerated because of the ascriptive category to which he belongs, where, for instance, age is an absolute release (for the very young) or recent motherhood (where a homicidal act may be defined as an act of infanticide, and not murder).[2] In other cases, much more complex and confusing, it is the specific situational environment that is the key determinant, as, for instance, where the violator acts in self-defense, or in response to a provocation, or as a consequence of threatening factors which he seeks to forestall, or else if he is not in full control of his actions (for various reasons ranging from innocent intoxication to unavoidable automatism) and is thus not fully cognizant of what is happening or what he is doing.[3]

A further aspect of criminal law is the formal, societal response toward those who are held to have violated society's norms. Modern penal law focuses very much on punishment, ranging from the ultimate penalties of capital punishment or life imprisonment, through fines and forfeiture, to probation and community orders. Many penologists have noted the close correlation between punitive practices and the larger patterns of a society's ethos, or alternatively, of its needs or even the interests of certain groups within the society.[4]

It is clear, then, that given the cultural and social differences between tribal communities and the state, some of the differences – relative to both normative beliefs and everyday behavior – will inevitably lead to conflict in the application of the law. The problems include the very substantive definition of what should be considered criminal, of the manner in which alleged criminal acts should be adjudicated, of special considerations that might be relevant, or of the nature of the societal response to violations of normative rules.

Pluralistic formulae would seem, at first glance, to be most problematic in this area, as the unique aspects of criminal law – prohibitions on certain forms of behavior or punitive reactions – raise the need for the strictest standards in the implementation of the law. Thus, guilt must be established beyond a reasonable doubt, due process must be enforced, and punishment must be subject to constitutional and human rights standards, factors which seem to leave little room for flexibility.

Yet criminal law has its flexible aspects, most notably in the sentencing stage, where there is the notorious problem of inconsistency with often only a limited degree of guidance through higher court precedents, and also with the possibility of creative decision-making by innovative judges. Further, there are extrajudicial, sometimes *sub rosa,* processes such as plea bargaining, which may link the willingness to admit to the crime with the prospect of a lenient sentence. In addition, there are theoretical arguments and practical projects aimed at seeking alternative dispute resolution, the latter an interesting development which, paradoxically, tends to make some aspects of law enforcement similar to the social control procedures of simple societies, including tribal communities of the modern world. Further, those defenses linked to the situational framework, such as self-defense or provocation, are closely related to the perceptions of the actor as filtered through to his awareness by the cultural norms of his society. A danger will be sensed, a provocation will be perceived, responses will be undertaken, according to the standards and the way of thinking of the surrounding milieu. Specifically in the criminal law itself the debate has raged endlessly as to whether or not the standard to be applied is subjective or objective, and to what extent that standard, particularly (but not only) if subjective, should be oriented to the belief system of a subcultural group, of which a tribe is one example.

In any event, since it is the criminal law that lays down the range of acceptable behavior, it is often here that the clash of cultures between the larger society and smaller groupings will find its most explicit expression. In its most brash form, it may be seen in the manner in which the social and cultural practice of polygamy becomes, by definition, the crime of bigamy, or the practice of scarification, aimed at creating beauty, becomes child abuse, constituting the crime of battery or assault, or the taking of a sacrament might constitute a violation of the substance abuse laws.

But perhaps no custom expresses the differing value-systems more than the practice of what is known as sorcery or witchcraft, and the various implications that flow from such belief. These are terms that are often used loosely and it is advisable to differentiate between the negative and the positive uses of what is known as 'witchcraft'; those practices which are aimed at causing harm to another, and those, in contrast, which are aimed at providing succor and treatment.[5] Succinctly put, it may be argued that the former should be eradicated while the latter should be allowed and even encouraged.[6]

But the issue of witchcraft is by no means exhausted by the provisions that are made for its control as against those who are its practitioners. Witchcraft is a word that conjures up some of the most negative images of non-western society. In fact, most of the litigation and the academic literature in this area deal not with those who practice witchcraft, but with those who respond to it, in an effort to evade its potential harm, a response that sometimes involves homicidal results. It is these cases, far more than the actual practice of witchcraft, that expose the depth of the clash of cultures, and that accordingly pose the most critical problems for just decision-making.

Within a culture that retains its belief in the existence and the efficacy of witchcraft, the fear of being subjected to its presumed potential harmful impact can become of overwhelming import to the prospective victim. The resultant response constitutes almost the cutting edge of culture conflict,[7] as an extreme pre-emptive defensive action is taken to forestall the feared consequences. A person who lives in a cultural milieu that believes in the power of witchcraft will sometimes take defensive measures to prevent the perceived danger. The most extreme reaction to ensure his own safety is to kill the person who is the source of his fear. In these circumstances, it is only by relating to the cultural background that it is possible to understand the killing of a person believed to possess magical powers and believed by the killer to be using them to cause direct harm to him or to those close to him. To understand is not necessarily to condone, but it certainly elicits the complexity of the issue. As the modern law allows for exceptions, in terms of specified conditions, to the blanket ban on killing, the question becomes whether, without conceding the correctness of the belief, consideration can be given to the surrounding circumstances – a belief by the killer that his victim was, in fact, threatening him and those close to him.

A number of avenues have been explored in an attempt to find modern law solutions to the problems caused by this tribal belief. The key legal argumentation is that the person committing the alleged crime acted, by his understanding, in self-defense, since the deceased person was engaged in activity that would, without a pre-emptive killing, have led to his own death or to the death of those close to him.

Self-defense is a recognized principle in any legal system, with the law recognizing the rationale of allowing a person to defend himself against the evil machinations of a potential adversary. It is permissible to kill a person brandishing a lethal weapon and threatening to use it; this is a clear-cut case almost instinctively recognized by anyone and incorporated into almost every legal system. However, there are more marginal situations, such as where a threat is not of physical harm, but to property,[8] or where there are alternative and less drastic solutions to the danger, or where the threat is not to the actor but to a third party,[9] or where those killed in self-defense are numerically far greater than the number saved by virtue of the drastic response. To determine whether the alleged crime will be forgiven and the exemption provided by the law activated, various rules have been laid down which focus primarily on the need to ensure that the action adopted was the lesser evil – whether it was better for the potential victim to save his own life, even by killing his tormentor, than to succumb to the latter's blatant threats.

It is manifestly clear that the issues are extremely tenuous, involve determining whether there was indeed a meaningful threat, and whether the response was attuned to such danger.

Of a similar nature is the more limited defence of provocation, used only for the specific crime of murder – where a person reacts not in defense, but in anger, moved emotionally to uncontrollable rage by some act of his protagonist. While the law affords some understanding of the passion which takes hold of the person, it does not provide total exoneration. The provocation, if proved, will lead to a lesser charge – of manslaughter or homicide instead of murder.[10] It is clear that the difficulties of determining if there was indeed a legitimate cause for self-defense become compounded in the case of provocation since it is not real outer danger that is at issue, but inner emotional torment. Even more so than in the case of self-defense, the question of the reasonableness of the response becomes crucial. Over the years the courts have used the idea of reasonableness to attempt to determine whether the response was within the bounds that most people would have chosen.

For the purpose of determining whether the criteria were met, the court uses the test of 'the reasonable person' and asks how he would have behaved in similar circumstances. The reasonable person, based on some sort of composite picture, is often presented picturesquely as the passenger on the 'Clapham Omnibus', an average person randomly chosen by chance, thrown into an acute situation to which he is obliged to respond. The problem, of course, is that the Clapham Omnibus travels in London, and so do its myriad of hypothetical passengers. How applicable is such a situation to the vastly different conditions in other parts of the world, over which the common law principles, as laid down by judges, have been imposed?[11]

Within England itself, the legal debate has been engaged on whether the criteria should be objective or subjective,[12] and whether there are gradations along the scale where the membership of a particular group or the possession of a particular quality (for example, a physical handicap) may make such a person, on average, more sensitive to provocation. For instance, in a classic example of what the French call *crime passionnel,* would a husband, responding violently to a situation of finding his wife in bed with another man and killing either or both, be entitled to raise the defense of provocation? In general, the answer is positive, but what if he was not a husband but only cohabiting with her? Would the change of status be relevant for determining the degree of the response to the provocation? Or what if they were only affianced?

In the case of tribal membership, would a particular movement, or the reciting of particular words, suggest that a spell was being cast by a witchdoctor or sorcerer? Could such an act, totally innocuous to someone else and certainly to our hypothetical bus passenger, constitute a provocation? Or, being informed that such a spell had already caused serious harm, for instance the death of one's child, would the information, quite meaningless to one who did not believe in it, allow for the defense of provocation?

Generally the defenses of self-defense and provocation are submitted to the court as alternatives – firstly, the claim is made that the accused acted in self-defense; alternatively it is argued that he was provoked. Where both defenses fail (as they usually do), further arguments inevitably present themselves. If the accused is considered to have had no valid reason to act because the belief in witchcraft has no basis in reality, then surely due consideration should be given to the accused's mistaken perception of reality. He should, so the argument goes, be entitled to the defense of mistake of fact which, unlike the mistake in law, does entitle the person in error to claim a legitimate legal defense. For surely, if the facts were as presumed by the accused, there might well have been an understanding of his pre-emptive act – either as self-defense or as provocation. If this latter argument is also rejected, then a further contention presents itself – if the dimensions of the incorrect understanding of social reality are so great that the mistake is not a reasonable one, then the accused's behavior can only be seen as the product of an unstable mind, which might justify a finding of insanity.

If this last argument too is rejected because his belief emerges not from within himself, but from the cultural milieu in which he lives, then we encounter the extreme paradox – that the accused cannot be considered insane as his beliefs are not idiosyncratic to him, but are shared by many of his fellow tribespeople, and so, within that context, he cannot be considered insane. For purposes of examining his behavior, the accused is not entitled to rely on the mores and customs of his tribal community. For purposes of determining his sanity, the very prevalence of the belief is used to deny possible mental illness that would avoid criminal culpability.

What emerges is an inherent illogic in the manner in which the defense is evaluated. The position is well described by Yoram Shachar: 'the greater the number of persons who believe in a wrong view of reality and share the view culturally, the lesser the chance each of them stands of getting absolved from criminal responsibility for acting on the basis of such a view'.[13]

While the problems of witchcraft may seem no more than an esoteric peculiarity, they crop up on occasion. It is not clear whether, within the framework of judicial confrontation, it is possible to expect a comprehensive understanding of the totality of the problem. In different parts of the world most of the cases tend to reject the various defenses offered, although occasionally, because of the unique circumstances of a case or the personal propensity of a particular judge, the defenses have been successful. There has also, naturally, been a certain amount of academic discussion on the issue, generally in order to expound on the problem itself, not necessarily in order to offer a solution. Often the debate on witchcraft is bound up with the larger debate on self-defense or provocation, or the manner in which the cultural climate or the general belief-system, or the average character structure of a community, may affect the response to a dangerous and provocative situation.

Occasionally, however, a strong stand is taken. Few have been as outspoken and insistent on the need for a reassessment of standard approaches as Kharisu Satiyar Chukkol, a Nigerian jurist, whose approach is unequivocally stated in the very title of his essay dealing not with witchcraft *per se,* but with what he terms 'Supernatural beliefs and the criminal law in Nigeria', where he categorically states: 'Contrary to all logic, however, our courts have persistently ruled that defenses founded on the belief of witchcraft should be rejected.'[14] Chukkol notes that the law and the courts may contribute substantively to enhancing the level of knowledge of a society, and so concedes that by insisting on a total denial of any validity to witchcraft, they may help to inculcate an understanding of reality. Moreover, he also takes cognizance of the danger of real criminals hypocritically exploiting the recognition of such a defense.[15] Nevertheless, in the final analysis, he argues for a close affinity to be sought, not just with physical reality (the lack of a causal nexus between sorcery and ensuing consequences), but also with the reality of community norms and the impact that they have upon the person's actions. He argues that the law:

> which operates in an African reality and seeks to regulate the conduct of African people ought to be applied in conformity with the prevailing social norms and values. A Nigerian threatened (or in some cases provoked) by the practice of witchcraft to kill his victim is hardly ever given a sympathetic hearing. Consistent with [the] prevailing ethos of his environment he may genuinely believe that some people are capable of harming him, his relations, or even his business by supernatural means. Left to him and an average member of his locality such people's machinations might be neutralized by all means at his disposal. Yet the law administered in his country's courts by his own countrymen term him a murderer should he strike back in self defense. The courts' stand is at best ambivalent for while they recognize the fact that there are Nigerians who believe in the existence of witches … they consistently rule that such beliefs where they exist cannot have any effect on the mind of an average Nigerian.

He further argues that

> African courts have clung rigidly to the letter of the imposed common law to the utter disregard of the prevailing beliefs among the indigenous population. Decades after colonial rule, and with Law Reform Commissions set up in many independent African countries, one would only hope that beliefs in supernatural powers and the existing criminal rules will be one area that will interest our law reformers. Yet from available evidence so far it does not seem probable that those haunted by witchcraft can have any early protection of the law.[16]

Most significantly, he takes issue with those African intellectuals who place the inculcation of modern western values above a sympathy for the average African, still swayed by his belief in the reality of witchcraft. Thus he points out that, while the Law Commission in Nigeria has non-lawyers in its ranks to allow for a broader perspective, they are still hidebound by the narrower interests of their members, all learned scholars in the disciplines of the social sciences – and so, as a result: 'That will leave possible witchcraft victims in the villages still with no effective protection.' Chukkol suggests specifically representation for the public at large on these commissions to make them more attuned to the reality of their society.

There is a need, according to him for 'people who one can truly describe as living "at close quarters" with indigenous customs and beliefs of the Nigerian people'.[17]

It would be easy to misunderstand Chukkol's intentions and to claim that he is not sufficiently cognizant of the harm wrought by witchcraft beliefs, and that his approach would lead to its continued practice. However, in fact, he is concerned that those who are adversely affected by witchcraft (the ones who perceive themselves to be its potential victims) are the ones who are being denied the protection of the law. He concludes by emphasizing that 'rejecting defenses founded on witchcraft as the courts do at present does mean punishing people whose minds are, for the most part, blameless. This is a clear negation of the fundamental principle of criminal responsibility' of the need for *mens res,* the criminal intent. Thus, 'any reform of the criminal law must take into account this irrefutable fact as no iota of justice can exist in a system of law which decides on issues of criminal responsibility in a complete cultural vacuum'.[18]

Chukkol is, of course, basically arguing on behalf of those who, far from having criminal intent, are themselves the victims of their mistaken beliefs. But, these beliefs are not some personal quirk for which the individual alone must bear the consequences and the responsibility for having delved into such aberrant and dangerous ideas. They are clearly embedded in the societal norms and they may easily be imbibed in the course of everyday living and interaction with others as part of a normal socialization process.

While, on the one hand, a modern state may wish to eradicate the belief in witchcraft and to punish those who practice it (as almost all have indeed done), the issue of a tolerance toward those taking what they presume to be a legitimate defensive action must be seen as a separate issue. Lack of tolerance can only undermine faith in the law – not among the educated, but among those very masses which it is the hope and the intent to educate. Meanwhile, of course, those who have, in all innocence, believed in the power of witchcraft to affect them, are being denied the protection of the judicial system when driven to extreme measures in order to protect themselves against perceived danger.

While Chukkol was writing at the academic level, a number of attempts have been made to incorporate just such an approach into the judicial system on the part of judges who displayed an understanding of both the overall cultural framework in which the act takes place and the personal pressures to which an individual may be subjected. But this understanding has, perhaps significantly, found most expression at the trial court level, where the judge is in direct contact with the victim/perpetrator and able to perceive, at close quarters, the belief-system which sustains him, the fear that grips him and the calculations that motivate him.

In contrast, in the more august forums of appeal hearings – removed from the thrust and parry of actually hearing the evidence unfolding in court and lacking the direct contact with the accused whose fate is at stake – the court tends to concentrate on the larger, theoretical issues, aware of its role in laying down precedent and in creating future norms, and these factors do not normally work in favor of the accused. For while it is apparently possible to allow maximum consideration of an individual's surrender to the pressures which daily life impose upon him, it is far more difficult to give sanction to such behavior as an acceptable norm of society, even though there are, as we shall show, many valid theoretical and practical factors actually working in that direction. An examination of decisions in three different areas – East Africa, Papua New Guinea, and Australia – will indicate this pattern of trial court willingness to recognize the realities of daily living in a particular case, and of appellate courts striving to lay down general rules for the society at large.

Robert Seidman, in his comprehensive anthology of criminal law in Africa,[19] presents a case of this nature that took place in Nyasaland (present-day Malawi) in the Fifties, which ended with an acquittal in the trial court and a conviction on appeal. The case is presented in a chapter dealing with the defense of 'Mistake of Fact' in a section entitled 'The Requirement of Reasonableness.'[20] The accused was charged with the murder of a cousin killed in the course of a family argument over familial obligations, after the deceased had said to him that he 'would not see the sun today'. As the trial judge explained this remark in its social context: 'the accused took the remark as an expression or act of witchcraft, and as meaning that the deceased had, or was about to, cast some kind of spell over him as a result of which he would die in the course of that day'. The British judge then noted his reliance on the African assessors (who sat on the bench with him) who 'are unanimous in their view that this was a definite expression of witchcraft, two of them going so far as to say that the mere pronouncing of these words would be thought to be sufficient to cause the accused's death'.[21] Examining the legal situation, the judge then held that:

> Whilst it is true that there is no English authority to be found dealing with the threat of witchcraft as raising a possible defence of self-defence, this does not, in my view, mean that there are no principles of English law which govern the position.

Going into detail as to the practicalities of the dilemma confronting the accused, the court stated as incontrovertible evidence that:

> the nearest witchdoctor who could prevent the spell was three days' journey distant, so that no other way of saving his life appeared to be open to the accused but to kill the deceased before the spell could take effect.[22]

Comparing this case with leading cases in which the accused was exonerated because the crime was committed in self-defense, the judge cuts through to the heart of the issue by stating that 'I find it difficult to accept the distinction drawn in some of the judgments between a physical and a metaphysical assault.' Then noting the larger implications of the impact of precedent, the court notes that:

> Some of the East African cases contain dicta pointing out the possible dangers of admitting self-defence as a valid defence in cases of alleged witchcraft. But I am of the opinion that it is not permissible on the ground of its possible dangers, to exclude a defence if it is valid in law.
>
> To my mind the important question of fact in the present case is whether the accused both genuinely and reasonably in all the circumstances believed that his own death was imminent, and the assessors who have assisted me in this case clearly take the view which (in view of the family circumstances disclosed) I see no reason to disagree with, that the accused's belief was both genuine and reasonable.

Applying overall principles of self-defense to the facts as determined, the court held that the homicide was excusable as the fatal blow was delivered because the accused felt it to be 'necessary for his preservation. For if the accused believes in the necessity, then even if such necessity does not in fact exist, there is a mistake of fact and not of law'.[23]

Supporting such a viewpoint is one of the leading figures in British criminal law, Glanville Williams, who, in an article written only a few years before this case, had persuasively argued that even an unreasonable mistake of fact should be recognized as falling within the legal purview of mistake of fact, creating the conditions for legitimate self-defense.[24] Williams's article deals with situations, hypothetical and real, that in some ways are even more removed from consensual perceptions, where belief in a ghost leads to a human being being mistaken for one and killed in order to remove the incorrectly perceived threat. As Williams argued, '... there are crimes (of which murder is one) where unreasonable mistake is a defence,'[25] and Williams notes the importance of such a defense, both for 'pockets of belief even in advanced communities' and because 'the common law has spread to backward territories where such beliefs are general'.[26]

On appeal against the acquittal heard in East Africa by British judges without the assistance of African assessors, the Supreme Court noted that the facts as determined could be accepted (particularly the genuine belief of the accused as to his imminent demise), and indicated that it would focus on the legal situation that arose therefrom.[27] The Court attached much significance to the reliance of the court on the African assessors and suggested that in so doing, the judge had reached an incorrect assessment as to the reasonableness, from a legal point of view, of the accused's action, for it became apparent that the trial court justice

> was thinking in terms of what might be regarded as reasonable in a person with the upbringing and background of an African. If this was so, then I think he was wrong in law ... [To] justify a killing in self-defence, the belief in the reality of the danger must not only be genuine, it must be reasonable. The test of reasonableness in itself implies an objective standard. The test of reasonableness is one that is constantly invoked in English law. In applying it, the standard is what would appear reasonable to the ordinary man in the street in England. The lives of considerable numbers of people are profoundly influenced by strange beliefs and phobias. But the existence of these peculiarities and the reactions that eventuate from them cannot be taken into account. It is the normal and the average that must be the guide.

The Appeal Court goes on to note the dangers of having a 'varying standard of reasonableness' which would 'vitiate the whole purpose of this test' and thus it 'cannot allow this standard to be varied in any way by the eccentricities of the particular individual who is on trial'.[28]

Then stressing the fact of applying English law, even in the context of Africa, the Court concludes that:

> bearing in mind that the law of England is still the law of England even when it is extended to Nyasaland, I do not see how any court, applying the proper test, could hold that a belief in witchcraft was reasonable so as to form the foundation for a defence that the law could recognise. Indeed the judgment that the court is ordinarily called upon to make as to what is reasonable, is, in this case, helped by what is, in effect, the legal recognition of the standard of the ordinary man. In the course of the last two centuries, all pains and penalties for witchcraft have disappeared from the English law.[29]

There are two factors emerging from this judgment which require further examination. Firstly, to what extent is the judgment a consequence of the colonial situation in which an imposed law, that of England, was applied in a dependent territory? To what extent do similar patterns of thought still prevail? To what extent does the state law still give priority to the normative legal standards of a foreign culture in determining, for instance, reasonable behavior, not just in Malawi, the successor state of Nyasaland, but elsewhere, or has independence allowed for a greater sensitivity and responsiveness to the surrounding local social environment? Secondly, is the law of England totally divested of involvement with superstitious beliefs (or, for that matter, even other value-judgments that are far removed from the law, yet have an impact on the manner in which the law is formulated, enforced and adjudicated)?[30]

A new state that has tried valiantly, but not necessarily successfully, to come to terms with consequences of the deep-seated belief in witchcraft, is Papua New Guinea. A Governmental Commission has thoroughly investigated the situation, making practical recommendations. A Sorcery Act has been promulgated, not without its ambiguities, involving a denial of its efficacy, together with a prohibition on its practice – a ruling which paradoxically takes some cognizance of its efficacy; and numerous cases have been brought to the courts.[31]

A further factor to be noted is the recognition of particularistic social factors that may be taken into account as part of the underlying principles recognized in constitutional practice. A key figure in this process is Bernard Narakobi, who is a former judge, a prolific writer on Melanesian Jurisprudence, and an active politician who has served, among other positions, as Minister of Justice.[32] As a judge, he was noted for his willingness to grant full recognition to local customs, even where it led to results not entirely in accord with prior precedent or accepted common law norms. However, on a number of occasions his decisions were overruled on appeal since the court was reluctant to grant some of the more problematic local customs the *imprimatur* of the land's highest court. But the issue is not just that of according recognition to questionable customs, it is also the issue of acknowledging the reality of daily social life as it is lived by citizens far removed not just from the intricacies of an alien court system, but also from the full impact of the larger society and its efforts to embrace progress, and most certainly from the higher courts of law, and even perhaps from ordinary effective law enforcement.

One case raises issues that go much beyond the opposing approaches adopted by the trial judge and the appellate court, and touches on the nature of the allegiance between citizens and state, and the capacity of the state to provide the kind of protection that will justify eliciting the requisite obedience to its law. It should be noted that the appeal case dealt only with the issue of penalty (even though some of the argumentation used by the trial judge, Narakobi, could have led, by logical deduction, to an acquittal). At the trial, and on conviction for murder, the lenient sentence of three months was imposed, as well as an additional payment of compensation (five pigs) in terms of traditional practices which, by statute, the courts are entitled to consider when imposing the penalty for a criminal conviction. On appeal,[33] the prison sentence was increased to five years, and the compensation was annulled as being beyond the power of the judge to impose.

This case, even though dealing only with the question of punishment, goes to the heart of the clash between traditional beliefs and the perspective of the modern legal system dedicated to an egalitarian rule of law that draws no distinction, especially in the field of criminal law, between persons.

Yet true justice must seek not just equality, but equity, specifically a flexible approach that will allow for exceptional approaches to cater for unusual situations and problems, whether of an individual or a group to which he belongs. While acknowledgment is often given to such idiosyncratic cases – perhaps the true 'hard cases'[34] which present real challenges for a fair judicial system – there is also an in-built reluctance to spread the largesse of special consideration too broadly lest, so the argument goes, the shared norms will be undermined. Nevertheless, some of these shared norms themselves obligate optimum, if not maximum, flexibility. Moral guilt, for instance, is the inner kernel and ultimate criterion of guilt. In some of the cases, it is specifically the quality of guilt that is lacking, the mental element of *mens rea,* of wishing in a sense to cause harm, to do evil, to break the law. Often there is a plain and simple clash between norms and the judge must decide which to favour.

In the case at issue, these inconsistencies are transparent. The Chief Justice, noting how deeply embedded the belief in witchcraft was, commented that in '… many communities in Papua New Guinea, belief in sorcery and its powers is very strong and we cannot brush it aside. My own people believe in it and great fear is caused by such belief.'[35] However, he went on to note that while 'the cultural setting of the respondent must be taken into account … it should not override the clear dictates of the Parliament'[36] which had allowed for a maximum penalty of life imprisonment with hard labor. The dilemma of the Court arises from its desire to bridge the gap between widespread beliefs that are incompatible with modern knowledge and the legal mandate to punish the perpetrator of serious crimes with sufficient severity, but, as we shall see, it is not the deficiencies of the belief-system alone that spawns the problem, but also the deficiencies of the legal system and the manner in which it is activated.

A fuller picture of social reality and the nature of social control emerges from the description of some of the events by another of the appeal court judges:

> There is no doubt that the respondents genuinely believed that the deceased was a sorcerer. They all came from the isolated area of Hewa behind Porgera … . These are and always have been strong mitigating factors … . But the respondents were aware of the Government law as they were taking the deceased to Porgera to face trial at the time that they killed her. It is true that she ran away and it may have been this which caused them to act on the sudden. But she had been caught and was being held when she was killed.[37]

Yet even this statement lacks some of the key ingredients without which the full nature of the respondents' torment cannot be understood. It is in a further judgment, that of Justice Kupi, that the full details of the accused's dilemma emerges. He writes:

> It is significant that at the outset, the respondents did not kill the sorcerer as is required by custom, but chose to take her to a Government station some five days' walk away. This, to my mind, is an indication of their knowledge of the law and Government influence on their lives. In my view their knowledge that a sorcerer should not be killed but reported to the police or the court is no different from any Papuan village which has over one hundred years' contact with the outside world and where fear of sorcery is still dominant. I do not suggest that the extent of Western influence is the same. All I am saying is that they know what to do with a sorcerer.[38]

Even though they may have felt under social pressure by others in the village to kill the sorcerer, '... the respondents exercised restraint from this pressure when they decided to take her to the Government Station .... The killing of a sorcerer is nothing less than taking the law into one's own hands.'[39]

However, what emerges from Justice Kupi's remarks is that far from a casual walk to the local police station (not to mention the possibility of a telephone call) to report her illegal activities as a sorcerer, the accused were involved in a five-day trek. We know nothing from the reported judgment of the circumstances of the trek, the problems that they encountered along the way, the arrangements they made for sleeping and eating, the measures they took for guarding the alleged sorcerer, how she managed to escape from their control, and what fears were induced by her temporary success. It seems to me that the issue of applying modern state law to this kind of situation involves not just the issue of witchcraft *per se*, but the very nature of social control, and the degree to which a citizen surrenders his right to self-help in return for the protection that the official and organized state authorities are presumed to offer him.

In the Nyasaland case, it was mentioned that the nearest witchdoctor, who could be asked to thwart the spell, was a three-day journey away. In the Papua New Guinea case, the distance to the nearest government station was a five-day walk, where there may be no alternative modes of travel – almost certainly no roads and quite possibly no navigable rivers. What kind of protection can the citizen expect in such circumstances, what kind of conception can he even have of governmental presence, what meaning can be attached to law and order, what expectations can he have of prompt and effective response to real or imagined dangers, what help can he anticipate against the potential evil that a sorcerer can wreak?

In such circumstances it is not just the belief-system that must be examined, but the total geographic environment. It is all very well for the court to make the accused beholden to the state laws based on the mere fact of seeking the intervention of governmental authority which indicates some minimal recognition on their part, but their desire to involve the central government in their problems must be understood in its total context for, in the final analysis, the looming danger of a sorcerer is immediate and present whereas the power and protection of the governmental authority is remote and vague. A sorcerer, escaping in the middle of a five-day journey, poses very real dangers for those who believe in her potency, while conversely, the presence of effective governmental control is highly dubious.

Justice Kupi correctly notes that the Sorcery Act 'makes provision for sorcery offenses. The deceased was entitled to be charged under that Act. Whether she was guilty or not she was entitled to the protection of the law.'[40] No doubt she was, but no less so were the accused, and given the details of distance and lack of effective governmental machinery in the vicinity, it could well be claimed that it was indeed the accused who had no 'protection of the law'; their efforts to gain such protection became undermined and their own safety became endangered the moment she effected an escape. To say so is not to deny the alleged sorcerer the right to be protected by law, but it is to claim no less a right for those fearful of her powers. The mere fact that she could, in fact, be charged with witchcraft, can certainly be interpreted by those who believe in it as an acknowledgment of her powers – and it is these powers that they were attempting to counteract.

In contrast to the conflicting decisions of trial and appellate courts in Papua New Guinea, there is a string of decisions dealing with similar issues, mainly in the context of provocation, which arose in the Northern Territory of Australia, in which generally there was no appeal and so the outlines of the considerations were laid down at the trial court level, generally in the course of giving instructions to the jury. One particular judge, Justice Kriewalt, was dominant, and his influence has been approvingly noted in a leading Australian textbook on criminal law. The authors, Norval Morris and Colin Howard, write:

> Kriewalt J tackled the problem of provocation among aborigines boldly, instructing juries that the terms used to describe what amounted to provocation at common law were to be understood in a relative sense, and were not necessarily to be applied to the reaction of an aborigine to a given stimulus in the same way as to the behavior of a white man under the same circumstances. In this manner, his Honour made a humane and sensible modification of the law to meet local conditions.[41]

In more general terms, they continue that:

> It is much to be regretted that none of his directions on provocation came up for consideration by the High Court. They are obviously important not only in Australia, or in any other courts where the common law has to be applied to indigenous and primitive peoples, but also to societies with such minority problems as are presented by Jamaicans in London and Puerto Ricans in New York.[42]

Some of these decisions lay down general rules as to how to treat the defense of provocation in circumstances where actions are taken that are consonant with tribal conduct, in fact possibly even of an obligatory nature, yet are in conflict with legal norms. On one occasion, Justice Kriewalt explained to the jury that:

> You may use these words, reasonable man, as meaning a reasonable native inhabitant of Australia. You may draw a distinction between the amount of provocation which is needed before the ordinary reasonable human being such as you are, would lose his self-control, and the lesser, if you think it applies ... degree of provocation needed before an aboriginal of Australia loses his self-control ... . You will apply the law in this case that you may adopt a lesser standard as amounting to provocation where a native is charged with murder than you would be entitled to draw where a white person is charged with murder.[43]

On another occasion, discussing retaliation to provocation, he noted that:

> Although I must lay down the law exactly the same for white people as for natives, the application of the rules of law by you may well be different. We all know that a white man cools down comparatively quickly. In the case of a native you may think it right to say that the effect of provocation lasts longer than in the case of a white person.[44]

In both these cases a verdict of manslaughter was returned.

Nevertheless, in slightly changed circumstances, where the issue dealt not so much with how to assess the behavior of Aborigines within the terms of the Western law, but how their own customs were to be regarded, Justice Kriewalt was far less indulgent of the Aborigine accused's conduct, explaining to the jury that 'It is no excuse for a native that he acts in accordance with his tribal law ... . Whatever your ideas may be about the wisdom of such a prosecution as this, although you may express those views outside the courtroom, inside the courtroom you must not give effect to them.'[45] Yet, despite these strictures, the jury in this case turned in an acquittal.[46] At issue was the impact of tribal custom on a person's conduct – in a two-fold sense. On the one hand the deceased had violated tribal law and was, therefore, to be punished; on the other, those who had killed him as part of a tribal sanction, were young men acting at the command of the tribal elders. Indeed, in situations such as this (where there was no possible defense of provocation, and the issue then became one of how to apply the law to a given state of facts), the court felt it had a duty to apply the law so as to serve as an educational factor for tribes only recently exposed to the norms and values of the larger society. In this case the accused had acted at the behest of the elders who wished for an extreme response of death, as the deceased had on two occasions revealed tribal secrets.

The court held that 'if this prisoner were not punished in some way all these tribes will believe that white law approves of the killing of a native who reveals tribal secrets',[47] although, of course, in many instances 'white law' approves of the killing of those who reveal the details of the white man's state secrets, treason being a capital crime in most modern states, including those which have abolished the death penalty for all other crimes.[48] It is also true, of course, that the punishment is rarely imposed in peace time, but then, also among the Aborigines, the court notes 'no witness could recollect any similar tribal killing in recent years'.[49] In the event a punishment of 18 months' imprisonment was imposed.

What emerges from these Australian cases is an attempt to apply different standards – of maximum consideration for the tribal milieu when what is at issue is a western rule that allows for legal consideration of reasonable behavior (as in the case of the defense of provocation), but a denial of such flexibility when the criminal law itself does not provide the framework for such consideration (as in the case of a tribal custom sanctioning the killing of a member for divulging secrets). From a strictly legalistic point of view, this differentiation is understandable. After all, it is the western legal system by which the process is being conducted. Nevertheless, from a larger jurisprudential point of view, certain deep philosophical issues remain to which we have already alluded, namely the issue of moral guilt. These are issues that must now be addressed.

A number of writers have suggested the need not merely to show consideration for tribal customs in terms of determining whether aberrant behavior is reasonable, but also consideration for such customs in the substantive and prior question of proof of criminal intent.

One of the first to explore this possibility in the context of problems facing newly independent countries was Robert Seidman.[50] Noting the reluctance of colonial courts to give due consideration to the special problems of beliefs in witches and murder arising therefrom, Seidman stresses that 'the African who believes in witchcraft is … faced by a fearful dilemma,' yet 'he sees nothing in the societal order to which he can appeal for protection' while 'his tradition approves of capital punishment for witches'.[51]

As others have also remarked, the judges themselves were, according to Siedman, often unhappy with their supposedly unavoidable dilemma, and so would recommend mercy, but Seidman argues this was because they themselves were imprisoned within a 'superstitious' belief-system – 'the historically-determined condition for the doctrine of *mens rea* is a system of pseudo-psychology that today is a superstition to which apparently only judges and lawyers subscribe'.[52] And then he explains that 'Reason and emotion are simply not independent entities. Man's personality is a unity.'[53] He concludes with a plea that the independent African states will remedy the errors of the past, and recognize the limitations of the criminal law in these matters.

> For a colonial court to apply law, which, except when relieved by executive clemency, seemed to rule by terror, was bad enough. It would be intolerable if the African nations sought to implement the radical social change now required by the same means.
>
> The solution lies in the abandonment of the concept of objective *mens rea,* a concept which has a specific historical origin and setting and reaches strange and unworkable results when wrenched out of it. The new African governments base themselves on doctrines of humanism, upon the dignity and worth of the individual personality. To retain the doctrine of *mens rea* in its received form, based upon the norms of rulers but not necessarily of the governed, denies that basic value.[54]

A more recent article by Robert Leikind gives a precise and pithy accounting of the nature of the problem:

> In the absence of finding that a defendant is morally culpable for a harm committed, the common law has traditionally insulated persons from criminal liability. As a result, determining what constitutes a morally culpable breach of societal norms has been an ongoing concern of the criminal law.
>
> Moral culpability refers to a voluntary breach of known norms which guide the conduct of a community ... . When members of a community breach established norms, their actions are perceived to involve some quantum of moral turpitude, precisely because they were expected to know their conduct was offensive.
>
> As a barometer of people's moral culpability, however, this expectation of knowledge is meaningful only to the extent that it is reasonable to assume that a person could have knowledge of the standard of conduct to which he is being held.

However, where a defendant is unfamiliar with the norms of the society 'finding the moral blameworthiness requisite to criminal guilt becomes problematic'.[55]

After discussing the inconsistency between the goals of the criminal law, focusing, on the one hand, on moral fault and, on the other, on the preservation of order in the context of a number of cases where there was culture conflict, Leikind addresses the specific matter of the indigenous defendant, noting that 'the tension between the goal of the criminal law which seeks to regulate social conduct and the ethical ideal that only morally culpable conduct should be punished becomes most acute where the norms and beliefs that informed the indigenous defendant's conduct are reprehensible to the adjudicating culture'.[56] Linking these latter problems of indigenous behavior with other instances of culture clash, Leikind seeks a solution to the problem in the context of a dispensation based on lack of knowledge of the law. He quotes an emerging legal situation where a number of common law jurisdictions have allowed a defense of ignorance of the law, under carefully controlled conditions, to prevent cynical exploitation of such a defense. The law, according to this approach, which is widely recognized in Continental law systems, can allow for 'non-culpable ignorance', since it basically reflects 'the defendant's incapacity to acquire the necessary information'[57] as to the legal situation.

While this suggestion contains the framework for resolving serious dilemmas – and deficiencies – in the criminal law, it is only a partial solution, for there are, as was noted in some of the cases, clashes that arise not only out of ignorance of the law in all innocence, but also situations where the law is known, but is rejected as having lesser moral compulsion than a contrasting or conflicting norm of the tribal culture. In fact, by adopting a broader approach dealing with ignorance of the law, and not a conscious flouting of the law, the criminal law continues what Aremu terms its 'failure … to grapple with the legal issues', raised by 'strong and deep-seated beliefs'. He argues for the need for

> a new judicial approach to (and new legislative provisions on) the issue of beliefs in witchcraft and the supernatural. Consequently, criminal responsibility under the Nigerian Criminal Code should reflect the fact that the majority of Nigerians still hold strongly to these beliefs. … To determine, as the courts have been wont to do, issues of criminal liability without a consideration of the effects of such beliefs on the parties involved is to decide the issue of criminal responsibility in a cultural vacuum and to ignore the basic tenet of criminal responsibility that *actus non facit reum nisi mens sit rea.*[58]

While Aremu is undoubtedly correct in this contention, it too fails to provide a broad solution, mainly because the very idea of *mens rea,* whatever its undoubted theoretical and historical import, has suffered serious erosion in the modern world because of the advent and increasing spread of the public welfare offenses and other criminally defined behavior based on strict liability.[59] While there is a dire necessity to resolve these issues, it would be advisable to seek a separate solution to the problem of offenses based on cultural differentiation, unlinked to any developments of the role and place of *mens rea* in the criminal law. There is a need for an approach that focuses specifically on the nature of the dilemma – a clash of normative cultural systems. One of the most promising approaches is one which suggests a 'cultural defense', raising the possibility of the grant of exoneration where a belief in a particular cultural norm would allow the court to consider excusing the commission of the crime.

A number of writers have raised the possibility, in a series of recent articles and notes – most of them as a reaction to cases in which a person's particular belief-system had led to a serious crime being committed, but the cases do not always deal with indigenous defendants. What is at issue often is the ultimate meaning of cultural pluralism for the legal system of a country which has many ethnic groups. Thus a Note in the *Harvard Law Review* (1986),[60] refers to two murders committed within ethnic and immigrant communities. In the one case, a Japanese-American, in response to hearing of her husband's adultery, attempted to commit 'oyako-shinjo', a parent–child suicide in terms of the traditional beliefs of her community. The children died, but she survived, and was then charged with their murder.[61] The second case was also a report of adulterous behavior when a Hmong tribesman from Laos killed his wife who had committed adultery, an alleged acceptable response within his tribal community.[62] The Note argues that, beyond arguments in mitigation of sentence, or attempts to use other defenses, such as insanity, there should be a specific 'cultural defence,'[63] not merely to provide consideration for the accused, but as a positive affirmation of deeply entrenched American values – individualized justice, cultural pluralism, general principles of fairness and equality toward minority groups with different cultures, and the commitment to an individual liberty free of conformist pressures. The Note, in fact, concludes that denial of a cultural defense would be to sacrifice important values of American society.

The most balanced way of introducing such a defense would be according to the traditional and tested criterion of the necessity defense, including the key test of the lesser evil, or what could also be called the 'greater good'. That is, instead of there being given automatic recognition to the mere existence of the particular cultural norm, the court would examine the validity of activating that norm and of behaving according to its dictates or direction in the context of the harm caused, taking into account alternative solutions that might be available to forestall the perceived threat, the precautions taken by the accused to minimize the harm he unavoidably was obliged to cause, and other recognized and acceptable considerations that are constantly used when the court considers the applicability of a necessity defense or one of self-defense.[64] For most practical purposes, the procedure would be identical to these other defenses, but in contrast to the present situation, the court would be able, by virtue of a new legal framework, to consider the cultural milieu, not as an addendum awkwardly appended to a broader defense of necessity or self-defense, but as a legal framework in its own right.

Such an approach would be a true expression of legal pluralism. It would certainly enable the courts to creatively and sensitively reach out for fair and meaningful solutions to the host of problems caused by social and cultural pluralism. Certainly, in trying to give content to such a framework, many of the older cases could be relied on for their earlier thoughtful appraisals. Bernard Brown quotes from a 1962 case in India which perhaps provides a succinct summary of the kind of thinking and reasoning required:

> What a reasonable man will do in certain circumstances depends on the customs, manners, way of life, traditional values, etc., in short, the cultural, social and emotional background of the society to which an accused belongs. In our country there are social groups ranging from the lowest to the highest state of civilization. It is neither possible nor desirable to lay down any standard with precision; it is for the court to decide in each case, having regard to the relevant circumstances.[65]

But I submit that the court could best carry out this function when, within the heterogeneous and pluralistic background described, it were given a direct and specific mandate to take account of cultural norms. Indeed, in answering to this challenge, the court would also be restoring the criminal law to some of its pristine purity where moral culpability and proven criminal intent were the *sine qua non* of criminality and its ensuing punishment.

At least two government commissions, in Papua New Guinea and in Australia, have given consideration to these issues. While noticing some positive advantages, they were both reluctant to unequivocally support such a legal reform.[66]

The prospects of an approach more amenable to the special cultural norms and cultural values of tribal groups would perhaps be enhanced if modern society could divest itself of some of its suppositions as to the qualitative differences between its rational form of society and its accompanying rational form of law, and the lack of rationality in what are considered more traditional and primitive societies. I have elsewhere attempted to address some of the larger theoretical issues involved in this matter, particularly focusing on errors in the work of Max Weber,[67] whose model of rationality in modern western society and law is possibly the most extreme manifestation of this trend – certainly the most influential in academic circles.

Jonathan Aleck[68] has also recently examined to what degree there is a dichotomous situation where law and rationality in western society can justifiably be contrasted with custom and irrationality in non-western societies. Focusing specifically on the question of sorcery, witchcraft and magic in Papua New Guinea, he writes that:

> To raise these issues is to engage questions central to an enduring debate over the properties of rationality and the vicissitudes of relativism in the interpretation of cultural variation. The far-reaching importance of this debate should not be underestimated, for it is one in which some of the major presuppositions of a rationalist, empirically based, scientific view of the world – which is to say, of course, a pre-eminently Western view – are challenged. At the same time, it is a debate which bears crucial implications for the practical disposition of a growing number of very real problems of law confronting societies in which conflicts of cultural diversity are fast becoming inevitable facts of political and economic life.[69]

Noting how the problems of enforcing the state law as against the common belief of citizens in remote areas are most marked in this issue of sorcery, and that far-reaching conclusions are then drawn as to the inherent incompatibility of these two cultures, Aleck shows how, when issues of this type arise in a purely western context, based on a belief system of a recognized member of that society, the court often finds the capacity to offer legal understanding of the background to aberrant behavior.

Aleck creatively examines a Californian case from 1987,[70] in which the parents claimed compensation for the death of their son – who had committed suicide – from a fundamentalist religious church of which he was a member, claiming that his adherence to their faith had led him to reject psychological treatment as he believed that his emotional problems could not be dealt with in a secular framework, but only through religious counseling. More specifically, they adduced evidence to show that the church inculcated a belief that in the event of failure to overcome one's sins, 'suicide was an acceptable and even desirable alternative to living'.[71] The parents failed in their attempt to show a causal link between the influence of the sect's teachings and their son's drastic action, but Aleck claims that there is significance to the case, not because of its outcome, but because it is an example – of which there are others, many not reported – where 'a 'modern' Western, rationalistically orientated, scientifically conscious and secular court was prepared to entertain their claim on the terms in which it was presented'.[72] The case, according to Aleck is:

> Apposite and appropriate, because it unequivocally involves a legally

> cognisable consideration of issues and affairs in which the intentional infliction of 'metaphysical' harm was claimed to have injuriously affected, and ultimately brought about the death of, the alleged 'victim;' and because such a claim was regarded as cognisable and justiciable by a common law court – something which, in principle, common law courts are assumed to have great difficulty doing, and something which at least some Melanesian judges appear to be loath to do.[73]

Aleck then examines closely the question of causation in law, showing how, within the western tradition, there is a greater and increasing willingness to countenance the impact of intangible factors, of outrageous conduct on the part of the alleged 'wrongdoer', and of emotional harm leading to physical consequences. Building on the work of G. White, W. Prosser and G. Calabresi, who traced the background to the development of Tort Law,[74] he concludes that 'the extension of tort law into the amorphous area of "emotional distress" represents ... the presence of a "new" and socio-culturally appropriate judicial perception about the boundaries of the common law.'[75] Applying this new approach to the larger picture of the common law, Aleck writes that:

> These are the intellectual matrices within which questions of legal causation are increasingly coming to be understood and within which, too, a growing number of common-law judicial decisions will likely be framed in the future. That the common law has shown itself amenable to what in many cases arguably represents a radical shift in the fundamental criteria by which the ideas and phenomena of cause and effect are determined to be tenable, is evidence enough of the epistemological elasticity of the common law tradition, and of its intrinsic capacity to adjust and to adapt to a wide variety of socio-cultural circumstances. Moreover, in doing so, it is developing within, rather than exceeding the operative parameters of that tradition.[76]

The thrust of Aleck's argument is that the belief system of the average Melanesian can well be seen, for legal purposes and within the overall perspective of the common law, as being essentially rational. Such a perception is crucial since there is obviously a close correlation between the manner in which reasonableness is evaluated and the rationality of the conduct being examined. In fact, Weber himself, the apostle of rationality in the modern world, allowed for some degree of 'irrationality' in the English legal system (part of his 'English problem') as these deviations seemed to be, according to him, 'reasonable'.[77] Be that as it may, the effect of perceiving rational behavior in a broader perspective, of allowing for causation based on metaphysical and emotional factors, and not just physical and tangible ones, has great significance for theoretical, philosophical, and jurisprudential issues. It provides further substantiation for my contention, as presented in the opening chapters, that the real problem of the culture clash between tribal and modern societies, is not the problem of custom but the problem of law – in this instance, that it is not so much a question of the validity of a custom that is the paramount issue, but of the capacity of the law to accommodate itself to the custom. As Aleck suggests, and in the light of what was earlier presented, it is specifically the common law, because of its traditions and because of its present make-up, that seems most appropriately suited to adapting itself to the challenge of strange customs, to the problematics of seemingly 'irrational' behavior, to the demands of legal pluralism.

Nevertheless, it must be noted that Aleck's article does not deal with the criminal law as such, but with tort. In other words, what emerges directly from his analysis is the need to allow, and essentially to encourage, those affected by traditional beliefs in sorcery to pursue their legal rights within the framework of the law of tort, to seek interdictions that might prevent the feared conduct, to seek compensation for harm already caused. It is of no little significance to note that the vast bulk of the cases do not indeed deal with civil remedies. Thus, Aleck's approach lays out the future contours as to how an acknowledgment of the understandable fears that sorcery holds, could lead to concerted efforts aimed at a resolution based on civil processes. But here, once again, we must return to the realities of society, to the lack of available lawyers capable of submitting a writ to the nearest court (perhaps a distance of several days away), to the pressures in situations where time may be of the essence. In the final analysis, where the civil law route of tort proceedings is not followed, the alternative is pre-emptive direct action – which leads to the criminal trial – even though one may also assume that, in some areas, given the lack of proximate police and forensic services, some major crimes, including murder, whether induced by sorcery or not, may go completely unreported – and this is clearly a problem of major dimensions in its own right.[78]

Thus, two parallel lines of action must be examined. The possibility, on the one hand, of allowing a cultural defense if recourse is had to an ultimate and extreme response, and alternatively, the prospects of providing satisfactory means of resolving interpersonal disputes, especially given the lack of sufficiently effective state law enforcement frameworks. It is this latter aspect that we shall be examining in the next chapter and especially focusing on the manner in which custom remains the real means of maintaining social order.

NOTES

1. See Paul Robinson, *Criminal Law Defenses* (St Paul, MN: West Publishing Co., 1984).
2. The killing of an infant, generally up to the age of one year, is defined as infanticide.
3. See interesting debate on provocation in *Criminal Justice Ethics* 15 (1996): Uma Narayan and Andrew von Hirsch, 'Three Conceptions of Provocation', p. 15; and Jeremy Horder, 'Reasons for Anger: A Response to Narayan and von Hirsch's Provocation Theory', p. 63.
4. Perhaps the most noted work is based on a Marxist perspective, see George Rusche and Otto Kirchheimer, *Punishment and Social Structure* (New York: Columbia University Press, 1939).
5. For a good discussion of the misuse of the term and its confusion in the context of traditional medicine, see Charles Good, *Ethnomedical Systems in Africa: Patterns of Traditional Medicine in Rural and Urban Kenya* (New York: The Guilford Press, 1987).
6. See discussion in Papua New Guinea Law Reform Commission Report on Witchcraft and Sorcery.
7. One of the first criminologists to explain the culture conflict basis of crime was Thorsten Sellin, *Culture Conflict and Crime* (New York: Social Science Research Council, 1938).
8. See Shawn Sullivan, *Killing in Defense of Private Property* (Missoula, MT: Scholar's Press, 1976).
9. Leon Sheleff, *The Bystander: Behavior, Law, Ethics* (Lexington, MA: Lexington Books, 1978).
10. There is also the possibility of a defense of diminished responsibility in these and other delicate and marginal situations.
11. For a good cross-cultural analysis of the Common Law idea of the reasonable man as applied in England, East Africa and Israel, see Michael Saltman, *The Demise of the 'Reasonable Man': A Cross-Cultural Study of a Legal Concept* (New Brunswick, NJ: Transaction Publishers, 1991).
12. For an interesting interpretation, linked to clear-cut cutural norms, see Hamar Foster, "The Queen's Law is Better than Yours': International Homicide in Early British Columbia', in J. Phillips, T. Loo and S. Lewthwaite (eds), *Essays in the History of Canadian Law* (Toronto: University of Toronto Press, 1994), p. 41. The customary law of the time was described as obligating those present at the accidental death to make known the fact of the death … . It was explained that 'If this is not done, it is taken as evidence that there has been foul play. The general custom … is that if anyone calls another to hunt with him, to go canoeing etc., and death occurs, the survivor always makes a present corresponding with his ability, to show his sympathy and good will to the friends of the deceased, and to show that there was no ill-feeling in the matter' (p. 42).
13. Yoram Shachar, 'The Insanity Defense and Culture', *Israel Yearbook of Human Rights* 15 (1985), p. 204.
14. Kharisa Satiyar Chukkol, 'Supernatural Beliefs and the Criminal Law in Nigeria', *Journal of Indian Law Institute* 25 (1983), p. 444.
15. Recently, grave concern has been expressed as to the dangers of witchcraft killings in South Africa. See, for example, articles by David Beresford, 'Spectre of Witchcraft Haunts South Africa', *Mail and Guardian,* 21 June 1996, p. 11; and Eddie Koch, 'Why People Burn Witches' on same page. There is clearly a danger of deliberate falsehoods being spread in order to create a climate that will lead to the demise of an enemy, done even with the consent of the community, with its prejudices against an alleged witch. However, given widespread concern about violent crimes in South Africa in recent times, it may be noted that Colin Sumner, in a general discussion, states that there is some evidence that witchcraft movements 'are a fairly close reflection of the disintegration of the rural, social structure' and suggests, in general, 'a relationship between underdevelopment and rural crime'. See Colin Sumner, *Crime, Justice and Underdevelopment* (London: Heinemann, 1982), p. 29.
16. Chukkol, 'Supernatural Beliefs and Criminal Law in Nigeria', p. 464.
17. Ibid.
18. Ibid., p. 470.
19. Robert Seidman, *The Criminal Law in Africa* (London: Sweet & Maxwell, 1966).
20. Ibid., p. 423.
21. *Regina v. Jackson*, [1956] R. & N.L.R. 66 (High Court, Nyasaland); appears in Seidman, *ibid.,* p. 425 at 426.
22. Ibid., in Seidman, pp. 426–7.
23. Ibid., p. 428.

24. Glanville Williams, 'Homicide and the Supernatural', *Law Quarterly Review* 65 (1949), p. 504.
25. Ibid., p. 492.
26. Ibid., p. 491. See also Williams, 'Provocation and the Reasonable Man', *Criminal Law Review* (1954), p. 740.
27. *The Attorney-General for Nyasaland v. Jackson*, [1957] R. & N.L.R. 443 (Federal Supreme Court), at Seidman, *Criminal Law in Africa*, p. 429.
28. Ibid., p. 431.
29. Ibid., p. 431.
30. At a more sophisticated level, one might consider the relevance for the situation in some tribal societies beset by belief in witchcraft, of the work of Stanley Cohen on *Folk Devils and Moral Panics* (Oxford: M. Robertson, 1980). See also the classic work on mass panic reactions to a radio broadcast by Hadley Cantril, *When Prophecy Fails* (Princeton: Princeton University Press, 1952).

    It is of some interest to note what a twentieth-century writer has written of witchcraft beliefs, including criminal trials of the alleged witches, in England up to as recently as the first half of the eighteenth-century. Ewen states: 'It is customary for the present generation of critical writers to express amazement at the credulity and ignorance of the seventeenth century witch persecutors, yet considered impartially such gullibility and want of understanding have their counterpart in the twentieth century in the delusions of the spirit seekers, and their trusting belief in the genuineness and integrity of the numerous charlatans and tricksters, who provide them with psychic manifestations.' S. L'estrange Ewen, *Witch Hunting and Witch Trials: The Indictments for Witchcrafts from the Records of 1373 Assizes Held for the Home Circuit AD 1559–1736* (London: Kegan Paul, Trench, Taubner & Co. 1929), p. 113.
31. For an example of a case based on the Sorcery Act No. 22 of 1971, see *R. v. K.J.*, [1973] PNGLR, 93, dealing with Sec. 20 of the Act, which allows a limited defense of provocation. The law provides a defense for an act committed in the heat of passion before there is time for the passion to cool, based on an honest and reasonable belief that the person who is the object of his wrath has committed, or is in the process of committing, an act of sorcery of such a nature – judged by reference to the traditional beliefs of the social group to which the accused belongs – as to adversely affect some other person to whom the accused is in a protective or obligatory relationship. For examples of pre-independence cases, committed before the promulgation of the act, in which the courts rejected various defenses, see *R. v. Womeni-Nanagawa*, (1963) P & NGLR 72, when a defense of insanity was rejected as, according to the Court, there are perfectly sane people in the country who believe in sorcery; *R. v. Mangakitai*, (1967–68) P & NGLR 180, when a defense of mistake of fact was rejected, since a superstitious belief could not be considered a reasonable belief, even if it was reasonably held; and *R. v. Ferapo Meata* (unreported case decided on 8 March 1967) in which a plea of self-defense was rejected as the accused was not faced with a direct assault.
32. See for example, Bernard Narakobi, *Lo Bilong Yumi Yet – Law and Custom in Melanesia* (Suva, Fiji: Melanesian Istitute for Pastoral and Socio-Econemic Service and University of South Pacific, 1989); and 'Adapting Western Law in Papua New Guinea', *Melanesian Law Journal* 52 (1983).
33. *Acting Public Prosecutor v. Uname Aumane and Others,* S.C.A. No. 14 of 1980 PNGLR (1980) 510 (note that in the report the headnote inaccurately is of Acting Public Solicitor. In Papua New Guinea, the Public Solicitor appears on behalf of the accused).
34. In recent years Ronald Dworkin has been the focal point of debate as to the important role and meaning of 'hard cases'. See his *Taking Rights Seriously* (Cambridge, MA: Harvard University Press, 1978).
35. *Aumane* case, p. 513.
36. Ibid., p. 513.
37. Ibid., p. 528, per Andrew J.
38. Ibid., p. 545, per Kupi J.
39. Ibid., p. 546.
40. Ibid., p. 546. See also *Regina v. Iu Ketapi* (1971) P and N.G.L.R. 46 – where, in a case not dealing with witchcraft, the court did give judicial consideration to the degree of accessibility and protection afforded by government agencies (for example, the police) in the area where the crime was committed.

41. Norval Morris and Colin Howard, *Studies in Criminal Law* (Oxford: Clarendon Press, 1964), p. 93.
42. Ibid., p. 93.
43. As quoted in ibid., p. 95, from unreported case of 27 July, 1953.
44. As quoted in ibid., p. 97, from unreported case of 21 March, 1956.
45. *R. v. Tiger and Captain,* North Territory Judgments, 1951–1976, 213 at 216. The decision was given on 5 November 1953.
46. There is a controversial aspect of jury trials in which the claim is made that a jury is entitled to return an acquittal verdict in conflict with the judge's directions, and that the defense lawyer may be allowed to tell them so specifically. See Mortimer Kadish and Sanford Kadish, 'The Institutionalization of Conflict: Jury Acquittals', *Journal of Social Issues* 27 (1971), p. 199; Thomas Green, *Verdict According to Conscience: Perspectives on the English Criminal Trial Jury, 1200–1800* (Chicago: University of Chicago Press, 1985); and Alan Scheflin, 'Jury Nullification: The Right to Say No', *Southern California Law Review* 45 (1972), p. 168.
47. *R. v. Aboriginal Charlie Mulparinga*, Northern Territory Judgments, 1951–1976, 219 at 222. The decision was handed down on 9 November 1953.
48. See my discussion of the use of the death penalty for treason in *Ultimate Penalties: Capital Punishment, Life Imprisonment, Physical Torture* (Columbia: Ohio State University Press, 1987), Chapter 10, 'Treason and Terror', p. 252.
49. *R. v. Aboriginal Charlie*, at n. 47, p. 223.
50. Robert Seidman, 'Witch Murder and *Mens Rea:* A Problem of Society under Radical Social Change', *Modern Law Review* 28 (1965), p. 46.
51. Ibid., p. 47.
52. Ibid., p. 59.
53. Ibid., p. 59.
54. Ibid., pp. 60–61. See also Robert Seidman, '*Mens Rea* and the Reasonable African: The Pre-Scientific World-View and Mistake of Fact', *International and Comparative Law Quarterly* 15 (1966), p. 1135.
55. Robert Leikind, 'Regulating the Criminal Conduct of Morally Innocent Persons: The Problem of the Indigenous Defendant', *Boston College Third World Law Journal* 6 (1986), p. 161.
56. Ibid., pp. 161–2.
57. Ibid., p. 183.
58. L.O. Aremu, 'Criminal Responsibility for Homicide in Nigeria and Supernatural Beliefs', *International and Comparative Law Quarterly* 29 (1980), p. 112.
59. See Colin Howard, *Strict Liability* (London: Sweet & Maxwell, 1963).
60. Note, 'The Cultural Defense in the Criminal Law', *Harvard Law Review* 99 (1986), p. 1293.
61. *People v. Kimura*, No. A-091133, Super Ct., 24 April 1985. The examples used are similar to some of the examples presented by Sellin in his discussion of culture conflict and crime; see n. 7.
62. The reference in the Note is to an article, 'Cultural Defense Fails to Mitigate Wife-Slayer's Sentence', *LA Daily Journal*, 29 November 1985, p. 15. See also A. Samuels, 'Legal Recognition and Protection of Minority Customs in a Plural Society in England', *Anglo-American Law Review* 10 (1981), p. 241.
63. But see also Alison Dundes Renteln, 'Is the Cultural Defense Detrimental to the Health of Children?' *Law and Anthropology: International Yearbook for Legal Anthropology* 7 (1994), p. 32. Her work deals mainly with child-rearing procedures, in terms of the cultural, or even religious, beliefs of the parents.
64. In a recent article I argue, following on some American feminist claims, that women (or children) should have a defense for killings committed in a situation of intra-familial and prolonged acts of violence, constituting an ever-present and potential danger of eventually leading to a fatal attack by the violent member of the family. Such pre-emptive action, while not fulfilling the 'justification' principle of self-defense, may well qualify for the 'excuse' principle – namely, while no prior permission may be given for the act, it may be retrospectively forgiven, if all the criteria of both the traditional self-defense (for example, the lesser evil) and the new approach (consistent danger posing an ultimate threat of death), are met. See Leon Sheleff, 'On Criminal Homicide and Legal Self-Defense', *Plilim (Israel Journal of Criminal Justice)* 6 (1997), p. 89 (in Hebrew).

65. Bernard Brown, 'The "Ordinary Man" in Provocation: Anglo-Saxon Attitudes and "Unreasonable" Non-Englishmen', *International and Comparative Law Quarterly* 13 (1964), p. 203.
66. See the Law Reform Commission, *The Recognition of Aboriginal Customary Laws,* vol. 1, pp. 317–24.
67. See Leon Sheleff, *Social Cohesion and Legal Coercion: A Critique of Weber, Durkheim, and Marx* (Atlanta, GA, and Amsterdam: Rodopi, 1997).
68. Jonathan Aleck, 'A "Rational" Perspective on Law and Sorcery in Papua New Guinea' (Part One), paper originally presented in the Research School of Social Sciences, Australian National University, Canberra, June 1990.
69. Ibid., p. 3.
70. The case is referred to in ibid., p. 22. The final decision in the California Supreme Court is cited as *Nally v. Grace Community Church of the Valley*, (1988) 763 p. 2d 948.
71. The quote is from the Court of Appeal decision as cited, *Nally v. Grace Community Church of the Valley*, (1987) 240 Cal Rpts, 215 at 223. See Aleck, n. 68, p. 24.
72. Aleck, see n. 68, p. 25.
73. Ibid., p. 26.
74. See the work of G. White, *Tort Law in America: An Intellectual History* (New York: Oxford University Press, 1985); G. Calabresi, *Ideals, Beliefs, Attitudes and the Law* (Syracuse: Syracuse University Press, 1985); and W. Prosser, 'Intentional Infliction of Mental Suffering: A New Tort', *Michigan Law Review* 37 (1939), p. 874.
75. Aleck, 'A "Rational" Perspective on Law and Sorcery in Papua New Guinea', p. 41.
76. Ibid., p. 44.
77. See Max Weber, *Economy and Society: An Outline of Interpretive Sociology* (New York: Bedminster Press, 1968); at p. 870, Weber writes that: 'natural law "reason" easily slipped into utilitarian thinking, and this shift expresses itself in the change of meaning of the concept of "reasonableness" ... [T]he English concept of "reasonable" contained by implication the meaning of "rational" in the sense of "practically appropriate".'
78. The 'dark area' of unreported crime is a regular problem in modern states. It takes on enormous proportions in rural, undeveloped areas, and may well include illegal practices linked to sorcery, namely that vindictive killings based on ordinary neighborhood tensions, may be explained as being pre-emptive actions against witchcraft. It devolves upon the court to be able to distinguish between genuine cases of witchcraft, constituting a perceived threat, and false pretensions of unfounded fears.

From Harm to Harmony

It is just a hundred years since the publication of one of the classics of sociology, Emile Durkheim's *The Division of Labor in Society*,[1] with its major thesis that the evolution of human society saw a legal development from repressive law to restitutive law. Durkheim adduced a wide range of historical evidence to sustain his thesis, including particularly from the work of Sir Henry Maine, an acknowledged expert in the history of law,[2] certainly in his own time, and during the period of Durkheim's writing, and even since then, despite some criticism lately made of his work. Maine too claimed that law underwent an evolutionary process, through which the emphasis moved from status to contract, that is, people's roles were determined initially by their status (generally ascriptive) while later societies offered freedom for individuals to carve out their rights and obligations through autonomous contractual measures. This aspect of Maine's work – a major theme, extensively used in later jurisprudential writings – was actually totally ignored by Durkheim, who drew on other statements by Maine, from which he quoted liberally to buttress up his own thesis. The essence of Durkheim's utilization of Maine is pithily stated:

> Maine had ... conjectured that, in comparing the different primitive laws, we would find the penal law to be as great as the societies were ancient. The facts confirm this assumption.[3]

However, this quotation, together with some other quotations, was presented in a truncated form. From some of the quotations key words are missing; from others, the quotation comes to an abrupt end precisely at the point where continued reading provides a clarification of the writer's intent, the import of which is to convey a message diametrically opposite to that which Durkheim infers. Thus, Maine explains his essential thesis in no uncertain terms: 'it may be asserted that in the infancy of jurisprudence, the citizen depends for protection against violence or fraud not on the law of crimes but on the law of tort'.[4]

Thus, according to Maine, far from ancient law being repressive (that is, emphasizing criminal law to resolve interpersonal strife) it seems to be characterized by largely restitutive measures. In earlier work I have drawn attention to these blatant errors in Durkheim's work, and suggested that much of his theoretical framework requires rethinking in the light of these errors.[5] In sociological terms, Durkheim draws a strong link between law and three other variables – society in terms of social solidarity, economics in terms of the division of labor, and religion in terms of threats of divine intervention for aberrant behavior.

Although in other major works, Durkheim creatively uses the anthropological knowledge of his time,[6] in *The Division of Labor* he completely ignores research in this branch of the social sciences. Yet, from the sociological perspective that he was pursuing – specifically the nature of social solidarity – it seems obvious that simple societies in the modern world, as researched by anthropologists, could well have provided him with the kind of information about the legal systems, the economic structures, and the religious patterns that he tried to glean from history. In particular, he would have found ample evidence to indicate a close correlation between the nature of law as described in anthropological writings, and the nature of law in ancient societies as described by Maine – if correctly understood (with full quotations and without distortions) – as being restitutive.

Further, from the sociological perspective – and especially within Durkheim's own theoretical framework of seeking to explain social solidarity by examining its interrelationship with other variables, particularly the economic division of labor – the rationale for such restitutive frameworks would have been seen to be tightly integrated within the very nature of social solidarity; especially as described by Durkheim himself. For briefly put, Durkheim claimed that modern law was restitutive (arising out of a social cohesion based on an integrative 'organic solidarity') because of the dependence of members of the society upon each other; a consequence of the intense division of labor in a heterogeneous society. This situation was the obverse side of a paradox, where, in smaller societies, the homogeneous nature of a society (lacking division of labor, where all of its members tended to perform similar tasks) led to a looser cohesion, which he termed 'mechanical solidarity'.

However, it seems that Durkheim erred in choosing the variable for determining the reasons for dependence – it was not the division of labor, an economic factor, that led to mutual interdependence and enhanced social solidarity, but the sociological factor of mutual interdependence in social life, which would serve as the basis for the 'organic' and more integrated social solidarity.

Briefly put, and working specifically within the Durkheimian theoretical framework of dependence leading to social solidarity, the members of smaller and simpler societies (whether in the ancient world or in modern times) were far more dependent on each other in social terms than are the members of modern societies dependent on each other in economic terms. Thus, social life demanded an interlocking participation in the performance of regular rituals (many of them religious in nature), annual cyclical ceremonies, occasional commemorations of the life-cycle, and ongoing participation in shared economic activities, such as harvesting or fishing expeditions, as well as constant physical presence entailing further interactions into the foreseeable future, of people linked together in a network of contacts, described by Max Gluckman as 'multiplex'.[7] All this could best be assured by seeking amicable resolutions to divisive friction.

Durkheim had argued that, in modern life, people's dependence in heterogeneous societies led to them seeking restitutive measures for harmful behavior, so as to ensure continued interaction in the future – but had ignored the fact that the very size of the society, with its heterogeneity, allowed for choice, a fact that diminished the dependence, and therefore allowed, and perhaps even encouraged, demands for repressive responses against people who had caused harm, and with whom there was no desire and no need for contact in the future.

On the other hand, the social needs of smaller societies, with the mutual interdependence for both special occasions and everyday mundane life, created the very conditions that Durkheim had described for ensuring continuity. Harmdoers and their victims were in dire need of reconciliation in order to ensure ongoing social functioning; and restitution to the victim was an essential aspect of this reconciliation. Failure to do so could lead to an intolerable situation of personal and subgroup animosities, causing a frenzied cycle of vengeful actions, an ongoing vendetta, which could disrupt the social fabric – and history provides examples of societal frameworks being disrupted or destroyed. In fact, in some respects, it was the constant lurking danger of such potential outcomes that provided some of the crucial catalytic thrust for opposite solutions of a moderate order, that would forestall the latent violence, defuse the open tensions and allow for reconciliatory procedures.[8]

Repressive measures of social control in such circumstances would exacerbate the tensions arising out of the conflict. However strong the reaction to harmful behavior (including even pressures for payback vengeance) the overriding needs of the society to resolve the issue satisfactorily (to all parties) would lead in a restitutive direction. This is true even of the most extreme of crimes, and even in cases where initial demands for revenge might well be the most intense. Thus, both historically, and often in certain circumstances in the modern world, the very cry for revenge would activate social processes leading to restitutive measures and ensuring reconciliation.[9]

On the contrary, it is often modern societies, more variegated in nature and more subdued in their immediate and direct demands, that seek a culmination in the extreme penalties, such as capital punishment and life imprisonment, specifically because there is no mediating process between the raw demands for vengeance and the moderating intervention to avoid vendetta situations. The ultimate penalty of life imprisonment is more characteristic of the modern world than earlier stages. The idea of prison was brought to many parts of the world – North America, Australasia, Africa – by the western civilization.[10] This is not to deny that in indigenous communities harsh penalties were also meted out, such as death sentences, corporal punishment and expulsion, but these were not the norm. They were often resorted to, in fact, only when the processes of reconciliation broke down, or in the case of flagrant recidivism.

The evidence of both ancient societies (in the work of Maine as well as other scholars such as A.S. Diamond and William Seagle)[11] and of present-day tribal societies, gives the lie to Durkheim's thesis. In fact, in countries such as Canada, Australia and New Zealand, where tribespeople form a disproportionate number of the prison population, and often suffer also disproportionately from its effects, innovative steps have been taken through legislation and judicial and correctional officials to allow for the incorporation of traditional punitive measures, either instead of imprisonment or within the prison system, and tribal elders and leaders have been involved in general discussions and specific decisions as to the most appropriate response to criminal behavior.[12]

In general, it must be realized that harmful behavior causing victimization, poses two differing possibilities for societal response – either restitutive in the form of tort remedies, such as compensation to the victim, or repressive measures, such as punishment through the criminal law to the wrongdoer (and it may be assumed that in referring to repressive law, Durkheim had in mind the criminal law, and not necessarily repression by a tyrannical regime).[13]

While I have no intention of examining the nature of repressive measures in the modern world, notice must be taken of the fact that in the past two or three decades, there has been much academic discussion and an appreciable amount of practical activity oriented to minimizing the activation of the criminal law and to allowing for tort-like remedies – of state-sponsored compensation to the victim, of decriminalization of certain phenomena, of imposing moderate punitive sanctions such as community work.[14] It is not only the Aborigines of Australia, the Maoris of New Zealand, the First Nations of Canada, for whom alternative means of social control – moderate and mediative – are now being sought.

It could even be argued that the development of law had been in a contrary direction to that suggested by Durkheim at the time of his writing, and that the decriminalization of many activities in recent years indicates how overly punitive it had been at the time of Durkheim's writing. But beyond any such debate, an analysis of both tribal law and modern law will indicate that, in its more positive form, tribal law is largely restitutive in seeking solutions to harmful behavior, while modern law, perhaps overly reliant on punitive measures, is groping towards alternative methods, which would replace much of its accumulated punitive ('repressive') measures with restitutive ones.

Much of the initial research into the legal systems of tribal communities was carried out by anthropologists, with jurists showing little interest in its intricacies, partly because of the initial assumptions, sponsored and sustained by the reigning ideas of legal positivism, that the customs being practiced were not law as such.[15] It was only the efforts of a number of leading anthropologists, which led to a grudging recognition that unwritten customs could be regarded as obligatory law, no less than formal legal systems based on statutes and codes.

Indeed, a number of anthropologists devoted some of their theoretical work to examining the parallels between the two kinds of systems – Hoebel[16] showed how the sophisticated jurisprudential model of fundamental legal concepts based on modern law (as set out by Hohfeld),[17] could be applied to the customary rules of indigenous people in North America; Max Gluckman[18] explained how much of decision-making in conflict situations among tribes in central Africa relied on very similar patterns and principles to those applied in the British common law, for instance the imagined conduct of the so-called 'reasonable man', so central to evaluating behavior in both criminal and civil law;[19] while Bronislaw Malinowski, in a series of works,[20] stressed the many parallels between simple societies and more complex ones, including their legal systems. Their work, *in toto,* together with that of other anthropologists, forced a reconsideration of the standard thinking of jurists, and, as I have recently argued, should lead also to a re-assessment of key sociological ideas, such as the work of leading sociologists – not just of Durkheim, but also of Max Weber, with his theoretical frameworks of the unique rationality of modern law and of modern society.[21]

In modern legal systems, ostensibly a distinction is made between two approaches – of punishing the wrongdoer or of compensating the victim. The punitive approach is spelled out in criminal law, the compensatory approach in tort law; the former is designated as part of the public law (together with such other branches of the law as constitutional law and administrative law), the latter is assigned to the private law (together with such other branches of the law as contract law, property law and family law). The criminal law is seen as dealing primarily with the nature of the relationship between the individual and the society; tort law is seen as being a matter between individuals – thus the sanctions of criminal law are generally punishment as penance for the damage done to the society as a whole, while the sanctions of tort law generally deal with obligating the harm-doer to recompense the victim.

These differences are deeply embedded in an elementary understanding of the way modern law operates. However, as many theorists have pointed out, the contradictory approaches are not inherent in the nature of things, but are an outcome either of chance historical developments, or of deliberate choice. In fact, for many harmful acts, the law provides a solution in both criminal and tort law. One may be sued in a civil court for an act that was the subject of a criminal trial, and no contentions of double jeopardy will be applicable and, as a general rule, the criminal trial will precede the civil one. However, the distinction between these processes can become blurred, as in some legal systems, for instance in France, where in a criminal trial, the possibility exists of the victim joining in the proceedings with full legal representation in the court and the right, in the event of a conviction at the end of the trial, to claim compensation.[22] Other systems allow the court to add to any punishment imposed, a compensation payment to the victim, for some at least of the harm caused, without the latter's representation in court. Further, and alternatively, in some civil cases, particularly in the United States, punitive compensation may be imposed on the defending party, beyond the actual damage caused, as a salutary measure for the defendant and for others, based on the same reasoning – of deterrence or retribution – as characterizes the punitive stage of the criminal trial.[23]

The fundamental fact is that the varying responses to harm-doing are based on choice, one which reflects some, at least, of the nature of society.[24] A decision must be made as to whether the damage wrought by harmful acts will be seen as primarily affecting the group as a whole (tribe, nation-state, province, realm) or the victim (whether the particular individual who was hurt, or the immediate and close group to which he belongs, for example, family, clan, neighborhood).[25] Value-judgments are being made, in some instances with ideological and/or utilitarian considerations. Thus, the development of the criminal law often symbolizes the existence of centralized power, and thereby also strengthens it, while specific punishments are used to the benefit of the central authority – such as money from fines adding to the royal or state coffers, or prison labor being used for exploitative purposes or innovative and dangerous projects – the digging of tunnels and mountain passes, or the sailing of galley-ships.[26]

Often the consequence of the expansion of the criminal law is the assigning of the victim into a peripheral role in the system of law enforcement – and, in modern western societies, it is only the existence of insurance systems and the welfare state that have provided the help that the victim of harmful conduct requires, and that in the past was provided by the wrongdoer.

In simpler societies, including tribal communities in the modern world, the victim is at the forefront of concern. Anthropological literature is replete with accounts of such activity. Sometimes these activities are seen as being primarily a form of self-help, based on the egoistic initiative of the victim,[27] but, in truth, for the most part it would seem that the victim responds within a normative system that has been created over time by the community structure. Often, in fact, the negotiations for compensation are orchestrated and mediated by go-betweens, leading and respected members of the community, or chiefs and big men, whose function it is to resolve the tensions in a satisfactory manner, satisfying to the parties involved, so that reconciliation may be attained, and also to the society as a whole, so that tranquillity may be restored and continuing harmonious living assured.

Simon Roberts describes the three key processes that may be activated in attempting to resolve disputes 'by talking'. He explains that research shows that 'the disputants may feel their way towards a settlement through bilateral negotiation; they may try to resolve the matter with the help of a neutral mediator; or they may submit the quarrel to an umpire for decision'.[28]

In many instances the overall process and particularly its culmination, may be accompanied by elaborate rituals signifying the conclusive nature of the settlement reached. The various parameters involved in these negotiations and attempts at settlement of the issues at stake are well described by P.H. Gulliver, who sums up that

> The whole pattern of discussion and negotiation, both in public assembly and in conclave, is permeated by pressures and counter-pressures, with the object of persuasion and constraint, in which reference to the commonly accepted norms of right behavior is but one factor. Ideally, but very often in practice, the dispute is resolved by an eventual mutually accepted settlement, to which either (*sic*) side concurs because it is felt to be the most advantageous one that can be obtained with an expectation of its proper fulfillment in the circumstances.[29]

Generally, to ensure that the settlement is effected, attempts are made to implement it immediately before the assembly or conclave disperses – or, alternatively, within a few days, also in the presence of a reconstituted conclave.

The assessment of these processes varies, and two experts of customary law, T.O. Elias, of Ghana, a leading jurist on African law, and Bernard Narokobi, of Papua New Guinea,[30] a leading jurist on Melanesian law, have adopted differing perspectives on this aspect of the law as seen in the context of modern law.

Narokobi opens his succinct discussion of 'the dichotomy between criminal and civil law' by a personal admission that he has

> never understood the sharp dichotomy between criminal and non-criminal law in English law, which seeks to draw a line between the two on the basis of objectives. The 'object of civil law is to redress wrongs by compelling compensation or restitution'. The 'victim' receives a benefit or avoids loss. In the case of crimes, the object is to punish the wrongdoer, offer deterrence to the community and exercise retribution. The victim gets nothing from the wrongdoer. ... Fines are paid to the state. In a nutshell, in civil law the person wronged is compensated while in crime the offender is punished.[31]

This situation causes a great deal of consternation among ordinary people, who see the system of justice as oblivious to their real needs. They are required to give evidence as complainant/witness, but may be given no special consideration by the court or the law enforcement and prosecutorial agencies. Discussing the operation of the national court system, Narokobi writes that

> Repeated demands for compensation by relatives of victims of homicide ... are the clearest example of the people's perceptions of right and justice as against the official perceptions which are nothing more than colonial reflections. Again and again victims of crimes attend courts at considerable expense and inconvenience .... Whether the accused is guilty or not, the victim remains 'guilty', as he or she is without redress.[32]

Narokobi describes the disadvantages which the victim incurs as a result of an official legal system that is based on typical western concepts, the result of the colonial years. He urges the need to incorporate some of the traditional approaches, and argues that even without legislation, the constitution of Papua New Guinea provides a firm base for such an approach. As part of his ongoing struggle to stress Melanesian jurisprudence in countries, such as PNG, Solomon Islands, Vanuatu, New Caledonia and Fiji, he writes, almost colloquially, that

> If an offender is to be punished for willful damage to the property of another, in the eyes of a classical Melanesian, it is absurd to lock him in prison and feed him and give him maximum protection while the person whose property has been damaged has to repair it, if he can, at his own expense.[33]

He notes that, although there is a possibility of instituting a civil action, this may be a costly procedure, and so he suggests that 'A tribunal which hears and determines guilt and proceeds to award punishment ought to have the power to order a type of punishment that will satisfy the victim as well as meet the broader objective of punishment.'[34] (As noted already, some common law jurisdictions allow this).

At a more general philosophical and jurisprudential level, he suggests that the constitution of Papua New Guinea 'offers ample scope for an integrated approach to law … . Respect for the individual and community independence were declared the basic principles of our society.'[35]

Narokobi notes that in many cases the court will actually take into account a willingness to pay compensation as a significant mitigating factor in determining the sentence to be imposed, but he also recounts a case where the judge rejected a proposal for reduction in the length of imprisonment in return for compensatory payment.[36] He stresses the need for law reform, which will allow for an integrated system in which punishment by the state and compensation to the victim will be linked. Of particular interest is his summation where, in terms of substantive law, he claims that traditional Melanesian principles will provide the required solution, while methodologically, he admits the advantages that might accrue from a proper understanding and a positive approach to the common law, in particular its technique and method.

He is of the opinion that:

> In principle, there is much that 'custom' can learn, not from common law, but from the common law approach. Thus a 'custom judge' can approach custom with a case-to-case method. From 'worthy customs' and 'noble traditions', from 'Christian principles that are ours now' [all the quotes are from the PNG Constitution], from human rights, from Statute, from analogies with foreign jurisdictions (including the common law of England, Australia, New Zealand, India, Israel, East Africa, Canada, the United States) and from the National constitution and its goals, directives and obligations he can evolve new 'underlying' or customary law for PNG[37] [the word 'underlying' is also taken from the constitution].

Narokobi's approach is, of course, in the best traditions of the common law, in which the judicial arm is an active and creative partner in applying the law, filling in lacunae, seeking just solutions, answering to real needs, laying down relevant precedents. This would be the way in which the best of customary law (in this instance, the concern for the victim) would be incorporated into the national legal system – true both to the substantive traditions of Melanesian jurisprudence and to the traditional procedures of the common law.

In substantive terms, it should be noted that many common law countries have, in recent years, been providing an increasingly relevant role for the victim – from victim compensation schemes, through parole considerations based on rapprochement achieved between offender and victim, to controversial victim impact statements (generally more vindictive, and not reconciliatory).[38]

In contrast to Narokobi's approach which stresses restitutive ideas, Elias concentrates on what he sees as being the punitive aspects of African law. However, it seems that the analysis that Elias presents is based on faulty premises – that include also a debate with a number of western writers, including Maine, whom he criticizes for not understanding the essence of the simple legal systems that he had studied. As already noted, Maine is, of course, writing not of modern tribal law, but of ancient law – even so Elias seems to have misunderstood Maine, though in a totally different manner from the errors that Durkheim committed, as pointed out at the beginning of this chapter.

Relying on one of the same quotations used by Durkheim, Elias focuses on the fact that Maine is stressing the tort nature (that is, restitutive nature) of the law in simple societies – correctly in my opinion – but then takes issue with Maine on the basis that such emphasis seems to indicate a lack of organized authority and to hint at private-style self-help, as well as an incapacity even to rule themselves in an organized manner – all blatantly incorrect assumptions, in my view, of the meaning of Maine's work.

Despite the time that has elapsed since Elias wrote, and given his stature as a leading jurist, and his great contribution to African jurisprudence, it behoves us to examine Elias's critique of Maine, as was earlier done with Durkheim, in order to dispel the misconceptions. In the case of Elias, he seems to have understood Maine's thesis correctly, but drawn incorrect inferences – in contrast with Durkheim, whose defective analysis emerged from his factual misunderstanding of Maine.

In a chapter dealing with the 'Distinction between Civil and Criminal Law',[39] Elias seems to have engaged in a debate with Maine of a totally fictitious nature, often using unnecessarily sharp language. Thus, whereas Maine had dealt with societies of bygone days, Elias is insistent on linking them with contemporary African societies, and then relating to Maine's thesis as though it was disparaging of African societies as such, whereas Maine is not concerned at all with African societies, and is in any case by no means disparaging of those ancient societies that he does examine. On the contrary, the thesis of his work indicates a respect for them; and inasmuch as he is guided or affected by modern-day life, it is the village communities of India (which he knew firsthand from years of service in India),[40] that sparked his interest for his historical studies, specifically because of his positive attitude to the manner in which the village people applied their customs, in a way that intrigued him.

Elias is reluctant to accept a widely held assertion that no distinction is made in African law between civil and criminal wrongs. 'The usual evidence cited in support', he writes, 'is that offenses like murder and theft, which are clearly criminal offenses according to English law, are generally treated by many African societies as matters for private redress by the wronged party or group rather than by the state or the custodian of public safety and welfare'.[41] Statements of this kind are, according to Elias, only partially true, and their prevalence is attributable to a number of factors, one of which is 'the great influence of Sir Henry Maine's writings'.[42] Elias then explains that Maine it was 'who first drew attention in his *Ancient Law* ... to what he regarded as the strange preponderance of criminal over civil law in *ancient* (identified for this purpose with *African*) law'[43] [emphasis in the original]. Leading off from this conjectural conjunction, of his own making, between ancient and African law, Elias then states:

> Maine had stressed the primitive belligerency of the savage, who are supposed to be always at war with one another and whose daily life is, because of the prevailing social chaos, supposed to be dominated by crime. Then he added the controversial point: 'Now the penal law of ancient communities is not the law of Crimes, it is the law of Wrongs, or to use the English technical word, of Torts.' The qualification here implied of the theory of warring savages, does not acquit him of the charge of responsibility for the fundamental fallacy. Like some others of Maine's not so happy generalizations, this is very confused and confusing, even as a description. It is apparently a contradiction in terms to say that a *penal* law is a law of *civil* wrongs; but what the jurist really implied is that penalties for *all* wrongs are exacted by the affected individual or his clan as a matter of private vengeance or redress[44] [emphasis in original].

While Elias has not misquoted Maine to the same extent as Durkheim, he has 'under'-quoted him. A fuller quote would have removed any doubts, for the 'apparent contradiction' – that Elias refers to – between a penal law and a civil wrong is indeed *only* apparent. Maine clarifies his deliberate use of these terms in conjunction, so as to dispel any presumed confusion. The explanation is simple; before the sentences quoted by Elias, Maine explained that the bulk of the law in ancient times was the criminal or penal law, but this reference to penal law 'has been used for convenience sake', since 'in fact the inspection of ancient codes shows that the law, which they exhibit in unusual quantities is not true criminal law' for 'the person injured proceeds against the wrongdoer by an ordinary civil action, and recovers compensation in the shape of money-damages if he succeeds'.[45] Discussing an early stage of one of the most sophisticated legal systems in the ancient world (the Twelve Tables of Rome – certainly not the work of 'savages', which Elias claims is Maine's attitude to the objects of his research, although it is a term Maine never used), Maine explains that 'offenses which we are accustomed to regard exclusively as crimes are treated as torts and not theft only, but assault and violent robbery'.[46]

The very use of the word 'torts' indicates Maine's full awareness that he is dealing with a recognized legal procedure, and not some anarchical situation of vengeful self-help. Thus the so-called contradiction in terms is a consequence of the fact that modern laws adopt the punitive approach of the criminal law to problems which ancient societies solved by the civil law (as similarly as most African societies, and also tribes in other areas).

Here was Durkheim's basic error, but Elias's error is of a different sort. He is concerned not that African law will be considered 'repressive' (Durkheim's term), but that it will be considered to be defective in maintaining adequate social protections. Elias seems to feel that applying the law of Wrongs is indicative of a lack of central authority, and perhaps a proof of self-help. But the law of torts is not self-help – it is a law that relates to a wrongdoer (bearing responsibility for willful or reckless wrong behavior) as a person who is a burden to the victim and not to the society at large – a judgment decision made by the society at large through its recognized means of laying down its normative rules. It *chooses* this approach not by default, but by design – it prefers the reconciliation of compensatory measures over the restrictions of punitive measures. A choice of this nature is largely true of most ancient societies and present tribal ones.

Elias goes on to criticize other writers for claiming the lack of a clear-cut distinction between civil and criminal law, which is then used, according to him, as a basis for pointing out the primitive nature of African societies; answering this position assumed to be held by these writers, he stirringly denies 'the fallacy that English (or even European) ideas of criminal law are incapable of application in Africa, because of the alleged incompatibility of the cultural and social attitudes of the African with the European'.[47] He then goes on to provide other examples of countries and cultures all over the world, which have recast their criminal law by adopting parts (or all) of English criminal law 'in order to meet the needs of a changed and changing social and economic order in these territories'[48] – there is thus, according to Elias,

> no reason at all to doubt that African law can and will make the same adjustment. It has, in fact, made encouraging progress in many developed communities in British Africa. English criminal law, often suitably modified to meet local requirements, is already operating there fairly successfully.[49]

These words were published in 1956, a few short years before 'British Africa' disappeared to be replaced by a group of independent nations, each having to build their own jurisprudence, and write their own criminal law, as applicable to the specific needs of their own people, even if they could creatively and sensibly utilize aspects of the British experience.

More important for the issue of the nature of civil and criminal law is the fact that Elias's book was published also only a mere few years before the deep soul-searching that was to characterize western thinking in criminology, penology, victimology and the sociology of law as to the 'overreach of the criminal law',[50] as to the neglect of the victim,[51] as to the need for victim compensation schemes,[52] as to new approaches to punishment,[53] as to the futility of the death sentence and the need for its abolition,[54] as to the burgeoning experiments in mediation processes in lieu of regular criminal trials,[55] as to the need for creative restitution,[56] as to the advantages of negotiated settlement of disputes.[57] In the midst of this process, Samuel Shuman was to ask, 15 years after Elias's work, whether 'criminal law is worth having' and to speculate 'what life would be like if the only remedies for harmful ... conduct were those available with the law of torts'.[58] Shuman claims that it should be possible to combine criminal and civil processes to provide both compensation and punishment, but neglects to consider what might be the major achievement of such a union – the possibility of using judicial processes to effect reconciliation between offender and victim, as is done in so many tribal societies that seek to move from conflict to reconciliation, from harm to harmony.

Indeed, today, outside of Africa, some modern societies are seeking traditional forms of reconciliation procedures, instead of punitive measures as a response to deviant behavior, with the model for these schemes being based partly on tribal practices, but with it being applied also to non-Aboriginal people. In Canada, the process is known as sentencing circles, in New Zealand and Australia, as family conferences, and the theoretical underpinnings and the practical manifestations will be discussed in the next chapter.

NOTES

1. Emile Durkheim, *The Division of Labor in Society* (Glencoe, IL: The Free Press, 1947).
2. Sir Henry Maine, *Ancient Law* (London: John Murray, 1919).
3. Durkheim, *Division of Labor*, p. 144.
4. Maine, *Ancient Law*, p. 330.
5. Leon Sheleff, 'From Restitutive Law to Repressive Law: Durkheim's "The Division of Labor in Society" Revisited', *European Journal of Sociology* 16 (1975), p. 16.
6. See, especially, Emile Durkheim, *The Elementary Forms of the Religious Life* (New York: The Free Press, 1965).
7. On multiplex relationships, see Max Gluckman, *Custom and Conflict in Africa* (Oxford: Blackwell, 1956). Involved in this development are also theoretical concepts of shame and its relief, community social expression and political empowerment, and empirical details of the enormity of the social problems confronting aboriginal groups and of their alienation from, their distrust of, and their suffering in the regular criminal justice and correctional frameworks. These issues will be addressed in the next chapter.
8. See, for instance, discussion in Leon Sheleff, *Ultimate Penalties: Capital Punishment, Life*

Imprisonment, Physical Torture (Columbia: Ohio State University Press, 1987), Chapter 13, 'Revenge and Retaliation', p. 352.

9. See discussion in Leon Sheleff, *Social Cohesion and Legal Coercion: A Critique of Weber, Durkheim and Marx* (Atlanta, GA, and Amsterdam: Rodopi, 1997), especially Chapter 7, 'On Compromise and Reconciliation.'
10. See, for instance, Harry Elmer Barnes, *The Story of Punishment* (Montclair: Paterson Smith, 1972), Chapter 6, 'Prisons: Their Rise and Development' (p. 113); and Chapter 7, 'The Nature and Evils of Imprisonment' (p. 150).
11. A.S. Diamond, *Primitive Law: Past and Present* (London: Methuen, 1971); and William Seagle, *The Quest for Law* (New York: Knopf, 1941).
12. See, for instance, Michael Jackson, 'Locking Up Natives in Canada', *University of British Columbia Law Review* 25 (1989), Part D – 'The Sentencing of Native People – Accommodation Within the Existing Structures', p. 255. Jackson writes:

    Within the last ten years in Canada, there have been a number of initiatives designed to make the criminal justice system more responsive to the concerns of native communities and more sensitive to the special circumstances of native offenders ...

    The Native Courtworker Program ... provides special services specifically to native people in conflict with the legal system (p. 255).

    See further detailed discussion in Chapter 16, 'For Shame'.
13. See, for instance, the discussion in Emile Durkheim, 'Two Laws of Penal Evolution', *Economy and Society* 2 (1973), p. 285.
14. See Leon Sheleff, 'A Critique of the Criminal Law', *Tel Aviv Studies in Law* 3 (1975), p. 113.
15. For instance, the idea put forward by John Austin that 'law was a positive command'; see Austin, *The Province of Jurisprudence Determined* (London: Weidenfeld & Nicolson, 1954).
16. E. Adamson Hoebel, *The Law of Primitive Man: A Study in Comparative Legal Dynamics* (Cambridge, MA: Harvard University Press, 1954).
17. Wesley Hohfeld, *Fundamental Legal Conceptions as Applied in Judicial Reasoning* (New Haven, CT: Yale University Press, 1928).
18. See, for instance, Max Gluckman, *African Traditional Law in Historical Perspective* (London: Oxford University Press, 1974).
19. For a critical discussion of the concept, see Michael Saltman, *The Demise of the 'Reasonable Man': A Cross-Cultural Study of a Legal Concept* (New Brunswick, NJ: Transaction Publishers, 1991).
20. See, for instance, Bronislaw Malinowski, *Crime and Custom in Savage Society* (London: Routledge & Kegan Paul, 1970).
21. Sheleff, *Social Cohesion and Legal Coercion.*
22. On the situation in France, see for instance, Colin Howard, 'Compensation in French Criminal Procedure', *Modern Law Review* 21 (1958), p. 387.
23. See, for instance, Kenneth Mann, 'State Punitive Civil Sanctions: The Growing Middle Ground between Criminal and Civil Law', *Yale Law Review* 101 (1992), p. 1795.
24. See, for instance, Svend Ranulf, *Moral Indignation and Middle Class Psychology* (New York: Schocken, 1964).
25. See Tom Hadden, 'Contract, Tort, and Crime: The Forms of Legal Thought', *The Law Quarterly Review* 87 (1971), p. 257.
26. See, for instance, Thorsten Sellin, *Slavery and the Penal Process* (New York: Elsevier, 1976).
27. See, for instance, Sally Falk Moore, 'Legal Liability and Evolutionary Interpretation: Some Aspects of Strict Liability, Self-Help, and Collective Responsibility,' in M. Gluckman (ed.), *The Allocation of Responsibility* (Manchester: Manchester University Press, 1972), p. 51.
28. Simon Roberts, *Order and Dispute: An Introduction to Legal Anthropology* (Harmondsworth: Penguin Books, 1979), p. 69.
29. P.H. Gulliver, *Social Control in an African Society: A Study of the Arusha-Agricultural Masai of Northern Tanganyika* (London: Routledge & Kegan Paul, 1963), p. 275.
30. T.O. Elias, *The Nature of African Customary Law* (Manchester: Manchester University Press, 1956); and Bernard Narokobi, *Lo Bilong Yumi Yet – Law and Custom in Melanesia* (Suva, Fiji: The Melanesian Institute for Pastoral and Socio-Economic Service and the University of South Pacific, 1989).
31. Narokobi, ibid., p. 123.
32. Ibid., p. 124.

33. Ibid., p. 124.
34. Ibid., p. 124.
35. Ibid., p. 125.
36. Ibid., p. 126.
37. Ibid., p. 127.
38. See my discussion in 'Victimology, Criminal Law and Conflict Resolution,' *South African Journal of Criminal Law and Criminology* 1 (1977), p. 31.
39. Elias, *Nature of African Customary Law*, Ch. 7.
40. Sir Henry Maine, *Village Communities in the East and West* (New York: Henry Holt, 1871).
41. Elias, *Nature of African Customary Law*, p. 110.
42. Ibid., p. 110.
43. Ibid., p. 100.
44. Ibid., pp. 110–11.
45. Maine, *Ancient Law*, p. 326.
46. Ibid., p. 329.
47. Elias, *Nature of African Customary Law*, pp. 128–9.
48. Ibid., p. 129.
49. Ibid., p. 129.
50. Norvål Morris, 'The Overreach of the Criminal Law', *Acta Juridica* (1977), p. 60.
51. See international journal *Victimology*.
52. See, for instance, J. Shapland, J. Willmore and P. Duff, *Victims in the Criminal Justice System* (Aldershot: Gower, 1985), Chs. 7–9, pp. 117–3.
53. Warren Young, *Community Service Orders: The Development and Use of a New Penal Measure* (London: Heinemann, 1979).
54. Hugo Adam Bedau, *The Courts, the Constitution and Capital Punishment* (Lexington, MA: Lexington Books, 1977).
55. See, for instance, Tony Marshall, *Alternatives to Criminal Courts: The Potential for Non-Judicial Dispute Settlement* (Brookfield, Vermont: Gower, 1985).
56. Albert Eglash, 'Creative Restitution', *Journal of Criminal Law, Criminology and Police Science* 48 (1958), p. 619.
57. See also L. Nader and H. Todd (eds), *The Disputing Process in Ten Societies* (New York: Columbia University Press, 1978).
58. Samuel Shuman, 'Responsibility and Punishment: Why Criminal Law', *American Journal of Jurisprudence* 15 (1971), p. 25.

For Shame

In the previous chapter, attention was drawn to the fact that Emile Durkheim had ignored much of the contrary empirical evidence of anthropology in claiming that law had evolved from repressive in nature to restitutive in nature. More recent theoretical perspectives in anthropology (and in a number of related disciplines) tend also to present an alternative thesis, as well as presenting a challenge to much of present-day penological practice. For anthropology's involvement in culture has led to a recurrent theme – developed particularly in the last fifty years, and incorporated more recently into psychological, penological and criminological thought – of a dichotomy between two different kinds of culture, reflecting personal feelings about one's own aberrant acts – one based on feelings of guilt, the other based on feelings of shame. In essence, societies that may be characterized as guilt-cultures are ones in which punishment is the appropriate response for harm caused, with the actor, however, aware of his aberration, on his own, irrespective of conviction for the offense, since the guilt which he senses stems from within himself; in contrast, cultures that may be designated as shame-cultures are oriented to the exposure of the wrongdoer to the opprobium of the community, and in particular to that of the victim and his immediate kin and only thereby does he have a sense of his wrongdoing, causing him shame. The consequences of punishment for guilt are often, albeit not necessarily purposively, the stigmatization of the culprit into the future; the consequences of exposure to shame are intended to facilitate the removal of the memory of the act so as to allow for reintegration of the wrongdoer into the community, concomitant with reconciliation between the offender and the offended. Guilt emanates from the autonomy of the individual, shame from the network of relations with others.[1]

One of the recognized presentations of these two contrasting approaches, was Ruth Benedict's description of Japanese culture, published immediately after the Second World War, and based on research conducted during the war itself in a concerted and conscious effort by a team of social scientists, to probe the psyche of the enemy, in order to understand their thought processes, and thereby perhaps predict and thus also forestall, some of their plans.[2] There was no directive in the mandate order under which Benedict worked (as far as can be gathered from her book), which obligated her to deal with questions touching so closely on punishment and related issues, so the very fact of her dealing with this variable (even though in brief) is indicative of how deeply these contrasting images of guilt and shame permeate the culture of a society in areas well beyond the purview of the law.

The contrast that Benedict drew between guilt and shame cultures is relevant not only for the society being examined (Japan) and the society in which, and for which, she wrote (the United States), but can well be adopted for distinctive differences between tribal societies (with a shame-culture) and modern western states (with a guilt-culture).

Before expounding on these two cultural frameworks in greater detail (and in particular on the impact of the shame ethos), with the intention of examining the relevance for social control and penological considerations, mention should be made of the recurrent dilemmas of penological theory and correctional practices (within the guilt culture of western society), as standard philosophical ideas – of deterrence, retribution, rehabilitation, prevention – compete with each other in intellectual discourse and then, in turn, displace each other as the reigning practices of criminal justice.[3] The frustrations are succinctly, if not quite accurately expressed, in Martiensen's challenging assertion, 'Nothing works'.[4] This particular research had focused on the failure of the philosophy of rehabilitation to achieve its stated goal, since recidivistic figures were so high. But, of course, other penological approaches, most particularly retribution, are not susceptible to empirical analysis – since they deal with intangibles of symbolically paying back (even through a tangible, such as imprisonment) for harm caused. This is a philosophical stance *par excellence* – either one accepts the premises or not; facts and figures can do little to substantiate its validity. Deterrence at the individual level (or prevention) may also be monitored with some minimum degree of accuracy, but for general deterrence, there is little prospect, given the sundry variables, of showing firm correlations between punitive measures and subsequent crime rates.[5]

However, a major problem of criminology and penology today goes beyond the question of which is the most effective (practically) or most favored (theoretically) punitive philosophy, to probing questions as to whether punishment, for whatever reason, is the desirable response – or where a punishment is indeed desired, whether the standard ones of prison or fines should not be replaced by others; or whether the judicial process of imposing the punishment should not be replaced by other socially-oriented processes. In these considerations and deliberations, some of the proffered solutions either draw upon or are reminiscent of patterns of the past or procedures widely practiced in present-day customary law systems. Thus, as briefly mentioned in the previous chapter, sentencing circles in

Canada are connected with traditional practices of many of the indigenous people and are largely oriented to them within the criminal justice system, while in New Zealand, the recently introduced family conference was modelled on Maori customs.

In this context Carol LaPraisie describes how in Canada the criminal justice system took ideas and practises 'based on traditional healing and talking circles and on the belief that traditional forms of dealing with disorder ... to facilitate reconciliation and peace, rather than for purposes of retribution and deferrence'.[6] Jean-Benoit Zegers and Catherine Price portray a similar situation in New Zealand: 'Various social factors were instrumental in bringing about the new Act. Determined efforts by Maori to put in place a system of justice in keeping with their cultural heritage precipitated the process of legislative reform. Maori communities perceived that the Westminster-style legal system discriminated against Maori and took little or no notice of Maori customs, values and beliefs.'[7] Thus, prior to setting up a system of family conferences, 'parliamentarians travelled New Zealand visiting Marae (meeting places) and Pacific Island centres hearing submissions'.[8]

Even where there has been no formal legal incorporation of tribal methods, interest has been shown in traditional means of dealing with aberrant acts, as, within criminology, and its subdisciplines of penology and victimology, the focus has shifted to the defects of many aspects of the criminal justice system, including the need to display more attention to the needs of the victim, involving both compensation and reconciliation between offender and offended. In the United States, a judge of the Navajo people has described the advantages of the tribal approach to wrongdoing, and the increasing interest recently being shown in tribal justice. Chief Justice Tom Tsu writes

> I regret that the outside world has never recognized that Navajos were functioning with sophisticated and workable legal and political concepts before the American Revolution. I regret even more that the ways we are different are neither known nor valued by the dominant society. Because we are viewed as having nothing to contribute, much time has been wasted. Let me be more specific. Anglo judicial systems now pay a great deal of attention to alternative forms of dispute resolution. Before 1868 the Navajo settled disputes by mediation. Today our Peacemaker courts are studied by many people and governments. Anglo justice systems are now interested in compensating victims of crime and searching for ways to deal with criminal offenders other than imprisonment. Before 1868 the Navajo did that.[9]

These different, almost opposing, approaches to social control and responses to wrongdoing are not merely technical procedures, but are deeply embedded in the nature of the culture. Indeed, the interest being shown, according to Justice Tsu, in Indian procedures of mediation by representatives of Anglo justice systems, eager to incorporate ideas such as victim compensation and reconciliation, may express no more than a forlorn hope of a panacea for rampant crime rates – just as the penalties of the modern criminal justice system may have disastrous consequences for members of some minority groups, alienated from the societal culture, yet recipients of its penological provisions – as will be discussed later on in the chapter. For the moment, it is necessary to focus on the distinction drawn between the two forms of culture, in order for the failings of unsuitable penological practices to be better comprehended.

Benedict explains that 'In anthropological studies of different cultures the distinction between those which rely on shame and those that rely on guilt is an important one.'[10] The key differentiation is that

> True shame cultures rely on external sanctions for good behavior, not, as true guilt cultures do, on an internalized conviction of sin. Shame is a reaction to other people's criticism. A man is shamed either by being openly ridiculed and rejected or by fantasying to himself that he has been made ridiculous. In either case it is a potent sanction. But it requires an audience, or at least a man's fantasy of an audience. Guilt does not. In a nation where honor means living up to one's own picture of oneself, a man may suffer from guilt though no man knows of his misdeed and a man's feeling of guilt may actually be relieved by confessing his sin.[11]

Benedict describes many differences in behavior between Japanese and Americans, which, according to her, may be attributed to the different perceptions each culture provides its members. She adds that, 'the primacy of shame in Japanese life means, as it does in any tribe or nation where shame is deeply felt, that any man watches the judgment of the public upon his deeds'.[12]

Benedict's work is fascinating, and has attracted a great deal of interest and she is widely quoted in many of the discussions dealing with the contrast between shame and guilt. But her analysis on this specific point is actually limited to only a few pages, is done in summary form and contains mainly generalizations and anecdotal material. Nevertheless, the contrast between guilt and shame – both in larger cultural terms and in the specific context of punishment – has continued to elicit interest, even though an early attempt to measure the tendency of non-western cultures to a shame approach found little empirical proof. Milton Singer, a social scientist, in a joint research project on children, carried out with a psychoanalyst, Gerhart Piers,[13] noted that of the five Indian tribes he described, only in one, the Navajo, were the children clearly part of a shame culture. In the remaining four tribes, there was little difference on the response in the shame-guilt axis, between them and a group of non-Indian American children from a mid-west community. Indeed, for two of these tribes, the Hopi and the Sioux, they had responses which were most similar to the non-Indian children. Despite this initial reservation on the validity of the guilt-shame issue, it has continued to arouse interest, and in recent years, assessments have been made of the value of inducing shame as a legitimate and effective punitive mechanism.

On the one hand, John Braithwaite has argued that judicious use of shame in social control may lead to constructive results, including reintegration of the offender into the community, and he uses the idea in a more comprehensive manner to expand existing criminological theories,[14] while, on the other hand, Toni Massaro examines critically a large number of sporadic efforts by innovative judges to use the induction of shame as part of the punishment, and warns of its limitations in a culture, which is generally considered not to be a shame culture.[15] The implication is that in a western guilt culture, shaming as a means of social control will be of only marginal value, and may even have detrimental effects.

Braithwaite argues for the positive impact that a carefully constructed policy of shaming, as an expression of punishment, could achieve, even though he is well aware of its possible negative spin-off effects. Nevertheless, he clearly opts for beneficial qualities, especially when seen in contrast to the stigmatizing impact of a guilt-oriented punitive system. In fact, his approach attempts to move beyond standard labeling theories,[16] which largely explain how the very act of punishment may be a causative factor in entrenching the punished person in his deviant ways.

Braithwaite suggests the need to avoid models of punishment that exclude[17] and stigmatize, which are the prevalent approach of punishment, yet without surrendering the capacity of society to cope with the problem of crime or to clarify to its offenders its unwillingness to tolerate their harmful behavior. The drawback of labeling theory, as presently enunciated, is its inability to offer a remedy for criminal behavior. It describes the negative consequences of punishment without offering an alternative, and particularly without a plan for meaningful reduction in crime. He suggests that judicious use of shaming presents a possibility of using labeling in a constructive manner – to label a person by shaming him, but to do so in a way that will not lead to his rejection by society, but by his return to its fold. Pithily expressed, Braithwaite explains that 'Reintegrative sharing is conceived as labeling that reduces crime.'[18] While the labeling theory encouraged 'A wholesome liberal tolerance of diversity … (and) the community learnt a lot about the dangers of overreacting to deviance that might be transient if left alone … at the same time, the labeling perspective fostered a debilitating nihilism that gave no advice about the limits of tolerating diversity.'[19]

Within this context (and referring also to the deficiencies of other leading criminological theories),[20] Braithwaite suggests that shaming provides a prospect of punishment that will have beneficial consequences.[21] Seeking 'a general principle of effectiveness in social control', he warns against punishment (in any context – home, school, community) that is 'cold and punitive' or conversely that is 'warm and permissive', and then argues that 'the strategy of first choice should be social control that is warm and firm, with shaming rather than pain-infliction providing the firmness needed in all but extreme situations'.[22] Because of the negative aspects of labeling, with its consequences of exclusion through ritual procedures of stigmatization (a judicial formal pronouncement of guilt and sentence, a debilitating prison experience, the restrictions imposed and sensed on re-entry to society), Braithwaite urges the advantages of a shaming approach: 'Reintegrative shaming actually has symbolic advantages over stigmatization because ceremonies of repentance have even more integrative potential than degradation ceremonies. A social policy of reintegrative shaming would not downplay rituals of blaming as does the inclusionary practice informed by labeling theory; it would seek to foster both blaming rituals and rituals of repentance and forgiveness.'[23]

Instead of avoiding a confrontation with the wrongdoer (which is the implied, or even explicit, message of labeling theory), Braithwaite's solution is 'to advocate vigorous moralizing about guilt, wrongdoing and responsibility which is informed by the theory of reintegrative shaming, in which the harm-doer is confronted with community resentment and ultimately invited to come to terms with it'. In such a situation, if the accused person is unable to prove his innocence, or even to suggest that 'his deviance is harmless diversity which should be tolerated', he will be expected to 'express remorse and seek to compensate for the harm he has done. It should be a society where retreat into a world of exclusion is difficult for either the accused or his accusers to accept.'[24]

Braithwaite concedes that shaming on its own can lead to unjust results, including even unfair stigmatization. The essence, then, of shaming, is that it must be done in a community context of caring aimed at the wrongdoer's subsequent inclusion in the very community that is inducing the shame. Thus, 'Reintegrative shaming is not only more effective than stigmatization; it is also more just.'[25] Such reintegrative shaming can best be achieved where community is strong – and so, Braithwaite also argues for the advantages of a communitarian society over an individalistic one.[26] Indeed the very individualism of a minimalist state, might well have the adverse consequencs of necessitating far greater social control in the realm of crime prevention and correction policies. However, even in an individualistic society, there may be expressions of communitarian efforts at crime control, for instance in local voluntary organizations, such as neighborhood watch schemes, widely found in an individualistic society such as the United States.[27] In sum, whatever the dangers of shaming, which may degenerate into stigmatization of marginal groups, Braithwaite is hopeful of new forms of community expression that will allow for both tolerance of diversity (the traditional stance of liberal stigma theorists) and reintegrative shaming.

Braithwaite's ideas obviously have relevance for a range of issues relating to indigenous populations both because of their disproportional involvement in the state criminal justice system, and for the fact that much of their communal approach to conflict resolution operates in a manner similar to reintegrative shaming. In fact, recent developments in state penological practice, bear strong resemblances to Braithwaite's thesis, especially as applied to some indigenous groups.

As noted, Canada, New Zealand and Australia are in the process of developing interesting and innovative programs, and some of the research on these programs makes specific reference to Braithwaite's theoretical perspective. Yet, interestingly enough, Braithwaite, an Australian himself, despite many positive references to other cultures (for example, Japan, Scandinavia)[28] makes only two passing and peripheral comments to Aborigines, ignoring the fact that amongst them, and other tribal communities, were examples of the very process he was advocating.

This may well be because amongst the Aborigines, there is also acceptance of corporal punishment, as in the case of 'spearing' (a fact that Braithwaite refers to indirectly in one of his marginal references to Aborigines),[29] but punitive approaches among the Aborigines were more diverse, and included also forms of reintegrative shaming; even spearing could be part of such an approach, especially where done symbolically, and under the watchful eye of prominent persons, such as tribal elders, in order to monitor its performance, and specifically prevent any harm.[30] Furthermore, other groups, who are not mentioned at all – Maoris or Indians, or the oft-quoted 'singing duels' among the Inuit of Canada,[31] intended to evoke embarrassment – present most vivid examples of Braithwaite's theorizing. If shaming is linked to the existence of community and the idea of communitarianism, then there is certainly a need to examine whether or not existing communities actually practice the shaming procedures described, and if so how, and with what degree of success.

In any event, about the time that Braithwaite's book was published, attempts to utilize an approach compatible with the theoretical perspective of reintegrative shame as well as the traditional procedures of tribal groups, were introduced in Australia and New Zealand (by legislation)[32] and in

Canada (by judicial innovation). According to some of the research and reviews of these projects, Braithwaite's work has been among the factors influencing these developments, although his initial work is considered by Jenny Burger[33] not to have had a major influence in New Zealand, since the Maori pressure there had been so intense, and had been so determinative in bringing about the change. However some of the subsequent research into these projects has been carried out by Braithwaite, and, in retrospect, he now seems fully cognizant of the degree to which traditional ideas have contributed to these new programs, including that of Pacific Islanders – thus in describing a stylized Samoan ritual of pardon and forgiveness, Braithwaite (together with co-author Mugford) suggests that 'There may be something to learn from the Samoans … on the conditions of successful reintegration ceremonies, namely the provision of a spatial-temporal dimension to the imperative for re-integration.'[34]

The full impact of tribal culture on this new approach to the criminal justice system is well set out by LaPrairie in her article; she writes,

> At opposite ends of the globe and at different stages of the criminal justice process, two models of popular and restorative justice have emerged, which, in varying degrees, reflect the disenchantment with the mainstream retributive system and the adoption of restorative justice. In New Zealand and Australia, these are family group conferences; in Canada they are sentencing circles. The former are based on traditional Maori concepts of conflict resolution and on recent theoretical work about the need to reintegrate and not ostracize offenders.[35]

Although the frameworks are not

> exclusively aboriginal … efforts have been made to accommodate some customary practices and concepts... There is some similarity in the use of traditional practices as each [the family conferences and the sentencing circles] recognizes shame and attempts to turn it to positive ends. Both involve an expanded vision of community … While not aboriginal-specific, sentencing circles have occurred in more aboriginal than non-aboriginal communities in Canada, and have involved more aboriginal people, in part, because of interest in self-government and a strong movement toward justice initiatives in aboriginal communities.[36]

In New Zealand, there is a similar larger use by Maoris than others, but in Australia, the pattern is somewhat different, with less Aboriginal involvement.[37]

Laprairie also provides a theoretical background to the process – 'The pursuit is for social rather than for strictly legal justice; the focus is on empowerment of those marginalized by mainstream legal systems; the object is to contextualize justice; the goal is to return the conflict to its rightful owners.'[38]

In dealing with the issues that are so central to Braithwaite's thesis – community reintegration and shaming – LaPrairie writes that 'Within the restorative justice paradigm, sentencing circles, by allowing greater participation in the criminal justice process, reflect less an issue of sentencing than a movement toward community health and healing, balance and harmony... The use of circles pre-supposes that community involvement in criminal justice decision-making assists in the building of community institutions, and has the capacity to bring about fundamental change in communities.'[39]

This assertion – of the interaction between the forms of the criminal justice system and the nature of the community – is connected directly to much of the motivation for the new approach, especially among the judges, who initiated it; they felt that their approach would help both in coping with the causes of crime and in the search for a cure, one which would contribute to preventing any recurrence of that crime in the future.[40]

The initiative of the Canadian judges was challenged as being outside of the mandate of their judicial office, but in a 1992 case, in the Yukon Territory,[41] the court held that, even without legislative backing, the circles would be allowed, provided the necessary surrounding factors were amenable to its use – a community prepared to devote the necessary resources and the willingness of both offenders and victims to co-operate. The system itself provides for the presence of the traditional participants in the criminal justice system (judge, lawyers for prosecution and the accused, various court officials), while additional persons involved might include members of the families of offender and victim, representatives of the community, probation officers, and the police. The 1992 decision confirmed a trend that had been developing for about a decade in courts of first instance among creative judges, sensitive to the special needs of indigenous people, but higher courts had, until then, been reluctant to confirm the experimental situations.

In an important, but little-noticed article, published in 1989, Michael Jackson describes some of the first gropings of the Canadian criminal justice system toward innovative approaches that were based on traditional concepts and processes of aboriginal communities.[42] He quotes extensively from a 1986 case, where the judge in the court of first instance, invited a Council of Elders (known as the 'Inumarit') to give evidence of the traditional treatment of offenders – in the case at issue, a young man was accused of a sexual assault on a minor, who happened to be his cousin. The judge, in imposing a light sentence, with only minimum imprisonment, and far different from the regular 'tariff' for such offenses, explained that he had taken into account community sentiment, as expressed by the elders, which indicated a willingness to receive the offender back into the community in a spirit of forgiveness and reconciliation.

On appeal,[43] the Court held that the penalty imposed was inadequate in the light of the precedents laid down, which called for a minimum sentence of three years. Even though willing to accept a shorter period of 18 months because of the special circumstances, the Court denied that there was room for incorporating traditional concepts, since the life-style of the accused and the victim was manifestly western. The Court even doubted the credentials of the Elders, since their Council had only recently been called into existence after a lapse of many years.

However, a minority opinion displayed full understanding both of the judge's approach and of the proof and import of tribal traditions. The judge described the special sentence hearing which attracted great community interest. About half the citizens of a community of some 400 people were in attendance throughout the 12 hours of evidence and submissions.[44] He also explained how the lower court judge had decided on the lenient sentence because

> he gave weight to the concerns of the community expressed to him by its elders ... and he took into account the unquestioned effectiveness of its traditional treatment of offenders.
>
> ... the primary concern of the community had been and still is to maintain its harmony and cohesivenessness, a concern undoubtedly traditionally considered crucial to the very survival of a small group in a harsh and isolated environment and now considered crucial to the survival of its cultural identity in the face of intrusion by a civilization foreign to it. Imprisonment, even banishment, were historically unknown as forms of punishments. Imprisonment is viewed not only as destructive of the accused himself, but as containing the seed of disharmony and division and hence destructive of the community itself. The traditional method of handling an offender is forced confrontation by the elders ... until a willingness to change for the better is manifested, and this is followed by relentless counselling until the offender is considered rehabilitated. The treatment is shown by the evidence to have achieved what must be the ultimate purpose in all punishment for crime, that is to say, protection of the community and rehabilitation of the offender. It has the added benefit of effecting reconciliation between victim and offender; a concept only now being advanced in our society by some criminologists.[45]

Indeed, a short time before, various researchers in victimology had raised the idea of seeking payment of restitution in the process of effecting reconciliation, and concepts such as creative restitution had become key factors in victimological debate.[46] There is a convergence of several academic and theoretical approaches with developing policy and experimental programs – but few can be considered as cohesive and integrated as those oriented mainly to tribal groups. In fact, many of these more recent concepts can best be understood, and also best applied, in the context of the overall culture of tribal groups.

The sum of these new approaches is that modern theoretical presentations and recent legal developments pertinent to modern criminal justice systems, are most likely to meet with practical success, when linked to traditional norms. As Zegers and Price explain (in discussing the Family Conferences in Australia and New Zealand): 'What were new concepts in the legislation were in fact familiar to Maori. The traditional Whanau conference involved notions of shame and reconciliation in order to heal the rift between the offender and the victim, the individual and the collective.'[47]

In concluding remarks they stress that even though the family group conference is based on legislation, and involves court officials, the role of the families is a major and meaningful one '… the family has been empowered. This is based on a model of Maori extended family (Whanau) decision-making, and recognizes New Zealand's cultural diversity. The new legislation', they claim, 'provides both services which are culturally sensitive and a process which is culturally appropriate.'[48] Beyond that, it challenges, in fact, the very basis of the standard adversarial legal system.

The question arises as to whether these new forms may be adopted elsewhere – after all, Braithwaite's ideas were not focused on nor intended specifically for aboriginal communities. He basically wished to replace the degradation ceremonies of the modern criminal justice system, based on a finding of guilt and an imposition of sentence (as so well described by Harold Garfinkel),[49] with a reintegrative ceremony, based on eliciting shame as a prior step to reconciliation. Can such a system based on the concept of shame function successfully in a culture based on guilt?

According to Massaro, a large number of individual, and idiosyncratic, attempts have been made by a varied group of judges in different jurisdictions of the United States to break out of the formalized punishment structure within which they work and to incorporate a host of shame-inducing devices into their sentencing procedures. The possibilities range from the opening example in the article of a 1989 judicial order for an accused to place a notice in a local newspaper spelling out his crime of child molestation, together with his picture and a suitable exhortation to others of his ilk to seek out professional help immediately,[50] to a community service order that included the obligation to wear identifying dress indicating that he was a convicted drunken driver.[51] The civil rights problematics of such humiliating publicity are apparently (for the moment at least) covered by their performance being a condition for receiving an alternative punishment (such as probation or community work) instead of imprisonment. The title of Massaro's article includes the word 'Shame', just as does the title of Braithwaite's book, but the nature of the shame-inducing procedures described are vastly different. In Massaro's article, the intention is to degrade, with possible consequences of stigma, and there is no necessary interaction with victim and members of the community, the very factors that are so crucial to Braithwaite's scheme. Nevertheless Massaro is well aware of the psychological and anthropological perceptions of shaming, including the fact that in the final stage of the process 'the shamed person must be afforded some means of regaining community esteem'.[52]

Lacking the total framework of community involvement, and lacking the necessary framework of a shame-culture, Massaro holds that these shaming techniques, for the most part, elicit mostly negative results (about which Braithwaite had warned). In addition, shaming may be considered to raise serious questions of fairness – thus, while

> Jurists and legislators have good reason to be frustrated by the failures of past attempts to find effective, humane, and economic punishment techniques … shaming sanctions are not the solution. We cannot wish away the absence of cultural conditions that might make shaming a meaningful cultural ritual. We likewise cannot ignore the profound harm that effective shaming, where it can be achieved, may attempt to fashion rational, humane, criminal punishment. They caution against widespread revival of the pillory and the stocks in the United States. Absent thoroughgoing changes in the nature of the modern state, in criminal court procedures and personnel, and in the dominant culture's conception of the relationship between the individual and the community, the modern shaming sanctions will not work. At best, they are likely to prove futile, even silly, responses to crime. At worst, they may become highly destructive, state-imposed assaults on human personality.[53]

But these categorical statements as to the dangers of shaming techniques without the moderating influences of an overall culture and a specific judicial mechanism (such as sentencing circles), cannot be considered within a vacuum. For, valid as the statements are in some respects, they ignore not just the futility of existing punitive practices, but also some of the destructive assaults on the human personality that are part of some state systems, both within the criminal justice system and in the larger societal framework, with its individualistic culture (linked also to guilt).

For the import of Braithwaite's work, it seems to me, relates not to punishment alone, but both to larger factors – within the society – and to more limited factors – within the criminal justice system. Braithwaite, like Masarro, is aware of the problematics of unbridled shaming, but hopes that a full-scale program will avoid the excesses. Specifically, he attempts to move beyond the sterile notion of the stigma of punishment. But a key factor of aboriginal life in many countries (as also for other minority and marginal groups) is the shame of the stigma imposed not by official punishment, but by one's identity. One of the major contributors to stigma theory, Ervin Goffman, takes due account of this 'tribal' factor – three types of stigma are described in his book – 'abominations of the body – the various physical deformities. Next there are blemishes of individual character'[54] – and here Goffman relates a string of defects linked to an even longer list of social disorders, such as imprisonment, addiction, suicidal attempts and unemployment. 'Finally', he writes, 'there are the tribal stigma of race, nation and religion, these being stigma that can be transmitted through lineages and equally contaminate all members of a family.'[55]

Included in this third category, but paradoxically, not mentioned by Goffman, is of course the tribal stigma of tribe – in many instances far more difficult to combat than the categories of race, nation and religion, especially in a modern world that is sensitive to these latter, including in its international covenants. In the United States, the plight of Native Americans is in many respects far more difficult than that of Afro-Americans; in Australia, it has been much easier for those with the status of convicts transported there[56] (and Goffman notes in a footnote comment how 'in recent history ... low class status functioned as an important tribal stigma')[57] to shed their stigmatized background than for Aborigines to be accepted, whether as individuals or as a group – and in a country with few people of African descent, they are known, (sometimes, but not always, derisively), as blacks; in Africa, the physical stature of a person (a small Pygmy or Khoi or tall Tutsi) is a key determinant of social status, generally of a detrimental or at least problematical, nature. To this inferior status is attached a stigma, which in turn, imparts a sense of shame. Here is shame in the raw, without the intervening caring of a reintegrative process. Braithwaite's analysis deals not just with how to respond to criminal acts, but directly confronts general criminological theories, not just stigma theory, but also others, such as subcultural, learning, social control, opportunity.[58] But, for certain sections of the population – those who carry their tribal stigma openly in the color of their skin and sense, within themselves, not guilt, but shame – may be found a possible partial explanation for the high rates of social problems, of crime, addiction, aggression, amongst so many aboriginal groups.

For many tribal communities, the imposition of stigma and the induction of shame are not issues relating only to the nature of the criminal justice system and its response to deviant behavior, but deep social and cultural factors that are themselves amongst the major causes of criminal behavior, and particularly those aspects of it that relate to alcoholism, disorderly conduct and violence. The stigma so often attached to aboriginal identity, and the shame associated with it, are integral parts of the aetiology of criminal and deviant behavior. Beyond this, there are even specific aspects of the culture that are not merely downgraded in value, but may even be formally criminalized. Thus, for instance, the partaking of a sacrament, such as peyote, falls under the rubric of drug abuse; scarification, a form of body adornment, becomes child abuse; spearing, a traditional form of punishment, often expressed in a symbolic or at least minimum manner, becomes an assault; polygamy, a recognized social phenomenon, becomes bigamy, a crime; the potlatch feast, in many respects so reminiscent of modern conspicuous over-consumption, is banned; traditional fishing and hunting practices are declared illegal, or confined to periods associated with leisure activities rather than with basic subsistence needs.

Bereft of traditions, dispossessed of land, denied political rights (or at least meaningful leverage on the system), the cumulative impact is in the denigration of the individual's self-image, and the consequent result, a disproportionate amount of crime, in fact so disproportionate that, as Jackson points out, it cannot be understood merely in terms of an existing situation – such as poverty – but as the end-result of the historic process of colonization.[59] In fact criminalization is only one aspect of a far more serious situation – of a range of social problems, including excessively high rates of infant mortality, suicide, alcoholism, and welfare dependence. Alcoholism, in and of itself, is a major causative factor in a significant number of criminal acts of violence, including killing. The seemingly complex trail, leading from large scale social and historical processes to individual deviant behavior, is actually a simple one to trace. For instance, as discussed in an earlier chapter, the sacramental drug of peyote may be banned, while alcohol is readily available; alcoholism leads to violence, which often necessitates law enforcement, including a judicial disposition; and then, in a final irony and indignity, the system places the individual in custody, either in pre-trial arrest, or as a direct punishment on conviction, or as an activated penalty on non-payment of a fine. In custody, the final drama is played out – inside an institution unknown in pre-colonial times, with procedures that are strange (including a lack of awareness as to rights, for instance of seeking probation at sentence, or requesting parole subsequently),[60] the possibility exists (again at a disproportionately higher rate than for non-aboriginal people) of dire consequences – from mental health problems to death – often by suicide.

Figures in Canada, Australia and New Zealand indicate the immeasurably greater likelihood of an indigenous person being imprisoned, and, within this framework, of his death. In Australia, concern over the increasing and disproportionate deaths of Aborigines, led to the appointment of a government commission, which in its opening statement of a document of over a thousand pages, stated unequivocally that 'an examination of the lives of the ninety-nine shows that facts associated in every case with their Aboriginality played a significant and in most cases dominant role in their being in custody and dying in custody'.[61] The Report also provides a historical description of the manner in which the Aborigines were dispossessed of their land and consequences that ensued for their culture and their economy, as well as an acknowledgment of prejudices of non-Aborigines to Aborigines and a general denigration of their culture.

It is possible to debate endlessly the issues that I have raised in this book, and that others have discussed in their analyses, as to the worth or the defects of the customs practised by different tribal groups, just as the various aspects of modern society have their proponents and detractors. But what cannot be denied is the heavy price paid at the personal level by those many individuals who have been the victims of the clash over values – those who, in their despair, have turned to drink in an orgy of self-destructive behavior, or those who have borne the brunt of new and legal norms imposed on a reluctant aboriginal population, or those who have led political struggles, which have been branded as seditious conduct.

In recent years, the full import of the impact of the criminal justice system on aboriginal life has become apparent – in selective patterns of law enforcement detrimental to the tribal people, in the imposition of penalties unknown to traditional tribal life, and, most particularly, in the unplanned, but not necessarily unforeseen, consequences of such punishments.

While the problem of deaths in custody is a world-wide problem – particularly acute in a political context – the figures for Aboriginal deaths in Australian jails and prisons seem to be abnormal. At a conference on Deaths in Custody, David McDonald presented a succinct account of the major findings in which one of the interesting aspects of its work was the fact that beyond the overall analysis, each of the deaths was subjected to an individual report, each serving almost as a memorial to the deceased, providing not just facts about the circumstances of the death, but data about the person's life; as McDonald notes, 'The Royal Commission is said to have been the most expensive in Australian history, but could well be seen as being 100 separate Royal Commissions: one into each of the 99 deaths and one more into the common underlying issues.'[62] The period covered was for a little less than ten years during the decade of the 1980s. The figures for the Aborigines is totally disproportionate to their number in the population, as much as twenty times, and also, slightly less so, than their number in the prison relative to others. The trigger leading to the appointment of the Commission was an abnormal increase in the number of deaths (large as it had been even until then), when 22 Aborigines died in custody in one year, most of them at the arrest stage. Of no little interest is the fact that the following year, after the Commission began its work, the number of deaths in custody of Aborigines fell to three.[63]

The fact of the majority of deaths in 1987 occurring in police custody, at the interrogation stage, is a pattern that is fairly consistent throughout the relevant years (the decade of the eighties). This is a particularly poignant fact, since many of those who had died, including those who had committed suicide, about one-third of the total, had been arrested for relatively minor violations, mainly involving drunkenness and disorderly conduct. As mentioned before, alcohol has, almost in a world-wide pattern, become a solace for so many indigenous people, struggling to keep their social bearings in a world that has deprived them of their land, their livelihood, their culture and their dignity – so it is particularly poignant that so many of the deaths should have causes in alcohol abuse, which is almost symbolic of the harm wrought by the contact between two different cultures, the degraded indigenous persons seeking escape from the larger tragedy of their people in a potent, debilitating product introduced by those who had conquered and dispossessed them. Indeed, given some of the judicial successes in recent years in civil suits against tobacco companies, one wonders why indigenous people – on an individual or group basis – do not make claims against liquor companies for the harm – personal and communal – that they have wrought on indigenous people. In an interesting comment, Marcia Langton claims that alcohol was used as part of a strategy, to entice the Aborigines to closer contact with, and dependence on, the settler population. She argues that the significant factor ignored in studies of Aborigines is the role of the British men who deliberately provided the alcohol 'to trick and debilitate those Aborigines who had survived the smallpox and the destruction into which they were forced'.[64]

Similar patterns prevail of alcoholism and suicide in other countries, but they have not been subjected to the same comprehensive analysis as in the Australian situation. However, in a specific reference to cultural factors as they impinge on the prison experience, Michael Jackson, has examined the phenomenon in Canada and describes some of the efforts to cope with it by emphasizing the positive aspects of the indigenous culture. Discussing 'Correctional Issues Affecting Native Peoples', he notes a recommendation in a Government Working Paper[65] for '... the development of a legislative scheme which recognizes native offenders as a particularly disadvantaged offender group and therefore deserving particular consideration'.[66] Some of the work done more recently has involved a recognition of the basic civil rights, including freedom of religion and the affording of opportunities to practise it. Jackson notes a situation where the introduction of religious practices, at the initiative of the prisoners, has become an important factor in the lives of the prisoners. He writes: 'Native prisoners who learn the ways of native spirituality discover, often for the first time, a sense of identity, self-worth and community.'[67] In fact,

> a sense of community emerges based not on the common element of criminality, but rather on a search for spiritual truths. In place of the alienation which prison typically engenders, native prisoners are able to experience a sense of belonging and sharing in a core set of values and experiences which link them with the outside native community. Native prisoners are able to experience feelings of value and self-worth … . Native spirituality, therefore, provides native prisoners not only with constructive links to each other but also with native people outside of prison and with their collective heritage. Native spirituality is seen … as an important element in dealing with problems of alcohol and drug dependency, violence and other forms of anti-social behaviour.[68]

The Australian Commission into the deaths in custody showed unusual sensitivity in focusing on each individual – so that it is not the numbers alone, but the life-histories of the victims that are fully documented and presented. Yet, beyond this individual aspect, there is a larger picture; the tragedies in the prison may (and perhaps must) also be understood in overall terms. Indeed, in many respects, they serve as a microcosm of the society at large. In his extensive discussion of suicide in Australia, Riaz Hassan notes that there is a higher rate of suicide among Aborigines than in the general population, even though formerly they 'had no history of self-destructive behavior'.[69] Viewing the situation in a general, sociological perspective, he argues that the higher figures are '… primarily due to the devaluation of their culture and self-identity, which has done irreparable harm to their social and cultural institutions … . This devaluation has accentuated a sense of anomie, hopelessness, despair and depression.'[70]

The final question that must be asked is what was the impact of shame attached to imprisonment in inducing the suicides that took place, as also the attempted ones that failed (that were not part of the Commission's mandate for enquiry). In another century, in another country, a government report laconically describes the efforts of a prisoner to hide from others the fact of his imprisonment. An 1876 Report in New Zealand describes the 'ludicrous' efforts made by a 'half-caste', in a prison work group, in order to 'hide his position from the Native passers-by'. It was clear to this government official that the prisoner's conduct indicated how preferable imprisonment was over a fine, since such a penalty would be meaningless for the culprit, as his relatives would normally pay, and so the criminal 'really suffers nothing'. The quoted case shows, in the words of the Report, 'that the Natives consider it a disgrace to be imprisoned, but a fine is nothing'.[71] As John Pratt comments, in presenting this material, Maori culture could still be expressed, where the European sanction was a fine, 'for fine payment could still be a shared one', but in contrast 'imprisonment carried particular shame'.[72]

Over a century later, the impact of shame would still be felt, with its tragic consequences for some, and its overall debilitating effect in general. Pratt himself, in his pioneering study of the penal system in New Zealand, notes the failures of the state penal system, and the possible positive aspects of the Maori approach to criminal justice; he concludes:

> the Western way of punishment, for all its cost (in human and financial terms) and its failings is still seen as the only legitimate way forward. And no doubt this will continue to be so, even in those countries, such as New Zealand, where the colonial past has meant that an indigenous system has been caught up in the web of historical development of the modern punishment framework.
>
> Indeed, in such countries, this is likely to be particularly so, since ... punishment does more than merely sanction behaviour; it makes an important contribution to the sense of identity and cultural well-being of a nation's citizens. The existing Western-based system will limp and stumble along, as it has always done ... it will continue to engulf a grey, amorphous mass of criminals ... . But now ... we can see a challenge alongside it. There are likely to be increasing demands for the reintroduction of culturally appropriate sanctions, of punishments in the Maori way.[73]

The comprehensive and comparative article by Jackson ends with the expressed hope that it will 'contribute to a better understanding by lawyers and judges of why the current system has to change and the directions in which it can change, if we are to have a criminal justice system, which does more than respond to dispossession and deprivation by locking up natives'.[74] Finally, he suggests that, 'In the area of alternative native justice systems, the importance, of legal pluralism within the Canadian Confederation must be recognized. It is not unrealistic to anticipate that models of aboriginal justice systems can be worked out in a Canadian context which, cognizant of the experience of other jurisdictions, can reflect the accumulated wisdom of both aboriginal law and the common law.'[75]

If the common law is indeed to serve as a model, then it might be noted that in an area that was not colonized, but with which a union was established (the union with Scotland in the early eighteenth century, as a unitary state and not a federation), legal autonomy was officially recognized, including separate penal laws and separate systems of criminal justice. Within this framework, the dominant partner, England, allowed such unusual concepts as a 'not proven' decision in a criminal trial, while major criminal law legislation is not automatically applicable in Scotland.[76]

This kind of legal system in the heart of the common law, is surely an indication of the possibility of a legal pluralism, that will allow for traditional indigenous practices and procedures in dealing with its deviant members, especially in the light of the crisis of modern penology, and the likely benefits to be derived from the mediation models and integrative systems of customary law.

In any event, there may well be other reasons for seeking extensive revisions in the criminal justice system, since there are many understandable reservations as to its capacity to mete out justice in a fair and satisfactory manner, when either the accused or the victim has an aboriginal identity. The most damaging evidence in this context is another governmental report,[77] this time a Canadian one, when the arrest, interrogation and trial of a member of the Mi'kmag Indian tribe, Donald Marshall Jr, was the subject of an intensive governmental investigation, arising out of serious allegations, which the Commission confirmed, that he had been wrongfully convicted, when a key factor in this miscarriage of justice had been the prejudiced attitudes adopted towards him by nearly all the actors involved – including crucial witness evidence that was colored by conventional negative assumptions as to the criminality of Indians, an incompetent defence based partly on similar assumptions, and an insensitive judiciary incapable of divulging the errors and discriminatory practices at the heart of the case.

As Archibald Kaiser succinctly describes the judicial failure:

> A monstrous injustice was perpetrated and then sustained over a period of fifteen years in the conviction and ongoing persecution of an innocent person. Finally ... even a government which had been blind to the need for reform in the crminal justice system could no longer resist the pentup provincial and national demand for a full inquiry into the circumstances of Mr. Marshall's conviction. The Nova Scotia Government also asked the Royal Commission to 'make recommendations' to help prevent such tragedies from happening in the future'.

Four years later,

> after extensive public hearings, several separate research projects, and a forum on 'native rights, racism, and the role of the Attorney General', the Commission published its seven volume study .... Many of its findings and recommendations were startling to a community which had been extraordinarily complacent when dealing

> with issues touching upon criminal justice. Within days of the release of the Report, the news media were deluged with apparently sincere apologies and promises from institutions that had previously been either somnolent or hostile. The appalling state of criminal justice in Nova Scotia as exemplified by the Marshall case had been explored and exposed.[78]

One of the lawyers who helped prepare the material that was presented to the Commission, Bruce Wildsmith, explains how difficult it was to overcome even the predispositons of the Commissioners who, in the initial stages of their investigation, were almost totally oblivious to the undercurrents of prejudice and discrimination at work.[79] In an appendix to his article, he provides parts of the transcript to show how reluctant the Commissioners were to allow any questioning which would suggest that racist attitudes against indigenous people lay at the roots of the judicial error. Yet, in the end, the cumulation of 93 days of public hearings, over 100 witnesses, almost two hundred exhibits, and the findings of research specially instituted, finally led the members of the Commission to the unequivocal statement that 'the evidence is once again persuasive and the conclusion inescapable that Donald Marshall, Jr was convicted, and sent to prison, in part at least because he was a Native person'.[80]

In mentioning this case, Shirley McMullen and C.H.S. Jayewardene, in the context of analyzing the criminal justice system, juxtapose it with a converse case, from the same period in Canada, in which a young Indian girl was murdered, and no genuine efforts were made to apprehend and try the culprits.[81] She was murdered in 1971, the same year that Marshall was tried, convicted and sentenced – the trial of those accused of her murder took place 15 years later, in 1986, the year in which Marshall was released from prison. Several years later, another governmental commission investigated her death, as well as that of another Indian (an activist who had been killed by a police officer).[82] Summing up these two commissions and several others that had been set up in other provinces for similar reasons, they summarize the findings as follows: 'In strikingly similar conclusions, all these Commissions of Inquiry acknowledged the existence of evidence of over-policing, of over-surveillance, of over-charging, and of the over-use of pre-trial detention. All of them also found evidence of under-policing, of cunctation in responding to Native calls to the police, and of police apathy in the investigation of crimes committed against Native people.'[83]

In recent years, there have been other instances of miscarriages of justice in many common law countries – in which other factors, for instance political and ideological, were the root cause of the errors, as well as examples of prejudicial attitudes against other disadvantaged groups, or even miscarriages which contained no discernible discriminatory practices. But while they offer a larger perspective for understanding some of the deficiences of the criminal justice system in general, they do not diminish the enormity of the personal tragedies of those caught up in the system, or the larger injustice being perpetrated on total communities of aboriginal people, and the urgency of pursuing an end to the prejudices, as well as an overhaul of the criminal justice system, including prospects of adapting it to the traditional patterns – mainly on behalf of aborigine groups, but also because of some of the intrinsic advantages of such systems for all.

NOTES

1. For a good collection of articles on guilt, see Roger Smith (ed.), *Guilt: Man and Society* (Garden City, NY: Doubleday, 1971) – see especially Margaret Mead, 'Some Anthropological Considerations Concerning Guilt', p. 117 (originally published in M. Reymert (ed.), *Feelings and Emotions*, New York: McGraw-Hill, 1950); and on shame, see D.L. Nathanson (ed.), *The Many Faces of Shame* (New York: Guilford Press, 1987); see also William Miller, *Humiliation: And Other Essays on Honor, Social Discomfort and Violence* (Ithaca, NY: Cornell University Press, 1993), especially pp. 138–69.
2. Ruth Benedict, *The Chrysanthemum and The Sword: Patterns of Japanese Culture* (London: Secker & Warburg, 1947).
3. See, for instance, H.L.A. Hart, *Punishment and Responsibility: Essays in the Philosophy of Law* (Oxford: Clarendon Press, 1968).
4. Robert Martiensen, 'What Works? Questions and Answers About Prison Reform', *Public Interest* 24 (1974), p. 25.
5. See, for instance, F. Zimring and G. Hawkins, *Deterrence: The Legal Threat in Crime Control* (Chicago: University of Chicago Press, 1973).
6. Carol LaPrairie, 'Altering Course: New Dimensions in Criminal Justice – Sentencing Circles and Family Group Conferences', *Australian and New Zealand Journal of Criminology* (Special Supplementary Issue on 'Crime, Criminology and Public Policy', ed. D. Dixon) (1995), p. 79.
7. Jean Benoit Zegers and Catherine Price, 'Youth Justice and the Children, Young Persons and Their Families Act, 1989', *Auckland University Law Review* – Symposium on 'Issues Relating to Family Law', 7 (1994), pp. 803–4.
8. Ibid., p. 804.
9. Chief Justice Tom Tsu, 'The Powers of Decision-Making in Tribal Courts', *Arizona Law Review* 31 (1989), p. 227.
10. Benedict, *Chrysanthemum and Sword*, 222.
11. Ibid., p. 223.
12. Ibid., p. 224.
13. Gerhart Piers and Milton Singer, *Shame and Guilt: A Psychoanalytic and a Cultural Study* (Springfield, IL: Charles C. Thomas, 1953), part II (written by Singer), Chapter 3, 'Psychometric Data on Shame and Guilt in American Indian Cultures'.
14. John Braithwaite, *Crime, Shame and Reintegration* (Cambridge: Cambridge University Press, 1989).
15. Toni Massaro, 'Shame, Culture and American Criminal Law', *Michigan Law Review* 89 (1991), p. 1880.
16. See Braithwaite's discussion of 'Labeling Theory', *Crime, Shame and Reintegration*, pp. 16-21. He particularly contrasts his approach with that of 'the first labeling theorist', Frank Tannenbaum, who pointed out the dangers of 'dramatizing the evil', since it would serve only to increase the likelihood of the evil taking place. Braithwaite argues conversely that 'low crime societies' are those that do 'dramatize the evil' (p. 17).
17. Braithwaite refers to Stanley Cohen's work on exclusionary and inclusionary modes of social control (pp. 155–7). See Cohen, *Visions of Social Controls: Crime, Punishment and Classification* (Cambridge: Polity Press, 1985).
18. Braithwaite, *Crime, Shame and Reintegration*, p. 20.
19. Ibid., p. 20.

20. See discussion on 'Subcultural, Control, Opportunity and Learning Theories', ibid., pp. 21–43.
21. Ibid., p. 152.
22. Ibid., p. 152.
23. Ibid., p. 156.
24. Ibid., p. 156.
25. Ibid., p. 161.
26. See ibid., section entitled 'Beyond Individualism', pp. 168–76.
27. Ibid., pp. 171–2. See also Leon Sheleff, *The Bystander: Behavior, Law, Ethics* (Lexington, MA: Lexingon Books, 1978).
28. See, for instance, Braithwaite, *Crime, Shame and Reintegration*, p. 169, where Braithwaite writes: 'Obligation to the group interdependences with the special quality of material help and trust ... are characteristics which have given the Japanese a contemporary advantage not only in crime control, but in making the best use of the talents of the populace in a post-industrial society'; – and 'It is hard to argue that liberal corporatist societies like Sweden, Norway, or Austria have less political or/and social freedom, less ferment of ideas, than individualistic societies like the United States'.
29. Ibid., p. 95. Braithwaite writes 'Australian Aboriginals might reject the white man's criminal justice system, might believe that it discriminates viciously against blacks, might have a different view of the punishments appropriate (e.g., support for corporal punishment), might view their traditional justice system as superior, but at least there is general agreement between Aboriginals and whites in Australia that the behavior criminalized by white man's law should be criminalized'. This generalization is aimed at suggesting that there is a consensus as to the core values of the criminal law ('almost all criminal laws to protect the persons and property of citizens are justified') despite dissension over other forms of deviance. But a generalization of this nature ignores the complaints of Aborigines in respect of their property rights, one of their major claims against the whites – and, in addition, of course, they were for long not even considered citizens.
30. See, for instance, Nancy Williams, *Two Laws: Managing Disputes in a Contemporary Aboriginal Community* (Canberra: Australian Institute of Aboriginal Studies, 1987).
31. Massaro, 'Shame, Culture and American Criminal Law', refers to 'informal adjustment of grievances', including the song duel in which 'the victim of the misdeed would compose a satirical song to mock the perpetrator and then challenge him to a public song duel'. Lowie describes the duel as follows: 'Drumming and chanting, [the challenger] throws his enemy's misdeeds into his teeth, exaggerating and deriding them .... The accused person receives the mockery with feigned composure and at the close of the challenger's charge returns in kind... The spectators follow proceedings with great interest .... Using these song duels, the Eskimos sought to preserve the social order without violence or other formal coercion' (p. 1911). The reference to Lowie is R. Lowie, *Primitive Society* (1920).
32. For New Zealand, see Children, Young Persons and Their Families Act, 1989. For earlier examples of the incorporation of Maori customs and the use of Maori chiefs in the nineteenth century, see John Pratt, 'Citizenship, Colonisation and Criminal Justice', *International Journal of the Sociology of Law* 19 (1991), p. 293. He writes that the Magistrates Courts Ordinance of 1846 'made provision for the appointment of Maori Chiefs to sit on the bench with Resident Magistrates to hear civil disputes that involved Maori'. However, he adds 'If such procedures (in which co-option of the Chiefs might legitimate for the rest of the Maori people) were designed to show some respect for "Maori customs" and "uses", they also constituted a more recognizable display of judicial and magisterial power for the Europeans.' However a major factor 'in its favour, it was a system without imprisonment; ... it was a system rooted in the local communities; it was a system that looked after the needs of victims'.
33. Jenny Burger, 'A Critical View of Conferencing', *Australian and New Zealand Journal of Criminology* (Special Supplementary Issue on 'Crime, Criminology and Public Policy', ed. D. Dixon) (1995), p. 100. She writes that the Act was a result of Maori pressure, 'based on "traditional" Maori concepts of conflict resolution. However, Braithwaite's original and compelling theory of "reintegrative shaming" was not a major influence on the New Zealand changes.'
34. John Braithwaite and Stephen Mugford, 'Conditions of Successful Reintegration

Ceremonies', *British Journal of Criminology* 34 (1994) p. 153. They write: 'Following an assault, the ... head of the extended family unit of the offender, will kneel on a mat outside the house of the victim family until he is invited in and forgiven. Sometimes that will take days' (p. 153).

35. LaPrairie, 'Altering Course', p.78.
36. Ibid., p. 79.
37. But see also interesting description of anti-alcohol program, carried out among Aborigines, partly based on Canadian experience – Kayleen Hazlehurst, *A Healing Place: Indigenous Visions for Personal Empowerment and Community Recovery* (Rockhampton: Central Queensland University Press, 1994).
38. Ibid, pp. 79–80.
39. Ibid., p. 80.
40. For a good description of these developments, especially in Canada, see Massaro, 'Shame, Culture and American Criminal Law'.
41. *R. v. Moses*, (1992) 11 CR (4th) 357 (Yukon Terr. Ct.).
42. Michael Jackson, 'Locking Up Natives in Canada', *University of British Columbia Law Review* 23 (1989), p. 215.
43. *R. v. Naqitarvik* (1986) 26 C.C.C. (3d) 193.
44. Ibid., p. 199.
45. Ibid., pp. 199-200. The dissenting judge (Mr. Justice Dalzil) also explained that 'The trial judge properly took into account the special circumstances disclosed in evidence of a small isolated group striving to preserve its cultural heritage by maintaining its cultural unity, not for the purpose of blocking the imposition of criminal law but by gradually introducing it by bridging the gap between traditional law and the new law. The crime-free record of the community obviously satisfied the trial judge that this community was much more successful in this than had generally been the unfortunate case in too many communities in the far North' (pp.206–7).
46. See Albert Eglash, 'Creative Restitution', *Journal of Criminal Law, Criminology and Police Science* 48 (1958), p. 619; and Stephen Schafer, 'The Proper Role of a Victim Compensation Scheme', *Crime and Delinquency* 21 (1975), p. 45.
47. Zegers and Price, 'Youth Justice and the Children', p. 804.
48. Ibid., p. 809. In this context also, a leading figure in Maori jurisprudence, Moana Jackson, has written: '... legal duties were manifest and included the ancestrally defined responsibility to maintain order and to protect the land by having a balance between the interlinked animal, plant, spirit and human worlds. The explanation for these rights and obligations, their philosophy, grew out of, and were shaped by, ancestral thought and precedent' (Moana Jackson, *The Maori and the Criminal Justice System* part 2 (Wellington: Department of Justice, 1988).
49. Harold Garfinkel, 'Conditions of Successful Degradation Ceremonies', *American Journal of Sociology* 61 (1956), p. 420.
50. Massaro, 'Shame, Culture and American Criminal Law', p. 1881.
51. Ibid., p. 1882. In this instance, the conditions of dress are specifically allowed by statute law in Nevada.
52. Ibid., p. 1883.
53. Ibid., pp. 1943–4.
54. Erving Goffman, *Stigma: Notes on the Management of Spoiled Identity* (Harmondsworth: Penguin Books, 1963), p. 14.
55. Ibid., p. 14.
56. See for instance, discussion of the fate of both the transported convicts and the Aborigines in the interesting analysis by David Neal, *The Rule of Law in a Penal Colony: Law and Power in Early New South Wales* (Cambridge: Cambridge University Press, 1991). He writes: 'The argument that I will develop is that the rule of law – a set of concepts encompassing legal rules, institutions, processes of reasoning and powerful symbols – played a prime role in changing New South Wales from a penal colony to a free society. The colonists used the imported rule of law ideology to settle the terms on which authority would be exercised in the colony and to force the colonial power to grant its penal colony the institutions and conditions of a free society' (p. xii of the 'Preface'). Later the contrasting positions of Aborigines and convicts are juxtaposed – on p. 79 Neal writes that 'Aborigines were excluded from the protections of the

rule of Law just as surely as they were from their land', while on the next page, he explains that the convicts used this concept of the rule of law to pursue their rights, as 'Through the legal system ... they explored these rights, and had them symbolically confirmed, for example, by testing their standing to sue in the courts, paradoxically, a right not allowed to people in England convicted of a felony unless in receipt of a royal pardon' (p. 80).

57. Goffman, *Stigma*, p. 14, n. 3.
58. See Braithwaite, *Crime, Shame and Reintegration*, particularly, Chapter 2 ('The Dominant Theoretical Traditions: Liberty, Subcultural, Control, Opportunity and Learning Theories' and Chapter 3 ('Facts a Theory of Crime Ought to Fit').
59. See Michael Jackson, 'Locking Up Natives in Canada'. p. 215, where he opens his article: 'Statistics about crime are often not well understood by the public and are subject to variable interpretation by the experts. In the case of the statistics regarding the impact of the criminal justice system on native people the figures are so stark and appalling that the magnitude of the problem can be neither misunderstood nor interpreted away. Native people come into contact with Canada's correctional system in numbers grossly disproportionate to their representation in the community. More than any other group in Canada they are subject to the damaging impacts of the criminal justice system's heaviest sanctions.'
60. See Jackson, ibid, pp. 283–4 where he writes of: 'marked differences between natives and non-natives in relation to the release system ... Native offenders tend to waive their rights to a parole hearing more often than do non-natives, choosing not to be considered for parole. Native prisoners are more unfamiliar with parole regulations than their non-native counterparts. In some regions of the country, native prisoners receive full parole at a significantly lower rate than non-natives. Following release, natives ... are more likely to be revoked for "technical violations" than for new criminal offence violations'.
61. *Royal Commission into Aboriginal Deaths in Custody* by Commissioner Elliott Johnston (Canberra, 1991), 5 volumes, p.1 of vol. 1. The report has elicited many differing responses, from those that welcomed its thorough investigation, and its honest revelations about a tragic situation, to those who criticized it, from many different angles – some claiming that the 30 million dollars spent were an unwarranted extravagance, others expressing disappointment over its unwillingness to be more specific in attaching blame, and its lack of recommendations as to direct, including possibly criminal, responsibility. See succinct summary of differing viewpoints in H. McRae, G. Nettheim and L. Beacroft, *Aboriginal Legal Issues: Comments and Materials* (Sydney: Law Book Co., 1991). See also Peter Brabosky (ed.), *Aboriginal Deaths in Custody*, as well as an account that pre-dated the Commission 'Aboriginal Deaths in Custody'. *Trends and Issues*, No. 12 (Canberra: Australian Institute of Criminology, 1988). See also report, 'Maori Deaths in Custody' – Issue No. 4 of *The Maori Law Bulletin;* from 1980 to 1988 there was a total of 50 deaths of Maoris in custody, compared to 45 deaths of Pakeha; and for Canada, see Luke McNamara, 'Aboriginal Justice Reform in Canada: Alternatives to State Control', in K. Hazlehurst (ed.), *Perceptions of Justice: Issues in Indigenous and Community Development* (Aldershot: Avebury, 1995), p. 5, where he writes, that although there was no commission on the scale of the Australian commission 'a similar phenomenon can be identified: the resort to independent enquiries to address fundamental questions about the impact of the social control institutions of the dominant culture on Aboriginal peoples'.

    In the United States, too, Laurence French draws attention to the fact that three Cherokees were found hanged in their jail cells during a three-month period in 1974–75; when there were no non-Indian deaths during the same time. All three were being held for minor misdemeanours. There were strong suspicions that they had been killed as an act of vengeance. See Laurence French, *The Winds of Injustice: American Indians and the US Government* (New York: Garland Publishing, 1994), pp. 140–41.
62. David McDonald, 'Australian Deaths in Custody: The Impact of the Royal Commission into Aboriginal Deaths in Custody', presented at International Conference on 'Deaths in Custody: Caring for People at Risk', held in Cambridge, April, 1994. In general, see D. Biles and D. McDonald (eds), *Deaths in Custody, Australia 1980–1989* (Canberra: Australian Institute of Criminology, 1992).
63. See David McDonald and Neil Thomson, 'Australian Deaths in Custody – 1980–1989', *The Medical Journal of Australia* 189 (1993), p. 581.
64. Marcia Langton, 'Rum, Seduction and Death: Aboriginality and Alcohol', *Oceania* 63

(1992–93), p. 203.

Similar situations were replicated elsewhere. See for instance the comment by Anthony Wallace in *The Long, Bitter Trail: Andrew Jackson and The Indians* (New York: Hill and Wang, 1993), at pp. 23–4: 'in order to lubricate the wheels of commerce, unscrupulous traders often sold or gave whiskey to a Native American population that had no experience with any drug more intoxicating than native tobacco or, in the Southeast, the "black drink", a ceremonial emetic ... there is no question that the behavioural and physical effects of alcohol ravaged native communities ...'

65. Correctional Law Reviews Working Paper No. 7, *Correctional Issues Affecting Native Peoples* (Ottawa: Solicitor General Canada, 1988).
66. Jackson, 'Locking Up Natives in Canada', p. 287. The Working Paper notes that 'it is very difficult for non-Native correctional workers to understand the social, cultural, spiritual and religious backgrounds of Native offenders and thus to understand the dimensions which affect many of them most strongly' (p. 8 of The Working Paper).

    In addition, McCrae, Nettheim and Beacroft, *Aboriginal Legal Issues*, explain that cultural factors 'may make imprisonment a harsher punishment for Aborigines, and also contribute to the high rate of suicide whilst in custody. For example, the experience of being locked up alone is particularly frightening and alienating for those used to living within a close network of kin.' They also note that 'Traditionally-oriented Aborigines worry ... about their inability to participate in dispute settlement procedures which grew from the acts which have caused their incarceration' (p. 281). In a 1969 case, the court explained a lenient sentence given to an Aborigine as it took into account that fact that the prison sentence would be tantamount to solitary confinement as the prisoner would be far removed from his normal environment, and would be unable to communicate with other people.
67. Jackson, 'Locking Up Natives in Canada', p. 287.
68. Ibid., pp. 287–8.
69. Riaz Hassan, *Suicide Explained: The Australian Experience* (Melbourne: Melbourne University Press, 1995), p. 128.
70. Ibid., p. 159. See also Alison Liebling, 'Vulnerability and Prison Suicide', *British Journal of Criminology* 35 (1995), p. 173.
71. The statements are from a 1876 Report from Officers in Native Districts, as quoted by John Pratt, *Punishment in a Perfect Society: The New Zealand Penal System* (Wellington: Victoria University Press, 1992), p. 59.
72. Ibid., p. 59.
73. Ibid., pp. 252–3.
74. Jackson, 'Locking Up Natives in Canada', pp. 298–9.
75. Ibid., pp. 299–300.
76. See R.A. McCall Smith and David Sheldon, *Scots Criminal Law* (Edinburgh: Butterworths, 1992), p. 4. Recently, of course, the Scottish Parliament has been reconstituted.
77. *Royal Commission on the Donald Marshall Jr. Prosecution* (Halifax: Government of Nova Scotia, 1989).
78. H. Archibald Kaiser, 'The Aftermath of the Marshall Commission: A Preliminary Opinion', *Dalhousie Law Journal* 13 (1990), p. 364.
79. Bruce Wildsmith, 'Getting at Racism: The Marshall Inquiry' *Saskatchewan Law Review* 55 (1991), pp. 97–9.
80. *Royal Commission*.
81. Shirley McMullen and C.H.S. Jayewardene, 'Systematic Discrimination, Aboriginal People, and The Miscarriage of Justice in Canada', in Hazlehurst, *Perceptions of Justice*, p. 27.
82. Ibid., p. 37.
83. Ibid., pp. 38–9.

Family Matters

An analysis of custom within a state in relation to family matters involves not only a clash between differing ways of life, the one recorded in modern law, the other regulated by unwritten rules, but also, in some instances, a clash between the interests of those encompassed within the family framework – between the husband and the wife, between the parents and the children, between the members of the immediate family and those in the larger extended familial framework or clan.

As for the husband–wife relationship, the two most significant factors concerning the legal framework of the relationship are those of polygamy and brideprice, the former dealing with the capacity to marry (can a married person take another spouse?), the latter with the formalities required to constitute a marriage (must livestock, property or a sum of money be transferred from the husband's parents to the wife's?).

It is clear that both issues raise a host of problems that are in conflict both with religious conservative *mores* dealing with monogamy, and newer and radical feminist ideas prevalent in the modern world as to the status and rights of women, as both polygamy and bride-price seem to be, *prima facie,* blatant examples of denigration of the value of women.

Within the western world, then, conservative and religious thought seems to be closely aligned with radical, feminist ideas – both approaches strongly condemn both polygamy and bride-price. But the total picture is, I submit, far more complex than a superficial glance would indicate.

Polygamy is not necessarily based on denying the dignity of status of women – in fact, in some instances, it involves a multiplicity of husbands, when it is known as polyandry, with the specific term polygyny being used for a plurality of wives. There is even some evidence to indicate that polyandry is far more prevalent than anthropological research would suggest – partly because instances of its existence have been ignored, denied or misunderstood.[1] Further, even where it could be shown that women's status was inferior in a tribal setting that allowed polygamy, it might well be that the connection between the form of marriage and the status of women was purely spurious. For instance, the fact that the form of marriage nominally and formally practiced in the western world for over a millennium is monogamous, provides no guarantee for a woman's status, rights or responsible roles. Theoretically, at least, it could be argued even that it is specifically the one woman on her own who would be far more susceptible to her husband's power – far more dependent upon him economically than where there were several women who might actually provide protection and succor for each other. Indeed, it would seem that legitimate suspicions may be raised as to the reasons why a strongly patriarchal society – such as the west was – should have opted so long ago for monogamy.[2]

The issue of polygamy should then be dealt with at two levels: (a) its conflict with older and more traditional values of western society, which saw the idea of having several wives as being not only in conflict with basic Christian values, but also as exemplifying the lustful and permissive nature of the society, with its host of accompanying social problems; and (b) its conflict with the newer normative patterns of sexual equality, its conflict with feminism which sees polygamy as relegating the woman to a subordinate role in society, as an appendage to the husband, with the wives in possible competition with each other for the favors, sexual and otherwise, of an all-powerful husband.

Other factors involve the fact that the exigencies of modern life, the economic pressures of maintaining a family, the reality of changing social patterns, have all contributed to a steady decline in the number of polygamous marriages. Certainly urban conditions make it much less likely (unless affected by the pressures and possibilities of migrant labor with the male in the urban area taking a second wife, with his first wife remaining in the rural area).[3] Similar considerations apply to bride-price, which is less prominent than it was, partly because of economic factors, which underline the possibility that such payments are being made in cash and not in kind. Linked to this is a factor of formal significance – whether bride-price was a mere casual practice, or whether it was an integral part of a marriage agreement, absence of which could render the marriage null and void, or at least voidable. It should also be noted that payment may also be made where the marriage ceremony is not a customary one, but religious or civil, demonstrating how strong the sentiments are in relation to it.

A discussion of these key aspects of marriage laws has also larger implications for the thesis that I am presenting – for this is one of the areas where the distinction between the nomenclature of tribe and alternative terms, such as ethnicity, becomes crucial. For there are almost no circumstances in which marriage customs of an ethnic group (as used in its traditional western conceptualization – such as ethnic Irish or Greek in the United States) would be given formal and legal recognition, unless, of course, linked to a religious group (Catholic or Orthodox), which would, in any case, make the specific variable of ethnicity irrelevant.

The fact is that in the case of tribe, the marriage ritual and its consequences is an essential part of tribal culture. This is not the case for ethnicity – where the rituals, for instance, revolve around culinary habits and musical accompaniment or ritualistic and even superstitious practices, but they do not touch on the validity of the marriage as such. In most instances, it will not be the ethnic affiliation that will determine the nature of the marriage (both its ritual and its legal consequences), but far more likely, its religious overtones. Thus, in most western countries, religious leaders are recognized as official marriage officers, together with judges and magistrates, but not 'ethnic leaders' of the ethnic community as such.[4] A religious minority will often be recognized for the purposes of conducting a marriage, but not an ethnic or language minority. If tribe is not *per se* to be regarded as a religious community, then its marriage procedures require special consideration of a form not afforded to the typical ethnic minority group. It is clear that here semantics affect legal and social reality.

Furthermore, even on the assumption that the key aspects of a marriage should be banned – polygamy and bride-price – there are other integral facets of a marriage, and the question then is whether they can be recognized or whether the member of a tribe should be forced to choose only between a civil and a religious marriage. What, for instance, if the marriage ceremony involves the taking of drugs as a sacrament in a country where drugs are banned?[5] Or an alternative possibility, often encountered – what if the commitment to tribal custom is so strong that it will be preferred over the legally offered choices? Thus, in Mozambique, where there is formal recognition of only one form of marriage, a civil monogamous marriage that must be registered, the vast majority of citizens apparently continue with traditional or religious forms of marriage, including those that recognize polygamy.[6] A tolerant legal system apparently allows it, but can the law cope with all the exigencies that arise as a result – for instance, the disposition of property on inheritance? In any event, the unified system of marriage, part of a unified system of law aimed at avoiding pluralistic principles with their consequent conflict of laws situations, sets up issues not just for tribe, but also for religion. Factually, there seem to be five forms of marriage, of which only one is formally recognized by the state, the others being two traditional, and two religious, Islam and Christianity.

As Gita Honwana, Francesca Dagnino and Albie Sachs note:

> Each of these systems has its own ceremonies and each creates its own patterns of family relations. It is not unusual to find the same couple married according to at least three of the systems, nor to find all the systems coexisting in the same area.[7]

So, the question may well be asked, why is preference then given in the law to a civil style of marriage? Perhaps either all five forms should be recognized, or no form at all. In any event, as the authors show, problems relating to marriage seem to be satisfactorily resolved through people's justice dispensed in People's Tribunals, irrespective of what form the marriage took. From a numerical point of view they note that:

> With only 10 per cent of marriages being registered, the remaining 90 per cent are largely regarded as *de facto* unions which for a great variety of legal purposes, especially in relation to the competence of the court, are equated to registered marriages.[8]

In essence, the position described seems not too different from the situation in many western countries where there is increasing cognizance of and protection for situations of cohabitation and what are known as 'common law marriages'.

From a substantive point of view, they note that 'in practice the courts at the local level refer to the parties as "husband" and "wife" simply on the basis of social acceptance and without paying regard to the payment of lobolo [bride-price] or the performance of certain religious rites'.[9] This may be an acceptable example of 'living law', but in a way it begs the question – should bride-price and polygamy be recognized? Indirectly, of course, it has been recognized, though the law has refrained from saying so openly. If it is because the constitution is committed to equal rights for women, and polygamy is considered to be a violation of that principle (which may be the case, even though the authors do not say so), then it may not be sufficient to allow only indirect recognition. What then if it involves also child betrothals, or other negative features? Is the state prepared to countenance such deviation from its revolutionary norms? It seems to me that a state cannot avoid answering these questions. Either it wishes to have a unified legal system, because, amongst other things it wishes to eradicate polygamous marriages, or it is prepared to recognize the pluralistic nature of the society, in which case it should do so formally and officially.[10] The situation in Mozambique certainly seems to be that there is recognition of both polygamy and bride-price. This, of course, could be interpreted as a good example of 'living law', but living law is in many respects a negation of a unified legal system and an affirmation of a pluralistic one.[11]

In any event the situation in Mozambique – of formal non-recognition, but of practical recognition – may well be preferable to situations where formal recognition is actually given, but the legal consequences are restricted. For often the recognition of tribal marriage is provided on a qualified basis and a differentiation is made between such a marriage, often given a different name to accentuate the inferior standing, and a recognized, civil or religious marriage. Leading off from this – if the reason for a lesser legal standing stems partly at least, from its polygamous nature, what if meanwhile the marriage is still monogamous? Should its status be determined by its factual situation, or by its future potential? These are not idle issues – for legal problems of this nature have often come before the courts, not only within the state involved, but also on a transnational basis, where a foreign court is asked to pronounce on the validity of a marriage that was either factually or potentially polygamous.[12]

Basically what happened in colonial times (and the position in some newly-independent regimes may be similar) was that, unable to eradicate what was perceived as the 'evil' of polygamy and bride-price, since the reality of social life took precedence for the tribesperson over the alien imposed law of a conquering power, the latter was forced to compromise, giving reluctant recognition, and then expressing the reluctance by limiting the overall validity of the recognition. Certain legal consequences flowed therefrom, and some of them seem to be a violation of universalistic values of equality, decency and downright fair play. This must be explained.

In parts of Africa, particularly southern Africa, once the initial attempt to do away with polygamy and bride-price had failed, once it became apparent that the compelling force of the living law, of the reality of daily life, of the sweeping impact of routine and ritual, were of more import than the legislative rules of a distant authority, a compromise was reached whereby 'customary unions' (that is, tribal marriages) would be recognized, but that their status and their legal consequences were to be subordinate to a civil or Christian marriage. One of the unfortunate consequences was that a subsequent marriage of the latter form would automatically nullify the customary union, without any need for prior divorce proceedings. In effect, the law was sanctioning 'bigamy' by allowing a person married by a recognized customary union to marry a second time. In some instances, many of the legal consequences of the first 'marriage,' the customary union, would also be automatically and retrospectively removed, which often affected the status of children and the disposition of property (although occasionally some minimum protection would be provided for the former wife and her children). As Leslie Rubin wrote of the situation that pertained for many years in South Africa, 'A customary union is automatically terminated if either of the spouses enters into a marriage with a third person.'[13]

One of the implications of the secondary status of the union, even while it was in effect, was that (until the law was finally changed in the 1960s), the widow of such a union would be denied some of the rights of a wife, such as compensation for the death of her husband killed in an accident. Rubin contrasts the approach of the tribal courts with the higher courts, with an example where the former was prepared to grant compensation, which was then denied on appeal.[14] He writes:

> In the absence of special statutory provision the Supreme Court takes no cognizance of a statutory union for the purpose of enforcing claims

> by an African woman. The native appeal courts have granted damages to the female partner in the union against the person causing her husband's death. The Supreme Court has refused to entertain such an action where the defendant is a European on the ground that, since there is no lawful marriage between the parties, there was no obligation in law upon the deceased to support the plaintiff. The result is an anomalous and unjust distinction between a white woman and an African woman as to the right in law to compensation for the loss of support which has in fact been provided by a deceased husband.[15]

It would be facile, but fallacious, to attach such grotesque results to the effect only of an apartheid regime, for the inferior legal status of an African tribal marriage pre-dated the apartheid regime, and was not unique to South Africa.

Indeed for many years the law in England adopted a similar negative approach to polygamous marriages entered into legally and formally, outside of Britain, denying the parties the full protection of the law – some of the decisions being in conflict even with widely accepted rules of private international law that lay down that the place of the performance of the marriage is determinative, or alternatively sometimes also the domicile of the parties at the time of the marriage. In fact, in one of the leading cases in the nineteenth century recognition was withheld on the basis alone of the marriage being only potentially monogamous.[16] And even this decision seems to have been based on an incorrect interpretation of the law in that particular place (in the state of Utah in the United States).[17] A similar approach in terms of tribal marriage is noted by Jack Simons, who writes that a potentially polygamous marriage in one case between a Rolong woman and an Englishman living in Bechuanaland – was declared invalid by the standards of the law in England.[18]

In any event, as Simons notes, the situation in England was vastly different from that in Africa. In the former the issue of polygamous marriage was a most rare event, 'an exotic phenomenon, a kind of legal oddity'[19] – and it is only recently that the courts have adopted a more open and flexible approach possibly because of the influx of people who come from cultures and countries that allow for polygamy. Contrariwise, in Africa polygamy was always a significant issue as it was a regular occurrence; in Simons's words, 'the South African society embraced a cultural pluralism. Most of its members practiced or aspired to polygamy as a matter of course.'[20]

Simons explains succinctly and pointedly that the thrust of judicial refusal to protect customary unions, despite some minimum legislative recognition of their validity, was their intolerance of African culture.[21] Once again, it should not be thought that this intolerance was special to South Africa.

In a series of interesting articles, G. Bartholomew has shown some of the inconsistencies of the judicial approach of many common law countries, of the difference between different common law jurisdictions, and of the manner in which prejudice of the judges affected their adjudication.[22] After contrasting the approaches of the English courts, which tend to deny recognition, with the United States courts which tend to allow it, he writes that 'Underlying the attitude of the English courts is the assumption that polygamy is not a form of marriage at all, although it may in some respects resemble it.'[23]

The American courts, he suggests, were more open to the idea of polygamy, whether within the country or outside of it, partly because of the unique nature of the legal situation that they formed with the bulk of the American Indians. At least in the field of marriage they tried to fulfill the terms of their recognition of the American Indians as sovereign nations[24] – and this, in turn, had an impact also on the way in which they related to polygamous marriages outside the country.

Going beyond the empirical analysis, he looks at the ideological background and then argues that:

> the difference between those who oppose the recognition of polygamy and those who support it ceases really to be a matter of law, it becomes simply a matter of prejudice.
>
> There is always a tendency for people to regard their own institutions as the embodiment of the good, the true, the beautiful, and it is this tendency which underlies the attitude of the English courts toward polygamy.[25]

However, what must be stressed is that the ideological issue applies not only to adjudication, but to jurisprudence. In the well-known debate on law and morality, Hart, adopting a liberal stance, chooses the example of polygamy[26] – basically its banning – as a test of the validity of his approach which argues for a clear distinction between law and morality, and for the right of the individual in the personal realm to be unrestrained as long as he causes no harm to others. Since it appears on the face of it that the ban on polygamy is a violation of these liberal principles (involving both interference with freedom of choice and an invasion of individual conduct), Hart attempts to show that the reason for the ban on polygamy (a ban which he seems to justify) is not because of its clash with the ethical value-system of the western world, but merely for the purpose of avoiding the 'nuisance' that he claims would ensue from its recognition, since there would be legal uncertainty.

It is difficult to understand the logic of this reasoning. Certainly, within pluralistic societies, it is the ban on polygamy which causes far more confusion, and few factors would be as likely to constitute nuisance and uncertainty as the fact of a recognized marriage, known as a customary union, being automatically annulled by the subsequent civil marriage of one of the spouses; or a decision by a foreign court that a marriage constituted elsewhere by citizens of another state was null and void. Furthermore divorce itself certainly constitutes a nuisance, affecting other people directly, yet most western countries gave up the attempt long ago to use a legal prohibition to control for this prevalence.

The idea of a 'nuisance' seems to be no more than a desperate attempt by Hart to find some kind of rationale for denying polygamy, when the liberal stance that he adopted seems to lead inexorably to its recognition. There can indeed be little doubt that what is at stake in the legislation, litigation and debate over polygamy is the moral values of a western society, and its underlying, ideological propensities. The ban cannot be justified in the presumably neutral terms of 'nuisance' as the end result of a careful utilitarian evaluation of its pros and cons.[27]

In fact, it is so much easier for Hart's protagonist in this debate, Lord Devlin, to justify the ban on polygamy (basically defining it as bigamy, and making its practitioners subject to criminal charges, even though no deceit was involved), since he undoubtedly relies on religious values, not just for marriage, but in general, as a binding force in the moral unity of a nation.[28] Yet even this stance is being challenged from within the religious framework by those who are more directly in contact with the reality of polygamy.[29] Thus, in Africa, some leading church figures have modified their former anti-polygamy stance. A Commission of the Anglican Church in southern Africa, appointed to investigate the issue, and conscious of the fact that in many areas no more than half of the members of the church marry in church (apparently because of the religious strictures against aspects of the traditional marriage), has recommended a reassessment. While anxious not to encourage polygamy, the Commission suggested the adoption of a tolerant attitude towards it – not to be regarded as a sin, nor to be totally proscribed, but at least to be tolerated as unavoidable, just as the Church has to accommodate itself to other social phenomena that are inconsistent with its teachings.[30]

Beyond that, the authors of the report attempt to provide a theological explanation for their position. 'Both monogamy and polygamy' they write, 'are manifestations of the reality of marriage as ordained by God;' however, monogamy is to be preferred as 'this reality appears within a more intense relationship'.[31]

Furthermore, the old debate as to polygamy cannot any longer be conducted within a social vacuum. In the nearly three decades since Hart wrote, much has happened to the institution of marriage. Whatever the nature of the theoretical position, new practical patterns are emerging that are threatening the traditional western style of marriage, from cohabitation to serial monogamy, a result of the high rate of divorce. Recently an alternative term to serial monogamy has been suggested, that of 'successive polygamy' (in contrast to 'simultaneous polygamy').[32] It is by no means clear which is the preferable form of 'polygamy', especially when consideration is given to the 'nuisance' consequences, particularly for the progeny of the dissolved marriage.

Added to this is the growing trend toward cohabitation where people enter into shared living arrangements without any formal ceremony sanctioning this, and may do it either as single people or divorcees, or separated from their spouses. The law has perforce had to give some recognition to such patterns of behavior, in order to protect the parties, including any children.[33] Yet, in the event of married persons, separated from their spouse, doing so, they cannot be charged with the crime of bigamy, since they are not officially married. In effect, of course, a situation of this kind is a sort of polygamy – in this case where a man may be considered officially as married to one woman, yet living with another, with whom he may even have children, who may bear his family name – and, in fact, even the woman (who is not his wife) may take his family name by formally so registering with the authorities, without indicating the reason for the change of name.

Mary Glendon[34] is among the most perceptive and articulate of writers probing these new patterns of inter-gender behavior, and her approach is of particular interest for those who wish to understand the problematics of polygamy in society, any society. Noting that it seems superficially that western societies have imposed '... an absolute prohibition of simultaneous marriage to more than one person' she goes on to argue that:

> this one-marriage-at-a-time rule behind which the legal systems of the West have seemingly thrown so much weight is not what a social scientist would call a general prohibition of polygamy. Polygamy, which is the most common form of marriage in past and present human society, can be simultaneously present or successive (in which the spouses are married one after the other). It is of course only simultaneous polygamy which is prohibited by the laws. They do not at all affect successive polygamy which is so popular in western industrialized societies that ... the law is fast changing to adapt to it. The legal systems here in question tend for the most part to reserve the use of the word 'polygamy' for that kind of polygamy which is not very popular in the West.[35]

Nonetheless, she notes that there is a growing willingness on the part of all the authorities to accord some kind of recognition to such 'polygamous' marriages, so that there are increasing jurisdictions that accord legitimacy to the children, benefits to the spouse, and legal protection to all.

Indeed, for Glendon, the real emerging problem of family law is specifically this issue of successive polygamy (serial monogamy) for modern legal systems. '... wrestling with the question of whether responsibility for successive spouses belongs to their one-time marriage partners or to society at large, not to mention the problems of children produced in the course of successive unions'.[36] Indeed, while many cultures that allow for polygamy 'are now moving toward the abolition of simultaneous polygamy' she suggests that 'It may be that the modern climates favoring polygamy are those of the affluent welfare states of the industrialized part of the world.'[37]

It should certainly not be forgotten that one of the main criticisms of polygamy is its presumed denial of status for women. The issue cannot however be resolved in some automatic assumption that polygamy is no more than a patriarchal ploy to allow the man promiscuous sex and a plentiful labor supply (both wives and children). For while polygamy seems to cater for the husband's needs, the reality is more complex.

In fact, very little is known as to how polygamy works in its daily operations, how it affects the lives of the women, how they interact among themselves, how they struggle to maintain their autonomy and dignity, and whether they succeed in doing so. For the most part, anthropology has been remiss in not probing more deeply into this key facet of most tribal life, in order to describe how its apparent complexities are resolved.

Rayna Reiter has pointedly stated the nature of this defect in anthropological research, arguing that,

> a great deal of information on women exists, but it frequently comes from questions asked of men about their wives, daughters, and sisters, rather than from the women themselves. Men's information is too often presented as a group's reality, rather than as only part of a cultural whole. Too often women and their roles are glossed over, under-analyzed, or absent from all but the edges of the description ... kinship studies are usually centered on males, marriage systems are analyzed in terms of the exchanges men make using women to weave their networks ... . These are instances of a deeply rooted male orientation which makes the anthropological discourse suspect.[38]

She herself refers to classic works by Margaret Mead and Ruth Lander from the 1930s as exceptions, but although these contain much material on women's lives, including sex and marriage, they contain no real references to polygamous lives beyond a passing reference to jealousy among the wives or their capacity to co-operate.[39] The articles in Reiter's book also fail to probe this issue adequately.

In similar fashion, Denise Paulme[40] suggests that one of the factors for lack of sufficient knowledge about women's lives in traditional settings is that so much of the anthropological research in the past has been carried out by men – apart from the impact of the latter's perceptions, there is also the understandable reticence of women to share their life experience with a male outsider, especially in the delicate area of married life.

The few instances of attempts to understand this aspect of life comes from women. Apart from Mead and Lander, Monica Hunter (Wilson) mentions, for instance, a tendency for adulterous behavior on the part of the woman in a polygamous marriage, behavior of which the husband is generally only vaguely aware.[41] Marjorie Shostak in her description of the life of Nisa, a !Kung woman has a short eight-page chapter on co-wives, which provides revealing insights including accounts of the frustrations and tensions, but tempered also with some advantages.[42]

Solang Faladé, much more recently, did try to examine the impact of a polygamous marriage, but unfortunately, her analysis relates to women from two tribes (Wolof and Lebu) living in an urban area, near Dakar, so that little can indeed be learned of polygamy under more customary rural conditions. She asks: 'Has any serious attempt ever been made to try and measure the psychological implications of polygamy, apart from the material problems that arise?'[43] But though she mentions the problems of relations among the co-wives, and the degree of trust and mistrust among them, she provides no detailed description herself from her research.

This is a surprising lack in anthropology in general, given the prevalence of polygamy and its conflict with the normative culture from which most anthropologists come. Be that as it may; what must be stressed is that, if women in such a social structure are in a subordinate position, it is not the fact of polygamy that provides the basis, but the larger social milieu and its cultural norms. To believe otherwise is to toy with an illusion that the removal of polygamy will also do away with the restrictions and handicaps under which women labor.

Further, it is to fuel the facile belief that monogamous marriage systems are a guarantor of freedom and rights of women. It is specifically here that serious reassessment is necessary. Polygamy *per se* does not necessarily enslave the women any more than monogamy does – everything depends not on the structure of the marriage, but the framework of ideas in the larger social and economic setting. If anything, polygamy potentially provides the woman with mutual support, in contrast to the isolation of the wife in a monogamous marriage, where one of her problems may well be her incapacity to receive the moral support she needs.

So much work on battered women indicates how it is precisely the isolation of the woman in a nuclear family that facilitates the husband's brutality; and the parallel need for the woman to have a female support group to which she can turn. Once again, though, there is a serious lack of reliable information. The aforementioned article on Mozambique does show that some of the marital problems brought before the local people's court dealt with family violence.[44] However the question of whether women in polygamous marriages in tribal societies are more exposed to family violence than the picture slowly and painstakingly being pieced together of the suffering in monogamous marriages in modern western societies,[45] is a question that, to the best of my knowledge, has still to be researched. Nevertheless, there is often an underlying assumption of polygamous marriages being generally problematic.

Thus, Thandabantu Nhlapo's opening sentence in an article on bigamy in Swaziland quotes approvingly the statement that 'Most of the sex inequalities in traditional society stemmed from the African concept of marriage.'[46] Yet, in a feminist analysis of the law of marriage in western society, Carol Smart explains that the 'central argument' of her book is 'concerned with the way in which law both creates marriage as a legal status with certain privileges, and sustains and perpetuates women's economic dependence within marriage and the family'.[47] In fact she specifically makes a disclaimer that it is the nature of marriage that causes the oppression; on the contrary, there are larger forces at work, beyond marriage, that hold women in subjugation.

Smart argues that even feminists and their sympathizers are often at fault in focusing only on the outer and visible framework, such as the legal framework or its actual implementation in law courts, dominated by male judges, often sexist and with other possible undesirable implications, for example, middle or upper class, and isolated from other aspects of social reality. Her book then becomes a systematic exposition of the many ways in which women are disadvantaged in a western society, presumed to be based on egalitarian principles and dedicated to the welfare of the wife/mother. There is, for her, no point in reforming family law without parallel transformations in other areas of the law, for example, employment, housing, tax, as well as naturally within society itself.[48]

Those who wish to understand the nature of polygamy and to sense the needs of the women, would do well to make a similar distinction – between the underlying social structure and the specific form of marriage. It is a little too easy, and somewhat unfair on the culture, to trace women's disadvantages to the institution of polygamy, while ignoring the similar disadvantages (relative to the kind of society and the economic standards) of women in monogamous (or successive polygamous) settings. It is not the structure alone that must be looked at, but the actual content.

In any event, however widespread the support for polygamy in tribal areas, the exigencies of the modern world are leading to its diminishing use. Industrialization, urbanization, Christianity, Western mores, are leading to a lessening of the practice, even where it is allowed, and it is sometimes sanctioned in countries in Africa and Asia with a strong Islamic influence.

In fact, what may be a problem more serious than polygamy for the rights of women is the growing phenomenon of desertion, with many of the newer states lacking the means, facilities and personnel to trace the husband, who leaves his wife (or wives) behind in the rural areas, and moves to the urban areas, entering into a new marital or cohabitation relationship in the town.[49]

What is emerging, then, as a new pattern of gender arrangements, both in western and non-western countries, is the practice of cohabitation. It certainly offers the male an opportunity, given his normally greater mobility, to practice an undisciplined 'successive polygamy'. The problem is liable to become exacerbated as migrant labor expands, both internationally and within state borders. In fact, in countries which have had longer experience of migrant labor, a very clear pattern of extramarital sexual relationships has emerged, as described by Philip Mayer for the South African situation.[50] However, in general, not too much is known about the full extent of these loose arrangements, but the recent increase in western countries of cohabitation has led to a new literature dealing with its social and legal ramifications. It is worth examining some of this work, for it too will enable us to better comprehend the nature of informal forms of marriage in the non-western world as well as phenomena that are increasing in the modern world.

In a sense the nature of marriage laws in the context of a multicultural world, in the context of opposing patterns of monogamy and polygamy, in the context of opposing patterns of formal and non-formal forms of marriage, has come full circle – since the name commonly used for judicial recognition of non-formal, non-legal marriage is 'common law marriage', the same common law that was applied in order to totally deny or substantively downgrade polygamy, while yet granting recognition, of a sort, to those in western societies who failed to comply with the ritual and legal demands of marriage as they set up their joint household. The historical analysis is used by scholars today to provide a basis for understanding the prevalent practice of cohabitation – but no less does it throw some interesting light on common law attitudes to polygamy.

Winifred Holland opens her book[51] on the legal aspects of cohabitation for unmarried couples with a description of the two 'quite different senses' in which the phrase 'common law marriage' is used. Firstly, in its more colloquial usage, it refers to cohabitation – to the relationship between an unmarried couple who choose to live together. Secondly, in its more technical and correct sense, it refers to a type of informal marriage in which some of the formal requirements of the marriage ceremony, which are normally required by the jurisdiction in which the parties are being married, have been omitted. In jurisdictions which recognize the common law marriage it may be difficult to state categorically whether a relationship is one merely of cohabitation or is indeed a common law marriage, because of the informality of the latter.[52]

What is of major interest is that the book then systematically examines all the legal implications of cohabitation, which parallel almost precisely all the problems that have traditionally concerned those who have attempted to assess the legal status of non-recognized polygamous marriages – such as rights to inheritance, to compensation benefits, to immunity from giving evidence against one's partner; in some the solutions are identical, in others differences may be noted.

The full range of potentialities is brought out in a wide-ranging survey edited by John Eekelaar and Sanford Katz.[53] It would appear that there is a world-wide trend toward seeking shared living arrangements outside a formal marriage ritual. Walter Weyrauch, discussing the situation in the United States, notes the 'extraordinary changes in American family law within the past decade', and argues that

> the law continues to be in flux and, consequently, in conceptual disarray. The demarcation between marriage and cohabitation has become obscure and the legal consequences less distinct. One cannot reliably predict whether a particular set of facts constitutes engagement, marriage, business partnership, sexual cohabitation, cotenancy, employment, or something else … .
>
> Parties may be unclear whether they are married or what other legal significance attaches to their relationship. Amorphous factual situations are often given structure only by the imagination of lawyers and judges who, without aid from a legislature that chooses to remain passive, shape the appropriate legal result by applying fictions.[54]

In similar fashion, H. Finlay suggests that there is

> an increasing coalescence of legal marriage and extramarital cohabitation … these two domestic institutions are gradually beginning to coincide in quality, the one from a position of extreme rigidity and inflexibility … the other from an apparent inchoation, bare of forms and formalities … as little by little, each sheds its more dominant characteristics and takes on some of the other's features, they will begin...to merge imperceptibly into one another.[55]

Cohabitation does not normally involve a polygamous situation, though it might be a part of successive polygamy, but the changes in the attitudes to marriage, and the corresponding legal approach of modern western legal systems to the challenge of these changes, must surely have an impact on attitudes to traditional marriage patterns, including, of course, polygamy. The only participant in the anthology to take note of this was also the only African to contribute an article. E. Nwogugu notes that specifically because of the prevalence of polygamy, in African societies cohabitation without marriage '... is usually frowned upon by the society as a violation of its traditional moral code. It is most revolting to people's religious belief and saps the foundations of the sanctity of marriage.'[56] As a result, children of such a union will be considered illegitimate, while most other marital rights and obligations between the parties are not applicable.

From the point of view of conservative and religious western views, there is a harsh irony here – namely that those Africans who are most insistent on maintaining the sanctity of marriage are those who practice polygamy.[57] The irony becomes even more acute when, as Nwogugu explains, the difference between mere cohabitation as a meretricious marriage and a proper marriage is the key ritual of bride-price, the other aspect of tribal marriage which is in conflict with western mores. He writes:

> Customary law makes a clear distinction between marriage and mere cohabitation. The touchstone of the distinction is whether or not bride price was paid in respect of the relationship. Where no bride price has been paid, the association is regarded as mere friendship, and the woman is not a wife *vis-à-vis* the man or his family. In turn the families of both parties have no formal part to play in the relationship with regard to its creation, sustenance or dissolution. In fact there are no regular links between the two families.[58]

So, it is bride-price, as a formal requirement, which paradoxically may save the marriage bond from being undermined by the world-wide trend to informal cohabitation. But Nwogugu draws attention to the aspect of a bride-price that places it in a role vastly different from the ideas that the term, possibly even inaccurately translated, conjures up. To use one of its more common terms, lobolo, it is not the buying of a woman, or even the payment of a dowry. It is to a large extent, a symbolic cementing of the bond between the larger family groupings, a pledge made between the parties;[59] it is also a sort of compensation to the wife's parents in a patriarchal society that the children of the woman will become a part of the husband's family; and it is on this basis that M. Jeffreys suggests that lobolo is really child-price.[60]

Simons describes other 'conventional reasons' given by Africans for adhering to the custom:

> They say that a lobolo compensates parents for the cost of raising and educating their daughter and for loss of her services; discourages a man from ill treating his wife, or her from deserting him, and therefore deters them from dissolving their marriage; obliges a woman's family to give her shelter and support in case of need; provides a form of social security; and constitutes an important part of

> the African 'heritage.' In the last resort they say that the custom is good because it is theirs and not the white man's.[61]

Nevertheless, Simons also argues that its drawbacks far outweigh any benefits, and claims that, despite increasing tolerance for it by White South Africans, including some church officials, it has become a negative factor, partly because it no longer takes place in its tribal setting, so that it is mainly a residual no longer relevant to changing conditions, in this case the move to the cities. He states that

> Operating in a money economy, lobolo has acquired some of the commercial qualities mistakenly attributed to it in its original setting. Lobolo is now, more than it ever was, 'the price of a woman'. The substitution of money payments for livestock has disrupted the network of reciprocal obligations that formerly linked families together and consolidated a marriage.[62]

Simons then is critical of lobolo not because of its inherent defect, but because it is largely no longer relevant to a changed society. If this is so then here is surely a real challenge to those who see customary, tribal law as being flexible, attuned to change in society, amenable to transformation in the rules. Simons even acknowledges that lobolo in the past might have contributed to 'Feminine dignity and the respect shown to women'[63] but claims that, in the modern world, there are other means of ensuring such respect.

He concludes by offering a number of reforms – 'to transform the "bride-price" into a genuine dowry' which would be given to the couple as a basis for the start of a new home; also, a ban on litigation in connection with lobolo claimed – 'But,' he adds, 'any changes must be made with the agreement of the Africans whose customs are being discussed.'[64] Many years later, analyzing the debate over lobolo in the context of the new constitutional structure of South Africa, Iain Currie warns against discussing the issue in terms of a contractual basis in law, while ignoring the still existing social aspects – for 'it is clear that a number of social and economic factors have encouraged the persistence of bridewealth ...' despite efforts at reform; to ignore these factors is to court 'potentially disastrous consequences'.[65]

Once again, the question of lobolo must be examined not just from the perspective of the particular customs *in vacuo*, but in the context of certain economic arrangements that characterize western marriages, or their alternatives. Simons hints at the latter possibility by his reference to dowry. Indeed if lobolo were to be seen primarily as dowry, the problem of the tribal custom would be easily resolved, since dowry is an acceptable, if non-obligatory, accompaniment of many marriages. Of course, there is also a key difference in that a dowry is essentially a payment made to the young couple setting out on their new joint life together, whereas lobolo is a payment from the parents of the husband to those of the wife.

But dowry too can be interpreted in negative terms – as being an economic inducement to the prospective spouse to enter into a marriage arrangement. Where the wife brings the dowry into the marriage, it could be seen as her 'bride-wealth', her investment, if you will, sponsored by her parents, to facilitate her entry into marriage.

Of course, one does not normally find such descriptions of dowry – because marriage is normally presented in its most favorable light – as an expression of love, as a holy union, as an affectionate framework for future progeny, as a voluntary binding agreement, till 'death us do part.' The latter phrase has been rendered no more than a hollow formula in the light of the divorce situation; but it is not the only aspect of marriage where reality is presented through the prism of ideological perceptions. It is the rising divorce rate that has also made people more aware of and sensitive to the material aspects of a marriage – for its dissolution means the inevitable allocation of shared resources. What was once the occasional unseemly struggle over a fair share of the inheritance among various family members, too often becomes a struggle *inter vivos* over separation or divorce.

While the most noticed issue is perhaps the custody of the children, the division of the joint property can be most hurtful and unpleasant. Recently, there has been a move to avoid confrontational negotiations, and to seek amicable settlements; but this more moderate and positive response must be seen as only a partial solution to the tremendous problems that property issues pose for divorcing couples.

In any case, some legal systems make provisions for ante-nuptial contract (the term 'contract' is the legal term used), in which during the marriage itself some (or all) of the property might be kept separately.[66] Contracts are now also increasingly being used as between common law spouses or those who are merely cohabiting together. In tribal societies, too, where the amount of lobolo was not precisely laid down in the customary framework, prior negotiations are entered into as to the amount to be paid. These are clearly different kinds of situations, but the differences should not blind us to the similarities.

While there is much documentation of the interesting phenomenon of lobolo, in its various forms and guises in tribal societies by anthropologists, there is almost nothing known of the process in western societies of the 'murky' and 'ugly' need to 'talk business' in the pre-marital period (while the parties are engaged). Who will pay for the wedding ceremony? What contribution will each pair of the parents make to the couple? Even an ever-increasing practice of having a 'bride's registry' is based on the cold calculation of invited guests contributing to the setting up of the house instead of allowing for the more personal gift, based more on the nature of the guest's relationship with the couple. A non-western anthropologist, perhaps even a western non-bourgeois anthropologist, might find these and other market-oriented aspects of many western marriages of great interest.[67]

But the real economic background may be found embedded in the casual remarks made by those involved in the total process of marriage – from the nuptial ceremony to divorce, with the latter aspect liable to provide more revealing statements. In fact, Smart, in her book, devotes a few chapters to describing the work and practices of the 'gate-keepers' of divorce – 'the law,' she explains, 'is not simply an essence which is encoded in statute, nor is it exclusively encompassed by case law and the discourse of high-ranking judges. The law is also what fairly low-ranking solicitors do every day and it is also something in which even the legally untrained (for example magistrates and probation officers) participate.'[68] After extensive quotes from interviews with solicitors (presumably all, or nearly all, male) she concludes that many solicitors operate on the basis of negative stereotypes of the wife, and assuring the husband the optimum terms for alimony and maintenance for children. A long quote tells of the advice given by the solicitor to his male clients as to how, by judicious payments and even presents, to keep his former wife sufficiently happy so as to enhance the prospects of her early remarriage – 'the sooner she's off your hands and into somebody else's the better,' he is quoted as saying.[69]

Nevertheless, however revealing some of these quotations from interviews are, it is in some of the examples from judgments of high court judges that the underlying market mechanisms of marriage (even though seen through the slightly distorted mirror of divorce) become clear. Lord Denning, in the process of laying down a rule-of-thumb that, of the two households to be set up from the previous common one, the wife would receive one-third of the property and the husband two-thirds, explained that 'The husband will have to go out to work all day and must get some woman to look after the house – either a wife … or a housekeeper … . The wife will usually not have so much expense. She may go out to work herself but she will not usually employ a housekeeper. She will do most of the housework herself, perhaps with some help. Or she may remarry, in which case her new husband will provide for her.'[70]

In another case, clarifying the need for the husband to pay maintenance for his ex-wife and their children (instead of them becoming a burden on the state), the judge explains that 'Husbands, even very young husbands, must realize that in matrimony they are taking upon themselves a financial burden, just as the wife may be taking upon herself a financial obligation if illness or disaster resulting in the inability to work should strike down the husband.'[71]

Both of these cases were decided as recently as the 1970s and though they deal with divorce the comments indicate clearly – at the time of the turmoil of a divorce – the sentiments that few would care to express at the time of the celebration of a marriage, and thereby they do clarify how marriage is seen by some.

In essence, what emerges is that modern monogamous marriages are bound up with economic considerations that differ more in degree and form than in kind and substance from the accruements of a customary marriage, including the use of lobolo. Indeed, in general, it might be said that while, on the one hand, feminist ideas present a real challenge to the validity of many tribal customs that seem to violate the rights of women (female circumcision, to be discussed in the next chapter, is an obvious example) there is also a certain amount of revisionist feminist writing that creatively places aspects of life within a full context, and interprets them far more favorably in terms of the status, needs, rights and privileges of women.

Thus, Eleanor Leacock writes that 'The analysis of woman's status in egalitarian society is inseparable from the analysis of egalitarian social-economic structure as a whole, and concepts based on the hierarchical structure of our society distort both.' She argues that

> the tendency to attribute to band societies the relations of power and property characteristic of our own obscures the qualitatively different relations that obtained when ties of economic dependency linked the individual directly with the group as a whole, when public and private spheres were not dichotomized, and when decisions were made by and large by those who would be carrying them out … a historical approach and an avoidance of ethnocentric phraseology in the study of such societies reveals that their egalitarianism applied as fully to women as to men.[72]

This equality, she explains in various examples, extended to all areas of life, allowing all, male and female, autonomy and control over their lives. In her discussion of polygamy she points out that

> Among gathering and hunting peoples, the married pair and their children are in no sense the basic unit of society as they are in contemporary class-structured society. The band, not the family, is the collective.[73]

She notes that with the assurance of care for weaker members of society, the young and the old, there would be less disruption for the children, for instance, in the event of divorce.

It should not be thought that divorce proceedings in customary marriages are automatically available; but often the divorce proceedings may be less acrimonious because the key debate as to the property took place around the idea of 'bride-price' in a more amiable spirit, prior to marriage, at a stage when it is not the property allotment that is the key consideration, but the establishment of an ongoing relationship between larger family units, oriented to enhancing overall solidarity. In any case, as J. Comaroff points out, there is much variation as to how the lobolo is paid and its effect on the marriage.[74]

In any event, it may be that the real problem of lobolo may relate not to its denigration of women, but to its link with the degree and nature of control that it symbolizes over the yet, unborn children. As already noted, Jeffreys suggested that a more accurate description of the phenomenon would be child-price. The question then becomes as to how much the 'payment' for the 'fruit of the womb' must be made by the husband's kinship group at the time of marriage. This may well raise other issues as to the rights of children, and the manner in which they are regarded by their parents, and indeed by adults in general, but that is another issue.[75]

NOTES

1. For a good survey of research on polyandry, including a debate as to its meaning and prevalence, see the special issue of *Journal of Comparative Family Studies* devoted to the topic of 'Women with Many Husbands: Polyandrous Alliance and Marital Flexibility in Africa and Asia' (Vol. II, No. 3, 1981), ed. Nancy Levine and Walter Sangree.
2. For a historical discussion of monogamy in the western world, see Jospeh Jackson, *The Formation and Annulment of Marriage* (London: Butterworths, 1969, 2nd edn), pp. 7–30; see also Edward Westermarck, *The History of Human Marriage* (London: Macmillan, 1925, 5th edn.).
3. In such circumstances, the man is liable to have a wife in the rural area and another in the town, though the latter might also have the status only of being a concubine.
4. In many common law countries, both judges and religious officers are given recognition as marriage officers, though religious functionaries in religions that allow polygamy (such as Islam) may be denied such recognition, where the legal policy is of monogamy.
5. In the United States some states have refused to allow the taking of the peyote drug in religious ceremonies of the Native American religion. See discussion above, Chapter 13, 'Holy Rites and Sacred Sites'.
6. Gitas Honwana Welsh, Francesca Dagnino and Albie Sachs, 'Transforming Family Law: New Directions in Mozambique' in Alice Armstrong (ed.), *Women and Law in Southern Africa* (Harare, Zimbabwe: Publishing House, 1987).
7. Ibid., p. 108.
8. Ibid., p. 116.
9. Ibid., p. 116.
10. It should, however, be noted that there may be a reason for having special legislation with regard to civil marriage, *viz* to allow for official registration of the marriage in a government registry, which does not necessarily apply to customary or religious marriages.
11. As discussed in Chapter 2 – see Eugen Ehrlich, *Fundamental Principles of the Sociology of Law* (Cambridge, MA: Harvard University Press, 1936).
12. As will be noted, legal systems with rules of monogamous marriages, sometimes refuse to recognize marriages legally performed in countries which allow polygamy, even if the marriage under consideration is not polygamous.
13. Leslie Rubin, 'The Adaptation of Customary Family Law in South Africa', in Hilda Kuper and Leo Kuper (eds), *African Law: Adaptation and Development* (Berkeley: University of California Press, 1965), p. 210.

14. *Santam v. Fonda*, 1960(2) S.A. 467(A.D.).
15. Rubin, 'Adaptation of Customary Family Law', p. 210. Although the law has since been changed to remove the anomaly, it is worth noting to indicate the discriminatory practices that formerly existed.
16. *Hyde v. Hyde*, (1866) L.R. 1 P. & D. 1307.
17. See G.W. Bartholomew, 'Recognition of Polygamous Marriages in America', *International and Comparative Law Quarterly* 13 (1964), p. 1022.
18. H.J. Simons, *African Women: Their Legal Status in South Africa* (London: C. Hurst, 1968), p. 250. The case referred to is *Zonyana v. Rex*, 1912 E.D.C. 361. For an extension of Simons's views, see 'South Africa's Family and Marriage Law Reformed: Towards One System for all South Africans', paper presented to seminar at Centre for African Studies, University of Cape Town, August, 1991.
19. Ibid., p. 151.
20. Ibid., p. 151.
21. Ibid., p. 151.
22. See, for instance, series of articles by G.W. Bartholomew, 'Polygamous Marriages and English Criminal Law', *Modern Law Review* 17 (1954), p. 344; 'Recognition of Polygamous Marriages in Canada'; *International and Comparative Law Quarterly* 10 (1961), p. 305. For other analyses of the early approach of English Law to the issue, see J.H.C. Morris, 'The Recognition of Polygamous Marriage in English Law', *Harvard Law Review* 66 (1953), p. 967; and W.E. Beckett, 'The Recognition of Polygamous Marriage Under English Law', *Law Quarterly Review* 48 (1932), p. 357.
23. Bartholomew, at n. 17, p. 1063. The attitude of the English courts is of great relevance because of their impact on courts of the empire and the commonwealth, both in colonial times and after independence.
24. Thus Bartholomew writes that 'The recognition accorded to American-Indian marriages was determined on exactly the same principles as if they had been foreign marriages': ibid., p. 1042.
25. Ibid., p. 1065.
26. See H.L.A. Hart, *Law, Liberty and Morality* (London: Oxford University Press, 1968).
27. See my critique of Hart's approach in 'Morality, Criminal Law and Politics', *Tel Aviv Studies in Law* 2 (1976), p. 190; and in Chapter 8 of *Social Cohesion and Legal Coercion: A Critique of Weber, Durkheim and Marx* (Atlanta, GA and Amsterdam: Rodopi, 1997); 'On Morality and Social Control', pp. 157–76.
28. Lord Devlin, *The Enforcement of Morals* (London: Oxford University Press, 1959).
29. Benezeri Kisembo, Laurenti Magesu and Aylward Shorter, *African Christian Marriage* (London: Geoffrey Chapman, 1977).
30. For examples of these approaches see Adrian Hastings, *Christian Marriage in Africa: A Report Commissioned by the Archbishops of Cape Town, Central Africa, Kenya, Tanzania and Uganda* (London: SPCK, 1973) – the Archbishops were of the Anglican Church; and Swquibo Dwane, 'Polygamy', in T. Verryn (ed.), *Church and Marriage in Modern Africa* (Groenkloof, SA: The Economical Report, 1975). See also discussion of 'African Polygamy and Christian Mission' in G. Forell and W. Lazareth, *Human Rights: Rhetoric or Reality* (Philadelphia, PA: Fortress Press, 1978), at pp. 54–5:

    > Western Christians have commonly considered monogamy to be the best expression of marriage. But this concept of marriage has produced serious problems for the church in the non-western world. This is especially true in those situations where it is demanded as a condition for baptism, that a polygamist of another culture should divorce one or more of his wives. Such an insistence on monogamy has worked against the stability of marriage, against the concept of fidelity, and against the most vital ties established between families and clans. Questions are increasingly raised: Should the proclamation of the gospel threaten human rights and family stability, disrupt social relations, and separate mothers from their children?

31. *Report of Commission of Anglican Church in Southern Africa*, p. 82.
32. See Mary Glendon, *State, Law and Family: Family Law in Transition in the United States and Western Europe* (Amsterdam: North Holland Publishing Co. 1977).
33. See for instance John Eekelaar and Sanford Katz (eds), *Marriage and Cohabitation in*

Contemporary Societies: Areas of Legal, Social and Ethical Change (Toronto: Butterworth, 1980).
34. Glendon, *State, Law and Family.*
35. Ibid., p. 38.
36. Ibid., p. 39.
37. Ibid., p. 40.
38. Rayna Reiter (ed.), *Toward an Anthropology of Women* (New York: Monthly Review Press), p. 12. For general anthropological discussion, see A. Radcliffe-Brown and D. Forde (eds), *African Systems of Kinship and Marriage* (London: Oxford University Press, 1950).
39. See Margaret Mead, *Sex and Temperament in Three Primitive Societies* (New York: William Morrow, 1935); and Ruth Lander, *The Ojibwa Woman* (New York: Columbia University Press, 1938).
40. Denise Paulme (ed.), *Women of Tropical Africa* (Berkeley: University of California Press, 1963), 'Introduction', pp. 1–2: she writes, 'It is well known that travelers in a foreign land, whether men or women, find difficulty in making contact with the womenfolk and in getting into conversation with them: and when, to the barriers of language and custom, are added those arising in a colonial situation between rulers and subjects, the difficulty becomes almost insuperable.' For general problems confronting a participant observer in research, see Robert Gordon 'The Field Researcher is a Deviant: a Namibian Study', in Pierre Hugo (ed.), *Truth Be in the Field: Social Science Research in Southern Africa* (Pretoria: Unisa, 1990). As an example of lack of depth in the analysis of women's life, a collection of 14 articles by E. Evans-Pritchard takes its title from one of the articles, *The Position of Women in Primitive Societies and Other Essays in Social Anthropology* (London: Faber, 1965), but is little more than a superficial survey, with anecdotal and speculative material mixed with a few references to the work of others. It was originally a lecture, with the addition of a comparison with 'women in our own society'. He discusses the 'independent social life of each, the clear division of labor between them, the authority of the man' (pp. 49–50), but no mention whatsoever is made of polygamy, and its impact on women in such societies.
41. Monica Hunter (Wilson), *Reaction to Conquest: Effects of Contact with Europeans on the Pondo of South Africa* (London: Oxford University Press, 1936), p. 203. For further brief discussions, see anthology edited by R. Glasse and M. Meggitt (eds.), *Pigs, Pearlshells and Women: Marriage in the New Guinea Highlands* (Englewood Cliffs, NJ: Prentice-Hall, 1969).
42. Marjorie Shostak, *Nisa: The Life and Words of a !Kung Woman* (Cambridge, MA: Harvard University Press, 1981), Chapter 7. This is by far the shortest chapter in the book.
43. Solange Falad, 'Women of Dakar and the Surrounding Urban Area' in Paulme, *Women of Tropical Africa*, p. 225. See also Wambui Wa Karanja, *Nigerian Market Women* (London: Routledge, 1988).
44. See Welsh, Dagnino and Sachs, 'Transforming Family Law'.
45. See, for instance, Constance Bean, *Women Murdered by the Men They Loved* (New York: Haworth Press, 1992).
46. Thandabantu Nhlapo, 'No Cause for Optimism: Bigamy and Dual Marriage in Swaziland' in *Women and Law in Southern Africa*, p. 125. The quotation is from Oladimeji Adegbte, 'The Concept of the Role of Law in African Societies', PhD Thesis, University of London, 1978, p. 187.
47. Carol Smart, *The Ties that Bind: Law, Marriage and the Reproduction of Patriarchal Relations* (London: Routledge & Kegan Paul, 1984), p. xi.
48. Ibid., *passim.*
49. This phenomenon also has potentially serious deleterious consequences for the children of the marriage, growing up in one-parent homes.
50. Philip Mayer, *Townsmen or Tribesmen: Urbanization in a Divided Society* (Cape Town: Oxford University Press, 1963), Chapter 16, 'Sexual Partnerships', pp. 252–69. See also Hunter, *Reaction to Conquest*, pp. 203–10, in section entitled 'Extra-marital relations'.
51. Winifred Holland, *Unmarried Couples: Legal Aspects of Cohabitation* (Toronto: The Carswell Co., 1982), pp. 14–15.
52. Ibid., pp. 14–15.
53. Eekelaar and Katz (eds), *Marriage and Cohabitation in Contemporary Societies.*
54. Walter Weyrauch, 'Metamorphosis of Marriage: Formal and Informal Marriages in the United States', in ibid., p. 265.

55. H.A. Finlay, 'The Informal Marriage in Anglo-Australian Law', in Eekelaar and Katz, *Marriage and Cohabitation*, p. 156. See also Paula Bonnell, 'The Domestic Partnership Act: "Cohabitants" Property Rights', *Harvard Women's Law Journal* 2 (1979), p. 49.
56. E.I. Nwogugu, 'Formal Marriage Law and its Underlying Assumptions in Nigeria' in Eekelaar and Katz, *Marriage and Cohabitation*, p. 121.
57. The writer also notes that even those married by monogamous marriages 'readily take additional wives without regard to the prohibition of polygamy' (ibid.). The situation described is in Nigeria, where, it must be remembered, there is, besides the influence of the West and Christianity, also a strong Islamic influence.
58. Ibid., p. 121.
59. Ibid., p. 118.
60. M.D.W. Jeffreys, 'Lobolo is child-price', *African Studies* 10 (1951), p. 145. See also discussion by Sebastian Poulter, *Family Law and Litigation in Basotho Society* (Oxford: Clarendon Press, 1976), pp. 153–4.
61. Simons, *African Women*, p. 94. See also Poulter, *Family Law*, who discusses the 'Functions of Bohali' (the Sotho word for lobolo) as validation of marriage, as determining status of children, as strengthening family bonds, as compensatory payment to bride's parents, and as tending to discourage divorce (Chapter 11, pp. 148–56).
62. Simons, *African Women*, p. 95.
63. Ibid., p. 95.
64. Ibid., p. 96.
65. Iain Currie, 'The Future of Customary Law: Lessons from the Lobolo Debate', in Christina Murray (ed.), *Gender and the New South African Legal Order* (Cape Town: Juta, 1994) – first published in *Acta Juridica* (1994).
66. The contract is intended, *inter alia*, to enable a woman to have greater freedom and to retain, during the marriage, control over property which she has brought into the marriage or was to earn after marriage. In the case where a wife (in the western legal system it should be remembered), was still considered a minor, and the shared marital property was under the sole control of the husband, she could also stipulate that she would have legal control over the property.
67. The 'bride's registry' is the practice of informing guests of the household goods, for example, sets of crockery and cutlery, that the couple have chosen for their new home, and each guest may then contribute so many plates, etc. In fact, this whole commercial process, as well as all the negotiations between the couple and their parents over all the expenses connected with the marriage ceremony, honeymoon costs and the expenses of setting up a home, could provide fertile material not just for novelists, but for anthropologists and sociologists. Of particular interest is the name given to the idea – a 'bride's' registry as though only the wife-to-be was interested in the goods intended for the joint household.
68. Smart, *The Ties that Bind*, p. 149. It should be remembered that most magistrates in the lower courts in England are lay persons, working on a part-time basis, such as one day per week.
69. Ibid., p. 190.
70. *Wachtel v Wachtel*, (1973) 1 All E R 829.
71. *Campbell v Campbell*, (1976) 3 WLR 572. Smart's book contains several other references in which economic accounting is placed high up on the characteristics of marriage. I have chosen the two quotations that most clearly relate to the judge's perceptions of the degree to which economics are an important part of a man's considerations in deciding to marry. Nevertheless the most blatant example of such cost accounting is in another quotation that Smart provides. For those who are concerned at the negative nature of lobolo payments because of their economic calculations as to the 'bride-price,' the following judgment by Sir George Baker should be of salutary significance. Dealing with a divorce settlement, and apparently rather taken aback at the proposal of putting a monetary value on the work of a housewife (at the stage of divorce it must be remembered) the judge stated:

    If the concept of earning is to be applied to a domestic situation, then it would be applied with all its normal consequence. One is that if the job is left unfinished you do not earn as much. A builder agrees to build four houses, he goes off to a job which he prefers to do, leaving them in varying stages of completion. Leaving aside any question of special contractual terms, the best he could hope to receive is the value of the work actually done, remembering also that the owner has to have the work completed. Is there any difference between four houses and four children? I think not. (*H v H* [1975] 2 WLR 131).

72. Eleanor Burke Leacock, *Myths of Male Dominance: Collected Articles on Women Cross-culturally* (New York: Monthly Review Press, 1981), p. 133. See also Karle Poewe, 'Universal Male Dominance: An Ethnological Illusion', *Dialectical Anthropology* 5 (1980), p. 111.
73. Leacock, *Myths of Male Dominance*, p. 125.
74 J. Comaroff (ed.), *The Meaning of Marriage Payments* (London; Academic Press, 1980), 'Introduction'. The writer also stresses the impact that a researcher's theoretical paradigm has on the manner in which social phenomena are understood, interpreted and presented. See also J. Ogbu, 'African Bridewealth and Women's Status,' *American Ethnologist* 5 (1978), p. 241; R.F. Gray, 'Sonjo Bride-price and the Question of African Wife Purchase', *American Anthropology* 62 (1960) p. 3; J. Goody and S. Tambiah (eds), *Bridewealth and Dowry* (Cambridge: Cambridge University Press, 1973); Adam Kuper, *Wives for Cattle: Bridewealth and Marriage in Southern Africa* (London: Routledge & Kegan Paul, 1972).
75. See, for instance, my discussion in *Generations Apart: Adult Hostility to Youth* (New York: McGraw-Hill, 1982).

Women and Children First

Few expressions so poignantly illustrate the weakness and powerlessness of certain categories of people as their acquiescence in actions that are harmful to themselves. Yet, as a corollary, it should not be forgotten that there are also few instances which so reflect feelings of superior paternalism than the arrogation of the right to unilaterally determine whether a particular action performed by others is harmful or not. These underlying premises should be constantly borne in mind when attempting to examine the nature of certain tribal practices imposed on defined groups, to evaluate the reasons for their existence and the results of their performance, and to assess the possibilities of modifying or eliminating them.

The most noted example of such phenomena is the custom of female circumcision, widely practiced in many parts of West Africa, and to a lesser extent, in a number of other places around the world.[1] It is girls or young women who are the recipients of these customary practices, having wide-ranging and long-lasting consequences for those who have undergone them.[2] This problematic custom is oriented to a group – based on gender and age – which is, for the most part, far removed from the decision-making and rule-enforcing centers of social and political power; thus, for instance, the concern evinced in emergency situations to save and care for women and children first, is really a distorted mirror reflection of their inferior status in the ordinary circumstances of everyday living.

As far as can be ascertained, the practice of female circumcision has the support of women in tribes to the extent that many, possibly most, are insistent that their daughters also undergo the customary practice. Opposition to the practice, because of the physical pain of the action and detrimental consequences, comes most likely still only from a minority of women in the tribes concerned, though their numbers are on the increase, while there is a small but influential band of outsiders, concerned for the physical welfare of the young girl, the social status of the female in the tribes affected and the negative message of the circumcision, who are at the forefront of the global onslaught on female circumcision. In fact, female circumcision has elicited in recent years a negative response far in excess of any reservations that have been expressed as to other customary practices and has grown more vehement with the passage of time, being sponsored today by as august a body as the World Health Organization (WHO), and spearheaded by feminist activists.[3]

There are few areas where the culture clash of modern, basically western values, with tribal customs is so noted as in this area; few issues, in which the gap between universalistic and particularistic principles yawns so precipitously as here.[4] Female circumcision is seen by its opponents as being medically dangerous, personally humiliating, psychologically devastating, sexually depriving and physically painful, leading to invariable anticipatory anxiety, and frequent subsequent anguish and occasional maiming or death;[5] yet, it is regarded by its proponents as being hygienically beneficial, traditionally acceptable, culturally obligatory and socially integrative, often part of a *rite de passage*, and even a prerequisite for marriage.[6]

Any discussion of the topic must also take cognizance of the fact that the term generally in use – female circumcision – does not deal with a uniform procedure, but with a variety, ranging from circumcision *per se* (the minimum expression involving the removal of the tip of the clitoris); excision or clitoridectomy, which involves the total excision of the clitoris, sometimes together with the labia minora; and infibulation or pharonic circumcision, in which part of the labia majora is also removed, and the remaining part may be partially sewn together, allowing only a small outlet for urine and menstruation.[7]

In an attempt to emphasize the negative nature of the phenomenon, there are those who forgo use of the neutral term, circumcision, and opt for the negative word 'mutilation'.[8] Others suggest that a clear distinction must also be made between male and female circumcision, with the former being of a far more benign nature.[9] However, although male circumcision is fairly widespread in the western world and elsewhere, and is obligatory in two of the three major monotheistic religions (Judaism and Islam), the topic of male circumcision has not been devoid of controversy – and a Jewish intellectual, radical journal, *Tikkun*, opened its columns a few years ago to protagonists, who presented opposing attitudes to the practice of male circumcision.[10] In a similar fashion, and in the same period, the *New England Journal of Medicine* carried opposing viewpoints in a symposium on the same question.[11]

The debate on female circumcision touches on delicate personal factors (relating to sexual organs, relations between the spouses and familial generational contacts) but, underlying it are also subtle ideological influences; women from the tribes, who have undergone the experience themselves, are regarded as having been co-opted to support a practice detrimental to their own interests, a typical example of false consciousness; those outside of the tribe, who wish to eradicate it are often considered as venting a form of cultural imperialism, attempting to impose their own value-system on others, while lacking a full understanding of the role and purpose of female circumcision within its tribal setting.

Thus, in a comprehensive and perceptive analysis, Allison Dundes Renteln notes:

> Feminists view women's support of the practice as a consequence of their having been victims of patriarchal systems and hence cite their attitude as an example of 'false consciousness'. But although many contend that this custom is the ultimate form of female oppression, women in many cultures favor its continuation. While it seems difficult for Westerners to imagine that the young girls are capable of consenting to it, it must be conceded that some believe they want to be circumcised in order to become part of the group. Educated women seem to be opposed to it, but some evidence indicates that even they succumb to social pressures to have the surgery performed. Regardless of the reason for their support of female circumcision, their willingness to continue the practice is a reality and one that must be squarely faced.[12]

One sees further instances of the ambivalence that characterizes the approach of the more educated (and the more articulate) in some autobiographical expressions of personal experience, as in the anonymous work of a Somali woman, who after describing several of the negative aspects of circumcision, nevertheless goes on to warn against outside pressures to ban it outright, and also to suggest that it be performed under medical supervision.[13] However the WHO is adamant in its opposition to such a compromise, and has issued several directives forbidding doctors to participate in any surgical activities related to the customary practices of circumcision[14] (even though such participation would minimize some of the harmful physical after-effects of the operation).

An even more critical stance against female circumcision has been taken by Fran Hosken,[15] whose work has been greatly instrumental in bringing the issue to a world-wide awareness, and who has argued that the WHO has not done enough to ensure its eradication. She has published several reports, each updating the previous ones, the first of which was published in 1978; she also publishes a newsletter – *Women's International Network: WIN*, which is a source of constant information about developments in regard to mutilation – and her use of this term has contributed to stressing its negative effects, as opposed to the more neutral 'circumcision'. In fact, in stressing the patriarchal basis of female genital mutilation, she makes a comparison not with male circumcision, but with penisectomy:

> From the point of view of anatomy, the clitoris and the penis are parallel organs, which is also confirmed by their embryonic development. Fertility is not impaired by either excision of the clitoris

> or excision of the penis; production of semen by a man continues. Conception and pregnancy of a woman proceeds much the same in excised as in normal women ... [but] orgasm for men who have had penisectomies clearly is not possible, nor is it possible for women who have had clitoridectomies.[16]

Hosken is quite clear as to the gender politics at the core of the problem, arguing that many myths are attached to the customary basis of the practice. She unequivocally demands that

> The male political leadership of Africa must be challenged to stop the terribly damaging customs of family violence including female genital mutilation by setting an example with their own families ... . The time has come for international agencies, anthropologists and international organizations to stop protecting violence against women and female genital mutilation as 'cultural traditions'.[17]

Hosken presents the issue directly as being one of human rights, and in describing various conferences that have been held to study the matter and seek elimination of the practice, she also notes the valuable role played by African women, who are active, on an individual and organizational basis, in striving to end the practice.

There can be no doubt about the necessity of a deep analysis of the meaning and function of female circumcision, and a penetrating assessment of the possibility of moderating its practice, and possibly of eliminating it altogether, but these probes can not be done from a perspective of an absolutist western stance that is, on the one hand, largely oblivious to the cultural (and occasionally religious) framework, within which it is encased, and, on the other hand, conveniently forgetful of problematics of a similar nature in its own culture. What is of vital importance is the necessity to facilitate needed changes, not as an externally imposed dictate, but as part of a gradual transformation compatible with the very nature of customary practices within an evolutionary framework. The lesson of the attempts to eliminate polygamy (as described in the previous chapter) should not be forgotten – both the power of its attraction as a fundamental factor in tribal cultures, and the existence of similar forms of marital (and non-marital) arrangements in the western world.

In terms of sexual violation of a woman's body, Robert Mendelsohn, a leading American gynecologist, has documented the exploitative practices of doctors, most particularly the performance of a hysterectomy, often done for unnecessary medical reasons, and sometimes even without the patient's prior acquiescence, in the course of performing another and unrelated operation.[18] The consequences are no less negative (though different) from the negative aspects of female circumcision. Mendelsohn claims that, in 1979, more than half-a-million women in the United States underwent hysterectomies unnecessarily. The operation is dangerous (according to Mendelsohn, more than 1,100 died from the procedure in 1975), while it has negative sexual effects. Mendelsohn quotes from a study that found 'reduced sexual drive in 60 per cent of the women who have had their uterus and both ovaries removed. Others have reported that after hysterectomy from 20 to 42 per cent of the women studied abstained from sexual intercourse ... much of the sexual dysfunction that propels women to psychiatrists and marriage clinics is a direct result of hysterectomy.'[19]

Furthermore, in a different area of concern affecting the variables of the pain and suffering that the girls undergo, modern society still does not know how to deal effectively and compassionately with those suffering from painful or debilitating terminal illnesses. Anachronistic ideas still dominate the public debate – and there can, in my opinion, be little doubt that only a paradigmatic sea-change in thinking will allow the kind of honest confrontation with the fact of the agony of those doomed to spend their last days in tortuous pain. I submit that an attempt to redirect social and moral thinking, in regard to active euthanasia as a result of the technological and medical advances of recent years, will require the same amount of efforts as is being demanded of tribespeople, who still practice female circumcision. Yet, the evidence to date is, in my opinion, indicative of a reluctance, or an inability, or even a dread, to contemplate, let alone carry out, any meaningful changes in attitudes, all this while oblivious to the pain and suffering of many patients who beseech their loved ones and their medical attendants to facilitate an end to their lives as the only relief from their physical agony.[20]

Much of this opposition stems from the lingering impact of religious studies, formulated in earlier ages, when medical circumstances were vastly different. In fact, some of the religious opposition to a frank and meaningful debate on euthanasia, reflects the desire of religious leadership to retain its controlling power over the rituals of death and burial, while some of the medical insistence as to its monopolistic decision-making authority, is an attempt to retain mastery over the dying process.

The significance and the dimensions of the demands being made on tribespeople in respect of female circumcision may perhaps best be appreciated within the context of the problem of euthanasia in the modern western world, partly because there are some tribes (not necessarily those that practice female circumcision) which have attempted to directly confront and cope with this issue, as will be discussed in the latter part of this chapter.[21] Indeed, one might well argue that the WHO may sooner than it thinks or desires, have to deal in depth with this problem, given increasing hints of surreptitious euthanasia being carried out without the patient's consent (for example, 'do not resuscitate' notices at the foot of the bed of some hospitalized patients), or, alternatively, requested euthanasia in one form or another being denied, because of what may well be 'false consciousness' contentions as to the sanctity of life.

Indeed, in her article Renteln realizes the value of similar comparative assessments in order to appreciate the problematics of attempting to outlaw female circumcision, and she draws heavily on examples taken from judicial decisions (particularly in the United States) dealing with parental opposition to medical treatment for their children, even in life-threatening situations (for instance, because of a religious belief in faith-healing)[22] – and the overall thrust of these cases is maximum judicial sympathy with the parents, even though the consequences for their children are potentially, and sometimes even factually, fatal. In some cases, the parents are acquitted, in others given a light penalty on conviction.[23]

In any event, female circumcision cannot be justified merely in terms of a *tu quoque* argument, but must, in the final analysis be measured substantively in terms of its own expressions and consequences. However, here it must be remembered that it forms part of a larger aspect of many societies – tribal and otherwise – as an aspect of *rite de passage,* that many young people, male as well as female, are forced to undergo.[24] While many of these prescribed rituals have clearly recognized positive aspects, some of the ritual exercises for males involve painful or dangerous or humiliating experiences, sometimes even with fatal consequences.[25]

Nevertheless, while such ritual passages in the life-cycle are generally aimed at contributing to the integrative forces of the society, a recent article has suggested that, for female circumcision at least, the true interests of the tribal group in seeking integrative measures, would be best served by its abolition; for arising out of such a ban would be greater equality for women in the tribe and a resultant greater feeling of satisfaction.

Robin Cerny Smith argues that if females were to be spared the various problems that are related to female circumcision, they would be able to take their places more easily in the tribal framework.[26] She poses the impact of the clash between opposing value-systems and the related conceptions of rights, and then probes the contrasting claims of tribal rights *vis-à-vis* individual rights. Smith avers that there is no overriding theory that would accord priority to either of these perspectives, and she personally opts in the situation for individual rights, especially since she feels that this would also enhance the tribal integration.[27]

However, writing in the *Harvard Women's Law Journal*, Kay Boulware-Miller focuses on the complexities of the overall issues involved in female circumcision. She notes that 'In African communities with strong cultural and traditional ties, the perceived need to be circumcised mitigates the hellish remembrance of the event. Little girls who are initially hurt, betrayed, and degraded by the operation later come to feel socially and morally acceptable because they have been circumscribed. As the girls grow into women, they may forget the pain and argue that the practice need not be banned.'[28] In a recent article in the women's feminist journal, *Signs*, Claire Robertson notes the danger in the increasing critique by Western feminists of African circumcision, as this emphasis on one problem may lead to a biased picture of African reality, in particular a diminution of the noted achievements of some African women, both in trying to combat female circumcision (and the data indicate with a fair amount of success), and in their positive activities in other areas, many of which might even be emulated.[29]

In similar fashion, Mary-Jane Ierodiaconou notes that 'the issue of genital mutilation raises complex strategic questions for feminists', especially for those who (for instance in the Australian situation),

> are committed to supporting multi-culturalism within the feminist movement. The increasing internationalization of feminism means there are a number of possible approaches, and that a feminist perspective should not be purely a white, middle class perspective. It may, for example, be an Eritrean immigrant women's perspective ... the women who are most affected by female genital mutilation must play a key role in determining policy approaches to the issue. Listening to these women may result in supporting views which are critical of some aspects of the culture concerned. This raises the potential conflict between cultural relativism and feminism ... .[30]

After analyzing different theoretical and ideological perspectives, and drawing on her own discussions with African women, Ierodiaconou comes to the conclusion that an express prohibition of the practice might well have a negative effect on the women she had spoken to. Hence she opposes a legislative ban on the practice, preferring a concerted educational approach, linked to an understanding that 'A contextualised feminist approach recognises that the women affected by the practice also hold the key to eliminating it.'[31]

The demand for the outright banning of female circumcision and the activities of the WHO are complemented by the Convention of the Rights of the Child, where reference is made to the need for all parties to the Convention to '... take all effective and appropriate measures with a view to abolishing traditional practices prejudicial to the health of children'.[32] Many argue convincingly that female circumcision would certainly fall under the rubric of this recommendation; indeed, it has even been suggested that this is the major intention of this clause.

However, while the major impetus for such formulae comes mainly from the Western world, it should be noted that, within the incipient human rights movement in Africa, increasing attention is being given to this issue. In fact, the African Charter on Human Rights provides a more detailed and focused framework for examining problematic aspects of customary practices. Thus, in the section devoted to 'Protection Against Harmful Social and Cultural Practices', it is stated that:

> States Parties ... shall take all appropriate measures to eliminate harmful social and cultural practices affecting the welfare, dignity, normal growth and development of the child and in particular:
> a) those customs and practices prejudicial to the health and life of the child;
> b) those customs discriminating to the child on grounds of sex or other status.

A Note in the *Harvard Law Review* describes how the indifference of governmental authorities to deal adequately with this and other similar issues, has led to the emergence of NGOs (non-governmental organizations) in Africa, whose purpose is to protect the young against harmful and exploitative practices. Thus the author states that

> Due to the lack of authoritative governmental intervention, non-governmental organizations, such as the Inter-African Committee on Traditional Practices Affecting the Health of Women and Children (IAC), have undertaken concrete efforts to abolish female circumcision, as well as other harmful practices such as body scarring, early-childhood marriage, and nutritional taboos.[33]

The Notes goes on to clarify the need to be able to appreciate that, with all due respect to the importance of relativistic considerations in laying down the parameters of human rights and the consequence of their violations, there is a need also to recognize those instances which transcend cultural boundaries and, the Note claims, female circumcision is one such example. Thus, relying on empirical investigation gleaned from

> first-hand accounts of the personal experiences of women in Nigeria, this Note presents the devastating health consequences of female circumcision, but analyzes the practice primarily from a human rights perspective. It argues that, although human nature is necessarily defined by cultural contexts, the decisions regarding which customs will be preserved in the name of culture or tradition must be oriented toward the promotion and protection of universal human rights in order to have legitimacy in any contemporary society.[34]

These aims of universalistic principles can best be incorporated into tribal culture if it is recognized that the 'concept of culture ... is a dynamic notion, not a static one. African culture incorporates things pre-colonial, colonial, and contemporary, as well as things social, economic, and political, and things both individual and collective'. On the basis of a dynamic culture, there is a need for a periodical re-examination of specific practices 'in light of contemporary values and knowledge, in order to ascertain whether the customs deserve to be perpetuated'.[35] The Note reminds us of a further factor – that at least some of the present customary practices are not even true expressions of the cultural past, and may well be

> ... based on myths that cannot validate either the initial existence or the continued persistence of an undeniably harmful tradition. Thus, although in other contexts there are legitimate claims to ethnicity and cultural continuity, arguments along these lines in defense of female circumcision more likely cloak pretextual justifications based on manipulations of a dying, lost, or even mythical cultural past.[36]

However, even without such overall universalistic guidelines, the issue of female circumcision is not one that is confined to the state in which the tribe is situated. Large-scale migratory processes have led to a situation where members of tribes that practice female circumcision have moved to a number of countries in Europe and America and some of these people have continued to practice circumcision on their daughters. The issue in such circumstances becomes then not how to cope with the problem in its totality within the original tribal setting, but how to react to an individual instance within an alien cultural framework that *prima facie* sees such action as being abusive, with the perpetrator being liable even to criminal prosecution.[37] One of the possibilities is to argue the cultural defense – for if it can be used to explain the 'necessity' (from a legal point of view) of homicidal acts,[38] surely it could be employed also as a possible argument in a less serious case, such as physical abuse.

In such circumstances, the whole question of a 'lesser evil' (or 'greater good') becomes relevant and crucial in terms of the future of the young girl – for instance, her sense of self-esteem or her prospects of marriage within the tribe. But, of course, the fact is that the defense, in this individual and alien context, becomes far harder to sustain on behalf of the parents (for instance, as accused in a criminal trial for harmful behavior) since the parents have, after all, physically removed themselves from the tribal territory, and indeed have also crossed national boundaries and even traversed continents. While such persons are clearly entitled to retain their tribal identity in the course of their travels to other climes (and, as discussed in an earlier chapter, this need for a sense of belonging can be felt even more intensively outside the tribal setting),[39] the scrutiny which will be focused on problematic practices will inevitably be ever more strict in a non-tribal setting. For instance, given the age range (generally of several years) within which circumcision can be performed, the inevitable question would arise as to why the parents should not wait until their return to tribal territory before exposing their daughter to circumcision? –

and if such return is not anticipated in the near future, then a reasonable conclusion is that the parents bear responsibility for the break in contact, and cannot continue to insist on their cultural right to persist in practices considered harmful by the society in which they have freely chosen to live (even if temporarily, if the period extends over many years).

Further, the length of stay raises the possibility that the daughter might evince a desire to remain in the foreign land (and if born there, might even be a citizen); and so, since one of the arguments put forward by supporters of the practice is that the absence of circumcision would adversely affect her marriage prospects, this argument could then be applied in a contrary manner – that her prolonged stay outside her tribal area would hamper her (after a circumcision) in being able to set up a family with a non-tribal member, which would be a distinct possibility for as long as she resided in Europe or elsewhere outside the tribal area. In a sense, the argument being made here is that the right to practice tribal customs, which are problematic by universalistic standards, must bear some clear-cut proof of the commitment of the persons claiming that right to their tribal affiliation, including connection with its geographical position.[40]

Until now, many of the cases in western countries dealing with female circumcision, have arisen in France. Renteln, who devotes much of her article on cultural defence to the topic of female circumcision,[41] notes:

> Female circumcision captured public attention in France when in 1982 the press reported fatalities resulting from the [circumcision] operation. Evidently some women from Mali and Senegal bring an 'exciseuse' (the person who performs the operation) to France once a year to perform the operation … . It is estimated that annually twenty-five thousand girls, approximately seven years old, have female circumcision surgery in France.[42]

While the original judicial responses, generally against parents, were lenient, for example, suspended sentences, in recent years more stringent punishments have been imposed, including prison sentences, some of them for lengthy terms.[43]

In the United States the issue has so far arisen most notably in terms of immigration policy – and whether young women seeking to avoid genital mutilation should be given asylum. Yet the treatment here may be a typical example of the myopic perceptions that Robertson had warned against. Thus, in an instance that became a *cause célèbre,* the *New York Times* (that had originally described the plight of one such woman, Fauziya Kasinga), greeted her release from detention for over a year with the front-page headline, 'US Frees African Fleeing Ritual Mutilation'.[44] The implication here is that the United States authorities had saved her from her unfortunate fate, whereas all that had transpired was that she was released from detention by the immigration authorities into the care of friends and supporters pending a final decision on her future. Thus, it seems that from a human rights point of view, the key issue being reported was not of genital mutilation, but immigration policy. The immigration judges are not required to pass on the existence, validity, justification or desirability of female circumcision – that is a separate issue. In this case, they are only required to determine whether someone fleeing that custom because it was to be forced upon her against her declared will, is entitled to sanctuary. For over a year Kasinga was kept in 'harsh confinement', sometimes shackled, sometimes in isolation, sometimes sharing a maximum security cell with a convicted criminal. The freedom referred to in the headline was from these conditions.

Subsequently, it should be noted, it was decided to grant her asylum. Even so, the procrastination in dealing with her case is in itself, a regrettable fact, especially in the light of the position adopted by the United Nations High Commission on Refugees, which recognizes the attempt to avoid forced genital mutilation as a legitimate claim for refugee status.[45] Yet, as Saba Bahar comments, 'Despite this recommendation and national legislation against the practice, few countries grant asylum to women on these grounds alone.'[46]

In fact, legislation against the practice is found not just in countries in the Northern hemisphere, and elsewhere in the 'Western' world, aimed basically at immigrant populations, but also in African countries, such as Burkina Faso, Egypt, Ivory Coast, Sudan, Guinea Bissau and Kenya. Bahar refers to such legislation in these countries to stress the fact that the issue must be dealt with at the national level, and cannot be seen as merely an internal family affair. Beyond the legislation, and in conjunction with grass-roots movements, a more recent development is the denunciation of the practice by some of its practitioners, as has occurred recently in the Gambia, and some of them have joined with popular movements working for its eradication.

While in France much of the criminal litigation deals with the problem of female circumcision, in England the thrust of public concern and judicial involvement has been oriented to scarification, the making of scars, generally on the face, partly for reasons of ritual and partly for aesthetic reasons – the enhancement of the child's beauty. This problem, too, should be analyzed in its dual context, with possible differences in the tolerance that can be shown toward the act, depending on whether it is performed in or near the tribal area where such markings are regarded favorably, or far removed in a foreign country, where the marks on the face suggest not beauty but cruelty (in the making of the scars) and ugliness (in the consequences). Here, too, there are the aspects of the immediate action – it causes pain; and the long-term effects – the fate of a child without the beautifying marks, or alternatively, the disfiguration that many will perceive outside of the tribal territory.

An important English case was *R v. Adesanya* in 1974, which dealt with the scarification of two young boys.[47] In this case, the court seems to have been fully sensitive to the conflict between differing value-systems, and this is reflected in the sentencing stage, when the judge gave an unconditional discharge. At the same time, the mere fact of conviction was clearly intended to send a message to members of this and other minority groups of the need for them to adhere to the standards of behavior of the country of residence, however strong their affiliation to their tribe was felt to be and however imperative the custom that they were performing.[48] Once again, the degree of tolerance shown may well be a function of the nature of their ongoing affiliation to the tribe, measured *inter alia* in terms of the duration of their absence from tribal lands, and their plans to return.

Further, a certain overall and comparative perspective is desirable – on the one hand, the fact that body-tattooing and body-piercing on all parts of the body and of all types, is considered a legitimate, even if an aberrant, form of body adornment[49] (though generally performed on adults, not children); on the other hand, it was during this same period that the British approach to corporal punishment in the schools (widely practiced and formally condoned) was subjected to strong criticism by the European Court of Human Rights, as being in violation of the universal principles of the European Convention on Human Rights.[50] In fact, during that same period, the United States courts had given similar approval to corporal punishment,[51] holding it to be compatible with constitutional rights, even when imposed without the protection of due process.

In the English case – of a Yoruban woman from Nigeria charged with abusing her children – the evidence indicated that her sons (aged 9 and 14) had acquiesced in the procedure. At the same time, the age disparity between the two boys again indicates the flexibility in the time that the scarification could be done – and again, the issue arises as to whether, in using the cultural defense, it is possible to prove the *necessity* of the action when time is not of the essence – indeed, the necessity defence examines whether alternatives are available, including a postponement of the act, so that the cultural defense (based on traditional necessity defense principles) can only be activated if it can be shown that there was no alternative (no time to wait, no other place to do the scarification, and so on) to performing the act when it was done. This takes the issue way beyond whether or not the court may show tolerance. It may well be that the court will be tolerant of the cultural imperative to practice scarification, but yet declare that, in the circumstances in which it was carried out, it was not justified. It should be noted that some of the articles dealing with the possibility of a cultural defense (for this and other phenomena) ignore this crucial aspect of the defense[52] – not just whether the particular custom may be allowed, but whether in the particular circumstances under review, there was indeed no alternative.

In any event, it seems a legitimate outcome that a court in Europe might apply stricter standards in measuring the possibility of criminality for a custom than would a court in Africa. Summing up the general situation in Britain, Sebastian Poulter has stated that there is a need for compromise in which 'Legal recognition must be afforded to many ethnic minority customs on grounds of practicality, common sense, individual liberty, religious tolerance and the promotion of racial harmony. However, a few restrictions and limitations must equally be imposed'.[53]

Furthermore, the problems of the young in many of the regions mentioned are not contained only within these practices – of circumcision, of scarification or of *rites de passage* (the latter for males, often dangerous, and often including painful and humiliating forms of circumcision). Genuine concern for the young in Africa, for instance, should involve also those harmful phenomena that have no connection with tribal customs – for instance, the recruitment of child-soldiers, especially in civil war situations (as in the ongoing strife in Liberia or Sudan). Girls specifically are at risk in a sexual manner as demeaning as circumcision, for example, where they are forcefully abducted, collusively sold, or cunningly enticed into the enslavement of prostitution – often as part of tourist offerings – and only recently have concerted efforts been made to eradicate the practice and penalize the offenders, including the customers.

In this context of sexual exploitation of young females, mention should also be made of the practice of *Trokos,* for instance in Ghana, where young girls are made into concubines for the delectation of tribal leaders, often presented as a religious task. This practice has received almost no attention in academic writing, by international human rights bodies, or by feminist groups, but the Ghana National Commission on Children has drawn attention to this problem, and has worked toward its eradication, basing itself also on a Report prepared specially by the Ghana Law Reform Commission.[54]

This discussion of problematic customs of tribal societies is based, to a large extent, on the vulnerability of the affected population groups – females and the young. There is another age group which is vulnerable, namely the elderly, and in recent years increasing evidence has come to light from all over the world of abuse inflicted upon the members of this group, some of it within a familial setting, and indeed in situations where children who were abused when they were young now mete out similar treatment to their parents in the latters' old age.

However, within this framework, there is one particular pattern of behavior that is not necessarily abusive in and of itself, but that has extreme consequences – the decision to apply to the elderly, in certain circumstances that are clearly defined, 'death-hastening behavior,' to use the terminology of Anthony Glascock in a perceptive and comparative analysis of such behavior. Specifically, Glascock examines the 'proposition that there are similarities between euthanasia and death-accelerating behavior …',[55] stressing that the problems of euthanasia in modern societies is not a new phenomenon, and that it is incorrect to conduct the debate under 'the implied assumption that we are the first society which has had to face this dilemma …'[56] Glascock goes on to argue that 'this situation is simply incorrect since people in other societies have also had to face the dilemma of how much effort should be used to cure a person's illness and to prolong the lives of people who are dying'. Consequently, he suggests that given the fact that:

> the ethical, moral, and legal uncertainties that surround these issues are not unique to American society; people in other societies have had to struggle with them just as we have. Therefore, it is useful to observe how people in less sociopolitically complex societies deal with these issues and to compare their solution to ours.[57]

Further, as noted in the early part of this chapter, the prospects of modern societies moving toward a solution of the problematic customs of female circumcision and scarification is connected to its ability to comprehend the deep-seated nature of beliefs that sometimes impede rational and compassionate discussion. My contention is that a similar factor of belief-system is impairing the capacity of modern societies to cope intelligently and compassionately with the host of problems spawned by medical advances in the modern world. The same mind-set that affects so many women in societies that practice female circumcision, affects many also in the modern world faced with the agonizing dilemma of the place of euthanasia (of death-accelerating behavior) in the modern world. Specifically, it seems that there is a need for an organization such as the WHO, which is so active in the struggle over female circumcision, to display at least the same amount of energy and concern over the fate of the elderly ill – in terms both of death-accelerating behavior carried out surreptitiously without full, informed consent, and, conversely, of the refusal to openly allow active euthanasia at the express request of the patient. As Glascock notes, 'Examples of death-accelerating behavior and euthanasia are becoming abundant in American society. Many of these examples show the contradictions that exist as Americans attempt to reach a consensus as to what behavior is the most appropriate for the decrepit elderly.'[58]

Drawing on extensive data from accumulated anthropological research, Glascock notes a conceptual problem that what should perhaps be considered euthanasia is given other terminology in the context of non-industrial societies. He suggests that the terms in use – of geronticide or gericide – are too narrow to encompass fully the nature of the phenomenon being described. Another term used is that of senicide, which has, of course, similar limitations – all three terms focusing only on the fact of the putting to death, while ignoring the motivations and the larger societal context – which are certainly conveyed by the term euthanasia, 'a good death'. In fact, precisely because these other terms are used, both the meaning of the act and its possible relevance for the modern world, have often been lost on the researchers.

In the examples examined, Glascock noticed a wide variety of behavior, ranging from abandonment (for instance, leaving the elderly behind as a nomadic group moves on to a new location) to an active killing carried out at the behest of the elderly person.[59]

What is most relevant is the fact that the practice of 'death-accelerating behavior' is carried out 'with supportive treatment'.[60] Noting the similarities between simple societies and advanced technological ones confronting dilemmas of 'decrepit elderly' (decrepit being the term used to indicate varying stages of illness in contrast to the 'intact elderly'), Glascock sums up his analysis as follows:

> First, examples of overt, direct killing of the elderly in America are still rare enough to produce sensational responses, particularly in news reports. In nonindustrial societies the killing, abandoning, and forsaking of the elderly, although emotionally demanding, do not take on the dramatic character found in American society. Death hastening is part of the culture of these societies; children have personally experienced the death of close relatives, as they age they may be called upon to hasten the death of one of their parents, and they in turn may ask their children to do the same. As a result, death-hastening is open and socially approved in nonindustrial societies. In America, on the other hand, the killing of the elderly is usually covert – the turning off of a life support-system, not undertaking a procedure to prolong life, or abusing the old person.
>
> Second, the people who decide and implement the killing or hastening are quite different in the two types of societies. In nonindustrial societies the decisions are made by the family, often with open discussions. In American society it is often unclear as to who decides – children, spouse, the old person, medical staff, courts of law, or some combination. Most often, the decisions appear to be made on an *ad hoc* basis, with the family brought in at the last minute and the elderly individual often not consulted at all. As … examples of recent legal cases in America show, when the decision is made and implemented by a single person, the consequences can be severe – he

> or she can be charged with premeditated murder. Thus, it is not surprising that people, especially hospital and nursing home administrators and physicians, are reluctant to take responsibility for accelerating the death of an elderly person. Social sanctions in the form of prosecution and lawsuits are applied inconsistently, with the result being that the killing and accelerating are done covertly and then covered up. In contrast, death hastening in nonindustrial societies is open and direct and people are willing to take responsibility because the rules are known and accepted by the social group.[61]

Based on this comparison of the situation in non-industrial and technological societies of the modern world, there is clearly an issue of major dimensions to be tackled. The first modern state to adopt a policy similar to that of some of the non-industrial societies examined, is the Netherlands,[62] and its policy has come in for much criticism, including the 'thin edge' argument, namely that its recognition of euthanasia may well lead (or has already led) to indiscriminate killing, carried out beyond the parameters established by the law. In some of my own work I have related positively to the issue of active euthanasia, and to the policies adopted in the Netherlands; this approach is, I submit, preferable to the presently prevalent passive euthanasia, which I consider to be a defective compromise.[63]

In any event, given the prevalence and the surreptitious nature of euthanasia, both active and passive, in the modern world (and it is far more prevalent than is officially known or acknowledged, or than Glascock's perception of its 'rarity'), I would suggest that bodies such as the WHO devote much thought to providing guidelines based upon an honest confrontation with the problem in terms of the dimensions involved, the financial implications, the cover-ups associated with it, the suffering of the elderly in terminally ill situations, or alternatively the surreptitious putting to death of those still desirous of living, and the implications for ethical standards of the sanctity of life and the dignity of the individual.

A direct and honest confrontation with this issue may also contribute to a more sensitive understanding of the dilemmas of those in tribal situations, reluctant to change their attitudes (on such issues, for instance, as female circumcision) in relation to deep-seated traditional beliefs that are not always compatible with the reality of the modern world. The issue of euthanasia is, in my opinion, no less important on a world-wide level, than that of female circumcision – but it would seem that for the latter, being a phenomenon only of tribal societies, it is easier to take a firm stand. Honesty and the exigencies of modern living demands that both issues be dealt with sensitively and courageously.

NOTES

1. See, for instance, Scilla McLean (ed.), *Female Circumcision, Excision and Infibulation* (London: Minority Rights Group, 1985).
2. See, for instance, Alison T. Slack, 'Female Circumcision: A Critical Appraisal', *Human Rights Quarterly* 10 (1988), p. 437.
3. See, for instance, World Health Organization, 'Female Circumcision, Female Genital Mutilation', *European Journal of Obstetrics and Gynecology and Reproductive Biology* 45 (1992), p. 153.
4. See William H. Meyer, 'Toward a Global Culture: Human Rights, Group Rights and Cultural Relativism', *International Journal on Group Rights* 3 (1996), p. 169.
5. See, for instance, Olayinka Koso-Thomas, *The Circumcision of Women: A Strategy for Eradication* (London: Zed Books, 1987).
6. See, for instance, Robert Myers, Francisca Omorodion, Anthony Isenalumhe and Gregory Akenzua, 'Circumcision: Its Nature and Practice Among Some Ethnic Groups in Southern Nigeria', *Social Science and Medicine* 21 (1985), p. 581.
7. See McLean, *Female Circumcision*, see also Nahid Toubia, 'Female Circumcision as a Public Health Issue,' *The New England Journal of Medicine* 331 (15 Sept. 1994), p. 712.
8. See, for instance, Kirsten Lee, 'Female Genital Mutilation – Medical Aspects and the Rights of Children', *The International Journal of Children's Rights* 2 (1994), p. 35; E. Dorkenloo and S. Elworthy, *Female Genital Mutilation: Proposals for Change* (London: Minority Rights Group, 1992); Lillian Passmore Sanderson, *Female Genital Mutilation: Excision and Infibulation – A Bibliography* (London: Anti-Slavery Society for the Protection of Human Rights, 1986); and Patricia Schroeder, 'Female Genital Mutilation – A Form of Child Abuse', *The New England Journal of Medicine* 331 (15 Sept. 1994), p. 739.
9. Note, 'What's Culture Got to do with it? Excising the Harmful Tradition of Female Circumcision', *Harvard Law Review*, 106 (1993), p. 1944. Several forms of female circumcision are discussed, including 'clitoridectomy, the form of female circumcision that is most comparable to its male counterpart, involves removal of the clitoral prepuce or tip of the clitoris' (p. 1946), and this seems to be the most moderate form.
10. See Section – 'Current Debate: Circumcision Decision', *Tikkun: A Bimonthly Jewish Critique of Politics, Culture and* Society, Vol. 5, No. 5, Sept.–Oct., 1990; Lisa Brave Moss, 'A Painful Case', p. 70; and Daniel Landes and Sheryl Robbin, 'Gainful Pain,' p. 72. I might add that in a town in Northern California, I once saw a protest poem posted on a notice board near the town library, entitled 'Circumcision,' written by Miriam Schwartz in 1994, which after describing the phenomenon in negative terms, ended with the words: 'Little boy, little boy, you're not a toy. Do what you can when you're a man. Do what you can.' In 1997, an organization was established in Israel to protest the widespread practice of circumcision. In fact, even secular Jews abide by the biblical dictate, even when they ignore most other religious traditions.
11. See symposium – Edgar J. Schoen, 'The Status of Circumcision of Newborns' and Ronald Poland, 'The Question of Routine Neonatal Circumcision' in section 'Sounding Board', *New England Journal of Medicine* 322, 3 May 1990, pp. 1308–15. Dr Schoen concludes that 'the benefits of routine circumcision of newborns as a preventive health measure far exceed the risks of the procedure' while Dr. Poland argues that while the risks are small, 'the benefits appear to be uncertain'. In May 1966, the *New York Times* carried an article on the changing patterns of male circumcision in the United States, from a high of 90 per cent of infant boys being circumcised in the late 1960s (in contrast to much lower numbers in other countries) to 60 per cent to 70 per cent in the 1990s (see reprint of article in *San Francisco Examiner-Chronicle*, Sunday, 19 May 1996, p. A-10: 'Circumcision Debate Comes Full Circle in US').
12. Alison Dundes Renteln, 'Is the Cultural Defense Detrimental to the Health of Children?' *Law and Anthropology: International Yearbook for Legal Anthropology* 7 (1994), p. 32. Another custom that has aroused concern is the practice of suttee in India – a widow jumping into the funeral pyre of her deceased husband. Although outlawed, there are still occasional reports of this practice – see, for instance, 'Root Committed Sati Voluntarily', *Bhubeneswan Sun-Times* (India), 15 Dec., 1988, p. 1.
13. Aman, *The Story of a Somali Girl*, as told to V. Burns and B. Boody (Hebrew translation, *Maariv*, 1994).

14. See, for instance, 'A Traditional Practice that Threatens Health – Female Circumcision', *WHO Chronicle*, Vol. 40, No. 1 (1986), p. 31.
15. Fran Hosken, *The Hosken Report – Genital and Sexual Mutilation of Females* (Lexington, MA: Women's International Network News, 1993, 4th revised edn).
16. Ibid., p. 16.
17. Ibid.
18. Robert Mendelsohn, *Mal(e) Practice: How Doctors Manipulate Women* (Chicago: Contemporary Books, 1981).
19. Ibid., p. 102.
20. Almost the only means of gauging the depth and the extent of the suffering is when a patient, or, more often, a family member, gives expression to the agonies undergone in a personal document – an article or a book. See, for instance, Bettyruth Walter, 'A Little Music', *The Pennsylvania Gazette* 18 (April 1983); Arthur Waskow, 'To Catch a Breath', *Moment* (April 1986), p. 46. The writers refer to suffering and torture.

    In general terms the *Journal of the American Medical Association* published a study in November, 1995, that revealed that fully 50 per cent of thousands of terminal patients interviewed at five major hospitals spent their final days in agony.
21. See, for instance, discussion by Anthony Glascock, 'By Any Other Name, It is Still Killing: A Comparison of the Treatment of the Elderly in America and Other Societies', in L. Sokolovsky (ed.), *The Cultural Context of Aging: Worldwide Perspectives* (New York: Berzin and Garvey, 1990), p. 43.
22. See Renteln, 'Is the Cultural Defense ...' at p. 48, in sub-section headed 'Fatalities: Faith Healing Cases'.
23. In the main case that Renteln discusses, the parents were found guilty of involuntary manslaughter and sentenced to probation for a period of ten years. See *Commonwealth v. Twitchell* (1993) 617 N.E. 2d 609 (Massachusetts).
24. See, for instance, the classic work of Arnold van Gennep, *Rites of Passage* (London: Routledge and Kegan Paul, 1960).
25. For examples, see Leon Sheleff, *Generations Apart: Adult Hostility to Youth* (New York: McGraw-Hill, 1982), p. 193.
26. Robyn Cerny Smith, 'Female Circumcision: Bringing Women's Perspectives into the International Debate,' *Southern California Law Review* 65 (1992), p. 2449.
27. Ibid., at pp. 2502–3. Smith writes of

    > the falsity inherent in defining a tribal group's identity and a woman's right to refuse female circumcision as being in opposition to each other. Tribal group identity may actually be strengthened if women have the power to refuse female circumcision ...
    >
    > As a Western feminist, I can simply point out that women may actually experience female circumcision as an oppressive practice – a viewpoint which is often invisible in the current legal debate surrounding female circumcision. The purpose of this Note is to reshape the debate so that the international community can resolve the female circumcision issue in a way that reflects the true experiences, oppressions, and needs of women and girls subject to circumcision. ... Then they [women and girls] may choose which traditions truly are necessary for tribal unity from their point of view and reject those traditions that continue to oppress them (p. 2503).

    It should be noted that Geraldine van Beuren draws attention to the fact that in 1991 the First Lady of Burkina Faso (where circumcision has been outlawed) related to it as akin to torture – see Annex 11 to the Report of the UN Seminar on Traditional Practices Affecting the Health of Women and Children, UN Doc. E/CN. 4/Sub.21991/48; as referred to in Geraldine van Bueren, 'Child Sexual Abuse and Exploitation: A Suggested Human Rights Approach', *The International Journal of Children's Rights* 2 (1994), p. 48. See also 'Proposals for a Children's Code' – A Report by the Ghana National Commission on Children (1996). This Report makes note of legislation in Ghana against female genital mutilation, and states that all the proposals for legislation 'stem from the Constitution which states in Article 39' that 'the State shall ensure that appropriate customary and cultural values are adapted and developed as an integral part of the growing needs of the society as a whole; and in particular, that traditional practices which are injurious to the health and well-being of the person are abolished' (pp. 58–9).

28. Kay Boulware-Miller, 'Female Circumcision: Challenges to the Practice as a Human Rights Violation', *Harvard Women's Law Journal* 8 (1985), p. 167. She also states that 'Although Western women often view female circumcision as a blatant violation of women's rights, many African women value the practice as an important cultural tradition. Because African women practice, defend and perpetuate female circumcision, a campaign to eradicate it must consider their views to be successful' (p. 155).
29. Claire Robertson, 'Grassroots in Kenya: Feminism, Genital Mutilation and Collective Action, 1920–1990', *Signs* 21 (1996), p. 615. For an interesting and searching analysis, which is also critical of outside intervention, see David Fraser, 'The First Cut is (Not) the Deepest: Deconstructing "Female Genital Mutilation" and the Criminalization of the Other,' 18 *Dalhousie Law Journal* (1995), p. 310. Thus, dealing also in large part with the issue from an Australian perspective, he writes:

    > ... women from the Horn of Africa who engage in the difficult battle to educate their communities in Australia are not truly consulted by the Family Law Court or the AMA [Australian Medical Association – L.S.] because these two powerful groups recommend, with the surrounding media uproar, the criminalization of the women involved in these practices (pp. 373–4).

    Fraser argues that widespread coverage of the issue in the media often reflects – and further fuels – a disparaging attitude to the other; in this case, African women. In the larger context, he argues that

    > what has to be interrogated here is not 'female genital mutilation' but the entire matrix of the 'Third World' and the quotidian involvement we all have in the continuation of the material oppression and construction of even more subtle and pernicious forms of oppression, domination and submission. When we learn that Somali women in refugee camps guarded by US Marines and the United Nations, fleeing civil war and starvation still ensure that their daughters are infibulated, can we make a claim to be engaged in the process of remembering the Other, of seeking justice when we speak in terms of moral indignation against the 'barbaric' practice of 'female genital mutilation' and leave the issue of the enormity of US and other Western aid funds in arms and 'population control' aside? What and whom are we forgetting then (pp. 375–6).

    Fraser then notes the efforts of Eritrean women freedom fighters to drastically diminish the role of circumcision as they reinvent their culture. Finally, as others have pointed out, in those parts of the world where female circumcision is practiced, there may well be a related, no less serious problem, of unwanted pregnancies including those which lead to death of the mother, or early death of the infant (because of overall social conditions and defective medical facilities); see, for instance, Priscilla Kincaid-Smith, 'The Fifth Freedom', *Bioethics* 9 (1995), p. 183. She writes of 'the misery, illness and death' of women 'denied the right to control their own fertility'. She claims that there may be as much as 500,000 pregnancy-related deaths each year (p. 184).
30. Mary-Jane Ierodiaconou, '"Listen to Us!" Female Genital Mutilation, Feminism and the Law in Australia', *Melbourne University Law Review* 20 (1995), pp. 562–3.
31. Ibid., p. 587.
32. Article 24(3) of The Convention on the Rights of the Child was adopted by the United Nations General Assembly on 20 November 1989, and entered into force on 2 September 1990. For a general discussion of this Convention in the context of tribal groups, see Rahera Barrett Douglas and Edward Te Kohu Douglas, 'The Rights of the Indigenous Child: Reconciling the United Nations Convention on the Rights of the Child and the (Draft) Declaration on the Rights of Indigenous People with Early Education Policies for Indigenous Children', *The International Journal of Children's Rights,* 3 (1995), p. 197.
33. See Note, 'What's Culture Got to do with It?', *Harvard Law Review*, pp. 1945–6.
34. Ibid., p. 1946.
35. Ibid., pp. 1959–60.
36. Ibid., p. 1961.
37. See, for instance, Female Circumcision Prohibition Act of 1985 in England.
38. See discussion above, Chapter 14, 'A Reasonable "Cultural" Defense'.
39. See discussion above, Chapter 9, on 'Belonging and Identity'.

40. For general discussion of the issues involved, see Hanny Lightfoot-Klein, *Prisoners of Ritual: An Odyssey into Female Genital Circumcision in Africa* (New York: Haworth Press, 1989).
41. Renteln, 'Is the Cultural Defense ...', p. 32.
42. Ibid., p. 32. Renteln refers to a French organization called 'Women's Group for the Abolition of Sexual Mutilation'.
43. See ibid., p. 33. For an example of the kind of arguments used in criminal proceedings, see the French case of the exciseuse, Ramata Keita, and the parents of a girl subjected to circumcision, as extensively documented in *Passages,* No. 3, 1992, pp. 1–3.
44. Celia Dugger, 'U.S. Frees African Fleeing Ritual Mutilation', *New York Times,* 25 April 1966, p. 1. The judge who originally heard her case apparently did not believe her story, but those working on her behalf claimed that she was part of a group in her tribe who were resisting genital mutilation. See *Fauziya Kasinga,* File A-73-476-695-Elizabeth, Interim Decision No. 3278 (B.I.A., 13 June 1996); and see discussion in Kathy Salamat, 'In re Fauziya Kasinga: Expanding the Judicial Interpretation of "Persecution", "Well-Founded Fear" and "Social Group" to Include Anyone Fleeing General Civil Violence', *Howard Law Journal* 40 (1996), p. 255.
45. See van Bueren, 'Child Sexual Abuse' who writes: 'where a girl flees a country because it is the only way to avoid circumcision, she will be entitled to refugee status on the grounds that she has a well-founded fear of being persecuted for reasons of membership in a particular social group' (p. 49).
46. Saba Bahar, 'Human Rights are Women's Rights: Amnesty International and the Family', *Hypatia,* 11 (1996), p. 11.
47. See Renteln, 'Is the Cultural Defense ...', pp. 29–31, for discussion of this unreported case, and the problem in general. The case is discussed in (1975) 24 ICLO 136.
48. It should be noted that Renteln suggests that the custom of scarification may well be on its way out, but clear evidence on this fact (as to the situation in Nigeria) was not provided.
49. For interesting discussion on tattooing, see publication by the Drawing Center in New York, based on exhibition – *Pierced Hearts and True Love: A Century of Drawings for Tattoos* (New York: Drawing Center, 1995); especially at p. 54, where mention is made of the discomfort and even pain involved in the process of tattooing, and also of efforts made to ban the practice in New York.
50. See *Tyrer v. UK,* 2 EHRR 1 Series A, vol. 26. See also, for a discussion of other cases, Sue Farron, *The UK Before the European Court of Human Rights: Case Law and Commentary* (London: Blackstone Press, 1996), pp. 61–9. In the *Tyrer* case, the British judge gave a lone dissenting opinion.
51. *Ingraham v. Wright,* 430 US 651 (1977); see also discussion in my book, *Generations Apart: Adult Hostility to Youth* (New York: McGraw-Hill, 1982), in chapter, 'In Loco Paternalism'.
52. On the nature of the necessity defence in general, see Paul Robinson, *Criminal Law Defenses* (St. Paul, MN: West Publishing Co., 1984). Attempts to expand the necessity defense have also been tried in the context of family violence – the right of the victim of the violence to take pre-emptive action, including killing, against the source of the violence – for instance, the wife killing her husband after years of suffering from his abusive actions, or children against cruel and violent parents.
53. Sebastian Poulter, *English Law and Ethnic Minority Customs* (London: Butterworths, 1986), p. v; see also Sebastian Poulter, 'African Customs in an English Setting'. *Journal of African Law* 31 (1988), p. 215.
54. See Report of Ghana Law Reform Commission, *The Impact of the Constitutional Provisions on the Customary Disabilities of Women in Ghana: Report on the Abolition of Ritual Slavery, Forced Labour and Other Related Practices* (1995). 'Trokosi' is defined as a custom whereby virgin females are made to serve fetish priests or priestesses as a pacification to the gods for an offence committed by a member of their family' (p. 12). The report gives details of the suffering of the young girls and their victimization. (My thanks to the Executive Secretary of the Ghana National Commission on Children, Mrs. B.A. Akuffo-Amoabeng, for providing me with this material.)
55. Glascock, 'By Any Other Name, It Is Still Killing', p. 43.
56. Ibid., p. 43.
57. Ibid., p. 43.
58. Ibid., p. 44.

59. Glascock provides four brief examples taken from the Human Relations Area Files – of the Chukchee (Northern Siberia), Lau (Southern Fiji), Bororo (Central Brazil) and the Yakut (North-Central Siberia). He discusses them under the respective headings of 'Killing', 'Abandoning', 'Forsaking – Denial of Food', and 'Forsaking – Denial of All Support'.
60. Ibid., p. 49.
61. Ibid., p. 55. It may be noted that the relatively small number of overt instances bear little relation to the total number of instances of euthanasia carried out *covertly,* or in ambiguous circumstances, which may be numbered in the thousands.
62. In the Netherlands, an open approach to the topic has facilitated the pioneering practices that had been instituted by the medical authorities, with support being provided by the legal profession, both prosecutors and judges, if the medical personnel acted according to the stringent monitoring regulations laid down in judicial decisions. A number of other jurisdictions have followed suit, for instance the State of Oregon in the United States – by referendum, or the Northern Territory in Australia – by legislation. In both instances, the law has been challenged in the court as being unconstitutional. In Australia, immediate attempts were made to enact federal legislation to override the Territory's Law; a number of legislators in the Territory also had second thoughts about their support of the law, partly, it should be noted, because of opposition to the law by Aborigines. However, this opposition must be seen in the context of general aboriginal apprehension of western medicine and the prevalent feeling that, even without the law, Aborigines are liable to be subject to faulty treatment, including 'allowing to die' procedures for the terminally ill. It should be mentioned that there is also a collective memory of a smallpox epidemic from the end of the eighteenth century, which devastated the population, causing many deaths, believed by some to be not just accidentally introduced by contact with the settlers, but deliberately induced by them. In any event, whereas in Oregon there has been no activation of the law because a legal challenge has been mounted as to the constitutionality of the legal situation created by the referendum, in the Northern Territory, the first instance of active euthanasia, carried out in terms of the strict monitoring provisions of the act, took place in September 1996, creating an intense public debate. A short while later, federal power was invoked in the Australian parliament to annul the law. For a brief description of some of the key factors, see editorial by Helga Kuhse and Peter Singer in *Bioethics* 11 (1997), p. iii.
63. See discussion in Leon Shelcff, *Ultimate Penalties: Capital Punishment, Life Imprisonment, Physical Torture* (Columbia: Ohio State University Press, 1987), chapter on 'The Medical Model', especially pp. 335–43.

PART IV:
SPECIAL TOPICS

19

Proving the Customary Rule

Courts are entrusted with the dual task of determining the facts of a dispute and then applying the relevant rule of law to those facts. Where a jury system is used, a division of labor normally operates in which it is the lay jury that determines the facts and the judge who is responsible for postulating the law. This differentiation of function indicates the contrasting nature of the judicial enterprise. Indeed, one of the major intellectual challenges of a trial lawyer is to be able to distinguish, on the facts, the differences between the case in dispute and a legal precedent that seems to be unfavorable to his client's cause, or conversely to draw factual parallels with a helpful precedent.

However, these contrasting factors become obfuscated when dealing with tribal custom as, while a custom is supposed to describe a legal situation, its existence in a regular non-customary court of law is not automatically taken for granted, but may have to be proved just like any other fact in dispute. That is, in a situation where the nature of a custom is crucial in the disputation of a particular case, the court of law is not necessarily presumed to have judicial knowledge of its existence. The parties may thus be expected to adduce evidence as to what the custom is and what is its obligatory force.

This procedure raises a host of theoretical and practical problems which go to the heart of the meaning of custom and to the possibility of using it in a modern setting, particularly if there are contrasting, and possibly conflicting, means of presenting the required evidence – from oral evidence by experts (who may be either respected and leading members of the tribe, or anthropologists who have done research in the relevant customs) to written expositions of the customs (which may be in the form of legal treatises, research reports, or impressionistic descriptions).

In theory, there is a transparent dilemma that is liable to arise on many occasions – a custom is presumed to be an expression of the people's will, forged in the crucible of daily living, known to all, including those who are called upon to adjudicate. This is indeed still the situation in those local and low-level courts (known by various appellations such as customary courts, chief's courts, local courts, community courts, tribal courts, village courts) whose sole or main activity is to apply the customary law. But the situation is vastly different when it is a regular state court that is called upon to pronounce on the nature of a custom, its validity in general, and its applicability to the case at issue. For the intervention of a non-customary state court means that the final determination as to a custom's existence will be made by a person possessing judicial authority, but not necessarily fully *au fait* with the social background whence the custom emerged.

The position becomes even more complicated when the customs are formally promulgated as a code, tending then to combine those characteristics that are associated with codes – of certainty as to its provisions coupled with rigidity as to its future development. A judicial decision in a court of law may also entail similar consequences, though limited, of course, only to those factors that were adjudicated in the trial. This impact will naturally be all the greater when the decision is on appeal – a factor further complicated as the court of first instance will generally be required to relate to the custom as a fact, while the appeal court will have to deal with it as a point of law.

The question must inevitably arise whether such procedures will not undermine the very validity of a custom – especially since the distinguishing mark of a custom is specifically that it stems from the life of the people, and is known by them, without the need for any official pronouncements. Once formally recognized by adjudication in a court of law, it could possibly lose its characteristic of responsiveness to changing social reality. However, it could be argued that this is the inevitable price that must be paid for the fact of recognition and for the willingness of the state to allow for customary practices to be incorporated into an official judicial system. On the other hand, it is also true that the procedure described applies also to customs of any type absorbed into a judicial system, as well as what, in fact, happens to custom within most of the customary law systems being analyzed.

Thus, courts of law have well-known procedures for examining customs of professional and business practices or of other corporate groups such as sporting and educational bodies, and once a custom of this type has been presented and accepted in the course of a judicial dispute, it tends to be regarded subsequently in a more definitive manner. This is true also of customary practices in international law once they have been the focus of judicial probing, whether in a court or by international arbitration.[1] Often, special tribunals are set up to adjudicate in defined matters – partly as a means of ensuring a large degree of independence for a certain kind of activity (for instance, international sport) from the jurisdiction of courts of law.[2]

More important, though, customary law exists not only in the minds and the lives of the people subject to it, but also takes on a more concrete form when subjected itself to judicial scrutiny within the normal customary framework. One of the ways in which the law traditionally developed and was brought to the cognizance of the people was through the pronouncements of those who sat in judgment to decide disputes. They not only determined the truth of the contrary allegations, they also laid down what the correct rule of law was and, in the course of so doing, would partake of what is known in modern jurisprudence as 'judicial law-making', a factor that allows for legal change in relation to social change.[3]

In the final analysis then, to a large extent, the courts will, at least in theory, be performing in a manner not too different from traditional practices. The key issue becomes then an empirical one, whether in practice they are succeeding in being true to the traditional framework within which the customs arise. This, in turn, depends on the nature of the mandate they are given, generally through some kind of legislation, as well as the quality of the judicial personnel and their attitudes toward the customary framework in general.

We have already seen that in Papua New Guinea, a general constitutional rule was laid down referring courts to the 'underlying law' where there was no legislative or judicial rule to hand.[4] This is almost a total commitment, and has often been described by a leading jurist as a search for a clear and singular legal identity, and for an integrated legal culture.[5] Similar, less precise formulations are being sought in countries such as New Zealand and Australia.[6] In all these places the separate communities are small, a fact that in some respects might militate against a unified jurisprudence, because of fragmentation of the society, but in other respects may actually facilitate it because no group will dominate. Certainly there seems to be sufficient unity in the culture in general to allow for the possibility of an integrated legal culture, even if not an identical legal system for all the groups.

The position of Africa is slightly different, partly because some of the groups are so much larger, partly because the historical development under colonial rule was different. For instance, in some places in Africa, attempts were made to lay down a code of law in certain areas, based on what was then known about the customs. Often it was done at the initiative of a particularly dominant administrator, as was the case with Lord Lugard in Northern Nigeria and Governor Shepstone in Natal.[7] In addition, local authorities might be empowered to make declarations as to what the customary law in their area was considered to be, or by-laws would sometimes be promulgated by local authorities or the Ministry for Local Government.[8]

However, since independence the situation and the considerations have changed. No longer is the issue to provide as much recognition for the local community law as would contribute to the ease of maintaining control for a foreign power, through the powers of the chief within the system of indirect rule.[9] Now the issue is how to express the yearnings for national unity while acknowledging the diversity of customs among the different population groups. Sometimes reluctantly, sometimes with an assertive pride in its indigenous culture, legislation has been enacted to indicate the role that custom would play in the unified legal system.

For example, in Nigeria, the law spells out how customary law is to be proved in a non-customary court. The Evidence Act provides that 'a custom may be adopted as part of the law governing a particular set of circumstances if it can be noticed judicially or can be proved to exist by evidence. The burden of proving a custom shall lie upon the person alleging its existence.'[10] The statute goes on to indicate the manner in which such evidence may be adduced, for instance chiefs and others having special knowledge of local customs (such as an anthropologist) are noted. Alternatively, reference may be made to books that are considered authoritative. Here there is a further problem, since the courts may have to make a prior decision as to whether the people whose customs are being examined, consider the book to be a faithful reflection of the customs.

Probably the most effective manner of ensuring that there will be an accurate and articulate expression of the custom is to use assessors to sit on the bench with the judge, their task being not always of adjudicating, but of assistance and advice.[11] The idea of assessors sitting on the bench with judges is a practice sometimes used in common law countries, and is not linked specifically to the issue of customary law.[12] Often they are lawyers themselves, assigned to help the judges in cases of particular importance, for instance murder. Often, mainly technical and budgetary factors are the major consideration of their use, their presence on the bench contributing greatly to easing the pressures on the judicial structure. Sometimes they may be non-lawyers chosen for their expertise where law interacts with some specialized aspect of life.[13]

In the specific context of customary law, assessors may be chosen to sit because of their knowledge of customary law. It is their task to help the judge form a reasoned and authentic picture of particular customs based not just on evidence submitted by the sides, but also on the informed opinions of the assessors sitting with him in the privacy of his chambers. Parenthetically, it might be noted that in the magistrates' courts in England, a reverse procedure is in effect where the lay judges are informed as to points of law by a legally qualified clerk of the court.[14]

The idea of lay justice could also be used in ordinary courts by relying more on the jury. However, while the jury system is considered as one of the distinguishing characteristics of the common law system, it is not always extensively used and there is almost no research reference to its possible contribution to resolving the issue of custom in non-customary law courts,[15] namely that the jury may be presumed to have underlying knowledge of the customs, just as assessors have, and therefore the need for outside evidence (written or oral) could possibly be minimized. It should also be remembered that not all common law countries use the jury system, since there were often extraneous, including political, factors that made the English reluctant to extend the system, and thereby lose some of their control over the administration of justice.[16] The jury system is considered an expression also of democracy, and in the colonial countries there was no full democracy, thus minimizing the pressures for its use since the political struggle was for national independence and the right to vote.

Since the jury system does have its deficiencies, there is no intention to open up a debate on this topic, except to note that the judicious use of the system could facilitate the possibilities of having an authoritative assessment of a custom by a state court. Non-customary courts are also entitled to accept a custom without specific evidence being adduced, where there has been prior judicial notice accorded to it, and the court may then act in terms of normal rules of precedent that are applicable. For example, in Nigeria the law provides that:

> A custom may be judicially noticed by the court if it has been acted on by a court of superior or co-ordinate jurisdiction in the same area, to an extent which justifies the court asked to apply it in assuming that the persons or the class of persons concerned in that area look upon the same as binding in relation to circumstances similar to those under consideration.[17]

Many countries still abide by principles in this regard originally laid down by the English. The leading case is a 1916 Privy Council case, Angu v. Attah,[18] taken on appeal from what was then the Gold Coast, in which it was stated that 'a customary law ... has to be proved in the first instance by calling witnesses acquainted with native customs until the particular customs have by frequent proof in the courts, become so notorious that the court take judicial notice of them'.[19] In proving the custom, a distinction must also always be made between customs that have the force of law, and other customary practices that are no more than folklore or habit or matters of convenience – not intended to be of binding impact.

A good summary of the position in general is provided by C. Ogwurike, who states that:

> customary law now means that part of the *corpus juris* which embodies those rules of traditional custom, which are discoverable by judicial enquiry and are enforceable because they conform to the current values in society as determined by the judge. If the validity of customary law rests on the assent of the native community, the mere existence of a customary rule will be enough to give it the force of law and the court will be compelled to enforce it. But the attitude of the

> court which picks and chooses between an enforceable customary rule and a non-enforceable one seems to have shifted the basis of its validity from the consensus of the community to the opinion of a handful of judges.[20]

There have also been other developments in which different legal principles have been enunciated. Most noted is the decision in Ghana to make proof of custom a question of law and not of fact, which means, *inter alia,* that its incorporation does not require the frequency rule. However, aware of problems that might arise in making a definitive decision, and aware of the binding nature of *stare decisis,* the law attempts to cope with any conceivable problematic situations by laying down contingency procedures. Thus, Sec. 50 of the Courts Act of 1971 states that:

> (1) Any questions as to the existence or content of a rule of customary law is a question of law for the courts and not a question of fact;
>
> (2) If the court entertains any doubt as to the existence or content of a rule of customary law relevant in any proceedings after considering such submissions thereon as may be made by or on behalf of the parties and consulting some reported cases, textbooks and other sources as may be appropriate, the court shall adjourn the proceedings to enable an inquiry to take place under the next section;
>
> (3) The inquiry shall be held as part of the proceedings in such manner as the court considers expedient and the provisions of this Act relating to the attendance of witness and testimony shall apply for the purpose of tendering of opinions to the court at the inquiry, but shall apply subject to such modifications as may appear to the court to be necessary.
>
> (a) the decisions as to the persons who are to be heard at the inquiry shall be one for the court, after hearing such submissions thereon as may be made on behalf of the parties.
>
> (b) the court may request a House of Chiefs or a Divisional or Traditional Council or other body possessing knowledge of the customary law in question to state its opinion which may be laid before the inquiry in written form.[21]

Derek Asiedu-Akrofi claims that 'in this way the doctrine of repugnancy in Ghana has been abolished'.[22]

The crucial role played by chiefs is worthy of mention as Ghana, like some other African countries, and countries in the Pacific region, has set up a constitutional framework which allows for representation of chiefs.[23] This represents a most interesting attempt to give effect to traditional custom. Ghana, in fact, laid down a model that was subsequently adopted in a number of other countries as well. The initial reference to such an institution for the chiefs was in the Draft Constitution which stated that the Chieftaincy in Ghana should be guaranteed and preserved,[24] and to this end a proposal was set forth for a House of Chiefs. Its constitutional function was mainly in the determination of custom and the laying down of guidelines for respecting it. To a certain extent this may be no more than lip-service acknowledgment, as much of the basis of the former power and prestige was removed, but it also represents a certain ambivalence – that the struggle for economic progress and political unity should not totally undermine the institution of chieftaincy, which in many ways is bound up with the cultural traditions of the people. In a sense, the legislation may be seen as an attempt to create a governmental institution that will have much symbolic force (similar in many respects to the British monarchy) but is clearly subordinate to the modern power structure of the president and the parliament.

In his book dealing with law and social change in Ghana, William Harvey devotes a whole chapter to the 'Status of the Traditional Authorities'[25] and concludes that the chiefs' status:

> is reduced to that of a stipendiary of the central government, dependent in fact for office on official recognition, limited to meeting in bodies many of which have no traditional base, under procedures and to perform functions defined by statute.

He finally expresses the opinion that it

> is difficult to see how the chiefs can long remain a significant factor in the social, political or governmental life of the country.[26]

Yet, more important perhaps, a formal means was established for declaring the customary law, admittedly different from what had traditionally been practiced, but an institution which, in theory at least, represented an attempt to modify existing procedures in response to the changes generated by the fact of independence.

In fact, the idea of a House of Chiefs at the regional level was a compromise between the new political leaders of the independent state of Ghana and those older traditional leaders who were basically being deprived of their former powers (often greatly entrenched through the policy of indirect rule). But beyond that, the solution worked out confirmed the basis for continued regard for customary law and institutionalized means for confirming it and – a matter of key importance – of modifying it. Indeed, the quasi-judicial function of the House of Chiefs reflects procedures that were applied earlier, where regular courts could submit, in interlocutory proceedings, questions to customary courts for their opinion as to the customary law on a particular point at issue.[27]

These procedures are, from a theoretical perspective, not so different from the authority invested in the European Court of Justice of the European Union, to state the law of the community when requested to do so by a national court.[28] However complicated this process seems to be, it works quite satisfactorily in Europe, and is designed in fact to allow for the avoidance of conflict of laws between two potentially different jurisdictions, in the case of Europe as between the law of the community and the law of its constituent parts, the sovereign nations who comprise it. It seems a sound framework in any situation where there is a likelihood of regular problems confronting a court in terms of its ability to determine the nature of law in an area outside of its declared authority and competence.

Parallel with the normal state courts, which are often confronted with such issues, are the special customary courts which have generally been set up in terms of specific legislation. These courts are limited in power, and in many respects resemble the attempts in modern societies to set up informal judicial mechanisms to guarantee a rapid and equitable justice, such as small claims courts. Customary courts serve very similar purposes of providing easy and rapid access to justice for ordinary people. The key issue then becomes the capacity of those entrusted with judicial capacity (whether judges in small claims, night or urban courts, or chiefs or headmen in customary, tribal or local courts)[29] to dispense justice in such a way as to assure ordinary members of the society that grievances will be dealt with equitably and in accordance with the prevailing norms and standards of the community.

Indeed, just as for ordinary courts of the lower levels, most customary courts do not propound deep and overriding principles of law and justice – they try only to resolve a specific empirical question. It is only the occasional hard case, or a particularly interesting case, or a case that for idiosyncratic reasons (such as the presence of an outsider – an anthropologist or even reporter) arouses interest, that leads to any lasting attention being paid to it. These courts may apply a custom without the need for specific proof, unless the members of the court consider that they are not familiar with the custom, in which case they are obliged to call evidence. It is, nevertheless, open to the parties to attempt to prove the changing nature of custom – that a custom recognized in the past had fallen into disuse, or that a new custom had come into being. However, a change in decision by a customary court raises problems, since the party adversely affected may claim that an injustice has been done. The suggestion has been made that there may be a need for prior announcement of a projected change so that people subject to the custom may be adequately forewarned.[30]

Such problems are not, of course, unique to customary courts. Any court breaking away from the doctrine of *stare decisis* and introducing a new precedent, sets up similar problems of doing an injustice to those who have acted upon the earlier ruling. Gordon Woodman, discussing the possibility of regular state courts ensuring constant update of their approach to customary law, suggests that judges could have devised 'a procedure whereby from time to time they collectively made formal declaration of the norms of customary law in particular areas. An analogy for this is the "practice statement", by which important principles have been established in some common-law countries',[31] that is, the judges issue a statement of their intentions to embark on a new approach in regard to a particular interpretation of the law; a policy used by the House of Lords in 1966 to declare and forewarn the public and legal practitioners that it would no longer be bound by its own decisions.

On the whole, though, in customary courts as in any lower courts of a state system, it is the facts that are of prime importance, and not the intricacies and niceties of the law. Nevertheless, an overall picture does inevitably emerge, and the question then arises – and with added force in recent years – whether it would not be advisable to have a summary statement of the customary framework. Some jurists or administrators have indeed published books of customary law that have acquired the status of definitive statements of the law – and this tendency can only grow as publication possibilities increase – from law journals providing a regular platform to publishing companies specializing in law.[32] Further, there are a number of institutions, both governmental and public, which have embarked on comprehensive publishing enterprises, such as the Restatement of African Law,[33] or Governmental Commissions into customary law,[34] which present an authoritative account of the law – again, similar to projects such as Halsbury's Laws of England or the American Corpus Juris Secundum or American Jurisprudence, or reports of governmental Law Commissions dealing with specific aspects of the law.

However much customary law is regarded as unwritten law, the fact that it is finally recorded does not change its essential nature. In fact it is not the unwritten aspect that is of its essence, but the fact that it is 'unlegislated' – that is, that the custom emerges out of the life and practices of the community and not by legislative writ. Once it is known, there seems to be no reason why it cannot finally be expounded in clear-cut written form, without thereby losing its quality of flexibility and spontaneity.

In the final analysis, just as for judging itself, it is the credentials of the person doing the summary and the manner in which he carries out his task, that is of prime importance. In addition, of course, there is a need for constant amending and annotating, as is done in the case of the English and American Restatements. This should certainly apply to any similar projects in Africa or elsewhere. Here, though, there is a real problem in terms of the capacity to finance such ongoing projects. There is the further problem that the laws of certain prominent countries will become dominant, especially in the case of Africa, where some countries might have the resources, intellectual and financial, which are lacking in other smaller less endowed countries, or even that within any country the larger tribe will elicit more interest and that their customs will often be taken as a measure or example of the custom throughout the country.

Linked to this is the question of striving for unity among the different customary systems of law.[35] There certainly seem to be many overlapping principles and institutions, so that the prospects of slowly building up a 'common law' for any country or region seems a feasible goal. However, in the process of building up a unified framework, there is always the possibility of noting exceptions to a general rule, or contrasting positions adopted by different tribes. Here, the American projects serve as useful examples since, given their federal structure, there are often differing approaches adopted by different states, and noting these differences is a major part of an authoritative overall analysis. In terms of the problems that a lack of unity causes (and customary laws do create such problems) it should be remembered that even a unitary state such as Britain has separate legal systems for its different peoples. One of the paradoxes of legal history is that the common law that has been exported all over the world, and had a major impact on the legal systems of vastly different and widely spread out countries, was never incorporated into the law of Scotland,[36] which still maintains a separate legal identity, with its own judicial structure (including a different nomenclature).[37] The Scottish law is admittedly not customary law, but it exists independently of the English common law and persists in its separate development, as it has done for almost 300 years.[38]

A further complicating factor is where the regular courts and the customary courts have concurrent jurisdiction. To what extent does a decision in one court constitute an absolute bar to any involvement by a parallel court in the other jurisdiction? To what extent does the rule of *res judicata* apply, namely that a definitive judicial ruling has been made which cannot then be challenged in any other court (except by way of appeal)? The problem of 'forum shopping' is well known in both private international law and in federal legal systems, where each party seeks to present his plea in the court that seems to offer greater prospects of success, thereby also giving the petitioner or plaintiff an advantage – and these kinds of problems arise also where there is a legal remedy in both the customary court and the regular court. Sometimes, though, the problem may emerge almost by error, where the plaintiff pursues his rights in the most convenient manner and only subsequently discovers that he would have been entitled to far greater rights and a better remedy in the alternative court.

William Twining[39] describes just such a situation which occurred in Kenya:

> The plaintiff, a Kikuyu, brought an action under the Fatal Accidents Ordinance in the Supreme Court on behalf of himself and the dependents of his deceased son, who had been killed by the defendant. The same plaintiff had already been awarded compensation of 106 sheep and 10 fat rams on behalf of his clan in proceedings against the defendant's father in an African Court. He now claimed unliquidated damages less the value of the compensation he had already been awarded. The Acting Chief Justice held that according to native law and custom the matter was *res judicata*, notwithstanding the fact that the parties to the proceedings were not the same and that under the Fatal Accidents Ordinance the award to the dependents would have been much greater. Under customary law there was a fixed tariff and this was considered as a final settlement for all. The result would have been different, however, if the plaintiff had elected to sue in the Supreme Court only.[40]

Yet different results have been forthcoming in other jurisdictions, especially where the customary law was applied without a formal court procedure. On a number of occasions courts in Australia have, in criminal proceedings, taken note of the fact that the accused was subject also to tribal sanctions for the crime that he had committed. In some cases where the customary punishment had already been meted out, the courts have given due consideration to the pain that had already been inflicted upon him.[41] In other cases, the courts have taken prior account of the fact that the accused would indeed be liable, whatever his formal punishment in a court of law, to further sanctions by the tribe in the future.[42] But the situation in Australia involves the application of the customary punishment without legal proceedings, since Australia does not recognize tribal courts.[43] It is of some interest to note that the courts have sometimes indicated that the tribal response seemed a more relevant and meaningful one than the court's options. Even so, where the tribal sanction involves spearing or some similar physical act, the court may relate to it as an assault.

In general, it might be observed that it would thus appear that paradoxically there is more likelihood, in some circumstances, of a customary rule being applied where there has been no formal recognition of a customary court structure, than where a separate court system exists. But the Australian situation – of non-recognition – has encountered one further problem that seems almost insurmountable, namely that many of the customs which may be the focus of a dispute, are secret and may not be divulged.

There have been instances where a thorough investigation of a case could not be obtained because of the inability of the tribe members to divulge tribal secrets. This occurred in a 1964 case known by the name of the victim as the *Chimney Evans* case.[44] Six members of a tribe were accused of killing another member who had stolen important and sacred relics (corroboree stones) and sold them to a white man several years before. He was well aware that in so doing he was violating tribal custom and had actually been a fugitive from the tribe ever since. This was seen as basically an internal matter for the tribe, and there was a great reluctance to cooperate with the authorities. It was mainly through evidence by officials of the Department of Aboriginal Affairs that the tribal background to the killing was brought to the attention of the court. These same officials also gave positive character evidence on behalf of the defendants. In general, the defense lawyers faced an almost intolerable task of defending clients who refused to co-operate fully with them, as they wished to withhold secret information from their lawyers as well as from the court.[45]

Once again, on a comparative basis, it should be remembered that there are many similar outcomes in a modern legal system which provide a bar to full disclosure of relevant facts, varying from protection offered to spouses not to give incriminating evidence against each other, through confidential information, either affecting state security or related to a particular protected profession (medical, legal, theological), to the exclusionary rule, applied most broadly in the United States as a bar against any evidence that is obtained by illegal means. The status of journalists seems to be the most ambiguous, and several journalists in different countries have chosen to go to prison on contempt of court charges rather than reveal to the court their sources of information.

This is an extremely delicate area of the law relating both to rules of evidence and basic human rights. One area that has yet to be adequately examined deals with information known to anthropologists to whom, because of the trust they have elicited and the time that they have expended, certain facets of tribal life become known, and the question arises as to the nature of that knowledge and what use may be made of it. How much of it may be divulged in the ordinary course of academic research and publication? How much may be revealed specifically in a court of law in order to help further the cause of justice? And who is to provide the researcher with the necessary dispensation that he is free to share the knowledge he has gleaned with others? On one occasion an anthropological account of the Pitjantjatjara, entitled 'Nomads of the Australian Desert', was challenged in a court of law as the writer had revealed tribal secrets.[46] The book was withdrawn from sale in the Northern Territory where the Pitjantjatjara live, after they had claimed that it had caused them 'dismay, concern and anger'. This is but one example of the delicate relations that may exist between those carrying out research and those who are its subjects, as well as the degree of good faith which must be displayed by the researcher.

There have also been instances where a particular tribal claim – for land use, or to block a proposed mining project or dam construction – has been opposed by the proponents of a proposed project since, so they argue, there is no recorded statement or document to substantiate the tribal claim. Indeed, suspicions have sometimes been aroused that the claim was artificially created only after the tribal leaders became aware of the potential value that could be derived from the claim, and hints have even been made as to exploitative extortion.[47] In fact, though, often the knowledge as to the sacred nature of a particular area is part of the secret lore and traditions of a tribe, and their contentions on behalf of preserving this sacred nature are only required in order to forestall the threats upon it that are being made by outsiders. Prior to that there is no reason to make public pronouncements in this regard. This is not to deny that, on occasion, false claims may have been made, but often these relate not to disputes with outsiders, but rather to conflicts within a tribe – as when a chief or a big man makes demands, in the name of custom and tradition, of their subjects, for land use, for tribute, for ceremonial status, which have no basis in fact, but which their present power enables them to obtain.

James Zion has suggested the need for a specialized study of the unique legal problems that arise from the attempt to give concrete expression to tribal custom.[48] Although focusing on what he terms the common law of Indian tribes in North America, his comments are valid elsewhere. He suggests that those working in the loose field of legal anthropology should be known by the name of 'ethnojurists', and their subject as ethnojurisprudence. He argues that neither 'anthropologist' nor 'ethnologist' is appropriate for the special kind of study that he has in mind. 'The work of the searchers is so recent in time,' he writes, 'that it is difficult to know what to call them … . The searchers are not all lawyers, although they are studying law, and yet they are so numerous that a special term is appropriate.'[49] He goes on to explain the broad range of knowledge and expertise envisaged in order to fulfill the aims that he poses and suggests that:

> Ethnojurisprudence is a study unlike any other. It requires a knowledge of law, anthropology, ethnology, political science, psychology, sociology and human relations. Its students travel from one discipline to another, trading ideas and giving support. The ethnojurist is likely to be an activist with distinct political goals and sympathies. Very often the ethnojurist is not a member of the culture he or she supports, and is very careful to define his or her role in terms of the desires of Indian leaders.
>
> The ethnojurist is often working in the dark. Legal anthropology is a fairly recent study, with few scholars and little in print for guidance. What has been published is often of limited use, because

> the classic studies of Indian law do not deal with the everyday modern legal problem.
>
> Ethnojurisprudence is frequently a very practical discipline. A tribal court wants to use the traditional common law in its proceedings and there is nothing to say how it is to be done. The lawyer-ethnojurist tries to explain to a Federal court precisely why a proposed dam will violate religious freedom, and is told by the Elders he can't explain 'why' because that would violate religious precepts. One needs to know a particular principle of Indian common law. The anthropological studies don't mention it and you have to find a 'reliable' source. Who is that person? How do you approach him or her? How do you ask the question in an understandable way? Should you approach a woman as well as a man because the question involves 'women's knowledge'? The ethnojurist asks not simply as a scholar or a scientist, but as a practitioner, advocate and adviser.
>
> The ethnojurist is an intercultural communicator, a reconciler of values, a fixer, an arranger, an author, and many other things.[50]

Zion then proceeds to enumerate the kind of activities that may devolve upon the ethnojurist, and how best to perform them. He draws on his experience of American Indian law to suggest solutions to problems, but much of what he writes has larger significance. Specific examples are, of course, endless, but it may be worthwhile to probe a few examples that have arisen elsewhere. Thus the issue of 'women's knowledge' has been addressed by two women working in Australia, an anthropologist and a lawyer formerly attached to the Aborigine Legal Clinic in Alice Springs. Diane Bell and Pam Dutton attempt to describe some of the problems women have, arising partly out of changing norms and mores, where aspects of life once the domain of women, are being breached, yet for them still 'much of the law is secret',[51] and cannot be divulged, certainly not to men who are not of their tribe, the normal situation, for instance, in a court of law.

Similar problems have arisen in respect of 'men's secrets'. On one occasion the male defendant objected to women being present in the courtroom, whether they were members of the jury in terms of law, or exercising their rights as citizens to be spectators at the proceedings. In discussing this case, and mentioning that the judge had acceded to the defendant's request, L.C. Green wonders 'what might have happened in a similar case in Canada affecting an Indian or an Inuit in view of the Bill of Rights and the ban on discrimination against women'.[52]

Similarly, in terms of intercultural communication, if ordinary lay people often find themselves confused when appearing in court because of the atmosphere and ritual, the terminology and rules of procedure and evidence, then these problems become accentuated tenfold when tribespeople are involved – whether in the capacity of plaintiff or defendant in a civil suit, or accused or complainant in a criminal case, or just as a witness for one of the parties.

Cognizant of the multitude of misunderstandings involving Aborigines in the legal process, particularly those accused of crimes, special guidelines were laid down in an Australian court judgment as to how interrogation should be carried out. These are known as the Anunga Rules (based on the case, *R. v. Anunga and Others*),[53] and take into account the many ways in which suspects are liable to incriminate themselves because they do not understand the import of questions or cautionary warnings as to confessions, as well as showing polite deference to authority figures which might well lead to them gratuitously agreeing with unjustified accusations being made against them. The guidelines include providing an interpreter where an Aborigine is not fluent in English;[54] wherever practicable, of ensuring that a 'prisoner's friend' is present who should be somebody who has the confidence of the accused and is able to give him sound advice; and taking great care when interrogating the accused, to be sure that the accused fully understands the import of the questions.

In many instances, the tribesperson will have a knowledge of the language of the court, generally English, but not sufficient to understand or appreciate the nuances of the language, let alone the complexities of legal terminology in a language that is basically foreign to him. Not always in such circumstances will he have legal representation. The theoretical framework of the common law is based upon an adversarial procedure between two sides, each presumed to be competent through judicious questioning and penetrating cross-examination, to elicit the truth. It is clear that most tribespeople lack this capacity, and without legal representation will be unable to mount an adequate defense.

In contrast to this are the procedures followed by some tribunals, such as the Maori Land Tribunal and the Waitangi Tribunal, to adhere as closely as possible to traditional procedures, so as to make the witnesses feel as comfortable as possible. Much of the evidence, dealing largely with memories that people have of customary practices in regard to land use, and including fishing and hunting rights, is presented in the traditional setting of the Maere, which is the meeting place where important tribal decisions would be made. The underlying assumption of the tribunal is that the evidence thereby gleaned – and carefully recorded – is a far more accurate recollection of past practices and presentation of present circumstances than would be elicited in more formal proceedings in an urban setting.[55] It is not clear to what extent such procedures could serve as a model for an ordinary court, but they do suggest alternative possibilities for those in the judicial system entrusted with the task of ascertaining the truth, determining the law, declaring the custom, and dispensing justice.

NOTES

1. On international law, see Martti Kaskenniemi, *The Structure of International Legal Argument* (Helsinki: Lakimiesliiton Kuslanus, Finnish Lawyer's Guild Publishing Co., 1989), Chapter 6, 'Custom'.
2. There is a recognized tribunal in Switzerland for arbitration procedures in sporting matters.
3. On judicial law-making, see, in general, Richard Wasserstrom, *The Judicial Decision: Toward a Theory of Legal Justification* (Stanford, CA: Stanford University Press, 1961).
4. See R. DeVere, D. Colquhoun-Kerr and J. Kaburise (eds), *Essays on the Constitution of Papua New Guinea* (Port Moresby, 1985); especially John Gawi, 'The Status of the Common Law under the Constitution', p. 1. He writes: 'Speaking generally, the underlying law, properly developed as a coherent body of substantive rules in a manner stipulated by the Constitution, was intended to become the common law and equity of Papua New Guinea as distinct from English common law and equity' (p. 3).
5. See, for example, Bernard Narakobi, 'In Search of a Melanesian Jurisprudence', in Peter Sack and Elizabeth Minchin (eds), *Legal Pluralism* (Canberra: Proceedings of Canberra Law Workshop, Australian National University, 1985), p. 215. He refers to the 'duty' of a judge 'to develop the underlying law'.
6. In New Zealand the search is for a bicultural jurisprudence, and in Australia for multiculturalism.
7. See Lord Lugard, *The Dual Mandate in British Tropical Africa* (London: Frank Cass, 1965).
8. See, for example, the Local Government Law of 1957 in the Western Region of Nigeria (Sec. 77). See also discussion in Antony Allot, *Essays in African Law* (London: Butterworth, 1960), pp. 95–6, and H.F. Morris and James S. Read, *Indirect Rule and the Search for Justice: Essays in East African Legal History* (Oxford: Clarendon Press, 1972), pp. 203–7.
9. See Michael Crowder and Obaro Ikime (eds), *West African Chiefs: Their Changing Status under Colonial Rule and Independence* (Ile-Ife: University of Ife Press, 1970). See also K. Busia, *The Position of the Chief in the Modern Political System of Ashanti* (London: Oxford University Press, 1958).
10. Sec 14(1) of Evidence Law (Lagos Laws, 1973, cap. 39); Evidence Law (N.N. Laws 1963, Cap 40); Evidence Law (E.N. Laws, 1963, Cap. 49).
11. See W.C. Ekow Daniels, *The Common Law in West Africa* (London: Butterworths, 1964), pp. 201–3.
12. See, for instance, J. Jearey, 'Trial by Jury and Trial with the Aid of Assessors', *Journal of African Law* 4 (1960), p. 133.
13. For instance, appointing an expert on taxation or ecology to sit as assessor when an issue in one of these areas arises.
14. See Michael Zander, *A Matter of Justice: The Legal System in Ferment* (Oxford: Oxford University Press, 1989), p. 118.
15. One of the few writers to discuss the jury is Daniels, *Common Law in West Africa*, pp. 195–201. See also Jearey, 'Trial by Jury'.
16. In Northern Ireland, for instance, juries were removed from criminal trials because of the tensions between the different religious communities; this change was based on a recommendation by a commission chaired by Justice Diplock. The formula is known as a 'Diplock Court'.
17. See 14(2) of the Evidence Act.
18. *Angu v. Attah,* P.C. (1874–1928), p. 43.
19. Ibid.
20. C. Ogwurike, *Concept of Law in English-Speaking Africa* (Lagos: Nok Publishers International, n.d.), p. 33.
21. Sec. 50 of the Courts Act, Act 372 of 1971.
22. Derek Asiedu-Akrofi, 'Judicial Recognition and Adoption of Customary Law in Nigeria', *American Journal of Comparative Law* 37 (1984), p. 571.
23. A number of countries in Oceania to have done so include Tonga and Fiji.
24. The President was to make solemn declaration to this effect by Article 14 of the Draft Constitution. These pre-state preliminaries have an importance, because of the crucial role Ghana played in subsequent developments, as it was the first African nation to be granted

independence after the Second World War.

25. William Burnett Harvey, *Law and Social Change in Ghana* (Princeton, NJ: Princeton University Press, 1966), Chapter 2, pp. 66–122.
26. Ibid., p. 122. This prognostication was made in 1966. Since then much has changed in Ghana. For an excellent analysis of the role of the chief in the context of political and social change, see Francis Mading Deng, *Tradition and Modernization: A Challenge for Law Among the Dinka of the Sudan* (New Haven, CT: Yale University Press, 1971).
27. Akintunde Olusegun Obilade, *The Nigerian Legal System* (London: Sweet & Maxwell, 1979), p. 90.
28. For the role of the European Court of Justice in determining the supranational European Law, see L. Neville Brown, *The Court of Justice of the European Communities,* 3rd edn. (London: Sweet & Maxwell, 1989).
29. On these informal courts, see R. Abel (ed.), *The Politics of Informal Justice* (New York: Academic Press, 1982).
30. See discussion in Deng, *Tradition and Modernization*, pp. 115–16, discussed under the heading 'Termination'.
31. Gordon Woodman, 'Customary Law, State Courts, and the Notion of Institutionalization of Norms in Ghana and Nigeria' in A. Allott and G. Woodman (eds), *People's Law and State Law* (Dordrecht: Foris, 1985), p. 149. For customary courts, see Martin Chauwuka Okany, *The Role of Customary Courts in Nigeria* (Enugu, Nigeria: Fourth Dimension Publishers, 1984).
32. The leading law journal is probably the *Journal of African Law,* which is published in London under the auspices of the London School of African and Oriental Studies. In Africa itself, a number of law faculties publish their own Law Journals, such as the *Zambia Law Journal.* Elsewhere Bar Councils have taken this responsibility, but there are still a number of countries which do not have their own Law journals. Indeed, nearly all the Anglophone countries bordering South Africa – Botswana, Swaziland, Lesotho, Namibia, and Zimbabwe – are heavily influenced by South African legal writing, both academic and in law reports, the reports for some of these countries appearing in the *South African Law Reports.* In Kenya there is a general law magazine which, while not academic, maintains a high level of critical discussion. Outside of Africa, the *American Indian Law Journal* is probably the most significant law journal devoted exclusively to indigenous law. Other journals place emphasis on this law, for instance *Arizona Law Review.* In Australia, the *Aboriginal Law Bulletin* maintains a high standard of critical general coverage of legal and political developments in regard to the rights of Aborigines. *The Journal of Legal Pluralism and Unofficial Law* is a leading comparative law journal, with articles dealing with customary law, while *Law and Anthropology* is an excellent annual publication. Other general comparative law journals that sometimes carry articles on customary law are the *Journal of Comparative and International Law* and the *American Journal of Comparative Law.* See also the *Melanesian Law Journal* (published by the Faculty of Law of the University of Papua New Guinea) for good coverage of Law in Papua New Guinea itself as well as in some of the neighboring Pacific States.
33. Examples of publications under the aegis of the Restatement of African Law include Volume 1; Eugene Cotran, *Kenya: The Law of Marriage and Divorce* (London: Sweet and Maxwell, 1968). For a discussion of the work of this project, see A.N. Allot and E. Cotran, 'A Background Paper on Restatement of Laws in Africa: The Need, Value and Methods of Such Restatement', in *Conference on Integration of Customary and Modern Legal Systems in Africa,* organized by University of Ife at Ibadan (New York: Africana Publishing, 1971), pp. 18-43.
34. One of the most recent comprehensive governmental studies of customary law is that carried out by the Australian Law Reform Commission, Report No. 31, *The Recognition of Aboriginal Customary Laws,* 1986, chaired by J. Crawford. In Papua New Guinea, there have also been a number of good reports – see, for instance Monograph No. 2 of the Law Reform Commission of Papua New Guinea, 'Customary Law in Papua New Guinea: A Melanesian View', edited by Richard Scaglion, and the earlier Report No. 7 of 1977, 'The Role of Customary Law in the Legal System', with Bernard Narakobi as the chairperson. The work of the Waitangi Tribunal in New Zealand should also be noted for the broad interpretation of their mandate, leading to a series of reports that probe deeply into the nature of Maori customary law – see, for instance, the booklet, *Environmental Management and the Principles of the Treaty of Waitangi – Report on Crown Response to the Recommendations of the Waitangi Tribunal 1983-1988* (Wellington:

National Library, 1988). In the United States, on the other hand, as James Zion notes (see below), attempts by the National American Indian Court Judges Association to carry out a project on the Indian common law have failed due to lack of governmental support. Nevertheless, there is a recognized textbook by Felix Cohen, *Handbook of Federal Indian Law* (Buffalo, CO: William S. Hein, 1980 [1942]); see also, William Canby, Jr, *American Indian Law* (St Paul: West Publishing Co., 1981).

35. It should be remembered that federal governments also have problems to achieve unity in the law. Even the 'common law' of the United States is fragmented with each state having its own common law, as a result of the controversial decision of the Supreme Court in *Erie Railroad v. Tompkins*, 304 US 64 (1938). A number of model Codes have been published with the intention of encouraging uniformity in the Law.
36. For a discussion on the possibilities of a change, see B. Levack, 'The Proposed Union of English and Scots Law', *Juridical Review* 20 (1975), p. 97.
37. For instance, a sheriff in Scotland is a judge in a lower court.
38. The recent setting-up of a Scottish legislature, will obviously accentuate even more the special nature of the legal system in Scotland.
39. William Twining, *The Place of Customary Law in the National Legal Systems of East Africa* (Chicago: University of Chicago Law School, 1963), p. 16.
40. Ibid., pp. 16–17. The case referred to by Twining is *Mwauru s/o Kamau v. Gatoto s/o Mwangi*, [1962] E.A. 528.
41. See, for instance, *R. v. Ward,* S.C. of W.A., Kalgoorlie, No. 119/1985 (unreported), where the judge, in passing sentence, said, 'I think I am entitled to pay some attention to the fact that he has already been punished to some extent by his own community and it is possible that he will be punished further by other members of the Aborigine community.' However, the court also added that 'Tribal punishment cannot dictate to this court what the court should do when sentencing … under the Law of the State.' The sentence itself was a light one, of six months for manslaughter, for the unintended death of a fellow tribesman, whom the accused had speared as a punishment for the accidental killing of a relative of the accused.
42. In general, including discussion of the *Ward* case (ibid.), see Roderic Broadhurst, 'Imprisonment of the Aborigine in Western Australia 1957–1985', in K.M. Hazlehurst (ed.), *Ivory Scales: Black Australians and the Law* (Kensington: NSW University Press, 1987), p. 168.
43. The Government Commission on *The Recognition of Aboriginal Customary Law*, recommended recognition of the customary law 'as far as possible', but maintained that this should be 'by existing judicial and administrative authorities, avoiding the creation of new and separate legal structures, unless the need for these is clearly demonstrated' (at p. 144) of Vol. 1 of Report.
44. See discussion of the 1964 *Chimney Evans* case by Elizabeth Eggleston, *Fear, Favour or Affection: Aborigines and the Criminal Law in Victoria, South Australia and Western Australia* (Canberra: Australian National University Press, 1976), pp. 289–93.
45 For an interesting discussion of how courts relate to secrets in general, based on United States cases, see Kim Lane Scheppele, *Legal Secrets: Equality and Efficiency in the Common Law* (Chicago: University of Chicago Press, 1988).
46. See *Foster v. Mountford and Rigby*, (1976) 29 FLR 233, 14 ALR 71; and Charles Mountford, *Nomads of the Australian Desert* (Adelaide: Rigby, 1976).
47. It might also be noted that in the aforementioned case of *Chimney Evans* (n. 44) it was suggested that at least some of the six accused may have been exploiting the tribal custom for their own ends.
48. James W. Zion, 'Searching for Indian Common Law', in Bradford Morse and Gordon Woodman (eds.), *Indigenous Law and the State* (Dordrecht: Foris Publications, 1988).
49. Ibid., p. 139.
50. Ibid., p. 139.
51. Diane Bell and Pam Dutton, *Law: The Old and New: Aboriginal Women in Central Australia Speak Out* (Canberra: Central Australia Aborigine Legal Aid Service), p. 22.
52. L.C. Green, *Law and Society* (Leiden: Sijthoff, 1977), p. 118 (from paper '"Civilized" Law and "Primitive" People', 1973). Green adds that the judge could, of course, order a hearing in camera, which would, however, solve the problem of spectators, but not of jury members. The case in question is *R. v. Gibson,* Judgment No. 1810, South Australia (12 Nov. 1973).
53. *R. v. Anunga and Others*, (1976) 11 ALR 412. See also *Between Jabarula and Suikart* in S.C. of N.T.

(No. 10 of 1984), 6.4.84 in Alice Springs.

54. For general discussion of the situation in Australia, see Kathy Laster, 'Legal Interpreters: Conduits to Social Justice?' *Journal of International Studies* 11 (1990), p. 15.
55. It might be noted that in both these bodies, much of the normative practices were laid down by Judge Durie, himself a Maori.

Academic Questions

Auguste Comte, one of the founding figures of the discipline of sociology, suggested that, since sociology touched on so many aspects of life, it could well be considered the queen of the sciences.[1] Few sociologists today would claim that distinction, and there are few in other professions who would wish to arrogate that title for their own discipline. But those involved in anthropology, both its physical and cultural sectors, might be closer to fulfilling that Comtean vision or mission. For anthropology goes beyond sociology (the study of society, an artificial creation) in dealing with humanity as such, its physical aspects, its place in nature, its evolutionary development, and its social and cultural aspect, both historically in ancient societies, and contemporaneously in societies of all types – initially mainly those present-day societies that are still 'primitive,' but today comparatively surveying societies of all types and sizes, including urban and modern.[2]

More than any other profession, anthropology is the meeting-ground of modern science and traditional tribes, a coming together that has been characterized by many ambivalent feelings and many ambiguous situations. There can be no doubt as to the tremendous contribution that anthropologists have made in conveying the richness and variety, the value and values of tribal life, in describing both the essential unity of the human race and the special uniqueness of some of its parts; but there can also be no escape from the host of problems that have arisen. Despite the sincerity of motivation for the research, the earnestness in which it is conducted, the empathy with which many of the researchers relate to their research subjects, or the sensitivity in presenting the material for a wider audience, anthropologists have occasionally been criticized or even castigated for a host of aberrations, ranging from inaccuracy of the facts to distortions in the interpretation.

Ethical concerns as to the limits within which researchers must work have occupied social scientists for many years; specific problems relate to how a necessary degree of objectivity can be attained, given the personal propensities, the professional pressures, the social influences, under which research is conducted – made even more acute when researchers (no matter how sensitive they are to their subjects, or even partial to their political claims), represent the perspective of one society while their subjects are of another, with differing normative rules and cultural standards. A number of writers have attempted to set up an intellectual framework within which the issues arising may be satisfactorily resolved. Thus, for instance, Karl Mannheim wrote of the parameters of the Sociology of Knowledge[3] and Max Weber of the search for *verstehen* (understanding);[4] later writers, such as Alvin Gouldner have written of reflexive sociology,[5] and in a much-quoted work, Peter Berger and Thomas Luckman have explored further dimensions in what they term the social construction of reality.[6]

Nevertheless, there have been instances in which anthropologists have been subjected to a barrage of accusations as to problematic aspects of their work, ranging from the divulging of secrets learned in confidence to the exploitation of tribal vulnerability in the name of science, at the price of violating basic rights, needs or interests of the tribes.

In recent years, one of the major issues has been that of the removal of skeletal remains and artifacts from graves for the purpose of conducting laboratory experiments or of mounting museum exhibitions. Initial hesitant objections have given rise to a massive wave of disapproval. The protestations of physical anthropologists, archaeologists and other related professionals as to the crucial importance of their work has been met with an ever-increasing insistence to immediately desist from further intrusions and removal of objects, and to a demand for return of past 'spoils'.

The compelling desire and need for further knowledge, in particular as to problematic aspects of the distant past, must always be tempered with a parallel obligation to display humility in the light of human limitations that place inevitable restrictions on what may be studied and how much may be learned; and to show respect and reverence for the materials being examined, both in and of itself, and inasmuch as it might affect present members of society, who might have a direct link, through proven ancestry, or even mythical sentimentality, to that material.

At times, in various scientific endeavors, calls have gone out to forgo the search for knowledge in a certain area, because the full implications of innovative ideas have not been adequately measured, or because of the potential dangers involved. One of the outstanding examples of such manifestation, was the call in the late 1970s by Nobel Laureate, Joshua Lederberger, for a temporary moratorium on certain areas of biological research, for instance in genetics, because society was not adequately forewarned and prepared to cope with the myriad of likely new issues that might arise.[7] In a sister science, physics, leading members of that discipline warned of the dangers that some of their own research might have caused, in terms of nuclear capacity.[8] In medicine, the ethical issues are so complex that guidelines have been laid down – the Helsinki Rules – both in terms of research and treatment.[9] There are limits that professions impose on their practitioners, such as forbidden methods for psychologists (some of it relating to sexual therapy),[10] or limits that the law imposes, such as when criminologists study illegal behavior.[11] Conversely, the law itself sometimes provides protection for particular individuals in terms of the privileged communications applicable in certain professions. Today much research is in any case hidebound by the exigencies of economic considerations.[12] Finally, the results of most research do not have the quality of infallible truth, a factor that should never be forgotten when laying down the boundaries of the permissible and the desirable in borderline situations.[13]

Skeletal remains undoubtedly capture untold secrets of the past, and encoded in the bones are often keys to an understanding of bygone eras and, as a result, also the modern age. The very diversity of population in the modern world, suggests research to examine whether the emergence of human beings was a one-time phenomenon or whether there were parallel developments in different parts of the world. Skeletal remains may be crucial for understanding basic factors about humankind.[14] Yet, such special advances cannot explain the immense number of skeletal remains that have been unearthed and are now on display in museums – when not tucked away in museum basements or cellars. The numbers in the United States have been estimated at several hundred thousand, with an emerging consensus (though no more than an estimate) of 600,000 examples held not only in museums and research institutes, but also in private collections.[15] As H. Marcus Price notes, 'The potential for conflict is substantial' and he explains that 'For many members of the aboriginal communities, these remains are symbols of spiritual and political power. For members of the scientific and museological communities, human remains yield data that can advance our understanding of human variation and evolution, thus benefitting all of humanity.'[16]

Price, however, also notes that the clash is not an absolute one, but must be seen in relative terms, where research itself can be considered to be an expression of respect. Furthermore, just as among religions with their different approaches (for instance, banning, allowing, favoring or obligating cremation)[17] so tribes do not have uniform approaches, some being more lax about protecting sites after the elapse of time than others. Even those groups that insist on protection of sites may agree to controlled exhumation for limited purposes. However, adamant stands have been taken, and Price writes that some

> Indian groups (such as American Indians Against Desecration) reportedly insist that all archaeology is desecration and that all prehistoric aboriginal remains and grave goods should be immediately returned to Indian communities for ceremonial disposition.[18]

The overall situation is still in some degree of flux, but the arrogance and obtuseness of many representatives of western society in the past is giving way to much more sensitivity and understanding. Thus, some museums have shown a willingness to return skeletal remains and burial artifacts to their tribal owners. Not always is such redress possible, because the precise provenance of the bones and artifacts may not be known, or because nomadic wanderings have led to sites being abandoned (sometimes only temporarily), or because of outside interventions – the building of dams and the consequent drowning of graves,[19] or the accidental unearthing of an ancient burial site in the process of innocent excavations prior to building.[20]

An anarchical situation that used to exist in the past, has now been replaced with guiding legislation, laying down the conditions to be met and the precautions to be taken, when relating to such potential research material. In the United States, for example, the major laws of recent years are the Archaeological Resources Protection Act of 1979, the National Museum of the American Indian Act of 1989, and the Native American Grave Protection and Reparation Act (NAGPRA) of 1990.[21] In sum, they mandate potential researchers to receive approval for their work from tribal authorities. Thus, NAGPRA requires the making of an inventory of collections in museums and institutions that receive federal support, and provides that the tribe, which is known to be linked to the remains, must be informed, and given the option of claiming back the remains. Any purchases or deals done in violation of these rules are prohibited.

In many instances, it is not possible to know the connection between the skeletal remains and any particular tribe. John Peterson explains some of the problematics in protecting skeletal remains, since

> Indian burial sites often fall short of the definition of cemetery when they are evaluated from the perspective of contemporary American burial standards. Several factors are attributed to this shortcoming. First, Indian burial customs varied widely over both time and space, and it was not uncommon for the dead to be placed in locations not specifically set aside for that purpose. Second, Indians often relied on natural features and oral tradition to denote burial locations rather than using specialized grave markers. Third, Indians often lost track of specific burial grounds because they were forced to relocate in response to, or under pressure from, government policy and Euro-American settlement. Finally, when a grave predates the historic period, there is a question of relationship between those remains and contemporary Indian groups.[22]

Some of the more critical issues are not so much concerned with ongoing problems that arise, but with the residual consequences of earlier times when there was little control over the disposition of remains and not sufficient respect shown for the legitimate concerns of tribes. Strong arguments have been raised for the return of skeletal remains and burial artifacts that were taken a long time ago. This is an issue that is actually not limited to skeletal remains and tribal rights, but is part of a far broader conflict, relating to general archaeological finds and cultural objects that have been removed over the years and transferred to museums and similar institutions in Europe from areas in other parts of the world, especially during the periods of imperial expansion.[23] International rules now govern much of this trade, and special efforts have been made to cope with those engaged in illegal practices, involving grave robbers and international smugglers. Some museums have voluntarily offered to return material that has strong symbolic meaning for the offended nation. However, it is clear that problems of skeletal remains and burial objects touch on even more sensitive factors, because of the claimed desecration of the memory of a human being, by disturbing the remains.

Because of the lengthy period since some of the remains were removed, where the determination of direct tribal connection is not always possible, general ethnicity becomes more important than specific tribal identity. That is, the claim is made on behalf of the Indians of the United States or the Aborigines of Australia and not any particular tribe. This is not an insurmountable obstacle, given the extra sensitivity that courts often display when dealing with protection from desecration of human remains in burial sites. John Winski, in his article dealing with the rights of repatriation of human remains and burial objects, draws attention to a number of cases, where standing was given to tribal groups, even when the question of tribal connection was not conclusively shown.[24] He quotes from cases, showing the broad degree of protection the courts offer in trying to assure respect for the dead and maintenance of their burial sites, including a flexible attitude to allow interested groups standing to bring suit. One particular case quoted involved the body of an Indian chief of the Comanche tribe, with an added complication of two rival groups from the tribe, each claiming direct familial connection. Chief Quanah Parker had been buried in a cemetery that was about to be condemned,[25] in order to allow the land to be used for other activities. A court order was sought for permission to disinter and rebury the bodies in the cemetery and two rival Indian groups claimed the right to determine the place of reburial for the Chief. The court found it unnecessary to determine which group was the rightful descendants of the chief, because it held that, in any case, the court had an overriding authority to protect the human remains of the dead, and could thus make the decision on its own. But the decision does indicate the special concern that the court displays toward burial sites. Winski sums up by arguing that

> there is no principled reason why ... liberal standing rules should not apply to Indian tribes as well. In fact, courts have not hesitated to extend these same types of considerations to protect American Indian burials. Under the ... broad standing rules, Indian tribes should have little difficulty in establishing their standing to maintain suit for wrongful interference with the right to disposition of the remains of tribal ancestors, or for interference with a property right to burial goods.[26]

More complicated situations arise when the removal was executed further afield. A recent newspaper article[27] tells the poignant story of a Griqua woman, from South Africa, who had been taken overseas, and put on show, naked, to European audiences, because of the unusual anatomical shape of the body, typical of many Khoi and San peoples.

After the death of the Griqua woman she was never given a burial, but her body was handed over to a Paris Museum, where it was kept on show for more than 150 years. Recently, the members of her tribal group demanded that her remains be returned for proper internment.

As in much of this process, at stake is more than just the question of respect for the individual, but the issue of group self-respect. As a spokesperson of the Griquas quoted in the article says: 'She's a potent symbol of the dismemberment and the dehumanization of the aboriginal people of South Africa.'[28] In fact, the symbolism in this case pertains not just to relations *vis-à-vis* the white people in Europe, but has to do with the status of the Griquas, a small marginal group in the new South Africa *vis-à-vis* other dominant population groups.

The most insistent demands that have been made in recent years for repatriation of skeletal remains, have come from the Aborigines in Australia.[29] Considered at first as examples of earlier human types, and far more isolated than most other peoples, they had aroused much scientific interest, and many skeletal remains were removed from their sites and transferred to Europe. For most Aborigine tribes, it is of major importance that the tribal member be buried in tribal territory, and even for many tribespeople, who no longer live in a tribal area, but maintain links with the tribe, a tribal burial is an ultimate affirmation of membership and belonging.

The organized activities by tribal people to put an end to the use of skeletons, and to demand return of skeletons long removed, has aroused much concern among anthropologists and archaeologists. There can be little doubt that, until the tribal people themselves raised the issue, researchers had not shown sufficient regard to the delicate implications that their scientific work posed for the societies involved. Much of the ruminations in academic writings began to appear only after the issue had been squarely placed on the international agenda by tribal groups.

Although there were doubtless many complaints voiced in the past, it was concerted and organized action that led to a transformation in attitudes.

In fact, two scientists involved in such research have given revealing descriptions in the journal *Antiquity* of their own coming to terms with demands being made over issues that they had formerly largely ignored. Thus Webb describes actions taken during the 1980s aimed at creating a dialogue between the scientists and the representatives of Aborigines in Australia.[30] He explains candidly that

> After listening to why people did not want research to continue, I could find no scientific argument to balance … their moral one. It is difficult to argue against the rights of any group of people to choose what should and should not happen to the skeletal remains. I find myself increasingly sympathetic to their point of view.[31]

Noting that permission was never sought to take the remains, he states that the

> … general opinion was that researchers had little respect for Aborigines. … Aborigine people were shocked by the amount of remains held in museums, the way they had been collected, and that collecting was allowed to occur in the first place.[32]

He adds that 'Grave-robbing could now be added to the long line of misdeeds inflicted upon Aborigines by white people.'[33]

However, all that said, Webb explains that, despite these past errors and the resentments that they aroused, there is nevertheless a 'strong interest among Aborigine people in gaining knowledge about their past'.[34] Some of them, in fact, are entering the profession of archaeology. Webb describes the understandings reached with some of the Aborigines in extensive discussions, and that, on an individual basis, some were prepared to concede the importance of the research, but that all such openness toward research was contingent on the Aborigines being accorded

> recognition that they are living descendants of *any* Aborigine skeletal remains, and as such should be consulted about research on those remains. Most feel that study of this sort should not be taken for granted or be seen by the scientists as a natural right.[35]

In particular, while there is understanding of research needs, there is little flexibility on the imperative need for ending museum displays, a viewpoint that Webb agrees with. He ends with a plea for a continued dialogue, linked to an awareness that 'Anthropologists are … being forced to re-evaluate the ethics and philosophy of the study of recent skeletal populations.'[36]

Webb's article evoked a positive response when I. Zimmerman described similar positive dialogues that had been undertaken in North

America.[37] In a revealing admission, he states that, at one stage, 'I was appalled at the attitudes of my profession. I came very close to leaving archaeology.'[38] He describes becoming 'radicalized' on the issue not just because of the demands of the Native Americans, but because of some of the attitudes of some of his colleagues, who were not always prepared to honestly relate to the Indians' demands, but would adopt 'appalling self-protective tactics and rationales ...'.[39]

In the final analysis, scientific research can, as Webb and Zimmerman indicate, only be carried out successfully and in basic human decency, if there is consent by the people for this research. The ground rules have now been set out by tribal groups themselves. In fact, at the beginning of the present crisis, the World Council of Indigenous Peoples made clear its position in a 1981 Declaration, which dealt with the total array of problems, of which skeletal and burial remains were examples. It states *inter alia:*

> Indigenous nations and peoples continue to own and control their material culture, including archaeological, historical and sacred sites, artifacts, designs, knowledge and works of art. They have the right to regain items of major cultural significance, and, in all cases, to the return of the human remains of their ancestors for burial in accordance with their tradition.[40]

In further clauses, the Declaration states:

> No technical, scientific or social investigations, including archaeological excavations, shall take place in relation to indigenous nations or people, or to their lands, without their prior authorization, and their continuing ownership or control.[41]

It will be seen that, beyond the special tensions associated with ensuring respect for the dead, there are other issues which go to the heart of tribal self-respect, and which have only recently been given the attention required. These deal with the creative expression of tribal people, in a group or an individual capacity, in which their achievements are used, without acknowledgment or consent. Here the demand is for recognition and, where appropriate, for adequate compensation.

Vivien Johnson has described various examples of exploitation of artistic treasures of the Aborigines, including, for instance, the design on the old Australian dollar note, which was taken from an aboriginal design.[42] In 1976, an Aborigine Artists' Agency was set up to seek recompense for illicit use of artistic material, or to work for removal from sale of the particular artistic object. Aborigine art is of a very special nature, unique in its manifestation, deeply rooted in ancient traditions, firmly connected to its religious and cultural base, some of it an expression of collective experience, which often complicates questions of copyright and compensation. Much work is needed in this area in order to prevent easy and profitable exploitation of folk art that often denies the individual creativity of the artist, or else ignores the larger collective spirit of the tribe that is embodied in the art, for instance masks that have deep and meaningful symbolic meaning, unbeknown to the purchaser.[43]

The anthropological issues do not relate only to physical aspects. There are also more amorphous issues, relating to the social and cultural trends of anthropology, and the moral obligations that field anthropologists bear toward the subjects of their research. On one occasion, an Australian anthropologist was sued for revealing secrets and distorting facts.[44] But a more complex issue arose in New Zealand recently, in a probing debate between those who believe that the anthropologist has a duty to partake in activist work on behalf of tribal groups, often powerless and exploited, seeking redress for past wrongs and present injustices, and those who claim that the services of anthropology (now a profession no longer studying only tribal groups) should be made available to any group seeking its assistance, including in conflicts with tribal groups, the traditional subjects of anthropology.[45] The issue came to the fore as a result of a legal clash over land rights in New Zealand, in which an anthropologist gave evidence, based on research, of the Pakeha (white) community striving to retain land on which they farmed, against counter-claims by a Maori tribe, Ngai Tahu. The anthropologist, Michele Dominy describes how she became involved in their dispute, brought before the Waitangi Tribunal, as a result of research that she had been conducting in a community of '365 sheep-farming families of European descent'.[46] She explains that

> these families, among whom I have been conducting ethnographic research, recognized in hearing Ngai Tahu testimony an expression of feeling for the land which resembled the farmers' own feelings for the land. They hoped that I would agree to provide a cultural perspective based on my research on the relationship of high country sheep station families to the land: this would be part of their submission … .[47]

to Waitangi Tribunal in opposition to the Maori claim. The request forced Dominy 'to explore the issues raised when an anthropologist is placed in a position where she has to offer her materials for the use of others in a context where the control and use of knowledge are politicized'.[48]

Dominy explains the unusual nature of her subjects' request. She also clarifies that her research community represented the kind of population rarely examined. 'The anthropology of colonialism,' she writes, 'has paid insufficient attention to the anthropology of white settler societies.'[49] In her evidence, she documented that the Pakeha in the high country 'have both a material and spiritual affinity to place which is evident in an examination of their behavior and symbolic forms.'[50]

She argues that her evidence was based on her research, ignoring the political aspects, including such issues as power relationships, and focused on the cultural aspects, dealing with the attitude, spiritual in nature, of the farmers to their land and the surroundings. She also clarifies the conditions under which she gave evidence: 'I prepared the evidence with the stipulation that I would not accept payment, which was offered, and that I would not change the content even if the farmers took exception to my testimony.'[51] In a sense she was acting within the framework that Mannheim's thesis allows – namely the choice a 'free-floating intellectual' has of opting for supporting the *status quo* (of ideology) or of seeking change (of utopia). She admittedly claims her objective stance, but that is specifically what Mannheim had denied as a possibility.[52] Dominy is well aware of the latent conflict with other anthropologists, and is at pains to explain that she had no quarrel with the Maori protagonists in this case. Her efforts were directed only to describing the special nature of the connection between the white farmers and their land and the surrounding environment – in terms apparently that paralleled opposing contentions being made on behalf of the Maoris.

Her thesis evoked several critical responses. Anthony Cohen raises the issue head-on in his opening sentence, stating,

> Michele Dominy's article poses a thorny ethical problem: as 'advocate' ... under what circumstance is it defensible to extend that advocacy to those who might be regarded by others (if not by themselves) as the privileged party in a dispute? An initial liberal response might be to say that *everyone* has the right to representation, and that it is not for the anthropologist to make judgments about the relative merits of competing claims.[53]

The real issue is, however, not of limited, neutral testimony in a court of law or a lands tribunal – it is the issue of committed advocacy, of identifying with the people who have allowed an intrusion into their lives and an exposure to others, and not just the anthropologists, of their way of life. When dealing with disadvantaged and dispossessed groups, inevitable questions arise as to what to do with the material, what moral obligation rests upon researchers to make representations on behalf of their subjects, to galvanize them (and others) into activism. The implication is that similar obligations do not apply when dealing with privileged or powerful groups, even if some of that privilege and power is being challenged.

Beyond this loom larger issues – of who owns the data? Cohen suggests that this is an issue which British anthropology has avoided, although it has been well explored by French anthropologists, partly because they have been forced to do so by their own informants.[54] In some respects, he is understanding of Dominy's attitude, partly because she limited her evidence to the factual ethnographic account, partly because there was no direct Pakeha–Maori confrontation, but both laid their claims against the state. Other writers, too, while circumspect about her action in giving evidence, are understanding of her dilemma and appreciative of the frankness with which she presents it. A statement, in the same journal, on behalf of the New Zealand Association of Social Anthropologists, notes that 'Many anthropologists living and working in New Zealand have chosen some degree of involvement in advocacy'[55] and goes on to describe the various contributions that they have made. This is all very commendable, and the activism of academicians, professional people, such as lawyers, social workers, historians, and fully fledged organizations, both of tribal people and concerned outsiders, was examined in an earlier chapter.[56] What is of import to note for the moment – and what is of major significance for some of the themes that are being presented in this book – is the manner in which Dominy both interpreted and presented her data within the parameters of the usual Maori discourse. In order to substantiate the competing claim of the Pakeha community – to be more exact, in order to develop correct perceptions of their innermost feelings – she used the kind of language associated normally with tribal people.

In his contribution to the debate, David Turner poses the issue forcefully,[57] by pointing out the importance attached to the variable of culture in Dominy's work. According to Dominy, the Pakeha have a spiritual attachment to their land. This is indeed central to Maori (and other tribal groups') concepts of land and an essential aspect of their modern claims. To use the language of spirituality is to accept their world-outlook, to acknowledge the philosophic underpinnings of their way of life. As already noted,[58] so much of conflict between modern, settler populations and tribal communities relates to land, partly because control of land (irrespective of who had possession) meant sovereign political power, partly because land is envisaged in such totally different manners by the two populations. Dominy, in presenting the Pakeha position within a traditionally tribal perspective, is making a significant contribution not just to the factual situation she describes, but to the larger framework of seeking an accommodation between modern society and traditional communities, and in specific instances of seeking a reconciliation between opposing groups.[59] The problem is, as Turner suggests, that her picture is not an accurate one of the social situation she researched:

> In relation to land, the spiritual is the substance of 'transcendent space' in a form above-and-beyond content sense. It is this to which continuities of humans are attached, not the land itself. Form above-and-beyond content is a *dimension* to the land, in some respects a

> vision beyond words. The substance of this vision – really 'on the other side', *beyond* this vision – is the realm of the spiritual.
>
> Within this perspective, the spiritual connection to land evidenced by Dominy on behalf of all the high country settlers is just not very 'spiritual' at all. Their relation to land is basically materialist … .
>
> In these respects the Maori relation to land seems similar to that of the settlers, but with an important addition. In Maori theology land, sea and sky are all *taonga,* something of value derived from the Gods. However, the jurisdiction that this afforded human beings over land, sea and sky was by no means eternal. There was no guarantee that one's jurisdiction would be respected by others. One could 'wrest' *taonga,* and land from another.[60]

This, then, is the heart of the issue. Is the conflict over land or is it over culture, over material possessions or over spiritual conceptions, over farming and agriculture or over aesthetics and religion, over formal legal title or over amorphous human rights? For Turner there is a very real danger that academic intervention may, by incorrect understandings and inaccurate definitions, complicate the issue:

> A definition in academic-discussive terms may very well limit the range of the possible, and therefore of the actual, that the author claims to re-present. This is no mere academic debate. The implications are enormous considering that we are dealing with the presentation of evidence that could irrevocably alter people's lives for better or for worse.[61]

Finally, since it is not just descriptions of social reality at stake, but binding legal decisions, Turner notes the additional complicating factor of law as it affects also anthropological discourse, the academic and practical, especially since 'the law itself has particular difficulty in dealing with what are in some aspects non-describable realities, and will always try to translate them into institutional realities'.[62] But, of course, true law, good law, whether traditional tribal or modern common, whether judge-made or equity, whether emanating from a court or a tribunal, will know how to deal also with the non-describable realities.

NOTES

1. Auguste Comte, *Sociologie*, 2nd edn. (Paris: Presses Universitaire de France, 1963).
2. In this chapter, references to anthropology will be made in the widest sense as used mainly in American anthropology (in contrast, for instance, to British, or other countries of the British Commonwealth) – including archaeology and physical anthropology.
3. Karl Mannheim, *Ideology and Utopia: An Introduction to the Sociology of Knowledge* (New York: Harcourt, Brace & World, 1936).
4. Max Weber, *The Methodology of the Social Sciences* (New York: The Free Press, 1949).

5. Alvin Gouldner, *The Coming Crisis of Western Sociology* (London: Heinemann, 1971).
6. Peter Berger and Thomas Luckman, *The Social Construction of Reality* (Harmondsworth: Penguin Books, 1984).
7. Since then, further developments have led to the beginning of a debate that would disallow human cloning – after the initial success in cloning a sheep in 1997 in Britain. For discussions on the problematics of genetic therapy, see a series of articles in *Bioethics*, vols. 9, 10 and 11 (1995, 1996, 1997); in general, see editorial 'Of Genes, Embryos, Human Individuals and Future Persons', in vol. 9 (1995), p. iii.
8. See, for instance, ongoing discussions in *The Bulletin of the Atomic Physicists.*
9. For a similar problem relating to research on animals, see Brigitta Forsman, *Research Ethics in Practice: The Animal Ethics Committee in Sweden, 1979–1989* (Göteburg: Center for Research Ethics, 1993).
10. In general, see Gerald Sjoberg (ed.), *Ethics, Politics and Social Research* (Cambridge, MA: Schenkman Publishing, 1967).
11. See interesting comment on the manner in which the law sometimes forces people to destroy loyalty to those with whom they have close or special relationships, such as family members, business partners, life-long friends – see Gordon Mehler, 'Informants, Rats, and Tattletales: Loyalty, Fear and the Constitution,' *Criminal Justice Ethics* 16 (1997), p. 2.
12. Reference is made here also to economic factors, because, in the neutral academic search for truth, the impact that funding has on what themes will be pursued is often forgotten.
13. In general, see Frank Heller (ed.), *The Use and Abuse of Social Science* (London: Sage, 1986).
14. In general, see Richard Leakey, *People of the Lake: Mankind and its Beginnings* (Garden City, NY: Anchor Press, 1978).
15. The figure of 600,000 skeletal remains appears in several of the main articles quoted in this chapter.
16. H. Marcus Price III, *Disputing the Dead: U.S. Law on Aboriginal Remains and Grave Gods* (Columbia: University of Missouri Press, 1991), p. 1.
17. For instance, Orthodox Judaism has a total ban on cremation, which Hinduism allows and encourages. Some trends in Islam protect graves only up to a certain point in time.
18. Price, *Disputing the Dead*, p. 2.
19. See discussion of several such issues, as brought out in judicial decisions, in Chapter 13, 'Holy Rites and Sacred Sites'.
20. Some legislation protects only recent graveyards, not ancient ones, whose whereabouts were unknown until uncovered by chance – although reports must generally be made about the discovery to the authorities.
21. See respectively 16 U.S.C. (1983); 20 U.S.C. (1989); and 25 U.S.C. (1990).
22. John E. Peterson II, 'Dance of the Dead: A Legal Tango for Control of Native American Skeletal Remains', *American Indian Law Review* 15 (1991), p. 129.
23. For the problems of taking important aspects of a culture out of a country, whether legally or illegally, see my discussion in *Social Cohesion and Legal Coercion: A Critique of Weber, Durkheim, and Marx* (Atlanta, GA, and Amsterdam: Rodopi, 1997) at Chapter 9, 'On Ecology and Crime'; see also Jeanette Greenfield, *The Return of Cultural Treasures* (Cambridge: Cambridge University Press, 1996); and Karl Meyer, *The Plundered Past: The Story of the Illegal International Traffic in Works of Art* (New York: Atheneum, 1977).
24. John B. Winski, 'There Are Skeletons in the Closet: The Repatriation of Native American Human Remains and Burial Objects,' *Arizona Law Review* 34 (1992), p. 187.
25. See *United States v. Unknown Heirs*, 152 F. Supp. 452 (W.D. Okla. 1957).
26. Winski, 'There Are Skeletons in the Closet', p. 213.
27. 'Quest for Remains of African Venus: Once a Circus Act, Now a Symbol of Outrage', *San Francisco Chronicle,* 24 February 1996, p. 1.
28. Ibid.
29. In general, see collection of articles in I. McBride (ed.), *Who Owns the Past – Papers from Annual Symposium of the Australian Academy of the Humanities* (Melbourne: Oxford University Press, 1985). See especially, A. Erh Soon Tay, 'Law and the Cultural Heritage'; J. Malvaney, 'A Question of Values: Museums and Cultural Property'; S. Sullivan, 'The Custodianship of Aborigine Sites in Southeastern Australia'; and D. Wilson, 'Return and Restitution: A Museum Perspective'.

30. S. Webb, 'Reburying Australian Skeletons,' *Antiquity* 61 (1987), p. 292.
31. Ibid., p. 293.
32. Ibid., p. 294.
33. Ibid., p. 294.
34. Ibid., p. 295.
35. Ibid., p. 295, emphasis in original.
36. Ibid., p. 295.
37. I.J. Zimmerman, 'Webb on Reburial: A North American Perspective', *Antiquity* 61 (1987), p. 462.
38. Ibid., p. 462.
39. Ibid., p. 463.
40. Declaration of World Council of Indigenous Peoples, 1981, Clause 11.
41. Ibid., Clause 13.
42. Vivien Johnson, 'A Whiter Shade of Paleolithic: Aboriginal Art and Appropriation', *Aborigine Law Bulletin* (October 1988), p. 4. See also, in the same issue of *Bulletin,* Kenneth Maddock, 'Copyright and Traditional Designs: An Aboriginal Dilemma', p. 8.
43. For good succinct discussion, see Howard Morphy, 'Aboriginal Art in a Global Context', in Daniel Miller (ed.), *Worlds Apart* (London: Routledge, 1995).
44. See *Foster v. Mountford and Rigby*, (1976) 29 FLR 233, 14 ALR 71. The book at the center of the dispute was Charles Mountford, *Nomads of the Australian Desert* (Adelaide: Rigby, 1976); see discussion in previous chapter, 'Proving the Customary Rule'.
45. For an example of anthropological evidence being rejected out of hand by a court, *inter alia,* because of alleged bias by the witness in favor of the indigenous people, see discussion of a Canadian case in the next chapter, 'Accounting for the Past'.
46. Michele Dominy, 'New Zealand's Waitangi Tribunal: Cultural Politics of an Anthropology of the High Country', *Anthropology Today,* 6 (April 1990), p. 11.
47. Ibid., p. 11.
48. Ibid., pp. 11–12.
49. Ibid., p. 12.
50. Ibid.
51. Ibid., p. 12. She also notes that, not being a New Zealander, she had no political agenda of her own, and thus it was easy to develop her contacts.
52. Mannheim explained that it is possible to strive for objectivity, but in the final analysis, there is no way of evading the impact of social factors impinging on the researcher; see *Ideology and Utopia.*
53. Anthony Cohen, 'In Reply to Dominy', *Anthropology Today*, 6 (June 1990), p. 7.
54. Ibid., p. 8.
55. 'Cultural Politics in New Zealand,' *Anthropology Today*, 6 (June 1990), p. 3. The statement is presented by M. Goldsmith, P. Herda, P. Laing, R. McKinlay, J. Metge, W. Norman, J. Park, J. Sluka, J. Simon, G. Smith – for the NZASA.
56. See Chapter 10, 'The Local Tribe in the Global Village'.
57. David Turner, *Anthropology Today*, 6 (June 1990), p. 6.
58. See above, Ch. 6, 'The Invention of Discovery' and Chapter 12, 'Land is Forever'.
59. See discussion in next chapter, Chapter 21, 'Accounting for the Past'.
60. Turner, *Anthropology Today*, p. 7.
61. Ibid., p. 7.
62. Ibid., p. 7.

Accounting for the Past

Making amends for past injustices and seeking reconciliation for former inequities are among the most crucial and excruciating factors facing societies that seek to acknowledge their errors and to plan their future on a new and more equitable base. For memories of old can never be totally erased, and the consequences of policies and practices now condemned will continue to have an effect on present circumstances. In any event, for some, the prejudices that once gave rise to discrimination will still persist, even if on a smaller scale and in more subtle expression; for others, the resentments that ensued will linger on, occasionally erupting in rage, more regularly evoking a dull cynicism at professions of remorse and proposals for reconstruction.

But any willingness to confront the past should be welcomed, while not minimizing the enormity of such a task. In recent years, in a different context, there have been examples of countries attempting to create innovative formulae and special forums for coping with their past as new democratic governments replace dictatorial and repressive regimes. Fundamental transformations in Eastern Europe, South America and Southern Africa have led to considerations, which favor a full divulging of the truth as to what happened as preferable to the meting out of any full measure of justice and imposition of punishment for those who bear responsibility for the harm caused.[1] In those areas of the world, the key change was in terms of political control, with ideological or military regimes being replaced. But the process – itself controversial in many of those countries for it often involved disputed pardoning and amnesty procedures[2] – may have some relevance for understanding the present attempts to recognize tribal aspirations. As noted in the discussion of the *Mabo* case in Australia, Jeremy Webber saw the judgment – with its radical revision of Australian history – as being a jurisprudence of regret,[3] an official acknowledgment of harm caused in the past, of a willingness to admit the fault, and of a desire to redress part, at least, of the grievances.

While Australia still lags behind some of the other countries that were formerly settler colonies in any formal establishment of official bodies to examine the past (though a Reconciliation Convention was held in May, 1997), and while the *Mabo* judgment itself is limited as an obligatory precedent (as discussed in Chapter 6), its deeper meaning contains the kernel of a fuller understanding of the nature of present-day relations between indigenous people and the descendants of the settler populations, as seen in their proper historical context.

Thus Webber advises us to read beyond the text itself in order to comprehend and to contemplate the partially hidden message being conveyed. He argues that 'treating *Mabo* as though it were simply the rectification of a mistaken interpretation of the common law of indigenous title begs the essential question: why should Australia follow that law? It has not done so for 200 years.'[4] While conceding the validity of many of the standard arguments in support of the decision (correction of past wrong interpretations of both common law and international law or an application of a basic Rule of Law idea of equality), Webber finds the need to probe deeper into a decision that, according to him 'deserves a more complete explanation of its moral structure, not only because *Mabo* is of profound importance to Australian law, but also because it is of general significance for an understanding of how justice can be achieved across cultures, especially across the indigenous/non-indigenous divide'.[5] The issues involved in the judgment are not merely legal, nor even historical inasmuch as the justices saw fit to reinterpret aspects of Australian history, nor even political, inasmuch as they reflect a changing political climate, but essentially philosophical, dealing with fundamental moral questions.

The value of Webber's work lies partly in the fact that he is a Canadian jurist, not just examining an Australian judgment, but pondering its larger connotations in a comparative setting. He draws on the theoretical work of a Canadian colleague, Gerald Postema, and refers to the evidence presented to a Canadian governmental commission.[6] Both in North America and in Australasia, there is a need for confronting the past, not only in terms of keeping faith with its commitments – thereby 'maintaining consistency, constancy, fairness and respect'[7] – but also in order to reflect on the shadow it casts as it lives on in the present while now judged to be wrong and in need of revision. As a result 'We therefore seek to act in the present in a way that gets us back on the right track, coming to terms with our past, rectifying its effects on the present (to the extent we can), and charting a future course that accords better with what we take to be good in our community's experience.' And at this point Webber succinctly expresses his belief that this 'is the nature of the moral enquiry underlying the recognition of indigenous title in Australia. The jurisprudence in *Mabo*, is, above all, a jurisprudence of regret.'[8]

Focusing on the facts at issue, Webber explains that the key factor was not merely the dispossession of land, the culmination of a struggle for control of property, nor even a battle for political power, but a human issue, including the denial of the very shared humanity of settler and Aborigine –

'The Aborigines' loss of land,' writes Webber 'has a substantial moral charge precisely because of the link between dispossession and the denial of the moral equality of Aborigines, their forcible exclusion from the Australian community, perhaps even the lack of respect for them as human beings. The reason to remedy the wrong is not simply to correct an injustice in the past, but to achieve ... reconciliation ... designed to heal what is now seen to be a profound flaw in the Australian national fabric.'[9] In fact, the taking of the land was facilitated by the prior negative definition of the Aborigines as 'remnants of a previous stage of human evolution, incapable of adaptation to a modern world or even of such civil virtues as gratitude or trustworthiness, that they were, when faced with advanced man, destined to be no more than a pathetic, dying race', living in societies that were 'primitive relics, trapped in the stone age, inevitably to be destroyed through the encounter with more advanced societies'.[10] It was these perceptions that allowed for the legal errors, 'that gave a veneer of legitimacy, or at least inevitability to the taking of indigenous land, and allowed non-indigenous Australians to reconcile the history of forced dispossession and degradation with the conviction that they had built a fair and just society'.[11]

A combination of factors in the post-war world, emerging from the consequences of ideologies of dehumanization, and seeking in all parts of the globe, decolonization, created the circumstances for a changed jurisprudence, particularly within a common law framework of activistic judges.[12]

The *Mabo* decision was given in a climate of concern for what had been done in the past, and at the time discussions were already under way – and have continued – for some sort of reconciliatory proclamation to be made and action to be taken at the appropriate time (for instance, in a rewritten constitution).[13] One suggestion was for a treaty to be signed between the representatives of the Aborigines and of the Australian government, although reservations have been expressed as to the use of the term treaty, since this presupposes some degree of sovereignty for the signatories. Nevertheless, the model is that which was used in North America and New Zealand,[14] where treaties were signed.

Within a year of the *Mabo* decision, Federal legislation, the Native Title Act of 1993, gave detailed expression to the major transformation brought about by the judiciary, including a fairly lengthy preamble outlining the background to, and the reasons for, the Act.[15] It evoked a fairly rapid response as groups of Aborigines made claims to the specially constituted Native Title Tribunal for their rights in land to be recognized – for many a complicated task, given the time that had elapsed.[16] On the other hand, many of the areas involved were in rich, or potentially rich, mining areas, or areas that had other sources of wealth, for example, tourist activities.

Since the *Mabo* decision allowed for legislative appropriation of the land, some of the states also passed land legislation attempting to foreclose possible Aboriginal claims, a legal situation giving rise to possible conflict and judicial challenges.[17] Further conflicts, of a quasi-judicial nature, arose in the course of administrative deliberations over the granting of mining leases in which the governmental authorities were held to a high standard of fiduciary trust. A newspaper report in August, 1996, noted a ruling with extensive implications for mining rights. The article, in *The Australian*,[18] claimed that a ruling against the West Australian Government for failing to negotiate in good faith on a claim for native title, means that 'more than 900 applications for mining leases in the state will have to restart their progress through the complex native title process'. Although this is no more than a journalist's assessment of the legal implications, it is, according to the report, based on a shared reaction to the ruling by 'Tribunal and senior West Australian Government sources [who] showed a rare degree of unanimity ... by concluding the decision would have big implications for mining leases in the State and, by implication, across the nation'.

Most of the other countries that were settler colonies of the British, have embarked on formal, legal programs designed to redress some of the past injustices, including violations of the treaties. It is by deliberate design that the formal process in New Zealand for working out the practical application of a 'jurisprudence of regret' is known as the Waitangi Tribunal, a quasi-judicial body, whose task it is to investigate grievances, provide a detailed report, and make recommendations to the government for possible measures of restitution and reconciliation.[19] It exists parallel to a more judicial body, the Waitangi Land Board, which makes specific allocations in terms of land ownership – and there is even an overlap in the membership of these two bodies.

But it is the Tribunal which is of particular interest, because of its overall impact in New Zealand, and as a possible model. When originally constituted, the Tribunal was seen as being little more than a marginal factor, and in the first few years of its existence, only minimal use was made to activate it. But with the years it has become a prominent force in New Zealand life, especially after amendments to the original legislation expanded its authority. The initial trickle of isolated petitions in the 1970s has become a constant stream of cases, leading in fact to a backlog in its work, given the methodical and thorough manner in which it operates, including an openness to varied evidence, often with visits *in situ* to areas under discussion.

The choice of Waitangi as the name is to evoke memories of a past – totally different from that of Australia – in which a conscious attempt was made to negotiate a *modus vivendi* between two different groups – the indigenous Maoris with their own rich narrative history of how they arrived by boats at the islands that they called (and still call) Aotearoa, and the settlers, with a royal mandate to peacefully seek permission for a British presence. This aspect of the New Zealand past – lacking in Australia – serves today as a point of departure for any reassessment of faults and failings, of any desire to redress the grievances. For it is not the Treaty as such that is the core of tension (except for some radical groups), but the subsequent developments – its disputed meaning, the violation of the treaty through dispossession of land, the many outbreaks of violence and wars of the nineteenth century,[20] even the judicial denial of the Treaty's obligatory nature.[21] But, in the attempt to reconstruct the past, it is to Waitangi that both population groups – indigenous Maori and Pakeha White settlers – have turned. And indicative of this mutual process and the support that most Maoris have accorded it, is the fact that a Maori Judge Durie, has been head of the Tribunal. For many, then, in New Zealand, whatever the original drawbacks in the treaty, or the manipulation and exploitation by the settlers of the original protective provisions on behalf of the Maoris,[22] it is increasingly being seen, in the words of a recent book, as the Magna Carta of the people, guaranteeing rights to all.[23]

The Tribunal cannot make any definitive and binding decisions; it is limited to making recommendations to the government with no more than persuasive power. Over the years the Tribunal has attained a respected position in New Zealand. The lack of obligatory authority has in no way harmed its status – in fact the non-binding nature of its reports has perhaps facilitated the broad range of its discussions and even the procedures with which it works. Thus in attempting to reconstruct the Maori rights, the Tribunal relies extensively on the verbal responses of older people recollecting childhood memories of hunting and fishing, of residence in one area or another, of religious rituals and of respect for sacred sites. The evidence is taken not only in the Tribunal's offices in Wellington, the capital, but the members often travel out to the area of dispute, and allow for the discussion to take place in a traditional manner in traditional meeting places (the Marae).[24] The Reports are also generally of a very distinctive nature, containing not only a presentation of the evidence taken and a careful analysis of its meaning within a legal framework, but are also often replete with apt quotations from literature or folklore, with a historical narrative that may incorporate stories handed down over the generations, and with a warm style of writing that shuns a calculated legal accounting as it reflects the ultimate human issues that are at stake.[25]

In its original form, the Act setting up the Tribunal provided only for an investigation of claims after a certain date, and in general it evoked very little response, but after an amendment extended the mandate of the Tribunal, and allowed it to probe into the more distant past, a wave of claims was presented to it. (It might be noted that the Waitangi Tribunal presented its first Report in 1987, the same year that other legislation made the Maori language one of the two official languages of the country[26] – a no less significant step in righting the wrongs of the past, signifying a recognition of a fundamental aspect of Maori culture).

The first claim had been made over a decade earlier so the investigation at that stage was conducted in a rather leisurely manner. The claim dealt with fishing rights and the Report stressed that 'It is appropriate these initial claims come from Orakei' for, according to the Report,

> The Maori people there were first to promote British settlement following the Treaty of Waitangi. They moved to protect the settlers from threatened attacks on the new town of Auckland, and rallied support for the Crown when New Zealand was on the brink of civil warfare. They led some of the earliest pan-tribal conferences that rank high in Maori history. They developed and through all adversity maintained a policy of respect for law, order and due process. Yet it was this group of Maori people who suffered at the hands of the Crown one of the worst cases of cultural genocide this country has known.[27]

Having presented this succinct summary of their suffering, the Tribunal's Report explains picturesquely that the tribe concerned, Ngati Whatsua,

> have been told often enough why they lost their land. ... The people's dispossession has been rationalized. Ngati Whatsua were conquerors too it has been said, and others have added they were recent immigrants to Auckland, they were a dying race, they wanted to sell. ...
>
> These things Ngati Whatsua have been told, but they were not the tales of Ngati Whatsua. They are the judgments of others, those who have assumed the prior rights of western development and have blamed the results on the inevitability of fate rather than admit to greed. It is time to hear the Ngati Whatsua side of the story, to listen and to understand.[28]

Then in a more matter-of-fact manner, the Tribunal declares categorically that:

> The story of Orakei is not a record of cultural misunderstanding at all. The wrongs that were done were not simply mistakes born of an early ignorance. They were breaches of a Treaty composed by the Europeans themselves. From reports to the House of Commons only shortly before settlement here began, Britain was well aware of the bad effects colonisation had had on native people elsewhere and had resolved that certain mistakes should not be repeated here.
>
> They were, but in New Zealand we were forewarned, the caveat

> of our forebear's concern being formalised in the Treaty of Waitangi. If ignorance of the law is no excuse, is disregard of that treaty any better?[29]

Having spelled out bluntly the overall historical account, the Report describes also the manner in which they ensured that their recounting of history would be a true reflection of what took place – 'In this report we have tried to balance a mass of official opinions and records with the story Ngati Whatsua know. To capture the latter we spent time with the people, shared their meals, listened to them and discussed with them at their Marae ...'.[30] Then follows an accounting of how deep were the roots of this Maori tribe in the region today of Auckland, 'their roots to the land were planted before the Normans invaded Britain'[31] and for this land they were prepared to fight, as indeed they did, for it harbored also the center of their religious life.

Further details of their history indicate the degree to which a formalistic rule of law allowed tribal land to be expropriated from the tribe and reallocated on an individual basis.[32] For a Native Land Court was set up to oversee the procedures of sale – yet the Native Lands Act was, according to the Tribunal, in violation of the Treaty; and by the decision of the Land Court, in recognizing the ownership of only some dozen tribe members (who then stood to benefit from the sale) while denying the rights of several hundred others, 'with the stroke of a pen the majority of a large and compact tribe were disinherited'.[33]

The Tribunal, in terms of a broad mandate, then focused not so much on compensatory payment but considered rather 'what might be done to re-establish Ngati Whatua as a tribe on its ancestral land in keeping with the original tenets of the Treaty of Waitangi'.[34]

The Tribunal then cannot undo all the wrongs of history, but it can – and does – serve as a forum for attentive hearing of the pleas and the plight of the Maoris, for a faithful recording of their memories and perceptions, and for an attempt to lay down a true account of what happened in the hope and expectation of helping with the healing of the wounds and laying a foundation for reconciliation as a basis for a shared and fair future.

In another Report, recognizing the sacred nature of a river, and the dangers of polluting the water's purity, in the course of technological exploitation of the resource, the Tribunal explained how the evidence had been gleaned – and there is much in its simple language to indicate how even such small procedural matters may contribute to the creation of a new understanding between the two peoples, the Maori and the Pakeha (the white settlers), that presently inhabit the country. The Report describes how:

> The Proceedings were held on the Marae [the Meeting Place] because the Tribunal was of the firm opinion that on their home territory the Maori people would be better able to express their

> feelings and make their concerns known. The Tribunal is completely satisfied that by adopting this procedure it was able to reach to the heart of the matter. This would not have been possible had the proceedings been held in a building such as a Courthouse or in proceedings conducted in the same manner as a court hearing.[35]

The method adopted by the Tribunal should not be seen as a minor procedural factor – rather it should be seen as a substantive contribution to evoking a climate which is conducive to mutual understanding across any cultural divide, and as a real and meaningful part of the jurisprudence of regret. The method may well be the measure of the seriousness and sincerity of the Tribunal's work.

Exactly how necessary it is to bridge any cultural gap, or how legalistic approaches and ethnocentric value-systems may affect the dispensing of justice, is well exemplified in an important case (in many respects the equivalent of *Mabo*) that has in recent years, made its way up through the various portals of the Canadian judicial system. The case deals with land claims of two small tribal groups (of several thousand people) in British Columbia for recognition of their ownership of a large tract of land (over 50,000 sq km) as part of their ancestral heritage. Their claims were dismissed by the trial court in a lengthy judgment of almost 400 pages, while a Court of Appeal ruling (of seven judges) did not accept the Aborigines' claim, but overruled much of the legal reasoning of the lone trial judge.[36] The case has much relevance for illuminating the nature of the approach adopted by the Waitangi Tribunal in attempting to go beyond the law – and physically outside of the courtroom – in order to attain as accurate an account of the past as possible, and the degree in which it lives on in the present.

In this particular battle of the Witsuwit'en and Gitskan people, the evidence given by three anthropologists on their behalf was rejected almost *in toto* by the judge, while the anthropologist of the government defendants was accepted. One of the anthropologists who testified in a lengthy written report as well as a witness in court, has responded in a book,[37] which contains her written testimony, as well as her reaction to the judge's severe critique of her evidence (and of that of her two colleagues). She is not alone in her reaction, as a number of other anthropologists have written their own comments, while the judicial analysis of the judge led to much debate in subsequent anthropological literature.[38]

In her book, Antonia Mills refutes the judicial contention that her evidence was not objective, because, as the judge perceived, she had become a partisan advocate for the aboriginal cause, to the extent even of hints at untruths. Indeed it may very well be that it was specifically her success in attaining the trust of the people whom she studied (an essential aspect of good anthropology) that caused the distrust of the judge.

However, far more important – for the purpose of this chapter – than the attitude of Judge McEachern to her presumed biases, is the analysis that Mills herself made of the ethnocentric perceptions of the judge and his inability to fully comprehend the meaning of the evidence being presented. In this case – in direct contrast to the High Court in *Mabo* in Australia decided a year later – there was not the slightest inkling of a jurisprudence of regret; and in direct contrast to the Waitangi Tribunal's work in New Zealand – there was no effort made to understand the narrative history and the present reality of the tribes.

As Mills writes:

> the absence of a written tradition proved to be a major factor in McEachern's decision in *Delgamuukw v. The Queen.* The presence of an oral tradition proved to be a stumbling block *vis-à-vis* McEachern's ability to hear the Gitskan-Witsuwit'en evidence. The Gitskan and Witsuwit'en have rich oral traditions which recount their origins and history; the recital of these traditions is very important for the transmission of rights to territory. ... Therefore it was important for the chiefs to present these traditions in court.
>
> At first the lawyers for the defendants (the province and the federal government) balked at hearing the Kungax [the oral traditions] because they are not written traditions and, hence, could be construed in the Western legal tradition as 'hearsay.' After deliberation, the judge agreed to make an exception in this exceptional trial and to hear testimony from the Gitskan-Witsuwit'en chiefs based on their perception of their history as recounted in their oral tradition.
>
> However, in his Reasons for Judgment, McEachern returns to the position that oral traditions constitute hearsay, which is not admissible as evidence. In his view only written documents constitute history, and, by uncritically accepting early historical accounts as unbiased, McEachern was able to persuade himself ... that prior to White contact and the fur trade the Gitskan-Witsuwit'en were so disorganized as societies that they had no established system of rights to territory.[39]

Mills notes that some of the written evidence – by White officials, for example – was highly suspect, whereas, some of the oral tradition – for instance of a great landslide in the area, recounted in the oral history – was scientifically substantiated by geologists.[40] Furthermore, order was attained, particularly after conflicts – by a ritualized feast, through which they forge their law. At the feast 'when eagle down is distributed the peace is binding and retaliation is stopped'.[41] Hence their phrase 'Eagle down is our law', and hence also the title of Mills's book.

But all this, according to Mills, was lost on the judge – 'The stumbling block seems to be that McEachern is not used to thinking of human society being organized unless it has a tradition of written law … . It is simply wrong to assert, as McEachern does, that societies without a written tradition were, and are, organized solely by "common sense subsistence practices".'[42]

Finally, Mills explains that she can

> appreciate that it is very hard for a judge schooled in British cum Canadian law to understand that societies which were aboriginal without written language, wheeled vehicles, or horses were and are indeed organized, and had and have both culture and law. Certainly, it is a different sort of law. Contrast [the] … statement 'Eagle down is our law' with Western concepts of written civil and customary law. However, we have a duty to try to understand that law, and to respect each First Nation's right to hold it. We cannot respect another culture's law until we understand it.[43]

The decision, as noted, was appealed, with mixed results, at the Court of Appeal. One of the chiefs – Chief Mas Gak – responded to the original trial and decision in sadness – 'sadness because our Elders had trusted their lives and beliefs to a court that showed no respect for the culture of the Gitskan and the Witsuwit'en. Sadness because so many of our people who taught us and gave us the strength to begin and continue this case have died. Sadness because we realize that by the time our dreams have been realized, many more of our Elders will have died without being awarded the respect and justice they deserve.'[44]

However, the question that inevitably arises is whether justice may be achieved within the formalistic framework of an adversial trial. It would seem that only through some non-judicial or quasi-judicial process can meaningful reconciliation be reached and justice be done. At the publication of Mills's book, after much of the trial court's judgment had been overruled without however granting the aboriginal claim, and after a change of government, the prospect arose that such a solution would be sought. As articulated by the government's lawyer before the court:

> This is a matter which must be resolved at the end by the treaty-making process … if there is going to be a just and lasting resolution of this problem, it is imperative that the parties be permitted to have a very direct and relatively free hand in crafting the ultimate outcome and not have solutions imposed on them by anyone.

In any event, the lawyer added, whatever the result, there would be hope for 'the beginning of a new era of relations between Aboriginal People and governments …'.[45]

Indeed, since then, a number of negotiated settlements have provided novel, and basically satisfactory, solutions to long-standing grievances. The model for any such negotiations arising out of initial court procedures was set up some years earlier in another part of Canada, and has been well described by another anthropologist, who also participated as an expert witness in the total process. Harvey Feit describes the need for an integrated approach, combining both judicial litigation and political negotiation, in fact that the best means of ensuring successful negotiation on behalf of aboriginal groups is through linking it with judicious utilization of alternative options.[46] The basic issue was vastly different, dealing not with the possibility of recreating the past, but with affecting the future, in this case, preventing a projected hydroelectric project on lands of the Cree Indians and Inuit in the James Bay area. Yet, the nature of the struggle is similar, and so are the methods. Feit's summary of a basically successful campaign certainly has wider implications that should be noted:

> A land claims agreement, however important it may be, should, I suggest, be seen as but one critical step in the process by which indigenous peoples can redefine their relations to encapsulating societies, and thereby attempt to ensure their own futures. The settlement establishes structures and means for a continuing relationship between the indigenous peoples and the government and it provides the resources with which the indigenous peoples can actively pursue their own interests … . Gaining recognition of aboriginal rights is a dynamic and continuing process in which land battles, political action, legislation, and negotiations must be used and coordinated. Any aboriginal … rights negotiation offers lessons that should be of use for the continuing efforts of all those engaged in seeking recognition of aboriginal rights. The critical evaluation of aboriginal rights agreements will be whether they enhance the ability of indigenous people to determine their own lives and futures, and whether they respond to the new opportunities for achieving those objectives.[47]

It would seem then that the intricate nature of historical land problems are such that only through negotiated settlement or arbitration procedures or a mediatory tribunal can fair outcomes be reached. In the United States, for instance, a special claims commission – a quasi-judicial body – was set up for a limited period of time and with limited success, since, despite the use of the name 'Commission', it seems to have been much more of a court; and as such, it was restricted in its capacity to resolve complicated issues, sometimes because of procedural factors. Before discussing its work, it is of worth to note a complex trial in a British court, which ended unsatisfactorily specifically because the Court, having displayed understanding of an aboriginal claim, came to the conclusion that it had no authority to order the requested compensation, and so recommended an *ex gratia* out-of-court settlement. This 1977 case (*Tito v. Waddell*)[48] has not attracted much attention outside of Britain, but as claimed by Gordon Bennett, is 'perhaps the most celebrated aboriginal litigation of recent years which gave rise to the longest trial in English legal history'.[49]

The case involves a claim made by a group of people, the Banabans, for royalties to which they were entitled for phosphate that had been extracted over a period of more than half a century from a small Pacific island, Ocean Island, that they inhabited, which had come under British control. They argued that, at the time that the phosphate was discovered (and almost simultaneously Britain took control), they had little knowledge of the commercial value of the mineral, and so entered into transactions in which they were exploited. It was the task of British officialdom – so they argued – to look after their interests in terms of a basic fiduciary trust that was owed to the people over whose island they had claimed control. (Parenthetically it should be mentioned that the independent Pacific island state of Nauru, with extensive phosphate holdings (mined by the same phosphate company), was until recently considered one of the richest countries in the world per capita, because of wise and judicious mining of the mineral.)[50] However, it should be noted that the court deals with only a limited aspect of the enormity of the tragedy of the Banabans, a small, powerless group of 2,000 people. Further facts about this affair are described in a fascinating and disturbing account by Martin Silverman, who writes:

> ... about the Banabans, the people of Ocean Island in the Gilbert and Ellice Islands Colony, whose island was put into ships and carried away to be made into fertilizer. Ocean Island would not be habitable after the projected exhaustion of its mineral resources, and the indigenous community was relocated on Rambi in the Fiji Islands, many miles from their Ocean Island home.[51]

The Court of Chancery held that the British government had indeed failed to discharge the obligations of good government, but since these were not legal fiduciary obligations, the court was 'powerless to give the plaintiffs any relief'.[52] Bennett argues that the decision was based on an unfortunate distinction that had been made in earlier cases between a higher trust and a lower trust on the part of a government – only the lower trust, as a formal legal agreement is enforceable in a court of law, whereas the higher trust is only of a desirable situation with no legal implications. Bennett claims that this distinction has no basis in law, and has been artificially constructed 'by the judiciary to save them wherever possible from the unwelcome task of enquiring too closely into the Executive's dealings with its aboriginal population; certainly, the English courts have usually tried to steer clear of the sort of political considerations to which such an enquiry would inevitably give rise'.[53]

Bennett suggests that a proper application of international law would have allowed an equitable decision on behalf of the islanders; but there is a larger legal paradox, since the Court of Chancery (which decided the case) had historically been the court to which citizens would turn precisely in order to attain just results that were not possible by the narrow rule of law as applied in the regular common law courts. In fact, the court was presumed to apply creative principles of equity as an expression of the King's conscience, in order to mete out justice, beyond the narrow dictates of the law.

The distinction between regular common law courts and special equity courts no longer exists, but one might have thought that some memory of its past history might have prompted the English judges to an activist stance that would have enabled them to provide the relief sought – an amount of several million dollars as compensation for decades of exploitation – especially since the people themselves had been forced to leave their island and had been transferred elsewhere as a result of the devastation of the island inflicted by the mining operations (once again, it might be noted how careful the authorities in Nauru have been in monitoring the extraction of phosphate on their island – for ecological and long-term financial reasons). Bennett concludes his analysis by arguing for the need for international law protection for 'indigenous litigants in their own countries'.[54] As discussed earlier, in Chapter 8, dealing with group rights, the international community has not been sufficiently sensitive to the special needs of many tribal communities.

Further, it may well be argued that financial considerations may well impinge on legal analysis – this certainly seems to have been the case in the failure of the Tee-Hit-Ton Indians in Alaska to be given the compensation they sued for, because the Court bluntly announced that the overall pecuniary consequences would be too great. James Falkowski explains that: 'The real reason for the Supreme Court's decision was buried in a footnote. Somehow the government got into evidence the fact that if the Supreme Court gave just compensation for the taking of unrecognized Indian title, estimated pending claims would be worth \$9 billion. This compares to the \$800 million paid for all the land purchased from the Indians in the United States. Really, this was purely an economic decision.'[55]

This case also has larger historical connotations. It was decided a year after the historic *Brown v. Board of Education* decision[56] which is seen as being one of the major benchmark decisions of the Supreme Court in finally depriving segregation policies of judicial and constitutional protection, and was indeed argued about the same time; so it appears that the new judicial approach aimed at redressing the grievances of the black population of the United States was not transposed to the Native American situation.[57] More important, from a practical point of view, the decision was handed down almost a decade after the Indian Claims Commission was set up to provide a recognized and formal forum for investigating and resolving the myriad of complex claims of Indians against the United States government – the Indian Claims Commission.[58] According to John Wunder, the Supreme Court was aware of the impact its decision might have on this quasi-judicial commission, and in particular was intent on spelling out unequivocally that the 5th Amendment protection of property did not apply to Indian tribes (preventing governmental taking without due process of law, which would include fair compensation.)[59]

For a number of reasons the Tee-Hit-Ton Indians (a small group of Alaskans) took their claim directly to the general Court of Claims (not that set up specially for the Indians), and when they lost, lodged an appeal to the Supreme Court. The result was that their failure in the highest Court of the land was to have an impact on the work of the Indian Claims Commission, and quite likely this was the intent of the Justices. According to Wunder, the *Tee-Hit-Ton* case '… left a powerful legacy in Indian law and the relationship of Native Americans to the Bill of Rights. Clearly, the Fifth Amendment did not apply to Indian claims of real property losses, which meant that takings could be sanctified by the Supreme Court without compensation.'[60] This was a clear message to the Indian Court of Claims that compensation to the Indians could almost be regarded as *ex gratia* payments, and that any decisions taken on final appeal to the Supreme Court would be examined without Fifth Amendment protections. 'Thus,' according to Wunder, 'the Tee-Hit-Ton holding and the workings of the Indian Claims Commission eliminated the Fifth Amendment as a possible right available to Native Americans'.[61]

This was not the only handicap that the Native Americans labored under in presenting their claims to the Commission – beyond the difficulties of proving the facts being argued often relating to events in the previous century; favorable decisions were often minimized by the denial of interest on the compensation awarded (dealing with tens of years) or the activation of offsetting arrangements where benefits provided (such as education or medical facilities) would be deducted from the compensation awarded.[62]

The work of the Indian Claims Commission is of major importance in analyzing America's attempt to redress Indian grievances, but, within a comparative context, it would seem that, despite the dedicated work of some of the commissioners, its work was done in an atmosphere devoid of the jurisprudence of regret.

This is all the more unfortunate, because the Indian Claims Commission is in many respects the first concerted attempt to provide a comprehensive solution to the host of claims being made by aboriginal peoples. Yet, it was not set up for the purpose of achieving a rapprochement between the indigenous population and the descendants of the settlers, but merely to seek a more efficient – and possibly less costly – way of achieving closure to the accumulated consequences of past policies. It was set up for a limited period of time, with restrictive resources and a minimal mandate. The idea of a special claims commission was based directly on the larger idea in America of a Court of Claims to handle financial disputes between the Federal Government and private individuals. When a number of Indian groups turned to this legal forum in gradually increasing numbers, it was finally thought desirable to set up a separate body – partly, as noted, to expedite matters, given the need for expert knowledge to determine the intricate and complicated historical and jurisprudential issues being raised.

The core of the problem was, in Harvey Rosenthal's words, the 'Despoliation of the land and its former possessors [which] was inherent in this mad, largely undisciplined, rush to the Pacific. The United States acquired about 443 million acres from 1789 to 1840 for some $31.3 million … and $53.8 million for Indian settlement further west. This cost to the government of about ten cents per acre compared very favorably to the value of $1.25 per acre that was the minimum purchase for lands of the public domain. Sale at this price would have brought the Indians $554 million.'[63] Rosenthal notes that the 'United States drove hard bargains,' but that 'Politically, morally, culturally, legally, and philosophically, America had all the tools and rationalizations it needed to remove the human blocks to its progress.'[64] In fact the bargain driven was even harder than Rosenthal states in the text, for, in a footnote, he adds that 'This figure of $554 million represents a minimum, for the price of public land from 1796 to 1820 was $2/acre and it was not reduced to $1.25 until 1820.'[65]

Rosenthal explains that

> By the 1890s the contest for America was over, and its possession signed, sealed and delivered. But, though the white man was contented with his record in these dealings, the Indian was not … the American right to buy always superseded the Indian right not to sell. Removal was forced removal. The white man's superior power allowed this policy, and *pro forma* use of the *de facto* treaty assuaged his Anglo-Saxon tradition and concern for the legalistic niceties.[66]

Given the formalistic emphasis to create an outward appearance of justness, the very title chosen by Rosenthal in his important portrayal of the work of the Indian Claims Commission, becomes problematic – 'Their Day in Court'. In fact in the end, on the final page,[67] Rosenthal suggests that they had no more than their hour, and are still seeking the remaining 23.

It was because the courts were largely closed to the Indians that the special Commission was set up – as Rosenthal himself notes. Thus, the more comprehensive Court of Claims created for the immediate purpose to allow citizens to file claims against the government was closed to the Indians for many years. The Supreme Court, in *Elk v. Wilkins,*[68] had declared that the Indians were not to be considered citizens – and were thus denied constitutional protections and indirectly barred from the Court of Claims. This decision, handed down in 1884, also contained a dissent by Justice Harlan, the same justice who was to be in lone dissent 12 years later in the infamous *Plessy v. Ferguson* case,[69] which provided the basis for segregation laws. Rosenthal quotes Harlan's brief, blunt summary of the consequences of the adverse decision – 'There is still in this country a despised and rejected class of persons, with no nationality whatever; who born in our territory, owing no allegiance to any foreign power and subject as residents of the States to all the burdens of government, are yet not members of any political community, nor entitled to any of the rights, privileges, or immunities of citizens of the United States.'[70]

Beyond this, the overall status of the Indians was very problematic, since the Allotment Act of 1887 (the Dawes Act, as discussed in an earlier chapter) was aimed at undermining the tribal framework and incorporating the Indians into the 'melting pot' of American society;[71] thus, payments to groups, about to disintegrate, seemed to be a futile gesture. However, the policy was only partly successful – the basis of tribal culture was seriously damaged – but the Indians continued to retain their identity. Finally, in 1924, the Indians were given citizenship on an individual basis,[72] which then became a turning point for a host of claims which were laid before the Court of Claims, although numerous problems remained – varying from proving jurisdiction to methods of calculating the compensation. The slow and lengthy process, the burgeoning backlog, a number of unfair decisions (for example, offsetting payments of compensation because of past benefits) led to the only viable solution – the institution of a special quasi-judicial body, the Indian Claims Commission, while leaving the Court of Claims as the appellate body. The Commission was intended to work intensively for a number of years in order to reach a final settlement of all issues and claims. The time allotted was not sufficient, and extensions were made to accommodate the tremendous pressures until the Commission was finally disbanded in 1978. Pending cases were referred back to the Court of Claims.

Rosenthal summarizes the achievements and disappointments of over three decades of work:

> The process of Indian claims resolution has been a lengthy one and the Indian Claim's Commission was simply an element of that process. Very few of the legal issues of Indian history have progressed to a point where a conclusion can be written to them. The legal

> history of Indian claims is certainly not one of these few ... The Commission did not fulfill its mandate to achieve a truly *final* settlement of ... claims. Drawn as it was and following the procedure it did, finality was impossible.[73]

And then Rosenthal moves on to the core of the problem – that compensation cannot suffice to redress all the grievances, to assuage the pain and resentment. He states that: 'A more innovative type of compensation, land instead of money, would not only have paid on the grievance but eliminated it. That this was never seriously considered is reflected in the early rejection of the commission format and the adoption of that of a claims court narrowly construed to redress property damages with money payments.'[74]

The basic fault, then, was a conceptual one. It is not the specific decisions adverse to the Indians or others only partly favorable that causes the resentment, but the fact that compensation, like the original payments, is no response to the harm inflicted. The issue for the Indians was not just one of land and property, but of culture and pride, of homeland and ecology, not just the diminution of the past, but of the future of tradition.

And for Western society, it is the very continued existence of the tribes that constitutes a problem; for tribal society 'presents a moral threat to settled myths. It keeps the past alive and presents questions for the future.'[75] The time is opportune, suggests Rosenthal, for a deep moral accounting, one which seeks not compensation but some minimum restitution; not resolution of financial matters but reconciliation; not closure of past debts but an openness for future contacts; not a formal judgment recorded by a court but an overall sense of justice done in negotiations.

Since this book adopts the perspective of the common law, it may well be that only in the system of equity – once parallel to the common law as a rival, but later incorporated into the common law as an essential expression of a complete legal system – is it possible to build the necessary framework.[76] Equity, for instance, offered possible answers that had eluded the common law – paradoxically one of the classic expressions of equity was the development of the trust as a means of safeguarding rights of vulnerable people, while one of the special remedies created was that of specific performance (and not just compensation). One doubts that the full framework of equity can be resuscitated in terms of the overall problems of the Indians or other indigenous peoples – but the rationale behind the framework (of seeking just solutions outside of the narrow terms of the law), and the principles that guided it (issues of coming to court with clean hands, and so on) may well serve as a lodestar. This seems to be what was lacking in the Indian Claims Court and to be an integral part of the Waitangi Tribunal in New Zealand. The past cannot be changed or relived – but just as its positive traditions must be respected, so its negative outcomes must be minimized. These are not just legal questions; they involve a moral stance, an honest confrontation, and a societal commitment.

NOTES

1. See, for instance, Yossi Shain and Juan Linz, *Between States: Interim Governments and Democratic Transitions* (Cambridge: Cambridge University Press, 1995). See also Ellen Lutz, 'After the Elections: Compensating Victims of Human Rights Abuses', in E. Lutz, H. Hannum and K. Burke (eds), *New Directions in Human Rights* (Philadelphia: University of Pennsylvania Press, 1989), p. 195.
2. Most controversy centered around legislation, such as the 'due obedience' laws enacted in several countries, which provided a legitimate defense to military, police and security personnel for crimes committed as a result of superior orders given. In general, see special issue of *Law and Social Inquiry*, vol. 20 (1995) – for example, articles by Luc Huyse, 'Justice after Transition: On the Choices Successor Elites Make in Dealing with the Past', p. 51; and Lynn Berat and Yossi Shain, 'Retribution or Truth-Telling in South Africa? Legacies of the Transitional Phase', 20 (1995), p. 163. See also Shain and Berat, 'Evening the Score: Layered Legacies of the Interregnum', *Estudios Interdisciplinarios de America Latina y el Caribe* 4 (1993), p. 57.
3. Jeremy Webber, 'The Jurisprudence of Regret: The Search for Standards of Justice in *Mabo*', *Sydney Law Review* 17 (1995), p. 5.
4. Ibid., p. 5.
5. Ibid., p. 6.
6. Gerald Postema, 'On the Moral Presence of Our Past,' *McGill Law Journal* 36 (1991), p. 1153.
7. Webber, 'Jurisprudence of Regret', p. 10.
8. Ibid., p. 10.
9. Ibid., p. 11.
10. Ibid., p. 13.
11. Ibid., p. 13.
12. See ibid., p. 14, where Webber notes the 'international context marked by increasing opposition to colonialism and racism. That opposition, which Australians have had a significant role in advancing, has caused a re-evaluation of the treatment of indigenous peoples everywhere, has shaken the presumption that there was something unique about Australia that excused dispossession, and has made the frank acceptance of racial inequality disreputable.'
13. In 1991, a preliminary meeting was held to examine the possibility of a new Australian constitution to be promulgated on the 100th anniversary of the present constitution of 1901. This constitution might possibly include a Bill of Rights, as well as a declaration of Australia as a republic within the Commonwealth, an idea that was later strongly supported by the former Labor Prime Minister, Paul Keating. Furthermore, there are ongoing negotiations between representative bodies of the Aborigines and Torres Islanders and governmental authorities to seek tangible and symbolic expressions of reconcilation. One suggestion mooted has been the adoption of the Aborigine flag as the official flag of Australia. Schofield, a columnist of the *Sydney Morning Herald* (28 September 1996, p. 24) suggests that such a gesture 'would be the most public sign of reconciliation and acknowledgment of the original ownership' of Australia. See also legislative action – Council for Aboriginal Reconciliation Act, 1991 (Cth.).
14. It should be remembered that the treaties signed in New Zealand, as in North America, were signed with groups of people not then considered citizens – whereas Aborigines in Australia received citizenship in 1966.
15. The Native Title Act of 1993; the major Federal case since *Mabo* is *Wik Peoples v. Queensland*, (1996) 134 ALR 637; (1996) 187 CLRI.
16. See Carolyn Cerexhe, 'Getting Talked out of Native Title', *Australian Journal of Human Rights* 4 (1997), p. 145.
17. For a general discussion, in comparative perspective, see Rajesh Choudree and Gregory

McIntyre, 'Restitution of Land in Two Jurisdictions: Australia and South Africa', *The South African Law Journal* 114 (1997), p. 187.

18. Nigel Wilson, 'Native Title Ruling Holds Back 900 Mine Hearings', *The Australian,* 8 August 1996, p. 11.
19. See I.H. Kawharu (ed.), *Waitangi: Maori and Pakeha Perspectives of the Treaty of Waitangi* (Auckland: Oxford University Press, 1989).
20. See, for instance, Keith Sinclair, *The Origins of the Maori Wars* (Auckland: Auckland University Press, 1957).
21. See for instance, *Wi Parato v. Bishop of Wellington*, (1877) 3 N.Z. Jur. (NS) 72, S.Ct.; which held that the Treaty of Waitangi was a 'simple nullity.' See discussion above, Chapter 6, 'The Invention of Discovery'.
22. For a good description of the growing sense of frustration on the part of the Maoris, and their political activism, see Andrew Sharp, *Justice and the Maori: Maori Claims in New Zealand Political Argument in the 1980s* (Auckland: Oxford University Press, 1990), especially Chapter 1, 'The Maori Demand Justice 1966–1988'.
23. Paul MacHugh, *The Maori Magna Carta* (Auckland: Auckland University Press, 1991).
24. The Marae was the traditional meeting place for members of a Maori tribe to get together for discussions and to make decisions.
25. See, for instance, H.B. Levine, 'The Cultural Politics of Maori Fishing: An Anthropological Perspective on the First Three Waitangi Tribunal Hearings', *Journal of Polynesian Studies* 96 (1987), p. 421.
26. Maori Language Act, 1987, No. 176, p. 2432: 'Whereas in the Treaty of Waitangi the Crown confirmed and guaranteed to the Maori people, among other things, all their taonga; And whereas the Maori language is one such taonga; the Maori language is hereby declared to be an official language of New Zealand.'
27. Orakei Report – Waitangi Tribunal, 1987, p. 1.
28. Ibid., p. 1.
29. Ibid., p. 1.
30. Ibid., p. 1.
31. Ibid., p. 1.
32. Ibid., p. 2.
33. Ibid., p. 2.
34. Ibid., p. 5.
35. Motuni Report – Waitangi Tribunal, 1983.
36. *Delgamuukw v. The Queen.* Reasons for Judgment, 1991, No. 0843, Smithers Registry.
37. Antonia Mills, *Eagle Down is Our Law: Witsuwit'en Law, Feasts and Land Claims* (Vancouver: UBC Press, 1994).
38. See, for instance, Symposium in Vol. 95 of *BC Studies,* edited by Bruce Miller, 'Anthropology and History in the Courts', and Frank Cassidy (ed.), *Aboriginal Title in British Columbia: Delgamuukw v. The Queen* (Lantzville, BC: Oolictian Books and the Institute for Research on Public Policy, 1992). See also article published before the first judgment – Peter Grant, 'The Gitskan-Witsuwit'en Land Claims: Pushing the Boundaries of the Recognition of the Content of Aboriginal Jurisdiction', *Law and Anthropology* 5 (1990), p. 121.
39. Mills, *Eagle Down is Our Law*, pp. 16-17.
40. See ibid., p. 18. Mills writes that in March 1992, the *National Geographic* 'printed a brief statement, along with a photo of Gitskan chief Lelt … entitled "Science Supports Ancient Legends".' The article describes the work of a geologist and biologist 'who rendered expert opinion reports on behalf of the Gitskan-Witsuwit'en. Their research indicated that a great landslide, recounted in the oral history, occurred about 3,500 years ago.'
41. Ibid., p. 38. It should be noted that the authorities had, over the years, attempted to put an end to this feast-making, so that many feasts were held 'underground.' See discussion of feasts in 'Prologue' of book, pp. 3–33.
42. Ibid., p. 25.
43. Ibid., p. 29.
44. See ibid., p. 186.
45. See ibid., p. 185. In the Foreword to Mills's book, Gitskan chief, Mas Gak (Don Ryan) notes, at pp. xii–xiii, that

while preparing for the Supreme Court of Canada, we have been attempting to get the Province of British Columbia to the treaty table. On Monday, 13 June 1994, the Gitskan/Witsuwit'en and the Province of British Columbia signed a political accord signifying mutual recognition and respect. The accord also called for the adjournment of our court case for one year to allow time for the parties to engage in substantive negotiations. The two parties will move immediately to get the federal government to join in this effort. The Gitskan and Witsuwit'en will return to the Supreme Court of Canada for a legal decision should political negotiations fail. On the other hand we may see the eagle down ceremony. Eagle down gives us optimism. We have kept the eagle down for thousands of years because it works. Eagle down is our law.

46. Harvey Feit, 'Negotiating Recognition of Aboriginal Rights: History, Strategies, and Reactions to the James Bay and Northern Quebec Agreement' in N. Peterson and M. Langton (eds), *Aborigines, Land and Land Rights* (Canberra: Australian Institute of Aboriginal Studies, 1983), p. 416. For further discussion of this affair, see the article by a member of the Cree – Billy Diamond, 'Aboriginal Rights: The James Bay Experience', in Menno Boldt and J. Anthony Long with Leroy Little Bear (eds), *The Quest for Justice: Aboriginal Peoples and Aboriginal Rights* (Toronto: University of Toronto Press, 1985), p. 265. The author argues that the original decision in favor of the Cree, with an order to desist immediately from work on the project, was one of the most important in Canadian legal history, even though a Court of Appeal soon intervened to suspend the injunction (pp. 270–1). However, this judgment of Justice Malouf 'was the key to the ... Agreement ... . The Crees hold today that the Agreement is based on the rights found to exist by Mr. Justice Malouf' (pp. 271–2). For a further Canadian example (this time in Manitoba) of a negotiated settlement, see Leon Mitchell, 'Using Mediation to Resolve Disputes over Aboriginal Rights,' in ibid., p. 286.

    For general discussion of further examples of successful aboriginal negotiations on land claims, see Constance Hunt, 'Aboriginal Decision-Making in Canadian Legal Institutions', *Law and Anthropology* 6 (1991), p. 25. Recent years have seen further far-reaching developments in terms of recognizing native rights and according autonomy status. For an example of what is considered to be 'the first Constitution of a Canadian Indian nation', see Albert Blaustein, 'Self-government for the Aboriginal Peoples of Canada: The Mi'kmaq Nation Starts Constitution-Making', *International Journal on Group Rights* 1 (1993), p. 225.

47. Ibid., p. 433.
48. *Tito v. Waddell*, (1977) 2 W.L.R. 496.
49. Gordon Bennett, *Aboriginal Rights in International Law* (London: Royal Anthropological Institute in association with Survival International, 1978), p. 9.
50. In recent years, Nauru has encountered economic difficulties as its reserves of phosphates dwindle and its investments overseas disappoint, while alternative sources of income are still lacking. Its population is a little over 10,000 people.
51. Martin Silverman, *Disconcerting Issue: Meaning and Struggle in a Resettled Pacific Community* (Chicago: University of Chicago Press, 1971), p. xiii. The distance between the islands was 1,600 miles. Silverman explains that 'their struggle is not only a "political" one in the narrow sense of the term. The Banabans are struggling to make sense out of their past and present and to give direction to their future ... . The notions about phosphate are intimately tied with the notion about land, and this fact informs the present social, political, and economic crisis of Banaban society' (p. 4).

    It should also be noted that in Fiji, the Banabans are considered a separate ethnic group. Their linguistic contacts are not with the Fijians, but with other people speaking the Gilbertese language. The Gilbert and Ellice Islands are now the independent state of Kirabuti. As for the Banabans, they presented a petition to the United Nations Committee on Colonialism, pleading for the independence of Ocean Island. The petition, presented by a Fijian lawyer, A.D. Patel, who is a leading Indian political figure in Fiji, was rejected (p. 333). Appendix 5 of the book (p. 343) provides some of the key factors in the original contract. In the Agreement of 3 May 1900, between the Pacific Islands Company and the King and people of Ocean Island, the company obtained the sole right to work the phosphate deposits for 999 years for a payment of 50 pounds sterling per annum. This aspect is barely hinted at in the judgment in the case of *Tito v. Waddell.* One wonders what might be the results of further judicial action, given the changed political, judicial and legal climate since the early 1970s; where, one may ask, is the jurisprudence of regret that Webber has written about, as discussed earlier on in this chapter? In general, see also H.E. Maude, *Of Islands and Men* (Melbourne: Melbourne University Press, 1968).

52. *Tito v. Waddell*, p. 616. This case may well represent the nadir of judicial activism in England, a total withdrawal from the great tradition of equity considerations and in fact, general common law development. For a recent and thoughtful discussion of the role of common law, in its typical and traditional form, in dealing with difficult and sensitive issues relating to aboriginal claims, see Peter Grose, 'The Indigenous Sovereignty Question and the Australian Response', *Australian Journal of Human Rights* 3 (1996), p. 40, especially at pp. 43–5, subtitled, 'Genius of the Common Law'. Grose argues that because of recent constitutional developments in Australia '... it is now *possible* for Australian case law to allow historical truths to intervene and for the guiding principle of the law to be the pursuit of justice. ...' (p. 45). These comments are readily applicable to other common law jurisdictions, including, of course, the font of the common law, England.
53. See Bennett, *Aboriginal Rights*, pp. 8–10. For a recent excellent discussion of the meaning of fiduciary obligations of the Crown to Aboriginal populations, see Leonard Rotman, *Parallel Paths: Doctrine and the Crown–Native Relationship in Canada* (Toronto: University of Toronto Press, 1996). See especially three cases brought by Native Americans in British Courts in 1982 in response to the new Canadian Constitution Act – *R. v. Secretary of State, ex parte Indian Association of Alberta*, [1982] 2 All E.R. 118 (C.A.); *Manuel v. Attorney General*, (1982) 3 All E.R. 118 (C.A.); *Noltcho v Attorney General*, [1982] 3 All E.R. 786 (Ch.). See also *Guerin v. Rex*, (1985) 13 D.L.R. (4th) 321 (S.C.C.).
54. Bennett, *Aboriginal Rights*, p. 10. The idea of trusteeship was one of the features of international law in the period between the two world wars. The intent there was to provide guidance to non-independent nations on the road to eventual independence. But the fate of minority tribal groups was not brought within the scope of this trusteeship.
55. James Falkowski, *Indian Law/Race Law: A Five-Hundred-Year History* (New York: Praeger, 1992), p. 107. The case discussed is *Tee-Hit-Ton Indians v. United States*, 348 US 272 (1955).
56. *Brown v. Board of Education,* 347 US 483 (1954).
57. The decision in *Brown v. Board of Education* was not, in the opinion of some commentators, as significant as it is often represented – neither in its asserted breakthrough on behalf of race relations, nor in the subsequent developments. For contrasting views, see Austin Sarat (ed.), *Race, Law and Culture: Reflections on Brown v. Board of Education* (New York: Oxford University Press, 1997).
58. See H.D. Rosenthal, *Their Day in Court: A History of the Indian Claims Commission* (New York: Garland Publishing, 1990).
59. John Wunder, *'Retained by the People': A History of American Indians and the Bill of Rights* (New York: Oxford University Press, 1994), pp. 115–18. The relevant parts of the Fifth Amendment read: 'nor shall private property be taken for public use, without just compensation'.
60. Ibid., pp. 117–18.
61. Ibid., p. 118. References to the Fifth Amendment protection are often associated with the constitutional right not to incriminate oneself – 'taking the Fifth Amendment' in popular parlance. But the Fifth Amendment also deals with other issues, including 'the taking' clause dealing with the protection against indiscriminate appropriation of property.
62. See, for instance the judgment in *United States v. Alcea Band of Tillamooks*, 341 US 48 (1950). In this case, the Court of Claims held that the Indians were entitled to $3 million in compensation for lands taken, at their value in 1855, almost a hundred years earlier, to which they added the right to an additional payment on interest of $14 million. On appeal, the Supreme Court denied the right to payment of interest. For the full facts of this case, see earlier decision, *United States v. Alcea Band of Tillamooks*, 329 US 40 (1946).
63. Rosenthal, *Their Day in Court*, p. 4. Similar financial possibilities exist in Australia – based not on land (for which, as noted there is now a Lands Tribunal to adjudicate on title claims) but on claims for welfare payments. These were, for instance, guaranteed to the Aborigines by sec. 70 of the Western Australian Constitution, 1899. However, this section was repealed six years later by ordinary legislation. This legislation has now been successfully challenged in the state Supreme Court, though an appeal was then lodged in the Australian High Court. Sec. 70 provided for 1 per cent of the state's gross annual revenue to be set aside for the welfare and

protection of Aborigines. The cumulated sum in the course of the intervening years is estimated at 540 million Australian dollars. See Ben Mitchell, 'Fresh Court Hope for Aborigines' $540m claim', *The Melbourne Age,* 10 August 1996, p. A6.

64. Rosenthal, ibid., p. 4.
65. Ibid., at footnote 2, p. 36.
66. Ibid., p. 5.
67. Ibid., p. 256.
68. *Elk v. Wilkins*, 112 US 94 (1884).
69. *Plessy v. Ferguson*, 163 US 537 (1896).
70. Rosenthal, *Their Day in Court*, p. 16, quoting from *Elk v. Wilkins.*
71. See discussion of Dawes Allotment Acts in Wilcomb Washburn, *Red Man's Land/White Man's Law: The Past and Present Status of the American Indian* (Norman: University of Oklahoma Press, 1995, 2nd edn), Part 3 – 'The Land', Ch. 6, 'Indian Land and its Allotment', p. 143.
72. Citizenship Act of 1924.
73. Rosenthal, *Their Day in Court*, p. 245. Emphasis in original.
74. Ibid., p. 245.
75. Ibid., p. 257.
76. For the role of equity in seeking just and even original solutions to almost intractable legal (and social) problems, see Richard Wasserstrom, *The Judicial Decision: Toward a Theory of Legal Justification* (Stanford: Stanford University Press, 1961), Chapter 5, 'Equity', p. 84. He writes: 'the concept of an equitable procedure of justification rests very largely upon the notion that the peculiar or unique facts of each case ought to be taken into express account and given primary significance in order to do justice in the particular case' (p. 114).

Beyond the Law

The essential thrust of this book has been to explore the possibility of using ideas of legal pluralism to allow for greater recognition of the customary laws of tribal groups in modern states. The advantages of legal pluralism are by no means limited to the needs of tribal communities, but offer possible solutions to intricate political problems, as well as explanations of existing legal structures. In many respects, for instance, a federal political system requires overlapping legal systems, while future developments in international and regional law are dependent on a willingness to recognize parallel jurisdictions, with shared power, in which the supranational court may have precedence over a national court. Both of these are examples of legal pluralism, even if only rarely is this concept used to describe such developments. But their importance lies in their proof of the viability of concurrent legal systems.

However, whatever the benefits, it cannot be denied that legal pluralism poses problems, and even dangers for a nation-state, just as federal systems, by their recognition of localized power, may have limited viability and the collapse in recent years of the Soviet Union, Czechoslovakia and Yugoslavia are vivid reminders of the fragility that underlies some political frameworks. Nevertheless it is not necessarily the federal structure, in and of itself, that is the causative factor, but the manner in which it is constituted, and the political and social culture in which it is sustained. The demise of the three sovereign states was triggered by many factors, not least the repressive nature of the regimes, the illegality in which some of the republics had been incorporated into the state (most notably in the cases of the Baltic states of the Soviet Union), the exploitation of a one-party state in a federal structure by local politicians, building up a regional power base, grounded in ethnicity (as occurred in Yugoslavia), the resentment caused by the pervasive presence of the central government (particularly in the Soviet Union) and the dominance of one ethnic group over another (as was the situation in Czechoslovakia).[1] Other federal states are in a delicate process of attempting to reassess their prospects of continued coexistence, and if so, under what conditions, for instance the situation of Quebec in Canada, or some states (particularly Kashmir) in India. But even unitary states, with centralized governmental organs and ostensible exclusive sovereignty, may suffer the tensions arising from clashes between different collectives, sometimes on a geographic and ethnic basis, as in the case of Britain (for instance, Northern Ireland) and France (for instance, Corsica), or, in recent years, in terms of geography and economics (as in the case of Italy, where a populist, regional movement in the north is raising the possibility of this richer region breaking away from its poorer neighbors in the south).[2]

In a similar manner, it may be argued that whether or not legal pluralism is divisive or integrative is a consequence not of its acceptance in ideological terms or of its existence in practical terms, but of the manner in which it is exercised and the content of the culture in which it is practiced.

The situation in the United States is of particular interest, since it serves as a model of an ideal federal structure, which not only has subsisted for over 200 years, but in a gradual process of settlement and expansion, has increased its constituent units from the 13 founding states to the 50 that make up its present framework. In many respects the United States is unique in that its federalism is based (for the most part) on a pure geographic basis, with no real ethnic differentiations, with the noted exceptions of the two states that are not part of its contiguous continental land-mass, Alaska and Hawaii, both of which have indigenous populations, different ethnically from the original indigenous populations of the United States, and with political, cultural and legal demands of their own.

Yet, specifically with those original population groups, the so-called Indians, the new nation decided to exclude them from its federal structure, and to enter into a compact that in some ways provided a different model of legal pluralism. Within their assigned areas, the Native Americans were entitled, subject to various restrictions, to maintain their own customary law. It was the federal nature of the United States government that, in practical terms, facilitated such a solution; since the individual states were reluctant to concede parts of their territory, it was the central government which, through treaties, provided the constitutional basis for the legal autonomy of tribes in their reserves, and then attempted, with only limited success, to protect these tribal lands against the inroads often threatened by the states.

Here was, indeed, a form of legal pluralism, but unlike the idea of federalism (in which the United States model was adopted by other countries, most notably for our purpose, by Canada and Australia), not one that has served as a model for others. On the contrary, in Australia the fact that there was no recognition of limited autonomous regions through treaties between the federal government and the various tribes, made it easier for the Australian judiciary to enunciate the doctrine of *terra nullius,* a jurisprudential assertion that would hardly have been tenable if the federal government had been signatories to treaties with the Aborigines.[3]

New Zealand courts might have declared the Treaty of Waitangi a nullity, but they never claimed a doctrine of *terra nullius*.

It was partly because of the Treaties with the Indians that Justice Marshall in the United States was able to define the Indian tribes as domestic, dependent nations (for treaties can only be made between nations, in contrast to contracts).[4] Such a definition was however an anomaly already at the time of its conceptualization, and has become something of an anachronism since. But, as Justice Marshall was well aware, the awkward definition (of a nation that was somehow not independent) reflected the dilemma of an even more awkward reality in the fate of the Indians. In fact, of course, the future was to provide ample evidence that the key word was not 'nation', but 'dependence', a dependence that was fully exploited, both by the individual states and the federal government itself, especially during the critical period of President Jackson's rule,[5] and then, in the post-Civil War years, when the demise of Indian tribes was foreseen and desired, and legislative and executive measures – including the denial and nullification of treaties – were taken to accelerate and guarantee this process.[6] Be that as it may, the reference to domestic dependent nations is still in current use, and the situation of nations having limited control, including governing bodies and courts, is still in existence – what has been called 'the nations within'.[7]

Yet much has changed in the intervening period. Not only has the doctrine of discovery been discredited, and not only is there little still left to be discovered (short of claims on Antarctica or in space, and the relevant international bodies are seeking trans-national solutions to these situations through binding treaties),[8] but the political climate has undergone transformation. The impact of the First World War led to a search to guarantee minority rights of groups, mainly in Europe or at its periphery (for instance, recognition of the rights of the Kurdish people and the concept of trusteeship for nations still on the path to future independence); the impact of the Second World War led to decolonization as a political fact, and the right to self-determination as an integral aspect of international law.[9] Within this transformed context, the inevitable question arises as to what is the status of 'the domestic dependent nations' of the United States, and linked to this, whether that appellation (and its linked status) applies also to other indigenous people in the United States who have different 'ethnic' characteristics – the Inuit of Alaska and the Native Hawaiians. Beyond that loom other questions – of the status, in a twentieth-century world that recognizes self-determination, of other indigenous peoples who were never even defined as domestic dependent nations, but who, a century or two after being 'discovered', are active actors on the domestic stage – and, to an increasing extent, the world stage as well. Some of them, indeed, have fulfilled the promise of self-determination in its utmost modern expression, as independent sovereign nations, recognized as such by the world community, including membership in that forum of sovereign states, the United Nations. These are not necessarily among the best-known examples of indigenous people – states such as Nauru, Western Samoa, the Marshall Islands, the Associated States of Micronesia, Solomon Islands, Kiribati, Vanuatu, Cook Islands, Niue, the Maldives – and some of them have forgone full sovereignty by retaining some link with their former rulers (for example in matters of defense, foreign affairs, judicial matters, or economics).[10]

Most of these countries are in the Pacific, far removed from the major concerns of the world's dominant nations and the world's media. Yet, amidst these sovereign states are similar inhabited islands, still under European control – New Caledonia, French Polynesia – and in the Caribbean, Montseratt, the Virgin Islands and Cayman Islands. If New Hebrides (formerly under joint British and French control) can become the independent state of Vanuatu, why should New Caledonia (under French rule) not become the independent state of Kanuka (as its indigenous people probably wish, but against the interests and will of the local French settlers)? If Western Samoa can become independent (in fact, the first Pacific nation to emerge from its post-war trusteeship status), what is to be the future status of American Samoa? Is it to continue to be part of the United States of America (though not (yet?) a fully fledged state), or do the ethnic links (and even some family links) with its geographic neighbors suggest a union between them, as happened in New Hebrides (and the Cameroons) where the divisive rule of more than one European power did not prevent a later political link-up?[11] And, leading off from this particular issue, arises the question of the future of other territories that have been incorporated into the United States without becoming a state, such as Guam, the Virgin Islands, Northern Mariana Islands. If in these areas some territories are already recognized sovereign states, and others are striving so to be, what are the implications of this political reality for even better-known indigenous peoples – the Maoris of New Zealand, the Aborigines of Australia, the First Nations of Canada, and the Indians of the contiguous Continental United States?

Much, though not all, of the concerns of this book have revolved around these latter groupings. The emphasis has been on the legal implications in the search for a viable and meaningful legal pluralism – but, just as in other cases of legal pluralism, already noted, inevitable political consequences may flow from its recognition. This fact must be acknowledged in any comprehensive study of the legal reality of tribal people and their customary law – and in this chapter attention will be drawn to certain events and processes which claim a solution for the problems of indigenous people in a recognition of their right to self-determination, which must involve also the option of total independence – as has been achieved by the tens of other similar peoples already enumerated. We shall relate to some of these factors, both because of their importance in and of themselves, and because they will help to clarify more fully the nature of the problems of indigeneity, as also the nature of legal pluralism, and perhaps of its value as a preferable option; in fact, far from being a divisive factor, of actually providing a framework that, given modern-day reality as a product of past historical events, provides a means of assuring a political unity while yet guaranteeing the rights of tribal peoples.

But even short of a fully-fledged sovereignty, there are political possibilities that need to be canvassed as they are corollaries of the legal situation. For instance, in recognizing the existence and the authority of tribal courts (one of the three major arms of a modern, organized political structure), a series of political issues inevitably arises – such as whether or not residual power to legislate is retained by the state, or whether or not the customary law is to be applied to non-tribal members. Beyond these legally related issues, are more direct political ones – such as whether or not there should be special representation on a 'communal' electoral roll for the indigenous people (as was accorded the Maoris),[12] or whether there should be special representation in Parliament for special areas,[13] or whether a special consultative assembly should be constituted to represent indigenous people.[14] Furthermore, there may even be a need for creative thinking which may move beyond social and legal pluralism into a political pluralism, that would acknowledge, for instance, different forms of sovereignty, as is being argued at present by a number of writers – for instance, Henry Reynolds has recently argued, in a book entitled *Aboriginal Sovereignty*, for a reassessment of both the legal and political frameworks extant in Australia, with the suggestion of a recognition of three separate nations within one state – European, Aboriginal and Torres Straits Islanders.[15] Given the intention to rewrite the Australian Constitution by the beginning of the next century (which would also be its Centennial), given the present process of reconciliation between Aborigines and other citizens in Australia, and perhaps given the growing support for a declaration of a republic, suggestions such as these may find a readier response in a fluid constitutional situation than in one clearly solidified.[16] Canada, too, while not preparing for any commemorative event, is in the throes of an ongoing political and constitutional crisis that involves French-speaking Quebec no less than increasingly insistent demands from its First Nations.[17] In a strange quirk of fate, the demands of the French population of Quebec for special consideration, because of its differentiated culture and historical roots,[18] finds a ready echo among the population of the First Nations, including those who live in Quebec itself.

Political and legal developments in the near future are also going to be materially affected by a Declaration of the Rights of Indigenous People, which is due to be presented for ratification some time during the present Decade of the Indigenous People that was introduced by the Year of the Indigenous People in 1993. The Working Group responsible for drafting the Declaration, appointed under the auspices of the United Nations, has taken evidence, examined representations made to it, and is in the process of formulating a Draft Resolution to be submitted for approval to the United Nations. Whatever form the draft takes, it will no doubt contain controversial items – not because that is the intent of the draftspeople, but because that is the nature and the complexity of the task that they have been assigned. Any illusions on that score may well have been dispelled when some of the members of the Working Group took part in a Conference of Pacific people[19] on this topic, held in Fiji in September 1996. The Conference, which had been addressed by the Prime Minister of Fiji, himself a member of an indigenous people, had representatives from sovereign states (such as Fiji, Solomon Islands, Western Samoa and Vanuatu) from representatives of indigenous peoples in non-sovereign territories (such as New Caledonia), and from representatives of people in areas that are parts of sovereign states (such as Maoris from Aotearoa-New Zealand, Native Hawaiians and West Papuans, namely that part of the island of Papua and New Guinea that is part of Indonesia).

Parenthetically, it may be noted that the West Papuan people have ethnic links as Melanesians with the rest of Papua New Guinea, and their present connection with Indonesia is a consequence of historical accident that they were ruled by The Netherlands, which also ruled over the various islands of the archipelago that today constitutes Indonesia (with the exception, of course, of East Timor, which had been ruled by Portugal, and which too, is seeking its independence).[20] As far as the political aspects are concerned, it should be noted that on the island of Bougainville, the local people are struggling to break away from Papua New Guinea for their ethnic links are with the Solomon Islands, with which they also form a fairly logical geographic link.[21]

In any event, whatever form the Declaration on the Rights of Indigenous Peoples takes, it seems most doubtful that it will provide an easy and acceptable formula for resolving the problems of New Caledonia and French Polynesia, of West Papua, East Timor, and Bougainville, of Western Samoa and American Samoa, of the Island of Hawaii in the United States and of the Torres Straits Islands in Australia. These are all political problems, but with intricate and inextricable links to the legal situation, and as such require a minimum consideration for a full understanding of customary law.

Furthermore, the recent developments in the Pacific and the future fate of some of its constituent elements, have an importance for international law and for the rights of indigenous peoples that goes way beyond their numbers in terms of population or their overall influence on the world scene. For they serve as possible models – specifically because of their smallness and marginality – for aboriginal groups in other parts of the world, especially (but not only) in North and South America and in the former settler colonies in the Southern hemisphere.

Indeed, in the very week that delegates from these Pacific Islands met in Fiji in the presence of members of the Working Group preparing the draft Resolution, by a strange coincidence another document, this time a finished document, was submitted to the Fijian Parliament by a Commission of three people, which provided a Review of the existing Fijian Constitution;[22] the document of over 700 pages, signaled a moment of hope that would lead to a new constitutional framework that would guarantee the rights of all peoples in Fiji – the slightly less than 50 per cent that were indigenous Fijians, and the almost equally slightly less than 50 per cent that were Indians, the descendants mainly of indentured laborers that had been brought from the Indian subcontinent in the nineteenth century (with the remaining less than 10 per cent being Europeans, Chinese and other Pacific Islanders).

The Constitutional Review Commission had been appointed to write 'finis' to a turbulent period in the history of Fiji, and enable it to regain its stature (real or mythical) as a model of harmonious coexistence between different ethnic groups, and its status as a member of the British Commonwealth, both of them lost as a result of the military coup which took place in 1987, the first military coup in the Pacific, and possibly the first to be carried out on behalf of indigenous people.[23]

The unique nature of the people and society of Fiji serves as a useful touchpoint for understanding some of the deeper underlying currents of indigenous concerns. In fact, a key factor to be noted was that, while the military coup elicited immediate strong, negative responses from the members of the Commonwealth, and in particular from Australia, New Zealand and India, it evoked a warm wave of sympathy and support among some indigenous leaders, particularly those with radical agendas of their own. Thus Andrew Sharp, in his important discussion of *Justice and the Maori*, writes of three leading radical Maoris who, in the wake of the coup,

> visited Fiji and amidst great publicity proclaimed their support for the revolution there in which over half (*sic*) the population (of continental Indian descent) had been stripped of political rights by an aboriginal movement claiming permanent hegemony. Aboriginal inhabitants of Fiji, their rights in place, must override those of subsequent comers. The three looked to the day when the Maori ... would reclaim similar rights of political domination. In the meantime, according to Maori

custom, they would keep the fires burning on the place they claimed and from which they had been forcibly evicted. They would continually remind the interlopers that the land was theirs.[24]

But in Fiji the basic situation was different from that of New Zealand,[25] in fact perhaps unique in the world, a uniqueness that provides an inverse mirror image of the complexities of the issues of indigeneity, of sovereignty, of human rights, of land ownership and possession, of majority and minority status, of democracy and justice.

The paradoxes are rife in any presentation of the situation. Thus,

(a) the dominant role of the indigenous population is noted in that the President of Fiji, to whom the Report was presented, was an indigenous Fijian, who had been Prime Minister up to the 1987 election when he had lost to a coalition consisting mainly of an Indian opposition party and of a newly constituted Labor Party led mainly by indigenous Fijians. The Prime Minister, Rabuka, elected in terms of the 1990 Constitution, was the military officer who had in 1987 led the military coup. The key, perhaps even the sole, reason for the coup, was to retain political power in the hands of the indigenous population, even though the Prime Minister proposed by the winning coalition was an indigenous Fijian himself (but considered to be in the manipulative power of the more dominant Indian politicians).

(b) In this situation, the terminology becomes inverted – (and serves to remind us of the problematics of terminology that we noticed in the opening chapters). The 'Indians' are not the indigenous population, but the 'real' Indians from South-East Asia. Nor, for that matter, are they colonial settlers, but the descendants of indentured laborers who had chosen to stay on after their contract of indentured labor had expired. On the other hand, reference to indigenous Fijians is almost always done without the adjectival addition. In papers and books, use of the word 'Fijian' is generally used in relation to the indigenous population, as in contrast to the Indians, and thus generally does not embrace all citizens or residents of Fiji.

(c) It is the non-indigenous population (mainly the Indians) who have the major complaints as to the land issue – since, nearly all the land was declared, in the middle of the nineteenth century, shortly after cession of the territory to Britain, to be retained in the ownership of the indigenous people.[26] At the same time, in a protective paternalism they were not to become part of the labor force, a decision which led to the need for indentured labor (brought in from India) to work in the newly-planted, extensive, and potentially profitable cane fields.

(d) The Fijians were characterized by an extensive use of chiefly power, concentrated mainly in the villages. To this day the Great Council of Chiefs is a prominent factor of political life in Fiji, with partial representation in the Upper House of the Parliament.

(e) Inasmuch as the ire of the Commonwealth and other democratic countries, at the coup, was focused on the denial of democracy (as the opposition parties had won the most seats by effective use of a coalition electoral pact), the interesting fact emerges that these two parties together, polled actually less than the former governing party (consisting almost entirely of Fijians). This, of course, is a common, and in some countries almost inevitable, consequence of a voting system that is not proportional. With only minor exceptions (generally in times of emergency, such as war or economic depression, when national unity governments are formed), the Prime Minister in Britain is elected on a minority vote (sometimes as low as 40 per cent of those participating),[27] while in presidential elections in the United States, the smallest majority in any state provides all the votes of that state to the winner, with no consideration of the size of the minority. Given such clearly non-democratic situations, some understanding, even if not approval, can be shown to a situation where the parties with a majority in the Parliament had received less votes among the people than their rival. Certainly, contentions as to the collapse of democracy in Fiji should be considered in the light of the very deficiencies of Westminster-style representation.

(f) Within the same framework of democracy as practiced in the British Commonwealth, the role of the Great Council of Chiefs in Fijian politics is surely no greater a diminution of true democracy rooted in the people than the role of the House of Lords in the Mother of all Parliaments. In fact, the chiefs probably have closer contact with the people in the villages than do most of the peers (especially hereditary peers) in the House of Lords with the common citizens of Britain.

(g) The Fijian Parliament had, from its inception, been based on partial communal voting, and a complicated system of cross-voting. The intention was to ensure that indigenous Fijians would not be denied their basic rights; this was an early attempt at ensuring that the indigenous Fijians would not, in a common poll, be squeezed out of political representation.

(h) The proportions between the two population groups was one of almost total parity – both being at approximately 46 per cent of the population. As between these two groups there is no real minority; the minorities are Europeans, Chinese, Rotumans, Banabans.[28]

(i) The question of customary law *per se* for Fijians is not a significant issue; those factors discussed in other chapters are hardly relevant – polygamy (and cannibalism) was eradicated by the church, the land was reserved *ab initio*, there were no practices such as genital mutilation and witchcraft, the traditional religion is no more than a museum relic, having been superseded by Christianity.

(j) The coup was carried out by a military leader (who was third in rank in the army, without consultation with his two superiors, one of whom was out of the country at the time), but with minimum bloodshed – although there was some public violence in the streets; however there had been similar violence preceding, and perhaps precipitating, the coup. The takeover was executed in the precincts of the Parliament itself, where the Prime Minister and members of his Cabinet were marched away by masked soldiers, under the watchful eye of the coup's leader, who then drove off to the home of the Governor-General (himself an indigenous Fijian) to report and to seek his aid in providing legitimacy for the coup.

Contrasting versions and assessments of the coup have been provided in academic writing. In a fascinating and very polemical analysis, Deryck Scarr[29] suggests that there was an inevitability about the post-election events, not just the coup, but also the public demonstrations against the new government by indigenous Fijians, fearful for the future of their heritage, some of them organized in the framework of extremist social movements. Scarr claims that the Indian politicians as well as many of the academicians critical of ethnic politics, had failed to appreciate the deeper underlying nature of Fijian society – whether in the sense of the aspirations and apprehensions of those of indigenous stock who were known as Fijians, or in the sense of the pluralistic nature of the political entity known as Fiji. While Scarr focuses on the political happenings, and provides a detailed description of the events, his work reflects also a positive appraisal of the role of indigenous culture within the western-style democracy that was set up. Thus, for him, the communal representation was an essential accommodation with the reality of Fijian society and politics, as was the need to ensure continued dominant participation of indigenous Fijians in government.

A contrary position is adopted by another Australian academic, Stephanie Lawson, who argues that Fijian politics failed the crucial test of a functioning democracy – a willingness on the part of those in power to hand over to their rivals in the event that such a transfer is the will of the people, as expressed in elections.[30] Beyond that, she sees two fundamental weaknesses in Fijian democracy – the existence of the communal electoral system and the predominance of the chiefly establishment, particularly of those in the eastern part of the largest island, where the capital city of Suva is also situated. As a corollary to these two factors, the pluralism of the electoral system is critically examined, not so much because Lawson sees it as being inherently defective, but because of the empirical manner in which it operated. She writes that

> In the case of Fiji, the plural society model so dominated political consciousness ... that virtually all political developments and activities were inevitably interpreted in the terms set by it ... the plural society syndrome was entrenched to the extent that it undermined ... the institutions that had allowed for succession of government ... there was in Fiji never any real consensus on the legitimacy of constitutional opposition ... .[31]

Thus, the attempt to take into account the needs of the two dominant groups in Fijian society (the indigenous Fijians and the Indians, particularly the former) is seen by Lawson as being a recipe for inevitable failure, whereas for Scarr, any attempt to avoid making full allowance for the unique ethnic nature of the society, is doomed to collapse. Lawson refers critically to Scarr's analysis,[32] while she, in turn, seems to be a typical example of the academicians (local and foreign), who, according to him, failed to understand and appreciate the society underlying the political structure.[33]

Unique as Fiji is in its societal base, far removed as it is in its geographic situation from many other nations, its crisis helps clarify the issue of indigenous culture, politics and law in the modern world. Indeed, part of the problematic situation in Fiji can best be understood in comparative terms. The need for balance between differing population groups is at the essence of most political structures. The very reason for a federal system is based on such considerations. In many situations, this is specifically the task of a Senate or Upper House of Parliament – weighted voting is used in order to give assurances to special population entities. In the United States, the State of Rhode Island (with a population of several hundred thousand and only one seat in the House of Representatives) is given the same two seats in the Senate as New York or California – a blatantly undemocratic device to help make democracy work, by protecting the interests of a numerically weak partner in a federal system. Enormous sums of money are spent in building artificial capitals (Canberra in Australia, Ottawa in Canada) as a moderating influence between the rivals for localized hegemony – Sydney and Melbourne, Toronto and Montreal. A Presidential candidate in the United States generally seeks a vice-presidential partner who will help to balance the ticket in terms of several variables.

In both Australia and Canada, there are enormous tracts of land that were never given full status as states (in Australia) or provinces (in Canada), because of the special nature of these geographic areas – in the extended desert wastes of the Northern territory[34] or the furthermost arctic regions of the Yukon or the Northwest. It is not by coincidence that in these areas, the aboriginal populations were (and in some places still are) a majority. Given the skewed nature of representation in Upper Houses, the implication of granting state status for the Northern Territory in Australia would be to provide this large tract of land with small population and mineral riches, with one-seventh of the representation in the Australian Senate[35] – while, in Canada, local autonomy was recently granted to an area inhabited almost exclusively by indigenous people.[36] Is the provision of communal voting in Fiji, or representation for the chiefs in the Senate, a greater deviation from pure Westminster-style democracy than the denial of statehood or representation in both Houses of Parliament to the citizens in those territories (that are not states), and that have significant numbers (even a majority) of indigenous people?[37]

There are two further points that must be borne in mind before the implications of Fiji's electoral system (and Fiji's coup) is applied to other situations. First, some ten years before the usurpation of power by a military leader in Fiji, there had been also what might well be considered a usurpation of power in Australia – on that occasion by no less a personage than the Governor-General, the Queen's representative, in an honored position of mainly symbolic value. In the course of a deep governmental crisis, where the Prime Minister was in a minority in the Senate, despite a safe majority in the more significant Lower House, he was unable to attain Senate ratification of his budget without which he would be unable to govern beyond a certain date, when no money would be available for everyday governmental operations.[38] The Governor-General suggested to the Prime Minister that he should resign, dissolve Parliament, and call for new elections. When the Prime Minister refused to do this, believing that he could still resolve the crisis, the Governor-General dismissed him, appointed the leader of the Opposition in his stead, on the understanding that immediately afterwards Parliament would be dissolved and a new election held. Prior to taking these actions, the Governor-General had consulted with the Chief Justice as to the constitutionality of his proposed moves, and had been assured that they were within the prerogative powers of his office.

This situation has been extensively examined and debated by Australian scholars, and the majority seem to be of the opinion that both the Governor-General and the Chief Justice acted beyond the powers of their office[39] – and, in that case, of course, the factual situation would be that there was an illegal use of power by the Governor-General, an unconstitutional intervention by the Chief Justice, and an illicit usurpation by the leader of the opposition, who agreed to lead an interim government until the upcoming elections.

While there are obvious differences between removing a Prime Minister from office at the barrel of a gun, and removing him by the stroke of a pen, there are also similarities inasmuch as legitimate authority is used, or rather abused, for ulterior ends. The illegal dismissal of the Prime Minister by the Head of State may be far more elegant and outwardly persuasive, while also far less dramatic or potentially dangerous than his physical removal from the Houses of Parliament, but in terms of unconstitutional usurpation of power, it may be far more serious – especially when evaluated within the parameters of democratic principles, the variable that serves Lawson as criterion for her analysis of Fijian politics. The fact that, prior to the sacking of the Prime Minister, the Governor-General had consulted with the Chief Justice does not by any means serve as a legal cover for his actions, but raises, it would seem, even more serious questions as to the propriety of the process. The function of judges is not to provide prior advice, but to examine actions retroactively (the fact that the Chief Justice had formerly been a member of the opposition party made his action all the more suspect). In fact, there was every likelihood of the Governor-General's action being challenged in court, which would not only make the Chief Justice ineligible to sit in judgment, but the position of those junior to him on the bench, untenable.

Furthermore, even if his advice was correct, which most constitutional experts believe it not to be, the Chief Justice would still have been acting improperly in offering it; the error in his advice, if so it be, only compounds the aberrations of both the leading figures. It should also be noted that the crisis itself arose because of the special representation (in many respects the equivalent of communal representation) given to the states – the Prime Minister was in a minority only in the Senate (with its skewed regional federal representation), but not in the Lower House, with its more direct representation of the people.[40] A leading Australian textbook notes that: 'By dismissing the Labor Party ministry in order to force a dissolution, the Governor-General discarded the ministry based on the popularly elected House of Representatives in favor of a ministry supported by the Senate with its heavy electoral bias. That action must be regarded as conceding substantial political influence to the Senate'[41] (a body based on sectional interests not much different from the sectional interests of communal voting). Further, the author argues that 'the Chief Justice of the High Court should not have accepted [the] invitation to advise [the Governor-General]. Not only could [his] political background be used to attack his impartiality, but his entry into such an intense political controversy could only damage the reputation of the Court' (no less a key pillar of a healthy democracy).[42]

The seriousness of the Governor-General's action may be appreciated in the light of very similar events in another Pacific island state, Vanuatu, also caused by an ongoing political crisis. In the course of a formal Presidential address to Parliament, the President of Vanuatu announced, without any prior consultation with the Prime Minister or members of his cabinet, that he was dissolving Parliament and calling for new elections, and shortly afterwards appointed a new interim Prime Minister and cabinet. The dismissed Prime Minister refused to obey the Presidential decree and held on to his position. The President (together with the new Cabinet Ministers that he had appointed) was then indicted on charges of sedition and conspiracy, found guilty and sentenced to six years in gaol.[43] Parenthetically, it may be noted that the Chief Justice of Vanuatu excused himself from sitting in judgment as he stated that he knew personally all of the accused.

The parallels between the crisis in Australia and Vanuatu are clear – the judicial proceedings in Vanuatu only emphasize how serious were the actions taken in Australia – and whatever the differences between a military coup (as was the case in Fiji) and unconstitutional usurpations by heads of State (as happened in Australia and Vanuatu), all constitute similar erosions of democratic principles.[44]

I mention these factors not to justify the military coup in Fiji, but to place it in its proper constitutional perspective. In fact, other aspects of Lawson's critique of Fiji's political structure should also be evaluated by similar comparative perspective – as when she describes how the chiefly establishments in the east have sought to entrench themselves in power, a further factor fueling her attack on communal politics[45] – but inasmuch as there may be validity in her descriptions and assertions, they amount to no more than the aberrations of many political figures in Europe and North America, and the manner in which they may, for instance, exploit their control of a political party, or their contacts with powerful financial interests or military figures, or even their ethnic background, in a way that undermines democracy.

In any event, in terms of democracy, the two parties in Fiji that constituted the government that was overthrown, had a majority only in the Parliament itself – they had actually polled less votes than the party that they had ousted; this is standard procedure in most Westminster-style political systems, but the logic of this skewed mathematics may well be difficult to fathom, and in fact, the need for a change to some form of proportional representation is a major plank in the British Liberal Party, consistently denied fair representation in Parliament because of the first-past-the-post constituency system.[46] Such a change is exactly what New Zealand executed in 1996, preferring a new proportional, multiparty system to the simple British form of constituencies which had caused several political stalemates.[47] It is possible, in fact, that a proportional representation system, which generally leads to coalition governments, and some form of consociational democracy, would be the system most suitable for Fiji.[48]

In New Zealand itself, a special communal roll for Maoris had long ago been set up, a factor which clearly did not resolve Maori demands, but certainly did not destroy New Zealand's democracy. In fact, at the time of the presentation of the Report on Constitutional Review to the Fijian parliament in 1996, the Parliament in India, now governed by a coalition of formerly dispossessed peoples, including tribal groups, far removed geographically and socially from the former political corridors of power of the Northern establishment and intellectual elite in Delhi and environs, was debating a resolution to reserve a third of the seats in the Parliament for women[49] – a further example, where special considerations of reality and an awareness of historical factors, lead to special voting arrangements, also in a sense the equivalent of communal voter rolls. Furthermore, it is now accepted practice that executive cabinets (where often real political power lies) are formed in terms of adequate balance between different population groups, based on region, religion, gender, ethnicity, age.

As another Australian academic, Ralph Premdas, has noted, there is a need to seek a balance within a properly-functioning political system – going beyond mere power brokering and extending the idea of consociational democracy. He writes of the need for a 'sharing of resources, status and power'.[50] He argues that 'While balance allows the areas of ethnic historical pre-eminence that have evolved in Fiji to be preserved, it does not insist on exclusivity or monopolies in the areas of dominance.'[51] In brief, then

> Balance assumes asymmetrical areas of dominance and sustains equality by requiring reciprocity. However, such exchanges are not imposed by love for another ethnic group but by informed self-interest … . Balance has been an evolving act, constantly needing the nurture of inter-ethnic consultation and cooperation. It is a dynamic concept that points to the need for revisions and adaptations to be made in response to changes in society.[52]

These words were written a year before the coup – but Premdas had even then noted that the very delicacy of balancing could well be undermined 'by chauvinistic ethnic leaders,' seeking hegemony – and he adds even the

> only on the needs of American Samoa … . As the ranking minority member on the House Subcommittee on Native American and Indian Affairs, I am now the leading Democratic spokesman on all national issues affecting the needs of Native Americans, Native Hawaiians and insular areas (Guam, Virgin Islands, Puerto Rico, the Freely Associated States of Micronesia, and American Samoa). This means overseeing $1.2 billion funding of national programs given to Native Americans, including management of Indian lands, claims, all matters regarding relations with the United States government and Indian tribes, Federal trust responsibility, and the sovereignty of American Indians. It includes all matters relating to Native Hawaiians, Micronesia and Antarctica … . American Samoa is fortunate to have a voice in this shared cultural experience … . And the contribution it makes to the needs of the region makes American Samoa much more than a puppet of the United States, as some in the region have suggested … . It is the people who now govern the affairs of Samoa.[100]

Here then is a further anomaly. A territory that is not a state is given representation in the legislature, and that representative is then obliged to oversee the interests of other similarly placed people. While I have suggested that there is room for co-operative endeavors among indigenous people in different parts of the world, this does not involve their representation of each other. The inevitable question arises – why should a Polynesian from American Samoa in the Pacific be charged with the responsibility of representing Native Americans living in the Continental United States – why is the right to special representation granted to some 100,000 Samoans (recently incorporated) but not to a million of the original inhabitants of the American continent? Further questions arise as to whether American Samoa is more linked – in every respect – to the United States, or to its ethnic neighbor, Western Samoa? Furthermore, whether Native Hawaiians, some of whom desire not statehood in the United States, but sovereign independence, will find their interests represented by an American Samoan? Some Native Hawaiians (now only a quarter of the population of their island) have made representations as recently as August 1996, that they prefer the prospects of sovereign independence to statehood in the United States. In a communication dealing with the UN Draft Declaration on the Rights of Indigenous Peoples, they write of their desire for decolonization as 'a people indigenous since time immemorial to our homeland …'. They add: 'we are not indigenous to the US. We are colonized by the US. Therefore, we seek negotiation with the US government … for peaceful decolonization …'[101] They refer to the fact that Hawaii was annexed after military occupation, by unilateral action by Congress. In fact, the document relies on an possibility of 'civil strife that will destroy the society'.[53] The strife broke out, but the society was not destroyed – an interim Constitution was drawn up in 1990, and then an overall review was made, culminating in the aforementioned Report on constitutional review. Among the key recommendations were a continuation of the communal roll, but greatly reduced in numbers (with indigenous Fijians being given 14 seats and Indians 12, while the bulk of the remaining members of Parliament (45 in all) were to be elected by all the voters on a common roll in 3-member constituencies. The Fijians are still protected to a certain extent, but the dominance in the Parliament is intended for those (of whatever ethnic group) who have been elected on a common roll. In addition, it is suggested that the President should be given the power to appoint up to six members of the Senate to represent communities or groups that might otherwise be considered to be under-represented. The Commission also recommended a continuation of the Chiefly Council, and that there should be both a President and a Vice-President, with the former reserved only for indigenous Fijians, and the latter for a member of any other ethnic group.[54]

The Report of the Commission was generally favorably received, but there were also criticisms voiced, including from those who felt that the rights of the indigenous population had been endangered.[55] However, whatever practical measures are adopted arising out of its recommendations, the ultimate message is not of some perfect electoral system or constitutional framework that will serve as a solution for Fiji's unique and complex situation, but an awareness of the fragile nature of heterogeneous societies and of the limitations of social pluralism. Furthermore, there is ample recognition of the need to preserve the rights of both of the major groups. However, the problem is that the rights they wish to preserve are of a differing nature – the Indians focusing on the traditional rights of liberal thought (the first-generation rights dealing with protection for the individual), and the indigenous Fijians on the newer rights presently being formulated (the third generation rights of groups and the protection of their heritage).

There is also a message for those elsewhere who seek a return to the hegemony they lost by conquest or dubious treaties. In Fiji the land of the original inhabitants was not taken away, nor were attempts made to force a loss of identity. But even so a crisis situation was reached. The election and the subsequent coup were the outer manifestations, but the underlying causes lay far deeper, in the fears of many Fijians that they, too, would some day lose their heritage in their own land. The fears may be unfounded, but they are real, not the product of xenophobic hysteria. They have to be related to and not ignored, which is what the constitutional commission appears to have done.

On the larger level, they also indicate the limitations of political solutions, including even of independence, or of guaranteed control of traditional land, because other forces at work (the arrival not of settlers, but indentured laborers, themselves victims of colonial policy) may complicate facile equations. These factors must be taken into consideration in the planning and rhetoric of aboriginal struggle.

Fiji's uniqueness and geographic isolation does not make its experience irrelevant for others. On the one hand, it is one of the examples of small states receiving independence; on the other hand, of the inability (short of draconian measures of wholesale transfers of population) to evade the impact of the past. Above all, it is a reminder that even political independence does not eradicate the fears for the future well-being of the indigenous heritage. A leading Fijian academician, Asesela Ravuvu, has summed up the situation in these somber terms:

> That the coup had taken place demonstrated to those who rely upon the democratic process and equality to protect them and their positions in Fiji, the possibilities and limitation of such ideas in resolving any political or social crisis in a multiracial society like Fiji. Life, freedom and happiness are bound up with changes in economic and social relationships. Before they place their hopes for survival upon the democratic process and on the idea of equality, they must make sure that these ideas will prove adequate to the difficult task of trying to live together harmoniously in a multi-racial society. Unless Fijians predominate socially, economically and politically in their own country, the future looks bleak and racial strife and unhappiness will be exacerbated.[56]

However disturbing such remarks may be in terms of the purest concepts of a liberal democracy, they may also be read as a *cri de cœur*, of the uncertain future that is the lot of indigenous people, whatever their political status. As a statement it serves perhaps as a useful antidote to the calm assurances that spokespeople for traditional liberalism still offer. Speaking a few years later at a special lecture in New Zealand (at the Robb Lectures of 1991), a leading scholar of international law, Ian Brownlie, argued that existing human rights standards are sufficient to safeguard the rights of aboriginal people.[57] His claim is that

> There can be little doubt that the normal application of human rights standards should take care of most of the legitimate concerns of indigenous peoples and if this is correct, then the continuing controversy over the definition of indigenous peoples is not of great significance, apart from the application of certain ILO Conventions, tied to the identification of either 'tribal' peoples or 'indigenous' peoples.[58]

Brownlie argues that most states are reluctant to accept legal responsibility based upon these categorizations since 'States are already bound by norms of general international law to respect the human rights of racial or religious groups,'[59] and in addition, in international law the principle of self-determination may be applied to 'distinctive groups in certain conditions, and these conditions do not make a capacity for self-determination depend on satisfying criteria of tribalism or indigeneity'.[60] Having simplified the issue of indigenous peoples to one of an internal implementation of universalistic human rights or the external grant of independence, having restricted the use of tribalism or indigeneity to the specific references to the updated Declaration of the ILO, Brownlie then goes on to castigate those writers who are 'specialists in human rights, rather than general international law, and specialists in indigenous peoples rather than human rights,' accusing 'some, at least, of these super-specialists' of suffering from 'super-tunnel vision'.[61] He explains that 'It does not seem to occur to them that their subject of special interest belongs to a much wider world of normative development, and ... a world in which the concepts lying to hand have more fluency and political inevitability'.[62] As an example, he refers to the Tibetans, whose struggle, he exclaims, is based not on indigeneity, but on principles of human rights and self-determination.[63]

Speaking in New Zealand, he even warns the Maori against the use of indigeneity; while he is prepared to concede possible benefits that might accrue from maintaining contact with the UN Working Group on Indigenous Populations, he nevertheless has reservations of exclusive attachment to 'the flag of the indigenous peoples'.[64] The world of indigenous people is a heterogeneous one, and so he argues, '... one should be wary about a classification which is so comprehensive, [since] each people has its own history and culture'.[65] There are only limited advantages to be derived from bracketing 'the Maori with the Inuit, the Australian aboriginal, the Central American Indian, or the Solomon Islander (who is independent)'.[66] In particular, the Maoris should not forget the concrete reality of their history, namely the Treaty of Waitangi, with its subsequent legislative offshoots. In any event, even the Treaty must be dealt with carefully as it may lead to discriminatory practices – in favor of the Maori; thus 'from a strictly legal point of view, the approach based upon the concept of indigenous people has the considerable drawback that it represents a claim not of equality but of priority and privilege'.[67]

With all due respect, this approach seems to contain a tunnel-like vision of its own, of unadulterated liberalism, which is oblivious to an emerging reality, well documented not just in textbooks, but in court judgments, which are granting increasing recognition to indigeneity – the book of the speech was published in the very year of the *Mabo* judgment in Australia, with its radical rejection of antiquated jurisprudence, and its first determined attempt to come to grips with specifically aboriginal rights.[68] It was published in the same year also as a worthwhile effort by Augis Fleras and Jean Leonard Elliott to draw strong parallels between the various 'Nations within' and the nature of 'Aboriginal–State relations in Canada, the United States, and New Zealand'.[69] In describing the various successes of recent years, emphasis is placed specifically on the uniqueness of the aboriginal claim, and the need for cross-fertilization of ideas and experiences, of success and failures, of similarities and differences, amongst these various indigenous populations.

The book deals with some of the latest developments, particularly in Canada (the focus of the book), including offering 'aboriginal leaders … full participation as distinct governments for the next round of constitutional talks', the appointment of 'a Royal Commission with a broad mandate and sweeping terms of reference,' whose function it is to review 'Canada's relationships with aboriginal people'[70] and the Agreements already signed on land claims (based on priority and indigeneity). Thus the 'three comprehensive land claims [that] have been settled to date: the James Bay and Northern Quebec Agreement – the first comprehensive agreement in Canada that also specified a set of aboriginal rights to self-governance in the context of a modern nation-state – in 1975; the Northeastern Quebec Agreement … in 1978; and the Inuvialiut Final Agreement in 1984. The latter conferred entitlement to 91,000 sq km of land in the Northwest Territories and Yukon on 2,500 Inuit.'[71] The book also refers to further agreements that seem likely in the near and also more distant future, as Canada embarks on its task of redressing the errors of the past. More than general and valued principles of human rights, whether in international documents or national charters, these achievements are a recognition of aboriginal rights of priority and a resuscitation of pre-modern documents, such as the Royal Proclamation of 1763.[72] Meanwhile the Tibetans, appealing in the name of human rights and self-determination, continue to strive unavailingly for their independence, and continue to suffer the burdens of harsh rule by their conquerors.

The key difference in the fate of the Tibetans (and other national minorities in China) and that of some of Canada's First Nations is not just in the democratic nature of the Canadian government, and its affirmation of human rights (for instance its recent Charter of Human Rights and Freedom, or international law declarations), but in an awareness of the 'rights' of 'priority' and 'privilege',[73] in an acknowledgment that the playing-field is not level, and never has been. Traditional liberalism flourishes in situations of level playing-fields, but is found wanting where the ball rolls smoothly for some, but is an uphill struggle against strong gravitational forces (of military power, economic exploitation, political manipulation, social discrimination) for others. Traditional liberalism, with its emphasis on rights and the individual, has much still to offer the world, but it must also find means of adapting its pristine principles to a present reality that is a product of past discrimination and dispossession.

One of the major dilemmas of the modern age is whether or not, and to what extent, affirmative action and reverse discrimination should be allowed.[74] Within this discourse, individuals jockey for positions as members of groups that were in the past either privileged[75] or disadvantaged[76] – but they seek a solution purely at the personal level. There is some relevance in the affirmative action debate for indigenous groups – but only up to a point; for beyond the individual level, the indigenous groups seek succor at the group level, in land issues, and in the political framework of group rights – not on the basis of language or religion (or ethnicity in its broadest sense), but specifically in terms of indigeneity, of priority and privilege, of tribal culture and customs.

Discussing the situation in New Zealand from a different perspective from that of Brownlie, Sharp writes not of rights, but of justice, and claims that the basic schism between Maori and Pakeha stems from their 'often contradictory conceptions of what justice demands'.[77] In debates over rights and even sovereignty, each group 'proposed to visit their own conception of justice on the other and thus still more systematically than before to render injustice to them'.[78] In fact, Sharp provides a partial answer to Brownlie's assertions – in making his opening gambit justice (and not, for instance, rights), in moving from that stance to an awareness that each side has different concepts of justice (and injustice), it is easier for him to realize that the definition of rights (like the formulation of law) is often an outcome not of philosophical abstraction but political reality.[79]

Perhaps Brownlie was warning against some of the more radical demands that were being made by some Maoris – for Maori sovereignty, either exclusive,[80] or shared. The shared sovereignty fits the pattern of bi-culturalism,[81] but it emerged not from an amorphous concept of rights, but from a reassessment of political reality as it was developing both in New Zealand, and elsewhere. This approach at least offered the prospect of a revival of Maori customary law – as expounded by a leading Maori jurist, Moana Jackson.[82] Picking on the same theme as Sharp, Jackson writes: 'without political authority, justice is a meaningless concept. Without the independent right to define justice and determine how it may be achieved, a people remain trapped in injustice.'[83] According to Jackson, the very everyday living of the Maori is dependent on regaining its political authority, a significant part of which is its own legal authority.[84] He argues that while there is a growing awareness and even acknowledgement among the Pakeha of the injustices of the past (in other words a critique of negative aspects in the past relationships of Maori and Pakeha), there is as yet no similar willingness to appreciate the positive aspects of Maori culture, including its legal aspect. He writes that the

> avoidance of the effects of colonization on the Maori soul, as distinct from its effects on Maori land or resources, prevents an honest appraisal of the role which the imposed law played and plays in the colonizing process. It thus also prevents any real analysis of why that law might now be unable or unfit to deal fairly and appropriately with Maori – the victims of the colonization of which it was a part and which it in turn legitimated.
>
> Yet the symbiotic relationship between imperial law and imperial political power is clear.[85]

Jackson's words need to be heeded if there is to be any real discourse between those who are concerned with protecting the enshrined values of western culture – its democracy and its liberalism, its concerns for equality and human rights – and those who are concerned with not just redressing the wrongs perpetrated by that very western culture and civilization, but of reviving their own traditional values, including those that pertain to political power and legal authority. In his article, Jackson provides a brief definition of some key Maori concepts, dealing with the care people should have for each other, the need for shared and reciprocal relationships, the nature of law as aimed at bringing people together.[86]

As already noted, many western jurists are re-evaluating aspects of conventional liberal thought – arguing for the incorporation of communitarian values.[87] This would entail some transformation in basic jurisprudential principles – but a recognition of an existing communitarian-style jurisprudence as practiced by indigenous people would entail a reconsideration of basic political ideas. For Jackson's concern is not whether or not western law becomes more communitarian, but whether traditional Maori legal principles will be given full recognition – as part not just of a legal pluralism, but in the framework of a shared sovereignty.

From a jurisprudential point of view, this is a total negation of Brownlie's ideas, from the political perspective, a total denial of Lawson's thesis. Yet, if the present attempts at redressing the wrongs of the past are to succeed, if the ongoing search for reconciliation is to bear fruit, then there must be a deep reassessment not just of practices and policies, but also of the underlying principles that sustained them. In earlier chapters, we have dealt with the possibilities of shared sovereignty (systematically presented by a group of Dutch scholars with their own particular agenda),[88] of group rights (as a third-generation right, still not fully recognized),[89] and most pertinently, of course, of legal pluralism (as an outcome of social pluralism). It is necessary also to deal with the implications of liberalism as a basic factor in modern thought, and its impact on resolving the various issues raised in this book.

Brownlie's fear of the consequences of acknowledging rights of priority and of privilege is an example of precisely the limitations of conventional liberalism. The universality of human rights (the essence of his argument) works best in a homogeneous world – but cannot always cope with the diversity of a heterogeneous world. An early attempt in the United States to do so on a partial basis led to disastrous consequences. In 1896, the well-known doctrine of 'separate but equal' was enunciated by the American Supreme Court, in a case that dealt with segregation on trains.[90] As long as the races were given equal facilities, there would, according to the Court, be no violation of constitutional protection of rights, in separating the races. The 'separate but equal' doctrine was nullified after almost 60 years,[91] but not before it had served as the legal basis for harmful, racist legislation and discriminatory practices. The doctrine failed because it ignored a basic fact of social life, that the segregation was desired by the dominant racial group because of its prejudices against those of a different race. On that basis separation was doomed to foster even further the inequality then prevailing.

Yet separation is not in and of itself an illicit demand. Nation-states arise, in fact break away from 'universal' empires, in order to be separate.[92] But the juxtaposition of 'separate' and 'equal' may well be rephrased. Not 'separate but equal' but 'equal but separate.' From a position of equality, peoples may pursue their separate ways, an equality based on respect, understanding, reciprocity – this is the separateness of a viable heterogeneous national culture, of a vital diversified world community; an equality that will give full recognition not just to universal principles of human rights, but also to unique aspects of cultural practices – and will, in some instances, even agonize over the need to reconcile the occasional conflicts that will arise between them.

As between independent, sovereign states, the separation is already in place. Within states is the political problem still awaiting solution. Here, too, an oft-quoted phrase of a judicial precedent may require both rephrasing and reinterpretation. I refer to Justice Marshall's categorization of the Indian tribes as 'domestic, dependent nations'.[93] This definition was, as I have noted, an anomaly in its time; it is an anachronism today – for it was formulated at a time when the Native Americans were not even citizens[94] – lacking such status, was there an alternative to their definition as a nation (except perhaps a term such as tribe, but tribes too cannot sign treaties)? In any event whatever noun is used, the adjectival 'dependent' must be discarded – perhaps an alternative term, 'distinct' – a distinct people – may be used, similar to the terminology suggested in Canada to categorize the unique situation of French-speaking Quebec.[95]

Within that context, all sorts of possibilities exist – of incorporating them within a regular federal system (as already noted); or of setting up special pan-tribal groupings to express their political and judicial distinctiveness. Thus, for instance, Deloria and Lytle, discussing the nations within, revive an earlier proposal of 'a national court to handle Indian matters' as a 'regular part of the federal judiciary'.[96] Their argument is based not just on the distinctive needs of the Indians, but on the similarities of such a specialized judicial forum to other specialized courts. They write:

> We already have various federal courts that deal with specific subject matter, and the justification for each of them is that they require a special knowledge and deal with a special body of law and hence relieve the regular courts from having to deal with technical subjects with which they might not have expertise.
>
> No area of federal law is more complicated or requires more expertise than federal Indian law. Hundreds of treaties, thousands of statutes, and hundreds of thousands of administrative rulings and actions are involved in federal Indian law. Over six hundred separate Indian communities are dependent in some manner on the vagaries of interpretation of federal Indian law, and literally billions of dollars and the lives of over a million people are at stake in Indian cases. There is sufficient justification for such an institution in both the scope of subject matter and in the amount of money presently spent in litigation on Indian matters by the federal and state governments and Indian tribal governments.[97]

The authors note that, in the past, such proposals had not aroused support in the Indian community, because of the fear that the judges appointed to such a court would be antagonistic to the Indians. But, a special court of this nature, based on respect for the Native Americans, and stemming from a concept of equality, including Amerindians themselves among the judges, would be a more attractive proposition.

Similar ideas need to be pursued in the political context – not just of federal representation, but of a separate pan-tribal body with defined functions, either purely as an advisory body or with certain legislative powers, pertinent to the needs of the Native Americans (and tribal and indigenous people in other countries).[98] As it is, at the Congressional level, representation has been given to some 'dependent' nations linked to the United States – island territories in the wide expanses of the Pacific Ocean or in the closer proximity of the Caribbean. The Delegate of American Samoa in Congress, Eni Faleomavaega, has written of his efforts to represent all indigenous people as part of his mandate.[99] In an interesting autobiographical account he writes:

> It is ludicrous to suggest that the office of the Delegate should focus

acknowledgement of the problematics of this action as set out in the Congress Apology Law of 1993. A Joint Resolution of the Senate and the House of Representatives declared:

> The Congress:
> (1) on the occasion of the 100th anniversary of the illegal overthrow of the Kingdom of Hawaii on 17 January 1893, acknowledges the historical significance of this event which resulted in the suppression of the inherent sovereignty of the Native Hawaiian people … .
>
> (3) apologizes to Native Hawaiians on behalf of the people of the United States for the overthrow of the Kingdom of Hawaii…with the participation of agents and citizens of the United States, and the deprivation of the rights of Native Hawaiians to self-determination;
>
> (4) expresses its commitment to acknowledge the ramifications of the overthrow of the Kingdom of Hawaii,. in order to provide a proper foundation for reconciliation between the United States and the Native Hawaiian people … .[102]

I would submit that, in this framework – or in a similar process of reconciliation being sought in Australia, or in terms of the work of the Waitangi Tribunal; or the Agreements being reached in Canada; or even the need to reassess some of the tribal struggles of the past in Africa – the prospects of reconciliation require not merely an apology for past actions (commendable as such developments are), but original thinking that will allow for newer concepts to be formulated and newer frameworks to be conceived, from which will emerge fuller expression of indigenous values, needs and interests – in the political arena (shared sovereignty, special representation) and in judicial fora (legal pluralism and parallel jurisdictions).

NOTES

1. As a good example of the collapse of one of these countries, see Leonard Cohen, *Broken Bonds: The Disintegration of Yugoslavia* (Boulder, CO: Westview Press, 1993). In this book stress is placed on the manipulation of power by regional political leaders.
2. For a few months this party was part of a tri-partite coalition government in 1995.
3. See discussion above, Chapter 6, 'The Invention of Discovery'.
4. See *Cherokee Nation v. Georgia*, 30 US (5 Pet.) 1 (1831) at p. 17.
5. See interesting analysis by Anthony Wallace, *The Long, Bitter Trail: Andrew Jackson and the Indians* (New York: Hill & Wang, 1993).
6. See Vine Deloria, Jr, *Behind the Trail of Broken Treaties: An Indian Declaration of Independence* (New York: Delacorte Press, 1974).
7. Vine Deloria, Jr. and Clifford Lytle, *The Nations Within: The Past and Future of American Indian Sovereignty* (New York: Pantheon Books, 1984).
8. See, for instance, Carl Christol, *Space Law: Past, Present and Future* (Deventer, Netherlands: Kluwer, 1991); and Sir Arthur Watts, *International Law and the Antarctic Treaty System* (Cambridge: Grotius Publications, 1992).

9. See, for instance, Marie Leger (ed.), *Aboriginal Peoples: Toward Self-Government* (Montreal: Black Rose Books, 1994); see especially, Pierre Lepage, 'Indigenous Peoples and the Evolution of International Standards: A Short History', p. 1; and Ted Moses, 'Seeking Justice at the International Level', p. 25.
10. For instance, the Associated States of Micronesia with the United States. For a general discussion of the small independent states in Micronesia, see R. Crocombe and A. Ali (eds), *Politics in Micronesia* (Suva: Institute of Pacific Studies of the University of South Pacific, 1983). For an interesting account of the legal aspects, see Brian Tamanaha, *Understanding Law in Micronesia: An Interpretive Approach to Transplanted Law* (Leiden: E.J. Brill, 1993).
11. See, for instance, Walter Lini *et al.*, *Beyond Pandemonium: From New Hebrides to Vanuatu* (Suva: University of South Pacific).
12. See, for instance, articles by Augie Fleras, 'From Social Control to Political Self-Determination? Maori Seats and the Politics of Separate Maori Representation in New Zealand,' *Canadian Journal of Political Science* 18 (1985), p. 551; and 'Aboriginal Electoral Districts in Canada: Lessons from the New Zealand Experience' in *Report of the Royal Commission on Electoral Reform and Party Financing* 2 (1991).
13. In the United States some island areas have been incorporated but not given status as states, for instance Guam, American Samoa and the Virgin Islands.
14. See, for instance, description of Australia's situation by Peter Hanks, 'Aborigines and Government: The Developing Framework', in P. Hanks and B. Keon-Cohen (eds), *Aborigines and the Law: Essays in Memory of Elizabeth Eggleston* (Sydney: Allen & Unwin, 1984), p. 19.
15. Henry Reynolds, *Aboriginal Sovereignty: Three Nations, One Australia?* (Sydney: Allen & Unwin, 1996).
16. Hanks, 'Aborigines and Government', refers to 'calls for the negotiation and signing of an Aboriginal Treaty, or a Makaratta, between the Australian Government and Australia's Aborigines, to provide a new foundation for the relationship between Europeans and Aborigines' (p. 19).
17. See, for an attempt at a new, overall accord, Michael Behiels (ed.), *The Meech Lake Primer: Conflicting Views of the 1987 Constitutional Accord* (Ottawa: Ottawa University Press, 1989).
18. See the suggestion to refer to Quebec as 'a distinct society' in ibid., Chapter 4, 'Deciphering the Distinct Society Clause', with contrasting viewpoints presented by Ramsay Cook, Stephen Allan Scott, and Jose Woehrling (pp. 137–208).
19. Pacific Workshop on the United Nations Draft Declaration on Indigenous Rights, held in Suva, Fiji, September 1996.
20. On East Timor, see David Robie, *Blood on Their Banner: Nationalist Struggles in the South Pacific* (London: Zed Books, 1989), Chapter 2, 'The Forgotten Wars', p. 41.
21. On Bougainville, see ibid; see also Peter Larmour, with Sue Tarua, *Solomon Island Politics* (Suva, Fiji: University of South Pacific, 1983).
22. The Commission was headed by a New Zealander, Sir Paul Reeves, and its two other members were Dr Brij Lal (an ethnic Indian, seconded for the 15-month period of the Commission's work from the Australian National University, where he is a Senior Fellow in Pacific History) and Tomasi Vakatora (an indigenous Fijian, who had formerly served as a Cabinet Minister). The 700-page report was presented unanimously.
23. For contrasting descriptions and discussions of the coup, see Deryck Scarr, *Fiji, The Politics of Illusion – The Military Coups in Fiji* (Kensington: NSW University Press, 1988); and Stephanie Lawson, *The Failure of Democratic Politics in Fiji* (Oxford: Clarendon Press, 1991).
24. Andrew Sharp, *Justice and the Maori: Maori Claims in New Zealand Political Argument in the 1980s* (Auckland: Oxford University Press, 1990), pp. 10–11. I have added '*sic*' to the quote as almost all accounts of Fiji indicate that the Indians are slightly less than half the population (as are the indigenous Fijians).
25. For an additional radical perspective on the New Zealand situation, see Jane Kelsey, *A Question of Honour?: Labour and the Treaty 1984–1989* (Wellington: Allen & Unwin, 1990). She writes about '… a struggle for economic and social power – one which has its roots in the historical contradiction between the economic, political, legal, social, and cultural systems of the coloniser and the colonised, the oppressor and the oppressed' (p. i from 'Preface').
26. See, for instance, description by Ahmed Ali, 'Fiji – Political Change, 1874–1960' in Brij Lal (ed.), *Politics in Fiji* (Honolulu: University of Hawaii Press, 1986), p. 1. He writes:

> The basic parameters of colonial policy were laid down at the time of cession, especially by Sir Arthur Gordon, the first substantive governor of Fiji (1875–80) .... The most significant aspect of Gordon's stewardship was his attitude towards the Fijian people. He interpreted his duty as a mission to safeguard the rights of the Fijian people from what he deemed the corroding effects of Western penetration .... For him, the Deed of Cession was a covenant wherein was enshrined the doctrine of the paramountcy of Fijian interests.... Gordon took a number of steps to ensure that traditional Fijian society remained undisrupted and maintained its distinct cultural identity. He thus sought to govern them through their traditional rulers .... He instituted the Council of Chiefs which became a regular gathering mainly of chiefs but also of their own people... . To further consolidate traditional Fijian society, Gordon forbade alienation of Fijian land, a practice rampant in pre-Cession days, and reviewed through a Land Claims Commission the validity of earlier sales to non-Fijians (pp. 1–2).

27. This is true even when one of the parties achieves a sweeping victory of seats in Parliament – even then it will generally not receive more than 50 per cent of the votes. Further, nearly half of the Members of Parliament are generally elected by a minority of voters in their constituency, because in practically all constituencies there are several candidates, and a simple majority is sufficient to be declared the victor – there is no second round run-off (as in France, for instance) or transferred votes (as in Australia).
28. The Rotumans are of a separate indigenous ethnicity, and live on the island of Rotuma. The Banabans were transferred to Fiji from an island in what is now Kirabati. See Martin Silverman, *Disconcerting Issue: Meaning and Struggle in a Resettled Pacific Community* (Chicago: University of Chicago Press, 1971); and the discussion of their plight in the previous chapter.
29. Scarr, *The Politics of Illusion*. See, for instance, Chapter 4, 'Talking to Convince Oneself – Politics Since 1970', p. 13.
30. Lawson, *The Failure of Democratic Politics in Fiji*, especially Chapter 1, 'Constitutional Opposition and Democratic Politics', p. 12. For her further critique of democracy in Fiji and other Pacific states, see Stephanie Lawson, *Tradition versus Democracy in the South Pacific: Fiji, Tonga and Western Samoa* (Cambridge: Cambridge University Press, 1996).
31. Lawson, *The Failure of Democratic Politics in Fiji*, p. 40.
32. Ibid., p. 9; she writes:

> Scarr's analysis takes entirely for granted the rhetoric promoted by the leaders and supporters of the coup and virtually endorses the notion that only the Alliance [the party mainly of the indigenous Fijians] and, by implication, the eastern chiefly establishment, had a legitimate right to rule Fiji. Indeed, Scarr goes so far as to assert that the Fiji Indians had no right to expect to be accorded any real political legitimacy in a land which is not theirs (p. 9).

33. Scarr, *The Politics of Illusion*. For instance, he refers to 'University of South Pacific-based ideologues, who were frequently expatriate' and states that 'In parts of the University of the South Pacific ... great and active political attention had lately been paid to the condition of the local Denmark. Fiji was found to be rotten' (in the pre-coup period) (p. 29). Scattered through the book are references to journalists, politicians and academicians from Australia and New Zealand, who failed, according to Scarr, to understand the nature of Fijian society and politics.
34. The Northern Territory of Australia, although not a state, has limited representation in Parliament – one senator and two representatives in the lower house. Admittedly, the territory has a much smaller population base than the other states, but then there is also a large disparity between the populations of the larger states (New South Wales and Victoria) and the smaller ones (Western Australia and Tasmania).

    See Colin Howard, *Australia's Constitution* (Ringwood, Victoria: Penguin Books, 1985). He writes:

> In 1978 the Northern Territory was given a large measure of self-government. This has led to the widespread impression that the Northern Territory has been converted into a state, or at least made equivalent to a state. So far as the constitution is concerned neither proposition is true. Although the Northern Territory now has its own legislature with extensive powers to regulate the internal affairs of the territory ... this change does not make it a state (p. vii).

35. It should also be noted that such an addition of states would also have far-reaching

constitutional implications – for instance, a simple majority of states is required to amend the constitution. With six states, this involves an entrenched majority (4 against 2), but a seventh state would change the ratio to 4 against 3.

36. Also, see historical discussion of recognition of partial independence during the French presence in North America – John Dickinson, 'Native Sovereignty and French Justice in Early Canada,' in J. Phillips, T. Loo and S. Lewthwaite, *Essays in the History of Canadian Law* (Vol. 5) (Toronto: University of Toronto Press, 1994), p. 17. He writes: 'The Iroquois, Algonquin, and Abenaki mission communities were sort of "republics" that functioned independently of French authority. Their inhabitants were not subjects but allies who remained closely tied to the French through commercial and military bonds' (p. 33).
37. It might also be noted that citizenship was given to Aborigines only in the 1960s.
38. More recently, a similar situation arose (of conflicting votes in both houses) in connection with legislation dealing with land rights of Aborigines, leading to a political crisis.
39. It might also be noted that the Governor-General involved, after completing his term of office, retired to exile in Britain, partly because of the unpleasant residue that remained after his actions – which had been taken against the party to which he had once belonged.
40. It had been an accepted convention that, in money bills, the Senate would defer to the lower house, so as to avoid the kind of crisis that had occurred.
41. Peter Hanks, *Australian Constitutional Law* (Sydney: Butterworths, 1994), 5th edn., p. 342.
42. Ibid., p. 341. Hanks also states: 'The Governor-General's intervention was justified by the Governor-General in a series of unargued (and inconsistent) assertions' (p. 342).
43. For a balanced account of the events and the trial, see the Report of the Australian Section of the International Commission of Jurists, written by its observer to the trial, Stuart Littlemore: *Mistake of Law? – The Vanuatu Sedition Trial* (Port Vila, 20 February–7 March 1989).
44. For details of the actions of the Governor-General after the coup in Fiji, and for attempts by the justices to intervene in an effort to deny the coup leaders any legitimacy, as well as the responses of the Great Council of Chiefs, see Scarr, *The Politics of Illusion*, Chapter 19, 'The Governor-General, the World and the Judges', and Chapter 20, 'The Great Council Intervenes'.
45. See Lawson, *The Failure of Democratic Politics in Fiji*, especially Chapter 3, 'Europeans, Fijians, and the Neo-Traditional Order in the Crown Colony System', at sub-sections, 'Chiefly Rule and Neo-Traditional Organization', pp. 93–104, and 'Chiefly Leadership and the Interpretation of Tradition', pp. 104–11.
46. For discussion of the British electoral system, see P. Pulzer, *Political Representation and Elections in Britain* (London: Allen & Unwin, 1967).
47. The New Zealand system was based largely on the German model, involving a combination of party lists with proportional representation, as well as multi-member constituencies. The first elections under the new system were held in October 1996. It is of interest to note the subheading given to the new system in a newspaper article describing how it works – the reference is to a system that 'unfairly punishes the Labour Party [one of the old, established parties – L.S.] and gives privileged status to minor parties' – see Malcolm Mackerras, 'Vote of No Confidence in Electoral System', *Weekend Australian*, 14–15 September 1996, p. 25.
48. Lawson, *The Failure of Democratic Politics in Fiji*, discusses what she terms 'The Consociational Alternative' (pp. 40–4), in terms particularly of the work of Arend Lijphart, a Dutch scholar whose model was based on the political system of the Netherlands, but fails to mention that the system itself is one that is almost the purest form of proportional representation, although she does note that its main characteristic is the formation of coalition government (pp. 41–2), and adds that a further characteristic is 'proportionality as the principal standard of political representation, civil service appointments, and allocation of public funds'. However, having presented this consociational model (without explaining its electoral operation), Lawson dismisses it, since it conflicts with her own underlying assumption of adversarial opposition leading to recurrent changes of power, namely the pure Westminster-style model of elections. She writes:

    > If, as I have argued, the operation of constitutional political opposition within an adversarial framework is a *sine qua non* of democratic politics, its virtual negation by the requirements of the consociational model, especially in terms of elite behaviour, must place the latter at a considerable distance from 'democratic' along the continuum to 'non-democratic' (p. 43).

49. See, for instance, report 'Women MPs in Indian Protest', *Weekend Australian*, 14–15 Sept. 1966, p. 17. The report states, *inter alia*, 'India's legislature broke up in an uproar yesterday after the Government was accused of trying to block a historic Bill reserving a third of parliamentary seats for women.' After describing various attitudes to the proposed legislation, the report concludes with the statement that 'There is only one woman in the [present] 35-member Government and women hold less than 10 per cent of the seats in the 545-seat Lok Sabha [the lower house of parliament].' Some countries in Europe do have similar provisions for minimum representation for women in elected assemblies.
50. Ralph Premdas, 'Ethnic Conflict Management: A Government of National Unity and Some Alternative Proposals', in Brij Lal (ed.), *Politics in Fiji*, p. 134.
51. Ibid., p. 134.
52. Ibid., pp. 134–5.
53. Ibid., p. 135. For a slightly different model, see in ibid., Robert Norton, 'Colonial Fiji: Ethnic Divisions and Elite Conciliation', p. 52. Norton, too, writing a year before the coup, refers to an existing stability based partly on the 'importance of traditional village society for Fijians', yet is aware that 'there is no reason to assume that this stability will endure ...' (p. 69).
54. The Report was tabled in September 1996. It takes account of the fact that, by the proposed electoral system, it is possible that no one party will have a majority, and suggests that the President should facilitate negotiations among the parties to set up a coalition government. In noticing that the President must be an indigenous Fijian (and the vice-President must be of another ethnic community) it should be remembered that some countries limit the range of those who might be Presidents on reasons related to birth – for instance the President of the United States must be born in America. Within a month after the presentation of the Report, a similar rule in Thailand led to the resignation of the Prime Minister, because of a number of allegations against him, including the fact that he had violated the rule limiting holders of this office to 'those born in Thailand'. See Associated Press report by Jiropern Wongpaithoun, 22 Sept. 1996.
55. See, for instance, front-page article, 'Cabinet Split: Constitution Review Commission Report Development', *Fiji's Daily Post*, 11 September, 1966, p. 1. The article notes that 'at least three Cabinet ministers spoke very strongly against it.... They felt that Fijians' political control had been significantly watered down.'
56. Asesela Drekeivaly Ravuvu, *Development or Dependence: The Pattern of Change in a Fijian Village* (Suva, Fiji: University of South Pacific, 1988), p. 195.
57. Ian Brownlie, *Treaties and Indigenous Peoples: The Robb Lectures, 1991* (Oxford: Clarendon Press, 1992).
58. Ibid., p. 62.
59. Ibid., p. 62.
60. Ibid., p. 63.
61. Ibid., p. 63.
62. Ibid., p. 63.
63. Ibid., p. 63.
64. Ibid., p. 72.
65. Ibid., p. 72.
66. Ibid., p. 72.
67. Ibid., p. 73.
68. Admittedly, the *Mabo* judgment was influenced by the norms of international law (for instance the decision of the International Court of Justice in the *Western Sahara* case), but in both cases the fact of indigeneity was most relevant.
69. Augie Fleras and Jean Leonard Elliott, *The 'Nations Within': Aboriginal–State Relations in Canada, the United States, and New Zealand* (Toronto: Oxford University Press, 1992).
70. Fleras and Elliott, *The Nations Within*, p. 116. They note that as late as 1969, a 'White Paper had proposed to abolish separate status' for Indians, yet 'Just over two decades later, aboriginal peoples are solidly entrenched as Canada's first citizens' (p. 118).
71. Ibid., p. 34.
72. See discussion of Proclamation above, Chapter 12, 'Land is Forever'.
73. Sec. 35(1) of the Canadian Constitution Act of 1982 recognizes special aboriginal and treaty rights.

74. See, for instance, discussion by Iris Young, *Justice and the Politics of Difference* (Princeton, NJ: Princeton University Press, 1990), especially Chapter 7, 'Affirmative Action and the Myth of Merit'. She writes that 'affirmative action programs challenge principles of liberal equality more directly than many proponents are willing to admit... . In particular, affirmative action challenges the primacy of a principle of nondiscrimination and the conviction that persons should be treated only as individuals and not as members of groups' (p. 192).
75. See, for instance, *Regents of the University of California v. Bakke*, 438 US 265 (1978).
76. See, for instance, *Brown v. Board of Education*, 347 US 483 (1954).
77. Sharp, *Justice and the Maori*, p. 1.
78. Ibid., p. 1.
79. Sharp, ibid., writes: 'legal justice must obviously come as close as it can to the two peoples' intuitions as to what is just and right. It is not enough that there simply *be* a legal sovereign and that it act. Its politics must be politics of peoples' justice' (p. 25, italics in original).
80. See, for instance, Donna Awatere, *Maori Sovereignty*, Broadsheet published in Auckland, 1984.
81. See Ian McDuff, 'Biculturalism, Partnership and Parallel Systems: The Context of Maori Rights,' in William Twining (ed.), *Issues of Self-Determination* (Aberdeen: Aberdeen University Press, 1991), p. 102.
82. Moana Jackson, 'Justice and Political Power: Reasserting Maori Legal Processes', in K. Hazlehurst (ed.), *Legal Pluralism and the Colonial Legacy: Indigenous Experiences of Justice in Canada, Australia, and New Zealand* (Aldershot: Avebury, 1995), p. 243.
83. Ibid., p. 261.
84. Jackson refers to the Maori concept of rangatiratanga, as a political authority, which 'means ultimately that justice for Maori is more than a discussion about legal pluralism or even about how a Maori legal system might operate parallel to that of the Pakeha. It requires debate about how rangatiratanga might be asserted so that Maori processes can once again control both the dream and the reality of justice itself' (ibid., pp. 261–2).
85. Ibid., pp. 250–1.
86. See ibid., p. 247. See also his description of the inter-relational base of Maori society, pp. 245–6; he writes:

    Maori society was, and still is, built upon three interrelated parts – iwi, hapu and whanau. The interrelationship was kin-based so that a new-born child was immediately part of a kinship collective. The interdependence of the members of the collective was thus inevitable and indissoluble. The individual could not resile from the collective obligations which that relationship imposed. Neither could the community resile from the individual rights which people within the collective gained simply through their community membership.

87. See discussion in, above, Chapter 8, 'The Right to Group Rights'. See also discussion of some Pacific Island States, in which their constitutions refer not just to the rights of citizens, but their duties – in *Victoria University of Wellington Law Review*, Monograph 4, 22 (1992). For instance, Part 2 of the Vanuata Constitution deals with 'Fundamental Duties'. Sec. 7 declares: Every person has the following duties to himself and his descendants and to others:
    a) to respect and to act in the spirit of the Constitution;
    b) to recognize that he can fully develop his abilities and advance his true interests only by active participation in the development of the national community;
    c) to exercise the rights guaranteed or conferred by the Constitution and to use the opportunities made available to him under it to participate fully in the government of the Republic;
    d) to protect the New Hebrides and to safeguard the national health, resources and environment in the interests of the present generation and of future generations;
    e) to work according to his talents in socially useful employment and, if necessary, to create for himself legitimate opportunities for such employment;
    f) to respect the rights and freedoms of others and to cooperate fully with others in the interests of interdependence and solidarity;
    g) to contribute, as required by law, according to his means, to the revenues required for the advancement of the Republic and the attainment of national objectives;
    h) in the case of a parent, to support, assist and educate all his children, legitimate and illegitimate, and in particular to give them a true understanding of their fundamental

rights and duties and of the national objectives and of the culture and customs of the people of the New Hebrides;

i) in the case of a child, to respect his parents.

These duties are non-justiciable but public authorities are required to encourage compliance, as is made clear in the following section – sec. 8 of the Constitution (see pp. 59–60 in Monograph 4 of VUWLR). For general discussion of the constitutional structure of the Pacific Island States, see the article on 'Law and Custom in Melanesia', by A.H. Angelo in the same issue of the journal (entitled 'Lo Bilong Yumi Yet'), who writes 'The constitutions of the Pacific territories typically make specific provision for the accommodation of customary land rights and traditional power structures' (p. 39).

88. See discussion above, Chapter 4, 'Whither the State?'.
89. See discussion above, Chapter 8, 'The Right to Group Rights'.
90. See *Plessy v. Ferguson*, 163 US 537 (1896).
91. See *Brown v. Board of Education*, 347 US 483 (1954).
92. In the context of liberalism, Anthony Smith writes that: 'Liberals have generally taken the view that, as mankind moved from a primitive, tribal stage of social organization towards large-scale industrial societies, the various primordial ties of religion, language, ethnicity and race which divided it would gradually but inexorably lose their hold and disappear … . Ancient customs and traditions would become obsolete …' – see *The Ethnic Revival* (Cambridge: Cambridge University Press, 1981). He adds 'It is, of course, easy to criticise the naive optimism and confidence of the liberal assumptions. Clearly, none of them has stood up well to the facts of historical development in the last century or more. The very economic and industrial trends that they assumed would undermine tribalism and nationalism, have instead tended to reinforce ethnic and national divisions and loyalties' (p. 3).
93. See *Cherokee Nation v. Georgia*.
94. Citizenship was given in 1924. It is of interest to note then in the infamous case of *Scott v. Sanford*, dealing with the rights of Black Americans in the pre-Civil War period, when slavery was still practised in the southern states, Chief Justice Taney commented that, in contrast to the Blacks, who could never get citizenship, Indians could do so by leaving their tribes and adopting a civilized form of life (*Dred Scott v. Sanford*, 60 US (19 How.) 393 (1856), at p. 404).
95. This phrase was used in the Lake Meech Accord, which was however not ratified.
96. Deloria and Lytle, *The 'Nations Within'*, p. 262.
97. Ibid., pp. 262–3.
98. See, for instance, Patrick Maklem, who suggests that 'Canadian Law could … explicitly recognize First Nations governments as a third order of government, on par with their federal and provincial counterparts' – Maklem; 'Distributing Sovereignty: Indian Nations and Equality of Peoples,' *Stanford Law Review* 45 (1993), p. 1311; a suggestion has also been made to give indigenous people direct joint representation at the United Nations.
99. Eni F.H. Faleomavaega, *Navigating the Future: A Samoan Perspective on U.S.–Pacific Relations* (KIN Publishers, in association with the Institute of Pacific Studies, University of South Pacific, Suva and East-West Center, Honolulu, 1995).
100. Ibid., pp. 40–1.
101. See communication of 21 August 1966 by Kekuni Blaisdell, Coordinator Ka Pakaakau to US Consultation with Pacific Indigenous Peoples – distributed at Conference on Indigenous Peoples in Suva, Sept. 1996.
102. See Public Law 103–150 – Joint Resolution of 103rd Congress, 5 January 1993. A similar action was taken by the Governor of Minnesota, declaring 1987 as a 'Year of Reconciliation' between the Dakota tribal communities in the state and the other inhabitants of the State – in commemoration of 125 years since the war against the Dakota people (part of a larger Sioux nation). See Proclamation of Governor Rudy Perpich, 19 December 1986. For an important and fascinating account of the conflict, focusing on the trials for murder of nearly four hundred Dakotans, and the executions of 38 of them, see Carol Chomsky, 'The United States–Dakota War Trials: A Study in Military Injustice', *Stanford Law Review* 43 (1990), p. 13.

PART V: CONCLUSIONS

History in the Making

Much of the essential thrust of my argument in this book is the need to reassess the manner in which western power and western law has ridden roughshod over the rights and dignity, the culture and customs, of indigenous people in all parts of the world. The ideas of multi-culturalism and of legal pluralism offer hope for a new agenda in which dispossessed tribal communities may regain some of what has been lost. In my description of various aspects of customary law, I have often been selective in my choice of examples (taken from a far larger pool of accumulated data), tending to stress the positive aspects, yet I have also not hesitated to deal with the problematics involved in some customary practices. At times I have contrasted these disturbing features with similar manifestations in western law, in the belief that such a comparative perspective is essential in order to ensure, at the least, a minimum degree of objectivity and, perhaps beyond that, the capacity for empathetic understanding of customs that may seem strange, or for relevant appraisals of practices that seem manifestly harmful by what may be considered universalistic standards.

Furthermore, the very redressing of wrongs caused by foreign intervention, such as the taking of land, is to a certain extent, a Sisyphean endeavor, since the complexities are such that not all of the past can be unraveled, on the one hand, while, on the other, a return to traditional practices may give renewed impetus to negative aspects of a society that was, in many instances, a patriarchal gerontocracy. Various of the customs were discriminatory in nature to women and the young – some of them had been incorporated into customary law, specifically because they favored the older male groups. Just as in the modern world law is often oriented to the needs and interests of the dominant class, so in tribal communities, custom may be a reflection not just of continuity with the past, but of a calculated and deliberate intention to entrench powerful social groupings. Tradition, so the argument goes for some critics, does not emerge from the people's will, in the course of their daily interactions, but from the dictates of the powerful, who create and cultivate traditions for their own narrow and sectarian ends.

Tradition, in fact, is invented – so argue Eric Hobsbawm and Terence Ranger and their co-writers in a collection of articles on this theme.[1] From a radical perspective, they describe the many manipulations in the modern western world that accompany a wide range of symbolic and ceremonial expressions, that can be traced not to a distant past, but to the more recent deliberate decisions and actions of those determined to artificially create a spirit of belonging and oneness.

Tribal communities are not immune to such processes. Discussing the situation in Africa, Ranger describes, on the one hand, how the artificial incorporation of European traditions served to consolidate colonial control and to provide a basis for the co-optation of some of the local people into positions of leadership, and, on the other hand, how local customs were exploited (or artificially created) to further the ends of the white settlers and the local leaders.[2]

As for the first aspect, Ranger describes how British tradition was transplanted – for instance, schools set up on the model of British education, or royal ceremonies celebrated in the colonies. Specifically, he writes of how the settlers 'drew upon European-invented traditions both to define and to justify their rules, and also to provide models of subservience into which it was sometimes possible to draw Africans'.[3] Thus, according to Ranger, 'The invented traditions of nineteenth-century Europeans had been introduced into Africa to allow Europeans and certain Africans to combine for "modernizing" ends.'[4]

As for the indigenous aspect, Ranger succinctly spells out the exploitation of custom for narrow particularistic ends:

> Codified and reified custom was manipulated by … vested interests as a means of asserting or increasing control … .
>
> Elders tended to appeal to 'tradition' in order to defend their dominance of the rural means of production against the challenge by the young. Men tended to appeal to 'tradition' in order to ensure that the increasing role which women played in production in the rural areas did not result in any diminution of male control over women as economic assets. Paramount chiefs and ruling aristocracies in politics which included numbers of ethnic and social groupings appealed to 'tradition' in order to maintain or extend their control over their subjects. Indigenous populations appealed to 'tradition' in order to ensure that the migrants who settled amongst them did not achieve political or economic rights.[5]

These are serious assertions that must be addressed. In a changing western world, where feminist concerns are having an increasing impact on people's perceptions of social reality, nothing would be more harmful and regressive than to inflict on women a subservience to men, and also on the young, a subservience to the older generation, at a time when western societies are slowly releasing them from many of the constraints that law (and for that matter, also custom) have imposed on them for so long. But even if the overly patriarchal nature of all, or most, tribal societies could be shown (and this contention is far more disputable than Ranger's tone would suggest), this would not of necessity lead to a denial of the role of tribe in the modern world, or the place of custom within the tribe. On the contrary, the prospects of avoiding the negative aspects of the past are always at hand, and must be considered. After all, democracy in modern societies was not discarded in its formative stage because it denied women the franchise until this century, and only even more recently lowered the voting age to allow 18-year-olds (subject to possible army conscription), to take part in elections.

As has been pointed out in the opening chapters, the essence of custom is its flexibility, and a static nature was attributed to it by westerners, partly because of the fictitious assumptions of the common law, based on English history, that courts could only grant recognition to a custom if it had been in immemorial use.[6] Yet it was part of the glory of the common law that it knew how to relate to this 'fictitious' statement for what it was – a legal fiction which never interfered with the capacity of creative judges to incorporate customs into the constantly developing law, and to adapt them, if necessary, to the need for just decisions – and beyond that, the capacity to change by a judicious use of equity principles in a specially constituted court, the Chancery Court.[7] In essence, though, equity law was formerly considered as separate from the common law, and as giving expression not to common customs of the people, but specifically, to the conscience of the King in situations where the common law solution was basically inequitable. However, the total legal system can only be understood in the joint context, and indeed, in the course of time, by legislation of 1873, these two separate legal systems that had existed concurrently, and often in intense rivalry for hundreds of years, were combined into one unified legal system.[8]

Thus, for instance, when the common law failed to present a palatable solution, the possibility always existed of turning to equity; over time, the decisions made in equity were molded together (just as had happened with the common law) into acknowledged precedents and recognized as having legal effect. Of particular interest is the development of the law relating to trusts,[9] as one of the singular characteristics of English law (in contrast to the civil law jurisdiction of Continental Europe) – one of the underlying causes of this development was the formulation of special frameworks for allowing women to inherit (through the use of trust procedures), when such rights were denied them by the common law.[10] Of course, the overall inferior status of women remained, including limitations on their rights to property (together with many other limitations) but, relative to general societal discriminations, a legal means was found to ensure women access to property bequeathed or transferred to them, through the adjunct legal system of equity. As explained in a leading textbook on equity,

> The position of a married woman at common law was a harsh one. She and her husband were deemed to be one person in law, and that person was the husband. She could neither acquire nor hold property independently of him.[11]

And so equity created, through judicial decisions of the court of Chancery, rules which protected the woman's rights to property, which came into her possession – for instance equity spoke of the 'separate estate', which was protected from sale or arbitrary use by the husband.

On the assumption that there are indeed many similarities between customary law and common law (with its emphasis on judicial precedent, including thereby also the recognition of custom in a far more extensive manner than was done in systems based on comprehensive codification – as in most of Continental Europe), then the question inevitably arises whether similar additions and adaptations can be incorporated into tribal legal systems, where they do not exist, or if they do exist, whether they can be emphasized so as to ensure continual change in the customs, including the enhancement of the possibility of refuting some of the critiques being launched against what are considered undesirable customs. In other words, while historically the common law was intrinsically flexible and adaptable to change, when it exhausted its creative potentiality, a means was found (by instituting a parallel legal system of equity) for ensuring further positive developments (I am ignoring, for the moment, that there were also additional factors involved in the creation of equity, such as the desire of the monarchy to recapture some of its power in the judicial sphere, that it had lost to an increasingly independent judiciary).[12]

The present period is an appropriate time to deal with such potential developments, for the resurgence of tribal pride in Australia, New Zealand and North America is taking place at the same time that radical arguments, including feminist ones, have become an integral part of general jurisprudential debate. Some very strong arguments have been made by feminist writers against customary law, because of the inferior status accorded women.[13] However, many similar criticisms have been made against modern law and the habitual practices of modern society. To a certain extent, modern law and modern society have been responding to the challenges posed by these critiques.[14] The question arises whether customary law, exposed to similar challenges, can also become responsive to them. Indeed, it is possible that the very fact of years of neglect of tribal law (so true in many places, notably Australia[15] and New Zealand) may have sharpened the need for more rapid change than was known in the past. The stagnation in its development, because of neglect, may allow for creatively selective application in the dimensions of the revival, including the possibility of updating in areas where criticism is persuasive and pertinent.

In such a process, the developments in South Africa are of particular interest and importance – first, because of the revolutionary change that it has undergone in recent years; second, because the very idea of a tribal entity and of personal tribal identity became anathema during the apartheid years when the regime, for its own purposes, accentuated tribal membership, including the setting up of tribal homelands, at the expense of recognition of a larger nation-wide affinity.[16] In the breakdown of apartheid and the creation of a new political system, including a written constitution, with a bill of rights, the society was perforce drawn into debate as to the place of tribe in the nation and custom in the law. Is there room in a newly constituted South Africa, shorn of its racist antecedents, for recognition of customary law, and if so, how is this compatible with the liberal principles of individual autonomy, human rights, gender equality and personal freedom?[17]

These issues have arisen before in many African countries, and different solutions have been arrived at. The South African situation is slightly different, because of the importance that the apartheid regime attached to tribal differentiation, this in an effort to undermine the cohesion of the anti-apartheid liberation movement, and as a justification for its ill-fated and short-lived program of separate homelands for the different tribal groups. During the years of struggle against apartheid, indications of tribal identity were often seen as being an affirmation of apartheid policies – the positive overtones of ideas of multiculturalism were not part of the political discourse of the South African resistance movement. However, in the post-apartheid era, there is an awareness of such multiculturalism,[18] ranging from the official recognition of 11 languages to the federal structure of the state which, while not based at all on tribal considerations, follows in part, for simple geographical reasons, the contour of tribal presence, and one province is known by the joint name of Natal-Kwazulu, the area which has the major, and almost exclusive, concentration of members of the Zulu people.

This softening of attitudes to the possibility of tribal differentiation, provides a unique opportunity for the reconsideration of the role of tribe to be undertaken in a spirit that will perhaps give tangible expression to the musings many years ago, of Tom Mboya, as discussed in the opening section of the book,[19] for accentuating the positive in tribalism and minimizing (or eradicating) the negative. In a climate of change and goodwill, of understanding and reaching-out, it should be possible (if by no means an easy task) to restructure the nature of tribal identity in the light of the new reality, which involves not only the demise of the apartheid regime, but also the active and prominent role played by many women – in politics, administration, education, business and culture.[20] It is possible that many of these women have no desire themselves to be linked to their tribal background, but that is not likely to be the general situation in the rural areas, where less sophisticated women are still very much living within a basically community framework, where their identity as Xhosa or Zulu, Tswana or Sotho, or other of the smaller groups, is in terms of daily life and ceremonial ritual, family and neighborhood frameworks, agricultural and commercial activities, no less real than their nationality as South Africans, with its recently acquired citizenship rights, and the legislation promulgated by its democratically elected parliament. For many of them, the local custom may be far more real and relevant than the official law of the state.[21]

Feminists, keen on ensuring the rights of women, may be well advised to consider a creative revamping of the woman's role in the tribe rather than an outright rejection of the customary law. One of the possibilities is, of course, a return to the 'repugnancy' provisions – that a custom will be recognized, subject to it not being in conflict with constitutional provisions.[22] But the situation contains many subtleties that cannot easily be encompassed within the legal formula of a constitutional document.

The role of women in South Africa in general, has been discussed in a number of recent publications. However, although reference is often made to a woman's position in customary law, such comments are often made *en passant*, and not in the form of detailed analyses. One of the better more recent examples is the 1994 issue of the legal annual, *Acta Juridica*, published simultaneously as a book, entitled *Gender and the New South African Legal Order.*[23] Although there is no article dealing specifically with women and customary law, reference is made to this issue on several occasions. In an 'Introduction' to the book, Felicity Kaganas and Christina Murray argue that, while the law generally does not cater to women's needs, 'For African women, there is an additional source of disadvantage under the law: customary law openly discriminates against them.'[24] They regret the general neglect of the topic of women in customary law (although they note Jack Simons's important survey written already in 1968).[25] Kaganas and Murray argue that:

> Change in the context of customary law is inhibited by the strong allegiance to tradition still prevalent among South Africans. In addition, South Africa's history renders prospective law reformers open to charges of cultural imperialism … . The prospect of change is made even less attractive by the fear that reforms to benefit women will undermine the very foundations of African society and bring the whole edifice crashing down.[26]

One of the other contributors to the book, Iain Currie, has suggested examining the future of customary law in the specific context of a practice considered generally to be an indication of inferiority, that of bridewealth or *Lobolo.*[27] He quotes from a 1981 study to warn against 'the potentially disastrous consequences of any interference in the institution of bridewealth, however well-intentioned it may be. It may be that the battle fought on behalf of one marginalized and vulnerable group of people, women – subject to customary law – may be won at the expense of another equally marginalized and vulnerable group.'[28] (His reference here is to elderly men, themselves in danger of being shunted off into the margins of the society).

In any event, in dealing with tradition, particularly in the context of women's rights, attention must be paid to Simons's admonition that part of the responsibility for the inferior status of women as generally understood, can be linked to both the impact of colonial conquest, and the interpretations given to tribal conduct by settlers and colonial administrators.[29] His opening statement is 'White South Africans of the last century resented the tribesman's way of life. They complained that he had too much land, leisure and sex.'[30] Particularly vehement attacks were launched against such phenomena as polygyny, lobola (bride-price) or exploitation of women at work. However, according to Simons,

> There is little substance to this indictment … . The pity shown on women was largely misplaced. They did not constitute a separate class, were not oppressed, and were not segregated behind a tribal kind of pariah … . All but a few Whites failed to gain an adequate insight into the African culture, or to make a fair assessment of its intrinsic qualities … . Identifying their quest for land, labour, trade and security, with a civilizing mission, they launched a crusade against tribalism under the banner of Christianity, feminine emancipation, and progress.[31]

In this comprehensive description of women's status in South Africa, Simons links some of these problems with overall oppressive measures in apartheid South Africa. Writing in the late 1960s, he concludes on an optimistic note – according to him, whereas in Europe general ideas of equality and democracy were current, while yet women were kept in a subordinate position, and whereas in much of Africa and Asia, an opposite situation prevails – women were given rights, for instance the franchise, before the incorporation of egalitarian and democratic ideas – he suggests that 'It may well be that feminine emancipation and political emancipation will go hand in hand in South Africa.'[32]

These possibilities are carefully examined almost thirty years later in a changed and changing climate of opinion by Tom Bennett,[33] as he analyzes the Interim Constitution set up in 1993. While basically supportive of most of the trends and the details in that Constitution, he is wary of placing too much reliance on written documents, including theoretically commendable bills of rights, that are not sufficiently attuned to everyday reality. In general terms he explains that

> An absence of rules and an emphasis on tradition do not necessarily mean that the individual will suffer mistreatment or abuse. Several writers ... contend that Africa has its own indigenous doctrine of rights, one which European colonists overlooked because they were too blinkered by a sense of superiority to realize that Africans too could evolve ethical systems.[34]

From the perspective of the legal system, the equivalents of such key western legal ideas as the rule of law, due process or equal protection of the law, may be found embedded inherently in the nature of the African judicial process; thus,

> African writers argue that whenever decision-making is consensual and society is not geared to profit-making ... a society has the makings of a system of ethics which is every bit as able as western law to serve the goal of human dignity,

while

> in an African tribunal the individual probably had a better degree of procedural fairness than in a western court, for African courts sought a reconciliation of the parties approved by the community. Because reconciliation required a slow but thorough examination of any grievances, litigants had every opportunity to voice their complaints in a sympathetic environment.[35]

Bennett describes the discussions about the role of the customary law in the new political structure of South Africa. Custom was largely ignored until, during the negotiations over the constitution's formulation, a group of chiefs suddenly became involved, and in return for their political support for the new political framework being etched out in the interim constitution, were promised a *quid pro quo* of maintenance of their position, even if their authority would be diminished.[36]

However, one of the key issues that stemmed from their intervention was the role of women; as put by Bennett: 'The African patriarchal tradition, in particular the system of patrilineal succession, had to be protected against the onslaught of a gender equality clause, which was a highlight of the bill of rights.'[37] In the event, limited powers were given to chiefs, as had been done in other African countries, by a Council of Traditional Leaders as a special 'new organ of government in which traditional leaders may debate all bills pertaining to their powers or to customary law'.[38]

While the future role of customary law in South Africa is still not clear, Bennett seems correct in his assertion that it will have a place in the new legal system. In general terms, Bennett notes the reluctance to acknowledge the role of chiefs in most of the countries in Africa that had won their independence, partly because of their collusive role in the pre-independence colonial regime – however, it was also realized that the institution of chieftaincy, even if not the individual chiefs 'still enjoys considerable public support'.[39]

Dealing with the theme of women's rights that constitutes a major barrier to an acceptance of tribal custom, including especially its patriarchal basis, Bennett (in agreement with Simons's comments) argues that women's status was better in pre-colonial times, and that their position was undermined by incorrect perceptions of key colonial figures, some of it incorporated into codes of law for the Africans – as a result, in Bennett's view:

> the law with which we now have to contend is a perversion of women's pre-colonial status; it is a poor reflection of current social practices; and it falls far short of modern human rights norms ... A nation-wide project is necessary to reveal the true position of women.[40]

In the final analysis, it will be the judicial system, and in particular the new constitutional court, that will have to resolve many of the issues that will arise – and judicial review of constitutional matters is often characterized by choices judges have to make when differing rights and differing values are in conflict. For Bennett, there must be a balancing of 'human dignity and democracy'; thus 'changing customary law on the basis of ... the Constitution would realize the goal of human dignity, but it might do so at the cost of the wider community's democratic right to express its views on reform'.[41]

Since so much of my own analysis has been based on the parallels between common law and customary law, may it be suggested that (in South Africa and elsewhere) where the customary law is in an impasse, because some practices (especially as regards women) are not compatible with progressive ideas of the modern era, that the courts become an active factor in adapting the customary law, just as in the courts of equity a means was found of resolving intractable problems of the common law, especially those in regard to women.

Such potential judicial developments are predicated on a prior ideological and political commitment. In the aftermath of apartheid, which exploited to the hilt the differences between the Black peoples of South

Africa in order to undermine the anti-apartheid forces, it will not be easy to create such a climate for change, as Bennett himself is well aware. But, even outside of South Africa, there are voices warning against the resurgence of tribal community and identity and the construction of pan-aboriginal strivings.

Some of these expressions are blatantly racist, as in the 'maiden' speech made by a new Member of Parliament in September 1996, in Australia, where defying age-old customs that such first parliamentary contributions should be non-controversial, she used the occasion for a verbal attack on Aborigines and their excessive demands on governmental policies.[42] The debate in the mass media in response raged partly over whether her remarks (including against immigrants from Asia) should be ignored or demanded a strong reply. Yet, there is much significance to such statements as a truer barometer of public sentiments than the exemplary governmental commissions or the reasoned and detailed academic analyses. They do at least serve as reminders of the enormity of the prejudices and resultant discriminatory practices that still exist.

Beyond that, however, there are also more refined descriptions that pose deep dilemmas that are often ignored by both activists and academicians partial to the need for recognition of tribal rights. A good example of writing that is sensitive to tribal traditions and to past injustices, but that warns against much of present-day activism, is a recent book by Fergus Bordewich, *Killing the White Man's Indian.*[43] It is in the subtitle, however, that the full thrust is presented – 'Reinventing Native Americans at the End of the Twentieth Century'. Bordewich uses the similar theme of invention that was referred to at the beginning of this chapter – in the case of the Indians, however, the traditions were not created *ex nihilo*, but had existed and after lapsing, are in the process of re-emerging. Thus, on the one hand,

> For the first time in generations, Indians were shaping their own destinies largely beyond the control of Whites. Talented tribal leaders were seeking innovative ways to define the place of tribes in the modern world. Inspired individuals were reinventing Indian education, rewriting tribal histories, helping to bring about a remarkable resurgence of traditional religions, and coming to grips with the alcoholism and social pathologies that blight reservation communities;

on the other hand,

> The ferment was not unalloyed … . Alongside inspired idealism … [was] ethnic chauvinism, a crippling instinct to confuse isolation with independence, and a chronic habit of interpreting present-day reality through the warping lens of the past.[44]

More than these negative undercurrents, however, was a deeper factor, namely that the resurgence of Indian culture presented a threat to 'traditional' American values – of equality, of promised possibilities for all, of shared, basic principles. As explained by Bordewich,

> The belief that Indians are somehow fundamentally different from other Americans, however romantically the idea may be expressed in terms of native 'tradition' or magical notions of affinity for the earth, implies a failure of basic American values, for it leads inexorably toward moral acceptance of political entities defined on the basis of racial exclusion.[45]

And then follows a warning which, it seems, confirms my contention as to the overall unwillingness to relate to tribal contentions. Bordewich is to be commended for postulating in such a focused and careful manner what really lies behind the reluctance to see tribe and tribalism as acceptable phenomena in the modern world; thus, not just values, but political power is the issue –

> Although the concept of tribal sovereignty has parallels in other ideologies of racial and ethnic separatism, it is potentially far more subversive, for Indian tribes, unlike the nation's other minorities, possess both land and governments of their own and have at least the potential to transform not only their hopes and creativity but also their biases into political power in a way that others never can. It should, moreover, be obvious to anyone that legitimizing segregation for Indians will set a precedent for its potential imposition upon black, Asian and Hispanic Americans.[46]

The prospects of such negative exploitation of Indian achievements to enforce imposed segregation upon others, seems rather far-fetched. It is specifically in tribe and tribalism wherein lies the uniqueness of Indian demands – that cannot be easily transposed to other groups, not even by those eager to exploit differentials for racist purposes.[47]

More serious, however, is Bordewich's argument that these 'concerns will surely be further exacerbated in the years to come as Indian identity becomes increasingly ambiguous,'[48] since the reality today is of increasing personal assimilation in the form of intermarriage as they are 'marrying outside their ethnic group at a faster rate than any other Americans' – thus,

> It is plain that the principle, or the pretense, that blood should be a central defining fact of being Indian will soon become untenable. How much blending can occur before Indians finally cease to be Indians? Unfortunately the implications of this demographic trend remain virtually unexamined. The question is sure to loom ever larger in the coming generations as the United States increasingly

> finds itself in 'government-to-government' relationships with 'Indian tribes' that are, in fact, becoming less ethnically Indian by the decade.[49]

These are legitimate concerns, and need to be addressed. Specifically they are voiced by someone whose argument is based not on negative assumptions, but on a perception (differing from that of pluralism which is the essence of my theme) that attempts to dispel the myths of the dominant culture as to who the Indian was; thus he writes that

> Until now, each age has imagined its own Indian: untamable, savage, child of Nature, steward of the earth, the white man's ultimate victim. Imagining that we see the Indian, we have often seen little more than a warped reflection of ourselves ... . Indians are not ... poignant vestiges of a lost age, but men and women of our own time, struggling to solve twentieth-century problems with the tools of our shared civilization.[50]

In many respects, the theme of my book attempts to provide an answer to arguments of this nature – but specifically in terms of these statements by Bordewich, I would suggest that the only way in which the shared civilization of which he writes, will really crystallize, is when the dominant part of that civilization – commonly known as the West – is willing not just to re-examine its imaginings of the Indians (and other tribal people), but also its imagination of itself as civilized conqueror, benevolent guardian of nature, liberal law-giver, the tribal person's ultimate savior. The aim of social and legal pluralism is not a regression to the past, but a recognition of the role that the past – every past – plays in the here and now, including the myths – all the myths – of a truly shared civilization.[51]

NOTES

1. Eric Hobsbawm and Terence Ranger, *The Invention of Tradition* (Cambridge: Cambridge University Press, 1983).
2. T. Ranger, 'The Invention of Tradition in Colonial Africa', in ibid., p. 211.
3. Ibid., p. 211.
4. Ibid., p. 247.
5. Ibid., p. 254.
6. The specific year that was considered the benchmark for determining immemorial use was 1189.
7. For a concise discussion of Chancery Court, see J.H. Baker, *An Introduction to English Legal History* (London: Butterworths, 1990, 3rd edn) Chapter 6, 'The Court of Chancery and Equity', p. 112.
8. See Judicature Act, 1873.
9. On the law of trusts, see Baker, *Introduction to English Legal History*, at pp. 328–35.
10. See, *Snell's Principles of Equity*, edited by P. Baker and P. Langan, 28th edn., 1982.
11. Ibid., p. 522
12. On equity in general, see John Pomeroy, *A Treatise on Equity Jurisprudence* (San Francisco:

Bancroft-Whitney Co., 1918).

13. See discussion above of feminist writers in Chapter 17, 'Family Matters' and Chapter 18, 'Women and Children First'.
14. For instance, marital rape is now recognized as a crime in most common law jurisdictions after hundreds of years in which the law permitted a husband to physically abuse his wife for the purposes of having sexual relations with her.
15. See Kenneth Maddock, 'Aboriginal Customary Law', in P. Hanks and B. Keon-Cohen (eds), *Aborigines and the Law: Essays in Memory of Elizabeth Eggleston* (Sydney: Allen & Unwin, 1984), p. 212.
16. By Act 46 of 1959, the Promotion of Black Self-Government Act, the Black population of South Africa was divided into nine tribal units, each one being entitled to its own national homeland, even when scattered widely in six different areas, as was the case for Boputhatswana. For an attempt to artificially create a 'tribal people', and then cede their territory to a neighboring state, while ignoring the wishes of the population, see T.W. Bennet and N.S. Peart, 'The Ingwavuma Land Deal: A Case Study of Self-Determination', *Boston College Third World Law Journal* 6 (1983), p. 23.
17. For general discussion of human rights issues in South Africa, written toward the end of the apartheid era, see symposium, 'Human Rights in the Post-Apartheid South African Constitution' in *Columbia Human Rights Law Review* 21 (1989). However, of the ten contributors, only Albie Sachs, later to be appointed a justice in the Constitutional Court, makes passing reference to this issue – in the context of 'whether cultural associations with an ethnic basis should receive constitutional protection'; see 'A Bill of Rights for South Africa: Areas of Agreement and Disagreement' (p. 28).
18. However, it should be noted that the term itself, multiculturalism, is rarely used in the South African debate, in comparison to its extensive use in places such as Australia. In fact, in popular parlance, the reference in South Africa is to the catchy phrase, 'Rainbow Nation'.
19. For discussion of Tom Mboya's views, see above, Chapter 2, 'Pluralism in the Modern World'; and his book, *Freedom and After* (London: André Deutsch, 1963).
20. In South Africa's first parliament under full franchise of all its citizens, one-quarter of all the members were women, a percentage far higher than has been achieved in any other African country in which democratic elections have been held, and which is higher than many of the older democracies, including nearly all the countries within the common law orbit.
21. On the impact of local customary law in South Africa, see Tom W. Bennett, *A Sourcebook of Customary Law for South Africa* (Cape Town: Juta, 1991).
22. See discussion in, above, Chapter 7, 'Between Recognition and Repugnancy'.
23. Christina Murray (ed.), *Gender and the New South African Legal Order* (Cape Town: Juta, 1994).
24. Christina Murray and Felicity Kaganas, 'Law and Women's Rights in South Africa: An Overview', in ibid., p. 16.
25. H.J. Simons, *African Women: Their Legal Status in South Africa* (London: C. Hurst, 1968).
26. Murray and Kaganas, 'Law and Women's Rights …' , p. 19.
27. Iain Currie, 'The Future of Customary Law: Lessons from the Lobolo Debate', in ibid., p. 146.
28. Ibid., pp. 167–8.
29. Simons, *African Women.*
30. Ibid., p. 15.
31. Ibid., p. 15.
32. Ibid., p. 287.
33. Tom W. Bennett, *Human Rights and African Customary Law* (Cape Town: Juta, 1995).
34. Ibid., p. 3.
35. Ibid., pp. 3–4.
36. See especially, ibid., at pp. 20–1.
37. Ibid., p. 21.
38. Ibid., p. 22.
39. Ibid., p. 69.
40. Ibid., p. 85.
41. Ibid., p. 95.
42. The member of Parliament, Pauline Hanson, is reported to have said *inter alia,* that the Aborigines are an unfairly advantaged group. Having only recently won an election as an

independent against the candidates of both major parties (running as an ex-Liberal party member in what was considered a safe Labor Party seat), there is no doubt that her sentiments are widely shared. For several weeks afterwards, her comments were widely discussed in newspaper editorials, opinion articles and letters to the editor, as well as radio talk programs. As examples, see editorial in *The Australian*, 'Free Speech Calls for Straight Talk', 25 September 1996, p. 12; and letter column in *Sydney Morning Herald*, 27 September 1996, p. 12, with about 20 letters devoted to her comments and the response to her by the Prime Minister and other politicians.

43. Fergus Bordewich, *Killing the White Man's Indian: Reinventing Native Americans at the End of the Twentieth Century* (New York: Doubleday, 1996).
44. Ibid., p. 11.
45. Ibid., p. 329.
46. Ibid., p. 329.
47. It should be noted that apartheid in South Africa did not stem from any division between the tribes – it was only well into the apartheid regime that the government set out its policy of separation and 'autonomous' Bantustans, based on tribal belonging. This policy was indeed aimed at undermining the unity of the Black people in South Africa – but it should be noted that this unity was forged at a crucial time in the 1950s during the leadership of Chief Luthuli of the Zulu tribe, a Nobel Peace Laureate, who bore his chiefly title without exploiting it, and whose membership of the Zulu tribe did not prevent his leadership of the African National Congress long before the Zulu-dominated Inkhata was set up as a political rival to the ANC.
48. Bordewich, *Killing the White Man's Indian*, p. 329.
49. Ibid., pp. 329–30. Bordewich draws on the work of a Cherokee Anthropologist – see Russell Thornton, *American Indian Holocaust and Survival: A Population History since 1492* (Norman: University of Oklahoma Press, 1990).
50. Bordewich, *Killing the White Man's Indian*, p. 343.
51. As for the myths of modern Western civilization, I have examined some of them in other books: for instance the myths of generational conflict, especially the use – and abuse – made in academic work of the Oedipus complex, based on a Greek myth, in *Generations Apart: Adult Hostility to Youth* (New York: McGraw-Hill, 1982); and the myths (and errors) of sociological analyses of legal situations, in *Social Cohesion and Legal Coercion: A Critique of Weber, Durkheim and Marx* (Atlanta, GA, and Amsterdam: Rodopi, 1997).

Community in Society

When all is said and done a tribe is one of the quintessential forms of a community, a group of people held together by tangible expressions of recurrent rituals, shared language, patterned conduct, recognized norms, and intangible feelings of belonging, identity, memories and aspirations. However difficult to define, however much exploited by alien, imperialist masters or calculating chiefs and headmen for their own ends, however tenuous their existence in a changing world of ideological and technological innovation, tribes are a reality – no less than states or empires, no less than ethnic or religious communities, no less than voluntary associations or trans-national corporations, no less than urban municipalities or regional unions. They are worthy of note and they are worthy of study. Their customs may be analyzed within a legal framework, their specific structures as part of political science, and their overall community life through the use of standard sociological procedures; and in fact the accumulated data of ethnograhic researches by anthropologists is in urgent need of the broader analyses of these sister disciplines.

This is particularly true of sociology, for one of its major concerns is, in the words of Robert Nisbet, a leading American sociologist, the 'quest for community'.[1] His book of this name opens with his explanation of the importance of understanding the manner in which political power impinges upon community – or to be more exact, 'the loss of community'. For as Nisbet goes on to explain 'of all symptoms of the impact of power upon human personality in the contemporary Western world the most revealing seems to me to be the preoccupation, in so many spheres of thought and action, with community – community lost and community to be gained'.[2] For Nisbet, the sovereign political state is 'pre-eminent', and the 'greatest single influence upon social organization in the modern West'. It is not just 'a legal relationship, a mere superstructure of power', but has penetrated deeply into social life, affecting, *inter alia*, 'kinship and local allegiances'. These factors are the underlying cause 'for the twentieth-century's obsessive quest for moral certainty and social community' and the consequent 'present-day problems of freedom and democracy'.[3]

There is, according to Nisbet, a very real need for some intermediate grouping between the individual and the society of which he is a member.

The specifics of such a framework are irrelevant – they may take any of several forms, but they are essential both for the well-being of the individual and for the welfare of the society.[4] Lest he be accused of overly conservative or even reactionary tendencies, Nisbet stresses that he is not intent on resurrecting older frameworks from the past, but of ensuring the relevance and importance of intermediary groupings regardless of the form they may take.

Nisbet avers that 'irrespective of particular groups, there must be in any stable culture, in any civilization that prizes its integrity, functionally significant and psychologically meaningful groups and associations lying intermediate to the individual and the larger values and purposes of his society'.[5] He discounts the possibility of voluntary associations, whether 'industrial corporations, governmental agencies, large-scale labor and charitable organizations', answering to these needs, because of their well-nigh inevitable 'impersonality'.[6] Neither these organizations, nor physical closeness to neighbors and fellow-workers, can overcome the sense of isolation and alienation that is the lot of the modern western individual. Thus, according to Nisbet, 'The quest for community will not be denied, for it springs from some of the powerful needs of human nature – needs for a clear sense of cultural purpose, membership, status, and continuity.'[7]

In a later book,[8] Nisbet chose community as one of the five most important unit-ideas for the study of society, as expounded by the great founding thinkers of the discipline of sociology, and indeed as the most important of them.[9] Community, for him, encompasses 'religion, work, family and culture; it refers to social bonds characterized by emotional cohesion, depth, continuity, and fullness'.[10] Each of the key unit-ideas (which are, in addition to community – authority, status, sacred and alienation) is linked to a conceptual opposite – in the case of community, this contrary concept is society.[11]

In contrasting these ideas of community and society, Nisbet is, of course, reiterating one of the classic conceptualizations of sociology, as first, and most fully, expounded in the nineteenth century by Ferdinand Tönnies;[12] the particular nuance attributed to these terms by Tönnies is exemplified by the fact that to this day, English-speaking sociologists, including Nisbet, tend to use the German form of these words, on the understanding that they have connotations in the original that are somehow not conveyed by the English translation – and so we have the sociological concepts of *Gemeinschaft* and *Gesellschaft*, for community and society. This dual contrast is an ongoing aspect of sociological work, with differing nomenclature being used – of primary and secondary, of mechanical solidarity and organic solidarity, of religious and secular.[13]

Thus, Nisbet writes that in understanding the nature of community 'the work of Tönnies is of greatest importance. Nowhere has sociology's contribution to modern social thought been more fertile, more often borrowed by other social sciences, especially with reference to the contemporary study of undeveloped nations, than in the typological use of the idea of community.'[14] However, here Nisbet seems to be remiss, for, as has already been pointed out, many works touching on community, ignore one of its major expressions – that of the tribe. In fact, Nisbet himself makes no reference to tribe in either of the two books that I have quoted, which deal so markedly with community. And this lacuna seems to be a constant pattern of sociological work – as though tribal groupings are the raw material only of anthropologists, and have no relevance for sociology.

In any event, much of Tönnies's writing explains the working of a *Gemeinschaft* (often in a favorable light which tends to shed a shadow on the *Gesellschaft*). *Gemeinschaft* groupings are characterized by the closeness and cohesion of the members, in many cases arising out of involuntary contacts and interactions, such as of family or even neighborhood. Tönnies describes the three key factors in a *Gemeinschaft* as being blood (for kinship relations), land (for neighborhood contacts), and mind (for friendship basis). *Gemeinschaft* tends therefore to be a more natural, deep and spontaneous framework, as compared to the artificiality, superficiality and laxity of the *Gesellschaft*.[15]

Nisbet points out that Tönnies was writing (in the nineteenth century) at a time when many historians and jurists were becoming aware of the importance of community for a true understanding of Europe's past (and the implications for its present). The Middle Ages were being seen in a more positive light than before, specifically because there was a better appreciation of the positive aspects, including democratic forms, that had existed then. Nisbet writes of 'the influence of the rediscovery of community upon the whole area of nineteenth-century historiography' and then he notes 'the veritable eruption of scholarly interest in the communal and traditional past of Europe … . One need but mention the names of Stubbs, Freeman, Maitland, Fustel de Coulanges, Savigny and von Gierke to suggest the degree to which historians of the first rank in the century gave themselves to the study of medieval communities and institutions.'[16] What Nisbet, however, neglects to mention is the fact that four of the above-named (Stubbs, Maitland, Savigny and von Gierke) were all leading jurists, and had discovered community in the process of describing the history of *law* – as had also other jurist-historians, most notably Maine, who is discussed as well by Nisbet and who had examined both ancient legal systems and village communities in India, where he had spent some time.[17]

In any event, Nisbet sums up this historiographical work as follows:

> The nineteenth century remains unexcelled even today in its institutional histories, and these are a part of the same awakening of

> interest in the medieval community that also affected the rise of Sociology. The largely adverse or hostile relationship that eighteenth-century historians had seen between medieval institutions and the modern electorates, assemblies, and liberties is now reversed; throughout the century we find historians searching for origins of democracy in the once despised contexts of folkmoot, manor, shire assembly, and estate.[18]

In discussing Tönnies, Nisbet draws attention to 'three major scholarly works in the mid-nineteenth century which, above any others ... provided the effective background for the typological use of community that we find in Tönnies and the Sociological tradition'.[19] Nisbet refers among lawyers to von Gierke and to Maine. von Gierke describes, *inter alia*, 'The organic unity of all communal and corporate groups before the law ... legal decentralization and the fundamental distinction between state and society', all of which contrasted with 'the *modern nation-state*, resting upon, first, the centralization of political power, and, second, the individual, with a consequent pulverization of all that had once lain in between'.[20] Maine's major contribution to legal history was the contrast he drew between 'status' in simple societies and 'contract' in modern western society.[21] (The third writer referred to by Nisbet, Fustel de Coulanges, also makes some reference to legal aspects of smaller communities as in Greek and Roman city-states.)[22]

Tönnies himself was influenced by these jurist-historians not only in his perceptions of community, but also, apparently in his attempt to understand the legal underpinnings of society, a task that was undertaken in a little-known book on Custom[23] (not referred to by Nisbet). In this short book, Tönnies describes the various meanings and stages of custom. At the beginning of the book he contrasts 'habit', which he attaches to an individual, seeing it as being basically individual-psychological, with 'custom', which is involved with groups and which he sees as being social-psychological.[24] He concludes that 'we can thus understand custom as a sort of legislative will, but we know that it is not – like the latter – formulated through a resolution, be it of an individual ruler or an assembly. Rather it is formed through habit and out of practice: it is based on tradition.'[25]

However, although custom has a force of its own, it cannot, according to Tönnies, withstand the impact of developing society, with its stress on fleeting fashions, stimulated and sustained by crass commercialization:

> Society, as the subject and supporter of fashion, stands in a certain contrast to custom. It is modern, cultural, cosmopolitan … . Trade, the production of goods … are the elements by which it extends its network over the whole populated earth. It desires movement and quick movement; it must dissolve custom in order to develop a taste

> for the new and for imported goods ... . Affection and fidelity to tradition, to one's own, to one's heritage, must necessarily give way. Commerce has ever a disintegrating effect.[26]

Parallel to the impact of society in undermining custom, is the role of the state – here not trade and commerce, but law and authority adversely affect custom. Thus, according to Tönnies the state 'wills to establish uniformity. Through ordinances and laws it fights custom where it seems noxious or only dangerous to it. The esteem of custom is diminished everywhere due to the state's absolute authority. The state serves progress, the development of independent personalities, but always at the expense of the folk and their *gemeinschaftlich* cooperative life.'[27]

Tönnies, despite his seeming partiality to both *gemeinschaft* and custom, warns that there is no need 'to lament this', yet he cannot deny a 'sense of the tragic in the course of things. Precisely because the progress is so immense, the collapse of tradition is highly charged with emotion.'[28] Thus, we see Tönnies's inevitable ambivalence – his desire to concede the good of 'progress', which is inevitable, yet his reservations as to the consequences. And so he continues with ambiguous, partly contradictory, statements: 'Within custom, individual rights are not stark and absolute; they are directed toward rather than against each other,' and 'Law becomes distinct from morality to which custom had bound it;'[29] then follows a more detailed statement, in which, building upon Schiller, he notes that custom

> makes man free and powerful. Where the police and their state act according to their own intentions, men become enslaved and impotent. They are guarded as if they were children. A people which is in the process of becoming spiritually more mature and stronger will again want to be its own master. It wants to recognize its own identity in the state, and to form itself into the state. It wants to again be self-ruling in the smaller groups.
>
> To the extent that a people succeed in this, a kind of renaissance of custom is possible.[30]

These words were written in 1909, and were formulated without any regard to tribal customs of the modern world. They referred to a historical situation that pertained to the Europe of yesteryear, and they expressed, hesitatingly, a vision of a resurgence of custom that would signify a rebirth of community, a democratic community free to lay down its own norms, without the restrictions of a dominant political authority.

Tönnies ignored, like most other sociologists, the tribal communities of his age – yet what he wrote is most applicable to them. The historical community that he described, and the future community that he envisaged, had room for democratic forms, within which the customs would be created. To a large extent this is true also of present-day tribes.

Lest it be thought that Tönnies is expressing no more than wishful thinking about a past (in Europe) that never really was, and a future that is utopian in the extreme, or lest it be considered that the tribe, as a modern example of community is also no more than a figment of imagination in the bureaucratic planning of a colonial administrator, or the research notes of an anthropologist, it is perhaps a salutary necessity to be reminded that, by a similar token the nation-state is, in Benedict Anderson's apt wording, 'an imagined community',[31] – 'imagined because the member of even the smallest nation will never know most of their fellow-members, meet them, or even hear them, yet in the minds of each lives the image of their communion'.[32] And because, it is 'imagined as a community ... the nation is always conceived as a deep, horizontal comradeship'.[33]

In a book on the invention of tradition,[34] as discussed in the previous chapter, Hobsbawm and Ranger and their participating colleagues present such 'imaginings' in the negative light of powerful societal forces manipulating the masses in order to create the myths that underlie nationhood, and preserve the essence of power, for the dominant groupings. There is much truth in their assertions, which include also some mythical aspects of tribal life in Africa in colonial times, although most of the chapter on Africa deals with the imported traditions. But, whatever the truth in this thesis, nation states – for all the fiction of their historical accounts – exist, and their rulers make laws and possess the machinery to enforce these laws.

This book argues that no less consideration should be given to the existence of tribal communities and the validity of their customs. Any imagining in the constituting of tribes as community is probably far less than in the constituting of states. No doubt, just as for nations and states, a certain amount of fiction may have facilitated the emergence of some of these traditions. No doubt just as for the 'mythical' judicial pronouncements – of 'terra nullius' in Australia, of the 'nullity' of the Treaty of Waitangi in New Zealand, of the existence of 'domestic, dependent nations' in the United States, of 'customary unions' in South Africa – some of the pronouncements of tribal members or of academic researchers are not precisely accurate; certainly the cohesion of the community has often been exploited by scheming chiefs, just as the framework of modern democracy has been exploited by powerful politicians.

But, all these possible defects cannot belie the fact and the force of tribes and of custom in the modern world – or of the prospects for their continued existence into the future. If tribes exist in nation-states as part of a social pluralism, then recognition must be accorded their customs as part of a legal pluralism. Pluralism, above all, provides assurances that there may be unity without uniformity, the building of a consensus without the imposition of conformity. Within society, there is room for community, and within the nation-state, there is room for tribe; alongside the law there is room for custom, and alongside the transformations of progress, there is room for the continuity of tradition.

NOTES

1. Robert Nisbet, *The Quest for Community* (London: Oxford University Press, 1969). The book was first published in 1953, issued as a paperback under the title *Community and Power* in 1962, and then reissued in 1969 under its original title. It is the latter edition which has been used.
2. Ibid., p. xxi – from the Preface to the first edition.
3. Ibid., p. xxii.
4. Ibid., p. 70. Nisbet writes 'It is, I believe, the problem of intermediate associations that is fundamental at the present time.'
5. Ibid., p. 70.
6. Ibid., pp. 71–2.
7. Ibid., p. 73.
8. Robert Nisbet, *The Sociological Tradition* (London: Heinemann, 1966).
9. See ibid., Chapter 3, 'Community', pp. 47–106.
10. Ibid., p. 6.
11. Ibid., p.7. The contrasting pairs are authority–power, status–class, sacred–secular and alienation–progress
12. Ferdinand Tönnies, *Community and Society* (East Lansing: Michigan State University Press, 1957).
13. See, for instance Emile Durkheim, *The Division of Labor in Society (*Glencoe, IL: The Free Press, 1947).
14. Nisbet, *The Sociological Tradition*, p. 71.
15. See Tönnies, *Community and Society*, p. 26.
16. Nisbet, *The Sociological Tradition*, p. 55.
17. Sir Henry Maine, *Ancient Law* (London: John Murray, 1919).
18. Nisbet, *The Sociological Tradition*, p. 55.
19. Ibid., pp. 71–2.
20. Ibid., p. 72. The reference is to Otto von Gierke, *Das Deutsche Genossenschaftsrecht* (1868).
21. See Maine, *Ancient Law*.
22. Fustel de Coulanges, *The Ancient City* (Garden City, NY: Doubleday Anchor, n.d.).
23. Ferdinand Tönnies, *Custom: An Essay on Social Codes* (New York: The Free Press of Glencoe, 1961), trans. A.F. Borenstein. The book was originally published in 1909, under the title *Die Sitte*.
24. Ibid., p.35.
25. Ibid., p. 42.
26. Ibid., pp. 133–4.
27. Ibid., p.137.
28. Ibid., pp. 137–8.
29. Ibid., p. 139.
30. Ibid., pp. 141–2.
31. Benedict Anderson, *Imagined Communities: Reflections on the Origin and Spread of Nationalism* (London: Verso, 1983).
32. Ibid., p.15.
33. Ibid., p. 16.
34. Eric Hobsbawm and Terence Ranger (eds), *The Invention of Tradition* (Cambridge, Cambridge University Press, 1983).

Select Bibliography

BOOKS

Abel, R., ed., *The Politics of Informal Justice.* New York: Academic Press, 1982.

Allott, Antony, *New Essays in African Law.* London: Butterworths, 1970.

____*The Limits of Law.* London: Butterworths, 1980.

Ambler, Marijane, *Breaking the Iron Bonds: Indian Control of Energy Development.* Lawrence: University Press of Kansas, 1990.

Anderson, Benedict, *Imagined Communities: Reflections on the Origin and Spread of Nationalism.* London: Verso, 1983.

Asch, Michael, *Home and Native Land: Aboriginal Rights and the Canadian Constitution.* Toronto: Methuen, 1984.

Austin, Tony, *I Can Picture the Old Home So Clearly: The Commonwealth and 'Half-Caste' Youth in the Northern Territory 1911–1939.* Canberra: Aboriginal Studies Press, 1993.

Australian Law Reform Commission, *The Recognition of Aboriginal Customary Laws.* Canberra: Government Publishing Service, 1986.

Baker, J.H, *An Introduction to English Legal History.* London: Butterworths, 1990.

Behiels, M., ed., *The Meech Lake Primer: Conflicting Views of the 1987 Constitutional Accord.* Ottawa: University of Ottawa Press, 1989.

Bell, John, *Policy Arguments in Judicial Decisions.* Oxford: Clarendon Press, 1983.

Belobaba, E. and E. Gertner, eds., *The New Consttution and the Charter of Rights.* Toronto: Butterworths, 1983.

Benedict, Ruth, *The Chrysanthemum and The Sword: Patterns of Japanese Culture.* London: Secker & Warburg, 1947.

Bennett, Gordon, *Aboriginal Rights in International Law.* London: Royal Anthropological Institute in association with Survival International, 1978.

Bennett, Tom W., *Application of Customary Law in Southern Africa.* Cape Town: Juta, 1985.

____*A Sourcebook of Customary Law for South Africa.* Cape Town: Juta, 1991.

____*Human Rights and African Customary Law.* Cape Town: Juta, 1995.

Berman, Harold J., *Toward Revolution: The Formation of the Western Legal Tradition.* Cambridge, MA: Harvard University Press, 1983.

Boldt, Menno and J. Anthony Long with Leroy Little Bear, eds., *The Quest for Justice: Aboriginal People and Aboriginal Rights.* Toronto: University of Toronto Press, 1985.

Bordewich, Fergus, *Killing the White Man's Indian: Reinventing Native Americans at the End of the Twentieth Century.* New York: Doubleday, 1996.

Braithwaite, John, *Crime, Shame and Reintegration.* Cambridge: Cambridge University Press, 1989.

Brookes, Edgar, *The History of Native Policy in South Africa.* Cape Town: Nasionale Press, 1924.

Brownlie, Ian, *African Boundaries: A Legal and Diplomatic Encyclopedia.* London: C. Hurst, 1979.

—— *Treaties and Indigenous Peoples: The Robb Lectures, 1991.* Oxford: Clarendon Press, 1992.

Burman, Sandra and Barbara Harrell-Bond, eds., *The Imposition of Law.* New York: Academic Press, 1979.

Burt, Larry, *Tribalism in Crisis: Federal Indian Policy, 1953–1961.* Albuquerque: University of New Mexico, 1982.

Calvocoressi, Peter, *World Politics Since 1945.* London: Longman, 1987.

Chalmers, D.R.C. and A.H. Paliwala, *An Introduction to the Law in Papua New Guinea.* Sydney: Law Book Co., 1984.

Chanock, Martin, *Law, Custom and Social Order: The Colonial Experience in Malawi and Zambia.* Cambridge: Cambridge University Press, 1985.

Clark, Bruce, *Native Liberty, Crown Sovereignty: The Existing Aboriginal Right of Self-Government in Canada.* Montreal: McGill–Queens University Press, 1990.

Clarke, Robin and Geoffrey Hindley, *The Challenge of the Primitive.* New York: McGraw-Hill, 1975.

Cohen, Felix, *Handbook of Federal Indian Law.* Buffalo, CO: William S. Hein, 1980 [1942].

Cohen, Jean and Andrew Arato, *Civil Society and Political Theory.* Cambridge, MA: Massachusetts Institute of Technology Press, 1992.

Constable, Marianne, *The Law of the Other: The Mixed Jury and Changing Conceptions of Citizenship, Law and Knowledge.* Chicago: University of Chicago Press, 1994.

de Klerk, Michael, ed., *A Harvest of Discontent: The Land Question in South Africa.* Cape Town: Institute for a Democratic Alternative for South Africa, 1991.

Deloria, Vine, Jr., *Behind the Trail of Broken Treaties: An Indian Declaration of Independence.* New York: Delacorte Press, 1974.

—— and Clifford Lytle, *American Indians, American Justice.* Austin: University of Texas Press, 1983.

—— and Clifford Lytle, *The Nations Within: The Past and Future of American Indian Sovereignty.* New York: Pantheon Books, 1984.

Diamond, A.S., *Primitive Law: Past and Present.* London: Methuen, 1971.

Diamond, Stanley, *In Search of the Primitive: A Critique of Civilization.* New Brunswick, NJ: Transaction Books, 1974.

Dooyeweerd, Herman, *A New Critique of Theoretical Thought.* Amsterdam: H.J. Paris, 1953.

—— *Roots of Western Culture: Pagan, Secular, and Christian Options.* Toronto:

Wedge Publishing, 1979.
Durkheim, Emile, *The Division of Labor in Society.* Glencoe, IL: The Free Press, 1947.
Edwards, Coral and Peter Read, *The Lost Children: Thirteen Australians Taken from Their Aboriginal Families Tell of the Struggle to Find Their Natural Parents.* Sydney: Doubleday, 1989.
Eekelaar, John and Sanford Katz, eds., *Marriage and Cohabitation in Contemporary Societies: Areas of Legal, Social and Ethical Change.* Toronto: Butterworth, 1980.
Egan, Sean, ed., *S.M. Otieno: Kenya's Unique Burial Saga.* Nairobi: Nation Newspapers Publication, 1987.
Ehle, John, *Trail of Tears: The Rise and Fall of the Cherokee Nation.* New York: Doubleday, 1988.
Elias, T.O., *The Nature of African Customary Law.* Manchester: Manchester University Press, 1956.
____ *British Colonial Law: A Comparative Study of the Interaction between English and Local Laws in British Dependencies.* London: Stevens, 1962.
Falkowski, James, *Indian Law/Race Law: A Five-Hundred-Year History.* New York: Praeger, 1992.
Fleras, Augie and Jean Leonard Elliott, *The 'Nations Within': Aboriginal–State Relations in Canada, the United States and New Zealand.* Toronto: Oxford University Press, 1992.
Fried, Morton, *The Notion of Tribe.* Menlo Park, CA: Cummings, 1975.
Ghurye, G.A., *The Scheduled Tribes.* Bombay: Bhaktal, 1963.
Glazer, Nathan and Daniel Moynihan, eds., *Ethnicity: Theory and Experience.* Cambridge: Cambridge University Press, 1975.
Glendon, Mary, *State, Law and Family: Family Law in Transition in the United States and Western Europe.* Amsterdam: North Holland Publishing Co., 1977.
Gluckman, Max, ed., *Ideas and Procedures in African Customary Laws.* London: Oxford University Press, 1969.
____ *The Judicial Process among the Barotse of Northern Rhodesia (Zambia),* 2nd edn. Manchester: Manchester University Press, 1973.
____ *African Traditional Law in Historical Perspective.* London: Oxford University Press, 1974.
Godelier, Maurice, *Perspectives in Marxist Anthropology.* Cambridge: Cambridge University Press, 1977.
Goffman, Erving, *Stigma: Notes on the Management of Spoiled Identity.* Harmondsworth: Penguin Books, 1963.
Goodrich, Peter, *Reading the Law: A Critical Introduction.* London: Basil Blackwell, 1986.
Gordon, Milton, *Assimilation in American Life: The Role of Race, Religion and National Origins.* New York: Oxford University Press, 1964.
Gower, L.C.B., *Independent Africa – The Challenge to the Legal Profession.* Cambridge, MA: Harvard University Press, 1967.
Gulliver, P.H., *Social Control in an African Society: A Study of the Arusha-Agricultural Masai of Northern Tanganyika.* London: Routledge & Kegan Paul,

1963.

——ed. *Tradition and Transition in East Africa: Studies of the Tribal Element in the Modern Era.* London: Routledge & Kegan Paul, 1969.

Hanks, P. and B. Keon-Cohen, eds., *Aborigines and the Law: Essays in Memory of Elizabeth Eggleston.* Sydney: Allen & Unwin, 1984.

Harring, Sidney, *Crow Dog's Case: American Indian Sovereignty, Tribal Law and United States Law in the Nineteenth Century.* Cambridge: Cambridge University Press, 1994.

Hart, H.L.A., *Law, Liberty and Morality.* London: Oxford University Press, 1968.

Harvey, William Burnett, *Law and Social Change in Ghana.* Princeton, NJ: Princeton University Press, 1966.

——*Introduction to the Legal System in East Africa.* Kampala: East African Literature Bureau, 1975.

Hazlehurst, K., ed., *Legal Pluralism and the Colonial Legacy: Indigenous Experiences of Justice in Canada, Australia, and New Zealand.* Aldershot: Avebury, 1995.

Hertzberg, Hazel, *The Search for an American Indian Identity: Modern Pan-Indian Movements.* Syracuse, NY: Syracuse University Press, 1971.

Hobsbawm, Eric and Terence Ranger, eds., *The Invention of Tradition.* Cambridge: Cambridge University Press, 1983.

Hocking, B., ed., *International Law and Aboriginal Human Rights.* Sydney: Law Book Co., 1988.

Hoebel, E. Adamson, *The Law of Primitive Man: A Study in Comparative Legal Dynamics.* Cambridge, MA: Harvard University Press, 1954.

Hooker, M., *Legal Pluralism: An Introduction to Colonial and Neo-Colonial Laws.* Oxford: Clarendon Press, 1975.

Hosken, Fran, *The Hosken Report – Genital and Sexual Mutilation of Females*, 4th revised edition. Lexington, MA: Women's International Network News, 1993.

Indian Rights – Human Rights: Handbook for Indians on International Human Rights Complaint Procedures. Washington, DC: Indian Law Resource Center, 1984.

Indigenous Peoples – A Global Quest for Justice: A Report for the Independent Commission on International Humanitarian Issues. Foreword by Sadruddin Aga Khan and Hassan bin Talal. London: Zed Books, 1987.

Jackson, Helen, *A Century of Dishonor: A Sketch of the United States Government's Dealings with some of the Indian Tribes.* Michigan: Scholarly Press, 1974 [1880].

Jackson, Moana, *The Maori and the Criminal Justice System.* Wellington: Department of Justice, 1988.

Johnston, Commissioner Elliott, *Royal Commission into Aboriginal Deaths in Custody.* Canberra, 1991.

Kawharu, I.H., ed., *Waitangi: Maori and Pakeha Perspectives of the Treaty of Waitangi.* Auckland: Oxford University Press, 1989.

Keane, John, ed., *Civil Society and the State.* London: Verso, 1988.

Kelsey, Jane, *A Question of Honour?: Labour and the Treaty 1984–1989.* Wellington: Allen & Unwin, 1990.

Kuper, Hilda and Leo Kuper, eds., *African Law: Adaptation and Development.* Berkeley: University of California Press, 1965.

Kuper, Leo and M.G. Smith, eds., *Pluralism in Africa.* Berkeley: University of California Press, 1969.

Lawson, Stephanie, *The Failure of Democratic Politics in Fiji.* Oxford: Clarendon Press, 1991.

Leger, Marie, ed., *Aboriginal Peoples: Toward Self-Government.* Montreal: Black Rose Books, 1994.

Lerner, Natan, *Group Rights and Discrimination in International Law.* Dordrecht: Martinus Nijhoff, 1991.

Llewellyn, Karl, *The Cheyenne Way – Conflict and Case Law in Primitive Jurisprudence.* Norman: University of Oklahoma Press, 1967.

Loos, Noel and Koiki Mabo, *Edward Koiki Mabo: His Life and Struggle for Land Rights.* St Lucia: University of Queensland Press, 1996.

MacHugh, Paul, *The Maori Magna Carta.* Auckland: Auckland University Press, 1991.

Magrath, C. Peter, *Yazoo: Law and Politics in the New Republic – The Case of Fletcher v. Peck.* Providence: Brown University Press, 1966.

Maine, Sir Henry, *Ancient Law.* London: John Murray, 1919.

Malinowski, Bronislaw, *Crime and Custom in Savage Society.* London: Routledge & Kegan Paul, 1970.

Manfred, Christopher, *Judicial Power and the Charter: Canada and the Paradox of Liberal Constitutionalism.* Norman: University of Oklahoma Press, 1993.

Mathabane, Mark, *Kaffir Boy: Growing Out of Apartheid – an Autobiography.* London: The Bodley Head, 1986.

Mazrui, Ali, *The African Condition: A Political Diagnosis.* London: Heinemann, 1980.

Mboya, Tom, *Freedom and After.* London: André Deutsch, 1963.

McBride, I., ed., *Who Owns the Past – Papers from Annual Symposium of the Australian Academy of the Humanities.* Melbourne: Oxford University Press, 1985.

McLean, Scilla, ed., *Female Circumcision, Excision and Infibulation.* London: Minority Rights Group, 1985.

McNeil, K., *Common Law Aboriginal Native Title.* Oxford: Clarendon Press, 1989.

McRae, K., ed., *Consociational Democracy: Political Accommodation in Segmented Societies.* Toronto: McClelland and Stewart, 1974.

Montagu, Ashley, ed., *The Concept of the Primitive.* New York: Free Press, 1968.

Morris, H.F. and James S. Read, *Indirect Rule and the Search for Justice: Essays in East African Legal History.* Oxford: Clarendon Press, 1972.

Morse, Bradford and Gordon Woodman, eds., *Indigenous Law and the State.* Dordrecht: Foris Publications, 1988.

Murray, Christina, ed., *Gender and the New South African Legal Order.* Cape Town: Juta, 1994.

Narakobi, Bernard, *Lo Bilong Yumi Yet – Law and Custom in Melanesia.* Suva, Fiji:

Melanesian Institute for Pastoral and Socio-Economic Service and University of South Pacific, 1989.

Nisbet, Robert, *The Sociological Tradition.* London: Heinemann, 1966.

—— *The Quest for Community.* London: Oxford University Press, 1969.

Norgren, Jill, *The Cherokee Cases: The Confrontation of Law and Politics.* New York: McGraw-Hill, 1996.

Nwabueze, B.O., *Constitutionalism in the Emergent States.* London: C. Hurst, 1973.

Obilade, Akintunde Olusegun, *The Nigerian Legal System.* London: Sweet & Maxwell, 1979.

Ojwang, J.B. and J.N.K. Mugambi, eds., *The S.M. Otieno Case: Death and Burial in Modern Kenya.* Nairobi: Nairobi University Press, 1989.

Orange, Claudia, *The Treaty of Waitangi.* Wellington: Allen and Unwin, 1987.

Paton, George, *A Textbook of Jurisprudence.* Oxford: Clarendon Press, 1972.

Peterson, N. and M. Langton, eds., *Aborigines, Land and Land Rights.* Canberra: Australian Institute of Aboriginal Studies, 1983.

Pevar, Stephan, *The Rights of Indians and Tribes: The Basic ACLU Guide to Indian and Tribal Rights.* Carbondale: Southern Illinois University Press, 1992.

Pommersheim, Frank, *Braid of Feathers: American Indian Law and Contemporary Tribal Life.* Berkeley: University of California Press, 1995.

Poulter, Sebastian, *English Law and Ethnic Minority Customs.* London: Butterworths, 1986.

Price, Marcus H., III, *Disputing the Dead: US Law on Aboriginal Remains and Grave Gods.* Columbia: University of Missouri Press, 1991.

Read, Peter, *The Stolen Generations: The Removal of Aboriginal Children in New South Wales 1883 to 1969.* New South Wales Ministry of Aboriginal Affairs – Occasional Paper, No. 1, n.d.

Regenstein, Lewis, *The Politics of Extinction: The Shocking Story of the World's Endangered Wildlife.* New York: Macmillan, 1975.

Roberts, Simon, *Order and Dispute: An Introduction to Legal Anthropology.* Harmondsworth: Penguin Books, 1979.

Robinson, Paul, *Criminal Law Defenses.* St Paul: West Publishing Co., 1984.

Rosenthal, H.D., *Their Day in Court: A History of the Indian Claims Commission.* New York: Garland Publishing, 1990.

Rowley, C.D., *Recovery: The Politics of Aboriginal Reform.* Harmondsworth: Penguin Books, 1986.

Royal Commission on the Donald Marshall Jr. Prosecution. Halifax: Government of Nova Scotia, 1989.

Sack, Peter, *Land Between Two Laws: Early European Land Acquisitions in New Guinea.* Canberra: Australian National University Press, 1973.

Sahlins, Marshall D., *Tribesmen.* Englewood Cliffs, NJ: Prentice-Hall, 1968.

Saltman, Michael, *The Demise of the 'Reasonable Man': A Cross-Cultural Study of a Legal Concept.* New Brunswick, NJ: Transaction Publishers, 1991.

Scarr, Deryck, *Fiji, The Politics of Illusion – The Military Coups in Fiji.* Kensington: New South Wales University Press, 1988.

Seidman, Robert, *The Criminal Law in Africa.* London: Sweet & Maxwell, 1966.

Sellin, Thorsten, *Culture Conflict and Crime.* New York: Social Science Research Council, 1938.

Sharp, Andrew, *Justice and the Maori: Maori Claims in New Zealand Political Argument in the 1980s.* Auckland: Oxford University Press, 1990.

Shattuck, Petra and Jill Norgren, *Partial Justice: Federal Indian Law in a Liberal Constitutional System.* New York: Berg, 1991.

Sheleff, Leon, *The Bystander: Behaviour, Law, Ethics.* Lexington, MA: Lexington Press, 1978.

____ *Generations Apart: Adult Hostility to Youth.* New York: McGraw-Hill, 1982.

____ *Ultimate Penalties: Capital Punishment, Life Imprisonment, Physical Torture.* Columbus: Ohio State University Press, 1987.

____ *Social Cohesion and Legal Coercion: A Critique of Weber, Durkheim and Marx.* Atlanta, GA, and Amsterdam: Rodopi, 1997.

Shivji, Issa, *The Concept of Human Rights in Africa.* London: Codesria Book Series, 1989.

Silverman, Martin, *Disconcerting Issue: Meaning and Struggle in a Resettled Pacific Community.* Chicago: University of Chicago Press, 1971.

Simons, H.J., *African Women: Their Legal Status in South Africa.* London: C. Hurst, 1968.

Smart, Carol, *The Ties that Bind: Law, Marriage and the Reproduction of Patriarchal Relations.* London: Routledge & Kegan Paul, 1984.

Soifer, Aviam, *Law and the Company We Keep.* Cambridge, MA: Harvard University Press, 1995.

Stanner, W.E.H., *White Man Got the Dreaming: Essays 1938–1973.* Canberra: Australian National University Press, 1979.

Stephenson, M. and S. Ratnapala, eds., *Mabo: A Judicial Revolution.* Brisbane: University of Queensland Press, 1993.

Tatz, Colin, *Aborigines and Uranium and Other Essays.* Richmond, Victoria: Heinemann, 1982.

Tönnies, Ferdinand, *Community and Society.* East Lansing: Michigan State University Press, 1957.

____ *Custom: An Essay on Social Codes.* New York: The Free Press of Glencoe, 1961.

Twenty-Five Human Rights Documents. New York: Center for the Study of Human Rights, Columbia University, 1994.

Twining, William, *The Place of Customary Law in the National Legal Systems of East Africa.* Chicago: University of Chicago Law School, 1963.

____ ed., *Issues of Self-Determination.* Aberdeen: Aberdeen University Press, 1991.

Vail, Leroy, ed., *The Creation of Tribalism in Southern Africa.* Berkeley: University of California Press, 1989.

Wallace, Anthony, *The Long, Bitter Trail: Andrew Jackson and the Indians.* New York: Hill & Wang, 1993.

Washburn, Wilcombe, *Red Man's Land/White Man's Law: The Past and Present*

Status of the American Indian. Norman: University of Oklahoma Press. 1995, 2nd edn.

Watson, Alan, *Legal Transplants: An Approach to Comparative Law.* Edinburgh: Scottish Academic Press, 1974.

Weisbrod, Carol, *The Boundaries of Utopia.* New York: Pantheon Books, 1980.

Wilkinson, Charles, *American Indians, Time, and the Law: Native Societies in a Modern Constitutional Democracy.* New Haven, CT: Yale University Press, 1987.

Williams, Robert, Jr., *The American Indian in Western Legal Thought: Discourses of Conquest.* New York: Oxford University Press, 1990.

Wunder, John, *'Retained by the People': A History of American Indians and the Bill of Rights.* New York: Oxford University Press, 1994.

LAW CASES

Africa

Gwao bin Kilimo v. Kisunda bin Ifuti, (1938) TLR 403.
Kweneng Land Board v. Kabelo Matlho and Pheto Motlhabane, Civil Appeal 10/91, Court of Appeal of Botswana, Lobatse.
Lewis v. Bankole, (1908) NLR 81.
Mariyama v. Sadiku Ejo, 1961 N.R.N.L.R. 81.
Mwauru s/o Kamau v. Gatoto s/o Mwangi, [1962] E.A. 528.
Otieno v. Ougo and Siranga, H.C.C. No. 4872 (1986) (Kenya).
Pluri v. Nkosi, 1941 NAC (N & T), 94.
R. v. Mchenji and Chargwi, 1917 SR 69.
Regina v. Jackson, [1956] R. & N.L.R. 66 (High Court, Nyasaland).
Santam v. Fonda, 1960(2) S.A. 467(A.D.).
The Attorney-General for Nyasaland v. Jackson, [1957] R. & N.L.R. 443.
Virginia Otieno v. Joash Ougo and Omolo Siranga, Civil Appeal No. 31 of 1987.
Viviers v. Klein, 1927 AD 449.

England

Campbell v. Campbell, (1976) 3 WLR 572.
Hyde v. Hyde, (1866) L.R. 1 P. & D. 1307.
Manuel v. Attorney General, (1982) 3 All E.R. 118 (C.A.).
Noltcho v. Attorney General, [1982] 3 All E.R. 786 (Ch.).
Tito v. Waddell, (1977) 2 W.L.R. 496.
Wachtel v. Wachtel, (1973) 1 All E R 829.

North America

Apsassin v. Canada (Dept. of Indian Affairs and Northern Development), 130 D.L.R. (4th) 193 (1995).
Badani v. Higginson, 638 F.2d 172 (1980).
Blatchford v. Native Village of Noatak, 111 S.Ct. 2578 (1991).
Braunfield v. Brown, 366 US 599 (1961).
Brown v. Board of Education, 347 US 483 (1954).
Calder v. Attorney-General of British Columbia, (1973) 34 DLR (3d) 145.
Cherokee Nation v Georgia, 30 US (5 Pet.) 1 (1831).
Church of the Lukumi Bobalu Aye, Inc. v. Hialeah, 508 US 520.
City of Boerne v. Flores, 521 US; 138 L. Ed. 2d. 624.
Coker v. Georgia, 433 US 584 (1977).
Crow v. Gullet, 706 F.2d. 856 (1983).
Davis v. Beason, 133 US 333 (1890).
Delgamuukw v. The Queen. Reasons for Judgment, 1991, No. 0843, Smithers Registry.
DeShaney v. Winnebago County Social Services Department, 489 US 189 (1989).
Dred Scott v. Sanford, 60 US (19 How.) 393 (1856).
Duro v. Reina, 495 US 676 (1990).
Elk v. Wilkins, 112 US 94 (1884).
Employment Division v. Smith, 485 US 660 (1988) (Smith I).
Employment Division, Department of Human Services v. Smith, 494 US 872 (1990) (Smith II).
Employment Division, State of Oregon v. Smith, 494 US 872 (1990).
Ex parte Crow Dog, 109 US 556 (1883).
Fauziya Kasinga, File A-73-476-695-Elizabeth, Interim Decision No. 3278 (B.I.A., 1996).
Fletcher v. Peck, 10 US (6 Branch) 87 (1810).
Frank v. State, 604 P 2d 1068 (Alaska, 1979).
Furman v. Georgia, 408 US 23 (1972).
Gallagher v. Crown Kosher Meat Market, 366 US 617 (1961).
Goldman v. Weinberger, Secretary of Defense, 475 US 503 (1986).
Guerin v. Rex, (1985) 13 D.L.R. (4th) 321 (S.C.C.).
In re: Adoption of Baby Boy D., 742 P. 2d 1059 (Okla. 1985).
In re: Kemmler, 136 US 436 (1890).
Ingraham v. Wright, 430 US 651 (1977).
Iowa Mutual Ins. v. La Plante, 480 US 9 (1987).
Johnson v. M'Intosh, 21 US (8 Wheat) 543 (1823).
Lone Wolf v. Hitchcock, 187 US 553 (1903).
Loucks v. Standard Oil Co., 224 NY 99.
Lyng v. Northwest Indian Cemetery Protective Association, 485 US 439.
Mashpee Tribe v. New Sebury Corporation, 592 F. 2d 575 (1979).
McBratney v. United States, 104 US 621 (1882).
Minersville School District v. Gobitis, 310 US 586 (1940).

Mitchel v. United States, 34 US (9 Pet.) 711 (1835).
Nally v. Grace Community Church of the Valley, (1987) 240 Cal Rpts, 215.
Nally v. Grace Community Church of the Valley, (1988) 763 P. 2d 948.
National Farmers Union Insurance Co. v. Crow Tribe of Indians, 471 US 485.
Northwest Indian Cemetery Protective Association v. Peterson, 795 F. 2d 688 (9th Cir. 1986).
Oliphant v. Suquamish Indian Tribe, 435 US 191 (1978).
People v. Kimura, No. A-091133, Super Ct., 24 April 1985.
People v. Woody, 394 P.2d 813 (1964).
Plessy v. Ferguson, 163 US 537 (1896).
R. v. Big M. Drug Mart, (1985) I.S.C.R. 295.
R. v. Moses, (1992) 11 CR (4th) 357 (Yukon Terr. Ct.).
R. v. Naqitarvik, (1986) 26 C.C.C. (3d) 193.
R. v. Secretary of State, ex parte Indian Association of Alberta, [1982] 2 All E.R. 118 (C.A.).
Regents of the University of California v. Bakke, 438 US 265 (1978).
Reynolds v. United States, 98 US 145 (1879).
Santa Clara Pueblo v. Martinez, 436 US 49 (1978).
Sequoyah v. TVA, 620 F. 2d 1159 (1980).
Sherbert v. Werner, 374 US 398 (1963).
Sparrow v. R., [1987] 2 WWR 577.
St Catherine's Milling Company v. The Queen, (1888) 14 App. Cas. 46 (PC).
State v. George Tassels, 1 Dud. 229 (1830).
Talton v. Mayes, 163 US 376 (1896).
Tee-Hit-Ton Indians v. United States, 348 US 272 (1955).
The Queen v. Drybones, (1970) SCR 282.
Thomas v. Norris, [1992] 2 C.N.L.R. 139 (B.C.S.C.).
Trop v. Dulles, 356 US 86 (1958).
United States v. Alcea Band of Tillamooks, 341 US 48 (1950).
United States v. Unknown Heirs, 152 F. Supp. 452 (W.D. Okla. 1957).
United States v. Wheeler, 435 US 313 (1978).
Walker v. Superior Court, (1988) 47 Cal. 3d 112.
West Virginia State Board of Education v. Barnett, 319 US 624 (1943).
Williams v. Lee, 358 US 217 (1959).
Wilson v. Block, 705 F.2d 735 (1983).
Wisconsin v. Yoder, 406 US 205 (1972).
Worcester v. Georgia, 31 US (6 Pet.) 515 (1832).

Oceania

Acting Public Prosecutor v. Uname Aumane and Others, S.C.A. No. 14 of 1980 PNGLR (1980) 510.
Bray and Ors. v. The Commonwealth of Australia, D 5 of 1995.
Coe v. The Commonwealth of Australia, 53 A.L.R. 403 (1979).
Foster v. Mountford and Rigby, (1976) 29 FLR 233, 14 ALR 71.

In re Toohey: ex parte Meneling Station (Pty) Ltd., (1982) 44 ALR 63.
Kruger and Ors v. The Commonwealth of Australia, High Court, M 21 of 1995.
Mabo v. Queensland, (1992) 175 CLR 1; 66 ALJR 408.
Milirrpum v. Nabalco Pty. Ltd. and the Commonwealth of Australia, (1971) FLR 141.
New Zealand Maori Council v. Attorney-General, [1987] NZLR 641.
R. v. Aboriginal Charlie Mulparinga, Northern Territory Judgments, 1951–1976, 219.
R. v. Anunga and Others, (1976) 11 ALR 412.
R. v. Jack Murrell, (1836) 1 Legge 72.
R. v. K.J., [1973] PNGLR, 93.
R. v. Mangakitai, (1967–68) P & NGLR 180.
R. v. Tiger and Captain, North Territory Judgments, 1951–1976, 213.
R. v. Toohey: Ex parte Northern Land Council, (1981) 56 ALJR 164.
R. v. Ward, S.C. of W.A., Kalgoorlie, No. 119/1985.
R. v. Womeni-Nanagawa, (1963) P & NGLR 72.
The State of Queensland v. Wyville, 90 ALR 611.
Wacando v. The Commonwealth and the State of Queensland, 148 C.L.R. 1 (1981).
Wi Parata v. Bishop of Wellington, (1877) 3 N.Z. Jur. (NS) 72, S.Ct.

Other

Advisory Opinion on Western Sahara, [1975] ICJR 12.
Belgium linguistics case, European Court of Human Rights, Ser. A No. 6 (1968).
Lovelace v. Canada, (R.6/24) HRC 36, 166.
Minority Schools in Albania, PCIJ, Ser. A/B, No. 64, 1935.
Tunisia v. Libyan Arab Jamahirija, IJC Rep. 1982, 18.
Tyrer v. UK, 2 EHRR 1 Series A, vol. 26.

Index